# Media Studies

## Volume 1

## Institutions, Theories and Issues

# Media Studies

## Volume 1

## Institutions, Theories and Issues

Edited by

Pieter J Fourie

This volume is part of a two-volume series:

*Volume 1: Media Studies: Institutions, Theories and Issues*
Edited by Pieter J Fourie

*Volume 2: Media Studies: Content, Audiences and Production*
Edited by Pieter J Fourie

First published 2001

ISBN 0 7021 5655 8

© Juta Education
P O Box 24309, Lansdowne, 7779
South Africa

*This book is copyright under the Berne Convention. In terms of the Copyright Act 98 of 1978, no part of this book may be reproduced or transmitted in any form or by any means, electronic or mechanical, including photocopying, recording or by any information storage and retrieval system, without permission in writing from the publisher.*

Subediting: Pat Hanekom
DTP and design: Charlene Bate
Cover design: Dallas du Toit
Printed and bound by: Creda Communications

# Contents

## Part A: Media Institutions

### Unit 1: A South African Media Map
Overview .................................................................................................................. 3
Learning outcomes ................................................................................................. 3
1.1 Introduction ..................................................................................................... 4
1.2 Broadcasting .................................................................................................... 6
1.3 The press ........................................................................................................ 34
1.4 Film ................................................................................................................. 75
Summary ................................................................................................................ 97
Research activities ................................................................................................. 98
Further reading ..................................................................................................... 100
Bibliography .......................................................................................................... 100

### Unit 2: Characteristics, Trends and the Political Economy of the Media
Overview .............................................................................................................. 105
Learning outcomes ............................................................................................... 105
2.1 Characteristics of the media business ........................................................ 106
2.2 Economic strategies ..................................................................................... 111
2.3 Economic trends and their impact on the media business ...................... 112
2.4 Critical political economy ............................................................................ 121
Summary .............................................................................................................. 126
Research activities ............................................................................................... 126
Further reading ................................................................................................... 127
Bibliography ........................................................................................................ 127

### Unit 3: Media Ownership and Control
Overview .............................................................................................................. 129
Learning outcomes ............................................................................................... 129
3.1 Introduction .................................................................................................. 129
3.2 Positions on ownership ................................................................................ 132
3.3 Levels of monopolisation ............................................................................. 137
3.4 Case study: Ownership and control of the press in South Africa ............. 139
3.5 The South African debate on ownership and control .............................. 148
3.6 Ownership and the future ........................................................................... 155
Summary .............................................................................................................. 159
Research activities ............................................................................................... 159
Further reading ................................................................................................... 160
Bibliography ........................................................................................................ 160

## Unit 4: The External Media Policy Framework: From Restrictive Policy to the Democratisation of Communication

Overview ............................................................................................................. 163
Learning outcomes ............................................................................................ 163
4.1 Introduction .............................................................................................. 164
4.2 The external media policy framework .................................................. 164
4.3 Regulators ................................................................................................. 166
4.4 The implications of regulating ............................................................... 182
Summary ........................................................................................................... 185
Research activities ........................................................................................... 185
Further reading ................................................................................................ 186
Bibliography ..................................................................................................... 186

## Unit 5: The Internal Media Policy Framework

Overview ............................................................................................................. 189
Learning outcomes ............................................................................................ 189
5.1 Introduction .............................................................................................. 189
5.2 Internal policy formulation .................................................................... 190
5.3 Influence of the external policy framework on the internal framework ............................................................................................... 194
5.4 Gatekeeping ............................................................................................. 196
5.5 Implications of gatekeeping .................................................................. 205
Summary ........................................................................................................... 205
Research activities ........................................................................................... 206
Further reading ................................................................................................ 206
Bibliography ..................................................................................................... 206

# Part B: Media Theory

## Unit 6: Mass Communication Theory

Overview ............................................................................................................. 210
Learning outcomes ............................................................................................ 210
6.1 Defining mass communication .............................................................. 211
6.2 Models of mass communication ............................................................ 222
6.3 Mass communication theory .................................................................. 229
6.4 Media theory and research .................................................................... 236
6.5 Public communication cultures .............................................................. 253
Summary ........................................................................................................... 259
Research activities ........................................................................................... 260
Further reading ................................................................................................ 261
Bibliography ..................................................................................................... 261

## Unit 7: The Role and Functions of the Media: Functionalism
Overview .................................................................................................................... 264
Learning outcomes ................................................................................................... 264
7.1 Introduction: Functionalism ............................................................................. 265
7.2 The political functions of the media: The case of pluralism ........................... 267
7.3 The functions of the press: Normative theory ................................................. 269
7.4 The functions of film: The case of entertainment ........................................... 277
Summary ................................................................................................................... 286
Research activities .................................................................................................... 287
Further reading ......................................................................................................... 287
Bibliography .............................................................................................................. 288

## Unit 8: The Effects and Power of Mass Communication
Overview .................................................................................................................... 290
Learning outcomes ................................................................................................... 291
8.1 Introduction: Categorising media effects ........................................................ 291
8.2 An overview of effect theories ......................................................................... 294
8.3 A cautionary note about effect theories and research ................................... 306
Summary ................................................................................................................... 308
Research activities .................................................................................................... 309
Further reading ......................................................................................................... 310
Bibliography .............................................................................................................. 310

## Unit 9: Media and Ideology
Overview .................................................................................................................... 311
Learning outcomes ................................................................................................... 311
9.1 Introduction ...................................................................................................... 311
9.2 A popular view of ideology .............................................................................. 313
9.3 Theories of ideology ......................................................................................... 313
9.4 Ideological struggles and conflicts of interpretations ..................................... 321
Summary ................................................................................................................... 324
Research activities .................................................................................................... 324
Further reading ......................................................................................................... 325
Bibliography .............................................................................................................. 325

## Unit 10: Media and the Production of Meaning: Semiotics
Overview .................................................................................................................... 326
Learning outcomes ................................................................................................... 326
10.1 Introduction: The field of semiotics ................................................................ 326
10.2 The history of semiotics ................................................................................... 328

| | |
|---|---|
| 10.3 The sign | 333 |
| 10.4 Sign system | 338 |
| 10.5 Code | 339 |
| 10.6 Meaning | 345 |
| Summary | 350 |
| Research activities | 351 |
| Further reading | 352 |
| Bibliography | 352 |

## Unit 11: Media and Culture

| | |
|---|---|
| Overview | 354 |
| Learning outcomes | 354 |
| 11.1 Introduction | 354 |
| 11.2 Culture and communication | 355 |
| 11.3 Social and cultural forms of expression | 356 |
| 11.4 Making sense of culture | 367 |
| 11.5 Cultural studies | 373 |
| 11.6 The cultural studies approach – a summary | 378 |
| Summary | 379 |
| Research activities | 380 |
| Further reading | 381 |
| Bibliography | 381 |

## Unit 12: Feminist Media Theory

| | |
|---|---|
| Overview | 383 |
| Learning outcomes | 383 |
| 12.1 Introduction: Basic assumptions | 384 |
| 12.2 The terrain of feminism | 385 |
| 12.3 Liberal feminism: A theoretical perspective | 386 |
| 12.4 Marxist and socialist feminism: A theoretical perspective | 389 |
| 12.5 Radical feminism: A theoretical perspective | 394 |
| 12.6 Psychoanalytical feminism: A theoretical perspective | 396 |
| 12.7 Postmodern feminism: A theoretical perspective | 401 |
| 12.8 Feminism and advertising | 404 |
| 12.9 Feminism in South Africa and media research | 406 |
| Summary | 409 |
| Research activities | 409 |
| Further reading | 410 |
| Bibliography | 410 |

# Part C: Critical Media Issues

## Unit 13: Media Imperialism: The New World Information and Communication Order

Overview ............................................................................................................... 414
Learning outcomes ............................................................................................... 414
13.1 Introduction ................................................................................................. 415
13.2 Cornerstones of the NWICO ........................................................................ 416
13.3 The history of the NWICO ........................................................................... 417
13.4 Reaction to the New World Information Order ............................................ 425
13.5 The NWICO today ........................................................................................ 426
13.6 South Africa and the NWICO: Blaming the watchdog continues ................. 428
13.7 Conclusions ................................................................................................. 438
Summary ............................................................................................................... 441
Research activities ................................................................................................. 441
Further reading ..................................................................................................... 442
Bibliography .......................................................................................................... 443

## Unit 14: A Critical Assessment of News

Overview ............................................................................................................... 446
Learning outcomes ............................................................................................... 446
14.1 Introduction ................................................................................................. 446
14.2 Language, signs, codes and the news ......................................................... 447
14.3 The selection of news ................................................................................. 452
14.4 The construction of news ............................................................................ 455
14.5 News and society ........................................................................................ 462
14.6 Conclusion ................................................................................................... 464
Summary ............................................................................................................... 464
Research activities ................................................................................................. 465
Further reading ..................................................................................................... 465
Bibliography .......................................................................................................... 466

## Unit 15: Representation: Race, Gender and Sexual Orientation

Overview ............................................................................................................... 468
Learning outcomes ............................................................................................... 468
15.1 Introduction ................................................................................................. 469
15.2 What are stereotypes? ................................................................................. 470
15.3 Case studies in representation .................................................................... 486
Summary ............................................................................................................... 502
Research activities ................................................................................................. 503
Further reading ..................................................................................................... 504
Bibliography .......................................................................................................... 504

## Unit 16: Media and Violence

| | |
|---|---|
| Overview | 508 |
| Learning outcomes | 508 |
| 16.1 Introduction | 509 |
| 16.2 Historical overview: Media violence debate and research | 509 |
| 16.3 Theoretical perspectives: Media violence | 511 |
| 16.4 Television violence research in South Africa | 517 |
| 16.5 A comprehensive circular process model for studying violence (Botha 1997) | 519 |
| 16.6 Preventative measures: How to curb the effects of television violence | 521 |
| Summary | 525 |
| Research activities | 533 |
| Further reading | 534 |
| Bibliography | 535 |

## Unit 17: Media and Terrorism

| | |
|---|---|
| Overview | 537 |
| Learning outcomes | 537 |
| 17.1 Introduction | 538 |
| 17.2 Terrorists and the media | 539 |
| 17.3 The role of governments and state departments | 543 |
| 17.4 Obligations and the nature of the mass media | 547 |
| 17.5 The public, the media and terrorism | 553 |
| 17.6 Policy formulation, terrorism and the media | 556 |
| 17.7 South Africa and the media/terrorism debate | 557 |
| Summary | 563 |
| Research activities | 563 |
| Further reading | 564 |
| Bibliography | 564 |

## Unit 18: Censorship and the Media

| | |
|---|---|
| Overview | 568 |
| Learning outcomes | 568 |
| 18.1 Introduction | 569 |
| 18.2 Censorship defined | 569 |
| 18.3 Major justifications for censorship | 572 |
| 18.4 Censorship in various media | 574 |
| 18.5 Media censorship in South Africa | 578 |
| Summary | 587 |
| Research activities | 588 |
| Further reading | 589 |
| Bibliography | 590 |

# Unit 19: Globalisation, the Information Superhighway and Development

| | |
|---|---|
| Overview | 592 |
| Learning outcomes | 593 |
| 19.1 Introduction: A theory and some characteristics of globalisation | 593 |
| 19.2 Globalisation, information and communication technology and development | 602 |
| 19.3 ICT planning and policy | 610 |
| 19.4 The future of ICT and globalisation: Four scenarios | 615 |
| 19.5 Conclusion: Problem analysis and solutions | 618 |
| Summary | 620 |
| Research activities | 621 |
| Further reading | 621 |
| Bibliography | 622 |

# List of Figures

**UNIT 1**

| | | |
|---|---|---|
| 1.1 | Corruption on the part of some IBA officials did much to dent the credibility of the Authority (*Sowetan*, 22 April 1997) | 17 |
| 1.2 | Resolving the financial woes of the SABC meant abandoning some public broadcasting principles (*City Press*, 6 March 1997) | 20 |
| 1.3 | e.tv's initial financial problems and licence contraventions placed the IBA in a compromising position (*Sowetan*, 4 December 1998) | 23 |
| 1.4 | Percentage of the population speaking each official language as their home language compared with the penetration of those languages by SABC public service radio stations broadcasting in those languages | 28 |
| 1.5 | The origins of commercial broadcasting in South Africa, *circa* 1997 | 29 |
| 1.6 | The structure of the South African press, *circa* 1985 | 47 |
| 1.7 | The structure of the South African press, *circa* 2000 | 64 |
| 1.8 | Control structure of Naspers (Naspers 2000) | 67 |
| 1.9 | Subpoenaing editors to appear before the SAHRC provoked an outrage by the press who saw the move as an infringement on press freedom (*Sunday Times*, 27 February 2000) | 71 |
| 1.10 | Perceptions of racism in the media – how the press measures up to radio and television (Survey ... 2000:2) | 73 |
| 1.11 | Newspapers perceived as being racist by survey respondents who felt newspapers were fairly to very racist (Survey ... 2000:2) | 74 |
| 1.12 | Film production in South African during the period 1960–1980 by language (Tomaselli 1989:263–268) | 80 |
| 1.13 | The total number of films produced and subsidised in South Africa compared with the number of production companies (Blignaut & Botha 1992:78–81) | 83 |
| 1.14 | Time line showing the influence of the changing nature of the South African sociopolitical environment on the development of the local film industry (adapted from Dodd 2000:50) | 85 |
| 1.15 | Proposed structure for the South African film industry (South Africa 1995:301) | 91 |

**UNIT 2**

| | | |
|---|---|---|
| 2.1 | Naspers and Independent Newspapers | 114 |
| 2.2 | Convergence | 114 |
| 2.3 | *Business Day* | 115 |

## UNIT 6

| 6.1 | Shannon and Weaver's (1949) information theory model | 225 |
| 6.2 | Westley and MacLean's (1957) model of mass communication | 226 |
| 6.3 | George Gerbner's cultivation model | 228 |
| 6.4 | Media epochs in human history (Wood 2000:245) | 251 |

## UNIT 10

| 10.1 | Jakobson's communication model (functions) | 336 |

## UNIT 11

| 11.1 | The built environment and the significance of context | 359 |
| 11.2 | Examples of architectural styles and the built environment | 360 |
| 11.3 | Sport as a form of social and cultural expression | 361 |
| 11.4 | Music as a form of social and cultural expression | 365 |
| 11.5 | Reading religion | 380 |

## UNIT 13

| 13.1 | *ANC Today – Online Voice of the African National Congress* | 435 |
| 13.2 | Africa2Africa | 437 |
| 13.3 | SABC Africa | 438 |

## UNIT 19

| 19.1 | Pre-modern compared to modern society (the concept of time, space and status) | 596 |
| 19.2 | Poverty in South Africa | 607 |
| 19.3 | Basic telecommunication services in South Africa | 607 |
| 19.4 | Internet usage in South Africa | 608 |
| 19.5 | Universal service | 610 |

# List of Tables

**UNIT 1**

| | | |
|---|---|---|
| 1.1 | Highlights in the development of M-Net | 15 |
| 1.2 | Number of radio receivers in selected African countries (United Nations 1997; 2000) | 24 |
| 1.3 | Number of television receivers in selected African countries (United Nations 1997; 2000) | 25 |
| 1.4 | Commercial radio stations operating in South Africa. Stations marked with an asterisk were previously part of the SABC | 30 |
| 1.5 | AMPS television viewing averages in South Africa (South African Advertising Research Foundation 1998:58) | 32 |
| 1.6 | Percentage of language allocation for SABC-TV channels broadcast during prime-time (18:00–21:00) (South African Broadcasting Corporation 1996:29) | 33 |
| 1.7 | Growth of black owned and operated newspapers for the period 1911 to 1930 (Cullen 1935:81) | 50 |
| 1.8 | Daily newspapers in selected African countries (United Nations 1997:119–120; 2000:117–118) | 56 |
| 1.9 | Readership of English dailies in 1 000s during the period 1998–2000 (South African Advertising Research Foundation 2000a) | 57 |
| 1.10 | Readership of Afrikaans dailies in 1 000s during the period 1998–2000 (South African Advertising Research Foundation 2000a) | 57 |
| 1.11 | Readership of English weeklies in 1 000s during the period 1998–2000 (South African Advertising Research Foundation 2000a) | 58 |
| 1.12 | Readership of Afrikaans weeklies in 1 000s during the period 1998–2000 (South African Advertising Research Foundation 2000a) | 58 |
| 1.13 | Readership of other weeklies in 1 000s during the period 1998–2000 (South African Advertising Research Foundation 2000a) | 59 |
| 1.14 | Film viewing figures of the total population for the period 1995–1999 (South African Advertising Research Foundation 2000) | 88 |

**UNIT 7**

| | | |
|---|---|---|
| 7.1 | Wright's model of functions | 266 |
| 7.2 | McQuail's typology of functions (McQuail 2000:79–80 | 267 |

**UNIT 16**

16.1  Average daily exposure to television (hours:minutes) ............................................................ 511

**UNIT 18**

18.1  Censorship legislation ............................................................................................................. 582
18.2  Laws that restrict the South African media .......................................................................... 586

**UNIT 19**

19.1  Problem analysis (Janssen 1996:347–348) ............................................................................ 620
19.2  Solutions to policy problems (adapted from Janssen 1996:322,342) ................................. 621

# Case Studies

### UNIT 1
| | | |
|---|---|---|
| 1.1 | Establishing the credibility of the IBA as regulator of broadcasting | 18 |
| 1.2 | The intricacies of the South African print media | 60 |
| 1.3 | The advantages and limitations of the South African film industry | 92 |

### UNIT 2
| | | |
|---|---|---|
| 2.1 | Public service broadcasting (PSB) | 118 |

### UNIT 4
| | | |
|---|---|---|
| 4.1 | Regulation: The telecommunication policy context in South Africa | 183 |

### UNIT 6
| | | |
|---|---|---|
| 6.1 | The South African media is racist | 248 |

### UNIT 7
| | | |
|---|---|---|
| 7.1 | Civic journalism defined | 276 |
| 7.2 | Rhetorical motifs in popular television genres | 283 |

### UNIT 9
| | | |
|---|---|---|
| 9.1 | Perspectives | 317 |
| 9.2 | How the mass media promote ideology | 323 |

### UNIT 12
| | | |
|---|---|---|
| 12.1 | *The Piano* (1993) | 399 |

### UNIT 15
| | | |
|---|---|---|
| 15.1 | South African Human Rights Commission: a chronology of the media racism enquiry | 488 |
| 15.2 | The role of the media in the representation of HIV/AIDS and AIDS sufferers | 497 |
| 15.3 | The media's portrayal of gays and lesbians | 500 |
| 15.4 | Media representation of women | 503 |

### UNIT 16
| | | |
|---|---|---|
| 16.1 | A critical analysis of *Teenage, Mutant Ninja Turtles* | 526 |
| 16.2 | *Yizo Yizo* | 529 |

### UNIT 18
| | | |
|---|---|---|
| 18.1 | *Cry Freedom* (1998) – a study of censorship in South Africa | 586 |

# Copyright

**FOR UNIT 1**

Editorial cartoon, *Sowetan*, 22 April 1997 (Figure 1.1)

Editorial cartoon, *City Press*, 6 March 1997 (Figure 1.2)

Editorial cartoon, *Sowetan*, 4 December 1998 (Figure 1.3)

Editorial cartoon, *Sunday Times*, 27 February 2000 (Figure 1.9)

Kobokoane, T. 2000. Satra and IBA successor must avoid woes of past, *Sunday Times Business Times*, April 23:4 (Case study 1.1)

A to Z: Spelling out the South African media maze. 1999. *Mail & Guardian*, 5–11 March:5 (Case study 1.2)

Greig, R & Thomas, R. 1999. So why don't we make Aussie films? *The Sunday Independent*, 26 September:12 (Case Study 1.3)

# Authors

Pieter J Fourie is a professor in communication science and head of the Department of Communication, University of South Africa.

Beschara Karam is a lecturer in communication science in the Department of Communication, University of South Africa.

Jennifer Lemon is senior lecturer in the Department of Communication, University of South Africa and coordinator of the same university's Institute for Gender Studies.

Lucas M Oosthuizen was, at the time of writing, senior lecturer in the Department of Communication, University of South Africa. Presently he is a private communication consultant.

Lynn Parry is senior lecturer in the Department of Communication, University of South Africa.

Magriet Pitout is an associate professor in communication science in the Department of Communication, University of South Africa.

Stefan Sonderling is a senior lecturer in communication science in the Department of Communication, University of South Africa.

David Wigston is a senior lecturer in communication science in the Department of Communication, University of South Africa.

# Introduction

## Why media studies?

The development of media studies as a field of academic inquiry with its own theories and methodologies is, both in South Africa and in the rest of the world, remarkable. A decade or two ago institutions of higher learning still tended to view media studies as "too concerned with the secular and the popular" and as such not worthy of serious academic study. Today universities and technikons fall over their feet to offer courses in media studies. The reasons are many. Here we highlight three of them:

- From an academic point of view, the omnipresence of the media and their role in society, culture, the economy, politics and education, in short their impact on everyday life and their role as a flagship of late twentieth and early twenty-first century culture can no longer be ignored.
- From the media industry's perspective, the industry itself increasingly acknowledges the need for their workers to have a sounder theoretical and methodological base.
- Last, but not least, media studies draws students, and institutions of higher learning need money generated by student fees.

Apart from these reasons, the following macro developments can be cited:

- Institutions of higher learning are forced to become more "relevant" in terms of social and industrial needs. In faculties of arts and humanities this means a focus not only on the canon of literature, philosophy, "high" art and the theories of sociology, politics, anthropology, and so on, but also the need to study the secular, including the study of the content and institutions of popular forms of symbolic expression such as the media and their role in defining everyday existence.
- Globalisation and all that it encompasses, including the central role of the media and information and communication technology in globalisation, its associated new economic order, and the impact of the "new" information revolution on every aspect of society – a revolution similar to that of the invention of the printing press and thereafter the telegraph has pushed media studies to the forefront.
- The growth of the media industry itself has given new importance to media studies. The fact that the media have become a major economic role player is evidenced by listings on stock exchanges and the coverage of the media by the media on the pages of their business sections, in radio and television programmes, in editorial articles, in articles about their power and importance as a pillar of democracy, and on the Internet. This has made the media industry itself a story and a culture in itself for itself. In short, the media industry's prominent self-reflection – reporting about itself and thus elevating itself to a level of importance – has contributed to a public awareness not known before of the centrality of the media in present day society and culture.
- The media form the backbone of the marketing, advertising and public relations industries. Without the media these industries will fail to grow and play a role as

important financial institutions and providers of jobs. At the same time their role as the main generators and communicators of our present-day consumer culture will, to the relief of many critics, be sized down remarkably. A sound knowledge of how the media work, think and disseminate meaning is, therefore, fundamental to these industries.
- From a communication science perspective the most important reason for the growth in and importance of media studies, is the recognition of the media as fundamental to democracy. To empower the media to sustain and develop democracy, to understand the complex relationship between the media and the state, and to develop a critical understanding of the media as complex political and ideological agents, demands a sound knowledge of media institutions and their practices and the ability to analyse media content against the background of scientifically tested theories and methods. This in turn will place discussions of the media on a scientific foundation.
- The last but no less important reason to be offered here for the growth of media studies concerns the media users or media audiences themselves. There is an increased awareness amongst a growing population of media users of the role of the media in their lives and the need to understand this role. Who are the people and institutions, how do they operate, and what are the content and quality of their products that play an important role in how we define ourselves, our society, our world and eventuality our perceptions of reality? The public's need to understand the media critically is acknowledged by educationists who increasingly introduce media studies as a school subject in which media institutions and media content are analysed alongside, and amongst others, works of literature and their authors. This gives recognition to the media as one of the, if not the most important disseminators of meaning and producers of symbolic forms.

The above reasons for the growth in media studies and recognition of the importance of the media have made media studies much more complicated than it used to be. Gone are the days when it was believed that knowledge of how to handle a camera or write a story constituted media literacy. Although this remains important, the academic study of the media entails much more. From a social science perspective, the one taken in this book (and in the companion volume), it involves, amongst others, a critical enquiry into the

- nature and practices of the media as power institutions
- political economy of the media
- functions and effects of the media
- media as producers and disseminators of meaning
- nature of media audiences.

In both volumes we have tried to cover a variety of approaches to these central topics in critical media studies. We use the term "critical" to distinguish our approach from the more practical approaches in which the emphasis is on media production techniques. Our approach is critical in the sense of trying to understand the media from various theoretical perspectives as major producers of meaning and as key role players in people's understanding, experience of and participation in politics, economics, society, culture, and their own lives and experiences of reality. Furthermore, our approach is analytical in the sense of trying to provide learners with the theoretical background on the basis of which critical questions and hypotheses about key issues related to the media can be formulated and investigated with applicable analytical instruments.

In terms of learning outcomes, a phenomenological knowledge of the nature of the media is a prerequisite for a responsible, theoretical and methodological grounded practice of any career in the media industry. Such a knowledge is necessary for the professionalisation of the media, and, with that, for the development of higher standards in media ethics and in the quality of media content (products).

Put in another way, our answer to the question: Why media studies? is that the media (television, radio, newspapers, magazines, film, video, compact discs, tapes and the Internet) are an integral part of our lives. This necessitates critical inquiry into the ways in which the media work. In short, the media are omnipresent. As such they impact on our perceptions and experiences of reality, of life, and on our relationships with each other. Secondly, the media have become major economic and political role players. An understanding of their power and responsibilities is essential for all citizens, politicians, the business sector, educators, in short, for all media users. Finally, workers in the media and communications industry (public relations officers, advertisers, communication consultants and directors in organisations) should have a sound and critical knowledge of the nature and working of the media. They are, after all, the people producing the popular meanings with which we are confronted on a daily basis. They are the people responsible for framing our ways of thinking about everyday matters, about products and about people. A critical understanding of how the media work can contribute to a more responsible approach to what they are doing, and hopefully to an improvement of the quality of media products.

## Structure of the book

The book is divided into two volumes. In Volume 1 the focus is on media institutions, media theories and some critical issues such as the media's representations of people, groups and reality in general. In Volume 2 we focus on approaches to the analysis of media content, the nature of media audiences and we provide an introduction to media production. Within the context of communication science the structure of the book is dictated by the communication triptych: communicator – message – recipient. In this case the communicators are the media institutions and their workers. The messages are the media content, and recipients are the media audiences (or users). The distinction between institutions, content and audiences, although strictly speaking not separable, also form the traditional fields of inquiry in critical media studies.

Each unit in the two volumes has the same structure: an overview of the learning material covered in the unit, the learning outcomes the learner should achieve, followed by the body of the text, a summary, research activities and references to further reading on the topic.

## The content of Volume 1

Volume 1 is divided into three parts and nineteen units.

### Media institutions

In the first part (Part A, units 1 to 5) the learner is provided with an overview of the media system in South Africa, a brief introduction to the nature of the media as business institutions, and an introduction to media policy.

Because of its changing nature, describing a country's media system, or providing a map of a media industry, is never an easy task. By the time of publishing, much of the figures, companies and even laws may have changed. David Wigston's purpose with the media map in Unit 1 of this volume is to provide learners with a historical context, a time line and a basis for keeping pace with the latest developments in broadcasting, the press and the film industry. (Advertising and the Internet are dealt with in other courses, as will be explained below.) Knowledge of the history and scope of a media industry, and skills to follow and develop an interest in the latest developments, are, amongst other reasons, necessary for an informed discussion of the power of the media, which is, if not manifest, a latent theme throughout this volume.

Similarly, a basic knowledge of economic trends such as commercialisation, privatisation, liberalisation, convergence and internationalisation is necessary for an understanding of the nature of the media as an industry and of their economic strategies. The purpose of Unit 2 is to provide such a basic knowledge without which learners will not be able to contribute to critical investigations and discussions of the political economy of the media and thus the close relationship between media, economy, politics and society and the impact of all this on the content of the media.

Being powerful political, economic and cultural role players, it is obvious that governments will seek to have some form of control and regulation of the media. This is discussed by Lucas Oosthuizen in units 3 to 5. In Unit 3 he looks at two structural approaches to the crucial issue of media ownership and control. He distinguishes between various levels of monopoly formation and discusses the development of the media ownership debate in South Africa. The unit is concluded with a brief look at the implications of structural, economic and political variables for the future debate on ownership and control of the media in South Africa.

In Unit 4, Oosthuizen discusses the values of freedom, equality and order as criteria for an external media policy framework. Against the background of these values he investigates the roles of governments, norms, pressure groups, advertisers, consumers, and the media profession itself as regulators of the media. He then provides the learner with an interpretation of media policy under the National Party government in South Africa compared to the media policy framework of the African National Congress (ANC) government. The unit is concluded with notes about the implications of external regulation and the role of codes of conduct.

As far as internal regulation is concerned, Oosthuizen introduces the learner to the important concepts of "gatekeeper" and "gate-keeping", in Unit 5. He then discusses charters, mission and/or vision statements, and news and programme policies as the basic documents of internal media policy. This is followed by a discussion of the influence of the external media policy frameworks on the internal media policy frameworks and the role of the different internal gatekeepers.

## Media theory

In Part A of the volume, having introduced the learner to the field of South African media and its history, as well as to policy aspects related to the control and regulation of the media, the second part (Part B, units 6 to 12) focuses on some of the key theories in media studies. The purpose of Unit 6 is to guide the learner towards a definition of the media as a form of mass communication, which in itself is a complex phenomenon, especially against the background of the development of information and communication technology. By way of asking a number of questions, the purpose of this unit is to introduce the learner to some of the complexities surrounding a definition of mass communication and the nature of the media as a form of mass communication.

In South Africa, as in other parts of the world, the media is constantly attacked (mainly by politicians) and blamed for almost everything that can go wrong. This leads us to questions about the role or functions of the media in society. There are many theories about this, ranging from positivist functionalist to critical theories. The purpose of Unit 7 is to provide learners with a theoretical foundation on which to base their arguments about the role of the media. A typology of media functions is provided, whereafter by way of case studies a closer look is taken at the normative theories of the press and a revision of these theories. As far as the entertainment function of the media is concerned, for many people the most important role of the media, we investigate answers to the question: What is entertainment?

The next question that arises is about the effects and power of the media. This topic is discussed in Unit 8. After establishing the strategic, scientific and ethical importance of the often controversial effects paradigm, learners are introduced to some of the theories related to the short- medium- and long-term effects of the media. The unit concludes with some criticism against the effects paradigm. Again the purpose is to provide learners with an introductory theoretical framework on which to base arguments and research on media effects.

Ideology is a key concept in media studies. Therefore the learner will encounter it in many of the units of this and Volume 2 of the book, even to such an extent that it may be experienced as repetitive. Keep in mind that each author discusses it from his/her perspective and within the context of his/her topic. In Unit 9, Stefan Sonderling's purpose is to provide the learner with an understanding of the concept "ideology" and the relationship between ideology and the mass media; to identify some of the theories of ideology and to explain how ideology is produced by powerful groups in society through the manipulation of language and the mass media in order to serve their own interests.

If ideology is about meaning and the creation and entrenchment of specific meanings, then media studies necessitates a closer investigation of how meaning is produced. This can be done from many perspectives, of which a favourite in media studies is the semiotic perspective. It can be argued that the underlying approach in this book is semiotic (especially in Volume 2) as we view the media as a unique sign system in which meaning is produced in specific ways. In Unit 10 learners are introduced to the basics of semiotics: the sign, the code and different kinds of meaning.

In Unit 11, Jennifer Lemon investigates the relationship between media and culture, which can be interpreted in two ways: media as culture and media as a reflection and portrayal of culture. The point of departure is that the media portray different forms of culture such as religion, architecture, sport, theatre, music, fashion and style. The relationship between culture and ideology is investigated and the assumptions of the cultural studies approach to the study of communication and media are briefly addressed.

Feminist media theory has developed as a key body of theory in media studies. Apart from emphasising the important role of women in the media and the role of women in defining reality through media content, a major contribution of feminist media theory has been to make us critically aware of the concept of "representation", be it the representativeness of different groups (race/gender) in a white male dominated media industry or how media content is a representation and interpretation of reality from a mainly white male dominant perspective. In Unit 12, Beschara Karam and Lynn Parry introduce learners to the main assumptions of feminist media theory and some of its central concepts.

To summarise: the purpose of the second part of this volume is to introduce learners to theories of the media as mass communication, the media's role and functions in society, their assumed powers and effects, the nature of the media as ideological agents, the way in which the media produce meaning, the media as a cultural phenomenon and feminist media theory as an example of criticism against the media as being white male dominated and the effects thereof on media content and its representation of reality.

## Critical media issues

In the last part of the volume (Part C) the emphasis is on media issues that we are confronted with on almost a daily basis. Apart from the critical issues of media ownership and regulation (discussed in Part A), the authors in this section of the book take a closer look at issues such as media and cultural imperialism, the problem of the media's objectivity in defining and covering "news", the way the media communicate with stereotypes and in stereotypical ways (which, in South Africa has given rise to the serious debate about the representation of race), the relationship between media and the occurrence of violence in society, the relationship between media and terrorism, the necessity for, but constant threat of, media censorship, and, finally, the role of the media in globalisation and its impact on development in developing countries. Again, the purpose of these units (units 13 to 19) is to provide learners with some theoretical background that could form the backbone of informed media policy and discussions.

## Contextualisation

Although both volumes of the book were developed and written for any course in media studies offered by any institution, their content forms the core of the Department of Communication of the University of South Africa's (Unisa's) two modules in media studies. In turn, these two modules form part of sixteen modules in communication science towards Unisa's BA (Communication Science) degree and as a major in communication science towards the BA, BA (Human and Social Studies) and Bachelor of Business Administration (BBA) degrees. In this regard it must be kept in mind that important topics such as media ethics, the role of the media in international communication, new media technology, political communication and the media, public relations and the media, and advertising and the media, are not covered explicitly in the content of these two volumes as these topics are dealt with in separate modules of the Unisa curriculum. Apart from the communication science modules, Unisa students of communication must also complete fundamental modules in writing and computer skills, research methodology and communication law.

Finally, in Volume 2 we deal with media content, audiences and production in the following units: text analysis, genre analysis, media and language, narrative analysis, film theory and criticism, reception theory, ethnography, the social psychology of media consumption, audience research, media and psychoanalysis, newspaper production, television production, radio production, film production, television as educational media, and radio as educational media.

*Pieter J Fourie*
November 2001

# Part A
# Media Institutions

### Unit 1
A South African Media Map

### Unit 2
The Characteristics, Trends and Political Economy of the Media

### Unit 3
Media Ownership and Control

### Unit 4
The External Media Policy Framework: From Restrictive Policy to the Democratisation of Communication

### Unit 5
The Internal Media Policy Framework

# A South African Media Map

*David Wigston*

## Overview

What do we understand by the concept "media"? Bennett (1982:30–31) says the concept media is made up of several layers of meaning. At the most basic level we understand that the concept refers collectively to the press, radio, television and film. But at other levels, this collective understanding of the concept can become misleading, in that the various media referred to by the concept only resemble each other in a superficial manner. To take as an example, the relationship between the state and broadcasting is very different from that between the state and the press on one hand, and the state and film on the other. In the case of broadcasting, the South African Broadcasting Corporation (SABC) held a monopoly from 1936. As a result, alternative points of view, particularly of a political nature, were excluded from programme content for many years. This led to the perception that the SABC was a government mouthpiece. Despite deregulation of the airwaves, the SABC still continues to dominate the broadcasting environment by virtue of its sheer size and seems unable to resolve its many problems. The press, however, has been dominated by commercial enterprises, which has resulted in a sometimes rough and rocky relationship with the government, while film simply cannot gain the critical mass necessary to become a meaningful force because of cultural demands and restrictions placed on the film industry by society and the state. To understand the concept media more fully requires that we look closely at the nature, processes involved and various relationships associated with the components that make up the concept media. This is the context of this unit, where we map out the organisation, various processes and inter-relationships associated with the media in South Africa. However, the social, economic and political forces that shape and determine the media are not static, but dynamic, constantly evolving and changing over a period of time with the result that the media map itself is also constantly shifting. To track these changes and to understand the *status quo* of the media in South Africa requires us to take a historical approach when charting the media in South Africa.

## Learning outcomes

At the end of this unit you should be able to
- list, chronologically, the important events in the development of the media in South Africa;

## MEDIA STUDIES

- identify specific historical periods for broadcasting, the press and film, and describe key events which took place in these periods;
- explain the relationship between society and the media and how this has affected the development of the media in South Africa;
- compare and evaluate the development of broadcasting, the press and film with each other in terms of their historical contexts;
- identify and describe issues and possible trends in the development of the South African media;
- evaluate the role played by regulation in the development of the media; and
- describe the current media environment of South Africa with regard to broadcasting, the press and film.

## 1.1 INTRODUCTION

Why do we need to study the history of the media? While the answer to this question is simple, the process of arriving at that answer is, by no means, simplistic. Our understanding of the nature and structure of the present media environment is largely influenced by what happened in the past. To take but one example: If the government of the day had accepted the recommendations of the Schoch Commission of 1948, then the structure of broadcasting in today's South Africa would have been very different. Whereas the Schoch Commission strongly recommended the decentralisation and the commercialisation of radio, the government opted to follow a monopolistic policy which resulted in the strong position of the SABC.

Similarly, it is largely assumed that tight government control of the media was the doing of the Nationalist Government. But history tells us that it was, in fact, the United Party, under the leadership of General Smuts who initiated this policy. Thus, if we are to consider the interactions of the various institutions within today's media environment, we need to deliberate on the reasons for and the roles played by those institutions within a certain context. In order for us to achieve this, we need to give serious attention to the historical development of the media in South Africa.

Media history is a fairly recent phenomenon in communications research, coming to the fore as a specialised study area only in the late 1970s. This growth is a direct result of the development of the Critical School of research that originated in Europe and later spread, in a modified form, to North America. Because of the Critical School's intense interest in the political economy of the media as an institution we find that a comprehensive and extensive literature exists for the European and American media. Here in South Africa, we are not so fortunate in having such a vast array of literature when it comes to studying the development of the media, but this is slowly improving as we become more conscious of the need to document development. However, we as yet have no detailed study of the South African media, such as Asa Briggs' four-volume history of the BBC.

Not that studying media history is without its difficulties, as no usable model has yet emerged enabling us to undertake an all-encompassing study of the media environment. Press models rarely describe broadcasting or film adequately and vice versa; their respective roles have been largely determined by politics and economics. Thus the three media we examine in this unit, namely broadcasting, the press and film, require distinct approaches. There are added practical problems. The physical output of the media is vast and largely ephemeral in nature. Browsing through press archives is physically much easier to do than for broadcasting where material is stored on audio- and videotape. We cannot access copies of early radio and television programmes, as for early newspapers and films, simply because there was no means of keeping a permanent record in the early days of broadcasting. With the invention of the tape recorder in the 1950s this problem was resolved, but the ephemeral nature of the broadcasting product has meant that much background material is often rapidly discarded. Thus, as an example, it is rare to find news bulletins preserved in archives. This means that for research purposes we cannot easily reconstruct what was reported, or how it was reported.

On the other hand, primary source material relating to the day-to-day operations of the institution, in the form of correspondence, memos and reports, is more readily found in broadcasting institutions than for film and the press, simply because of the bureaucratic nature of broadcasters. But, warns Briggs (1980:7), we should not place any reliance on this as a source of data, as access to this documentation is dependent on access to institutional archives. And, often vital documents can simply go missing. Thus, our knowledge of media history tends to be made up of secondary sources gained largely from memoirs, the press and annual reports.

When studying media history, we ideally need to engage in what Dahl (1978:132) terms "deep-drilling" as this does more justice to the subject than adopting an all-embracing episodic approach that is more chronological in nature. "Deep-drilling" implies looking at the resulting interactions between technology, politics, economics and culture at a particular point in time in order to try and untangle the shifting relationships between the media institutions, the government and the public. This approach is detailed and can provide us with a better understanding of the ethics and distinctive qualities of the media. A major drawback of such an approach is that is does tend to break up the continuity of development.

With this point in mind, by virtue of the constraints of time and space, and as this is probably your first encounter with the history of the South African media, we follow an episodic approach in this unit. We need to keep in mind, while working through this unit, that an obvious weakness in adopting an episodic approach is the exclusion of detailed institutional and political history as well as management analyses, audience research and gate-keeping studies. Obviously, we needed to take some decisions regarding what we included and excluded in this brief history of the South African media. Thus, if you are familiar with the particular history of broadcasting, the press or film in South Africa, you may disagree with us regarding the emphasis of certain events over others. But then you need to keep in mind that the purpose of this brief history is an introductory one, and we hope that it will inspire you to further your own in-depth investigations.

## 1.2 BROADCASTING

The historical development of broadcasting in South Africa is also largely the history of the South African Broadcasting Corporation (SABC), simply because the SABC held a monopoly on the airwaves until fairly recently as any other forms of broadcasting were not permitted. The early development of broadcasting in South Africa followed a similar pattern to elsewhere in Europe and North America. Radio began with a few enthusiastic amateur radio hams, followed by several experimental broadcasts and only later by regular programming on a more organised basis. We can divide the history of broadcasting in South Africa into seven periods. These periods are based on those originally devised by Tomaselli, Tomaselli and Muller (1989:24), whose list extends from 1924 up to 1971, where four specific periods are identified. To provide a broader and more comprehensive overview of the history of broadcasting in South Africa, we have expanded on, and amended this original list. Briefly, the periods are as follows:

- 1919–1936: The establishment of radio in South Africa
- 1936–1948: The South African Broadcasting Corporation
- 1948–1960: Post-World War II expansion
- 1960–1971: A period of transformation
- 1971–1981: A period of challenge
- 1981–1992: The rationalisation of broadcasting
- 1992–present: The restructuring of broadcasting

We must remember that when we delimit historical periods in the development of the media that we cannot be too categorical about the exact date when a period begins or ends. Determining the specific year in which any particular period begins or ends, is usually an arbitrary decision; periods tend to merge with one another rather than begin or end abruptly. Therefore, when we consult other authors on the historical development of broadcasting, we may find that they may have differing opinions about the grouping of periods and the importance of events during those periods. With this point in mind, let us consider the key events in each period associated with broadcasting in South Africa.

### 1.2.1 From 1919 to 1936: The establishment of radio in South Africa

*Amateur broadcasts*

We can identify three prominent amateurs who offered broadcasts following the lifting of restrictions on the use of radio following World War I. They are:

- John Samuel Streeter, who broadcast gramophone concerts on a weekly basis, first from Sea Point and then from Observatory, Cape Town.
- Reginald Hopkins, who broadcast pianola music together with messages from his home in Wynberg, Cape Town.
- Arthur Sydney Innes, who broadcast programmes of gramophone recordings from his radio station, known as 20B, located in Observatory, Johannesburg.

The programmes provided by these amateur operators were popularly received and reportedly heard well into the Karoo. However, listeners had to build their own receivers in order to hear the programmes. As the popularity of radio as a means of entertainment grew, so too did the realisation that radio was becoming more than just a pastime for a few select enthusiasts, and radio moved into the next important stage in its development.

## Experimental broadcasts

A series of sixteen concerts were broadcast from South African Railways headquarters in Johannesburg, beginning 18 December 1923. The aim of these concerts was to raise funds for the Empire Exhibition. Each of the Railway broadcasts lasted two hours. As few people owned receivers, arrangements were made for group listening at the Railway Institutes located at Witbank, Germiston and Pretoria. Western Electric, who saw the experiments as a business opportunity, provided the transmitting and receiver equipment. Although intended for a specific audience, the broadcasts could be heard throughout the country by those who had access to receivers.

## The first regular broadcasts

Following the popularity of the amateur and experimental broadcasts, the government called for applications for licences to provide regular and sustained radio broadcasts. However, the licences were limited to one per metropolitan area. Regular broadcasts began in Johannesburg on 1 July 1924, when the Associated Scientific and Technical Societies (AS&TS) took over the equipment used for the Railway broadcasts and began broadcasting as Station JB. Licences were also granted to the Cape Peninsula Publicity Association which began broadcasts from Cape Town on 15 September 1924, and the Durban City Corporation, which followed with broadcasts on 10 December 1924. The three radio stations tried various schemes to raise capital and improve their financial positions, such as the sale of advertising on air. But despite these efforts, these three stations only remained operational for some two years before being forced to consider closure, largely due to a lack of financial sustainablity.

## The African Broadcasting Company

In 1927 the Johannesburg millionaire, IW Schlesinger, took over the broadcasting operations of the three fledgling radio stations with the consent of the government, amalgamating them to form the African Broadcasting Company (ABC). This brought about the centralisation and standardisation of production. However, the use of landlines to distribute signals to Durban and Cape Town resulted in sub-standard quality programmes, while the growth in income from listeners' licences was dismal. A crisis point was reached in March 1929 when expenditure soared.

To avert yet another financial crisis, the *Blue Free Voucher Scheme* was introduced. This was an arrangement between ABC and the retailers of radio sets, whereby ABC stopped leasing radio sets to listeners while the dealers offered new sets at a discount. Part of the discount went to paying the licence fee. The scheme was highly effective in generating income, but by 1935 the ABC was again in financial difficulty. At the same time, the government considered broadcasting as too important to be left to commercial organisations. An investigation by Sir John Reith of the BBC, which resulted in the Reith Report, recommended that the ABC be developed as a public corporation free of government control or political motivation. An emphasis was to be placed on high quality programming. Also, the difficulties of broadcasting to the whole of South Africa had to be resolved.

### 1.2.2 From 1936 to 1948: The South African Broadcasting Corporation

*Formation of the SABC*

Reith's report was debated in Parliament and resulted in the Broadcasting Act, no. 22 of 1936 which was passed on 1 August 1936, the same day on which the South African Broadcasting Corporation (SABC) began to function as an entity. The SABC was modelled largely on the BBC, with the exception that the SABC was not subject to regular commissions of inquiry. An amount of £150 000 was advanced by Sanlam as capital for the new SABC.

*Broadcasts in Afrikaans*

Up to this point, programming was predominantly in English, but section 14 of the Broadcasting Act of 1936 provided for Afrikaans broadcasts. However, providing programmes for Afrikaans listeners by means of a bilingual service proved problematic. At this time, the majority of Afrikaners lived in rural areas and the medium-wave signal just did not reach these areas of the country satisfactorily. To try and resolve the problem, a short-wave service was introduced. Although initiated by efforts to provide a service for Afrikaans listeners, this short-wave service was technically inferior and quickly became a point of contention. The signal would fade suddenly and was subject to severe distortion by summer thunderstorms, while the listener was required to make several frequency changes during the course of the day. The division of time between English and Afrikaans was in a ratio of 8:2. The minimal amount of time devoted to Afrikaans-language programmes, in addition to technical problems, did not encourage listeners to tune-in (Tomaselli et al 1989:37).

The re-enactment of the Great Trek in 1938 was a stimulus in the development of Afrikaans broadcasting. Audience demand for coverage of the event quickly revealed the many shortcomings in the organisation of a nationwide service. The solution, it was felt, was to split the service. And so, in 1938, the short-wave service carried only Afrikaans programming, becoming known as the B Programme (today's RSG), while the medium-wave service continued with English programming, under the somewhat superior sounding moniker of the A Programme (today's SAfm). Thus, we can say that from its very beginnings, the development of the new SABC was shaped, not only by the geographic size and nature of the country and the limitations of technology, but also the ideology of the time.

### 1.2.3 From 1948 to 1960: Post-World War II expansion

#### *Introduction of news services*

As with the growth of radio in the United States and Britain, there was a strained relationship between the fledgling radio stations and the South African press over the presentation of news. In an agreement with the press, Station JB could only broadcast news that had already appeared in print. The SABC, in 1936, reached an agreement with the South African Press Association (SAPA) to provide four news bulletins a day. The SABC had no control over the content or organisation of these bulletins until the SABC created an internal news department in 1950. This also signalled the end of relaying news bulletins from the BBC in London. The first SABC-produced news bulletin was aired at 07:00 on 17 July 1950. As the news department expanded, so the number of bulletins offered was increased, reaching six per day in October 1950.

#### *Commercialisation*

By 1946, as with the ABC and its predecessors, the SABC was beginning to experience financial difficulties. Two methods were tried to relieve the financial burden: one was to exempt the SABC from paying income tax; a second was to reduce the Post Office share of the licence fee to one percent. These moves were to little avail, and the only way out was to consider a move to commercialisation and sell advertising time on air. The revenue received from the sale of advertising on one station would then subsidise the remaining stations. The Schoch Commission was appointed in 1946 to investigate the matter, as part of a number of other broadcasting issues.

The resulting report was presented in February 1948 and recommended that commercial broadcasting be established alongside that of the SABC. The commercial station would then be taxed at ten percent of its gross revenue, which would be used to subsidise the SABC. The SABC would then continue to produce quality programmes reflecting high culture. Other than from advertising agencies and the SABC, there was little enthusiasm for the introduction of a commercial service (Tomaselli et al 1989:42–44). In the meanwhile, a Nationalist Government had come to power and it saw things differently. Rather than permitting the introduction of independent broadcasting, the recommended commercial service was to be part of the SABC. The purpose now was not to provide additional income as originally intended, but rather to expand the transmitter network and provide for additional Afrikaans programming (Tomaselli et al 1989:37).

Thus, Springbok Radio was launched on 1 May 1950 as a bilingual commercial service. Springbok Radio soon proved to be highly popular with listeners, and is particularly remembered for the abundant number of soap operas, comedy shows, quiz shows and dramas that made up its programme schedule. However, with the coming of television to South Africa in the late seventies, many of these programmes moved to the newer medium, resulting in an audience loss for Springbok Radio. While unable to compete with television, Springbok Radio closed down in late 1985, but commercial radio had become firmly established as part of the South African broadcasting environment.

## Programming for black listeners

Despite the point that in his report, Reith made mention of special programmes for language groups other than English and Afrikaans, at no point was this ever given consideration by the government. It was only during the course of World War II that an initial, but unsuccessful, attempt was made at providing night-time programming for black listeners. This was done using telephone lines to compounds, hostels and major townships. There was also an additional morning broadcast three times a week on the English and Afrikaans medium-wave services. Following the end of the war in 1945, the service was withdrawn. The system was costly to maintain, while income from black listeners could not provide sufficient revenue to keep the service going. This service is generally assumed to have been a pro-English propaganda exercise as a war-time contingency measure (Tomaselli et al 1989:39–41).

Starting in 1949, a half-hour programme was transmitted daily on the English and Afrikaans medium-wave services in IsiZulu, IsiXhosa and Sesotho. In August 1952 a redifussion service (relaying of programmes by cable from a central receiver) was installed in Orlando, south of Johannesburg. Loudspeakers were hired out to subscribers and installed in their homes, and sixteen hours of programming were provided daily. Over the next seven years the service was extended to neighbouring townships. The service peaked in 1956 with fourteen thousand subscribers and then declined as forced removals to the new townships took place (Tomaselli et al 1989:51–53). The SABC was keen to extend the service to all townships, but was prevented from doing this by the government. Tomaselli et al (1989:52) offer three possible reasons for this. The installations were expensive and gave an image of permanency when the black townships were considered merely a temporary phenomenon. There was conflict between the Director-General, Gideon Roos, and the SABC Board and the implementation of FM services was imminent. As an interim measure, the daily half-hour programme on the medium-wave services was extended to a full hour.

### 1.2.4 From 1960 to 1971: A period of transformation

## Introduction of FM

In order to provide listeners with better reception and more channels, plans were begun in 1960 for the introduction of FM (frequency modulation) services, which provided for improved radio reception over a distance of about 60 kilometres. This would allow for six additional radio channels, sufficient for the three existing stations (i.e. the English and Afrikaans Services and Springbok Radio) while also allowing for the creation of three new regional channels. However, the cost was enormous (R40-million was provided by the government) and this almost crippled the SABC financially. The network required the installation of some 500 new transmitters, complete with towers for the antennas, across the country (de Villiers 1993:130). On 25 December 1961, the three existing services began FM broadcasts from the SABC tower in Johannesburg, followed shortly by Radio Zulu and Radio Sesotho. The first regional radio service, Radio Highveld, was started on 1 September 1964. This was followed by Radio Tsonga and Radio Venda on 1 February 1965, Radio Good Hope on 1 July 1965 in Cape Town and Radio Port Natal (later to become East Coast Radio) on 1 May 1967 in Durban. These regional stations operated according to a strict programme formula that consisted mainly of middle-of-the-road music, advertising and abbreviated news bulletins. Initially these channels brought in many new listeners without any loss to the existing radio services.

## Station automation

The three regional stations, Radio Highveld, Radio Good Hope and Radio Port Natal, were fully automated in 1969. Announcements, advertisements and music were all recorded well in advance on separate tapes and then played automatically throughout the day and night in a predetermined order. The sequence was regulated by means of inaudible pulses on the recording tape.

Theoretically, station automation reduces the costs of running a radio station. An automated radio station requires exceptionally few personnel thus cutting costs by reducing salaries and expenses. Some 115 SABC staff members were made redundant by station automation, which helped to reduce the financial burden brought about by the introduction of FM broadcasts. The SABC's decision to introduce station automation also had an ideological benefit. Automation allows for greater control of programme content by station management. This meant that all programme content could be checked to comply with policy before being broadcast. This coincided with a new programming policy that actively promoted national interests. The end result was blandness in programme quality that ultimately cost the SABC dearly in terms of listener numbers, particularly when the independent stations of Capital Radio and Radio 702 came on air.

## African language services

The first full-scale radio stations aimed at black listeners only came into being with the introduction of FM transmissions. The service was collectively known as Radio Bantu. The first FM transmissions in Sesotho (Radio Sesotho) and IsiZulu (Radio Zulu) were broadcast on 1 January 1962, and from 1 July 1962 the same programmes were presented in North Sotho (Radio Lebowa) and Setswana (Radio Setswana). On 1 February 1963 IsiZulu transmissions were introduced in Natal, while on 1 June 1963,

# MEDIA STUDIES

Radio Xhosa began broadcasting from Grahamstown. As the FM network expanded throughout the country, so programming on the medium-wave services was phased out. Only when the FM network was completed was the redifussion system finally closed down. Programming consisted primarily of traditional choir and jazz music until the early 1960s when jive was added. Discussions were limited to topics lacking overt political content. News was patronisingly insular, in that content emphasised local news, almost to the exclusion of international events. The SABC made the presumption that an emphasis on local items best served the needs of black listeners (Tomaselli et al 1989:73). In 1960 the Bantu Programmes Control Board was created, through which all programme content was controlled by thirty-five white staff with a knowledge of black languages, in order to prevent any disparaging comments from being made on air regarding government policies (Tomaselli et al 1989:60).

## 1.2.5 From 1971 to 1981: A period of challenge

### Introduction of television

During the 1950s and 1960s, the Nationalist Government vehemently opposed the introduction of television on moral and ethical grounds. In 1971 the Meyer Commission was appointed to investigate the possibility of introducing television to South Africa. One of the findings of the Commission was that in a country with a diverse culture and multiplicity of languages, such as found in South Africa, television should be used "to advance the self-development of all its peoples and to foster their pride in their own identity and culture" (Mersham 1993:175). As this thinking was in line with the ideology of the government, the proposals of the Meyer Commission were accepted. On 27 April 1971 the government announced that the SABC was to provide a television service. The SABC's first test broadcasts began on 5 May 1975 and a regular service was introduced on 5 January 1976. The service initially provided 37 hours of programming a week on one channel in English and Afrikaans. Advertising on television began in January 1978. A second SABC service, TV2/3, began on 1 January 1982, splitting into two separate channels on 30 March 1985. Gradually additional stations came on air: Bop-TV on 31 December 1983, M-Net on 1 October 1986, Trinity Broadcasting Network (a religious television service) in the Ciskei (now part of the Eastern Cape) on 3 December 1986, and e.tv much later on 1 October 1998.

### The coming of independent radio

The government's policy of creating the so-called independent national states of Transkei, Bophuthatswana, Venda and Ciskei created a loophole that permitted independent radio to begin. Simply put, South African legislation was not valid in these independent states. Therefore, protective laws granting a monopoly to the SABC were not binding in these states. As a result, stations such as Capital Radio, Radio 702, Radio Bop and Radio Thohoyandou came on the air, providing their transmitter sites were located in one of the independent homelands. However, programmes and signals were directed at the major urban areas within South Africa. These stations made a major impact on radio listeners as they often presented alternative points of view and programming not heard on SABC stations at that time. In addition, the independent stations made big inroads into SABC radio audiences simply by providing better quality programming.

### 1.2.6 From 1981 to 1992: The rationalisation of broadcasting

This ten-year period saw two major investigations into South African media, each putting forward differing points of view. It is also during this period that we note the beginnings of major changes to the broadcasting environment in South Africa. For example, in anticipation of future developments, the SABC embraced Thatcherite policies by commercialising the corporation through a division into various business units.

#### *The Steyn Commission, 1981*

The Steyn Commission (South Africa 1981) was an extensive investigation into the media. The resulting report was highly criticised as pandering to government ideology. Yet, the Steyn Commission made four important recommendations regarding broadcasting:
- Government control of the SABC needed to be relaxed in order to ensure the autonomy and impartiality of the broadcaster.
- The SABC Board should be opened to all interest groups and not be limited to white members only, while the Board would no longer be responsible to any particular minister, but rather the head of state.
- The Department of National Education should work in close collaboration with the SABC in order to realise the full potential of broadcasting in education.
- The creation of independent radio within South Africa should be allowed. This last recommendation was not received favourably as the government considered independent broadcasting to be detrimental to the national interest.

#### *Bop-TV*

Bop-TV came on the air on 31 December 1983 as an initiative of the Government of Bophuthatswana. Initially, the station used the SABC's distribution network (now Sentec) to transmit their signals. By airing popular international programmes and avoiding a pro-government approach to their news, Bop-TV attracted a fairly large number of white viewers away from the SABC's TV1 (now SABC2). In retaliation, the SABC blocked the signals for Bop-TV so that the station could only be received in Soweto, on the pretext that the service was originally intended only for Bophuthatswana citizens living in the townships. When it became obvious that Bop-TV was also more popular than TV2 and TV3, the focus of the signal was narrowed even further to areas of Soweto where Tswana-speaking residents were concentrated (Mersham 1993:183).

Over the years, Bop-TV has tried to expand its service to a larger part of South Africa but owing to opposition from the SABC it has had little success. In 1988 Bop-TV hired transmitters and began broadcasting by satellite. On 1 March 1998, Bop-TV was formally incorporated into the SABC. However, there is still uncertainty regarding the future of the service, which continues to remain available only to a narrow audience located in the townships.

## M-Net

M-Net began broadcasting on 1 October 1986 as the first over-the-air subscription television service in the Southern Hemisphere. M-Net came into being as a direct result of growing concern by the major newspaper groups over the rampant commercialisation of the SABC. This translated into a considerable loss of advertising revenue for the press. For example, the adspend (the amount of money advertisers are prepared to spend on advertising) in the press dropped from 86 percent in 1977 to 51 percent in 1990, while that for radio and television rose from 17 percent to 44 percent for the same period. A proposal for a subscription television service, managed and owned by a consortium formed by the major English and Afrikaans newspaper groups, was put to the government in 1984 by the management of Nasionale Pers. As a concession, the Government approved of the proposal, provided the channel limited itself to providing entertainment programmes and did not broadcast news. Effectively the new service was then not in competition with the SABC as an information provider, over which the government exerted a strong influence. The name "M-Net" was selected as an acronym for "media-network", indicating the original ownership of the service by the various press groups. Since its beginnings as an individual subscription service in 1986, M-Net has undergone radical change and immense growth. In 1990, M-Net was listed on the Johannesburg Stock Exchange (now the Johannesburg Securities Exchange) which introduced a large number of individuals as shareholders. However, the major press groups still retain the majority of shares. The following year, in 1991, M-Net began an aggressive penetration of the international market to become a truly global organisation, beginning with the acquisition of a stake in FilmNet, a service that operates in Belgium, the Netherlands and Luxembourg. Soon after that, in 1992, M-Net launched an international service into Africa. From its beginnings as a subscription service in 1986, M-Net has undergone radical change and immense growth. Some of the developments are indicated in Table 1.1.

## The Viljoen Commission, 1991

Coming a decade after the Steyn Commission, the purpose of the Viljoen Commission (South Africa 1991) was to investigate the future direction of broadcasting in South Africa. The major recommendations made by the Commission were the following:
- The setting up of an Independent Broadcasting Authority.

# A South African Media Map

- Commercial broadcasting should be subject to fewer restrictions than public broadcasting.
- The ownership of radio and television stations should be limited.
- The SABC should become a public service broadcaster.
- The deregulation of broadcasting should begin with the introduction of community radio services.

### Table 1.1 Highlights in the development of M-Net

| | The Development of M-Net |
|---|---|
| 1986 | • M-Net begins an encrypted over-the-air subscription service |
| 1990 | • M-Net listed on the Johannesburg Stock Exchange. Shares are offered to all existing subscribers |
| 1991 | • Global acquisitions begin with the purchase of a stake in FilmNet, which allows access to Belgium, the Netherlands and Luxembourg |
| 1992 | • M-Net launches the long-running South African soapy, *Egoli* |
| 1993 | • M-Net splits into two companies: M-Net, which is responsible for programming, and MultiChoice, which is responsible for managing the subscriber database |
| 1994 | • MTN established with M-Net/MultiChoice as one of the major shareholders through a subsidiary company, M-Cell<br>• Acquires Telepiu |
| 1995 | • Entry into the Greek market<br>• MultiChoice lists on the Johannesburg Stock Exchange as a separate entity and becomes the dominant partner<br>• M-Net's international service is launched into Africa, via satellite |
| 1996 | • Scandinavia, Central Europe, Africa and the Middle East are added to the MultiChoice market<br>• MultiChoice now known as MultiChoice International Holdings or MIH<br>• DStv platform launched offering 28 TV and 46 audio channels, using direct broadcast satellite technology |
| 1997 | • MIH stake in Europe, worth some $2-billion, sold to competitor Canal Plus in order to apply the acquired funds to acquisitions in Thailand<br>• MIH enters the Internet business with the launch of M-Web |
| 1998 | • MIH merges with its Thailand competitor, UTV, to form UBC |
| 1999 | • M-Net launches a new Afrikaans channel, KYKnet, featuring magazine and youth programmes, Afrikaans films, drama series, news and a late-night talk show<br>• M-Net licence amendment takes effect, with the introduction of a 2 percent levy on the company's annual revenue |

The Viljoen Commission was also not without its critics. From its very inception, the Commission was labelled as being unrepresentative of the broader South African community. This led to concerns that, as with the Steyn Commission, the findings would be within the ideology of government and that the strong bias towards the promotion of the Nationalist Government by the SABC would continue. However, these fears were allayed when the report was released and clearly indicated that dramatic changes were on the cards for broadcasting in South Africa.

### 1.2.7 From 1992 to the present: The restructuring of broadcasting

*The beginning of community radio*

Following the release of the Viljoen Commission's report, there was extensive lobbying for the restructuring of broadcasting. Following a period of hiatus, a number of new stations came onto the air with a limited geographic range and for a limited period of time, usually about three weeks, with a temporary broadcast licence issued by the Department of Home Affairs. These stations were usually linked to some or other cultural event, such as the Rand Easter Show. The first radio station to operate legally under the new dispensation was that of Festival FM. This station broadcast for only ten days, from 09:00 until 18:00, as part of the Grahamstown National Arts Festival, beginning 27 June 1991. The purpose of the station was to provide information regarding the Festival in the form of news bulletins on the half-hour. The rest of the time was filled by interviews with Festival performers, celebrities and music. With hindsight, the organisation of Festival FM can be seen to have been, at best, haphazard. No audience research was done and as the announcers were students, the music selection was limited to pop and heavy metal genres. The limited selection of music quickly alienated many listeners.

The temporal state of community broadcasting continued until 1995 when the Independent Broadcasting Authority (IBA) finally issued a number of temporary licences that allowed stations to broadcast for a period of one year. Some ninety stations went on air, covering a wide range of interests from religious and campus stations on one hand, to wildlife and community development on the other. (See Unit 13 in Volume 2, for a more detailed discussion of community radio in South Africa.)

*The establishment of the IBA*

The creation of the Independent Broadcasting Authority (IBA) was an outcome of the Multi-Party Negotiation Forum, held at the World Trade Centre (now Caesars, a hotel and casino complex) during 1993. The purpose of creating the IBA was to distance the SABC from Government in order to give the SABC greater credibility as a purveyor of news and information, particularly regarding the upcoming democratic elections in South Africa during 1994. The role of the IBA was to generate policy regarding broadcasting, to issue broadcast licences and to regulate and monitor the activities of broadcasters.

The IBA was placed in a unique regulatory position where it had firstly to establish the criteria for licence applications before it could actually start to function as a regulator. This action resulted in the Triple Inquiry Report, which was only published some two years later in 1995. The report concerned itself with three basic issues:

- The protection and viability of public broadcasting – it was recommended that the financially lucrative regional radio stations operated by the SABC be sold off.
- The percentage local content of radio and television stations – although differing percentages were recommended for the different types of broadcasting, broadly speaking the recommendation was that local content constitute at least 50 percent of programming by the year 2000. This target was never reached, however, and became the subject of further discussion in 2001.
- The establishment of criteria regarding cross-media ownership – no one person may own more than one television station, two FM and two medium-wave radio stations. This was to encourage diversity in ownership. However, a newspaper may not have an interest in both a radio and television station at the same time. There were further limits placed on newspaper ownership of radio and television stations. For example, a newspaper that exceeds 15 percent of the total distribution within its circulation area may not have any financial interest in a radio or television station in that area.

Additionally, the Report recommended that radio stations owned by the former TBVC states (Transkei, Bophuthatswana, Venda and Ciskei) were to merge with the SABC, or be sold, or that the frequency be considered for a community station.

**Figure 1.1 Corruption on the part of some IBA officials did much to dent the credibility of the Authority** (*Sowetan*, 22 April 1997)

Despite bringing about major changes to the broadcasting environment, the IBA was often heavily criticised. For example, the IBA was seen as being exceedingly slow in concluding investigations and issuing licences because the Authority was reluctant to draw on expertise in the industry. The fact that the IBA was required to establish policy as well as regulate that policy was seen by many as a serious conflict of interest that affected the objectivity of the Authority in its activities. The Authority was also dogged by a number of scandals involving impropriety in the activities of some key personnel, as illustrated in the cartoon in Figure 1.1. All told, these aspects had a negative impact on the Authority's credibility and further delayed the issuing of new licences. A discussion of this, and other problems, is furthered in Case study 1.1. On 1 July 2000, the IBA was amalgamated with the South African Telecommunications Regulatory Authority (Satra) to form the Independent Communications Authority of South Africa (ICASA).

**Case study 1.1:** Establishing the credibility of the IBA as regulator of broadcasting

### Satra and IBA successor must avoid woes of past

The new regulatory institution needs to start with a clean slate, writes THABO KOBOKOANE

In 1997 the Independent Broadcasting Authority faced a crisis of financial mismanagement as well as allegations of political interference after it announced Midi Television was the winner of a free-to-air TV licence.

Two years later, relative calm has returned to the IBA, but a crisis is unfolding at sister regulator, the SA Telecommunications Authority (Satra), as the adjudication over the lucrative third cell licence becomes a farce.

Crisis is, clearly, nothing new to either body. The question is how government avoids similar problems befalling the new regulatory institution that is to replace Satra and the IBA, as well as ensure its credibility.

First, the new Independent Communications Authority of SA must have a clean slate. This means that the embarrassment that has become the third cell licence should be resolved speedily. Irrespective of what happens now, the damage to the credibility and reputation of SA regulatory and licensing institutions has been done and the longer it goes on, the messier it gets.

Second, and more pressing for government, is how to avoid the same pitfalls in the future. Past problems at Satra and the IBA should be seen as growing pains – these are sometimes unavoidable for start-ups – but should on no account be repeated.

The new body will potentially preside over the adjudication of a fourth cell licence, the issuing of another television licence, and new private radio stations. So it can't afford to get things wrong.

Councillors of both Satra and the IBA have made impassioned pleas in their submissions to the Parliamentary Portfolio Committee on Communications for the independence of the new body to be guaranteed. This suggests both these institutions did not, and are not enjoying this independence.

A previous councillor of the broadcasting regulator, who declines to be named, cites interference by the Department of Communications in the affairs of the IBA. The extent to which it is prevalent, if at all, remains unknown unless present and previous councillors break their silence.

IBA Chairman Mandla Langa says: "There have been trying times in the IBA's attempts to execute its mandate, but in all of these instances there have thorough debates with the department of Communications."

Part of the problem – and this is true for new institutions – is that there has been a lack of clarity about the difference between the role of the IBA and that of the Department of Communications. Issues have been fudged because of overlapping responsibilities.

For example, it is not clear whether it was the Cabinet's prerogative to decide that no operator had exclusivity over the GSM 1800 spectrum, a decision many felt fell within the gambit of Satra.

Satra, which has held hearings on the matter, is yet to announce its findings. If they conflict with government's view, it will cause confusion in the marketplace.

The choice of councillors, particularly the appointment of a chairman, will remain a key issue.

The first batch of councillors at the IBA were always going to find the going tough. After all, they were negotiating new and unfamiliar territory in which the rules were not clear-cut. When the auditor-general uncovered widespread abuse of credit cards and lack of financial management at this institution, one councillor resigned, taking collective responsibility for the mess.

Beginning with the leadership of Felleng Sekha and now Langa, the IBA has since stabilised.

Sekha, in particular, is credited with laying most of the ground-work for restoring the credibility of the IBA.

More importantly, Sekha was never shy of speaking out, even against those in government. Sekha's shortcoming may have been her lack of political support, something which Langa seems to enjoy. Both also have a strong broadcasting background.

The new batch of seven councillors will have to balance the interests of broadcasting and telecommunications, which means they will have to have strong experience in both industries. Concern has been that telecommunications will swamp broadcasting interests.

Just as important to bear in mind is the revelation this week by Langa that most of the private radio stations licensed by the IBA have yet to make money.

This goes for e.tv as well, which recently signed an agreement with Rembrandt under which the industrial giant will take an indirect 26% stake in Midi television, e.tv's parent.

(*Sunday Times Business Times*, 23 April 2000:4)

## Restructuring of the SABC

As part of the new dispensation for broadcasting in South Africa, and in order to meet the challenge brought about by many new competitors, the SABC entered into a lengthy, and as yet incomplete, phase of restructuring in order to fulfil its new role as that of the nation's public broadcaster. Despite a much hoped for turn around of the SABC, the Corporation continues to endure many problems. For example, the SABC experienced yet another financial crisis, aggravated largely over the preceding decade by the growth of a culture of non-payment of television licence fees initiated by disadvantaged communities as protest against the Apartheid system. Piracy peaked at 57 percent of all viewers during 1997, resulting in a revenue loss of some R900-million a year to the SABC (South African Broadcasting Corporation 1999:9). In addition, the Astrasat project, an analogue free-to-air satellite service that began operating during July 1996, was finally abandoned in February 1998 as a dismal failure, resulting in a write-off of R143-million.

As part of the restructuring process, six of the SABC's seven highly successful and lucrative regional commercial stations had to be sold to the private sector. It was hoped that the income generated from the sale of these radio stations could be used to offset the financial difficulties that beset the Corporation. But it was a bitter pill for the SABC to swallow when the income from the sale of these radio stations went to the Treasury instead. With the assistance of outside consultants, McKinsey and Associates, the SABC managed to turn around its financial deficit and recorded a budget surplus of R122-million by the end of March 1999 (South African Broadcasting Corporation 1999:9). But this turn-around came at a price – local content was decreased while the use of English was increased to maximise advertising revenue (Duncan, 2000). This situation is graphically illustrated in the cartoon in Figure 1.2.

**Figure 1.2 Resolving the financial woes of the SABC meant abandoning some public broadcasting principles** (*City Press*, 6 March 1997)

The SABC still has to deal with the problem of credibility, particularly as a provider of news, notwithstanding having a large and efficient news department. In addition, the matter of low staff morale remains a thorny issue, despite the fact that the SABC has undergone an effective period of transformation and has advanced a large percentage of black personnel. The Corporation has also been rocked by a number of scandals, including that of corruption and maladministration, which has resulted in a rapid turnover of management.

## e.tv

The brief history of e.tv clearly illustrates how important politics and economics are in the operation of the media. From the announcement in April 1998 that the Midi group was awarded the first free-to-air commercial television licence in South Africa, the station has been awash with criticism and controversy, beginning with allegations of political interference in allocation of the licence (Kobokoane 1999a:1). The major shareholders of Midi included at that time Hosken Consolidated Investments (HCI) (26%), Vula Communications (25%) and Time Warner (20%), the balance made up of a number of minority shareholders, namely the Mineworkers Investment Company (4%), the SA Clothing and Textile Workers Union (4%), with the remaining 21 percent spread between Mopani Media, RM Productions, Medumo Media, Youth Development Trust, Disabled Employment Concerns and African Pioneers Investment Trust (Klein 1999a:3; Kobokoane 1999a:1).

Broadcasts started on 1 October 1998 and e.tv aimed for 15 percent of market share and 10 percent of adspend within the first year of operation, rising eventually to 30 percent by 2007. Within its first week of operation the station was highly criticised for reneging on its initial promises of providing indigenous programming, and instead focused largely on American material (Pokwana 1998:23). In addition to these harsh comments from the critics, the IBA threatened to withdraw e.tv's licence. However, the matter was referred instead to the Broadcasting Monitoring and Complaint Commission (BMCC), which was then a subdivision of the IBA, where e.tv could account for the violations of its licence agreement (Hlophe 1999:6). The seven contraventions cited included:

- not enough black African language, information and children's programming (each counting as a separate violation)
- the length of broadcasts
- airing more advertisements than permitted
- not providing a structure for public complaints
- not keeping proper records.

A further dispute also arose between e.tv and the IBA over the station's delayed commencement of news bulletins, which were scheduled to begin 1 December 1998. The delay was attributed by e.tv to dilatory customs officials who refused to clear shipments of equipment needed for the news service. However, the IBA considered the postponement of e.tv's news service as being unfair to the public, as the licence was issued on condition that the station would cater to the needs of all South Africans. The dispute between e.tv and the IBA on one hand, and public criticism of programming on the other hand, overshadowed a third crisis which threatened the introduction of news bulletins when journalists threatened to stage a walkout. This situation resulted from strained relations between e.tv journalists and management relating to a number of problems. Staff made claims that contracts did not comply with labour laws; editorial positions were filled by incompetent staff; quality control was inefficient; and that they were threatened by the CEO, Mr Jonathan Procter, for no reason (Malefane 1999:8) and warned of a possible 20 percent salary cut (Nxumalo & Hlope 1999:13).

The news service finally took to the air on 1 February 1999, and was strategically placed one hour ahead of the flagship bulletin presented by the SABC on SABC3 at 8 pm (Freedom of Expression Institute 1998). The presentation was seen as refreshingly informal from that offered by the SABC, where the news anchor (a person acting as the main presenter in a programme that has many components) sat, in a relaxed manner, on the edge of a desk located in the newsroom, with working journalists in the background and presented the news in a conversational style (Banda 1999:3; Hagen 1999:1; Wrottersley 1999:5). A strong plus is the fact that viewers regard e.tv as truly independent and objective in its news coverage (Klein 1999a:3).

The strained relations between e.tv and the IBA over the station's licence conditions continued, fuelled by the opinion on the part of e.tv that some of the licence conditions were unenforceable (Banda 1999b:14). The strained relationship between the two bodies even became the subject of an editorial cartoon, illustrated in Figure 1.3. By February 1999, while the issue concerning licence conditions had not yet reached any form of resolution, a financial crisis had brought the station to the brink of bankruptcy – e.tv's monthly expenditure of R15-million could not be offset by an advertising revenue of R7-million (Klein 1999b:3). This financial dilemma came to a head as the minority shareholders failed to come forward with their allocation of the capital, leaving HCI to shoulder a larger than expected financial burden (Kobokoane 1999a:1). As a result of their inability to raise the necessary finances, these minority shareholders would lose their shareholding to HCI. A proposal was put to the IBA for an amendment to the shareholder structure, which would leave HCI with a much larger share of Midi. The IBA rejected this initial proposal arguing that the licence had been granted to Midi simply because of the number of empowerment groups within its structure.

Tensions also grew between HCI and Vula Communications, who by May 1999 had only met half of their financial obligations to the Midi Group. This led to a number of spats that boiled over into a power struggle for control of the consortium (Kobokoane 1999b:1), resulting in the resignation of Jonathan Procter, CEO of Midi Television, with immediate effect (Koenderman 1999c:33). Procter's position was taken over by Marcel Golding, the chairman of HCI (Hills 1999:1).

# A South African Media Map

**Figure 1.3 e.tv's initial financial problems and licence contraventions placed the IBA in a compromising position** (*Sowetan*, 4 December 1998)

HCI then submitted a subsequent proposal to the IBA whereby a special purpose vehicle (SPV), known as Sabido, would be created to house the interests of the shares owned by minority groups until such time as they could raise the necessary capital over a period of three to five years. This revised application by HCI put pressure on the IBA, who as regulator, was bound to uphold legislation, but at the same time could not allow the Midi Group to disintegrate. With hindsight, it was blatantly clear that from the very beginning e.tv could never meet the requirements of its licence and formally applied to the IBA for amendments. On the ensuing dilemma facing the IBA regarding this issue, Moerdyk (1999a:15) writes:

> If on one hand it [the IBA] simply dismisses e.tv's application and forces the station to stick to its original commitments, there is very little chance that South Africa's showcase of black empowerment broadcasting will be able to survive.
>
> And if e.tv folds it is highly unlikely that any of the original consortia will again be prepared to risk gambling millions of rand on another pitching process and would probably be even more unlikely to gamble investing in a television enterprise so strangled by regulation.
>
> On the other hand, if the IBA makes concessions to e.tv it will be seen to be a travesty of justice second to none. Particularly those who lost the race for the licence and claimed at the time that e.tv ... knew full well that ... many conditions would have to be amended to ensure viability.

The IBA created a major problem for itself by initially insisting on such stringent operating conditions for the new station and for not allowing market forces to

# MEDIA STUDIES

determine issues such as local content, advertising quotas and programming (Moerdyk 1999a:15). In a face-saving exercise, Midi TV withdrew some of the more controversial aspects regarding local content quotas and use of independent production companies in its application for amendment to its licence (Magardie 2000:7). While the requested amendments to its shareholding structure were granted in December 1999, the problems regarding programming remained unresolved. This meant the station now had three shareholders, Sabido (70%), Time Warner (20%) and Vula Communications (10%) (De Ionno 2000:1). The request to amend human resource obligations, so that more coloured and Indian personnel could be employed, was rejected on the ground that the station needed to reflect the population of the entire country (Magardie 2000:7). The IBA's solution to the whole problem was dictated by a need to preserve black empowerment (Lloyd 2000:22).

Despite all the tensions and problems, both within the Midi Group, and with the IBA, e.tv has proved a success and from a rapid growth in ratings has demonstrated that it has firmly entrenched itself within the South African media environment, gaining a loyal viewership, and is posing a serious threat to the SABC's dominance of free-to-air services.

## 1.2.8 The South African broadcasting environment

The penetration of radio and television receivers among the South African population can be considered as among the highest in the continent. The way in which South Africa compares with other Africa countries regarding the penetration of radio is briefly indicated in Table 1.2, while television is indicated in Table 1.3. The importance of radio and television as a medium in South Africa is clearly indicated by the high concentration of radio per one thousand inhabitants, matched only by that of Egypt.

**Table 1.2 Number of radio receivers in selected African countries**
(United Nations 1997; 2000)

| | \multicolumn{6}{c}{Number of Radio Receivers (Thousands)} |
|---|---|---|---|---|---|---|
| | S Africa | Nigeria | Egypt | Kenya | Zimbabwe | Zambia |
| 1980 | 8 000 | 7 000 | 6 000 | 650 | 240 | 135 |
| 1985 | 10 000 | 14 500 | 12 000 | 1 600 | 500 | 500 |
| 1990 | 11 450 | 18 700 | 17 000 | 2 000 | 832 | 650 |
| 1995 | 13 100 | 22 000 | 19 400 | 2 600 | 1 000 | 800 |
| 1996 | 13 400 | 22 700 | 20 000 | 3 000 | 1 100 | 1 000 |
| 1997 | 13 750 | 23 500 | 29 500 | 3 070 | 1 140 | 1 030 |

| | \multicolumn{6}{c|}{Receivers per 1 000 inhabitants} |
|---|---|---|---|---|---|---|
| 1980 | 274 | 97 | 137 | 39 | 34 | 24 |
| 1985 | 303 | 175 | 241 | 81 | 60 | 78 |
| 1990 | 337 | 215 | 302 | 85 | 84 | 90 |
| 1995 | 350 | 222 | 311 | 96 | 92 | 98 |
| 1996 | 351 | 224 | 315 | 108 | 100 | 119 |
| 1997 | 355 | 226 | 317 | 108 | 102 | 120 |

**Table 1.3 Number of television receivers in selected African countries** (United Nations 1997; 2000)

| | \multicolumn{6}{c|}{Number of Television Receivers (Thousands)} |
|---|---|---|---|---|---|---|
| | S Africa | Nigeria | Egypt | Kenya | Zimbabwe | Zambia |
| 1980 | 2 010 | 550 | 1 400 | 62 | 73 | 60 |
| 1985 | 3 000 | 1 000 | 3 860 | 100 | 178 | 90 |
| 1990 | 3 700 | 3 500 | 5 700 | 225 | 260 | 210 |
| 1995 | 4 500 | 6 100 | 6 850 | 500 | 320 | 260 |
| 1996 | 5 000 | 6 500 | 7 500 | 700 | 350 | 270 |
| 1997 | 5 200 | 6 900 | 7 700 | 730 | 370 | 277 |
| | \multicolumn{6}{c|}{Receivers per 1 000 inhabitants} |
| 1980 | 69 | 7,6 | 32 | 3,7 | 10 | 10 |
| 1985 | 91 | 12 | 78 | 5,0 | 21 | 14 |
| 1990 | 109 | 40 | 101 | 9,6 | 26 | 29 |
| 1995 | 120 | 62 | 110 | 18 | 29 | 32 |
| 1996 | 131 | 64 | 118 | 25 | 32 | 32 |
| 1997 | 134 | 66 | 119 | 26 | 33 | 32 |

## Legislation relating to broadcasting

Legislation pertaining to broadcasting in South Africa is made up of a set of four Acts, which have to be read in conjunction with each other. The policy relating to broadcasting is embodied in this legislation. Any attempt to modify the policy by, for example, the introduction of regional television, will require a review of this legislation.

We briefly describe the purpose of each Act below, relative to broadcasting.

- Independent Broadcasting Authority Act, no. 153 of 1993

  This Act originally intended to provide for the regulation of broadcasting activities through the establishment of an authority, independent of the State, known as the IBA, now the Independent Communications Authority of South Africa (ICASA). The IBA Act also required the IBA to conduct several investigations into broadcasting, which resulted in the Triple Inquiry Report of 1995, which we discussed earlier. Today, much of the IBA Act of 1993 has become superfluous with the promulgation of the Broadcasting Act of 1999 and the ICASA Act of 2000. For example, aspects of the IBA Act that relate to matters regarding the administration, management and planning of the IBA have been repealed, while in matters relating to the regulation and licensing of broadcasters, the Broadcasting Act of 1999 takes precedence. The IBA Act is still relevant with regards to the code of conduct for broadcasters and the activities of broadcasters and broadcasting during election periods.

- Telecommunications Act, no. 103 of 1996

  The main purpose of this Act is to regulate telecommunications activities through the formation of the South African Telecommunications Regulatory Authority (Satra). Within the ambit of broadcasting this Act provides for the control, planning, administration and management of the frequency spectrum by ICASA under the standards and requirements of the International Telecommunications Union (ITU). The Telecommunications Act of 1996 requires ICASA to prepare, and constantly review, a frequency plan that determines how the frequencies are allocated and used, to protect users from interference by other users and to introduce new technologies.

- Broadcasting Act, no. 4 of 1999

  In general terms, the Broadcasting Act of 1999 is the dominant piece of legislation within the broadcasting environment and its purpose is fourfold. Briefly, the purpose of the Act is:

  - To provide a Charter for the SABC. The Broadcasting Act of 1999 firmly establishes the SABC as a public service broadcaster and outlines the objectives of the SABC. However, the Act also permits the SABC to operate a public commercial broadcasting component as a separate entity. The public broadcasting component is charged with providing services in all the official languages, as circumstances permit. In addition, the SABC is required to cater for the cultural and multilingual diversity of South Africa; provide impartial, balanced and fair journalism; formal and informal educational programming; and national and minority sports programmes. Funding of the public service component is provided by advertising, sponsorships, grants and donations in addition to the collection of licence fees. The public commercial services are required to subsidise the public service component. The Act limits the SABC Board to eleven members appointed by the State President on the advice of the Communication Portfolio Committee of Parliament.
  - To establish the Frequency Spectrum Directorate, whose duty it is to manage the radio frequency spectrum for efficient usage.

- To establish the South African Broadcasting Production Advisory Board, which is to advise the Minister of Communication on the development and production of radio and television programmes, commenting, for example on aspects such as local content.
- To establish a human resources capacity in broadcasting policy development.

The Broadcasting Act of 1999 also provides for a three-tier system of broadcasting services, that is public, commercial and community broadcasting which are discussed below. A further distinction is made based on the mode of delivery, namely free-to-air and satellite-free-to-air for basic broadcasting services; and satellite encrypted, terrestrial encrypted, direct-to-home delivery or cable for subscription services. The Broadcasting Act of 1999 is to be read in conjunction with the IBA Act of 1993.

- Independent Communications Authority of South Africa Act, no. 13 of 2000
 The Independent Communications Authority of South Africa (ICASA) Act simply provides for the establishment and functioning of a regulatory authority for both broadcasting and telecommunications through the amalgamation of the IBA and Satra, in order to perform the duty of those former authorities as detailed in the relevant legislation. The ICASA Act calls for the appointment of six full-time councillors who serve for a period of four years, with elections to be held every second year for three positions on the council.

## The three-tier system of broadcasting

Legislation, in the form of the IBA Act of 1993 and the Broadcasting Act of 1999, clearly distinguishes between three types of broadcasting licence. These licence types are largely defined in the legislation in economic terms rather than in terms of the service to be provided. We briefly discuss each type of broadcasting.

- Public broadcasting
 The mandate of the public broadcaster is to serve the various diverse cultural and language groups that make up the country. Public broadcasting is a concept of broadcasting which emphasises quality programming and is defined in legal terms as a service provided by the SABC or any other statutory body or person who receives all or some income from licence fees and can include a commercially operated service. Public broadcasting is not primarily market driven. Providing for a public service for each of the eleven official languages places an enormous burden on the SABC. The SABC is obliged to provide a terrestrial radio service to 80 percent of listeners. In 1992, when transformation began, only two stations, that is SAfm and RSG, could fulfil this requirement. To meet these requirements requires the installation of additional transmitters, which is a costly exercise. To date, Umhlobo Wenene FM, Motsweding FM and Phalaphala FM have been upgraded and the SABC claims these stations can now reach 80 percent of their potential audience.

## MEDIA STUDIES

An interesting picture emerges when we consider the penetration of the official language groups by the various public service radio stations operated by the SABC. This is illustrated in Figure 1.4. Although Ukhozi FM (isiZulu) and Umhlobo Wenene FM (IsiXhosa) show very large average daily listener numbers – 2,980 million and 2,368 million respectively (South African Broadcasting Corporation 1999:25), the penetration of these language groups only averages 32 percent.

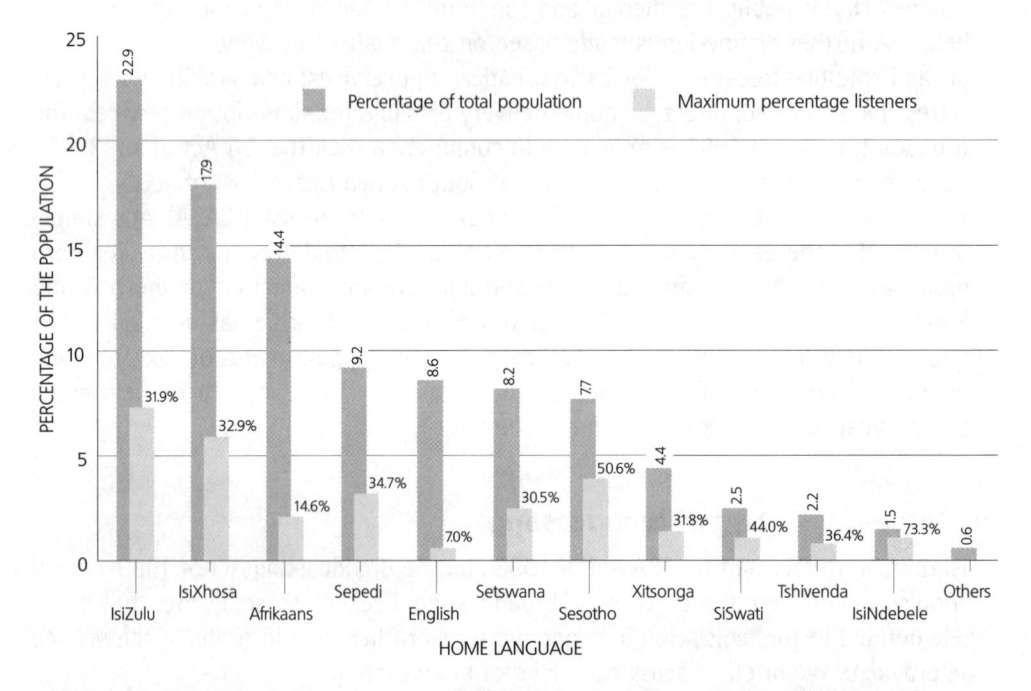

Figure 1.4 Percentage of the population speaking each official language as their home language compared with the penetration of those languages by SABC public service radio stations broadcasting in those languages

Only two of the eleven public service stations can claim to have a listenership of over 50 percent of all speakers of that language, that is Lesedi FM (Sesotho) with 50,6 percent penetration and Ikwekwezi FM (isiNdebele) with a remarkable 73,3 percent penetration. However, IsiNdebele speakers account for only 1,5 percent of the total population of South Africa. The low penetration of English- and Afrikaans-speaking groups by SAfm and RSG can be explained by the large number of alternative commercial stations available, broadcasting in English and Afrikaans, as indicated in Table 1.4 on page 30.

- Commercial broadcasting
  Commercial broadcasting is defined as a service operated for profit. Being financed through advertising revenue, commercial broadcasters need to have a high success

# A South African Media Map

rate with their programming structure in order to deliver an audience to potential advertisers. This means that commercial stations are free to take advantage of new ideas, trends and developments in programming as they are purely market-driven. (This aspect is discussed in more detail in Unit 13, Volume 2.) Similarly, they can alter, or even abandon, any programme format that fails to deliver the required audience statistics. Currently only two television services are considered as commercial services, that is M-Net and e.tv. The three SABC channels are still subject to negotiation and while they are public services in name, they remain commercial in operation.

It was only during late 1997 that greenfield licences (a licence issued to a new radio or television station) were issued for eight radio stations across the country, whereas four radio stations were grandfathered (a station that has been given a licence because it existed prior to the establishment of the IBA); the rest being part of the SABC. Figure 1.5 indicates the origins of the various commercial stations. From this chart, which excludes the eleven SABC public radio stations, we can clearly see the dominance of the SABC in the broadcasting environment. Since the greenfield licences were issued by the IBA in 1997, no new commercial stations have come on air. Licences are issued for a duration of six years, subject to renewal. Table 1.4 lists the commercial radio stations operating in South Africa.

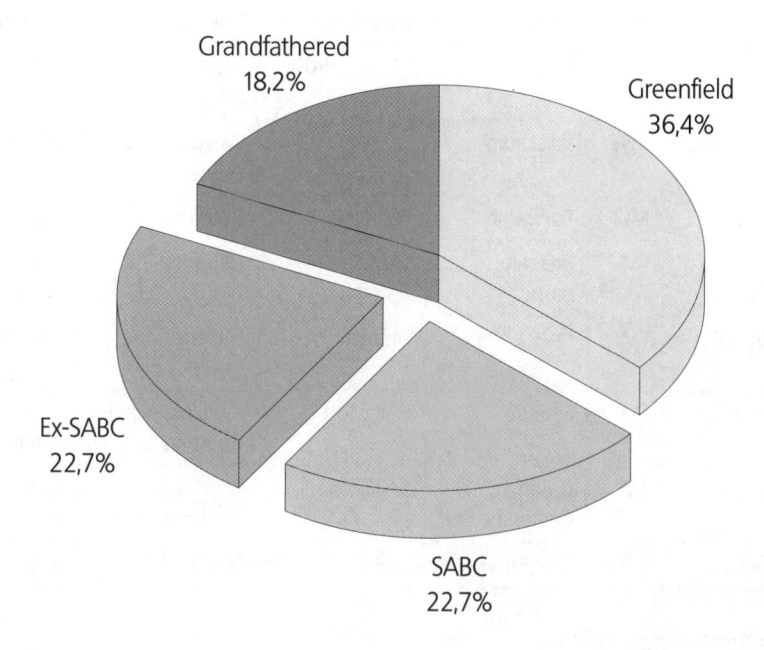

**Figure 1.5 The origins of commercial broadcasting in South Africa, *circa* 1997**

# MEDIA STUDIES

**Table 1.4 Commercial radio stations operating in South Africa**
Stations marked with an asterisk were previously part of the SABC

| Station | Format | | Operator | Area | Language |
|---|---|---|---|---|---|
| 5FM | FM | CHR | SABC | National | English |
| Cape Talk | MW | Talk radio | Primedia | Western Cape | English |
| CKI Stereo | FM | MOR | SABC | Eastern Cape | English/isiXhosa |
| Classic FM | FM | Classic | Classic | Gauteng | English |
| East Coast Radio* | FM | MOR | Kagiso | KwaZulu-Natal | English |
| Goodhope FM | FM | MOR | SABC | Western Cape | English/Afrikaans |
| Highveld Stereo* | FM | MOR | Primedia | Gauteng | English |
| Jakaranda Stereo* | FM | Golden oldies MOR | Newshelf | Gauteng | English/Afrikaans |
| Kaya FM | FM | Soul, R&B | Moribo | Gauteng | English |
| KFM* | FM | MOR | Crescent | Western Cape | English/Afrikaans |
| Metro FM | FM | Urban contemporary | SABC | National | English |
| OFM* | FM | MOR | New Radio | Free State | English/Afrikaans |
| P4 | FM | Jazz | Makana Trust | Western Cape Natal | English |
| Punt Geselsradio | MW | Talk radio | | Western Cape Gauteng | Afrikaans |
| Radio 702 | MW | Talk radio | Primedia | Gauteng | English |
| Radio 2000 | FM | Beautiful music | SABC | National | English/Afrikaans |
| Radio Algoa/ BRFM* | FM | MOR | Umoya | Eastern Cape | English/Afrikaans |
| Radio Lotus | FM | Ethnic | SABC | KwaZulu-Natal Gauteng | English/Hindi/ Tamil |
| Radio Bop | FM | Urban Contemporary | SABC | North West Gauteng | English |
| Radio Sunshine | FM | Religious | SABC | North West | English/Setswana |

- Community Broadcasting
  The concept community is defined as being a geographically founded community or any group of persons or sector of the public having a specific, ascertainable common interest.

Community broadcasting service means a broadcasting service which:
- is fully controlled by a non-profit entity and carried on for non-profitable purposes;
- serves a particular community;
- encourages members of the community it serves or persons associated with or promoting the interests of such community to participate in the selection and provision of programmes to be broadcast in the course of such broadcasting service;
- may be funded by donations, grants, sponsorships or advertising or membership fees, or by any combination of the aforementioned.

Thus far, community services have been limited to the issuing of licences for community radio stations only. Although 100 temporary community licences were granted over the past four years, by March 1999 only 79 community stations were on the air (Independent Broadcasting Authority 2000:131-132). A number of stations were granted licences but never started up, while others had to stop broadcasting because of financial constraints. This points to the unstable nature of some community radio broadcasters and the desperate need for skilled management and broadcasters. In 1997 applications were invited for four-year licences and 252 applications were received. However, by July 2000 the process of issuing four licences was still incomplete as a direct result of problems experienced by the IBA prior to its merger with Satra. Many community radio stations exist on a "hand-to-mouth" basis and the lengthy delays in finalising their long-term licences has resulted in financial failure of the radio station (Duncan 2000). Short-term licences are still granted for periods up to thirty days to cover special events such as Deepavali and the Grahamstown National Arts Festival.

## *The SABC model*

The Broadcasting Act of 1999 has four distinct implications for the organisation and operation of the SABC. These are as follows:
- The SABC is governed by a Broadcasting Charter, which is monitored for compliance by ICASA.
- The structure of the SABC is made up of two distinct groups, that of public and commercial broadcasting services.
- The commercial services are to subsidise the public broadcasting services.
- The SABC is to become a limited liability company with the State as the shareholder.

Collectively, the process of implementing these four points is known as corporatisation of the SABC. At the time of writing, the SABC is examining ways of implementing the corporatisation processes in order to split the corporation into two operating entities. As a result, the effect of corporatisation on the organisation of the three SABC television channels remains unknown. SABC radio still remains the dominant force in the South African broadcasting environment, commanding 81 percent of the total adult radio listenership (South African Broadcasting Corporation 1999:24).

- Commercial and community radio
  Here we find Radio 2000, a nation-wide facility service used for religious, educational and sports broadcasts, simulcasts of television programmes and popular music. There are also two national music format stations, 5FM and Metro FM. Radio Lotus, in Durban and Johannesburg, and Good Hope FM in Cape Town provide for community needs. These stations are considered to be extremely successful in terms of listener loyalty and revenue generation, which is used to cross-subsidise the public service stations. Radio Sunshine, a commercial gospel station, broadcasts in English and Setswana.
- Public service radio
  The public service portfolio contains the stations with the largest listenership; some 63 percent of the SABC's total listenership. These stations include Ukhozi FM (IsiZulu), Umhlobo Wenene (IsiXhosa), Lesedi FM (Sesotho), Radiosondergrense (RSG)(Afrikaans) and SAfm (English). Six stations in the public service portfolio predominantly serve rural audiences. Hence, developmental information is given priority as listeners often do not have access to alternative forms of media. Stations in this portfolio include Ligwalagwala FM (SiSwati), Ikwekwezi FM (IsiNdebele), Motsweding FM (Setswana), Phalaphala FM (TshiVenda), Thobela FM (Sepedi) and Munghana Lonene (Xitsonga).
- Television
  The SABC's television service, consisting of three channels, broadcasts in eleven languages, reaching a daily audience of about 12 million viewers. Table 1.5 compares the daily television viewing figures in South Africa for the period 1994–1998. The division of programming for the eleven language groups is indicated in Table 1.6.

**Table 1.5 AMPS television viewing averages in South Africa** (South African Advertising Research Foundation 1998:58)

|  | 1994 | 1995 | 1996 | 1997 | 1998 | |
| --- | --- | --- | --- | --- | --- | --- |
|  | % | % | % | % | % | '000 |
| SABC1 | 35,0 | 33,5 | 26,2 | 32,1 | 33,5 | 8 613 |
| SABC2 | 22,6 | 22,5 | 20,1 | 23,2 | 24,1 | 6 199 |
| SABC3 | 1,9 | 2,3 | 9,1 | 11,7 | 11,5 | 2 961 |
| M-Net | 9,9 | 10,0 | 9,5 | 9,5 | 9,6 | 2 465 |
| Bop-TV | 0,8 | 0,9 | 0,5 | 0,8 | 0,6 | 160 |
| Mmabatho TV | 0,1 | 0,1 | 0,1 | 0,2 | – | – |
| TOTAL Satellite channels | – | – | – | 0,3 | 0,8 | 201 |

SABC1 emphasises the Nguni family of languages (IsiZulu, IsiXhosa, IsiNdebele and SiSwati) while remaining programming is in English. SABC1 focuses on nation-building projects based in the community. For example, the *Soul City* drama project was a successful venture at edutainment with a strong focus on health and social issues. SABC1 is aimed at younger viewers and it has an average daily adult audience of 8,613 million (South African Broadcasting Corporation 1999:16).

SABC2 can be considered unique in that it presents programming that addresses the needs of four separate languages groups, namely the Sesotho family of languages (Sesotho, Setswana and Sepedi), Xitsonga, TshiVenda and Afrikaans. Additional programming is in English or is multilingual. The average daily adult audience is 6,199 million.

SABC3 moved from being a channel that was mainly educational in orientation, to one with a bias for family entertainment and more specialised and niche programming that proved popular on the previous NNTV. Programmes shown on this channel tend to be more diverse with programmes originating from Britain, the United States, Canada and Australia. SABC3 is predominantly in English with very few multilingual programmes. A major drawback of SABC3 remains the restricted terrestrial transmitter reach of the channel. SABC3 reaches only 56 percent of the total population against 72 percent for SABC1 and 76 percent for SABC2. This problem is considered as serious, since SABC3 carries the main flagship English news bulletin of the day at 20:00. To help resolve this problem in the short term, certain SABC2 transmitters are switched with those of SABC3 at 18:30 on weekdays.

**Table 1.6  Percentage of language allocation for SABC-TV channels broadcast during prime-time (18:00-21:00)** (South African Broadcasting Corporation 1996:29)

|  | SABC1 | SABC2 | SABC3 | Average |
|---|---|---|---|---|
| English | 29,17 | 23,61 | 97,22 | 50,00 |
| IsiZulu | 17,01 | – | – | 5,67 |
| IsiXhosa | 16,67 | – | – | 5,56 |
| Afrikaans | 1,04 | 20,20 | 0,40 | 7,21 |
| Sepedi | 0,35 | 9,71 | – | 3,35 |
| Setswana | – | 8,92 | – | 2,97 |
| Sesotho | 0,35 | 8,92 | – | 3,09 |
| Xitsonga | – | 0,79 | – | 0,29 |
| Setswana | 1,04 | – | – | 0,35 |
| TshiVenda | – | 0,79 | – | 0,26 |
| IsiNdebele | 1,04 | – | – | 0,35 |
| Multilingual | 33,33 | 27,08 | 2,38 | 20,93 |

## Satellite services

Satellite services are dominated by DStv, a subscription service that began operations in October 1995 as part of MultiChoice Africa, a spin-off company from M-Net. The DStv bouquet comprises 45 video channels, six data channels and 51 audio channels. The service also includes several one-way interactive data channels for weather, games and astrology. Following the failure of the SABC's Astrasat service, the SABC launched two pay-TV channels on DStv on 16 November 1998. These are SABC Africa, which offers 24 hours of news and information and Africa-2-Africa, which is an entertainment channel. In addition to the two pay channels, SABC 1, 2 and 3 are also distributed from the DStv digital platform. In so doing, the SABC television channels can be received in 44 African countries (South African Broadcasting Corporation 1999:22).

## 1.3 THE PRESS

Of the three media we discuss in this unit, the press has the longest history. Unlike broadcasting, which we looked at in the previous subsection, which closely allied itself to government ideology, there has always been a strained relationship between the press and the government in South Africa. The resulting tension has manifested itself in the form of constant threats in the form of restrictive legislation. However, the degree of this tension has ebbed and flowed according to political developments in the history of South Africa, beginning literally with the arrival of Jan van Riebeeck at the Cape in 1652. Roelofse (1996:70–71) identifies five enduring themes that run through the history of the press in South Africa. These themes are as follows:

- There is tension and conflict between government and the press.
- Divisions in the press are based on language.
- Further divisions in the press are based on race.
- The state sees the press as a threat to peace and security.
- Efforts by journalists to circumvent undemocratic laws.

As a result of the divisions identified in the second and third themes mentioned above, the development of the press does not follow a single path. This makes it difficult to identify distinct periods as we did for broadcasting in the previous subsection. Rather, we need to divide the history of the press in to four distinct strands, each of which follows its own developmental pattern. These strands are:

- The English press
- The Afrikaans press
- The black press
- The alternative press

We look at the development of each of these in turn, but we first need to consider the roots of the press in South Africa.

### 1.3.1 The early years in the Cape Colony

Locally produced newspapers did not appear in South Africa until a century and a half after the occupation of the Cape by van Riebeeck in 1652, simply because the Dutch East

## A South African Media Map

India Company perceived the press as a potentially revolutionary instrument. News and views had to be channelled through newspapers, such as the *Post van der Neder-Rijn* and the *Suid-Hollandsche Courant* which were published in the Netherlands (Fourie 1994: 291). It was only after the Dutch ceded the Cape to British military rule in 1795 as a reprisal for the Dutch's alliance with France during the French revolutionary wars that the first local publication began. The *Cape Town Gazette and African Advertiser/ Kaapsche Stads Courant en Afrikaansche Berigte* was first published on 16 August 1800, by Alexander Walker and John Robertson who were also renowned for being corrupt slave-dealers. The public complained about the price of the newspaper and argued that Walker and Robertson overcharged for advertisements (de Kock 1982:22). The paper appeared mainly in English and was printed on a government-owned press at the Castle. Only official notices and advertisements were printed in this newspaper which was strongly controlled by the governor, Lord Charles Somerset. Needless to say, only colonial interests were represented in this newspaper. When the Cape reverted to Batavian rule in 1803, the title was changed to *Kaapsche Courant*, but reverted back to its original bilingual title in 1806 when the British re-occupied the Cape. Private newspapers were prohibited except for those published by missionaries in the hinterland (Diederichs 1993:73).

### The struggle for freedom of the press

The first non-government newspaper was *The South African Commercial Advertiser*, which first appeared on 7 January 1824 in Cape Town, owned by George Greig but with Thomas Pringle and John Fairbairn as the editors. This move broke the twenty-two year monopoly of the Government Press at the Cape (de Kock 1982:53). Although this paper was published mainly in English, it also made provision for Dutch news and advertisements. The paper consisted of eight pages of which four were filled with advertisements (de Kock 1982:42). The freedom of the press enjoyed by this first unofficial publication was of brief duration. A feature of the *Commercial Advertiser* was its extensive coverage of events in the law courts. In one particular case concerning the malpractice of the disposal of slaves by the local customs officer, Lord Somerset interceded in the proceedings of the case in order to predetermine the outcome. Somerset, fearing that his actions would be extensively reported by the *Commercial Advertiser*, simply confiscated the eighteenth edition and ordered publication to be suspended. Although the page proofs were returned, Pringle and Fairbairn had to submit their paper for censorship. Refusing to comply, the Government then sealed the press and banished Greig from the colony for subversion and sedition (de Kock 1982:46–47).

Some two months after starting the *Commercial Advertiser*, Thomas Pringle and John Fairbairn, who are now honoured as South Africa's first journalists, also started a bilingual periodical known as *The South African Journal and Het Nederduitssch Zuid-Afrikaansch Tydschrift* together with the Reverend Abraham Faure. The first edition of *The Journal* appeared on 5 March 1824 when a thousand copies were reluctantly printed by the Government Press. *The Journal* immediately became unpopular with the authorities as the content related to constitutional matters, such as the curbing of despotic power, and in later issues, the freedom of the press. By mid-May 1824, Pringle and Fairbairn were warned that they could only continue publication provided they stopped criticising the authorities. Pringle, refusing to submit to an authority that misinterpreted his work, closed down *The Journal*.

Greig returned to the Cape, and the *Commercial Advertiser* was revived again on 31 August 1825 after a drawn-out battle with the colonial office in London. But not for long, as the British government suspended publication 19 months later. Fairbairn, as editor, reprinted an article from *The Times*, which depicted Lord Somerset as vindictive, but gave no acknowledgement that the article had appeared previously in another newspaper. Somerset complained about the article to Bathurst, the British secretary of state for the colonies. Ten months later the licence for the *Commercial Advertiser* was cancelled (de Kock 1982:68–69). After a lengthy appeal, the newspaper was revived for a third time, on 3 October 1828.

And so continued the struggle to secure the freedom of the press. We can single out three factors that influenced the granting of press freedom from strict government control. These are (Roelofse 1996:72):

- Lord Somerset's departure from the Cape on 5 March 1826
- The appointment of General Richard Bourke, who favoured a free press, as governor
- Fairbairn's dogged pursuit of matters relating to the press with the British government

It became clear to the British Government that conflict at the Cape could not be resolved unless the press was free of government restrictions. With Somerset now out of the way it became possible to make this a reality. On 30 April 1829, Ordinance No. 60 was signed. Regarded by Cutten (1935:21) and de Kock (1982:65) as the Magna Carta (a document that provides liberty and political rights) of the South African press, it formally announced the independence of the press. While most of the proclamation related to rules and regulations, the government could only take action against publications if it could prove that they had made irresponsible statements. Over the following decade a number of new newspapers and journals, such as the following, started up in the Cape Colony:

- 1830: *De Zuidafrikaan* (in April)
- 1830: *The Cape of Good Hope Literary Gazette* (in December)
- 1831: *The Grahamstown Journal* (in December)
- 1837: *The Moderator and Mediator*
- 1838: *Eastern Province Government Gazette* (from 12 June)
- 1838: *Price Current*
- 1838: *De Ware Afrikaan* (from 4 October)
- 1838: *De Honingbiji*
- 1840: *Cape of Good Hope Shipping Lists*
- 1840: *The Cape Times* (not to be confused with the present *Cape Times* which began in 1876)
- 1857: *The Argus*

A second major event that strongly influenced the development of the press in South Africa was the arrival of the British settlers in 1820, who brought both printing presses and expertise with them. As a result, by the end of the nineteenth century, there was hardly a town of any size that did not have its own newspaper. Many of the editors of these smaller newspapers lived in the frontier towns, and unlike Fairbairn and Pringle who explored more philosophical issues of press freedom, championed the cause of British settler and Dutch farmer alike (Diederichs 1993:74). The English left an indelible stamp on the development of the press in South Africa. Apart from promoting the struggle to establish press freedom in South Africa, Roelofse (1996:73) identifies three other important contributions made by the British. They established:

- the conventions of excellence and professionalism on which South African journalism is based. The early English editors had strong journalistic backgrounds and were highly skilled and combined this with a fierce belief in human rights and a strong sense of independence;
- commercialism and a free-market approach to the production of a newspaper, realising that circulation and income from the sale of advertising space was vital to the financial wellbeing of a newspaper;
- a tradition of Britishness in South Africa. Although at odds with colonial officials, the first editors still maintained strong bonds with Britain, and in so doing benefited from the associated expertise. However, this obedience to the throne ultimately led to alienation by the Afrikaner and black South Africans who saw this as colonialism. English journalists also tended to ignore the plight of black South Africans and their claims to independence, autonomy and political participation.

## The beginnings of the Afrikaans press

Unlike the English press, the Afrikaans press remained passive for a long time. Roelofse (1996:74) ascribes this to the inherent understanding of freedom by the Afrikaner. For the Dutch Afrikaner, the concept of freedom stemmed from the authority of and obedience to the state. While for the English, freedom was seen as being located within the individual while the state functioned as a mere extension of that freedom in order to serve their interests and to guarantee that freedom. As a result of these differing views, we can say that the English placed a higher value on freedom of the individual than did the Afrikaner. This distinction continued to influence the approaches adopted by the press right through the twentieth century (Roelofse 1996:74).

The Dutch/Afrikaans press was established largely as a reaction to the liberal views of Fairbairn in the *South African Commercial Advertiser*, particular regarding issues such as slavery, the tensions between the Dutch farmers and the Xhosa and the work of missionaries. However, the founder of the Afrikaans press was not of Dutch descent, but an eccentric hunchback Portuguese Jew, Josephus Suasso de Lima, who had been sacked from the Dutch East India Company for the misuse of documents. In 1826 de Lima established a weekly newspaper *De Verzamelaar*, which had, according to Roelofse

(1996:74), no real historical significance other than being the first publication exclusively in Dutch. Publication continued for some 22 years, dogged by financial difficulties and was eventually snapped up by de Lima's one-time failed business partner and now opponent, Charles Etienne Boniface (de Kock 1982:94).

Publication of *De Zuid-Afrikaan*, the first newspaper to speak for Dutch/Afrikaner interests began on 9 April 1830, by Christoffel Joseph Brand, an advocate unpopular with the local authorities for his ability to defend cases against the government in the law courts with some success. The first editor was Boniface, a French musician and playwright who lead a bohemian-like existence, but managed to last only two months in the position leaving hastily for Natal when sued for libel. His successor, JR Stapleton, departed after six months. By 1831 eighty sponsors had to be found to keep the paper going (de Kock 1982:88–89). The paper was formed largely as a reaction to the apparent indifference of the English press to the Afrikaner's needs and the attempted anglicisation of the Afrikaner by the government. Fairbairn, of the *Commercial Advertiser*, and *De Zuid-Afrikaan* clashed bitterly over issues such as that of slavery and the Voortrekkers. Roelfose (1996:74) identifies three enduring trends in the history of the South African press that were initiated by *De Zuid-Afrikaan*, namely:

- a commitment to Africa through the name, and the cause of Afrikaans-speaking Africans, the Afrikaners;
- an open and visible opposition on a political and cultural level between the English and Afrikaans press which has endured until fairly recently;
- to actively promote the cause of the Afrikaans language and those that speak the language.

*De Zuid-Afrikaan* merged with *Ons Land* in 1894, which ceased publication in 1930 as a result of competition with the Nasionale Pers newspaper *Die Burger*, which started in 1915 (Engelbrecht 1972:40; Fourie 1994:291).

Whereas *De Zuid-Afrikaan* championed the rights of the Afrikaner in a British colony where Dutch was barely tolerated, *Die Afrikaanse Patriot* promoted Afrikaans as a language, being the mouthpiece of the *Genootskap van Regte Afrikaners* (Association of Genuine Afrikaners), later known as the *Afrikanderbond*. The first issue appeared in Paarl on 15 January 1876. Although there were only 50 subscribers for the first edition of the monthly newspaper, it drew an immediate reaction from the community. The paper was harshly criticised for promoting what was then considered a "kitchen" language (de Kock 1982:90). The Synod of the Dutch Church forbade children to read it and teachers were reprimanded for writing articles for publication. The *Cradocksche-Afrikaner* said of it scathingly "Semi-educated Griquas will surely be delighted with this paper" (Cullen 1935:36). Because of the intense opposition to written Afrikaans, subscribers and contributors had to write, in a clandestine fashion, via *De Zuid-Afrikaan* in Cape Town (de Kock 1982:91). The paper was the effort of the Reverend Stephanus Jacobus du Toit, founder of the *Genootskap*, and his older brother Daniel François du Toit who later edited *Die Afrikaanse Patriot* for a short period. The paper was by no means a propaganda sheet, but a complete newspaper supplying news and market prices in addition to letters, prose and poetry (de Kock 1982:90–91). In its second year, the paper became a weekly and by the third year subscriptions rose to 3 000 when it gained support from Afrikaners living in the British annexed Zuid-Afrikaanse Republiek. However, the newspaper lost a great deal of its readership after 1892 as a result of Du Toit's support of Cecil John Rhodes against Paul Kruger. Influential members of the *Genootskap* resigned and withdrew their capital in an attempt to change the policy of the paper, without much success, and eventually the paper went out of business in 1904 (Cullen 1935:3; de Kock 1982:91). Today, *Die Afrikaanse Patriot* is considered to have played an important part in the establishment of Afrikaans as a language (Diederichs 1993:74).

Roelofse (1996:75) has identified a number of crucial differences in the development of the Afrikaans and English press during the nineteenth century, which had an enduring effect well into the twentieth century. The Afrikaans newspapers were

- not the result of professional journalist practice – the editors were in most cases, ministers of religion committed to Calvanistic ethics rather than professionally trained journalists, such as Abraham Faure and SJ du Toit;
- not primarily considered as commercial ventures – the Afrikaner cause weighed more heavily than profits; a trend that only changed in the 1970s when Nasionale Pers expanded into the Transvaal and as a result many of the early Dutch and Afrikaans newspapers folded;
- seen as cultural and political crusaders, where promotion of the Afrikaans language, political independence and the perceived threat of black nationalism became enduring themes;
- committed to Africa and the role of the Afrikaner in South Africa – whereas the English press reported diligently on British affairs, the Afrikaans press focused on the affairs of Afrikaners and South Africa.

## Further developments of the press in South Africa

The first newspaper in Natal was *De Natalier*, a four-page weekly, mostly in Dutch with some smatterings of English, that appeared on 15 March 1844, edited by Boniface, previously with *De Zuid-Afrikaan*, who left the Cape hastily when faced with a charge of libel. *De Natalier* did not last very long, closing in 1846, following libel action. The newspaper was quickly replaced by *The Natal Witness*, then a bilingual weekly paper, which today is the oldest newspaper in South Africa still in publication (Cullen 1935:40; Leahy & Voice 1993:90). A large number of smaller newspapers sprung up in Natal in the period 1850–1859, but few of these caught the imagination of the people and most were defunct by 1860 (Cullen 1935:41–42). On the contrary, the country newspapers of Natal were few in number and did not show the characteristic bilingualism evident in the Cape and Transvaal newspapers. Of the more important Natal newspapers, the *Natal Mercury* appeared in 1852, while *The Daily News* first appeared in Durban under the name *Natal Mercantile Advertiser* on 3 January 1878.

## MEDIA STUDIES

The first publication to appear in the Transvaal, was the *Government Gazette*, which was published by Cornelis Moll in Potchefstroom, beginning 25 September 1857 (Cutten 1935:50; Diederichs 1993:74). The name was changed two years later to the *Gouvernements Courant der ZAR*. However, the first Transvaal newspaper, *De Oude Emigrant*, was established 15 October 1859, also in Potchefstroom, then the capital of the Zuid-Afrikaanse Republiek. Three years later *De Emigrant* began, edited by AF Schubert following the collapse of *De Oude Emigrant* nine months earlier, which was seriously considered to have brought the profession of journalism into disrepute with its insulting articles (Cullen 1935:50). From 1863 the *Staats Courant* was published from a building on Church Square in Pretoria. The *Transvaal Argus* was set up in 1866 with Fredrich Jeppe as editor in Potchefstroom. Two years later it was renamed the *Transvaal Advocate*. As this paper was published in English, its circulation was limited and constantly suffered from economic problems and soon collapsed (Cullen 1935:51-52). The first Transvaal newspaper of any significance appeared on 8 August 1873 when *De Volkstem* was formed, later to become *Die Volkstem* in 1922 and continued publication until closure in 1951 except for a brief period, during the Anglo-Boer War, in 1880 (Leahy & Voice 1993:90; Cullen 1935:54). Within a short time after the establishment of Johannesburg in 1886, a number of newspapers appeared that had close ties with the mining industry. The first is considered to be the *Diggers' News*, sold at sixpence a copy from the printing work in Market Street from 24 February 1887 and consisted of four pages mostly filled with advertisements. A day later *The Mining Argus* appeared. The offices of the bi-weekly *Argus* consisted of a stretch of canvas over a wooden frame and copy was sent to Pretoria by horseback where the paper was printed. During the journey some of the copy often got lost, resulting in a loss of revenue for advertisements not printed. The *Standard and Transvaal Mining Chronicle* began in March 1887 and later amalgamated with the *Digger's News*, to be followed by *The Transvaal Observer*. The well-known daily, *The Star*, which originated in Grahamstown as *The Eastern Star*, moved to the Rand and appeared as an evening newspaper renamed *The Star* on 3 April 1889. *The Star* was to become the biggest daily in South Africa and continued to have the biggest circulation up to 1991, when overtaken by the *Sowetan*.

*The Friend of the Sovereignty and Bloemfontein Gazette* was the first newspaper in the Free State, beginning publication on 10 June 1850. Four years later, when the Free State achieved independence the paper changed its name to *The Friend of the Free State*, later shortened to simply *The Friend*. This newspaper had the great distinction of being edited, for a short period during the British occupation of the Free State, by none other than the famous author Rudyard Kipling. The paper closed in 1985 after 130 years of publication. A *Gouvernements Courant* was published in 1857, followed five years later on 29 October 1862 by *De Tijd*, the first Dutch newspaper in the Free State, which continued publication for thirteen years. The publication of newspapers in the Free State did not reach the same levels of development as with the Cape, Natal or Transvaal, and it was not until 11 March 1876 that the third newspaper appeared under the title *De Express en Oranje Vrijstaats Advertentieblad*. *De Express* was eventually closed down by the military authorities in 1900 because of its strong connection with the English during the Anglo-Boer War then raging (Cullen 1935:47). Other newspapers that started up in the Free State included *The Daily News* which started July 1882, *De Burger*, *The Independent* and *Fakkel*.

## The Newspaper Press Union

Following the early years of struggle for press freedom in the Cape, direct government control no longer posed a treat to the press in the 1880s. But in its place there was indirect control through subtle pressure on the press. A new libel law had been passed. Unless newspapers could prove that a libellous statement, even if true, was in the public interest, they would be given a heavy fine. Apart from the fact that this posed a serious threat to the freedom of the press, it also forced many smaller newspapers to close down, as they simply could not pay the fines. Government advertising was withheld and high tariffs for telegraphic services were charged, essentially tying off the main artery that supplied the newspapers with the news. In addition, the government exploited the continual petty squabbling among newsmen in order to keep the press fragmented. Added to these difficulties, the press also had to face a number of logistical problems such as long distances and poor infrastructure, and a limited audience who had to be served in two languages (de Kock 1982:108-109). All that was established by Pringle and Fairbairn was disappearing. Newspapers had not discovered the value of cooperation amongst each other, such as the pooling of news or collective bargaining to reduce telegraphic tariffs, in order to combat these problems. The very survival of the press was at stake.

Francis Joseph Dormer set out to resolve this situation. Having given up his teaching position in Cape Town, Dormer found himself reporting on the Frontier and Zulu Wars for the *Cape Argus*, later to become its sub-editor and then editor in 1878. On 1 July 1881, Dormer bought the *Cape Argus* for £6 000, with cash provided by Cecil John Rhodes. Dormer then set about to reorganise the newspaper. Dormer, who was astute, rapidly summed up the position of the press.

The only way the press could protect their hard won liberty and not be done out of their earnings was to unite in a common front. Organised by Dormer and RW Murray, a colleague from the *Cape Times*, twenty-six newspapermen met in the council chambers of the Grahamstown Town Hall on 27 November 1882. Here the Newspaper Press Union (NPU) was formed with the purpose of promoting and protecting the common interests of the South African Press. That Dormer had persuaded English and Afrikaans newspaper owners and editors to meet together, including that of *Die Afrikaanse Patriot* was an achievement (de Kock 1982:10).

The National Press Union undertook to fight for the amendment of libel legislation and to establish a protective fund to help newspapers that ran into financial difficulties. The independence of the press was emphasised in the inaugural address. In its long history, the NPU has changed, and not always for the better. For example, in 1912, following an application for membership by John Tengo Jabavu, black editors and newspaper owners were barred from membership, a decision only reversed in 1975 (Roelofse 1996:79).

### 1.3.2 Into the twentieth century

If the nineteenth century belongs to the press pioneers, writes de Kock (1982:118), then the twentieth century was one of unimaginable expansion. The new century began with Britain and its two colonies, the Cape and Natal at war with the two Boer Republics, which lasted from 1899 to 1902. The resultant animosity between the English and Afrikaners did little to resolve the differences between the English and Afrikaans press. It was in these difficult conditions that new newspapers were established that would ultimately lead to the creation of a large industry dominated by four major press groups (Roelfose 1996:79). While the Argus Group had already been established in the previous century, the first two decades of the twentieth century saw the foundations being laid for Nasionale Pers and Times Media. The fourth monopoly, Perskor was to arrive on the scene only in the 1970s. Today these groups control most of the mainstream newspapers in the country (see Figure 1.7 on page 64).

### *The Afrikaans press groups*

The development of the Afrikaans press during the first half of the twentieth century is deeply intertwined with politics and we need to view this development within the context of the complex sociocultural history of the Afrikaner. From this complex history, Muller (1987:120) identifies three significant political events:

- General Hertzog's breakaway from Louis Botha in 1912 and the establishment of the National Party in 1915. There was also strong resistance by the Nationalists against Smut's decision to participate in World War I.
- Dr DF Malan's withdrawal of the "gesuiwerde" or purified Nationalists from the pact that fused the white political parties into the United Party under Smuts and Hertzog.
- Hertzog's split with Smuts and South Africa's entry into World War II as a British ally. In the second elections following the war, Smuts' United Party was swept out of power by the Nationalist party who held on to power until the 1994 democratic elections.

Apart from the establishment of the National Party, 1915 is significant in that it saw the beginnings of three major Afrikaans-language newspapers. *Het Volksblad* was the first to appear in March, having evolved from the Dutch weekly *Het Western*, which began publication in 1904. *Het Volksblad* initially remained a weekly, publishing out of Potchefstroom, becoming a daily on its move to Bloemfontein in 1925 and holds the claim to being the oldest Afrikaans newspaper (Muller 1987:120). As the paper was not nationally distributed, it did not make much impact politically. Four months later, in July 1915, *De Burger* appeared in Cape Town, later to become *Die Burger* and the flagship title in the Naspers Group in addition to being considered the voice of Cape nationalism. The newspaper was originally established by wealthy professional men who needed a means to air their political views as well as a potential business enterprise for their capital, under the leadership of JHH de Waal. De Nasionale Pers Beperk was registered as a company in May 1915 for this purpose. As a result of *De Burger's* efforts at promoting Afrikaner nationalism, the paper did not receive a warm welcome from anglicised Cape Town, where there was a call, in 1917, for an advertising boycott of the paper. The editor was Dr DF Malan who was later to become Prime Minister. The third paper to appear in 1915 was the bi-weekly *Ons Vaderland* in Pretoria, with General Herztzog and his two main supporters, TJ Roos and NC Havenga as the main shareholders. The paper changed its title to *Die Vaderland* in December 1931.

While returning from the National Party congress held at Middleburg in 1935, Hofmeyer and Malan devised a scheme to launch a new newspaper, *Die Transvaler*, to be published by Voortrekkerpers, which was registered as a company in March 1936. The purpose was to provide a northern counterbalance to the highly influential *Burger*. The first edition appeared in October 1937. Oddly, the first editor to be appointed was a social psychology professor who hailed from the Cape, HF Verwoerd. According to Muller (1987:125) this was Hofmeyer's biggest mistake. In the very first editorial, the new editor rebuked the Jewish community for meddling in Afrikaner financial affairs and suggested that all Jews be deported. Such outspoken views antagonised not only Hofmeyer, who resigned from the board after two years, but also the English and largely Jewish entrepreneurs in the Transvaal. The result was an advertisement boycott of the newspaper, similar to that experienced by *Die Burger*, resulting in financial losses. Thus, on the eve of World War II we find *Die Burger*, an influential newspaper in the south of the country serving nationalist and capitalist interests, while *Die Transvaler* was beginning to find its republican feet under the editorship of Verwoerd (Muller 1987:126).

## *The Press and apartheid*

Whereas in most countries, the press is usually categorised according to various political affiliations, the South African press, from its very beginnings in the Cape Colony, has been organised in terms of race. Thus we find the English press, initially in opposition to the Dutch, then the Afrikaans press, the black press, the Indian press and so on. Roelofse (1996:85) writes: "while race has since the beginning of our press history been one of the defining characteristics of the South African press, race and racism reached its zenith in the period 1948 to 1990 – the apartheid era". On coming to power in 1948, the government immediately implemented various policies that strengthened the position of the Afrikaner, most of who lived in the urban areas and who were desperately poor. The government also made moves to neutralise the rising aspirations of black South Africans, who were perceived as a serious threat. This was achieved through a form of social engineering that became known worldwide as apartheid. When the National Party came to power, a broader and fundamentally political classification of the South African press became established. Newspapers were either pro-government or in opposition. Within this scenario, any efforts at editorial independence were bound to fail, as the government labelled newspapers as either supportive or oppositional.

Given the close bond between the Afrikaans press and politics established during the first half of the twentieth century it is not surprising that, under apartheid, the Afrikaans press found itself in a unique and privileged position. Not only did journalists from the Afrikaans newspapers find themselves at Nationalist Party meetings, but they were also given special treatment at Party congresses as civil servants responsible for the distribution of information. In the end, this proved to be self-defeating, as Roelofse (1996:87) writes:

> Their close links, however, worked against good journalism in that they did not expose or investigate graft or corruption, even when they knew something about it. They became victims of self-censorship in exchange for favours from prominent people in government.

A crucial aspect in the successful control of South African society lay in the use of propaganda, which attempted to sell the government as the state, whereby any attack on the government was considered as unpatriotic or even treasonable. Worldwide condemnation of apartheid resulted in the fact that South Africa remained high on news agendas for a sustained period of time, with negative consequences. This resulted in efforts by the government to control the flow of information in order to sustain the apartheid system. By the mid-1970s the Nationalist Party felt it had become necessary to take action to counter the negative information regarding South Africa being distributed worldwide. At the same time, it was felt that something had to be done about the unpatriotic and rebellious English press. Gradually there emerged a strategy for controlling the press, based on propaganda and political action such as (Roelofse 1996:87–88):

- declaring a commitment to press freedom in parliamentary debates;
- accusing the press of being disloyal towards South Africa and of being in collusion with South Africa's enemies, usually the communists;
- threatening the press with legal action unless the press sorted itself out;
- appointing commissions of inquiry, usually pro-government, to investigate the press;
- discussing possible regulatory legislation with press owners; and
- encouraging the press to draw up codes of conduct and to set up control bodies.

Through this strategy, the government could lay claim to placing a high premium on press freedom, while at the same time getting the press to regulate itself through the application of self-censorship. This resulted in a great deal of uncertainty in newspapers as to what could be printed and what could not. In the end, newspapers decided to play it safe and ignored news that would provoke the ire of the government. As a result, news in the mainstream press regarding rising black aspirations went unreported while political news focused almost exclusively on the *status quo*.

## The Information Scandal

During 1978 and 1979 the apartheid government was rocked by a major scandal when the press revealed that the Department of Information had engaged in a clandestine propaganda exercise to "sell apartheid to the world" (Hachten & Giffard 1984:230). Using millions of rand illegally, the Department had, without approval of the government, begun a campaign to influence public opinion on a global scale. To this end, the Department had established a pro-government English morning tabloid aptly titled *The Citizen*, subsidised a news magazine *To the Point*, tried to buy out the SAAN group, the *Washington Star* and a fifty percent stake in United Press International Television News (UPITN) in an effort to manipulate the flow of news on South Africa. The scandal was quickly dubbed Muldergate by the press, as Dr CP Mulder, then tipped as the next Prime Minister, was the minister responsible for the Department of Information. The event saw the end of his political career as well as that of John Vorster who was obliged to retire as Prime Minister (Roelfose 1996:90). The scandal led to the introduction of legislation which required newspapers to seek permission from the Advocate General before they could expose corruption in state administration. In this way, the government tried to muzzle the press, but the move drew such a sharp reaction that the legislation was suitably amended.

The Information Scandal marked a turning point in the cosy relationship between the Afrikaans press and the apartheid government. "It destroyed the blind faith of a significant number of Afrikaners traditionally loyal to the cause of the National Party, the so-called verligtes" (Roelofse 1996:90). The event also split the Afrikaans press, with the Cape-based Nasionale Pers condemning the government openly, while Perskor attempted to protect the National Party leadership. "In fact", writes Roelofse (1996:91), "on the very morning of the day Dr Connie Mulder's involvement in the affair was admitted, *Die Transvaler* carried a front page lead denying his involvement. *Beeld* and *Die Burger* did not make the same mistake." Following the scandal, the Afrikaans press began to express misgivings about the government and apartheid with an increasing frequency, producing cracks in the apartheid system that ultimately led to self-destruction.

## The Steyn Commission of Inquiry

With criticism against apartheid policies on the increase following the Information Scandal, the government felt some response was needed, particularly given the importance of the media, especially the press, in supporting apartheid. With press-government relations at a low ebb, the Steyn Commission of Inquiry into the media was appointed in June 1980 as a further attempt to control the flow of news and information. This presented an apparently legitimate way of dealing with, what was to the government, a troublesome and disloyal press. The brief of the Commission was to "inquire into and report on the question of whether the conduct of, and the handling of, matters by the mass media meet the needs and interests of the South African community and the demands of the times, and, if not, how they can be improved" (Hachten & Giffard 1984:77). This mandate was later expanded to propose legislation to implement its recommendations. The Commission was led by a senior judge, Marthinus Steyn, and produced an extensive report, of nearly 1 400 pages, on 1 February 1982, that found many shortcomings in the media. The recommendations were considered controversial (Jackson 1993:23). These included the following aspects (Hachten & Giffard, 1984:83–84):

- Professionalisation of the media, through the registration of licensed journalists. Any journalist convicted of subversive activity would be automatically disqualified – a move which would have silenced most black journalists.
- Establishment of a press council to set the norms and standards for objectivity and fairness, particularly when reporting on matters relating to the peace, order and safety of the country – effectively prohibiting any reporting on the rising black consciousness.
- Breaking up the major press groups, particularly that of Argus and SAAN, by prohibiting anyone to hold more than ten percent of the shares – under the guise that monopolies were a threat to press freedom.

From its very beginnings, the Commission was controversial. Journalists, even from the Afrikaans press, refused to be associated with the inquiry. It is not with surprise that the final report was met with indignation by both pro- and anti-government newspapers. The English press rejected the report, in which nearly two-thirds was devoted to a description of the political environment, including Soviet global aspirations and black consciousness as part of the onslaught against the country. The report was quickly shown up as being seriously flawed in its selective use of data, factual inaccuracies and plagiarism.

Oddly, the government did little to implement the draconian recommendations, despite the fact that the proposals supported the government point of view. Hachten and Giffard (1984:85) speculate that intervention by the Reagan administration of the United States of America persuaded the government to rethink the Commission's recommendations. A second factor that persuaded the government to think otherwise was the fact that, as with the Information Scandal a few years earlier, the English and Afrikaans press stood together in their condemnation of the report. However, legislation was introduced in June 1982 establishing a new media council that forced all newspapers to join the Newspaper Press Union. A key aspect of the new legislation required all newspapers to submit themselves to the media council of the Newspaper Press Union in the event government determined that disciplinary measures were necessary, or have their registration cancelled. This move was seen as an attempt to bring right-wing newspapers, such as *Die Afrikaner* and *Die Patriot*, under some sort of control (Hachten & Giffard 1984:85).

## Pressures on the press

Over the last quarter of the twentieth century, the South African press probably underwent greater challenges and changes than during any other period in the history of the media in South Africa. As a result, the organisation of the press at the end of the twentieth century is different from that of two decades earlier, as demonstrated in a comparison of Figure 1.6 with that of Figure 1.7 on page 64.

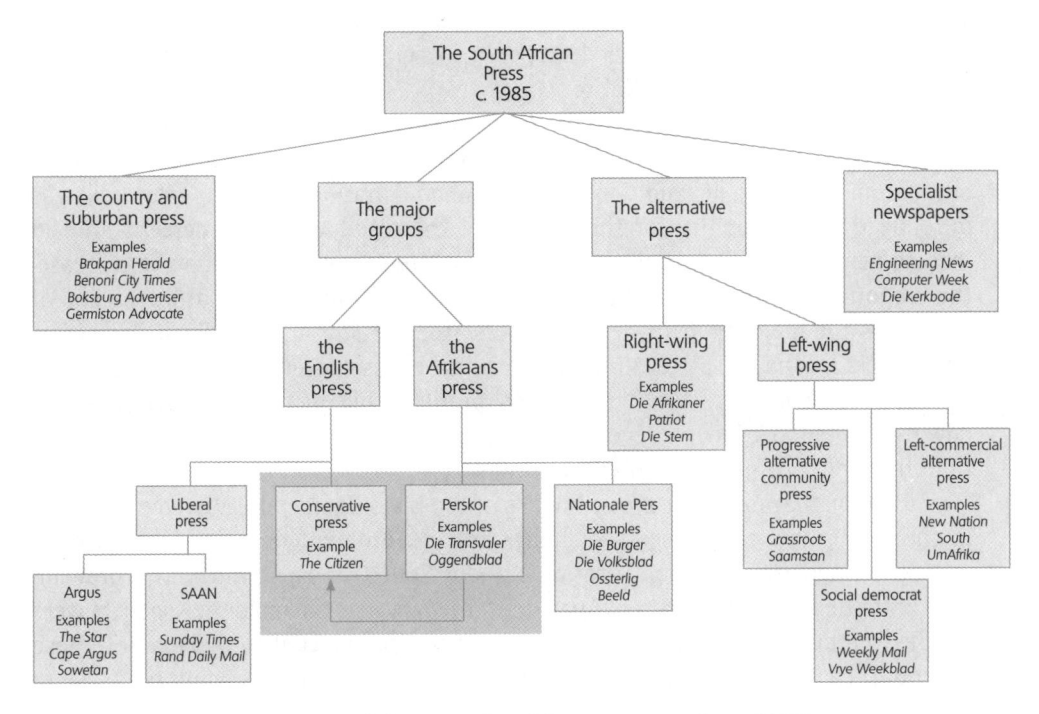

Figure 1.6 The structure of the South African press, *circa* 1985

Jackson (1993:6–10) identifies five specific areas that were the cause of added pressure to the press during the period from 1976 to 1990.

- *Pressure from the government*: The most specific challenge was the declaration of the State of Emergency by the government on 21 July 1985. However, it was the second State of Emergency that followed on 12 June 1986 that was the most restrictive on the press. Effectively, it placed large areas of the country as off-limits to the press. The purpose was to control what the government saw as incorrect or distorted images from being disseminated abroad. In reality it controlled the flow of accurate information to the South African public. Special powers were granted to the ministers of law and order and home affairs to close any newspaper they wished, either temporarily or permanently. The State of Emergency was only lifted on 2 February 1990 by President FW de Klerk.

- *Pressure from television*: The flighting of advertising on South African television, beginning in January 1978, had a major impact on the finances of the press, highly dependent on the income from sale of advertising space. Advertisers turned to the newer medium of television with the result that newspapers' share of total adspend dropped dramatically from 46,1 percent in 1975 to 26,6 percent in 1987. Television on the other hand accounted for 30 percent, to which radio added another 11,6 percent (Jackson 1993:7). To counter the effect of loss of advertising revenue to television, the four major newspaper groups joined forces and launched a television service of their own, in 1 October 1986, on a subscription basis, known as Electronic Media Network, or simply M-Net for short.
- *Pressure from the economic downturn*: Compounding the loss of advertising revenue to television, the economic downturn of the mid-1980s led to a further cut in advertising spending. In addition to a spiralling inflation problem, sales tax was introduced in the country for the first time. The result was a 26 percent drop in income from advertising. While the number of literate blacks was on the increase, the proportion of white readers continued to drop, with the result that by the end of the 1980s the majority of readers of papers, like *The Star* and the *Rand Daily Mail*, were black. This had disastrous financial results because despite the large circulation figures, the *Rand Daily Mail*'s readership profile could just not attract potential advertisers; the low income levels of blacks at that time made them less attractive than the high income represented by whites.
- *Pressure from the alternative press*: The rise of the Mass Democratic Movement (MDM) in the 1980s saw a coalescing of many anti-government organisations with an associated increase in the politicisation of many South Africans, who were a growing market for news and information. Apart from the fact that the major newspapers were unable to provide coverage of events and information relevant to this market, these potential readers viewed the major newspapers with suspicion as being too close to the government, and too concerned about making profits and maintaining white readership to be concerned with labour and life in the townships. This led to the rise of an alternative press. While posing little threat to the dwindling advertising revenue, the alternative press emphasised the fact that the major newspapers were out of touch with reality in South Africa. A more significant threat imposed by the rising alternative press was the challenge it presented to the English press, that had traditionally seen itself as the voice of the opposition in the country. More and more, the alternative press took over the function as critic of the government.
- *Pressure from the public*: By the end of the 1980s there was a growing apathy in the reading public towards a constant diet of negative news. There was a feeling among readers that the press was making a bigger issue out of unrest situations of the times than needs be. In addition, the ceaseless attacks by the government on the English press had resulted in a form of disdain on the part of the public regarding the values of a free press. Simply put, the press had become stigmatised with a negative image as the bearers of bad news created from living in a society obsessed with secrecy and intolerance.

## 1.3.3 Development of a black press

Newspapers for black readers only appeared shortly after Ordinance No. 60 came into being in 1829, granting press freedom to the Cape Colony. Hachten and Giffard (1984:145) identify four periods in the historical development of the black press in South Africa. Briefly, these periods are as follows:

- 1830–1880: The missionary period
- 1880–1930: The independent élitist period
- 1930–1980: The white-owned period
- 1980–1995: The multiracial period

Roelofse (1996:82) has since added that from about 1995 we are moving into a fifth period in which the mainstream press and traditionally white newspaper groups are beginning a phase of restructuring where they are incorporating black financial interests.

### From 1830 to 1880: The missionary period

The origins of the black press in South Africa is closely linked to the establishment of mission stations in the Eastern Cape and the work between missionaries and local blacks. Not only did the missionaries teach literacy; they also provided the skills and equipment necessary for publishing. In the process they also transferred the basic tenets of Western culture which is reflected in the first black newspapers (Johnson 1991:16). Initially, publications were limited to spelling and religious books, such as *Morisa Oa Molemo*, produced by the London Missionary Society, in Tswana, at Kuruman in the early 1930s. The first newspaper intended for black readers was *Umshumayeli Wendaba* (which means Publisher of the News), printed at the Wesleyan Mission Society in Grahamstown from 1837 to 1841. The Lovedale Missionary Institute produced *Ikwezi* (Morning Star) between 1844 and 1845, with *Indaba* (The News), a bilingual Xhosa/English newspaper following in 1862. *The Kafir Express*, also a bilingual paper, appeared in 1870. The Xhosa section *Isigidimi Sama Xosa* (The Xhosa Messenger) became a separate newspaper in 1876, and is considered important as it was the first newspaper to be edited by blacks. Commenting on the implications of the work of the missionaries, Johnson (1991:16) says a widening gap soon emerged between those who had received a missionary education and the rural-based majority who had not, resulting in the formation of a minority black élite infused with Western values.

### From 1880 to 1930: The independent élitist period

The training provided by the missionaries created an élite group who felt a need for newspapers independent of missionary control. The central figure here can be considered the 25-year old John Tengo Jabavu, who in 1884, resigned his position as editor of *Isigidimi Sama Xosa* in 1884 to found *Imvo Zabantsundu* (African Opinion) at King William's Town, the first newspaper written, owned and controlled by black people

(Cullen 1935:81). The paper rapidly developed into an influential expression of black opinion, promoting principles of non-violence and working together with liberal whites in an effort to bring about reforms, but soon ran into problems, including financial difficulties and internal tensions, and experienced intense competition from *Isigidimi* (Johnson 1991:17).

While *Imvo* was in decline, a new paper emerged in November 1897, *Izwi la Bantu*, which strongly opposed Jabavu on the issue of an organisation to represent black rights. With AK Soga as editor, *Izwi* was considered far more radical than *Imwo* demonstrating a socialist approach towards capitalism and a need for blacks to improve their lot. *Ilanga Lasa Natal* (The Natal Sun) was the next important newspaper to emerge for black Zulu readers; started in 1903 by John Dube. In 1912 Dube was elected the first chairman of the South African Native National Congress (SANNC), which later was to become the African National Congress (ANC) in 1923. With the exception of Jabavu, all pioneering black journalists were involved in the beginnings of the SANNC. One of the first activities of the newly formed organisation was the establishment of a newspaper to serve as a mouthpiece, *Abantu-Batho* (The People) (Johnson 1991:19). Other publications from this period were also associated with the establishment of political movements. For example, Mahatma Ghandi, the founder of the Indian National Congress in 1894, launched the paper *Indian Opinion* in 1903 as a weekly from Durban, which was immensely popular (Hachten & Giffard 1984:146).

Table 1.7 Growth of black owned and operated newspapers for the period 1911 to 1930 (Cullen 1935:81)

|      | Cape | Natal | Transvaal | Free State | Total |
|------|------|-------|-----------|------------|-------|
| 1911 | 4    | 3     | 1         | 0          | 8     |
| 1916 | 6    | 6     | 2         | 0          | 14    |
| 1921 | 5    | 7     | 3         | 3          | 18    |
| 1926 | 5    | 4     | 4         | 3          | 16    |
| 1930 | 2    | 7     | 7         | 3          | 19    |

## From 1930 to 1980: The white-owned period

Despite their important contribution to political awareness, most black newspapers lacked capital, equipment, skilled workers and a reliable distribution network. Bertram Paver, an ex-farmer and itinerant salesman saw potential profits to be made from the aspiring black market. Lacking any enthusiasm from commerce, Paver decided that the only way to prove the viability of the black market was from the inside, and this he decided could be achieved by becoming involved in publishing (Johnson 1991:21). The Bantu Press Ltd was formed and inaugurated a national newspaper *Bantu World* in April 1932. The establishment of *Bantu World* is important as it represents a move from a local to a national black press, in addition to redefining the role and strategy of the press. *Bantu World* was modelled, as a tabloid, on the British *Daily Mirror*. While Paver tried to avoid the image of white control over a black staff he was not always successful as a new controlling factor began to emerge, that of economics (Johnson 1991:21). Fourteen months later the Bantu Press was taken over by the Argus Company, which continued to control the company until 1952, quickly becoming the first monopoly in the black press with publications throughout southern Africa, with ten weekly newspapers, in addition to handling advertising for twelve different publications in eleven languages (Hachten & Giffard 1984:147). By 1962, the *World* had become a daily, and from then until its banning on 19 October 1977, became a significant voice in black journalism. Shortly after the Soweto uprising of June 1976, Percy Qoboza was appointed as the first black editor without white supervision.

The next important development came in May 1951 when Jim Bailey, the son of mining magnate Abe Bailey started the *African Drum*, followed in March 1955 by the *Golden City Post*. With these titles, Bailey started a new trend in journalism, by using a formula of sport, sex and crime to establish a popularist press which appealed to the broad mass of literate black South Africans. In October 1951, the *African Drum* was shortened to *Drum* and moved from Cape Town to Johannesburg, under the editorship of Anthony Sampson and Tom Hopkinson, who brought Fleet Street experience to the publication. Roelfose (1996:83–84) identifies a number of significant contributions made by *Drum*:

- It became the forerunner of the alternative press that was active during the final years of apartheid, in that it fearlessly conducted investigative journalism and addressed the social and political grievance of blacks.
- It focused world attention on South Africa by exposing abuses such as exploitation of blacks on many white farms, the appalling prison conditions and the Sharpeville massacre.
- It restored pride in the black population by focusing on sociocultural issues that interested sophisticated blacks.
- It highlighted the contributions made by world-class black musicians and writers to South African culture.
- It developed modern and colourful English for black urbanites.

In addition to providing a lasting impact on black journalism, by 1969 *Drum* had a weekly circulation of 470 000, larger than most of South African periodicals (Hachten & Giffard 1984:149). Although *Drum* was never banned, like many of its journalists, as a result of the politics of mid-1960s the periodical was withdrawn in 1965, only to reappear later in a milder form, without the aggressive reporting of political issues that had earlier been so meaningful to urban blacks (ibid).

## *1980–1995: The multiracial period*

With the urbanisation of blacks, increasing numbers started reading whatever newspapers were available. In this manner, many of the so-called white newspapers found, as the 1960s moved into the 1970s, that they gained a substantial black readership with the introduction of regular township editions. At the same time, most white newspapers had saturated their markets. In 1976 there were ten newspapers in a market of two million readers in the Gauteng area (Hachten & Giffard 1984:150). While the introduction of television at the beginning of 1976 translated into reduced circulation figures.

Black journalists who were originally hired for the township editions or as stringers (freelance newspaper correspondents) now began to move into more regular positions on the major newspapers. Papers such as the *Rand Daily Mail* took the lead in integrating more black news into all parts of the paper. By the time the *Rand Daily Mail* closed in 1985, almost 80 percent of its readers were black (Roelofse 1996:84). A problem that now emerged was the limited number of skilful and adequately trained black journalists. A 1977 study found that there was one journalist per 1 171 white people, but only one black journalist for 51 961 blacks (Hachten & Giffard 1984:151). The need for adequately trained black journalists is still an acute problem in the media.

Another victim of the political turmoil of the apartheid years was the *Post*, which closed at the end of the 1970s because its registration had lapsed following industrial action and the government's unwillingness to agree to re-registration. This ironically led to the birth of South Africa's largest daily newspaper, the *Sowetan* (Roelofse 1996:84–85). The Argus group produced a knock-and-drop (local newspaper delivered free to suburban homes) newssheet known as the *Sowetan Mirror*, which was distributed in the townships. This newssheet absorbed some of the thirty journalists who lost their jobs due to the closure of the *Post*. On 2 February 1981, the tabloid was transformed into a daily tabloid to fill the void left by the *Post*, edited by Joe Latekgomo, former deputy-editor of the *Post* (Hachten & Giffard 1984:152). The *Sowetan* was sold by the Argus group to the black business group New Africa Investments Limited (NAIL) in 1994 indicating a move out of the fourth phase and into the fifth phase of development.

### 1.3.4 The alternative press

During the second half of the twentieth century, social and political struggles characterised South Africa. Most of the mainstream press provided limited or no coverage of these diverse political and social activities (Oosthuizen 1991:46). In South Africa, the mainstream press is usually considered to be the publications of the four major press groups, which at that time consisted of the titles published by Times Media, the Argus group, Nasionale Pers and Perskor. An alternative press usually becomes active when the political, economic, social or cultural views of certain social groups are excluded from the popular media market, or the group itself has no voice. Although the alternative press particularly came to the fore in the late 1970s after two Argus newspapers, *World* and *Post*, were closed by the government, the alternative press in South Africa has a much longer history. The emergence and development of the alternative press tends to parallel the struggle against apartheid. Louw (1989:26-27) and Johnson (1991:24) identify three distinct phases in the historical development of the South African alternative press. Briefly these periods are as follows:

- 1930s – 1960s: A period characterised by opposition and resistance
- 1960s – late 1970s: A period characterised by the rise of black consciousness
- 1980s – mid 1990s: A final period characterised by the intensity of the struggle and peaking of the alternative press

## From the 1930s to the 1960s: A period of opposition and resistance

The first phase in the development of the alternative press, according to Johnson (1991:25), begins within the context of general resistance. It was during the 1930s that white control of the black press was consolidated, while the ANC entered a period of inertia following adoption of a policy to shun militancy. This resulted in a few pockets of black-owned newspapers, such as *Inkundla*, to represent an independent liberal voice. Despite being viewed as a radical left publication by the authorities of the time, *Inkundla* was actually moderate in its views, providing a mix of politics, sport, the arts and general-interest features. However, the paper did openly support the ANC and played a key role in the election of Albert Luthuli as the Natal President of the ANC. *Inkundla* closed in 1951. We can consider *Inkundla* as a transition journal because it was independent, relatively liberal, but with a wide and sympathetic coverage of the ANC.

Other publications from this period include *Fighting Talk* (1942-1963) which campaigned for soldiers' rights and warned of the advances of Nazism. While *The Africanist* (1953) and *The Guardian*, which began publication in 1937, became the *New Age* in 1954, which in turn became *Spark* in 1962, closing in 1963, promoted the cause of the ANC. This publication has the distinction of being renowned as an example of a radical newspaper (Johnson 1991:27). In turn, *The African Lodestar* (1949) promoted the multiracial Communist-orientated Youth League that eventually was to become the Pan Africanist Congress (PAC) in 1959. This first phase was a complex period in the development of resistance, where alternative publications reflected on the development of political movements against a background of ongoing internal conflict and political apathy. Most alternative publications had been silenced together with movements such as the ANC and PAC. There followed a significant lull in resistance.

## From the 1960s to the late 1970s: A period of rising black consciousness

The alternative press emerged again in the late 1960s as part of an expression of rising black consciousness, taking the form of massive labour strikes such as those during 1973 which were part of the opposition to white domination. Reaction from the state came in the form of repressive tolerance where leaders were allowed to release tensions as long as it was restricted to rhetoric (Johnson 1991:28). The rise of black consciousness, both as an ideology and strategy, prompted the re-emergence of independent non-commercial alternative publications, such as the *SASO Newsletter* of the South African Students Organisation, which was founded in Durban during 1970, and was crucial in spreading black consciousness ideology. The *Newsletter* was aggressive, bringing racial issues to the foreground of the black political agenda and set the trend for similar publications such as *Black Review*, which started in 1972 and *Black Viewpoint*, which was edited by Steve Biko. The *UBJ Bulletin* was produced by the Union of Black Journalists in 1975, a breakaway group of black dissident journalists from the multiracial South African Society of Journalists, and was banned after only two issues. Although limited in publication, it is generally regarded as being representative of black consciousness at its peak (Johnson 1991:29).

It is ironic that the very success of the rising black consciousness was its own undoing. As the uprising spread across the country, it brought mass participation (Louw 1989:27). Following on from the Soweto riots of 1976, the passive attitude of the government changed dramatically, leading to the banning of organisations, publications and leadership, which brought to an end the second phase through the creation of another vacuum. According to Louw (1989:27), this phase was primarily characterised by a top-down approach to resistance, where intellectuals became leaders and the alternative press started to play a significant role in the mobilisation of black people.

## From the 1980s to the mid 1990s: The climax of the alternative press

Developments in the 1980s were related to the emergence of the Mass Democratic Movement (MDM) and the United Democratic Front (UDF) in 1983 and the re-emergence of an alternative press was associated with the rise of these freedom movements. Unlike the second phase, the third phase was marked by a bottom-up style of resistance where mass and democratic participation at grassroots level in the struggle and resistance movements took place, resulting in mobilisation of the people. The alternative press, which was varied, was to play an important part in this resistance. Louw and Tomaselli (1991:7–13) divide the alternative press of this phase in to three categories. The Nationalist government, however, viewed the alternative press as a single entity, being seen as part of the greater total onslaught concept (Hachten & Giffard 1984:3).

- The *progressive-alternative press*, which is also known as the people's media, expressed the struggle at community level as part of the great national struggle. Community issues were central to the purpose of the alternative press, which formed part of the process of popular resistance. Examples of publications here are *Grassroots, Saamstaan* and *Al Qualam*. As resistance grew, it was still ignored by the conventional press. To accommodate this deficiency, a left-commercial press emerged after 1983 as a hybrid development of the capitalist and progressive-alternative presses, but with a focus on left-wing activities.
- The *left-commercial press* was closely related to establishment press, concentrating on the coverage of national news, financing themselves through the sale of

advertising space, while the community newspapers reverted to coverage of grassroots community issues. *New Nation* was formed in Johannesburg in 1986, *South* in Cape Town and *New Africa* in Durban, both during 1988. Not even the states of emergency could prevent their development, simply because the emergency had become a "way of life" where activists exploited legal loopholes (Louw & Tomaselli 1991:9-10). When leaders were detained, new ones simply took their place. In many respects, according to Louw and Tomaselli (1991:10), the experiences of the left-commercial press is similar to that of the Afrikaans press which mobilised Afrikaner nationalism during the 1930s. At one stage *New Nation* and *South* were banned for periods of between one and three months. Circulation figures were not very high, averaging about 20 000 per issue, although *New Nation* did have a readership of 67 000.

- The *independent social-democrat press* differed from the conventional press in its approach, form, and especially content. The aims of the social-democrat press were financial independence, support of broad democratic ideals and the maintenance of their independence from any specific political movement. The ideal of accuracy in reporting was also important. Whereas most publications grew out of the various resistance groups, the *Weekly Mail* grew out of the closure of the *Rand Daily Mail* in 1985. Former *Rand Daily Mail* journalists found themselves stigmatised and unable to find gainful employment. The solution was to start their own newspaper, and in this way the *Weekly Mail* pioneered a commercially viable leftist-press (Louw & Tomaselli 1991:12-13). Wending Publikasies was established in 1988 and the Afrikaans weekly, *Vrye Weekblad*, appeared on 4 November 1988. *Vrye Weekblad*, under the editorship of Max du Preez, was the only left-wing Afrikaans alternative newspaper and soon became known as a newspaper that did not hesitate to criticise the shortcomings of the government of the day, despite the restrictions on the press, sometime with dire consequences. For example, in 1992 *Vrye Weekblad* had 37 criminal charges, eight libel suits and five urgent court interdicts against it (Faure 1995:127).

After FW de Klerk, the then State President, launched his reform initiatives in February 1990, the position of the alternative press, which had often carried exclusive news of the struggle, gradually deteriorated. The mainstream press now started to cover news of the recently unbanned political parties and trade unions. The alternative press therefore lost their exclusivity in respect of certain news events. Another setback came in the withdrawal of overseas funding for alternative newspapers following the dismantling of apartheid. This made it even more difficult for alternative newspapers to survive, since their working class readers are, on the whole, poor and there is little incentive to attract advertisers. Clearly some adjustments had to be made. The *Weekly Mail* merged with *The Guardian Weekly* with effect from 3 April 1992 to become the *Mail & Guardian*. The *Vrye Weekblad* changed its periodicity in May 1992 from that of a weekly newspaper to that of a fortnightly glossy news magazine with the emphasis on providing background articles, but with little success, finally closing down on 2 February 1994 (Diederichs 1993:86).

## 1.3.5 The South African newspaper environment

If we look at Table 1.8, where the number and distribution of newspapers for a number of selected African countries are compared, it is clear that while South Africa is a media-rich country in African terms, it is by no means the leader in the area of the press. However, South Africa does lead by a long way in terms of the number of newspapers that are available and in circulation statistics for the Southern African Development Community (SADC) region. The breakdown of the various titles and readership is given in tables 1.9 to 1.13. If we were to generalise from an overview of these tables, it would seem as if most newspapers show an increase in their circulation figures. Koenderman (2000a:94) warns that we need to exercise care when interpreting All Media and Products Survey (AMPS) figures. As the population base that is used for the surveys on which these circulation figures are based has been updated, the latest figures given in tables 1.9 to 1.13 should be treated with particular care. To take as an example, the *Pretoria News* (see Table 1.9), we need to ask if it is really credible that readership has increased by 36 percent, while circulation has only increased 7 percent? Alternatively, the figures show that *The Citizen* enjoyed a readership increase of 16 percent while circulation actually declined by 6 percent. These discrepancies come from the fact that, in order to match contemporary demographics, the universe (all possible elements that can be included in a research sample) used for AMPS has been increased by 11 percent or some 2,75-million people.

**Table 1.8 Daily newspapers in selected African countries**
(United Nations 1997:119–120; 2000:117–118)

|  | Number of titles |  |  |  | Circulation Total 000 |  |  |  | Per 1 000 inhabitants |  |  |  |
|---|---|---|---|---|---|---|---|---|---|---|---|---|
|  | 1980 | 1985 | 1990 | 1996 | 1980 | 1985 | 1990 | 1996 | 1980 | 1985 | 1990 | 1996 |
| South Africa | 24* | 24 | 22 | 17 | 1 400 | 1 440 | 1 340 | 1 288 | 51* | 47 | 39 | 34 |
| Nigeria | 16 | 19 | 31 | 25 | 1 100* | 1 400* | 1 700* | 2 740* | 17* | 18* | 20* | 27* |
| Egypt | 12 | 12 | 14 | 17 | 1 701 | 2 383 | 2 400* | 2 400* | 39 | 48 | 43* | 38* |
| Kenya | 3 | 4 | 5 | 4 | 216 | 283 | 330* | 262 | 13 | 14 | 14* | 9,4 |
| Zimbabwe | 2 | 3 | 2 | 2 | 133 | 203 | 206 | 209 | 19 | 24 | 21 | 19 |
| Zambia | 2 | 2 | 2 | 3 | 110 | 95 | 99 | 114 | 19 | 15 | 14 | 14 |

* Estimated

# A South African Media Map

Table 1.9  Readership of English dailies in 1 000s during the period 1998–2000 (South African Advertising Research Foundation 2000a)

| English daily newspapers | Jan–Jun 1998 AMPS 1998 '000 | Jan–Jun 1999 AMPS 1999A '000 | Jul–Dec 1999 AMPS 1999B '000 | Jan–Jun 2000 AMPS 2000A '000 |
|---|---|---|---|---|
| Business Day | 86 | 155 | 133 | 146 |
| Cape Argus | 389 | 371 | 387 | 351 |
| Cape Times | 278 | 247 | 260 | 355 |
| The Citizen | 585 | 651 | 756 | 897 |
| Daily Dispatch | 199 | 159 | 182 | 218 |
| Daily News | 349 | 370 | 337 | 367 |
| Diamond Field Advertiser | 47 | 44 | 48 | 45 |
| EP Herald | 145 | 126 | 131 | 181 |
| Evening Post | 96 | 72 | 77 | 116 |
| The Mercury | 196 | 246 | 241 | 249 |
| Natal Witness | 115 | 112 | 118 | 141 |
| Pretoria News | 119 | 132 | 130 | 202 |
| Sowetan | 1 552 | 1 558 | 1 807 | 2 145 |
| The Star | 603 | 665 | 610 | 855 |

Table 1.10  Readership of Afrikaans dailies in 1 000s during the period 1998–2000 (South African Advertising Research Foundation 2000a)

| Afrikaans daily newspapers | Jan–Jun 1998 AMPS 1998 '000 | Jan–Jun 1999 AMPS 1999A '000 | Jul–Dec 1999 AMPS 1999B '000 | Jan–Jun 2000 AMPS 2000A '000 |
|---|---|---|---|---|
| Beeld | 411 | 432 | 459 | 469 |
| Die Burger | 472 | 523 | 479 | 600 |
| Die Volksblad | 110 | 112 | 106 | 127 |

© Juta & Co

## MEDIA STUDIES

**Table 1.11  Readership of English weeklies in 1 000s during the period 1998–2000** (South African Advertising Research Foundation 2000a)

| English weekly newspapers | Jan–Jun 1998 AMPS 1998 '000 | Jan–Jun 1999 AMPS 1999A '000 | Jul–Dec 1999 AMPS 1999B '000 | Jan–Jun 2000 AMPS 2000A '000 |
|---|---|---|---|---|
| The Citizen (Saturdays) | 581 | 733 | 600 | 796 |
| Daily Dispatch (Saturdays) | 112 | 167 | 111 | 97 |
| East Cape Weekend | 175 | 105 | 98 | 150 |
| EP Herald (Saturdays) | 114 | 113 | 106 | 153 |
| Independent on Saturday | 273 | 303 | 288 | 338 |
| Mail & Guardian | 120 | 174 | 163 | 192 |
| Natal Witness (Saturdays) | 120 | 118 | 112 | 144 |
| Pretoria News (Weekend) | 63 | 84 | 87 | 73 |
| Saturday Star | 357 | 547 | 439 | 503 |
| Saturday Argus (Weekend) | 328 | 388 | 363 | 397 |
| Sunday Independent | 86 | 166 | 119 | 184 |
| Sunday Times | 2 345 | 2 666 | 2 517 | 3 212 |
| Sunday Tribune | 547 | 568 | 281 | 687 |
| Sunday Argus (Weekend) | 249 | 290 | 290 | 304 |

**Table 1.12  Readership of Afrikaans weeklies in 1 000s during the period 1998–2000** (South African Advertising Research Foundation 2000a)

| Afrikaans weekly newspapers | Jan–Jun 1998 AMPS 1998 '000 | Jan–Jun 1999 AMPS 1999A '000 | Jul–Dec 1999 AMPS 1999B '000 | Jan–Jun 2000 AMPS 2000A '000 |
|---|---|---|---|---|
| Die Burger (Saturdays) | 368 | 514 | 471 | 570 |
| Naweek-Beeld | 175 | 218 | 198 | 238 |
| Rapport | 1 578 | 1 700 | 1 762 | 1 762 |
| Die Volksblad (Saturday) | 80 | 74 | 103 | 112 |

# A South African Media Map

**Table 1.13  Readership of other weeklies in 1 000s during the period 1998–2000** (South African Advertising Research Foundation 2000a)

| Other weekly newspapers | Jan–Jun 1998 AMPS 1998 '000 | Jan–Jun 1999 AMPS 1999A '000 | Jul–Dec 1999 AMPS 1999B '000 | Jan–Jun 2000 AMPS 2000A '000 |
|---|---|---|---|---|
| *City Press* | 1 563 | 1 856 | 1 709 | 2 381 |
| *Ilanga* (Mondays) | 806 | 1 021 | 1 038 | 1 440 |
| *Ilanga* (Thursdays) | 724 | 891 | 932 | 1 313 |
| *Post* | 299 | 352 | 314 | 314 |
| *Soccer Laduma* | 356 | 559 | 561 | 1 104 |
| *Sunday World* | – | – | 148 | 323 |

The second half of 1998 was not particularly good, as most newspapers recorded poor returns with possibly the lowest circulation figures over the past five-year period. Only three of the 16 major dailies showed an increase, while combined sales dropped by 4,3 percent compared with the previous year. In an industry that functions on tight margins, this figure is significant (Koenderman 1999a:123). This downturn was partly attributed to the economic downturn experienced at that time, as the general state of the country reflects in the performance of a newspaper. But, says Moerdyk (1999b:15), the reason for poor returns was also largely due to a lack of focus. Those titles that did manage to hold their own were those with extensive marketing campaigns, such as with the Independent Newspapers group in Gauteng. In an aggressive marketing campaign, Naspers' *City Press* dropped its cover price from R3,20 to R2,00 for a week and launched a competition with R1-million in prize money (Haffajee & Shapshak 1999:4). When the circulation figures of weekly titles are added, circulation shows a decline of only 0,6 percent, which, says Koenderman (1999a:123), suggests that people were buying weeklies rather than dailies simply for economic reasons. Poor circulation statistics continued into 1999 and while the newspaper industry was struggling economically it was also subject to more corporate restructuring than in any other sector of the economy. Case Study 1.2 attempts to set out some of the many changes that have taken place within the press industry in South Africa over the past few years. While Naspers and Times Media were expanding, Independent Newspapers were cutting back, retrenching staff in order to become more efficient by removing unnecessary costs. Staff saw things differently as a plan to remove dead wood in order to make room for the implementation of affirmative action policies. A consequence was low staff morale (Haffajee & Shapshak 1999:4).

The complex nature of the South African press is summed up in Case study 1.2, which is representative of the *status quo* in the first quarter of 2000. The case study also hints at the rapidly changing nature of the press in South Africa.

# MEDIA STUDIES

**Case study 1.2:** The intricacies of the South African print media

## A to Z: Spelling out the South African media maze

### A
An alphabet soup. That's what the print media industry is becoming. Ownership is changing every day. Shares have changed hands in each of the four major newspaper publishers and they seem to continue to do so as black shareholders buy in. New titles are hitting the news-stands with regularity and new media personalities are being sculpted. This is a short guide.

### B
BDFM. The company owned jointly by Times Media Limited and the United Kingdom-based Pearson Group. It owns *Business Day* and *Financial Mail*, both of which are showing steady circulation growth.

### C
Caxton. This company, owned by Terry Moolman, merged in 1998 with Perskor in a R3,4-billion deal. It sold off its shares in *Rapport* and now owns *The Citizen*. All eyes are on Caxton to see what it is planning to do with *The Citizen*, whose bland coverage is surprisingly popular, especially among horseracing enthusiasts. Caxton has cornered the knock-and-drop market but the jury is still out on its ability to run a daily that will go head-to-head with the *Sowetan* and *The Star* in Gauteng.

### D
Dynamo Investments. Oscar Dhlomo's company, which owned 51% of the shares in *City Press*, has sold its equity stake back to Nasionale Pers.

### E
*Elle*. With the departure both of its editor, Shona Bagley, and her deputy, Heather Robertson, *Elle* has appointed Nadine Rubin as its editor. The 27-year-old debuted at *Cosmopolitan* and has most-recently been working in New York.

### F
Football. Soccer-mad South Africans are the target readership of the new Times Media Limited title, *Sportsday*, which will focus on quality soccer coverage. At the same time, the *Sunday Times* is investing in new soccer writers.

### G
Government Communication and Information System (GCIS). This body has replaced the old South African Communication Service. It will sculpt policy (and possible legislation) to guide and encourage media diversity.

# A South African Media Map

**H**
Hacks. An impolite term for a noble profession, journalists are naming their price in a newspaper war. Speak to any editor – they all bemoan the rapid staff turnover newspapers are suffering.

**I**
Independent Newspapers. The biggest newspaper publishers on the continent are based in South Africa with head offices in Dublin, Ireland. Owned by Heinz king, Tony O'Reilly, the company has 14 titles around the country. It is run by chief executive Ivan Fallon and is regarded as an establishment voice close to the ruling African National Congress. The new owners have started the daily *Business Report*, which is slotted into all the morning titles. There is strong market talk that a daily *Sports Report* will follow.

**J**
Johnnic. This black-controlled holding company has significant media interests through its shareholding in TML and Omnicor. It is chaired by Cyril Ramaphosa and owned by the National Empowerment Consortium (NEC), a loose grouping of black business interests.

**K**
Fred Khumalo. The 32-year-old editor of the *Sunday World* which launches on Sunday. Hailing from KwaZulu-Natal, Khumalo has said that there is no black-owned, managed and run newspaper that is a force to be reckoned with in South Africa. That is what he's promising. It will have an initial print run of between 150 000 and 200 000 newspapers.

**L**
Libel. Over the past few years, irate public figures have asked the courts to intervene and punish newspapers for stories they claim are defamatory. Few have won their cases.

**M**
Moolman, Terry. The king of the knock-and-drop empire is about to break into the mainstream industry he has hankered after. Moolman is now co-owner of *The Citizen* and is still brawling with Independent Newspapers despite a *détente* in their relationship. In terms of the peace deal, Moolman has given the nod to Independent Newspapers' plans for its own knock-and-drops. In turn, Independent has given Moolman a ticket into the big time.

**N**
Nasionale Pers. The Afrikaans-owned media concern is one to watch. Under the hand of its new managing director, Koos Bekker, it has invested in its newspaper and

matched this with state-of-the-art development of its Internet projects. The group was keen to get into the English market, but now seems content to invest in its flagship weekend title, *City Press*.

New Africa Investments Limited (Nail). This holding company is building up significant media interests. Its media division is headed by former broadcasting executive Zwelakhe Sisulu. With TML, it is the co-owner of two newspapers: the *Sowetan* and *Sunday World*.

## O

Tony O'Reilly. The Irish baked-bean king [Heinz] turned media magnate is no stranger to these shores. Not content with owning the biggest newspaper publishing business on this continent, he this week announced intentions to base his new online operation in Cape Town, which he sees as being the world's newest Silicon Valley.

## P

Penta Publications. Sold two years ago by Independent Newspapers to businesswoman Pearl Mashabela. The company owns several magazines. The best-known of them are *Living Africa, De Kat* and *Tribute*. The editors of each of these titles have quit in the last month, amid talk that there is a cash flow crisis at the company. Electricity has been cut several times (once during the Christmas party) and salaries paid late. But Mashabela says all is well.

## S

South African Press Association. The national wire agency is selling off its radio news division, Network Radio Services, for a rumoured R1,8-million to recoup its huge losses. Network provides news bulletins to community and commercial stations. It is likely to bought by its MD, James Lorimer.

## T

Times Media Limited. Now controlled by NEC, this group owns the *Sunday Times* and has joint holding of the *Sowetan* and *Sunday World*. It has diversified and has a growing electronic media arm that produces news for radio current affairs and the daily television programme *Business Tonight*.

## U

Unbundling. While the call to smash the media monopolies was popular in anti-apartheid days, it has proven somewhat more difficult in practice. Faced with rising print costs and shrinking advertising revenue, more media companies are going for economies of scale and they are consequently getting bigger. Black companies like Dynamo and Kagiso have shrugged off their print interests.

# A South African Media Map

**V**

The virtual newspaper. The jury is still out on how popular the virtual newspaper is. "The Daily Me" is the name given to a new kind of read when Internet newspapers customise a newspaper for browsers. Its major drawback is that it cannot be read on the toilet.

**W**

Bronwyn Wilkinson. On March 15, Wilkinson will become the country's first female newspaper editor. She takes the helm of *Sportsday*, itself a coup as there are so few women sports journalists in the country. The newspaper is owned by TML and is aiming for daily sales of 40 000.

**X**

X-rated. Increasingly, South African newspapers are getting racier on the outside and more intelligent on the inside. Major Sunday reads (*Sunday Times, City Press* and *Sunday World*) will feature more showbiz and sex. At the same time, to attract wealthier black readers, they all feature more economic analysis, personal finance and political coverage inside the paper. *City Press* had a bare-breasted Page 3 girl for a while, but she's been scrapped.

**Y**

Youth. The key to rising newspaper circulation. The Print Media Association has a school project to encourage a reading culture. Most newspapers report that young readers are drawn to sports coverage and showbiz news.

**Z**

No snoozing. With new titles being launched and ownership changing, no editor or publisher can be caught napping. The Internet is the new wave in publishing, more immediate than its older print sister and beyond the reach of censors. Most major newspaper companies are investing heavily in the Internet, with classifieds a growing trend.

(*Mail & Guardian*, 5–11 March 1999:5)

Diversification of the media was also a priority of the newly elected government, and the major newspaper groups were looking for possible partnerships with empowerment groups. The diversity that could be found in broadcasting is still lacking in the press, and this is a matter of concern to the government. The four press groups continued to focus exclusively on the readership they always had and were not seen to be venturing into newer markets. The government was also particularly keen to avoid the formation of monopolies that own both publishing and distribution interests. Over the last 25 years, the South African press had become characterised by the formation of cartels that own the major newspapers. This trend intensified over the past few years, with the result that the four major groups are more interested in their immediate competition than in

# MEDIA STUDIES

increasing the number of newspapers. This is clearly evident in the statistics quoted in Table 1.7, which show a decrease in the number of newspaper titles available in South Africa over the eleven-year period between 1985 and 1996.

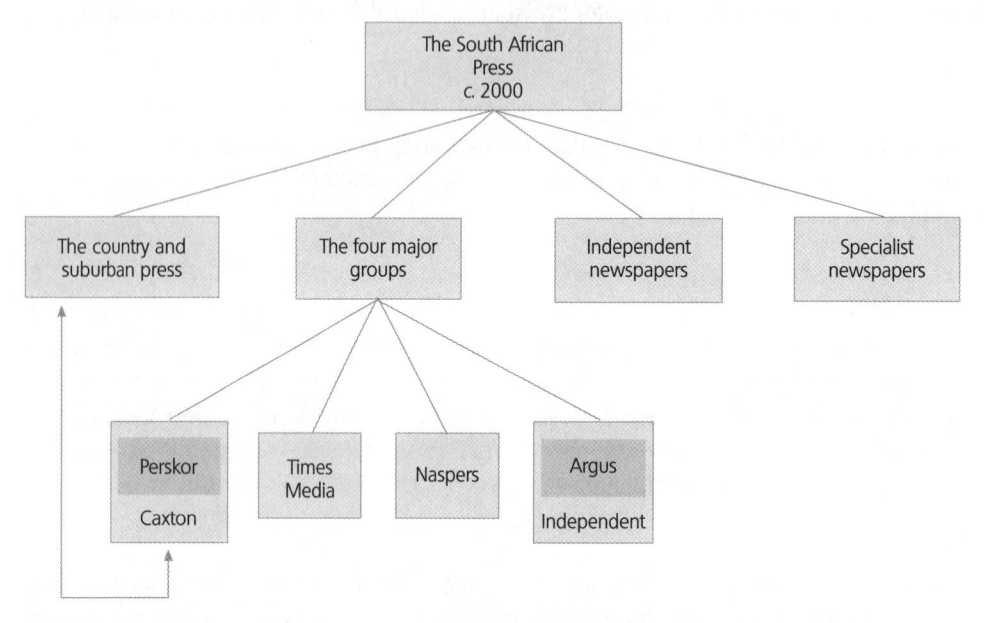

**Figure 1.7 The structure of the South African press, *circa* 2000**

## The four major press groups

The South African press is dominated by the publications and associated business of four major groups. However, there are smaller companies that produce publications as well as a number of so-called independent publishers or agencies that are responsible for newspapers such as the *Mail & Guardian*. During the 1980s, ownership of newspaper titles began to consolidate, driven by the economics of centralised production on one hand and the competition brought on by the introduction of television on the other (Diederichs 1993:78). Although we can regard the ownership of the South African press today as highly centralised, it is much less so than prior to democratisation of the country in 1994. Since 1994, the press has been characterised by dramatic and ongoing changes in ownership, which is beginning to challenge the assumption that the South African press has always been in the hands of the few. As examples, both the Argus Newspapers and Times Media were subsidiaries of the Anglo American Corporation. These ongoing changes are part of the greater transformation of the South African sociopolitical environment, with the focus on black empowerment. However, transformation has not been without criticism, as it is seen as benefiting only the wealthy élite within the black sector of the broader South African community. We look briefly at each of the four major press groups.

# A South African Media Map

- Independent Newspapers
  Independent Newspapers can trace its ancestry back to Francis Dormer who established the Argus Printing Company in 1889. When first established, this company had close links with the powerful mining magnate, Cecil Rhodes. The company retained its ties to the mining industry until it was sold to Independent Newspapers though ownership as an Anglo American subsidiary, JCI. The first step Argus Newspapers took to decentralise ownership was the selling off of its controlling interest in the *Sowetan* in 1993 to New Africa Publications, a subsidiary of New Africa Investments Limited (NAIL). Argus ties with the Anglo American Group ended when Tony O'Reilly, owner of Independent Newspapers of Ireland, bought a 31 percent share in Argus Newspapers in 1994 (see also Case Study 1.2). O'Reilly's Independent Newspapers is a global player, owning 65 percent of the newspaper industry in Ireland, is the fourth largest newspaper group operating in Australia and has a 24,99 percent interest in the British newspaper *The Independent*. O'Reilly is also a director of the *Washington Post*. A possible advantage of O'Reilly's takeover of the Argus Group is that South African groups cannot prescribe what can or should be published in Independent publications. Secondly, the change of ownership is seen as a means of upgrading the quality of English-language journalism in South Africa. The buy-out by Independent required a resolution of the intricate cross-ownership between Argus and Times Media of each other's titles. For example, Times Media owned 30 percent of Natal Newspapers and the *Cape Argus* and 45 percent of the *Pretoria News*, which now became 100 percent Argus owned (Argus buys TML ... 1994:13). Titles in the Independent Group include:
  - *Sunday Independent* (Johannesburg)
  - *The Star* (Johannesburg)
  - *Saturday Star* (Johannesburg)
  - *Pretoria News* (Pretoria)
  - *Sunday Tribune* (Durban)
  - *Daily News* (Durban)
  - *The Mercury* (Durban)
  - *The Independent on Saturday* (Durban)
  - *Cape Argus* (Cape Town)
  - *Cape Times* (Cape Town)
  - *Diamond Filed Advertiser* (Kimberley)

  *The Star* is considered as the flagship title of the group and publishes four different editions daily, from early morning to late afternoon. This enables the paper to distribute the latest news to readers at various stages throughout the day. *The Star* is also available in an international edition, known as *The Star and SA Times* which is distributed in London and Syndey.

- Times Media Limited
  Like the Argus Group, the roots of Times Media Ltd also lie in mining, when mining magnate Sir Abe Bailey bought the *Rand Daily Mail* in 1902 and the *Sunday Times* in

1906. These two newspapers shared staff and facilities. In 1937 the *Sunday Express* was also added to the group. Out of this grouping evolved South African Associated Newspapers (SAAN) in May 1965. SAAN published the internationally acclaimed *Rand Daily Mail* and *The Sunday Times*. SAAN was forced to close the *Rand Daily Mail* and later, *The Sunday Express* after both titles lost R23-million within a period of 15 months (Diederichs 1993:80). Concentration of ownership was further reduced in 1996 when a black empowerment deal was struck between the Anglo American Corporation and the National Empowerment Consortium (NEC), whereby a group of 28 small shareholders bought a 35 percent share. To ensure independence, a 50 percent controlling interest in the leading TML titles, *Business Day* and *Financial Mail* was sold to the UK publisher, Pearsons. This means that Johnnic, which is controlled by the National Empowerment Consortium, no longer has a say in the running of these two publications.

Titles in the TML group include:
- *Sunday Times* (National) (co-owner)
- *Business Day* (Johannesburg) (co-owner)
- *Eastern Province Herald* (Port Elizabeth)
- *Evening Post* (Port Elizabeth)
- *Weekend Post* (Port Elizabeth)
- *Algoa Sun* (Port Elizabeth)
- *Our Times* (Jeffreys Bay)

TML also owns five regional newspapers in the Border region of Eastern Cape through a subsidiary, Dispatch Media.

- Naspers (Nasionale Pers Limited)
Nasionale Pers was originally established in Cape Town in 1915 and catered for the interests of the Afrikaans community through *Die Burger*, the first Afrikaans daily. Until the 1950s the activities of Nasionale Pers were limited to the Cape and Free State. It was the industrial development and subsequent urbanisation of the then Transvaal, now Gauteng area, during the 1960s that led to the establishment of the Sunday newspaper *Die Beeld*. *Die Beeld* later merged with *Dagbreek* to become *Rapport*. The establishment of *Beeld* as a daily title in 1974 broke Perskor's monopoly of Afrikaans-language newspapers in the Transvaal. *Die Volksblad* of Bloemfontein is also part of the Naspers group. Naspers is also a major shareholder in the Sunday newspaper *City Press*, published in Johannesburg. The *Oosterlig*, which was published in Port Elizabeth, closed in 1994. Naspers also has extensive interests in rural and suburban newspapers throughout the country. The control structure of Naspers is illustrated in Figure 1.8, where the directors of the company retain control through the issue of high-voting unlisted shares, which carry 82,8 percent of the voting rights compared with the 17,2 percent of the listed N shares (Naspers 2000).

# A South African Media Map

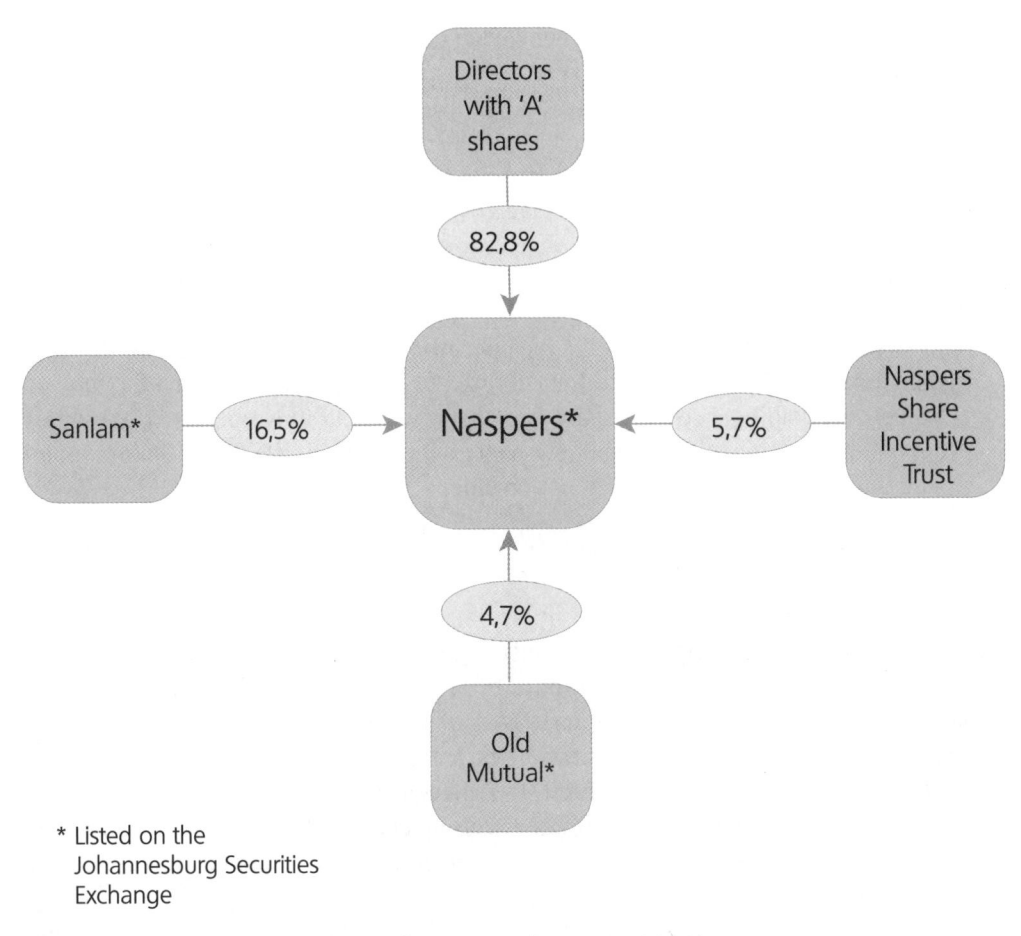

**Figure 1.8 Control structure of Naspers** (Naspers 2000)

\* Listed on the Johannesburg Securities Exchange

- Caxton Limited
  To understand the current structure of Caxton Limited we need to begin a brief look at Perskor, formed in 1971 by the amalgamation of the Afrikaanse Pers, founded in 1932, with that of Voortrekkerpers, founded in 1936. As with Nasionale Pers, politics played an important role in the established of Perskor newspapers. *Die Transvaler* was launched in 1937 with the exclusive purpose of promoting Afrikaner nationalism and culture. HF Verwoerd was the first editor and this newspaper became the mouthpiece of the Nationalist Party in the Transvaal. The establishment by Nasionale Pers of *Beeld* in 1974 as a daily newspaper led to direct competition with *Hoofstad* and *Oggendblad* in Pretoria and *Die Vaderland* and *Die Transvaler* in Johannesburg. Unable to maintain viability in the face of competition, *Hoofstad* and *Oggendblad* closed in 1983, followed later by *Die Vaderland* which was transformed into a regional newspaper, *Noord-Transvaler Metro*, which also closed down in1998.

A black empowerment deal was concluded during 1996 when Perskor, which then was partly owned by Nasionale Pers (24%) and Rembrandt (27%) merged with Kagiso Publishers to form a new consortium, Persebel. In this manner, Kagiso gained a partnership in all the titles produced by Perskor of which *The Citizen* was then the biggest. Together the new consortium published some 250 titles. A slump during 1998 in the educational market impacted detrimentally on the finances of the textbook and stationery divisions, resulting in yet another rationalisation of the Perskor group. Another merger resulted, this time with CTP Holdings and Caxton Limited, with the new conglomerate taking the name of Caxton. (See also Caxton and Moolman in Case Study 1.2.) As part of the merger, Perskor's country and regional newspapers were sold to the Penrose publishing group, in which Caxton has a 70 percent holding. Perskor's share in *Rapport* was sold to Naspers in 1999. Apart from numerous regional and local newspapers, the flagship title in the Caxton group is *The Citizen*, which is distributed nationwide.

## *The rural and suburban press*

There are around 450 local, suburban and rural newspapers in South Africa. Most of these are tabloids serving specific towns, districts or suburbs, containing local news and advertisements. Because of their local nature, suburban and rural newspapers tend to avoid national politics and are bilingual. Most of the papers that fall into this group appear once a week. About 70 of these titles are what is known as knock-and-drop newspapers that are financed through the placement of advertisements by local businesses. The newspapers are distributed free of charge in certain suburban areas. There has been a general increase in the number of these regional, township and suburban publications (Diederichs 1993:82).

The growth of these local newspapers may be ascribed to their exclusive and comprehensive coverage of local news. For example, five daily newspapers are available in Pretoria, yet a market also exists for the knock-and-drop newspaper known as the *Record*. On the East Rand we find *The Brakpan Herald, The Benoni City Times, The Boksburg Advertiser* and *The Germiston Advocate*. The big daily newspapers simply cannot cover local news for every small town or area. The smaller newspapers retain their popularity because they are able to carry news that is of interest and relevant to that community. Papers can run up to thirty-two pages in length and often have extensive classified sections for local sales and services. They also cover events such as local council decisions, schools activities, local society meetings, churches, sports meetings, local crime and development programmes.

Many of these publications have a long history and are rich in tradition. For example, *Grocott's Mail* in Grahamstown, the oldest of these papers, has existed since 1830 and still remains an independent publication. Other local papers are linked directly to one of the four large press groups or indirectly to companies in which they have shares, such as Caxton or CTP Holdings. The association with the large press groups dates back to the introduction of television in 1976 when national advertisers switched to the newer medium, withdrawing much of their adspend from the big dailies in the process. As the major newspapers became more and more dependent on local advertisers this brought them into direct competition with local newspapers, in which they also began to invest.

## Freedom of the press

When we consider the concept of freedom of the press within South African circumstances, we need to do so within the context that we cannot find absolute freedom of the press anywhere in the world. What we can find, however, are degrees of freedom, with balance and counterbalance built into the respective system. Basically, freedom of the press is governed firstly by the constitution and then by the legislation of a particular country. The purpose of the constitution of a country is to protect the individual, the community and the state. Therefore, the right to the freedom of speech cannot be permitted to interfere with other rights as indicated by the following extract from section 16 of Chapter 2 of the Constitution of South Africa, which was adopted on 8 May 1996.

1  Everyone has the right to freedom of expression, which includes –
   a  freedom of the press and other media;
   b  freedom to receive and impart information and ideas;
   c  freedom of artistic creativity; and
   d  academic freedom and freedom of scientific research.
2  The right in subsection (1) does not extend to –
   a  propaganda for war;
   b  incitement of imminent violence; or
   c  advocacy of hatred that is based on race, ethnicity, gender or religion, and that constitutes incitement to cause harm.

As this constitution is still relatively new, the interpretation of these sections may differ and is often subject to testing in the Constitutional Court. This is especially true of section 16, since these rights are also subject to a number of other rights. The constitution lays down guidelines that we can use to determine what is permissible in the reporting of:

- accidents and disasters
- crime
- civil unrest
- judicial proceedings
- official corruption and abuse of power
- politics
- consumer affairs
- sex offences and scandals
- security and national security

There is very little legislation that relates specifically to the press and the work of journalists. One such law is the Newspaper and Imprint Registration Act of 1971 which requires that newspapers published at intervals of less than thirty days have to be registered (Grogan & Barker 1993:230). This means that journalists are subject to the same laws as are ordinary citizens with regard to their rights of acquiring and disseminating information. Today, the laws tend to regulate the press rather than restrict them as during the apartheid era. For example, there is legislation in place to regulate the registration of newspapers, advertising and activities by the media during an election. However, we still have a number of laws which restrict the press in their reporting of certain events under specific circumstances, mostly for reasons of national security, such as the following:

- Defence Act, no. 44 of 1957
- Internal Security Act, no. 74 of 1982
- National Key Points Act, no. 102 of 1980
- National Supplies Procurement Act, no. 89 of 1970
- Petroleum Products Act, no. 120 of 1977
- Armaments Development and Production Act, no. 57 of 1968

The freedom of speech is accepted in South Africa as a fundamental right, but subject to two limitations. Firstly, we cannot exercise our right to the freedom of speech if our action infringes on the rights of others. Secondly, we cannot say something that is prohibited by another law. Thus, we can say that the freedom of speech in South Africa is limited by the competing rights of others and the proscriptions of criminal law (Grogan & Barker 1993:230).

## Hearings into racism in the South African media

The South African Human Rights Commission (SAHRC) was established under Chapter 9 of the Constitution to promote a culture of human rights and to monitor and evaluate the observance of these human rights. The catalyst that set off the controversial investigation into racism in the media came from two professional bodies, the Black Lawyers Association and the Association of Black Accountants of South Africa, who requested the SAHRC to investigate the *Mail & Guardian* and the *Sunday Times* for alleged violations of the fundamental rights of black people (Glaser 2000:374). It was particularly felt that the *Mail & Guardian*, in its anti-corruption investigations, unfairly targeted black professionals. From this the SAHRC decided that a full-scale investigation into the causes of, and the media's handling of, race and incidence of racism was necessary. An interim report was released in November 1999, which was met with harsh criticism for being methodologically flawed.

During February 2000, the SAHRC issued over 30 differing media organisations with subpoenas (an order to attend court or a hearing), where editors were required to explain at public hearings how they handled various racial issues. Editors who refused to appear before the SAHRC were threatened with a stiff fine or six months' imprisonment, while documents could be forcibly seized. There was a strong reaction to this move by the SAHRC. Very quickly the issues of racism in the media were overtaken by accusations from within South Africa and abroad, regarding the violation of press freedom, which threatened to side-track the investigation. The SAHRC was considered to have gone beyond its powers by calling for the media to appear before it and to account for their style of reporting. In turn, the SAHRC accused those media organisations that were subpoenaed of misinterpreting the situation. Without any doubt, the SAHRC was taken by surprise at the intensity of the backlash, some of it even coming from within the SAHRC itself. In negotiations with the media, through the South African National Editors' Forum (SANEF), the SAHRC withdrew the subpoenas, but continued to threaten the media with them (Pityana 2000:531). The hearings continued through March and April 2000. Ideological cracks soon appeared between black and white editors in SANEF when black editors opted to attend the hearings because they felt the issue of racism in the media was important enough to warrant examination, in that after six years following the 1994 democratic elections, the power structures in the media had remained unchanged (Bhengu 2000:3; Pityana 2000:531).

**Figure 1.9 Subpoenaing editors to appear before the SAHRC provoked an outrage by the press who saw the move as an infringement on press freedom** (*Sunday Times,* 27 February 2000)

The final report, released on 24 August 2000, produced few surprises. Basically, "the report characterised all South African media as 'racist institutions' that display insensitivity and a 'reckless disregard for the effect of racist expressions'" (Taitz 2000:2). The findings can be summarised as follows (Lawrence 2000:36; Nkutha 2000:2):

- The media are racist in that they reflect persistent patterns of racist expressions.
- The media offer a "unipolar" (or unicultural) worldview, largely because they do not reflect South African cultural diversity.
- While the mainstream media do not indulge in blatant racial hatred or incitement to racial violence, there is much evidence in the press of condemnation of hate speech.
- Racism occurs at the institutional or structural levels where there are racial imbalances in the editorial staff of most media institutions.

A number of recommendations were also made. These include (Lawrence 2000:36; Taitz 2000:2):

- the establishment of a statutory regulatory framework for all media, controlled and funded by the industry;
- the aggressive recruitment and training of black staff;
- regular workshops be held for journalists to promote equality and human dignity through immersion in different cultures;
- the establishment of a cadet training programme;
- the dilution of the concentration of media ownership; and
- the establishment of a Media Diversity Agency.

The report drew a mixed reaction. While most of the recommendations were well received by SANEF, the creation of a so-called independent regulatory authority for all media came in for severe criticism, based on two fundamental issues. Firstly, the regulation of broadcasting differs markedly from that of the press, argued by the fact that the frequency spectrum needs to be managed as a national asset and that the SABC is a public corporation. (We discussed the disparity between various media in the overview to this unit.) Secondly, the control of such an authority could easily be taken out of the media's hands by a future government, with grave consequences for media freedom (Lawrence 2000:36). How many of the recommendations will ultimately come to fruition and in turn make a meaningful contribution to the resolution of the racism issue remains a moot point. Depending on one's perspective, this investigation into racism in the media was viewed either as a travesty of media freedom (Glaser 2000:373–393) or as a watershed in the development of South African democracy in that it was a non-juridical approach to promoting and protecting human rights (Pityana 2000:525). Whatever one's views, the hearings sent shockwaves throughout the media. As far as the press was concerned, the problem was not the revelation that there is racism is the press, nor that the SAHRC tried to counter it, but that the SAHRC was seen as having set itself up as the final judge in deciding what was or was not racist, that it was equating criticism of the government with racism and that it was using its statutory powers to force the media to appear before it (Glaser 2000:374).

Independent of the SAHRC investigation, *Business Day* commissioned a survey, conducted by ACNielsen Customised Research, to establish the views of the public regarding racism in the press. The findings were released in July 2000, ahead of the SAHRC report. According to the ACNielsen survey, the media was seen as racist by 37 percent of whites, 30 percent of coloureds, 17 percent of blacks and 14 percent of Indians. The higher figure among whites was attributed to a greater sensitivity to racism because whites "are traditionally the ones accused of being racist" (Survey ... 2000:2). Among those who believed the media to be racist considered the press to be the biggest culprit, as reflected by the statistics illustrated in Figure 1.10. Oddly, it was found, blacks did not label white newspapers as being racist, nor vice versa. However, the findings did reveal that a newspaper that targets a particular race, or cultural group, is likely to be perceived as being racist, as suggested by the statistics illustrated in Figure 1.11. An interesting aside to emerge from this survey is the absence of any respondents naming the *Mail & Guardian* as being perceived of as racist. Yet, it was the accusation that the *Mail & Guardian* was racist in its reporting that launched the inquiry.

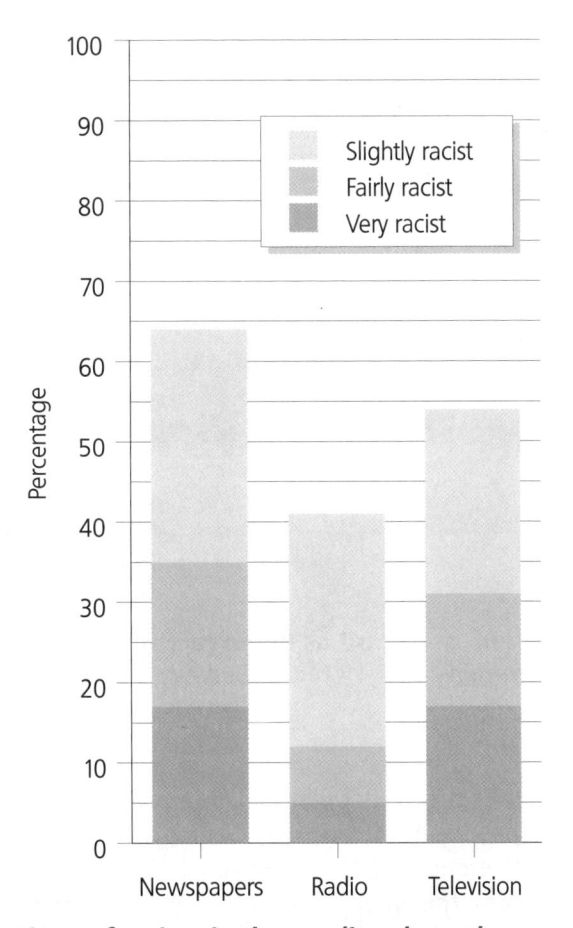

**Figure 1.10 Perceptions of racism in the media – how the press measures up to radio and television** (Survey ... 2000:2)

## MEDIA STUDIES

The ACNielsen survey came to the conclusion that two factors can influence the public's perceptions of racism in the media (Survey... 2000:2):
- Past impressions play a large part in the creation of perceptions, even though a newspaper may have changed radically from the apartheid days when they did serve a racist purpose. Negative perceptions tend to remain entrenched.
- A newspaper (or any other medium) that targets a specific racial group is more likely to be accused of being racist.

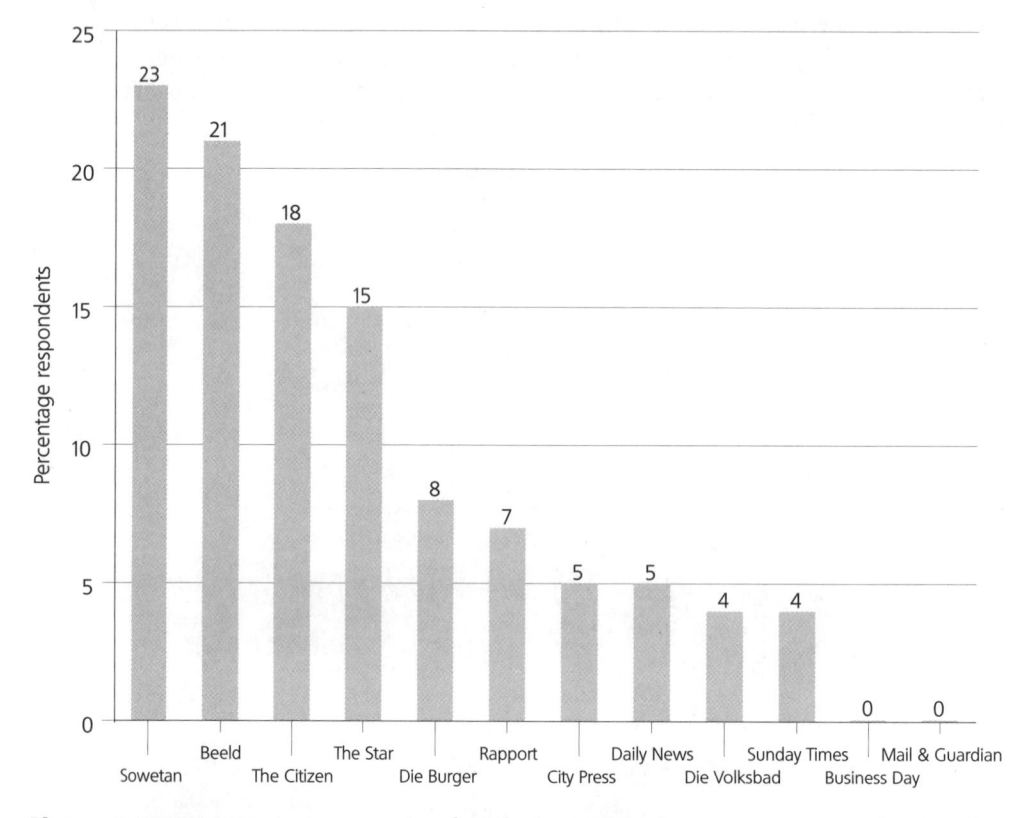

**Figure 1.11 Newspapers perceived as being racist by survey respondents who felt newspapers were fairly to very racist** (Survey ... 2000:2)

### Ombudsman

With the establishment of the Press Ombudsman (a government official appointed to investigate complaints) during 1996, the press has moved away from an era of government regulation and government induced self-regulation towards a regulation by the press itself in order to serve the interests of the public. This move is also in line with the expected role of the press in a social democratic society as articulated by the normative theory of social responsibility. During the period July 1997 to June 1998, the office of the Press Ombudsman received 83 complaints from a variety of people and interest groups. This is in stark contrast to the previous situation when the majority of complaints to the preceding Press and Media Council were largely from the government or government departments. The power of the Press Ombudsman is limited to enforcing publication of the necessary reprimands and corrections. Huteau (2000:44) explains the procedure:

> Complaints against the press are lodged by private individuals or institutions first with the ombudsman, who will try and settle the matter. If this fails, the complaint becomes a formal one. The complainant can appeal against the ombudsman's decisions to the appeal panel. At each stage, discussions between the conflicting parties are held.

## 1.4 FILM

In this brief overview of the film industry in South Africa, we need to remember that, as with all forms of industry, the driving force is a combination of politics and economics. Therefore, we need to approach our historical overview from a sociological perspective, in which we need to look closely at ownership and control. Two aspects of the industry are relevant here. On one hand we need to look at the actual production of the film, while on the other hand we need to give serious consideration to the distribution of those, and other, films. It is important to our understanding of the film industry in South Africa today that we have an understanding of how the manufacture and distribution of films in South Africa were organised in the past. As with broadcasting and the press, the effects of apartheid ideology had a strong effect on the development of the film industry in South Africa. However, in adopting a sociological approach, we also need to take note of the following. First, we need to give consideration to the efforts and idiosyncrasies of individual producers. Second, filmmaking has not taken place in isolation. A large percentage of the films screened in South Africa were, and are, products of Hollywood. Thus, the local industry has been particularly influenced by the ideology of Hollywood.

Our aim, then, in this section is to briefly review film in South Africa over the past 100 years. To this end, we base our discussion on the chronology devised by Louw and Botha (1993:161–167). However, Louw and Botha do not identify distinct periods in the development of the film industry in South Africa, but rather examine the development decade by decade. Botha and Van Aswegan (1992), who provide a more detailed account of the historical development of the film industry in South Africa since 1960, also tend to group events into periods based on the decade. We have rather opted to group meaningful events within the development of the film industry in South Africa, and in so doing have established a loose distinction of seven periods. Briefly, we can summarise these periods as follows:

- Prior to 1910: The beginnings
- 1910–1926: The silent era

# MEDIA STUDIES

- 1926–1939: Arrival of the talkies
- 1939–1950: Rise of Afrikaner nationalism
- 1950–1960: An industry evolves
- 1960–1984: Industry boom
- 1984 onwards: An industry in crisis

### 1.4.1  Prior to 1910: The beginnings

Between 1895 and 1909, it was mainly British and American films that reached many parts of South Africa by means of mobile bioscopes. Early projection devices were used around the Johannesburg gold fields from 1895 onwards as part of a sideshow. The first cinema was built in Durban by Electric Theatres Limited in 1909. The first ever newsreels were filmed at the front during the Anglo-Boer War (1899–1902) and gave the medium a form of respectability.

### 1.4.2  From 1910 to 1926: The silent era

The first South African film was *The Great Kimberley Diamond Robbery* (1910), while the first Afrikaans (Dutch) film was *De Voortrekkers* (1916), influenced largely by the work of DW Griffith. Other notable films from the period include *The Splendid Waster*, *The Artist's Dream*, *A Zulu's Devotion* and *The Silver Wolf*, all made in 1916. In total, over 1 350 South African feature films had been made since 1910, of which forty-three films, some of them epic in scope, were made between 1916 and 1922 by IW Schlesinger's company, African Film Productions.

With a very limited local production, the South African film industry concentrated on distribution of British and American productions through the building of cinemas. Competition between the four major distribution companies (Wolfram's, Union Bioscope, Tivoli Theatres and Bijou) became so intense that the film distribution industry ended up facing a financial crisis. As he was to do later with radio in South Africa, American-born industrialist, IW Schlesinger bought up the various distribution companies and consolidated their operations in to African Films in 1913. The development of the film industry in South Africa can then be largely ascribed to the efforts of Schlesinger. In the same year, 1913, African Films began making the regular newsreel, *The African Mirror*, which became the world's longest running newsreel. For the next 43 years the Schlesinger organisation held the monopoly on film distribution from the Cape to the Zambezi (Louw & Botha 1993:159).

### 1.4.3  From 1926 to 1939: Arrival of the talkies

The addition of sound to film had a dramatic impact on the industry, not only in the United States, but also locally. This caused some initial problems for Schlesinger, as he could not secure a local franchise for the new films. But, by 1930 Schlesinger owned African Consolidated Theatres and African Consolidated Films. In 1930 African

Consolidated Films founded the Killarney Film Studios in Johannesburg, which produced various films that were distributed in South Africa and overseas. Some notable titles produced by these studios include *Allan Quatermain*, *King Solomon's Mines*, *Prester John*, *Rhodes of Africa*, and *They built a Nation* (Louw & Botha 1993:159). *Sarie Marais*, the first South African film with sound, was produced in 1931, after which local films gained in popularity.

### 1.4.4 From 1939 to 1950: Rise of Afrikaner nationalism

It was during the 1930s that we first see the stirring of an alternative film industry in South Africa, which resulted in the politicisation of Afrikaans films during the 1940s. Afrikaner nationalism was on the rise and there were strong feelings against the cultural imperialism of the South African film industry as organised by Schlesinger. Dr Hans Rompel established a film production organisation known as the *Reddingsdaadbond-Amateur-Rolprent-Organisasie* (*RARO*) (which roughly translated means Rescue-action-league Amateur Film Organisation). As an alternative film industry, RARO objected to the Anglo-American cultural imperialism prevailing in South Africa as a result of the showing of numerous overseas films. The first film produced by RARO was *'n Nasie hou Koers* in 1939, and as with more contemporary alternative film, the content emphasised political and emotional events. RARO films were distributed by the Volksbioskope-maatskappy. It is, however, rather ironical that the Volksbioskope-maatskappy had to include Hollywood productions in their distributions merely to remain financially viable. RARO and the Volksbioskope-maatskappy eventually closed down when the Nationalist party won the general election of 1948.

Although some of the films were overtly political, such as *Lig van die Eeu* (1942), which was financed by the Dutch Reformed Church, and *Simon Beyers* (1947), most of the films produced were covertly nationalist in the guise of social melodramas, such as *Donker Spore* (1944), which was also the first filmed version of an Afrikaans novel. This period also saw the rise of popular film actors, such as Al Debbo and Frederik Burgers who made a name for themselves in the film, *Kom saam Vanaand*. Others actors who came to the fore during this period include Hendrik Hanekom, Johan Fourie and Wena Naudé.

### 1.4.5 From 1950 to 1960: An industry evolves

In was during the 1950s that Jamie Uys began to make a name for himself as a director. He was also involved in Zoltan Korda's *Cry the Beloved Country* (1951), based on the book by Alan Paton. Uys fulfilled many of the roles in the production of a film, including producer, scriptwriter, director, photographer as well as lead actor, producing films such as *Daar doer in die Bosveld* (1951), *Fifty-Vyftig* (1953), *Daar doer in die Stad* (1954) and *Geld soos Bossies* (1955). The Debbo-Burgers team continued to entertain with slapstick comedy. While many of the films produced during this period were melodramas and comedy, several films with a more serious theme appeared, such as *Son of Africa*, *Hans die Skipper* and *Inspan*.

The 1950s saw Hollywood in a crisis as the novelty of the then new medium, television, swept across America. But in South Africa, cinema attendance remained high. This meant that South Africa gained importance for the distribution of Hollywood-made films. It was this fact that prompted Twentieth Century Fox to invest directly in South Africa by buying out the Schlesinger conglomerate in 1956. Between 1956 and 1969, over 75 percent of the distribution of films in South Africa was controlled by Twentieth Century Fox. In opposition to Twentieth Century Fox was a small independent film distributor, Wonderboom Inry Beleggings (WIB), which was based in Pretoria. WIB was soon to change its name, and in so doing was to become a major force in the local distribution and screening of films, not only within South Africa, but, by the turn of the century was also destined to become a global player in the field. This company was Ster-Kinekor, which we discuss in more detail in a later section.

### 1.4.6 From 1960 to 1984: Industry boom

As the audience for mainstream films during this period was largely limited to white Afrikaners and because of the State's policy towards the film industry, the South African film industry continued to produce films that were limited to comedies, melodramas and the glorification of army life; basically a continuation of the themes of the 1950s, but on a more lavish scale. For the most part, the industry concentrated on producing bland middle-of-the-road formula films. Ideologically, it was initially cinema for whites only, and moreover, predominantly Afrikaans (Botha & Van Aswegen 1992:9).

Unlike the films of the 1950s which attempted to bolster Afrikaner culture, the films of the 1960s were poor imitations of Hollywood genres. The period is also dominated by the work of a few producers, such as Elmo de Witt, Franz Marx, Koos Roets, Daan Retief, Jan Scholtz, Tommie Meyer and Jamie Uys (Botha & Van Aswegan 1992:9). There were a few attempts by films to examine the phenomenon of apartheid. These included the Emil Nofal-Jan Rautenbach film *Die Kandidaat* (1968) and *Katrina* (1968) and Jans Rautenbach's *Pappa Lap* (1970). These films quickly came up against censorship and Afrikaner resistance, however, and could not succeed in making a real and lasting cultural contribution (Fourie 1994:314). Jans Rautenbach's *Jannie Totsiens* (1970) can be regarded as an expressionistic psychodrama and one of South Africa's few avant-garde films to date. Elmo de Witt's *Debbie* (1965), dealing with premarital sex and the difficult circumstances of a pregnant teenager, not only touched on a sensitive issue of the sixties, but also emphasised the inadequacy of the outdated censorship system of the Publications Board (Louw & Botha 1993:165).

For the most, the films of this period show little creativity on the part of the producers. Nor do these films move beyond the concept of mediocre entertainment. The themes portrayed in film show little relevance to the social reality of South Africa of the times, and presented to the audience an idealised and distorted image of life in South Africa. Botha and Van Aswegan (1992:11) suggest that the closest mainstream films ever came to investigating the sociopolitical situation in South Africa were the comedies produced by Jamie Uys which dealt with the relationship between English and Afrikaans speaking South Africans. Although these were so-called boom years for the industry, the writing was clearly on the wall. Apart from the indifferent attitude by producers to the realities of South African society, producers were also out of touch with the demands made on the medium by the advent of television. In order to compete with the newer medium, the international film industry became more comprehensive in scope. South Africa continued to churn out family entertainment, a function by then largely taken over by television. The norms and values of Afrikaner society at the time were also largely to blame for maintaining the mould. To attain anything resembling healthy box-office returns, films had to subscribe to the conservative norms and values of the Afrikaner. This was tantamount to moral censorship that had to be considered by the producer before the film was made.

Of the 60 films made between 1956 and 1962, 43 were in Afrikaans, four were bilingual and the remaining 13 were English. The state subsidy can also be largely blamed for the *status quo* of the industry as it undermined the production of sociocritical films. By this stage it had become a complex, yet pointless exercise as it regarded filmmaking as neither a culture nor an industry, which pointed directly to attitudes of the government of the day (Botha & Van Aswegan 1992:14). The subsidy system only rewarded box-office success. Only once a film had earned a specific amount of money at the box office did it qualify for the subsidy, which paid back a percentage of costs. In an attempt to promote the production of films in Afrikaans, in order to promote the growth and spread of the Afrikaans language, the subsidy for Afrikaans films was higher, up to 70 percent, than for English productions, which could gain a maximum 60 percent subsidy.

The white Afrikaans audience for the local cinema was relatively large and very stable, guaranteeing nearly every Afrikaans film a long enough run to break even as long as it provided light entertainment (basically escapism) and as long as it idealised perceived Afrikaner reality and beliefs (Botha & Van Aswegen 1992). This idealistic conservatism was characterised by an attachment to the past, to ideals of linguistic and racial purity and to religious and moral norms. The images of Afrikanerdom by Rautenbach in *Jannie Totsiens* or Devenish in *The Guest*, which depicted an Afrikaner intellectual's struggle with drug addiction, certainly did not meet the expectations of audiences. The audience rejected these films and instead flocked to those that portrayed Afrikaners as chatty, heartwarming and lovable people. Their conception of sociopolitical reality was confined to the conventions of Afrikaans soapies about mismatched couples, most of whom had to overcome obstacles on the path to true love (Botha & Van Aswegan 1992:11–12).

It was, in fact, the soapie genre that formed the nucleus of films produced during the later half of this period, sparked by the huge success of films like *Hoor my Lied* (1967) and *Jy is my liefling* (1968). Beginning with *Die Geheim van Nantes* (1969), long-running radio serials started to provide inspiration for many films (Botha & van Aswegan 1992:11–12). The introduction of television to South Africa in 1976 did not dampen the

## MEDIA STUDIES

enthusiasm for the soapie genre, and in fact, several successful television programmes provided themes for films, such as *Bosveldhotel* and *Nommer Asseblief*. Similarly, films with a military theme, such as *Kaptein Caprivi*, *Aanslag op Kariba* and *Ses Soldate*, were cast in the same mould. There was no critical evaluation of war as found in American films such as *Apocalypse Now* and *The Deer Hunter* (Botha & Van Aswegan 1992:4). The Afrikaans films ignored the sociopolitical turmoil of the period, and certainly the realities experienced by black South Africans. Botha and Van Aswegen (1992:12) state that most Afrikaans films communicated by means of obsolete symbols that had little multicultural communication value. These films painted a one-sided and stereotypical portrait of the Afrikaner, leading to a misconception about who and what the Afrikaner was. Furthermore, the insulting portrayal of blacks as a servant class in these films was a visual symbol of the deep-seated apartheid ideology.

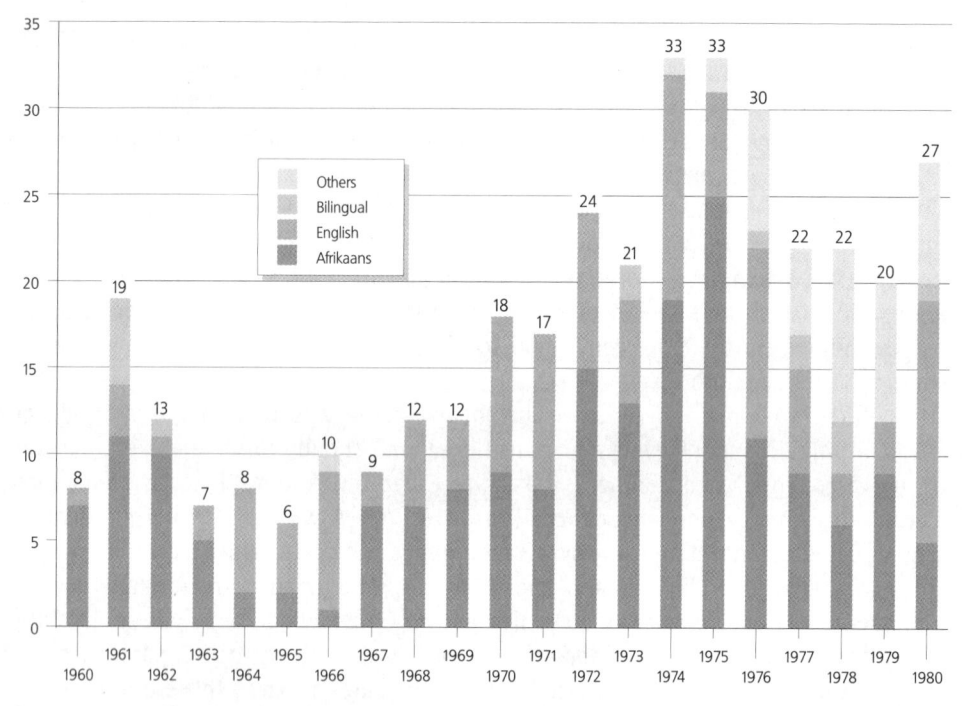

**Figure 1.12 Film production in South African during the period 1960–1980 by language** (Tomaselli 1989:263–268)

Despite the restrictions placed on the film industry, a few producers managed to make exceptional films. Manie van Rensburg entered the field of Afrikaner culture through political satire. His film, *Die Square*, which was a significant satirical statement, was banned by the Publications Control Board. In 1975 Jamie Uys received the Golden Globe award for the best documentary film, *Beautiful People*, and followed this with another successful production, *The Gods must be Crazy* (1980). After Jamie Uys's film, *Funny*

*People*, which was based on *Candid Camera*, the theme was overused and abused in the 1980s, especially by Leon Schuster. Apart from Rautenbach and Van Rensburg, another outstanding South African filmmaker was Ross Devenish who made three internationally praised films, *Boesman and Lena*, *The Guest* and *Marigolds in August*. After struggling for almost a decade to make films in South Africa, Devenish left the country to work in England. Filmmakers such as Devenish and Rautenbach found it difficult to make the kind of film that deals critically with sociopolitical issues.

An attempt to create a black film industry under apartheid during the 1970s resulted in the making of a large number of shoddy films in ethnic languages that were screened in churches, schools and community and beer halls. It was contrary to government policy to allow black cinemas in the urban white areas, since this would concede citizenship to urban blacks. The urbanisation of blacks was portrayed in these films as uniformly problematic and homeland life as more fitting. At this stage, black and white audiences were treated differently. Audiences were separated, each with its own set of rules and operations, films and cinemas. Any film that managed to be made which in any way reflected South African society in turmoil was banned by the state, or received no distribution whatsoever, and thus did not qualify for any film subsidy. A true national film industry did not, therefore, emerge through the Afrikaans and made-for-blacks films.

### 1.4.7 From 1984 onwards: An industry in crisis

In the 1980s, film attendance dropped to its lowest level as a result of the popularity of television and a scarcity of good films. Bensusan's film, *My Country My Hat* (1983) was one of the few creative films that made an innovative contribution to sociopolitical satire (Botha 1993:166).

Since the late 1970s and early 1980s, a group of film and video producers and directors who were not affiliated to established film companies in the mainstream film industry, made films and videos about the sociopolitical realities of the majority of South Africans (Botha & Van Aswegen 1992; Blignaut & Botha 1992). Some of these films were shown at local film festivals such as the Durban and Cape Town International Film Festivals and, from 1987 until 1994, at the *Weekly Mail* Film Festival. Other venues included universities, church halls, trade union offices and private homes. Most sociopolitical films experienced censorship problems during the State of Emergency during the 1980s, and many were banned.

These films were made on small budgets and were either financed by the producers themselves, or by progressive organisations such as the International Defence and Aid Fund for South Africa for a United, Democratic, Non-racial South Africa, and overseas television stations. These films were chiefly the product of two groups that emerged simultaneously: a group of white university students opposed to apartheid, and black workers who yearned for a film or video form using indigenous imagery that would portray their reality in South Africa, that would give them a voice and space in local films. Together with numerous documentaries, community videos and full-length films such as *Mapantsula*, short films and even animation work marked the beginning of a new, critical South African cinema.

Initially, this new cinema was based on audio-visual material that reflected the realities of the black majority of South Africa in their aspirations and struggle for a democratic society. But, since the beginning of the 1990s, other marginalised voices were added to these documentaries and short films (e.g. those of women, gays and lesbians, and even the homeless). It is from these films and videos that the symbols and iconography of a national South African film industry can be drawn, rather than from the diversions produced by the Afrikaans cinema of the 1960s and 1970s, or the made-for-blacks cinema of the 1970s. Most of the new critical local films, features or short films can be described as progressive film texts in the sense that the majority of them are consciously critical of racism, sexism or oppression. They deal with the lives and struggle of the people in a developing country and are mostly allied with the liberation movements for a non-racial, non-sexist South Africa. Some of these films (short, features and documentaries) also deal with events which were conveniently left out of official South African history books or actuality programmes on national television under control of the Nationalist regime. Films such as these have therefore become guardians of popular memory within the sociopolitical process in South Africa.

According to Tomaselli (1988:226), 1986/1987 can be regarded as the turning point in the South African film industry. Only then did several feature films begin to critically examine the South African milieu, apartheid and colonial history. Tomaselli calls this the "new wave" in the South African film industry. Martin Botha and Adri van Aswegen labelled it an alternative film revival, a cinema that gave a voice to those who were previously marginalised by apartheid (Botha & Van Aswegen 1992). These films touched on issues of black-white conflict and friendship (*Jock of the Bushveld*), the poor treatment of black farm workers by certain farmers (*A Place of Weeping*), the effects of war on whites (*'n Wêreld sonder Grense*), terrorism (*City of Blood*) and the trauma of racial conflict (*Saturday Night at The Palace*) (Louw & Botha 1993:167).

Approximately 944 features were made during the 1980s, as well as nearly 998 documentaries and several hundred short films and videos (Blignaut & Botha 1992). Although most of the features were mediocre, at least 20 to 30 remarkable indigenous local feature films were made. They included *Mapantsula*, a vivid portrayal of the State of Emergency in the late eighties; *On the Wire*, about the psychological scars left by the war in Namibia and Angola; *The Road to Mecca*, a film on the life of artist Helen Martins; Andrew Worsdale's *Shotdown*, a political satire; the evocative Afrikaans dramas with strong female characters – *Fiela se Kind*, *Die Storie van Klara Viljee* and *Paljas*; *Jobman*, a strong anti-apartheid drama set in the years after Sharpeville; and Manie van Rensburg's masterful portrayal of Afrikaner nationalism during the 1940s in *The Fourth Reich*. Directors such as Jans Rautenbach, Manie van Rensburg, Ross Devenish, Katinka Heyns, Darrell Roodt and Andrew Worsdale are evidence that there is indeed great talent in the South African film industry. Van Rensburg's *The Native Who Caused all the Trouble* and *The Fourth Reich* are films that built on the foundation of the post-1987 new wave (Botha & Dethier 1997).

## A South African Media Map

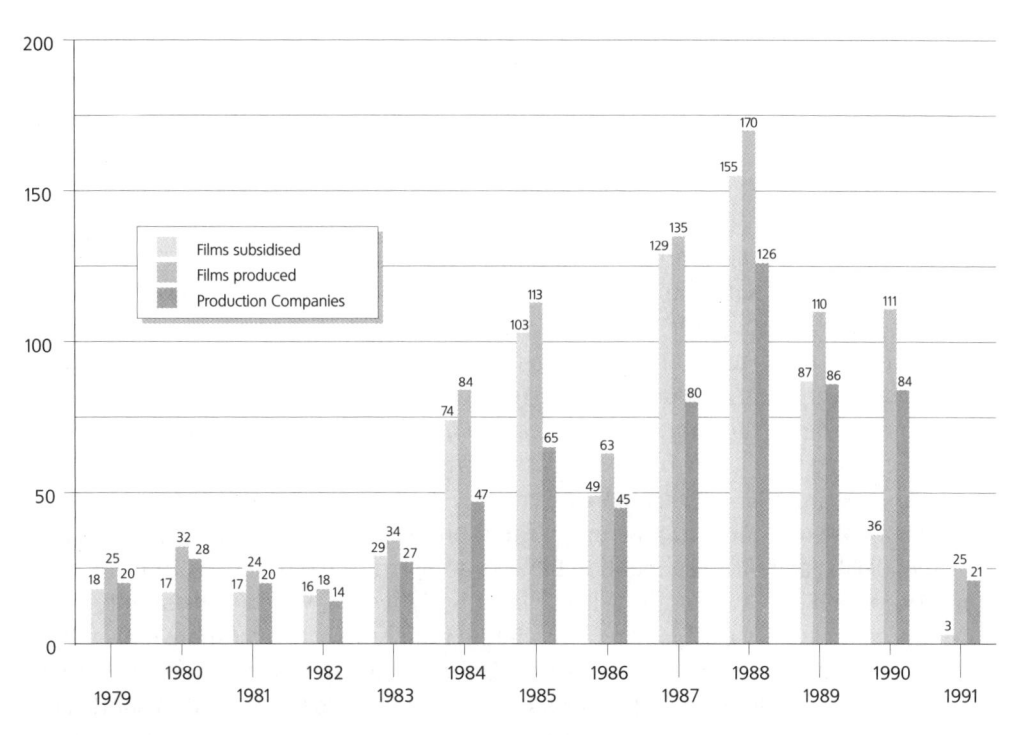

**Figure 1.13 The total number of films produced and subsidised in South Africa compared with the number of production companies** (Blignaut & Botha 1992:78–81)

During the 1990s, further developments within the local film industry stimulated the production of, especially, short films, a significant development in the growth of the local film industry. M-Net initiated a project entitled "New Directions" to give talented first-time South African and other African filmmakers and scriptwriters a break into the film industry. By 1999 M-Net's MagicWorks had completed 20 short films and two features. This project is a showcase for new talent in this country, and has led to some outstanding short films such as *Come See the Bioscope, Angel* and *Salvation*. First-time directors and screenwriters, some of them female and black, have explored a diversity of themes. Director Khalo Matabane and scriptwriter Mtutuzeli Matshoba, for example, created an award-winning comedy *Chikin Biz'nis – The Whole Story* about the vibrant South African informal economic sector, which provides millions of unemployed urban South Africans with alternative livelihoods. Russell Thompson and Patrick Shai explored South Africa's culture of violence in *The Pink Leather Chair* and *Stray Bullet*, while directors Dumisani Phakathi and Tamsin McCarthy highlighted intimate relationships against the background of the new South African democracy in *An Old Wife's Tale* and *Cry Me A Baby*. Relevant social problems such as drug abuse (*Stimulation*) and abortion (*The Apology*) were also explored in these M-Net short films.

Another important development was the historic democratic elections of 1994. The year 1994 could also be regarded as a landmark for the South African film industry. A comprehensive study by the research institution the Human Sciences Research Council (HSRC) into the restructuring of the entire South African film industry was completed and forwarded to the Department of Arts, Culture, Science and Technology (see Botha, Mare, Langa, Netshitomboni, Hgoasheng, Potgieter & Greyling 1994). This report, of 400 pages, received widespread praise throughout the local film and television industry. The HSRC research team recommended that state aid to the local film industry should be administered by a statutory body referred to as the South African Film and Video Foundation (SAFVF). The research team argued that commercial viability should not be the sole criterion for government support of locally made films. All types of films, including short films, should benefit from state subsidies, and a developmental fund should be used to support first-time filmmakers from previously marginalised communities. A government-appointed Task Group used this report extensively during 1995 to draft the White Paper regarding a post-apartheid film industry. The White Paper was completed by 1996 and the National Film and Video Foundation Bill was accepted by Parliament in 1997.

In March 1995, the old South African film subsidy system, which was based on box-office returns, ceased to exist, and an interim film fund came into operation. R10-million was annually distributed among various projects, which included funding for short film-making. In 1998, for example, R110 000 was allocated to the development of short films and R1-million for the actual production of short films. During 1999 the proposed National Film and Video Foundation was established to support the local film industry, including short film-making.

Regional initiatives further encouraged short film production. The Cape Film and Video Foundation and the South African Scriptwriters Association (SASWA) in collaboration with the Department of Arts, Culture, Science and Technology, funded three short films, entitled *Kap an Driver*, a beautiful exploration of racial relations in the "new" South Africa; *On the Rocks*, about an affluent white man's encounter with Cape Town's homeless people; and *Stompie and the Red Tide*, also about Cape Town's homeless. The Southern African International Film and Television Market (*Sithengi*), held every November in Cape Town, has become an important forum for locally made features and short films.

*Sithengi* 1998 highlighted an important Pan-African short film initiative called *African Dreaming*. The array of six short films is a major co-production, the first of its kind on the continent, which uses talent from Mozambique, Namibia, Senegal, Tunisia, Zimbabwe and South Africa. International funding came from the South African Broadcasting Corporation (SABC), the Hubert Bals Fund in the Netherlands, Cable Channel La Sept/Arte in France, YLE TV2 in Finland, HIVOS and NCDO in Holland, the CNC in France, the French Ministry of Cooperation and Video Lab in South Africa. Deals and contracts were coordinated by one of South Africa's leading producers, Jeremy Nathan, through his company Catalyst Films. The South African film, *Mamlambo*, a love story between a black boy and a Chinese girl, gave first-time female black director,

# A South African Media Map

Palesa Nkosi, a chance to direct a film. In many ways short film-making in South Africa provides previously marginalised people a voice.

Most of the short fiction and non-fiction films during the early 1980s were political texts, that is, instruments in the anti-apartheid struggle. Only later during the 1980s were other themes explored by various marginalised filmmakers (e.g. gay and lesbian equality within South Africa's conservative and homophobic society). Current post-apartheid cinema is very much a cinema about marginalised people (e.g. the homeless of Cape Town in a documentary such as *Pavement Aristocrats: The Bergies of Cape Town* or the short M-Net fiction film, *Angel*, which deals with a homeless couple. Possibly the most notable South African production of 1998 was *Paljas*, produced by VideoVision Entertainment, and directed by Katinka Heyns. It was intended as an artistic rather than a commercial film, although opinions are divided about its artistic merits. What made it remarkable was that it was an Afrikaans-language feature chosen as the official South African film for consideration at the Cannes Festival – a sign of hope for a more open and culturally tolerant future.

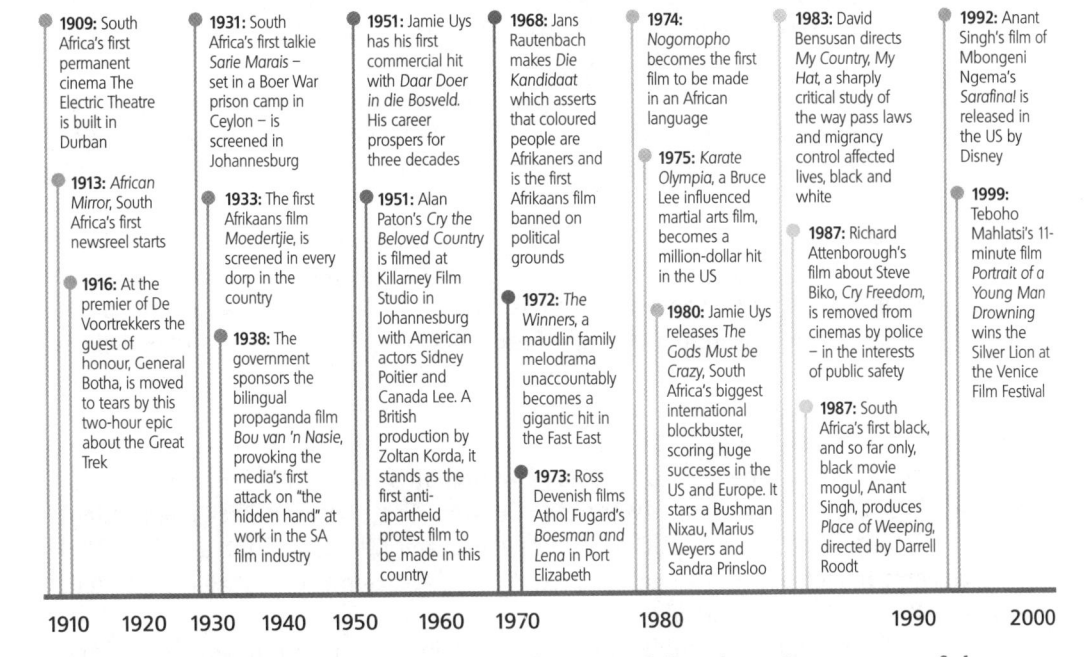

|  |  |
|---|---|
| 1909 | South Africa's first permanent cinema The Electric Theatre is built in Durban |
| 1913 | *African Mirror*, South Africa's first newsreel starts |
| 1916 | At the premier of De Voortrekkers the guest of honour, General Botha, is moved to tears by this two-hour epic about the Great Trek |
| 1931 | South Africa's first talkie *Sarie Marais* – set in a Boer War prison camp in Ceylon – is screened in Johannesburg |
| 1933 | The first Afrikaans film *Moedertjie*, is screened in every dorp in the country |
| 1938 | The government sponsors the bilingual propaganda film *Bou van 'n Nasie*, provoking the media's first attack on "the hidden hand" at work in the SA film industry |
| 1951 | Jamie Uys has his first commercial hit with *Daar Doer in die Bosveld*. His career prospers for three decades |
| 1951 | Alan Paton's *Cry the Beloved Country* is filmed at Killarney Film Studio in Johannesburg with American actors Sidney Poitier and Canada Lee. A British production by Zoltan Korda, it stands as the first anti-apartheid protest film to be made in this country |
| 1968 | Jans Rautenbach makes *Die Kandidaat* which asserts that coloured people are Afrikaners and is the first Afrikaans film banned on political grounds |
| 1972 | *The Winners*, a maudlin family melodrama unaccountably becomes a gigantic hit in the Fast East |
| 1973 | Ross Devenish films Athol Fugard's *Boesman and Lena* in Port Elizabeth |
| 1974 | *Nogomopho* becomes the first film to be made in an African language |
| 1975 | *Karate Olympia*, a Bruce Lee influenced martial arts film, becomes a million-dollar hit in the US |
| 1980 | Jamie Uys releases *The Gods Must be Crazy*, South Africa's biggest international blockbuster, scoring huge successes in the US and Europe. It stars a Bushman Nixau, Marius Weyers and Sandra Prinsloo |
| 1983 | David Bensusan directs *My Country, My Hat*, a sharply critical study of the way pass laws and migrancy control affected lives, black and white |
| 1987 | Richard Attenborough's film about Steve Biko, *Cry Freedom*, is removed from cinemas by police – in the interests of public safety |
| 1987 | South Africa's first black, and so far only, black movie mogul, Anant Singh, produces *Place of Weeping*, directed by Darrell Roodt |
| 1992 | Anant Singh's film of Mbongeni Ngema's *Sarafina!* is released in the US by Disney |
| 1999 | Teboho Mahlatsi's 11-minute film *Portrait of a Young Man Drowning* wins the Silver Lion at the Venice Film Festival |

**Figure 1.14** Time line showing the influence of the changing nature of the South African sociopolitical environment on the development of the local film industry (adapted from Dodd 2000:50)

## 1.4.8 Distribution and screening of films in South Africa

In the 1950s, television dealt the USA film industry a severe blow. At the time South Africa, which did not have television, was seen as a particularly important market for

Hollywood's film industry. This situation made Twentieth Century Fox decide to become directly involved in South Africa and buy out the whole Schlesinger Empire in 1956. Between 1956 and 1969 Twentieth Century Fox owned more than three-quarters of the South African film distribution network. Since 1962 Afrikaner capital became a significant factor in the film industry when the insurance company Sanlam acquired a major interest in Ster Films, a small distribution company with the explicit intention of providing cinema predominantly for Afrikaner patrons. Ster Films built three movie-theatre complexes in Pretoria, Johannesburg and Durban with finance again provided by Sanlam. But Ster Films just could not compete with the strength of the Twentieth Century Fox distribution network. This placed Sanlam's investment in the three movie complexes at great risk. Ultimately matters came to a head in 1969 and it was a case of either lose the investment or become more deeply involved. And so Sanlam bought out Twentieth Century Fox and merged this operation with Ster to form Satbel (the Suid-Afrikaanse Teaterbelange Beperk). Despite the original intention to provide Afrikaans films as a counter to American culture, with the merger Ster-Kinekor became the conduit for Hollywood into South Africa with control of 76 percent of all distribution. The remaining 24 percent being controlled by UIP-Warner (Louw & Botha 1993:160). In 1984 Sol Kerzner bought the Satbel group from Sanlam.

Film screening in South Africa is dominated by Ster-Kinekor and Nu Metro, which between them have 307 (283 without Ster-Moribo) screens in the major cities and suburbs and 152 in the rural towns. According to Botha (1996), there were about 202 independent cinemas in South Africa in the 1990s (although some were in the process of closing down). These independent cinemas are largely second-run cinemas (screening films that have already played the major networks), playing double-bill shows at minimal ticket prices. The independent films of the 1980s, which were critical of apartheid, were chiefly distributed through these independent venues and so the makers of such films seldom had their work being distributed by the main distribution companies. Independent theatres did not qualify for the state subsidy of box-office income (Botha 1996).

The distribution of films in South Africa is dominated by UIP Warner, Ster-Kinekor (representing Columbia Tristar, Twentieth Century Fox, Disney; the independent producers Castle Rock, Rysher, UGC as well as Polygram, Miramax, Rank and Majestic) and Nu Metro (major licences include Disney, Warner, Fox Home as well as independent licences such as New Line and Morgan Creek).

Primedia Entertainment bought Ster-Kinekor from Interleisure in July 1997, and Nu Metro was bought by CNA Gallo (now Millennium Entertainment Group Africa) in 1996. It is worth pointing out that the local production industry feels that these two distribution and screening companies do not give the same publicity or marketing and screening opportunities to domestic productions as they do to imported films, particularly American productions. Nu Metro consists of Nu Metro Theatres, Nu Metro Video, Nu Metro Distribution and Nu Metro Games. Primedia owns the Ster-Kinekor Group with 360 cinemas in addition to cinemas in Europe and the Middle East. Ster-Moribo was formed as a joint venture and as a 50/50 partnership between Ster-Kinekor and Moribo, a subsidiary of the black-owned company Thebe Investments. Ster-Moribo's primary focus is to bring the experience of the big screen to suburbs in disadvantaged communities. Over 18 million people visited Ster-Kinekor theatres and 850 000 visited the newly created Ster-Moribo cinema chain in 1995.

Video-based cinema cuts two-thirds off the cost of entry in comparison with normal cinemas. This has given Maxi-Movies, a video-based cinema company, the opportunity to develop new markets in traditionally black areas in South Africa and in other countries in Africa, where there has been no formal film exhibition beyond Zimbabwe. Maxi-Movies has twelve screens in South Africa and is installing two screens in Mozambique, four in Zambia (Lusaka), four in Zimbabwe (Bulawayo), three in Uganda (Kampala); the company also plans to open a cinema in Malawi. Ster-Moribo purchased 60 percent of the equity of this video cinema franchising business. According to Amos (1996:4), one of the interesting aspects of the South African market is that a film seen by 500 000 to a million people on the cinema circuit usually goes on to be a major seller on the video rental circuit. The South African video distribution industry is worth more than R200 million and sells more than 500 000 tapes annually.

The top local films that have earned the highest income yet for South African cinema theatres are:

- *Panic Mechanic* (R4 257 074)
- *There's a Zulu on my Stoep* (R8 583 336)
- *Sweet 'n Short* (R6 886 843)
- *The Gods Must be Crazy 2* (R6 408 377)
- *Oh Shucks it's Schuster* (R5 732 530)

The ten films that earned the highest income for South African cinema theatres during 1999 were:

- *The Matrix*
- *Star Wars Episode 1*
- *Notting Hill*
- *The Mummy*
- *Entrapment*
- *Tarzan*
- *Enemy of the State*
- *A Bug's Life*
- *The Spy Who Shagged Me*
- *Deep Blue Sea*

The top selling film of all time in South Africa and internationally is *Titanic*, which has grossed over a billion US dollars worldwide. The film viewing figures for the total population during the period from 1995 to 1999, are compared in Table 1.14.

The figures shown in Table 1.14 indicate how frequently people go to the cinema in South Africa. From these figures it is alarming to note there is a declining tendency in cinema attendance. We need to ask ourselves whether cinema theatres are still popular with South Africans? In order to increase audience attendance, do we need to build more cinemas? To answer these questions, we need to undertake an in-depth survey of patrons to find out their feelings. However, one point is certain, which is that future audience development is crucial to ensure a bigger market for locally made and African films.

Table 1.14  Film viewing figures of the total population for the period 1995–1999 (South African Advertising Research Foundation 2000b)

| Drive-in or four-waller | 1995 % | 1996 % | 1996 in '000 | 1997 % | 1998 % | 1998 in '000 | 1999 % | 1999 in '000 |
|---|---|---|---|---|---|---|---|---|
| Up to 7 days: | 3,4 | 3,1 | 806 | 2,8 | 2,7 | 691 | 2,2 | 563 |
| Up to 6 weeks: | 9,3 | 9,1 | 2 331 | 5,2 | 9,3 | 2 396 | 7,8 | 1 063 |
| Up to 12 weeks: | 12,5 | 12,4 | 3 191 | 8,7 | 12,6 | 3 251 | 11,1 | 2 860 |
| Up to 6 months: | – | 15,7 | 4 043 | 15,9 | 16,0 | 4 112 | 14,9 | 3 838 |
| Up to 12 months: | 17,5 | 19,5 | 5 005 | 19,6 | 20,0 | 5 147 | 19,2 | 4 948 |

### 1.4.9 The state of the film industry in South Africa

Developments within the film industry since November 1998 suggest that South Africa is securing a foothold in the international market and that our work is on the verge of international recognition. South Africa has more than 100 film, television and video production companies. These companies specialise mainly in advertising, educational, documentary, news, journal, sport, children's and other television programmes for the SABC, M-Net, e.tv, government institutions and private companies. In spite of the large number of companies, it is no exaggeration to say that, as far as the production of full-length feature films is concerned, the South African film industry is still lagging behind countries such as Australia, New Zealand, Canada and France (Botha 2000)(see Case study 1.3).

For a number of years production companies have had to concentrate chiefly on producing television programmes in order to survive. But from the high quality of domestic television pictures it would appear that there is considerable film talent in South Africa. Internationally, however, the film industry is no longer dependent on cinema theatres to draw an audience. Instead of competing with television, the film industry uses television in all its forms, namely video, cable TV, satellite TV and subscription TV. The market has become bigger, more segmented and more diversified. Today, certain films are only made for viewing on television. Film, however, still has the advantage of the big screen and unlike watching television, going to the cinema is still considered a social event in South Africa. The integration of the film industry with that of television-cable-satellite-video industry has made it almost impossible to say where film ends and where one of the other components begins. On a positive note, this integration has expanded the market for the film industry. As there is growth in the number of television channels, so the demand for films will increase until equilibrium is reached between production and consumption.

One of the most positive developments in the early 1990s was the perception within all sectors of the South African entertainment industry that film and video have a valuable role to play in creating social cohesion in South Africa. In this manner, film and video can play a valuable role in promoting democratisation and development. But, a number of significant issues need to be addressed regarding problems in the industry before film can make any deeply meaningful contribution to the development of South Africa. We discuss briefly some of these issues and possible solutions.

In 1991 the Film and Broadcasting Forum (FBF) was established to address the problems of the industry. It was widely considered to be an important step in the consultation process that resulted, in the creation of a single national film body during 1993, motivated by common interests. In composition, the FBF represented the widest possible cross-section of people from the industry, from producers through to directors, writers, actors, musicians, technicians, agents, management and studios. It also included both progressive and more establishment-orientated groupings, some of whom had previously not been very cooperative. The constructive process of cooperation resulted in the creation of the Film and Broadcasting Steering Committee and, finally, the Film and Television Federation (FTF) in 1993. For the first time in the history of South African film, the industry was unified and could face the problems in the industry with some form of consensus, such as the problem regarding the lack of skills and training. This lack results from the fact that we have an inadequate educational infrastructure as far as the film and video industries are concerned. There are problems regarding educational standards, the level of trainer competence, affirmative action policy and the skills required by the film industry. In addition, there is no national film school with international standing and our film training institutions tend to operate in isolation from one another (Botha et al 1994).

A sustained level of government and private sector aid to the post-apartheid film industry is necessary to ensure the continued existence of South African cinema. Even the highly developed First World film industries outside the United States, such as in Canada, Australia, New Zealand, France and the Scandinavian countries, cannot survive without ongoing support from the state. This does not mean that financial support to the local film industry is thrown into a bottomless pit. As in the case of Burkina Faso, one of the poorest countries in the world, but boasting a vibrant film culture, the South African public could, in terms of development, cultural reconstruction, progress and eventual prosperity for the country as a whole, reap the benefits of a healthy film industry.

Commercial viability should never be the sole criterion for state support of locally made films. All types of films, as in France and Burkina Faso, should benefit from financial investment from a film commission or statutory body. The underlying assumption should be that a diversity of film types would make for a healthier film industry; France being an excellent example here. A film industry that places the focus exclusively on maximising profit will inevitably become shallow and lacking in artistic credibility. In general, the dilemma of the local film industry can be attributed to the fact that film is seldom looked upon as a cultural industry. Although film can be regarded as a commercial product, it should also be seen as a product of culture, such as indigenous literature, theatre, the plastic arts and music.

The HSRC study (Botha et al 1994) recommended that the proposed Film and Video Foundation support all aspects of the film and video industry. The audio-visual industry needs to be seen as an organic whole, where each part contributes equally to the overall success of this industry. Production, distribution, exhibition, training, archives management, research and information, visual literacy programmes and the promotion and marketing of locally produced films and videos are essential elements in the successful relationship between film and the public. Botha et al (1994) also suggested that there should be five permanent functions of the Foundation as a statutory body:

- a department of production and distribution;
- a department of marketing and co-productions;
- an education department;
- an audio-visual research department which includes an extensive database; and
- a department of development and cultural support.

An Arts and Culture Task Group (ACTAG) was formed in August 1994, with the purpose of counselling the minister of the Department of Arts, Culture, Science and Technology on the formulation of a policy for the film industry. The aim of this group was to set out relevant objectives for the film industry while at the same time complementing the Reconstruction and Development Programme. In so doing, the policy needed to reaffirm and promote the rich and diverse expression of South African culture so that all citizens are guaranteed the right to practise their culture, language, beliefs and customs, while enjoying freedom of expression and creativity. ACTAG recognised that the film industry has a crucial role to play in the forging of social cohesion and the process of democratisation and development in South Africa simply by being an important part of the cultural domain of the country (South Africa 1995:282).

One of the long-term aims of the restructuring of the South African film industry was to put it on a sound commercial footing with the intention that it becomes internationally competitive. It was hoped that spin-offs from this process would include increased tourism and promotion of South Africa as an ideal venue for film production (South Africa 1995:283). A chart of the proposed South African film industry was drawn up and is illustrated in Figure 1.15.

In November of 1995, four months after the final ACTAG document was published, a Reference Group was appointed to write a White Paper on film, using the ACTAG document as the foundation for this paper. The first draft of the White Paper appeared at the beginning of 1996, and a revised version was published later in the year. The White Paper proposed that the South African film and video industry be administered by

## A South African Media Map

a proposed statutory body known as the South African Film and Video Foundation (SAFVF). This move was based on the fact that countries that have successful film industries, like Australia and Canada, have a national statutory body to oversee the industry (South Africa 1995:286). The statutory body would fall under the Ministry of Arts, Culture, Science and Technology, but as can be seen in Figure 1.15, a number of links with other government ministries are proposed. The functions of the statutory body would include the following:

- liaison with the film and television industry;
- protect free market mechanisms;
- maintain relations with foreign filmmakers;
- support production, distribution and exhibition of films;
- facilitate training and accreditation; and
- liaise with archives.

A film commission would be part of the statutory body, which should promote local films, publicise the achievements of local filmmakers by drawing attention to cultural and entertainment value, and promote awareness of the film industry among the public, both local and international, through the vehicle of film festivals.

It is proposed that under the auspices of this statutory body, a Film Finance Division be instituted to provide the following functions:

- discretionary low-cost loans and outright grants;
- financial guidelines for local and foreign high-risk ventures;
- seed funding;
- finance for the development of scripts, projects and experimental films; and
- bursaries for the study of film and video in order to provide skills.

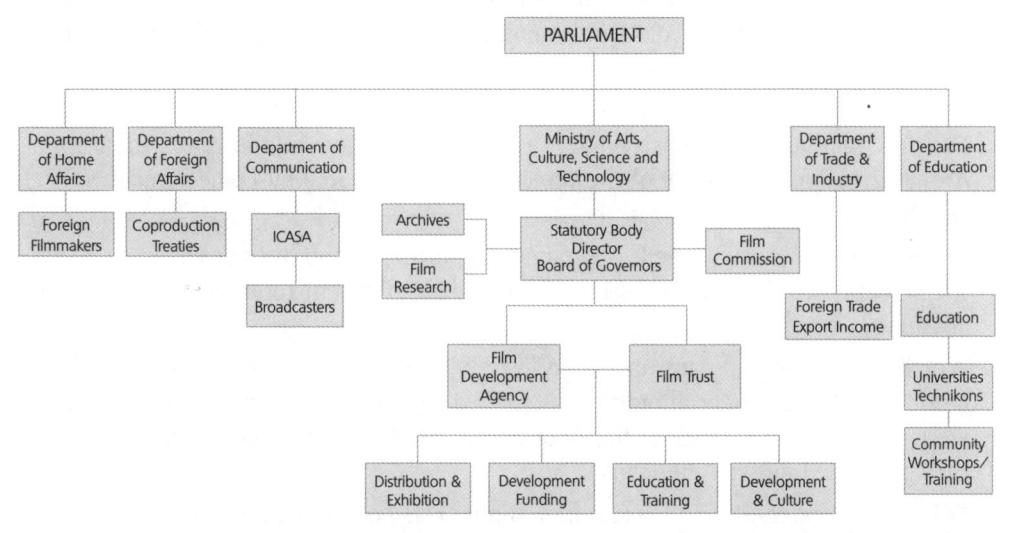

**Figure 1.15 Proposed structure for the South African film industry** (South Africa 1995:301)

One of the long-term aims of the proposed Foundation is to help place the South African film industry on a sound commercial footing and to enable it to become internationally competitive. This, in turn, should promote South Africa as a tourist attraction and as a location for foreign film productions and the filming of television advertisements. It will also enable South African audiences to see their own stories and their personal interpretation of experience reflected on local screens. Despite all these efforts, the South African film industry stubbornly refuses to gain impetus. We can identify a number of factors that simultaneously promote and retard the development of the industry. These are summed up in Case study 1.3.

**Case study 1.3:** The advantages and limitations of the South African film industry

### So why don't we make Aussie films?

The developing SA film industry faces problems, but there are encouraging signs, write Robert Greig and Howard Thomas.

You go to a South African film. Or you don't. Someone is bound to ask: "Why don't we make movies like the Australians?"
Here are 14 reasons:

**Money:** Movie-making is the auto-industry of the arts: its needs lots of money and diverse skills. Few movie industries can do without state funding and/or massive private investment. Australia's central government and its state spend about R1,8 billion a year on its industry. Our central government spends R11 million.

**Audiences:** The more money a film earns at the box office, the greater the chance of other movies being made. Our cinemas can accommodate 5 million out of a population of 45 million – about 11 percent. Australia's attendance last year was 8 million out of 19 million, 42 percent.

**TV:** The film and TV industry have a close production relationship. Thanks to Afrikaner nationalists' terror of the demon box, we were Johnny-come-latelies to TV. The Australian public had TV in the sixties.

**Irreverence:** Democracy breeds irreverence for authority and this goes hand-in-hand with creativity. When did you see a South African film that took the mickey out of anything?

**Worthiness:** South Africans have long lived with an issue – apartheid – which they brandished like a beggar brandishes a crippled leg. Imagine if most Australian films were about the hard times of the Aborigines or if American films largely eulogised the vanquished native Americans.

**Cultural homogeneity:** To make a film, filmmakers have to be clear who the film is for. This implies either that the filmmaker is culturally certain or, in making a film for one group, feels okay about being attacked for not ignoring it for another. South

Africans know they are South Africans but have a nagging feeling some South Africans are somehow more entitled than others.

**Cultural cringe and cultural strut:** Australians worked out some of these feelings on inferiority and the counterpart, bragging as themes in their seventies movies. We hanker – and need – foreign bucks and thus foreign approval.

**Writers:** A movie script is the equivalent of an architectural plan for a building or a skeleton of a body. Without it, the structure sprawls. Traditionally, South African writers have stood outside the movie-making process, noses pressed to the glass. Australian writers are part of the film crew. Our writers are expected to write, deliver scripts and go home to play. The script gets mauled around by the producer who wants it more commercial, the director who wants something else, the actor whose role doesn't shine enough and the camera operator... Then the editor says the film is too literary and cuts out scenes with dialogue. South Africans fear that writers might be "intellectual". Australians may be anti-intellectual but know than anti-intellectual film characters require good scripts, along with direction and performance.

**Movie-making is good business:** The film industry is an industry: it earns foreign exchange and employs people. The Australians treat it seriously as an industry, not a group of way-out creative people spending money. Only recently has the Department of Arts, Culture, Science and Technology established a working relationship for films with the Department of Trade and Industry.

**Training:** We have only just appointed a national film and video foundation, with a mandate to start a film school (Australia has had one for yonks).

**Tax breaks:** Movie-making, from an investment point of view is high risk: one in 10 Hollywood films makes a profit. Film investors – the local ones are leery – can be enticed by lower costs, and ours are becoming less competitive. The Department of Finance has rigorously ruled out tax breaks. See state funding.

**Labour:** Most countries protect their skilled film labour pool: you can't work elsewhere unless you have a good reason and a permit. It's a contentious matter because job protection can also insulate an industry from ideas and competition. Equally, it can force foreign filmmakers to expose locals to new ideas.

What are we getting right?

**State backing:** The state is taking movies seriously within its financial constraints. It is hosting initiatives for the industry to speak with a common voice and command its own destiny; setting up links between interested departments (arts and culture and trade and industry); and putting films on international trade agendas. The ministry of trade and industry, hosted by Investment South Africa and UCLA, will be making a presentation to the Hollywood entertainment industry at le Meridien on September 27. This US-South African Business and Finance Forum, taking place in New York and Los Angeles, marks the first official government visit to promote business in the entertainment sector in Los Angeles. President Thabo Mbeki will be in attendance at the New York presentation. The entertainment presentation will be made by South Africa's most prolific independent producer, Distant Horizon's Anant Singh, and Dave Erwin, who has been involved in financial planning in the industry.

**Tradition:** South Africans have been making films for nearly 100 years.

**Actors:** We have a strong body of actors who are used to making transitions from stage to screen.

**Local audience interest:** South Africans are in a phase of intense self-interest. This makes for receptive audiences.

**Industry backing:** Exhibitors – Ster-Kinekor, Nu Metro – are bending the rules to make South African films succeed. On its first two weeks' showing, *A Reasonable Man* under-performed; a foreign movie would have been pulled off the circuit. It was kept running, and business improved.

**Directors:** Thanks to SABC's use of outside firms to supply material, the industry has developed considerable film-making skills.

**Foreign interest and backing in principle:** This takes various forms: from a promise by Richard Attenborough to facilitate script development, to funding commitments, to large attendances – there were 1 000 delegates from more than 40 countries at last year's *Sithengi*, the southern African international film and television market in Cape Town.

**African connection, Western infrastructure:** The South African blend of African location and Western economic structure is attractive to foreign business – as well as the African outlook of many media businesses, like M-Net.

**Script-writing:** Courses are burgeoning in the country.

**Short films:** Short films, often for TV, are a growth area in South Africa. They give emerging filmmakers a low-risk point of entry into feature-making.

**Competition:** Maybe filmmakers don't really like the fact that they are up against international industries and muscle. But we've seen what happens when a local film industry is sheltered: dreck.

*Howard Thomas is editor of South African Screen News Bulletin. (The Web site is www.screenafrica.com)*

(*The Sunday Independent*, 26 September 1999:12)

### 1.4.10 Current local production

The first annual Southern African International Film and Television Market (*Sithengi*) was held in November 1996 in Cape Town. The focus of *Sithengi* is on co-productions and joint ventures in southern Africa, and to establish contact between filmmakers and buyers. *Sithengi*, in effect, exposes filmmaking on the African continent to the world and also hosts the All-Africa Film Awards. The market is indicative of an increasing growth in film and television production in southern Africa. The 1998 Southern African Film and Television Market was touted as the most successful local market to date. Although the 1998 market was mainly a television-based event, rather than a feature film market, it included the Newcomer's Competition, which was an important boost to new directors. This competition is an opportunity for any filmmaker to submit, free of charge, their short documentary, short drama or music video. Today, *Sithengi* has become an important focal point of the local film industry, functioning as an arena for local and international film professionals to enter into dialogue through forums, workshops and seminars and exchange information and knowledge.

At both the 4th *Sithengi*, and the 22nd Cape Town International Film Festival, the real strength of a post-apartheid cinema was clearly demonstrated. South Africa's short films and documentaries, which won numerous international awards during 1998 and 1999, overshadowed its attempts at feature filmmaking. Two documentaries towered above the rest: Greta Schiller and Mark Gevisser's historical overview of gay lives under apartheid in *The Man who Drove with Mandela*, and Francois Verster's portrait of the homeless in *Pavement Aristocrats: The Bergies of Cape Town*. Schiller and Gevisser's film received the Documentary Teddy prize at the 49th Berlin International Film Festival for its unique contribution to gay history. Verster's grim study of a marginalised people was selected for the 18th Amiens International Film Festival and won a major documentary award in South Africa.

Wynand Dreyer's trilogy of documentary films about ordinary lives on the Cape Flats are lyrical and moving documents. In South Africa itself, he has received praise for *Ravensmead, A Piece of Life, A Piece of Death* and *Steel upon Steel*. Another multi-award winner was Zola Maseko's *The Life and Times of Sara Baartman*, which deals with the tragic true-life story of a young South African Khoi woman who was taken to Europe and exhibited as a freak in London and Paris in the early nineteenth century. Maseko's short film, *The Foreigner*, a heartbreaking indictment of xenophobia in contemporary South Africa, also won various international awards, including a second prize at the Festival di Cinema African in Milan. Among the other short films, Gavin Hood's *The Storekeeper* stood out. This was a devastating portrait of South Africa's culture of violence. Without relying on dialogue, Hood tells the story of an elderly man who owns a small, isolated shop in rural South Africa. After several burglaries, he takes the law into his own hands with shocking consequences. Hood's film won as overall best short film at the Nashville Independent Film Festival. It also won the bronze for best dramatic short at the Houston International Film Festival. Hood's feature debut, *A Reasonable Man*, is a vivid portrait of conflict within a multicultural society and won an award at a major international film festival.

This renaissance in documentary and short films has resulted from funding by the Department of Arts, Culture, Science and Technology. During 1998 more than R2 million from the Interim Film Fund was allocated to the production of documentaries. Short films received more than R1 million. But, post-apartheid feature film-making, however, remains disappointing and we still seem unable to equal the renaissance in independent filmmaking of the late 1980s and early 1990s. The least said, for example, about Bernard Joffe's *Letting Go*, a poorly made account of a black woman's return from exile, the better. Russell Thompson's *The Sexy Girls*, about gangs on the Cape Flats, suffers from a poor script and weak characterisation. And Herman Binge's *Pride of Africa*, about intrigues on a luxury steam train in 1925, is simply boring. Even worse, Robert Benjamin's sentimental ghost story, simply entitled *The Ghost*, merely imitates certain aspects of the far superior American movie, *Ghost*.

Apart from Hood's *A Reasonable Man*, only two other feature films are worth noting. Neal Sundstrom's *Inside Out*, a reasonably good romantic comedy about a Jewish South African bit-part actress who lands up directing a Nativity play in a small rural town, and Khalo Matabane's delightful Soweton comedy, *Chikin Biz'nis – The Whole Story*. This film celebrates the ordinary experiences of black South Africans, especially those who are trying to make a living in the informal market as chicken salesmen. Fats Bookholane's performance in the lead, as well as Mtutuzeli Matshoba's witty script, has deservedly been awarded prizes at FESPACO, the Pan African film festival in Burkina Faso.

The 5th *Sithengi*, held 13 to 16 November 2000, was considered as more subdued than in previous years. This was despite an increase in attendance, but marked by a lack of screenings of new South African projects. Despite the fact that the growth rate in the broadcasting industry is quoted at 6%, three times that of the national economy, feature films are just not being produced in this country (Worsdale 2000). While funding continues to remain problematic, the industry seems unable, or sometimes even reluctant, to shrug off the ideological baggage from the so-called boom years of the sixties and seventies. In retrospect then, it becomes a moot point to say that South Africa has an indigenous film industry.

### 1.4.11 Western Cape: the Mecca of a future film industry?

Western Cape has become the success story of the local film industry. Broadly inclusive of production for film, television, video, photography and related media, the film industry has experienced significant growth in Western Cape since 1994. The presence of world-class production facilities and crews, combined with a stunning diversity of locations, has developed this province into a premier production destination. Local investors have recognised the potential for industry growth in Western Cape and have ploughed significant resources into the acquisition of high-end post-production capability, in terms of both technology and the training of local technicians as skilled operators. As international awareness of this vibrant industry increases, through annual events such as *Sithengi* and the Cape Town Film Festival, Western Cape Province has attracted the attention of world famous actors and directors including Wesley Snipes, Danny Glover, Angela Bassett, Quentin Tarantino, Sidney Poitier and Michael Caine.

The film industry's activities in Western Cape centre mainly on the facilitation of in-bound international productions. The largest single source of revenue generation is the

# A South African Media Map

co-production of television advertisements; a total of 450 were made during 1999 to the value of R106 513 000. As a result of the industry's growing expertise and expanding facilities, Western Cape is also seeing an increase in the production of South African film and television material, such as Jack Lewis's three-part documentary series on gay history, entitled *Apostles of Civilised Vice*, and John Badenhorst's made-for-TV film, *Slavery of Love*. Award-winning documentaries and short films were also produced during 1998 and 1999 by directors such as Francois Verster and Wynand Dreyer.

Factors that suggest that the rapid growth and development of the film industry in Western Cape are likely to be sustainable, include the following:

- The relocation of *Sithengi* to this province.
- Studio complex developments by Sasani – a media conglomerate in South Africa.
- Facilities for production, which were upgraded by The Refinery.
- The establishment of national broadcaster e.tv in the province.
- The establishment of the South African Film Finance Corporation, the Cape Film Commission and the Cape Film Office to promote and develop the regional film and video industries.
- Extensive training initiatives can be found in Western Cape.

## Summary

Within the context of Africa, South Africa can be considered as a media-rich country as evidenced by its highly developed media environment. However, to understand the organisation and interrelationship that exist in the current media environment, we need to consider how the media evolved by studying its historical development. We need to look at the three strands that make up the media, that is broadcasting, the press and film, individually, although development took place simultaneously. The reason for adopting such a diverse approach is simply because the supporting theories and models are not readily interchangeable between the three strands.

We began by looking at the developments that have taken place in broadcasting. The history of broadcasting in South Africa is largely that of the SABC. With the coming of democracy to South Africa in 1994, so the broadcasting environment underwent a radical change with the establishment of an independent regulator, charged with the task of overhauling the broadcasting environment. Today, the broadcasting environment is made up of a three-tier system, consisting of public, commercial and community broadcasters. To fit in to the new dispensation, the SABC was selected to become the public broadcaster. To accommodate this challenging position, the SABC has been required to undergo an extensive and ongoing restructuring process. Despite the number of considerable changes that have taken place, we can say that theoretically the monopoly of the SABC has been broken. But, if we look at the number of radio and television stations that the SABC continues to own and operate, then it is clear that the SABC still continues to dominate the broadcasting environment.

# MEDIA STUDIES

Next we looked at the press. Of the three media groups we considered here, the press has the longest history of all, dating back to the days of the Cape Colony. Unlike broadcasting, which was largely shaped by the needs and wishes of government, historically the press has always operated as a commercial enterprise. This has led to repeated clashes and conflict with the authorities, dating back to the British occupation of the Cape and which continues well into the new democratic South Africa. These clashes have resulted, at times, in censure, censorship, bannings and even the closure of certain newspapers. Over the past twenty-five years, the press has been, and continues to be, dominated by four cartels that own most of the major newspaper titles throughout the country. Of the three media strands that we considered in this unit, it is the press that is the most dynamic, as the organisational structures and shareholders are constantly changing, particularly as a result of effects to accommodate efforts at empowerment by the historically disadvantaged groups. Despite moves in this direction, we can say that ownership and control of the media does not yet adequately reflect the heterogeneous nature of South Africa's society.

Finally we considered the development of the film industry in South Africa. While film shows the greatest growth potential, the industry also happens to be stagnant. Following an artificially induced boom in the local film industry during the 1970s and 1980s, feature film production has declined to a few mediocre titles a year. Despite numerous efforts on the part of the Government to stimulate the industry, it stubbornly refuses to develop to its full potential. Reasons for this are numerous, including *inter alia*, ideological baggage from the apartheid era and a chronic lack of skills and training facilities.

## Research activities

1 You have been appointed to teach a media studies class at a local community college. As part of the curriculum you are required to teach media history. However, you find that your students are staying away from your classes because they feel there is no value in studying the past. How would you motivate them regarding the value of history to our understanding of the current media environment?

2 You are part of a team involved in running a stand promoting South Africa at an Expo in a city in the United States. Many of the visitors to the stand question you about the lack of diversity in the South African media. It appears that their understanding of the South African media environment is based on dated propaganda from decades ago. How would you explain attempts by the media to accommodate the diverse number of cultures and languages that can be found in South Africa?

3 As part of the same team mentioned in the activity above, and because of your knowledge of the South African media, you are asked to design a time-line comparing the development of the press with that of broadcasting and film in South Africa which can then be enlarged and displayed on the stand.

# A South African Media Map

4 You have been nominated as a candidate for the position of a councillor to serve on the (fictitious) South African Media Regulatory Council. You are required to appear before a panel of judges at a public hearing where your suitability for the position is to be evaluated. As part of the hearing you are expected to air you views on the relationship of the State with the media. Before you can do this, you need to establish the nature of the relationship of the present government with the media and how this has changed, if at all, from previous governments. In formulating your position on the matter, you need to take into account the influence and effect of the State on the development of the media in South Africa. Prepare notes that you can use at your public hearing.

5 You have been appointed to host a group of Russian journalists visiting South Africa for the first time. As Russia experienced the collapse of Communism at about the same time as the democratisation of South Africa, these journalists have expressed a keen interest in how the media environment has changed as a result of political events in the country. Prepare a brief that you can hand to these visiting journalists in which you highlight important developments over the past decade and then conclude with a description of the current media environment in South Africa.

6 As a budding film producer, you wish to embark on your first major production, but do not want to run the risk of having a major box-office failure on your hands. You realise that the greater majority of films made in South Africa have been lacklustre and of a mediocre standard. In order to avoid a repeat of the same, you decide to investigate the reasons why so few South African films exhibited high artistic and cultural standards, before you begin with your production. What are your findings?

7 As part of an investment team, and because of your detailed knowledge of South African media, you have been asked to address your colleagues in a seminar concerning the problems and issues regarding the contemporary South African media environment, so that potentially awkward questions from foreign investors can be given meaningful answers.

8 You are visiting a prominent university overseas as part of a cultural exchange programme. During a seminar, the topic of government repression of the press during the 1980s comes up. It quickly becomes obvious to you that the audience has a limited and generalised view of events, in that they see government repression of the media as an isolated incident within the broader context of the media history of South Africa. You feel strongly that the record needs to be set straight. Without being partisan, respond to the discussion by placing events of the 1980s within a deeper historical context by elaborating on the often-fraught relationship between the South African press and the government on one hand, and differences between the various press groups on the other, that can be traced back to the colonisation of the Cape and continues into the current day.

## Further reading

### Relating to the press
Hachten, WA & Giffard, CA. 1984. *Total onslaught: the South African press under attack.* Johannesburg: Macmillan.
Mervis, J. 1989. *The fourth estate.* Johannesburg: Jonathan Ball.
Tyson, H. 1993. *Editors under fire.* Sandton: Random House.
Manoim, I. 1996. *You have been warned: the first ten years of the Mail and Guardian.* London: Viking.
Tomaselli, K, Tomaselli, R & Muller J. 1987. *Narrating the crisis: hegemony and the South African press.* Johannesburg: Richard Lyon.
Tomaselli, K & Louw, PE (eds). 1991. *The alternative press in South Africa.* Bellville: Anthropos.

### Relating to broadcasting
Louw, PE. 1993. *South African media policy: debates of the 1990s.* Bellville: Anthropos.
Rosenthal, E. 1974. *You have been listening ... The early days of history of radio in South Africa.* Cape Town: Purnell.
Tomaselli, R, Tomaselli, K & Muller, J. 1989. *Currents of power: state broadcasting in South Africa.* Bellville: Anthropos.
Van der Merwe, C. 1995. *Electronic media management.* Johannesburg: Africa Growth Network.

### Relating to film
Botha, M & van Aswegen, A. 1992. *Images of South Africa: the rise of the alternative film.* Pretoria: Human Sciences Research Council.
Blignaut, J & Botha, M. 1992. *Movies – moguls – mavericks: South African cinema 1979–1991.* Cape Town: Showdata.
Tomaselli, K. 1989. *The cinema of apartheid.* London: Routledge.

## Bibliography

Amos, G (ed). 1996. Ster Kinekor. Supplement to *Business Day*, September.
Argus buys TML minority holdings. 1994. *Pretoria News*, 12 March:13.
Banda, R. 1999a. It's news, but not all good news, at e.tv. *Cape Times*, 18 January:3.
Banda, R. 1999b. IBA, e.tv relations sour over licence. *The Star*, 25 February:14.
Barrel, H, Ngobeni, E & Kindra, J. 2000. Media are racist ... if you say so. *Mail & Guardian*, 25–31 August:4.
Bhengu, C. 2000. White editors walk out of HRC hearings. *Sowetan*, 8 March:3.
Bennett, T. 1982. Theories of the media, theories of society, in *Culture, society and the media*, edited by M Gurevitch, T Bennett, J Curran & J Woollacott. London: Routledge: 30–55.
Blignaut, J & Botha, M. 1992. *Movies – moguls – mavericks: South African cinema 1979–1991.* Cape Town: Showdata.
Botha, MP. 1996. *An introduction to South African cinema.* Unpublished report.
Botha, MP. 2000. South Africa, in *International film guide*, edited by P Cowie. London: Faber & Faber.
Botha, MP & Dethier, H. 1997. *Kronieken van Zuid-Afrika: de films van Marie van Rensburg.* Brussels: Vubpress.
Botha, MP, Mare, L, Langa, Z, Netshitomboni, R, Hgoasheng, K, Potgieter J & Greyling M. 1994. *Proposals for the restructuring of the South African film industry.* Pretoria: Human Sciences Research Council.

Botha, MP & van Aswegen, A. 1992. *Images of South Africa: the rise of the alternative film.* Pretoria: Human Sciences Research Council.

Briggs, A. 1980. Problems and possibilities in the writing of broadcasting history. *Media, Culture & Society* 2:5-13.

Cutten, TEG. 1935. *A history of the press in South Africa.* Cape Town: National Union of South African Students.

Dahl, HF. 1978. The art of writing broadcasting history. *Gazette* 24(2):130-137.

De Ionno, P. 2000. e.tv tightens empowerment belt. *The Star,* 10 January:1.

De Kock, W. 1982. *A manner of speaking: the origins of the press in South Africa.* Cape Town: Saayman & Weber.

De Villiers, C. 1993. Radio: chameleon of the ether, in *Mass media for the nineties: the South African handbook of mass communication,* edited by AS de Beer. Pretoria: Van Schaik:125-146.

Diederichs, P. 1993. Newspapers: the fourth estate – a cornerstone of democracy, in *Mass media for the nineties: the South African handbook of mass communication,* edited by AS de Beer. Pretoria: Van Schaik:71-98.

Dodd, A. 2000. Movies: portrait of a young industry growing. *Sunday Times,* 2 January:50.

Donaldson, A. 2000. Focus on SA's ailing film industry. *Sunday Times Metro,* 5 November:4.

Duncan, J. 2000. Talk left, act right: what constitutes transformation in South African media? [O]. Available: http://www.und.ac.za/und/ccms/jane.htm
Accessed on 2000/08/08

Emdon, C. 1998. Ownership and control of media in South Africa, in *Media and democracy in South Africa,* edited by J Duncan & M Seleoane. Pretoria: Human Science Research Council and Freedom of Expression Institute.

Engelbrech, JCR. 1972. *Die pers as massakommunikasiemedium.* Pretoria: Human Sciences Research Council.

Faure, C. 1995. Ondersoekende joernalistiek en sosiale verandering: 'n ontleding en evaluering van die agendastellingsrol van *Vrye Weekblad.* DLitt et Phil thesis, University of South Africa: Pretoria.

Faure, C. 1996. The alternative press, in *Introduction to communication – course book 5: journalism, press and radio studies,* edited by LM Oosthuizen. Kenwyn: Juta:264-281.

Fourie, PJ. 1994. Zuid-Afrika, in *Nederlandstalige en Afrikaanstalige media,* 2nd edition, edited by N van Zutphen & J Nootens. Brussels: Vlaamse Raad:279-341.

Freedom of Expression Institute. 1998. Roundup. *FXI Update* December:11-15.

Glaser, D. 2000. The media inquiry reports of the South African Human Rights Commission: a critique. *African Affairs* 99(396):373-393.

Greig, R & Thomas, H. 1999. So why don't we make Aussie films? *The Sunday Independent,* 26 September:12.

Grogan, J & Barker, G. 1993. Media law: to tread cautiously on different beats, in *Mass media for the nineties: the South African handbook of mass communication,* edited by AS de Beer. Pretoria: Van Schaik:229-244.

Haffajee, F & Shapshak, D. 1999. Gloves off in the battle of the paperweights. *Mail & Guardian,* 5-11 March:4.

Hagen, H. 1999. e.tv news at last. *The Citizen,* 18 January:1.

Heard, J. 1998. What a rush as e.tv goes into orbit. *Sunday Times,* 4 October:5.

Hills, C. 1999. Midi Television's Procter resigns. *The Citizen,* 9 June:1.

Hlophe, N. 1999. e.tv invests R100m in news shows. *The Star,* 12 January:6.

Huteau, J. 2000. Media self-control, the south's new option. *Unesco Courier* April:43-45.

Independent Broadcasting Authority. 1995. *Report on the protection and viability of public broadcasting services, cross media control of broadcasting services, local television content and South African music (Triple inquiry report).* Johannesburg.
Independent Broadcasting Authority. 2000. *Annual report for the financial year ended 31 March 1999.* Sandton.
Jackson, GS. 1993. *Breaking story: the South African press.* Boulder, CO: Westview.
Jayiya, E. 1999. e.tv owners embroiled in squabbles. *The Star*, 24 September:3.
Johnson, S. 1991. An historical overview of the black press, in *The alternative press in South Africa*, edited by K Tomaselli & PE Louw. Bellville: Anthropos:15-32.
Keane, J. 1991. *The media and democracy.* Cambridge: Polity.
Klein, M. 1999a. Midi's e.tv says it is catching up with competitors. *Sunday Times*, 18 April:3.
Klein, M. 1999b. Lean and mean is the new motto at cash-strapped e.tv. *Sunday Times Business Times*, 4 July:3.
Klein, M. 1999c. We're doing best thing for e.tv, says Golding. *Sunday Times*, 19 September:4.
Kobokoane, T. 1999a. Funds crisis drives e.tv parent into a corner. *Sunday Times Business Times*, 2 May:1.
Kobokoane, T. 1999b. Midi row about 'bull-in-kraal' Marcel Golding. *Sunday Times Business Times*, 23 May:1.
Kobokoane, T. 1999c. Legal row looms over e.tv shake-up. *Sunday Times*, 13 June:1.
Koenderman, T. 1999a. Circulation bloodbath. *Financial Mail* 152(7):123.
Koenderman, T. 1999b. e.tv begins to make headway. *Financial Mail* 152(7):124.
Koenderman, T. 1999c. Now for some stability. *Financial Mail* 153(10):33.
Koenderman, T. 2000a. The last word ... *Financial Mail* 1 September:94.
Koenderman, T. 2000b. Print circulation in trouble. *Financial Mail* 18 August:75.
Laurence, P. 2000. Racism in media neither quantified nor specified. *Financial Mail* 1 September: 36.
Leahy, PE & Voice, P. 1992. *The media book, 1991–92: your guide to getting the most from media: for marketing, advertising, public relations and media professionals.* Bryanston: WTH.
Lloyd, T. 2000. And may they all live happily ever after ... *Financial Mail* 14 January:32.
Louw, PE & Botha, JR. 1993. Film: the captivating power of fleeting images, in *Mass media for the nineties: the South African handbook of mass communication*, edited by AS de Beer. Pretoria: Van Schaik:151–169.
Louw, PE. 1989. The emergence of a progressive-alternative press in South Africa with specific reference to Grassroots. *Communicatio* 15(2)26–32.
Louw, PE. 1993. *South African media policy: debates of the 1990s.* Bellville: Anthropos.
Louw, PE & Tomaselli, KG. 1991. Developments in the conventional and alternate presses, 1980–1989, in *The alternative press in South Africa*, edited by KG Tomaselli & PE Louw. Bellville: Anthropos: 5–4.
Magardie, K. 2000. e.tv has to find local content. *Mail & Guardian*, 7–13 January:7.
Makoe, A. 1999. Black Wednesday – a day of bannings, a day to remember. *The Star*, 18 October:11.
Malefane, M. 1999. SAUJ warns e.tv of channel collapse. *The Citizen*, 15 January:8.
Manoim, I. 1996. *You have been warned: the first ten years of the Mail and Guardian.* London: Viking.
Mathiane, N. 2000. Self-scrutiny needed, forum told. *Business Day*, 25 August:5.
Matloff, J. 1996. Issue of free press now divides old allies who fought apartheid. *Christian Science Monitor*, 10 July:9.
Mda, Z. 1998. On the small screen: e.tv offers nothing to tempt viewers away from the SABC. *Sunday Times*, 4 October:20.

Mersham, GM. 1993. Television: a fascinating window on an unfolding world, in *Mass media for the nineties: the South African handbook of mass communication*, edited by AS de Beer. Pretoria: Van Schaik:173-197.

Moerdyk, C. 1999a. IBA will get egg on its face over e.tv. *Saturday Star*, 11 September:15.

Moerdyk, C. 1999b. Publications get boldface economics lesson. *Saturday Star*, 20 February:15.

Moerdyk, C. 1999c. Sales of papers rise in Gauteng. *Saturday Star*, 7 August:15.

Muller, J. 1987. Press houses at war: a brief history of Nasionale Pers and Perskor, in *Narrating the crisis: hegemony and the South African press*, edited by K Tomaselli, R Tomaselli & J Muller. Johannesburg: Richard Lyon:118-140.

Naspers. 2000. [O].
   Available: http://www.fm.co.za/reports/giant2000/naspers.htm
   Accessed on 2001/03/22

Nkutha, Z. 2000. HRC says SA media is racist. *Sowetan*, 25 August:2.

Nxumalko, F & Hlophe, N. 1999. e.tv newsdesk may face staff walkout. *Saturday Star*, 16 January:13.

Oosthuizen, LM. 1989. *Media policy and ethics*. Cape Town: Juta.

Oosthuizen, LM. 1991. Suid-Afrikaanse mediabeleid: die media se bondgenoot is soek. *Communicatio* 17(1):38-47.

Oppelt, P. 1999. The ecstasy and the agony. *Sunday Times*, 3 October:19.

Palmer, J. 1999. Weeklies grow while dailies' figures drop. *Business Day*, 24 August:21.

Parker, J. 1999a. News comes too late to help e.tv's case. *Business Day*, 12 January:2.

Parker, J. 1999b. Internal disputes at e.tv denied by Midi Television. *Business Day*, 21 January:4.

Philp, R. 1998. Grooming the couch potato. *Sunday Times Lifestyle*, 25 November:21-23.

Pityana, B. 2000. South Africa's inquiry into racism in the media: the role of national institutions in the promotion and protection of human rights. *African Affairs* 99(397):525-532.

Pokwana, V. 1998. e.tv line-up fails to satisfy viewers. *City Press Showbiz*, 11 October:3.

Pollak, R. 1981. *Up against apartheid: the role and the plight of the press in South Africa*. Carbondale, Ill: Southern Illinois University Press.

Pople, L. 2000. 'Europa gaan nie Kersvader speel'. *Naweek-Beeld*, 11 November:3.

Roelofse, JJ. 1983. *Towards rational discourse: an analysis of the report of the Steyn commission of inquiry into the media*. Pretoria: Van Schaik.

Roelofse, K. 1996. The history of the South African Press, in *Introduction to communication – course book 5: journalism, press and radio studies*, edited by LM Oosthuizen. Kenwyn: Juta:66-118.

Rosenthal, E. 1974. *You have been listening ... The early days of history of radio in South Africa*. Cape Town: Purnell.

Silverstone, R. 1999. *Why study the media?* London: Sage.

South Africa. 1981. *Report of the commission of inquiry into the mass media*. Pretoria: Government Printer. Chairman: M Steyn.

South Africa. 1993. *Independent Broadcasting Authority Act, no 153, 1993*. Pretoria: Government Printer.

South Africa. 1995. *Report of the Arts and Culture Task Group*. Pretoria: Government Printer.

South Africa. 1996. *Telecommunications Act, no 103, 1996*. Pretoria: Government Printer.

South Africa. 1999. *Broadcasting Act, no 4, 1999*. [O].
   Available: http://www.polity.org.za/govdocs/legislation/1999/act99-004.html
   Accessed on 1999/09/03

South Africa. 2000. *Independent Communication Authority of South Africa Act, no 13, 2000*. Pretoria. Government Printer.

South Africa. Department of Arts, Culture, Science and Technology. [Sa]. *Film development strategy.* [SI].
South Africa. Government Communications. 1998. *The media.* [O].
　　Available: http://www.gov.za/yearbook/media.htm
　　Accessed on 2000/06/26
South Africa. Task Group, Broadcasting in South and Southern Africa. 1991. Report of the task group on broadcasting in Southern Africa. Pretoria: Government Printer. Chairman: C Viljoen.
South African Advertising Research Foundation. 1998. *SAARF AMPS 1998 (Jan-Dec) and trends 1994-1998.* Condensed pocket edition. Sandton.
South African Advertising Research Foundation. 2000a. *Readership of newspapers in 1 000's.* [O].
　　Available: http://www/saarf.co.za/topnewspapers.htm
　　Accessed on 2001/01/15
South African Advertising Research Foundation. 2000b. *SAARF AMPS 1999A: Yesterday/Cinema attendance.* [O].
　　Available: http://www/saarf.co.za/cinema
　　Accessed on 2001/01/15
South African Broadcasting Corporation. 1996. *Annual report and financial statements, 1995/96.* Johannesburg.
South African Broadcasting Corporation. 1999. *Annual report and financial statements, 1998/99.* Johannesburg.
Steyn, R. 1994. The transition process and the South African media. *Editor & Publisher* 127(2):44.
Survey: nearly 25% say media is racist. 2000. *Business Day*, 18 July:2.
Switzer, LS & Switzer, D. 1979. *The black press in South Africa and Lesotho.* Boston: GK Hall.
Taitz, L. 2000. Media not off the race hook, says Pityana. *Sunday Times*, 27 August 2000:2.
Tomaselli, K, Tomaselli, R & Muller J. 1987. *Narrating the crisis: hegemony and the South African press.* Johannesburg: Richard Lyon.
Tomaselli, K & Louw, PE (eds). 1991. *The alternative press in South Africa.* Bellville: Anthropos.
Tomaselli, K. 1989. *The cinema of apartheid.* London: Routledge.
Tomaselli, R, Tomaselli, K & Muller, J. 1989. *Currents of power: state broadcasting in South Africa.* Bellville: Anthropos.
United Nations. Department for Economic and Social Affairs. Statistical Division. 1997. *Statistical yearbook*, 42nd edition. New York.
United Nations. Department for Economic and Social Affairs. Statistical Division. 2000. *Statistical yearbook*, 44th edition. New York.
Van der Merwe, C. 1995. *Electronic media management.* Johannesburg: Africa Growth Network.
Vermeulen, A. 1999. Rembrandt and e.tv minorities in talks on funding. *Sunday Times Business Times*, 10 October:1.
Wigston, DJ. 1996. A historical overview of radio, in *Introduction to communication – course book 5: journalism, press and radio studies*, edited by LM Oosthuizen. Kenwyn: Juta:283–326.
Worsdale, A. 2000. *Sithengi again a learning curve.* [O].
　　Available: http://www/mg.co.za/mg/art/film/0011/001127-sithengi.html
　　Accessed on 2001/03/20
Wrottesley, S. 1999. Nice e.studio, shame about the news content. *Cape Argus*, 18 January:5.

# Characteristics, Trends and the Political Economy of the Media

*Pieter J Fourie*

## Overview

In the previous unit you were provided with an overview of the South African media system. In this unit we take a closer look at the business nature of the media. In critical media studies, one of the main concerns is that the media are increasingly practised as businesses with the emphasis on profit; and practised less as the production of culture with the emphasis on meaning and quality. Nevertheless, we cannot deny that in our information and entertainment society, the media as business entities with related businesses (among them advertising, entertainment and the Internet) are big. A basic knowledge of the nature of media as businesses is thus essential for criticism as practised in critical media studies.

In this unit we look at some of the business characteristics of the media – broadcasting, film and the press as business entities – some economic strategies in the media business, some trends in the media business and how they impact, for example, on public service broadcasting. Finally, we consider the assumptions of critical political economy.

## Learning outcomes

After completing this unit you should be able to
- describe the basic characteristics of the media as business entities;
- distinguish between direct and indirect competition in the media business and give your own examples of such competition;
- name and give your own examples of how media products are sold to the public;
- name and give your own examples of how media audiences are sold to advertisers;
- explain and give examples of the main economic trends in present-day capitalism and how they affect the media industry; and
- describe and critically debate the underlying assumptions of political economy.

## 2.1 CHARACTERISTICS OF THE MEDIA BUSINESS

From an economic perspective the purpose of the media business, like any other business, is to make a profit. Entering the business requires a basic knowledge of at least some of the main characteristics of the media as a business (or industry). McQuail (1994:168–169) lists the following characteristics. The media

- are hybrid businesses;
- depend on fixed costs;
- depend on creativity and this involves a lot of uncertainties;
- cannot rely on the multiple and recycled use of their products;
- tend towards concentration;
- are difficult to enter (capital resources); and
- depend on public interest.

What do we mean by the above characteristics?

Hybridisation means that the media are hybrids in respect of markets, products and technology. There are different kinds of media producing different kinds of products for different markets in different ways with different technologies. If you wish to enter the media business this means that you should have a sound understanding of the reasons why you want to start a media business. You must have a clear reason, purpose and goal with, for example, a community newspaper, should you wish to start one. Furthermore, you must know and understand the nature and possibilities of the medium: what is involved in the production of, for example a newspaper? (cf. The production units in Volume 2 of this book for more about this and related topics on production.) Just as important as the above is a knowledge of the audience you wish to reach.

Secondly, the media business involves high fixed costs. By this we mean, for example, licence fees, office and production facilities, the salaries of skilled workers, production costs which can involve expensive technology such as computer hardware and software, printing equipment, broadcasting technology, photographic, film and video equipment and stock, and distribution costs.

Thirdly, the media business involves creativity and uncertainty. Media products differ from other products such as, for example, a hamburger, a pair of shoes, or groceries. They are first and foremost a product of the human mind, for the human mind. The production of media content and media products involves creativity both in terms of creating media content, representing reality (cf. Unit 15 on Representation) and planning. The media business involves a sound understanding of the human mind and spirit, of reading the signs of the times, and so on. Because media content is a product for the human mind (for the readers, the listeners and viewers who may differ in terms of their needs, tastes, culture and education), media as businesses involve a lot of uncertainty, despite sophisticated market research. For example, despite market research it remains difficult to predict the popularity of a film, a television or radio programme, or a specific edition of a newspaper. The media business is thus often referred to as a high-risk business.

# Characteristics, Trends and the Political Economy of the Media

Fourthly, media products can seldom be used in a multiple way and/or recycled. Although huge numbers of the same media product can and are usually produced, and although the production process can be standardised, many media products have a once-off use and must be changed on a daily basis. For example, thousands of the same copy of a newspaper can be printed and distributed on the same day. However, each day the newspaper must be different in terms of its content and news coverage. A day-old newspaper is only of historical value. As far as content is concerned, the same applies to the other media. A television station cannot screen the same programmes day-after-day. People usually watch a specific film only once. Compared to this, a pair of shoes, a car, or a fridge, can have user-value for many years. Some exceptions are books, films and compact discs (CDs), but even they may remain unused on a shelf once they have been read, watched or listened to. This characteristic, namely that media products cannot be easily re-used, further contributes to the risk factor in the media business.

A fifth characteristic is that the media business tends towards concentration (cf. 2.2 and 2.3, and Unit 3 on ownership). From an economic point of view, including the need to reduce the risks mentioned above, it makes sense that a newspaper owner will want to enter as many media fields as possible, for example, the newspaper owner will have broadcasting interests and vice-versa so that one business subsidises the other. To further substantiate this point, in the case of Naspers (one of South Africa's big media companies) the success of some of its newspapers carries the possible losses of other newspapers in the same group; Naspers' successful broadcasting interests in M-Net (a South African subscription television station), and DStv (a South African owned digital satellite television platform) can subsidise Naspers' publishing and newspaper interests.

A sixth characteristic is that without large capital resources the media business is *difficult to enter*. In South Africa we have experienced, for example, the complex process of setting up a free-to-air television network such as Midi Television, which owns e.tv. According to regulations, financially committed shareholders had to be found. This involved a lengthy and costly procedure before a costly licence to broadcast was awarded. Although not on the same scale, even the setting up of a local or community newspaper or radio station involves high costs, not excluding the cost of employment.

Finally, one should be constantly aware of the fact that the success of media depends on public interest. It is easier and safer to start a shoe or a food factory than a media business. The owner of a shoe factory or a grocery shop has the assurance that everybody needs shoes and food. However, people can do without the media, or may not even be interested in the media. For example, setting up a student newspaper on campus is doomed to failure if students have no interest in such a newspaper; starting a football magazine in a country where people are not interested in football, will fail; starting a newspaper in an underdeveloped community were people cannot read, is doomed to fail. This emphasises the need for thorough audience research before one can think of entering the media business (cf. Unit 9, Audience research, in Volume 2).

The above are only some of the characteristics of the media as a business. From these characteristics it is clear that the media business is a risky business.

# MEDIA STUDIES

Why then is the media business, almost globally, one of the biggest and fastest growing industries? The answer is that economic trends (see 2.3), the development of information and communication technology (ICT), globalisation, and increased consumerism have created a favourable environment for media owners. In general, this environment is characterised by a shift in emphasis from providing quality (in the case of media the quality of information and entertainment) to providing quantity (in the case of media the quantity of information and entertainment); from providing a service to the public to selling a product; on accessing the biggest possible audience (readers, viewers, listeners), even in the case of growing niche markets.

## 2.1.1 Selling products and accessing audiences

In the media business two products are sold: media products and media audiences. The key to media profits is to access the largest possible audience(s) (Grossberg, Wartella & Whitney 1998:93–117).

### Access to audiences (or how to sell media products)

Media owners can gain access to audiences in a number of ways, or we could say they sell their products in a number of ways and through a combination of ways. Ways of selling their products include, amongst others, the following: direct sales, subscriptions, licence fees, subsidies and advertisers.

- Direct sales: People go to a newsstand and buy a newspaper, or a book, a CD, video, and so forth. They go to a cinema theatre and buy a ticket for a specific movie.
- Subscriptions: People subscribe for a period of time to newspapers, magazines, a book club, CD and/or video club. They also subscribe to television networks such as, for example, to M-Net and DStv. In the case of DStv they receive access to a number of specialised television programme networks such as news channels, documentary channels, entertainment channels, sport and music channels. In the case of subscriptions, people pay a weekly, monthly or annual rate.
- Licence fees: People pay a licence fee for radio and television stations, other than subscription services. Licence fees usually apply to public broadcasting services such as those television and radio services offered by the SABC (South African Broadcasting Corporation) or any other public broadcasting organisation. Licence fees are usually low. Different countries apply different methods of accessing licence fees from the public. Not paying licence fees is usually against the law and punishable.
- Subsidisation: Many media products are subsidised by organisations and by the government, especially in developing countries, and distributed free of charge. Here we can think of the in-house journals and newsletters of organisations, community newspapers, scientific, cultural and educational journals, and other media products such as videos, films, sound cassettes, and so on. Usually the main purpose of these

## Characteristics, Trends and the Political Economy of the Media

products is to inform and educate the public about topics and matters not necessarily in popular demand and not offered by the mainstream media. In South Africa we are investigating the setting up of, for example, a Media Development and Diversity Agency (MDDA). MDDA's task will be, amongst others, the subsidisation of local and community newspapers and radio in under-developed and poor communities.
- Electronic/digital delivery: Lately many media products are delivered electronically through the Internet. Almost all the big newspapers, media companies and their products, can be accessed through the Internet. In this case, audiences subscribe to an Internet service through an Internet service provider (ISP). (See the discussion of convergence under 2.3.)
- Knock-and-drops: By this we mean newspaper and other printed material usually delivered free of charge to homes in suburbs and communities. We often also refer to these products as "junk mail". In this case the advertisers cover the costs in full.

The above are only a few ways that media owners can use to sell their product, get it to the public, or access their audiences.

Obviously, the main reasons for selling their products are to

- finance production costs, and
- make a profit.

It is understandable that media owners will try to access the biggest possible audience. The size of the audience determines the advertising income. For example, a popular TV programme with a big audience will sell at a much higher rate to advertisers than a programme with a small audience.

### Access to advertisers (or selling audiences to advertisers)

We have already explained that the production of media products is expensive. The above means of selling media products are not sufficient to finance production costs. For example, in 2000 it cost R18 to produce a single copy of one of South Africa's largest newspapers, *Beeld* (largest in terms of readership figures). However, the price paid for a copy of *Beeld* at a newsstand was only R2,30.

The bulk of costs in terms of financing production and making a profit, are financed by selling the consumers/audiences to advertisers. This is done by means of selling *space* to advertisers in newspapers, journals, magazines and in all other printed material, and selling *time* in the case of broadcasting. Small wonder then that there is fierce competition between the different media, for example, between the print media and the broadcast media, to get the biggest share of the so-called "advertising cake".

Advertising and marketing are specialised fields that cannot be dealt with here. Suffice to say that for media owners advertising income implies careful and almost scientific planning in terms of reaching the right audiences and markets for their products; to pitch a product on the right level for the right market. For example, advertising baking products in the middle of a sport broadcast will be far less successful (if at all) than advertising beer. Advertising an expensive car or real estate in a campus newspaper will have less impact than advertising it in a publication for a higher-income group, unless the intention is not to sell the product, but to create an awareness and a need in a potential market.

An increasing result of this is market segmentation, in other words focusing the product on a specific group, be it the youth, a low or high income-group, women, men and niche markets.

As far as broadcasting is concerned, different time slots costing different prices are sold to advertisers and sponsors of events. Here the issue is finding the right audience and the biggest audience for a specific product, and at the right time of the day. Product manufacturers will usually go for prime-time – that time of the day (usually in the evenings) when the largest audience can be reached and/or when the most popular programmes are broadcast. In defining prime-time, broadcasters have to distinguish between the markets the advertisers wish to reach and they have to calculate the popularity of programmes or programme types (genres). For that they use ratings, which are done with specialised measuring methods and techniques. (See Unit 9 in Volume 2 on audience research.)

Procuring advertisements in order to cover production costs and to make a profit, to gain access to media consumers (audiences/users), and to sell such access to advertisers (the producers of goods and services) involves competition between media owners.

## Competition

As far as competition is concerned we can distinguish between direct competition and indirect competition.

- Direct competition: By this we mean competition within the same medium. For example, different newspapers compete with each other for the same markets; different radio and/or television stations compete with each other for the same markets and even within the same station there may be competition between different programmes. Different film producers compete with each other. The same accounts for the production houses of CDs, books, comics, and the like.
- Indirect competition: This involves competition between different media. In other words, competition between radio, television, film, the print media, the Internet, and so on. When a new medium enters the market, such as for instance the Internet, it usually causes a flutter in the dovecote and means that older media have to adapt. Television and its growth in popularity initially threatened the existence of radio, the film industry and the print media. These "older" media had to adapt by creating new needs, offering new and unique content and new formats in order to survive and attract new markets. At the time of writing, they all have to adapt to the threats posed by the Internet. However, it seldom happens that a new medium completely replaces or supplants an existing medium. An exception is the compact disc (CD) industry, which almost completely replaced the record industry.

# Characteristics, Trends and the Political Economy of the Media

We began this section by saying that the media business is a profit-making business. We also explained that it is a high-risk business. To reduce the risks there are a number of strategies.

## 2.2 ECONOMIC STRATEGIES

For selling their products and gaining access to the largest possible audiences, media owners have adopted economic strategies (for example Grossberg, Wartella & Whitney 1998:109-117) such as the following:

- Vertical integration: This means to integrate the production process or to control the entire production and distribution process. Big media organisations usually own their own printing and distribution divisions, sometimes they are separate companies affiliated within the same group; broadcasters own their own production facilities or production houses, either as part of the company or affiliated, and are responsible for their own signal distribution. Lately, control over the production and distribution processes goes hand in hand with concentrated media ownership (see 2.3). This provides media owners with the opportunity to gain access to the audiences of different media and affiliated media companies. (See the reference to the AOL Time Warner merger in 2.3.) *eg. Metro story on Barbara & BBC show*
- Horizontal integration: This means to create a product for multiple media use and distribution. For example, a radio soap opera provides the basic screenplay for a television soap opera, which can be reworked for a film. A television programme can be syndicated and shown over various channels in various countries, distributed via satellite. Comic strips are syndicated and published in thousands of newspapers and magazines all over the world. The same article is sold to various magazines, as is the same photograph. The popular South African cartoon, *Madam & Eve*, first published by the *Mail & Guardian* is now also a popular television situation comedy.
- Rationalisation of consumption: Earlier we said that the media business is a risky business because it depends on the popularity of a product, which is determined by consumers. Popularity is always difficult to predict. Media owners tend to reduce this risk by focusing on a product with proven success or the best chance of appeal to audiences. In television this is known as the L-O-P (Least-Objectionable-Programme) formula (Grossberg, Wartella & Whitney 1998:113). Closely related to focusing on a product with proven success, is opting for a popular genre. Television producers will, for example, rather produce a soap opera, which is a genre with proven success, than produce an avant-garde programme with a limited chance of popularity. Media owners also focus increasingly on niche markets. In other words, they produce a product for a specific group with a specific interest.

The above is a brief overview of three of the strategies followed by media owners. Although such strategies may be commendable from an economic perspective, critics, especially in the field of critical media studies, argue that these strategies are responsible for much of the shallowness we are experiencing in media content. Despite the claim of catering for diverse markets and offering more diversity, a closer analysis reveals that audiences actually get more and more of the same. The extra-ordinary in media content is a rarity. In news and in the print media these strategies can lead to superficial reporting and writing of articles; and in broadcasting to sound bites which may be catchy and sensational, but empty and rhetorical. It is exactly these kinds of strategy that are contributing to the demise of quality broadcasting. In short, the argument is that media content, being product and audience centred instead of content and quality centred, has became nothing more than a consumer product with limited value. We will return to this kind of argument in the discussion of critical political economy (2.4).

We end this section with a quotation from Grossberg, Wartella and Whitney (1998:115):

> The media involve the production of goods for a profit: hardware as well as software. The media are a major source of advertising and thus of the promotion of other goods. And the media package and commodify the audience so they can sell it to advertisers. The audience has to be large, but it also has to be the right kind of audience, and it has to be in the right frame of mind.

The above characteristics and strategies of the media business are, to a great extent, the result of broader trends in the economy.

## 2.3 ECONOMIC TRENDS AND THEIR IMPACT ON THE MEDIA BUSINESS

Although they have always been present and are almost characteristic of capitalism, the following economic trends have intensified over the past decades:

- Concentration
- Convergence
- Commercialisation
- Liberalisation
- Privatisation
- Internationalisation

The purpose of the following section is to briefly discuss these trends.

### Concentration

Concentration happens when the means of production in market sectors are owned increasingly by fewer and larger groups. One of the best and latest examples of concentrated media ownership is the merger of America Online (AOL) and Time Warner, in January 2000. This merger created a $350 billion empire. The new company is called AOL Time Warner and, at the time of writing, it incorporated the ownership of some of the

## Characteristics, Trends and the Political Economy of the Media

world's biggest film production studios, television stations such as CNN, TNT, the Cartoon Network, to name a few, record and CD companies, thirty-three magazines including *Time*, book publishing companies, and cable television networks. It includes online services such as Netscape, Compuserve, MovieFone, and Internet Messenger. For Time Warner the merger included possibilities such as the development of the emerging Internet movie business and the digital delivery of movies-on-demand, more interactive television, online radio stations, broadband outlets, and so on. For AOL it meant access to Time Warner's cable customers and speedier Internet and television services (*Time* 2000:39–50).

Immediately after the merger, *Time* magazine (part of the new company) reported extensively on the merger. In an essay "Is big really bad? Well, yes" Victor Navasky (2000:48) wrote:

> ... [the trend – PJF] that fewer and fewer corporations would come to dominate the media environment, resulting in the free-enterprise equivalent of [being something similar – PJF] to a Ministry of Culture. It has to do with mega-communications conglomerates that are bigger than the economies of [developing – PJF] countries whose [so-called – PJF] monopolistic information policies we [the USA – PJF] condemn as a violation of democratic values.

The fact is that these concentrated media markets can of themselves be a threat to democracy, as will be discussed or referred to in following units of this book.

In South Africa, the media also tends to concentration. Two examples are the highly successful Naspers, as well as Independent Newspapers (cf. Unit 1 for an overview of South African media companies).

---

**Naspers and Independent Newspapers**

At the time of writing (July 2000), Naspers (cf. http://152.111.1.74/) owned newspapers such as the big Afrikaans daily *Beeld*, and the Sunday paper *Rapport*, numerous regional newspapers, and a whole list of some of the most popular South African magazines. Through the company MIH Holdings Limited (the MIH Group) it holds the leading share in the televison station M-Net and has expanded to more than 40 countries throughout sub-Saharan Africa, the Middle East, the Mediterranean and across Asia. Naspers owns leading South African book publishers such as Tafelberg and Human & Rousseau, book clubs such as Leisure Books, bookstores and educational publishers such as Van Schaik Publishers. It owns National Private Colleges (NPC) with distance education colleges such as Lyceum and Success. Through its division Nasprint, Naspers specialises in printing using the latest printing technology. Finally, Naspers has also entered the world of the Internet and related technology with more than a 50% stake in M-Web. Apart from this, Naspers has ties with other leading South African companies.

Independent Newspapers claims to be the leading newspaper group in South Africa. With, at the time of writing, more than 14 daily and weekly newspapers, such as *The Star*, it aggregated weekly sales of 2,8 million copies, received close to 50% of the total adspend (money spent on advertising) in the paid newspaper market, and reached 63% of English

# MEDIA STUDIES

newspaper readers. Besides this, the company also publishes free delivery weekly community newspapers and has interests in magazines, book publishing and broadcasting (cf. http://www.inc.co.za/corp/independent.html).

Figure 2.1   Naspers and Independent Newspapers

## Convergence

Convergence is used in the sense of the coming together of information and communication technologies (ICTs), especially the merging of telecommunications and traditional media technologies, to create new ways of producing, distributing and using knowledge, information and entertainment. Mansell and Wehn (1998:13) argue that the technological convergence in the ICT sector means that there are very few clear boundaries between these sectors. The telecommunications network provides the electronic platform for the development of new communication and information services including database access, the Internet, Pay TV, High Definition Television (HDTV) and multimedia. All this is made possible by the digitisation of the information and media content and the introduction of a new variety of interactive services (ibid:132).

### *Radiosondergrense* and convergence

A good example of convergence and its impact on traditional mass media is the SABC's Afrikaans radio station RSG (*Radiosondergrense*). In October 2000 it became the first radio station in the world to go multi-media and thus available on radio, television (a channel on DStv), the Internet (http://www.rsg.co.za) and on WAP-cellphone. The station's programmes can now be accessed worldwide on the Internet. Convergence allows listeners to become user (audience) and producer in terms of immediate interaction with the station (feedback). The Internet site enables listeners to tune into the frequency, search archives, advertise local events, post comments, visit celebrities' home pages and interact with DJs in the studio. In short, RSG is no longer just a radio station, "but a purveyor of information; ... not a simple extension of existing media, but encourages each media platform to reflect audience interaction; its free-to-air channel on the Dstv satellite bouquet and Internet portal is revolutionising this medium and language, offering advertisers value for money" (Hunter 2001:16).

Figure 2.2   Convergence

A further example of the impact of convergence on the traditional media is the fact that almost all the big South African newspapers are now also available on the Internet. A good example is the weekly newspaper *Mail & Guardian*, now available daily on the Internet as the *Daily Mail & Guardian*, with news updated daily and even hourly, including an African service providing news, opinion and features from Africa. Another

## Characteristics, Trends and the Political Economy of the Media

example is DStv, South Africa's main satellite television provider. Apart from providing numerous specialised television channels to subscribers, DStv also provides free interactive data services such as GameZone and BrainDomain, allowing viewers to play games, test their skills, and so forth.

In short: "The Internet's fusion of some of the capabilities of traditional media could lead to new modes of usage. The main differences will be interactivity in communication and the facility to time-shift consumption of information" (Mansell & Wehn 1998:130).

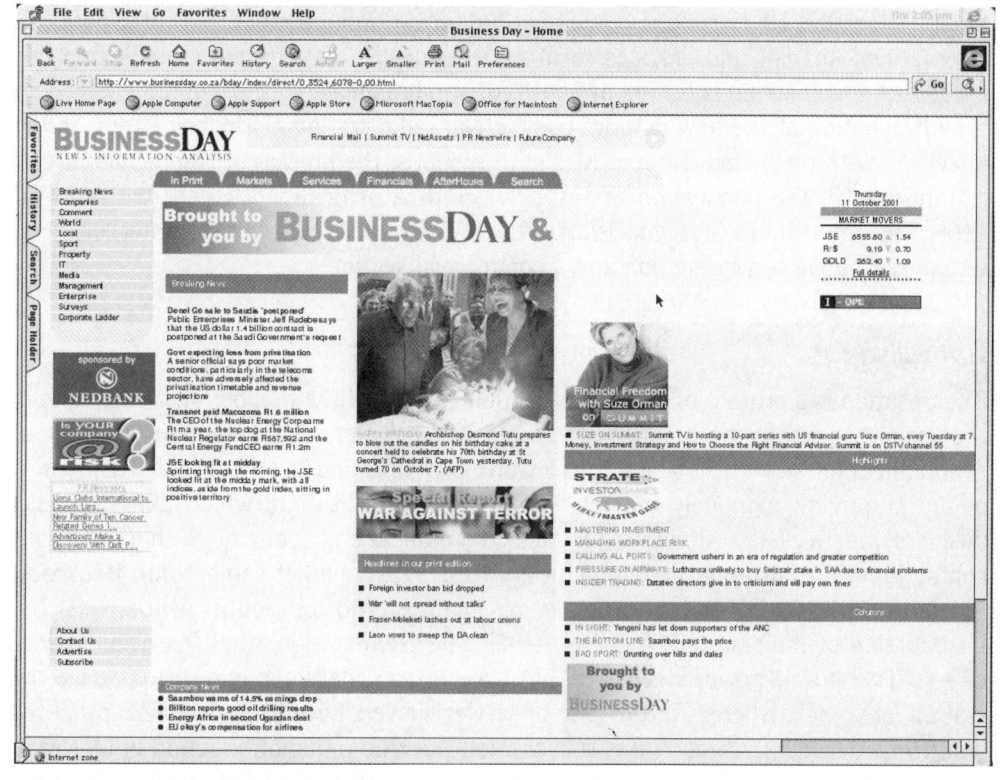

**Figure 2.3** *Business Day*

Apart from the fact that convergence leads to new methods of media production, distribution, and access, and demands new computer-related skills from media workers, convergence also has many social and legal implications, especially in the field of media policy, which is the topic of another module in the Unisa (University of South Africa) Communication Science syllabus.

## Commercialisation

Mosco and Rideout (1997:168) define commercialisation as the process that takes place when the state replaces forms of regulation based on public interest, public service and related standards, such as universality, with market standards that establish market regulation. In the communications industry this has meant greater emphasis on market position and profitability. In other words, the emphasis is no longer on providing a universal service to the public such as, for example, public service broadcasting with the emphasis on information and entertainment of a high quality. To the contrary, the emphasis is now on the marketability and thus popularity of media content. The result is commercial broadcasting with an overload of popular programme genres and content such as talk shows, popular music, games, sport and advertisements. Everything depends on audience size, advertising revenue, and producing programming that anticipates an international market and linkages to other revenue-generating media (ibid). One can argue that the commercialisation of South African broadcasting started in the '50s with the introduction of the now defunct commercial radio station, Springbok Radio, and in television with the introduction of M-Net in the '80s. The process of commercialisation continues with the publication of the new South African Broadcasting Act, no. 4 of 1999. This Act provides for the division of the SABC (public service broadcaster) into two sections: a public service section and a commercial section.

## *Liberalisation*

Liberalisation is a process of state intervention to expand the number of participants in the market, typically by creating or easing the creation of competing providers of communication services. Usually, this involves establishing a private competitor in a public or private monopoly market. Unlike commercialisation, which aims to make business practices the standard for the communications industry, with or without competition, liberalisation aims specifically to increase market competition (Mosco & Rideout 1997:170). A good example of liberalisation in South Africa was the introduction of the country's first free-to-air television station, Midi Television, owner of e.tv. (Free-to-air means viewers do not have to pay additional money to receive the station (or signal), whereas in the case of M-Net viewers have to pay a subscription fee and own a decoder.) Although it is subscription television, the introduction of M-Net in 1986, the first South African television broadcaster besides the SABC, can also be seen as a step in the direction of liberalisation. The same accounts for the separation of the SABC in terms of the new Broadcasting Act (4 of 1999) in to two operational entities, as mentioned above. Another example of liberalisation in the communications industry, was, at the time of writing, legislation to introduce a second fixed-line telecommunications operator, besides Telkom.

## *Privatisation*

Mosco and Rideout (1997:173) define privatisation as a process of state intervention that literally sells off a state enterprise such as a public broadcaster or a state telephone company. They explain that privatisation takes many forms, depending on the percentage of shares to be sold off, the extent to which any foreign ownership is permitted, the length, if any, of a phase-in period, and the specific form of continuing state involvement, typically constituted in a regulatory body, in the aftermath of privatisation.

According to Mosco and Rideout (ibid) the main reasons for privatisation are:

- the rise of governments that are ideologically committed to private control over economic activity
- the attraction, if only a once-off event, of revenues for government coffers
- the pressures of transnational businesses and governmental organisations such as the International Monetary Fund
- because commercialisation is, at best, an inadequate first step towards market control.

Some of the criticism against privatisation is

- the loss of sovereignty for nations selling off to foreign firms, and
- the consequent loss of local control over national policy.

A good example of privatisation in the South African media was the SABC's sale of public radio stations to private owners. Another example, as a first step in the privatisation of Telkom, was the sale of a 30 percent strategic equity stake in Telkom to the US company SBC Communications International Inc and Telekom Malaysia Berhad (at the time of writing).

## *Internationalisation*

Internationalisation involves the processes of states creating their own wide range of teaming arrangements or strategic alliances that integrate them in different degrees of internationalisation. A first degree of internationalisation is usually regional alliances such as, for example the Southern African Development Community (SADC). Other examples include institutional planning organisations (Group of Seven), and interstate agreements such as the General Agreement on Tariffs and Trade (GATT), and the International Monetary Fund (IMF). Internationalisation requires some degree of interstate coordination. It shifts communication responses from national policy applications to ones where bilateral, trilateral and multinational trade agreements require structural policy changes. The danger of internationalisation is that it can challenge national sovereignty and raise questions about national identity. All countries, but particularly those whose markets are too small to sustain substantial indigenous production for the local market, are faced with declining capacity for independent governance and cultural formation (Mosco & Rideout 1997:174–177).

The fact that the new South African Broadcasting Act (4 of 1999) has special clauses related to the protection of and support for local content in broadcasting, is a clear indication that South Africa, as almost all other countries, needs to ensure that South African audiences are not bombarded with programme content from foreign countries, especially the USA that dominates the market, to the detriment of own culture(s). In media studies this problem is known as media-imperialism and/or cultural imperialism (cf. Unit 13 on the NWICO – New World Information and Communication Order).

We conclude this segment by saying that the above economic trends are closely related to the development of capitalism, which in its turn is closely related to the development of democracy. In both capitalism and democracy the development and use of information and communication technology (ICT) play a key role. Put in another way, lately capitalism, democracy and ICT can hardly be separated. There is almost a causal relationship between them and they are almost interdependent. Within democratic societies and against the background of the growth of capitalism, governments can hardly continue to play "big daddy" over business, including the media business, that is, as business becomes increasingly globalised. The result is that governments tend towards deregulation, the setting up of statutory bodies to oversee liberalised and privatised businesses, and entering into international trade agreements.

The same is happening in the media business. As the country's public service broadcaster, the SABC has (since 1994), and as already mentioned, sold off a number of its commercial radio stations to private companies. The Independent Broadcasting Authority (IBA) has been established as a statutory body to oversee the business of South African broadcasting, including the issuing of public service, private (or commercial) and community broadcasting licences. Against the background of the convergence between broadcasting and telecommunications technology, the IBA has merged with the South African Telecommunications Regulatory Authority (Satra) to form the Independent Communications Authority of South Africa (ICASA). The new Broadcasting Act (4 of 1999) makes provision for the separation of the SABC in a public service section and a commercial section. There is growing competition between the SABC and new private broadcasting companies and community broadcasters in South Africa, with more commercialised (popular) programming as a result – programming often far removed from the public service broadcasting ideal to foster good taste and programming of a high quality. In the field of telecommunications Telkom has been partially privatised. At the time of writing the continued privatisation of Telkom and the privatisation of other parastatals such as Eskom were on the table.

### Case study 2.1: Public service broadcasting (PSB)

The above trends and their impact on media can best be illustrated by taking a closer look at what is happening, almost worldwide, in public service broadcasting.

In most parts of the world, broadcasting and especially public service broadcasting (PSB) is undergoing radical changes. In general there is a shift to private broadcasting. These changes can be attributed to a number of factors but mainly to the economic trends discussed above, namely concentration, commercialisation, and so on.

It is generally accepted that British broadcasting served as a model for the establishment and functioning of public service broadcasting in almost all the rest of the world, including South Africa. After becoming aware of the power of broadcasting in moulding public opinion and thus its power as a political instrument, and after lengthy investigations into the role of broadcasting in a society in the 1920s, Sir John Reith was appointed as the first director general of the newly established British Broadcasting Corporation (BBC) in 1927. Reith, who also played a leading role in the formation of the South African Broadcasting Corporation in the '30s (Rosenthal 1974:150–159), formulated a "manifesto" for public service broadcasting which is historically seen as the philosophy underlying the nature of public service broadcasting. This manifesto boiled down to a plea for

- the maintenance of high programme standards;
- the use of radio (at that stage television was not yet available) for cultural education, distribution of knowledge, and the elevation of public taste;
- brings into the greatest possible number of homes all that was best in every department of human knowledge, endeavour, and achievement;
- the preservation of a high moral tone and the avoidance of the vulgar; and
- to lead public taste rather than to pander to it.

The service was to be universal, meaning available to all the citizens in a country, at the lowest price possible. It was to be free of commercial pressure (advertising) and funded by licence fees and government subsidisation (Scannell 1990:13).

In the educational, social and political fields, Reith saw broadcasting as a powerful tool for the creation of social unity, consensus and enlightened and reasonable public opinion. In short, Reith saw public service broadcasting as a cultural, moral and educational instrument for spreading knowledge, raising standards and improving behaviour; as a kind of social cement to keep society together and build a nation; as the role and function of broadcasting in the government's task to uplift the working class morally, politically and culturally. In order to realise this, Reith was an advocate of a monopolistic and non-commercial broadcasting service under the control of the government (Scannell 1990:15–29).

Throughout the years, this view led to what can be termed the principles of public service broadcasting (in its pure or idealistic form): Public service broadcasting

- is a universal service;
- universal in its appeal;
- provides for minorities, especially for those disadvantaged by physical or social circumstances;
- serves as a platform for public debate;
- is committed to the education of the public;
- encourages competition in good programming rather than competition for audience numbers; and

- liberates rather than restricts programme-makers (in other words, should experiment with new programme formats rather than follow recipes such as for the production of soap operas) (Tracey 1998:26-27).

Despite criticism that public service broadcasting has often been misused for state propaganda, also in South Africa, few can deny the high standards and quality programming that prevailed in public service broadcasting. Critics, such as Tracey (1998: 50-60; 259-278) argue that the above discussed economic trends, especially commercialisation, privatisation and internationalisation, have contributed to the decline of public service broadcasting. It has transformed broadcasting to mediocrity, market centredness, and predictability.

Public service broadcasting is in growing competition with private and commercial broadcasters. It is now ruled by a corporate philosophy in which the emphasis is on

- competition and beating the competitor;
- cuts in production costs - to produce programme content at the lowest cost;
- exploitation of new markets for what is bound to be an increasingly fragmented market; and
- co-productions and facility sharing.

All this has resulted in a lowering of standards.

As far as the future, survival and necessity of public service broadcasting are concerned, Tracey (ibid) argues that because of globalisation, public service broadcasting should and can play an even bigger role in helping societies to define their particular characters. A prerequisite for being able to do this is a coherent and stable belief system in the value and future of public service broadcasting among public broadcasters themselves and among policymakers. Only against the background of such a belief system will public service broadcasters and policymakers be able to define their missions and will they be able to confront organisational and structural change, new policy environments, new proposals for funding and new programme philosophies. Only against the background of a sound belief system in the value of public service broadcasting will broadcasters be able to face the threats of downsizing, funding, and competition (cf. Tracey 1998).

Tracey also warns that broadcasting policy should not take "trends", politics and economy as its point of departure, but that it should be based on a clear understanding of what kind of society it is supposed to serve. "If a society has not decided its own preferred character in a broad sense, it will find it exceedingly difficult to determine its character in the particular sense of its broadcasting" (ibid:278). This is where the impact of globalisation becomes relevant. It is not the impact of globalisation on economy and politics that should concern us, but its impact on the potential of societies to define themselves and their institutions, and to formulate coherent policies based on what a society wants to be (cf. Unit 19 on globalisation).

In the previous sections of this unit we briefly discussed some of the characteristics of the media as a business, economic strategies to reach the largest possible audiences and ensure profit, and economic trends closely associated with the development of capitalism. In short, what we have done was to describe some of the aspects of the capitalist mode of production. It is this mode of production and its impact on the significance of the media as a cultural product that is questioned and investigated in critical political economy.

## 2.4 CRITICAL POLITICAL ECONOMY

Critical political economy can best be described as one of many paradigms used in media studies to understand and investigate the power of the media. (By paradigm we mean a model, frame of reference or perspective from which something is viewed.)

The best way to understand political economy is to begin with a practical example. For many years the South African media was owned and managed mainly by privileged white individuals and groups. Since the fall of apartheid there have been regulations to create an environment for black and previously disadvantaged groups and individuals to own media, and to manage media. For instance, in the case of South Africa's first free-to-air television station, e.tv, the then IBA ruled in terms of the law that previously disadvantaged groups (black people, the disabled, youth, civic organisations, and unions) should own some percentages of the company's shares.

One may ask why such regulations are necessary, and what impact will they have? These are the kind of questions asked in political economy. Apart from the fact that ownership may contribute to the economic empowerment of previously disadvantaged groups, an answer to these questions may be that it is to ensure that the "voices" of previously disadvantaged groups will be heard, seen, and read. All this has to do with the political, economic and symbolic power of the media (see 2.4.1).

By allowing and empowering previously disadvantaged groups to own and manage the media, it is hoped that South African audiences will also be exposed to new, previously ignored and silenced perceptions and interpretations of South African society and South African realities.

Political economy will investigate, for example:
- what the impact of mainly white media ownership was on the South African society, media content and on democracy;
- what the impact of the new rules related to media ownership is on South African society, media content and on democracy, in other words whether the empowerment of previously disadvantaged groups contributes to new voices and perceptions being heard, published and seen, and if not, why not.

A single definition of political economy is almost impossible. It is an umbrella term for all those theories and analytical approaches which have the purpose of understanding how economic and political relationships, interests and affiliations determine the nature and functioning of social institutions (including the media as a social institution), and the impact or lack of impact of these relationships on social transformation and development.

Critical political economy developed out of Marxist-based social theory. In this theory it is believed that all means of production, including media production, determines the nature of a society. Economy is the base of all social structures, including institutions and ideas. In a capitalist society the idea of making a profit (as we have discussed in the above sections) drives production. Profit is closely related to the cost of labour. People are responsible for labour. Thus, it is argued in Marxist theory, the working class is oppressed by those individuals and groups in a society who own the means of production and whose sole purpose is to make a profit. Only when the working class rises up against dominant groups, can the means of production be changed and the liberation of the worker be achieved (Littlejohn 1992:245-246). (See Unit 9 and Unit 11 for a more in-depth discussion of Marxist theory and especially for a discussion of the relationship between media and ideology.)

In media studies, an underlying political economy proposition is that the economic and political control of the media determines the content and thus the ideological power of the media. By ideological power we mean the power (and means) to form, direct and influence the thinking of people. This power is mainly vested in those who own the media and who have the financial means to own and manage media.

Initially media studies emphasised the analysis of media content with the purpose of showing how information and entertainment reflect interests of the dominant classes in a society - their political, economic and cultural ideas and values. Although such an analysis is valuable, founding scholars of political economy in media studies, such as Murdock and Golding (1977) argued that in order to understand the power of the media one should rather start with a concrete description and analysis of media ownership. Therefrom can one have proof how such ownership impacts on media content (Murdock & Golding 1977:17; Curran, Gurevitch & Woollacott 1982:23-24).

Such an analysis, complex as it may be, will show that despite their claim of being objective messengers and the providers of "innocent entertainment", media owners are primarily interested in financial profits, or, in the words of Murdock and Golding (1977:37) "in maximising audiences and revenues". Their primary interest is to uphold the principles of the capitalist mode of production in order to guarantee profit.

Put in another way, political economy argues that the media and the way media markets operate is part of the capitalist economic system with close links to the political system in a country. The predominant character of what the media as a cultural industry produces (information, entertainment and advertisements) can be accounted for by the exchange value of different kinds of content, under conditions of pressure to expand markets, and by the underlying economic interest of media owners and decision-makers (Garnham 1979; McQuail 1994:82).

As an industry, the media adheres to the four standard features of the capitalist mode of production (Inglis 1990:114):
- mass production and the distribution of commodities

- capital-intensive technology
- managerial organisation of highly specialised divisions of labour
- cost-effectivity as the criterion of success, in other words the maximisation of profit.

To a great extent these interests determine what we read in newspapers, hear over the radio, see on television and in movies, and get on the Internet.

The consequences of this mode of production are, amongst others (McQuail 1994:82):

- the reduction of independent media sources
- concentration on the largest markets
- avoidance of risks
- reduced investment in less profitable media tasks (such as investigative reporting and documentary film-making)
- neglect of smaller and poorer sectors of the potential audience.

All this results in what Murdock and Golding (1977:37) describe as the consolidation of groups already established in the main mass-media markets and the exclusion of those groups that lack the capital base required for successful entry.

> Thus the voices which survive will largely belong to those least likely to criticise the prevailing distribution of wealth and power. Conversely, those most likely to challenge these arrangements are unable to publicize their dissent or opposition because they cannot command resources needed for effective communication to a broad audience (ibid).

### 2.4.1 Power

From the above description of some of the propositions of critical political economy it is clear that the concept "power" is central and needs some clarification.

There are many definitions and theories of power. Thompson (1995:12–18) distinguishes between four kinds of power. They are: economic power, political power, coercive power and symbolic power.

Economic power, as described by Thompson, stems from human productive activity resulting in the production of goods that can be consumed or exchanged in a market. Productive activity involves the use of and creation of raw materials, tools of production, for example land, consumable products and financial capital. These resources can be accumulated by individuals and organisations for the purposes of expanding their productive activity; and, in so doing, they are able to increase their economic power (ibid).

For example, as an economic industry the media produces goods, ranging from newspapers, books, videos, films, magazines, news, CDs, and so on. The bigger a media company is and the more it is able to expand its productive activity to include, for example, not only newspapers but also Internet services, computer software, programmes for television and radio studios, and so forth, the bigger is its economic power. Small wonder that we constantly read about the expansion of media companies such as, for example, M-Net into the field of film production, Naspers into the fields of book publishing, broadcasting, the Internet and educational industries, and PrimeMedia into the fields of broadcasting, film distribution, and advertising.

Political power involves the activity of coordinating individuals and regulating the patterns of their interaction. One may argue that all of us are in one or another way involved with political power. This may be within our circles of friends, family or work where there are certain patterns and rules of interaction. However, Thompson (ibid) argues that certain institutions are primarily involved with political power. Such an institution is the state which in its various forms (ranging from the classical Greek city-state, African tribal traditions of governance, to the nation-state) has as its purpose and goal to govern citizens. This is done with a complex system of rules and procedures that authorise certain individuals to act in certain ways. These rules and procedures are encoded in laws that are enacted by sovereign bodies and administered by a judicial system. Thompson also argues that for the state to command authority it is dependent on its capacity to exercise some influence over coercive and symbolic power.

Coercive power involves the use, or threatened use of physical force. This form of power is usually associated with military (such as the army) and para-military (such as the police and related security forces) institutions. These institutions are used (or misused) for the purposes of external defence and conquest, and for the purposes of internal pacification and control or suppression.

Symbolic power is the real and potential power vested in all cultural institutions such as the church, educational institutions and the media. These and related institutions possess the power to influence people's thinking and behaviour. They produce symbolic forms of expressions that guide people to understand and think about the world in certain ways.

For example, religious doctrines entrench certain norms and values of what is right and wrong. Educational institutions, such as schools and universities, produce and transmit knowledge against the background of certain educational philosophies and points of departure such as, for example, Christian-National education or liberal education.

In the case of the media, fictional films, documentaries, news, radio programmes, newspaper and magazine articles, popular music, advertisements, political comment, all provide us with interpretations of the realities in which we may find ourselves. This happens not only in or through the genres of political journalism. To the contrary, popular music such as rap, soul, hard rock and so on, says a lot about the human spirit of our times – its values, beliefs, joys and anxieties. One may subscribe to these interpretations or not. A cartoon such as *Madam & Eve* says a lot about racial relations in South Africa. It comments in a humorous and often sharp way on the processes of transformation in South African society. Advertisements, with their various and most of the time unrealistic and glamorous messages, are central in creating and sustaining our present consumer culture.

From the above it is clear that the media have an inherent power to form and guide our perceptions and interpretations of reality. It is therefore not strange that governments seek to control the media in one or another way. Apart from restrictions on the freedom of the media, in undemocratic countries (often severe restrictions), government control is usually effected by means of the regulation of ownership. Ownership, regulation and related policy topics are dealt with in units 3, 4, and 5.

In sum, the underlying propositions of political economy are the following (McQuail 1994:83):

- Economic considerations and interests control media content.
- Media developments tend towards concentration.
- Global integration is taking place in the media industry.
- Media content and audiences are commodified.
- Media diversity decreases.
- Opposition and alternative voices are marginalised.
- Public service media are declining.

Scholars claim that these propositions and the need to investigate them are becoming even more relevant against the background of the economic trends such as concentration and liberalisation, as discussed above.

## Criticism against critical political economy

As is the case with all theoretical and research paradigms, political economy is not above criticism. The Marxist thesis that production is determined by the dominant (capitalist) class and that the output of mass media is ultimately controlled in the interest of that class (the media owners); that media content serves to legitimate and reproduce media owners' ideologies, interests and power as opposed to those of subordinate classes, is rejected by liberal pluralists. They argue that such a view is too conspiratorial and tends to oversimplify economic and market realities.

From their perspective, the economically concentrated power of media ownership does not give media owners total control over output (content). To the contrary, the power of ownership is counter-balanced by the plurality of competing interests represented by diverse groups of shareholders and consumers, professional managers and producers, advertisers and trade unions, all of whom are refereed by the state (O'Sullivan, Hartley, Saunders, Montgomery & Fiske 1994:55). In other words, in a company such as Naspers there are diverse shareholders. Against the background of empowerment, shareholders from previous disadvantaged groups are increasing. The company caters for diverse tastes and cultures among their consumers. Its various products, ranging from newspapers, to books, television, magazines and the Internet are managed by professional managers and journalists who will resist interference from the owners as well as interference from advertisers, who in turn will not be prescribed to by media owners. Apart from this, a company such as Naspers has to compete with other media groups in the same markets and society with different ideological

# MEDIA STUDIES

perspectives on South African politics and realities. Finally, the public has the freedom of choice between different media products from different media groups. This entails pluralism. Pluralism is to create as many voices as possible for as many and diverse audiences and their diverse needs, tastes and cultures (cf. Unit 7 on the roles and functions of the media).

## Summary

In this unit we discussed the characteristics of the media as a business entity. We emphasised that it is a hybrid business with high fixed costs, involves creativity and therefore uncertainty; that the use of its products is usually not multiple, that it tends towards concentration, and depends on public interest. We then argued that the media business is about selling two products: media products and media audiences. The bottom line is the bigger the audience, the bigger the profit. We referred to some strategies to increase profit. As far as broader economic trends are concerned we referred to concentrated ownership, convergence, commercialisation, liberalisation, privatisation and internationalisation. Finally you were introduced to some of the underlying propositions of political economy. In this paradigm it is, amongst other issues, argued that media ownership determines the ideological content of the media. We concluded with the liberal pluralist view that propositions of political economy are too conspiratorial and oversimplified.

## Research activities

1. After collecting information (either on the Internet, media reports (usually in the business sections of newspapers), by visiting your local library, or by visiting a media group's head office), draw a diagram of the structure of a media group's business interests and affiliates. On the basis of this write a short essay in which you express your views on the impact of concentrated ownership on the quality of media content and on media audiences.
2. Interview a journalist and/or media owner about his/her perceptions concerning the basic characteristics of the media business, and his/her approaches to gaining access to audiences.
3. Find your own examples of each of the following trends in the media business: concentrated ownership, privatisation, liberalisation, internationalisation, convergence, commercialisation.
4. Write a short essay in which you express your views of the propositions of critical political economy (whether you agree with it or not) against the background of the liberal pluralist view.

## Further reading

Branston, G. & Stafford, R. 1996. *The media student's book*. London: Routledge.
Curran, J & Gurevitch, M (eds). 1996. *Mass media and society*. 2nd edition. London: Arnold.
Grossberg, L, Wartella, E & Whitney, DC. 1998. *Media making. Mass media in a popular culture*. Thousand Oaks, CA: Sage.
McQuail, D. 2000. *McQuail's mass communication theory*. 4th edition. London: Sage.
Mosco, V & Reddick, A. 1997. Political economy, communication and policy, in *Democratizing communication? Comparative perspectives on information and power*, edited by M Bailie & D Winseck. Cresskill, NJ: Hampton Press.
O'Sullivan, T & Jewkes, Y. 1997. *The media studies reader*. London: Arnold.
Thompson, JB. 1995. *The media and modernity. A social theory of the media*. Cambridge: Polity Press.
Tracey, M. 1998. *The decline and fall of public service broadcasting*. Oxford: Oxford University Press.

## Bibliography

Curran, J, Gurevitch, M & Woollacott, J. 1982. The study of the media, theoretical approaches, in *Culture, society and the media*, edited by M Gurevitch, T Bennett, J Curran & J Woollacott. London: Methuen:11–29.
Garnham, N. 1979. Contribution to a political economy of mass communication. *Media, Culture and Society* 1(2):123–146.
Grossberg, L, Wartella, E & Whitney, DC. 1998. *Media making. Mass media in a popular culture*. Thousand Oaks, CA: Sage.
Hunter, Cheryl. 2001. RSG explores converging frontiers. *Saturday Business Report*, 24 February 20001:16.
Independent Newspapers Homepage.
    Available: http://www.inc.co.za/corp
    Accessed on 2000/09/20
Inglis, F. 1990. *Media theory. An introduction*. Oxford: Blackwell.
Littlejohn, SW. 1992. *Theories of human communication*. 4th edition. Belmont, CA: Wadsworth.
Mansell, R & Wehn, U. 1998. *Knowledge societies: information technology for sustainable development*. Oxford: Oxford University Press.
McQuail, D. 1994. *Mass communication theory. An introduction*. 3rd edition. London: Sage.
McQuail, D. 2000. *McQuail's mass communication theory*. 4th edition. London: Sage.
Mosco, V & Reddick, A. 1997. Political economy, communication and policy, in *Democratizing communication? Comparative perspectives on information and power*, edited by M Bailie & D Winseck. Cresskill, NJ: Hampton Press.
Mosco, V & Rideout, V. 1997. Media policy in North America, in *International media research: a critical survey*, edited by J Corner, P Schlesinger & R Silverstone. London: Routledge.
Murdock, G & Golding, P. 1977. Capitalism, communication and class relations, in *Mass Communication and society*, edited by J Curran, M Gurevitch & J Woollacott. London: Edward Arnold.
Naspers Homepage.
    Available: http://www.153.111.1.74
    Accessed on 2000/09/20
Navasky, V. 2000. Is big really bad? Well, yes. *Time* magazine, 24 January 2000:39–50.
O'Sullivan, T, Hartley, J, Saunders, D, Montgomery, M & Fiske, J. 1994. *Key concepts in communication and cultural studies*. 2nd edition. London: Routledge.

Rosenthal, E. 1974. *You have been listening ... The early history of radio in South Africa*. Cape Town: Purnell.
Scannell, P. 1990. Public service broadcasting: the history of a concept, in *Understanding television*, edited by A Goodwin & G Whannell. London: Routledge.
South Africa. 1999. *Broadcasting Act, no. 4 of 1999*. Pretoria: Government Printer.
SA advertising shapes up to tougher times. 1999. *Sunday Times Business Times*, 1 August.
Thompson, JB. 1995. *The media and modernity. A social theory of the media*. Cambridge. Polity.
Tracey, M. 1998. *The decline and fall of public service broadcasting*. Oxford: Oxford University Press.

# Media Ownership and Control 3

*Lucas M Oosthuizen*

## Overview

In this unit we look at two structural approaches to ownership and control. We distinguish between various levels of monopoly formation and discuss the development of the ownership debate in South Africa. We conclude by looking at the implications of structural, economic and political variables for the future debate on media ownership and control in South Africa.

## Learning outcomes

After completing this unit you should be able to

- explain the two dominant theoretical positions on media ownership;
- explain the different levels of monopolisation;
- analyse and evaluate ownership of the South African press;
- make recommendations about media policy formulation pertaining to ownership and control; and
- contribute to the future public debate about ownership and control of the media in South Africa (or the country of your residence).

## 3.1 INTRODUCTION

In this unit we focus on the issues of ownership and control. Ownership and control are primarily media policy issues and are not new to the field of mass communication.

As early as the turn of the century, German press theorists were already dealing with the concentration of ownership that was developing in the German economy and with the implications of ownership for what they viewed as a fairly omnipotent press (cf. Hardt 1979). These theorists argued that because of economic ownership, press content predominantly reflected the interests of the owners and therefore the economic *status quo*. Ownership, in their view, also made the press prone to manipulation. This argument later formed the basis of Marxist critique against the ownership and control of the press.

In most Western countries, economic growth after the advent of the Industrial Revolution soon led to the formation of strong economic groups and conglomerates that also had an effect on newspaper ownership. Newspapers – as the first mass media – formed the vantage point for the media ownership debate. In the second half of the

1900s there was a general increase in newspaper chains – where single companies increasingly owned newspaper titles in different cities. Some of the controlling companies also had wide interests in other economic sectors and therefore formed part of conglomerates. At the same time, newspaper titles were on the decrease, which meant that competition between newspapers was on the decline, leading to bigger control by single companies of the newspaper market – referred to as monopolisation.

The first signs of monopolisation in the newspaper market of the United States of America (USA) appeared at the turn of the century. Around that time Joseph Pulitzer established himself as a proprietor of several newspapers with a mass circulation (Hiebert, Ungurait & Bohn 1991:224). Pulitzer and one of his main rivals, William Randolph Hearst, soon built up journalistic empires through aggressive promotion of their newspapers. In the first thirty years of the twentieth century, newspaper circulation in the USA increased dramatically. The number of daily newspapers reached a peak in 1910 with 2 200 titles. Although the circulation of newspapers soared in the next 20 years, the number of dailies was down to 1 932 by 1930 and kept falling. At the same time, economic pressures and mounting competition spurred the consolidation of ownership, which was reflected in the formation of newspaper chains (Hiebert et al 1991:226).

The concentration of ownership of newspapers in the USA reached astronomical proportions in the early eighties. The 50 largest newspaper chains accounted for some two thirds of the daily newspaper sales. Outright monopolies (with no competition) existed in 97,5 percent of the cities, while the circulation of 73 percent of daily papers was controlled by chains (Oosthuizen 1989:26). Where a total of 2 042 daily newspapers in 1900 had 2 023 owners, the number of daily titles decreased to 1 730 dailies in 1980, owned by 760 owners (Bagdikian 1983:8). Competition between papers in the same market also decreased. In 1990, dailies had competing titles in only 21 cities, as compared to 700 in 1920 (Marshall 1990:481).

Meanwhile, concentration of ownership and monopolisation also became issues in Britain and Europe. In the late sixties, for example, economic problems in Holland resulted in numerous mergers. As a result, newspaper owners were reduced from 60 to 24. In the early eighties (Martin & Chaudhary 1983:244–247), 70 percent of newspaper circulation in Britain was in the hands of only three companies. In Germany, Axel Springer controlled 25 percent of the daily newspaper circulation and 80 percent of that of the Sunday papers. By 1987 Springer's group enjoyed a market share of 28,58 percent of daily newspapers in Germany (Humphreys 1990:84–85) with near complete regional monopolies in Hamburg (86,4 percent) and West Berlin (71,4 percent). In addition, four groups (with Heinrich Bauer Verlag as market leader) accounted for 66,7 percent of the popular illustrated magazine market in the country.

Axel Springer is a typical example of what Tunstall and Palmer (1991:105) refer to as media moguls. Before his death in the late 1980s, Springer and others, like Robert Hersant of France, Rupert Murdoch of Australia, and Silvio Berlusconi of Italy, represented the new generation of entrepreneurs who owned and operated large media

## Media Ownership and Control

companies or empires in Western Europe. Like the American WR Hearst before them, these media moguls' political connections and electoral support led to a fair amount of public controversy and anxiety among politicians.

Amongst others, the controversy emanated from the following:

- *Alleged partisan support to political parties during election campaigns by newspapers of a specific empire:* According to Tunstall and Palmer (1991:107), the Australians Keith Murdoch and his son and successor Rupert, for example, played a pertinent and sometimes leading role in every national election in Australia between 1931 and 1987. In time, the Murdoch company also acquired newspaper interests in Britain and America. Rupert Murdoch's newspapers were also highly partisan in British national elections in the 1970s and 1980s and no less so in city, state, and national elections in the USA. Springer and Hersant were both belligerent right-wing partisans in the German and French mass press respectively. This partisan support made especially the opposition parties nervous. Berlusconi ended up leading the centre-right Freedom Alliance into a general election in Italy in April 1996. He later led the country as prime minister.
- *The possibility of influencing the national political agenda through ownership of prestige newspapers:* For example, by the eighties Springer owned *Die Welt*, Hersant *Le Figaro* and Murdoch *The Times of London*. All leading Italian dailies were controlled either by Berlusconi or other industrialist media moguls (Tunstall & Palmer 1991:107).
- *Allegations that moguls seek favours from politicians in return for electoral and agenda-setting support:* As Tunstall and Palmer (1991:107–109) indicate, this political-business bargaining and deal-making has been especially prevalent in Italy where Berlusconi acquired effective control of three television stations in the 1980s. According to Tunstall and Palmer (1991:108), Murdoch's purchase of *The Times*, the *Sunday Times*, and *Today* in Britain depended on favourable Thatcher interpretations of ambiguously worded monopoly law. Even more favourable Australian government decisions allowed Murdoch to control 60 percent of the Australian daily newspaper circulation, despite his acquired American citizenship. Between 1983 and 1987 Murdoch also acquired extensive interests in the American print and audiovisual market. Murdoch's ventures have therefore grown into a multimedia enterprise stretching over a number of continents. He has interests in, amongst others, British satellite television (BSkyB), the Fox network in the USA, Star TV in Asia and Vox-TV in Germany. Other newspaper companies have also developed audiovisual media activities (De Bens and Østbye 1998:11) or have acquired such interests.

Judging from the remarks by Tunstall and Palmer (1991:111), the development of multimedia enterprises has been better curtailed in the United States than in Europe. A long tradition of antitrust legislation and action in the USA secured a wider spread and a larger number of significant media companies. In the 1980s, Bagdikian (1983:xv, 7–8) estimated that the majority of the American media (newspapers, magazines, radio, television, books, and movies) were controlled by 50 giant corporations. These corporations were interlocked in common financial interests with other massive industries – which is also fairly common in Europe. Berlusconi (Mazzoleni 1991:169), for example, initially made his money in the construction business. Most of the European newspaper publishers are also involved in other media concerns (cf. Tunstall & Palmer 1991; Humphreys 1990). The European companies are, even compared to American standards, quite large and this has facilitated take-overs of American media companies by European companies and media moguls (Tunstall & Palmer 1991:111).

Antimonopoly legislation and other forms of regulation that address or redress the concentration of media ownership are, of course, examples of media policy. From the point of view of the media, media policy is usually regarded as all the restrictions imposed on the media by governments. The type of policy that is formulated by a government depends largely on the nature of the social structure (and, in particular, the political structure or dispensation) in that particular country (cf. Oosthuizen 1989). However, such policy – which would include media policy formulation about ownership and control – is also increasingly influenced by global trends and developments.

Some of these developments that are of particular importance for media concentration include:

- *The trend to deregulate the audiovisual sector.* This has enabled publishers and investors from outside the media to enter the broadcast market; and, in some countries, has also allowed for existing print media operators to take the gap and move into the more lucrative broadcast market.
- *The globalisation of the economy.* This has made it possible for media companies that have become too big (in terms of antitrust legislation) in their own countries, to diversify into related business in other countries. Where restrictions are placed on foreign ownership, it reinforces concentration on a national level.
- *New media* – like the Internet – while creating new markets, could also impact negatively on the survival of the traditional media.
- *Preferred business strategies* – that include the formation of trusts and strategic alliances – have further increased the concentration process (Meier & Trappel 1998:38–39).

These trends and developments are now informing the traditional positions on ownership and control. They have led to increasing cross-ownership of the media (e.g. companies holding interests in press and television); increased foreign ownership of local media; pressure on regulators not to oppose take-overs (where such take-overs would prevent the closing down of traditional media), and so forth.

## 3.2 POSITIONS ON OWNERSHIP

Traditionally, policy formation regarding ownership and control has mainly emanated from democratic and Marxist perspectives.

### 3.2.1 The democratic position

Democracy is associated with the liberal tradition which views humans as free and as having the right to self-determination. Human freedom for which democracies make provision includes freedom of speech, religion and movement, as well as the freedom to form economic associations (cf. Ruddock 1981; Oosthuizen 1989:6). In addition, democracy makes provision for one law that is applicable to all, and the right to counteract the tyranny of rulers by ensuring independent legislative, executive and judicial authorities.

The whole point of democracy as ideology is therefore to promote social and political conditions in which people can exercise choice and become freer. Opportunities to cast off repressive measures imposed by bad governments, to have regular elections where free choice of representation may be exercised, and to gain knowledge about alternatives and discuss these freely and openly, all form part of this endeavour. But democracy, of course, also implies that the individual has a duty to tolerate the views of others. Individuals and groups also have the responsibility not to jeopardise the liberties of others (Roelofse 1983:4–5; Oosthuizen 1989:7).

From this anthropology and political system/ideology we can deduct a specific conception of communication and a particular role for the mass media in society. Communication is viewed as a means for the free expression of ideas. But, in order to determine their own lives, people are also dependent on access to information and freedom to communicate (Fisher & Merrill 1976:29).

The mass media in a democracy have the responsibility of providing citizens with the necessary information so that they can take informed decisions about matters such as who to vote for at the ballot box. Therefore, freedom of information and protection of diversity of opinion (called pluralism) are major determinants of media policy in a democracy.

Ideally, the media in a democracy should therefore be able to freely provide information (without authoritarian restrictions) to the populace and should compete for the support of media users in a free market. Citizens in a democracy – on the other hand – should ideally have unrestricted access to information (freedom of reception) as well as the means to impart such information (freedom of expression) (Meier & Trappel 1998:42–43). Freedom and diversity of the media is therefore inextricably linked in a democratic policy framework.

From a democratic perspective, the main objection to concentration of ownership is that it diminishes the diversity or pluralism of news. According to Merrill (Fisher & Merrill 1976:128), the assumption is that a democracy is best served by a diversity of communication in the marketplace, and that a diversity of competing voices can provide the public with a range of information and opinions on which to base their decisions (Oosthuizen 1989:26; Dennis & Merrill 1984:61).

When news media have to close down or merge (in other words, become fewer) or are increasingly placed under centralised control where there is no competition (concentration), it is assumed that pluralism declines. Some critics even regard this diminishing of pluralism as a sign of the failure of libertarian theory.

Under such conditions, common belief holds that:
- competition is distorted;
- existing media corporations acquire the ability to deny market access to new independent entrants; and that
- it ultimately leads to monopoly-formation, which is undesirable on both economic and social grounds (cf. Meier & Trappel 1998:45).

Increasing concentration has triggered two types of explicit policy formulation. The first was the granting of subsidies to help newspapers, in particular, to survive. Subsidies have, for example, been awarded in the Nordic countries – Sweden and Finland – to keep party papers going, while in France the government has subsidised daily newspapers with circulations lower than 200 000 which derive less than 30 percent of their revenue from advertising. It is interesting to note that direct subsidies in Norway, Finland and Sweden seem to have had the desired effect. In these countries there are more newspapers than in Denmark – where no direct subsidies are in place (De Bens & Østbye 1998:14). In Holland, direct subsidies were, however, not able to halt the concentration process.

Other indirect forms of subsidies include reduced distribution costs by way of lower postal and telegraph rates and tax concessions (e.g. abolishing value added tax (VAT) on the sale of newspapers). In the early eighties, the British press reaped an estimated benefit of 200 million pounds from such concessions (Martin & Chaudhary 1983:248; Tunstall 1983; Oosthuizen 1989:27). In Germany, tax concessions were granted particularly to smaller publishers (Humphreys 1990:102). De Bens and Østbye (1998:13) point out that research in the United Kingdom has indicated that most of the regional dailies would disappear were they not exempt from VAT. The circulation figures of regional newspapers in the UK would drop by an estimated 10 percent if they had to pay VAT.

The second policy measure that has been introduced is the creation of institutions to *monitor* and *prevent* the formation of monopolies. In Britain (cf. Robertson 1983), the Press Council has the responsibility of publicising developments that may give rise to greater concentration of ownership and monopolies. The government can – but is not obliged to – refer newspaper take-overs to the Monopoly Commission. In Germany, the Cartel Office deals with concentration of ownership. Since 1976, the general cartel law in the country has made specific provision for the press. This law stipulates that when press companies with a total turnover of 25 million Deutschmark amalgamate, such a merger becomes notifiable for merger control to the Federal Cartel Office because of possible market dominance. This critical threshold (in terms of gross turnover) is much higher for other companies – in other words, less strict. However, Humphreys (1990:102–103) points out that the Federal Cartel Office has not been that interventionist in preventing mergers, especially if such intervention would result in the collapse of a newspaper. In other instances, mergers have – for obvious political reasons – not been viewed as unfavourable by the government in power and have been allowed to go ahead. For example, when the *Westdeutsche Allgemeine Zeitung* (with a circulation of 700 000) merged with two smaller newspapers, the creation of a virtual social-liberal newspaper monopoly was acceptable to the social-liberal SPD government. Newspapers in Germany are also compelled to provide the Federal Statistic Office with relevant information with the aim of establishing the real extent of press concentration. This includes information about the legal form of the company, type and number of the workforce, turnover, costs, circulation, sales, advertising rates, and so on (Humphreys 1990:104).

It is interesting to note that Italy, West Germany, France and Britain have all evolved bodies of specific press monopoly legislation. In Italy, one owner is restricted to 20 percent of press sales. In the case of West Germany and France, lengthy press monopoly debates focused on the role of Springer and Hersant. Tunstall and Palmer (1991:109) say that, in both cases, policy that emanated from these debates was weak and full of loopholes. In their opinion, this is also the problem in Britain.

### 3.2.2 The Marxist position

The necessity of policy formulation to curtail ownership and control also emanates from the Marxist critique of capitalist society and, in particular, the ideological nature of this society. Let us look at the views of Marx in broad terms.

In Marx's conception of reality, the economic structure or base structure forms the basis of society. As a result, economic relations determine the history of society. Virtually all the other factors – also called the superstructure – are based on the economy. The capitalist class is in a dominant position in capitalist society because it owns property and exercises control over income. This makes it the dominant economic force in society, so that its dominance is also reflected in other sectors of society.

Ideology resides in the ideas that express the interests of the ruling class. These ideas represent an invalid mental representation of experience (false consciousness) for subordinate classes, because it does not represent their real interests. Ideology is therefore false because it stands for ruling class interests only and not those of the whole society. Furthermore, self-interest has blinded members of the ruling class to the fact that it is historically inevitable that their class will be destroyed. The dialectical nature of society fuelled by class conflict will see to that.

Ideology is closely related to interest- or class-bound thought. People are placed in different classes in society on account of their social and, in particular, economic differences. Their class positions theoretically give them different views of reality. Because the class (the capitalists) that controls the means of production also controls the means of mental production (such as schools, churches and the media), the ruling class subjects other classes to its own view of reality. This subjection leads to false consciousness among the subordinate classes (Oosthuizen 1990:39–40).

We have already seen that in classical Marxism the economic base structure forms the basis of society. This view of reality regards the media and ideology as part of the superstructure. The economic dominance of the capitalists also leads to their domination of the superstructure.

In the process, the media become ideological since they maintain existing power relations (the inequality between the proletariat and the bourgeoisie). The media perpetuate these relations because of economic ownership, and spread ideology that legitimises the interests and actions of their owners. Generally speaking, the application of the base/superstructure model to the mass media generated a continuing concern with the ownership and control of the mass media, and later on also with production.

In subsequent reformulations of Marx's concept of the base/superstructure, the relationship between the two (in terms of absolute dependency or relative autonomy of the superstructure) has been reworked. We need not go into these reformulations. For the purpose of this unit, it will suffice to understand that the concentration of ownership is unacceptable from a classical Marxist position. The underlying assumption that is made here is that economic ownership leads to the control of content that promotes the interests of the ruling class at the expense of the masses. Theoretically, Marxist theory also places advertisers in a very strong position because advertisers present the main source of income to the media. Advertisers therefore form part of the base structure with potentially the same influence as the owners.

The implications of classical Marxism for media policy formulation are reflected in the Soviet media theory. This theory was developed from the postulates of Marx and Engels with the rules of application mostly stemming from Lenin. In terms of ownership and control, it makes provision for

- control of the media by the working class; and
- the banning of private ownership (McQuail 1987:118–119).

The functions of the media in Soviet society also differed markedly from those in democratic society. The media were expected to serve society positively through socialisation to desired norms; education; information; motivation and mobilisation (McQuail 1987:119). With the dismantling of Communism, the media in the former East Bloc have started moving closer to the democratic position.

The inability of the media in capitalist societies to perform similar positive functions is sometimes also ascribed to the influence of ownership control. It is interesting to note that the rekindling of the Marxist debate in Europe in the sixties was accompanied by demands from journalists in Germany in particular (Humphreys 1990:106) for so-called codetermination rights or management participation.

These demands were clearly aimed at curtailing the influence (control) of publishers on editorial decisions and content. Journalists also demanded codecision rights on matters such as editorial staff policy and even in the economic affairs of media firms. These demands for what they called "internal press freedom" slot in neatly with the Marxist idea of curtailing ownership control.

The democratic and Marxist positions on ownership provide the broad structural frameworks that serve as background for media policy formulation on ownership and control of the press. Once we start looking at the levels of monopolisation, it becomes obvious that the media policy debate on ownership and control is also infused with economic principles.

## 3.3 LEVELS OF MONOPOLISATION

In most democratic countries, the media are capitalist ventures operated by private parties with the aim of generating profit.

The primary basis of the capitalist or free-enterprise economic system is that allocative decisions (about who gets the resources, goods or services) are made on the basis of the economic forces controlling operations of the market (Picard 1989:11). The market system basically makes provision for free competition between producers and between consumers in the market. The system is believed to be self-regulatory (i.e. no or minimal control is required) because the decisions that are taken are based on supply (what the producer can produce at what price) and demand (what the consumer wants and how much the consumer is willing to pay for it). Both parties (consumers and producers) are regarded as equal. Under ideal conditions the system is supposed to generate capital which can be used for new production which in turn contributes to the growth of the national economy and the quality of life of all concerned. As Picard (1989:12) points out, the classic assumptions about this market-based system and its success have been challenged time and again because of certain problems in the system.

Of particular importance in this section are the remarks by Karl Marx (Picard 1989:13) that the accumulation of capital in the market system leads to the creation of bigger firms that have unequal power over smaller firms. In the process, competition diminishes between producers, unequal power is created between producers and consumers, and the benefits of the market system diminish. This can also happen in the case of newspaper groups, where larger firms purchase small firms and merge to become even bigger. As McQuail (1992:35–36) explains, the economic freedom of the press is viewed as essential, but market freedom also leads to concentration of ownership, reductions in diversity and commercial failure, leading to closure.

By forming trusts and cartels, larger newspaper firms get into the position where they can control the supply of raw material (e.g. paper) and the production and price of products (newspapers). They are therefore in an unequal position with regard to smaller newspapers. In order to redress this imbalance in the market system, governments then formulate policy to restrict anti-competitive actions and the formation of trusts and cartels.

In ideological terms, the free market idea is also linked to communication in democracies. The basic argument is that it is most beneficial for society when diverse ideas compete for acceptance. Newspapers – and other mass media – are the institutions that must bring these ideas to the populace. The more diverse the newspaper market, the better are the newspapers that will reflect this required diversity.

In a democracy, all people are theoretically free to start a newspaper. It is, however, not always easy to enter the market, especially if the position of competitors is so well entrenched. The classification of monopolies deals with various levels of competition or noncompetition (monopoly). Let us discuss these levels in broad terms.

Litman (1988:4–14) distinguishes between four scenarios that are represented as market structures on a continuum. On the one extreme lies *perfect competition*. Here a firm is one of a large number with an insignificant share of the market. The absence or presence of such a firm is therefore scarcely noticed. According to Picard (1989:75), perfect competition, in nearly every case, involves undifferentiated, homogeneous products for which buyers have no brand name preference. The output of each firm and the wages of workers are relatively low and the companies tend to be labour- rather than capital-intensive. The price is set through the market alone via the intersection of industry supply and demand. The firms must therefore take the price as a given (they become price takers) which means that they must conform to the existing market price and must only decide on the quantity of the output (Litman 1988:4; Picard 1989:75). Put another way, when there is perfect competition there are many competitors or sellers of a product. Because of the competition and the ease of entrance into the market, a firm is therefore not in a position to raise its price, because that could mean losing the entire product supply to the other competing companies. No media industries – or, for that matter, few industries in general – operate in the perfect competition market structure (Picard 1989:76).

At the opposite end of perfect competition lies *perfect monopoly*. The monopoly firm has no competition because it encompasses the whole market for a specific product (Litman 1988:6). In other words, one firm provides the product. The following characteristics can usually be identified in such a market structure:

- Barriers to enter the market, as well as capital requirements, are high.
- The industry is capital- rather than labour-intensive.
- Output, as well as wages, are high.

Under such circumstances the producer can set the price and, therefore, becomes the price maker. In addition, the producer also has total control over how much to manufacture and the decision whether to maximise output and revenue (Picard 1989:76). Power, therefore, vests in the monopolist, and not in the market (Litman 1988:8). Although no media industries operate under perfect monopoly conditions (Picard 1989:78), it is clear that the South African Broadcasting Corporation (SABC) came very close to it under National Party rule. In the case of radio, some substitution of products was available in the form of stations that broadcast from so-called self-governing territories. With television, however, no such substitutes existed prior to the introduction of the pay channel M-Net and the late night broadcasting of programmes from channels such as Cable News Network (CNN). In the case of newspapers, a local newspaper (i.e. the only newspaper distributed in a particular city or town) might have a near perfect monopoly in some aspects of their product market. In other words, being the only purveyor of local news and the carrier of local advertisements can put such a newspaper in a potentially powerful position. Some limited substitution would, however, be possible (e.g. using a regional or national daily newspaper as a source of news or as an advertising vehicle).

The structure closest to a monopoly (but further from perfect competition) is the *oligopoly* market structure. In the case of an oligopoly, there tends to be a relatively stable structure with a few firms (typically three to six) sharing the market. As Picard (1989:77) remarks, these firms also know each other and watch each other's conduct. Rivals seek to maintain their relative standing in the market. They must therefore react to any action taken by other firms – which all face similar industry conditions and economic stimuli (Litman 1988:10). Entry into the market is difficult (barriers are high), and the products are not typically highly differentiated (Picard 1989:77).

The respective oligopoly firms seek to distinguish themselves by carving out a market niche and obtaining a loyal following of customers. Within this grouping of a few firms, the distribution of market shares may be balanced or dominated by one or two industry giants (Litman 1988:10).

The fourth type of market structure is that of *monopolistic competition*. It lies between perfect competition and oligopoly. Picard (1989:78) states that, in the case of monopolistic competition, there are typically a number of firms in the market with some differences in terms of production capabilities and location. Some product differentiation is usually present, and the market and other firms influence quantity and pricing decisions. Although prices may differ, they will usually be set within the price range of competitors. According to Litman (1988:8), a monopolistic competitive firm is one of many such firms in the industry. They typically produce similar but not identical products. This type of competition (Picard 1989:78) is evident in the (American) motion picture exhibition industry, as well as in the publishing industry.

## 3.4 CASE STUDY: OWNERSHIP AND CONTROL OF THE PRESS IN SOUTH AFRICA

In South Africa, at the time of writing, five companies primarily dominate the newspaper market. A few introductory notes on these companies are given, to put you in the picture.

### 3.4.1 Independent Newspapers and Media

By far the biggest of the newspaper groups, Independent Media acquired its local newspapers in 1995 when it took over 35 percent of the Argus company from local industrial giant, Johannesburg Consolidated Investments (JCI), part of the Anglo-American mining group. Anglo virtually built the English press in South Africa (Emdon 1996:196). According to Louw (1993:162), the gold mining industry started dominating shareholding in Argus as early as 1910 and by the 1950s Anglo and JCI controlled 34 percent of the shares. When Anglo and JCI merged in 1960, they directly controlled 40 percent of the Argus company.

# MEDIA STUDIES

By 1990 Argus was selling more than 50 percent of all daily newspapers in the country. Newspapers in the Argus stable by that time included *The Star* (Johannesburg); *Argus* (Cape Town); *Pretoria News*; *Daily News* (Durban); *Natal Mercury* (Durban); and *Diamond Fields Advertiser* (Kimberley) (Louw 1993:160). Other interests of the company included an 18 percent stake of M-Net; de facto control over Times Media Limited (TML); an 18 percent share of Radio 702; stakes in CNA/Gallo; control over the magazines *Style, Leadership*, and *Pace*, and so on (Louw 1993:165). In 1994 Argus obtained the shares of Times Media Limited in the *Pretoria News* (a 45 percent stake), as well as Times Media's holding of 30 percent in the *Natal Mercury* and the *Daily News*, and also, in the Cape Joint Operating Agreement, the *Cape Times*. This gave Argus total control of the English-language newspaper market in Western Cape and KwaZulu-Natal, as well as a 72 percent stake of the market in Gauteng (Emdon 1996:197). In terms of Louw's implied reasoning (that ownership leads to control), this also put the controlling shareholders in a potentially powerful position. As he points out, the Argus company became the voice of mining capital as early as 1910 and continued to be the voice of the interests of Mining-Finance Capital (JCI/Anglo and Barlow Rand) up to the early 1990s (Louw 1993:163). When Independent therefore took over the JCI/Anglo shares, international financial interests became part and parcel of the ownership debate.

Independent forms part of an Irish publishing conglomerate, known as Independent Newspapers plc (INP), owned by Irish businessman Tony O'Reilly. INP owns about 65 percent of the Irish press, and, with substantial interests in newspapers in Britain (24,9 percent stake in the British newspaper *The Independent*), Australia and New Zealand, O'Reilly is fast becoming a media mogul in his own right. In March 1995 Independent Newspapers increased its shareholding of the old Argus Newspapers from 34,9 to 58,23 percent. The company now known as the Independent Newspaper Corporation (INC) still had INP (through Abbey Communications registered in the Netherlands) as main shareholder (58,2 percent) in 1996. The other most important shareholders were SA Mutual (12,1 percent) and nominees known as Eighty One Main Street Nominees Limited (8,0 percent) (McGregor Information Services 1995:210).

In 1999 the company delisted to become a private company with close to 100 percent of the shareholding held by PLC. O'Reilly's total investment in South Africa at the time was reported to be in the region of R1,3 bn (Berger 2000:2). At the time of writing the local company was trading as Independent Newspapers and Media (SA) and still controlled 14 daily and weekly newspaper titles in South Africa as well as local newspapers in the Cape. Its position in the market still made Independent the most important publisher of English dailies and weeklies in the country. In terms of the company's own estimates it was reaching about 2,8 million readers per week in the year 2 000; was taking up close to 50 percent of the advertising expenditure of paid for newspapers in the country and was reaching 63 percent of the English newspaper readers with its publications. Other interests of Independent included a stake (estimated at about 14 percent) in Kaya FM as well as a controlling interest in Internet Online (a site specialising in E-Commerce).

### 3.4.2 Times Media

Times Media, formerly known as South African Associated Newspapers (SAAN), also has historical ties with mining. According to Louw (1993:167), this group was founded in 1906 when the wealthy Sir Abe Bailey gained control of the *Rand Daily Mail* (founded in 1902) and the *Sunday Times* (founded in 1906). Bailey made his fortune in mining. The *Times* and the *Mail* shared staff and the same printing facilities and, although they traded as separate companies, soon gave shape to what Louw refers to as the Bailey group. In 1920 this group reached an agreement with Argus to split the market and to "consult" on advertising. Argus would, in accordance with this agreement, not compete in the morning market, while the Bailey group would leave the afternoon market to Argus. This agreement stood for 60 years.

The Bailey group extended its interests in 1934 when it bought the *Sunday Express* from another mining magnate, Schlesinger. SAAN was founded in 1955 (15 years after the death of Bailey) when the *Rand Daily Mail* and *Sunday Times* officially amalgamated to form SAAN. The *Rand Daily Mail* and the *Sunday Express*, in particular, served as staunch critics of the policies of the National Party (NP) government.

In the seventies, SAAN became financially vulnerable and the NP government tried to buy these two papers from the Bailey Trust. A rescue operation by the Adowson Trust kept the two papers out of government hands. The Trust acquired 20 percent in SAAN, which after subsequent restructuring left Argus with 40 percent of the shares in SAAN by the 1980s. This put Anglo-American and JCI in de facto control of SAAN (Louw 1993:167–169). Both the *Rand Daily Mail* and the *Sunday Express* were closed in 1985, and 1986 saw the launching of *Business Day*. SAAN was subsequently restructured in 1987 and its name changed to Times Media Ltd (TML). By 1990 TML owned *Sunday Times* (Johannesburg); *Cape Times* (Cape Town); *Financial Mail* (Johannesburg); *Business Day* (Johannesburg); *Eastern Province Herald* (Port Elizabeth); *Evening Post* (Port Elizabeth); and *Weekend Post* (Port Elizabeth), and also had 50 percent of the shares in the *Pretoria News* (Louw 1993:166). It subsequently sold its stake in both the *Pretoria News* and the *Cape Times* to Argus. In 1995 TML acquired the controlling share in the Eastern Cape's *Daily Dispatch*. Other newspapers in the TML stable include *Our Times* (Jeffreys Bay), as well as the *Algoa Sun* (Port Elizabeth).

By 1996 TML was still part of the Omni Media Corporation, controlled by Anglo-American through Johnnic. In the same year the Black empowerment group, the National Empowerment Consortium (NEC) – a coalition of about 40 black businesses and trade unions, took over control of Johnnic. Since then they have started to unbundle from a broad industrial company to an infotainment group with primary interests in media, entertainment and information technology.

By 1998 the company had a 46 percent stake in the publishing and printing group Caxton; a 92 percent interest in Times Media Limited; a 33 percent interest in Millennium Entertainment Group or MEGA (who owns Gallo – formerly CNA/Gallo – and Nu Metro); a 24 percent interest in M-Net Supersport; a 33,4 percent stake in MIH Holdings (holder of

MultiChoice – the digital television platform manager); a 32 percent interest in the Internet company M-Web; and a 30,4 percent stake of M-Cell (who controlled a substantial part of the cellular operator MTN – cf. http://www.suntimes.co.za/98/06/28/). The stake in M-Cell later increased to 51 percent. The group subsequently also acquired a stake of 50 percent in the newly launched black Sunday newspaper, *Sunday World*.

At the time of writing indications were that Johnnic would make a joint bid for the second fixed telephone line operator in South Africa in 2001. Possible partners that were mentioned at the time included Transtel, MTN and Eskom. By the turn of the century Johnnic's core business and future plans therefore clearly reflected the general trend of the convergence (or merging) of media content, information technology and telecommunications.

The take-over of Johnnic by the National Empowerment Consortium coincided with the internationalisation of media interests in the group. United Kingdom-based Pearson's bought half of *Business Day* and the *Financial Mail* from Times Media (Berger 2000:3). This effectively minimised the say of Johnnic in the running of these two publications. Pearson's also went on to set up the large Internet publishing operation I-Net Bridge with TML.

Six magazine titles, including *Elle* and *Longevity*, made up TML's magazine interests by the year 2000 – which represented a market share of only 1 percent.

### 3.4.3 Naspers

By far the biggest of what have been referred to as the Afrikaans press groups is Nasionale Pers Beperk (NPB) or Naspers as it is lately known. It was founded in 1915 when *De Burger* (later *Die Burger*) was established as official mouthpiece of the National Party in the Cape. NPB created its second daily newspaper in 1925, when Bloemfontein's *Die Volksblad* was turned into a daily. The Port Elizabeth-based *Die Oosterlig* was acquired in 1937. In 1965 NPB ventured into Transvaal and established the Sunday newspaper *Beeld*. This paper was turned into a daily in the seventies and was distributed mainly in the Gauteng area. As Louw (1993:171) points out, the inception and, in particular, the financing of NPB formed part of an exercise in *Volkskapitalisme* or people's capitalism. Small investors contributed to a savings and press fund to finance *Die Burger* in order to empower Afrikaners. The same model was used to finance other Afrikaans ventures, such as Sanlam (a life assurance company). In this way NPB's link with Sanlam was established and, according to Louw (1993:171), Sanlam came to be a dominant influence over NPB policy.

NPB was listed on the Johannesburg Stock Exchange (JSE) in 1994 and was renamed Naspers Ltd on 17 August 1998. Like the other press groups, Naspers also has diverse media and publishing interests. By the late nineties, Nasionale Pers owned newspapers such as *Die Burger* (an Eastern Cape edition of this paper replaced *Die Oosterlig*); *Die Volksblad* (Bloemfontein); *Beeld*; *City Press* (a black Sunday newspaper) and *Rapport* (an Afrikaans Sunday newspaper). Although Nasionale Pers newspapers have been in competition with those of Perskor for many years, Naspers had a virtual monopoly in the Afrikaans daily and Sunday newspaper market by the turn of the century – it owned an estimated 37 local and regional papers.

Naspers calculated its market share in the South African magazine market (based on sales per issue) on 65,3 percent (made up by 16 solely owned Naspers titles) at the time of writing. An additional 3,4 percent could be added to that for four joint ventures. Magazine titles of the group included the biggest seller in South Africa, the consumer magazine *Huisgenoot* (with an average circulation of close to 500 000) and its English counterpart *You*. By the year 2000, Naspers was selling more copies of *Huisgenoot* per annum than the combined magazine sales of their closest competitor, Caxton.

Other media interests of Naspers included shares in Electronic Media Network or M-Net (28,6 percent in 2000), MIH Holdings or MIHH (55,8 percent); M-Web Holdings (52,8 percent); SuperSport International Holdings (28,6 percent) and M-Cell (5 percent) (Profile's stock exchange handbook, Jan 2000 to Jun 2000:323). These interests were complemented by extensive involvement in book and educational publishing.

Naspers was also extending its international interests (as subscription television platform and service provider) by the end of the nineties. The aggregate subscriber base serviced by the television platform operations of the MIHH group increased to more that 1,9 million subscribing households in 1999. About 1.3 million of these subscribers were resident in Africa and the Middle East, close to 350 000 were in Greece/Cyprus and 300 000 in Thailand. In the same year MIHH also listed its indirect subsidiary – MIH Limited or MIHL in which it had an interest of 58,98 percent – on the Nasdaq National Market in New York and on the Amsterdam Stock Exchange (Annual Report MIH Holdings Limited 1999:2). As a result, America Online, News Corporation and Time-Warner acquired shares in MIH's OpenTV (Berger 2000:3). OpenTV offers operating systems, development tools, applications and related technical services for interactive televison. The listing of MIHL has not only given the group access to international capital markets, but is also seen as the catalyst that will enable the group to become a world-class provider of media technologies and services over a variety of electronic platforms, including the Internet and interactive television (Annual Report MIH Holdings Limited 1999:2). The convergence of interests in media, information technology and telecommunications was therefore also evident in the Naspers group at the start of the new millennium. MIHH was looking to extend its television platform and online Internet service opportunities in South East Asia and China as part of its future strategy (Profile's Stock Exchange Handbook, January 2000 to June 2000:309).

M-Net (the subscription television provider) was serving 1,2 million subscribers in 41 countries across Africa and on adjacent islands by the year 2000. Naspers, at the turn of the century, was clearly an international fully integrated media company. By 1999 most of the company's turnover was generated by television platforms (R3,6 billion); followed by magazines (R840,2 million); and newspapers (R628 million) (cf. Naspers Annual Report 1999). Apart from the media interests mentioned above, the company also had interests in distance learning (with controlling shares in Lyceum and Success colleges). At the time of writing their acquisition of Educor was being investigated by the Competition Commission.

As far as its press interests are concerned, Naspers can no longer be regarded as an exclusively Afrikaans press group. At the time of writing the group was handling an equal number of English and Afrikaans magazines and books. When Nasionale Pers made its shares freely available on the stock exchange in 1994, the ownership structure also changed from almost exclusively Afrikaner to more diverse ownership. In terms of an organisational clause, the power of single shareholders was also restricted. The main shareholder in 1995 was Nasionale Pers Investment Ltd (49,7 percent) and the other major shareholder was Servgro International, a company controlled by Sanlam (11 percent) (McGregor Information Services 1995:276). Prior to the changes in ownership in 1994, Sanlam-Santam controlled five of the seven top shareholders in NPB's ownership structure. In Louw's (1993:172) view this led to the exercising of hegemonic influence by this grouping and, *inter alia*, also through the people represented on the board. In terms of stipulations that restrict the votes of shareholders, NPB was far less likely to be influenced by the key shareholders than in the case of the English-language newspapers under TML and INP – at the time still a public company (Creamer 1996:66).

By the year 2000 the major shareholders in the company were: Standard Bank Nominees Ltd (18 percent); CMB Nominess Ltd (16,4 percent) and Nedcor Bank Nominees Ltd (15,2 percent). The control of the company was therefore effectively in the hands of the directors.

### 3.4.4 Perskor/Caxton

Perskor (for Afrikaanse Pers Korporasie), like NPB, historically also had strong links with the National Party (Louw 1993:174). Perskor's flagship for many years, the *Transvaler*, was started in 1935 to do the same for Afrikaner Nationalism in the north as *Die Burger* did in the south. Under the editorship of Dr HF Verwoerd, the *Transvaler*, however, became a central voice for northern Nationalism (Louw 1993:175).

Perskor came about in 1971 when Afrikaanse Pers (publishers of *Die Vaderland*) merged with Voortrekker Pers (publishers of the *Transvaler*). By 1991 Perskor owned the following major newspapers: *Die Vaderland* (Johannesburg); *Transvaler* (Pretoria); *The Citizen* (Johannesburg); 50 percent of *Rapport*; *Imvo Zabantsundu* (King William's Town). The group also had extensive interests in magazine publishing through its control of Republican Press (publishers of titles like *Scope, Thandi, Farmer's Weekly,* and *Bona*). In terms of newspapers, Perskor's stake of the daily market continued to shrink after 1991, with the closure of *Die Vaderland* and the *Transvaler* in 1988 and 1992 respectively. Prior to that, Perskor also closed down two other dailies in Pretoria, namely *Hoofstad* and *Oggendblad*. By 1996 Perskor had only one daily newspaper left in the market, namely *The Citizen*. Apart from publishing regional newspapers in Gauteng, North-West, Mpumalanga, Free State, Eastern Cape and Northern Province, Perskor's other interests included television (a 12,2 percent share in M-Net and MultiChoice), book publishing (e.g. Educum and Lex Patria), commercial printing and ink manufacturing.

Ultimate controlling shareholders of Perskor by 1996, were Dagbreek Trust, Rembrandt and Nasionale Pers. Van Rijn Investment Corporation (Rembrandt) had the largest share (27,1 percent), with Nasionale Pers and Afrikaanse Pers Fonds with 24 percent and 7,2 percent respectively (McGregor Information Services 1995:99).

Negotiations between Perskor and Kagiso Trust, a black-controlled company with interests in educational publishing, culminated in the merging of Kagiso publishers and Perskor in 1996.

With Perskor's newspapers (*The Citizen* was the only daily left in the group), magazines, and printing interests and Kagiso's educational publishing interests, many observers regarded this merger as a match made in heaven.

However, due to a slump in the educational market, Perskor again had to rationalise during 1998. They closed down the *Noord-Transvaler Metro* as well as *Imvo* and then went on to find a stronger partner to merge with in printing and publishing concern Caxton Limited. Caxton published a score of community newspaper titles in South Africa at the time.

The new company is known as Caxton Publishers and Printers. Control lies with CTP Holdings in which Johnnic's Omni Media Corporation is the major shareholder (43 percent).

The group has relinquished joint ownership of the Afrikaans Sunday newspaper *Rapport* to Naspers. Newspapers are now grouped under the Penrose stable. The flagship of the Caxton group is the English daily, *The Citizen*, with a circulation figure of close to 130 000. Other interests include about 30 regional and community newspapers, *Weekend Post* taken over from TML, as well as magazines such as *Bona*, *Country Life*, *Essentials*, *Garden & Home*, *Living & Loving*, *Thandi*, *Your Family*, *Joy*, (monthly), *Rooi Rose* (fortnightly) and *Farmer's Weekly*, *Keur* and *Personality* (weekly, since closed). By the year 2000, Caxton calculated its share of the South African magazine market to be 11,8 percent (made up by 15 titles).

### 3.4.5 Kagiso

Kagiso went on to acquire an interest in Jacaranda Radio (42,5 percent – the same stake as Nail (see 3.4.6), with the French company EDT owning 15 percent ) and control of East Coast Radio (91 percent) and an interest in Radio Oranje/OFM (24,9) through Kagiso Media Ltd. By the year 2000 it had won Map's award for the Best Black Empowerment Performer on the JSE. The group's other media interests included a national radio advertising sales house Radmark (33.3 percent – the other two partners Nail and EDT have an equal stake), the publishing of academic and professional books through Butterworths, specialist magazines like *Computer Week* through Systems Publishers and an Internet-based placement service with the name of *Job Navigator*. The company also managed consumer exhibitions (e.g. Rand Easter Show) as well as trade exhibitions (such as Saitex). At the time of writing they were working on an Internet strategy to enhance their media business through the combination of Internet and the more traditional media, like radio. Kagiso sold their shares in Caxton in 1999.

### 3.4.6 Nail

Another new kid on the block, so to speak, is Nail (New Africa Investments Limited). In 1992 the Argus Group announced that it was going to unbundle the shares of the *Sowetan*. At that stage the *Sowetan*, targeted at black readers in Gauteng, already had by far the biggest readership of all newspapers in South Africa. Before this unbundling could be put into effect, the controlling share in the *Sowetan* was bought by Nail, a black-owned and controlled conglomerate headed by Dr Nthato Motlana. Nail subsequently bought the *New Nation* (Emdon 1996:197), formerly a funded alternative weekly, but closed down the paper in 1997.

Nail was listed on the JSE in 1994 as an investment holding company with the aim of ensuring black empowerment. It has interests in the financial sector (control of Metlife, The African Bank and Africa Merchant Bank). Its other media interests at the time of writing included shares in the television company Urban Brew (50 percent), Jacaranda FM (37,2 percent) and *Sunday World* (50 percent through the *Sowetan*), control of the magazine *Leadership* (100 percent), a controlling share in the film company Philofilms (60 percent), and a 60 percent stake in Rapidphase (a cartoon production company). The company also had a 23 percent stake in Kaya FM.

### 3.4.7 Newspaper ownership

In order to get an idea of the extent of newspaper ownership concentration, take a look at the following calculations about the circulation and sales of daily and weekly newspapers in the country.

By the middle of the nineties, Independent, Times Media, Perskor and Nail were responsible for 92 percent of the circulation of daily and weekly newspapers. Of these companies, Independent Newspapers (36,5 percent of total circulation and 40,8 percent of total sales in rand value) was by far the market leader. Independent was followed by Nasionale Pers (Naspers) (with 19,6 percent of circulation and 16,2 percent of total sales), New Africa Investments (11 percent of total circulation and only 5,5 percent of total sales), Times Media (10,9 percent of circulation with 21 percent of the sales), and Perskor (9,5 percent of circulation and only 4 percent of sales). The joint venture of Perskor and Naspers, the Sunday paper *Rapport*, accounted for an additional 4,5 percent of circulation in 1994. The efforts of independent publishers amounted to only 5,2 percent of the total circulation, with the remaining circulation (2,8 percent) generated by the joint publishing of *Ilanga* by Independent Newspapers and Mandla Matla (cf. Emdon 1996). The reason for the difference between the percentages for circulation and sales (in rand value) is the result of differences in price per copy. Although the above situation changed somewhat by the year 2000 (as a result of the Caxton/Perskor merger and Naspers' acquisition of

*Rapport*) such a breakdown would of course only give you an indication of the potential symbolic power of these groups (telling stories as they see them).

In terms of economic activity (potential economic power), it is of far greater importance to look at advertising income as a prime indicator. As you would know by now, advertising represents the main source of income for newspapers. By the year 2000 the dominance of especially four companies in the advertising market were still clearly visible. In terms of advertising expenditure, Independent was the clear leader in the daily newspaper market (the group generated close to 51 percent of the advertising expenditure or adspend). Naspers – with a monopoly in the Afrikaans daily newspaper market – generated 22 percent of the adspend, Times Media 9,6, and Caxton – with only *The Citizen* in their stable – was responsible for 5,07 percent of the market. Other owners only accounted for 12,34 percent (with Nail's flagship the *Sowetan* responsible for a 7,08 percent portion of this tally). In broad terms, the five companies were therefore capturing close to 95 percent of all the advertising in the daily newspaper market (period April 1999 to March 2000).

In the weekend newspaper market, Times Media with the *Sunday Times* as flagship had close to 40 percent of the advertising market, followed by Naspers (owners of *Rapport*) who accounted for 29 percent; Independent with 25 percent; and Caxton with less than 1 percent. In real terms, these four groups were therefore responsible for 94 percent of the adspend between them (period April 1999 to March 2000) in the weekend newspaper market.

With close to thirty solely owned community newspapers, Caxton was the clear leader in the community newspaper market. At the time of writing the group accumulated close to 52 percent of the advertising expenditure in this sector. Naspers had less than half this share with 21 percent. Capro – representing independent and jointly owned newspapers – handled 18,7 percent of this market and Independent just over 8 percent. Between Caxton, Naspers and Independent they therefore serviced in the region of 81 percent of the community newspaper advertising market (period April 1999 to March 2000).

In terms of circulation and advertising revenue, the newspaper industry therefore reflected strongly concentrated ownership and market activity.

### 3.4.8 The type of market structure

What type of market structure would the newspaper industry in South Africa represent? As Litman (1988:14–15) indicates, it is difficult to place the American daily newspaper industry within one of the structures (types of monopolies) outlined above. In South Africa, this is also not an easy task. The main reason is that we seldom find only one (monopoly) newspaper in a particular location. Even two newspapers competing in the same market (duopoly) is rare.

In broad terms, the situation in South Africa in 2000 probably had more in common with the oligopoly structure than any of the other three. As we have seen, relatively few companies formed the whole newspaper industry in the country. Independent clearly dominated both circulation and adspend in the English daily newspaper market while Naspers did the same in the Afrikaans newspaper market (albeit with a smaller share of the circulation and advertising stakes); Times Media had a marginal advantage above Naspers and Independent in the weekend newspaper stakes; while Caxton clearly dominated the community newspaper market.

Under these conditions, entering the market could obviously be quite difficult The launching and closure of the *Mail* (daily edition of the *Weekly Mail*) in September 1990 clearly underscored this point. Joint editor of the *Mail* Anton Harber said at the time that they did not realise that it would be so difficult for an independent newspaper to enter the market (Grange 1990:6). He alleged that centralised control and impatience on the part of the big companies made the launching of a newspaper an uncertainty. Although members of the mainstream press did not agree with Harber (Oosthuizen 1991:45), we can surely take note of his views. Another factor that made Harber's entry into the market more difficult was, of course, the cost involved in the launching of the paper. Commentators at the time calculated that he started the venture with between one and four million rand. This was not enough. This is the type of expenditure for which any new entrant into the market will have to make provision. We get back to this point below.

As far as pricing is concerned, a quick scanning of the cover price of different newspapers directed at the same market does not really reveal obvious price-fixing, but interdependence could possibly be present. In 1994 the cover price of *The Citizen* was 90 cents. In 1996 the price per issue of this paper – with a 60 percent black readership – stood at R1,20. *Sowetan*, directed mainly at blacks in Gauteng had a cover price of 80 cents in 1994 and the price per issue stood at R1,10 in 1996. In 2000 the *Sowetan* was selling for R1,90 and *The Citizen* for R1,80. The price per issue in both cases was markedly cheaper than that of other dailies like *The Star* (R2,40) and *Beeld* (R2,30). In terms of price, both these pairs of newspapers seemed to be keeping track of each other. Joint operating agreements (cf. Independent and TML in Johannesburg) and cross-shareholding (like the 43 percent stake of Omni in CTP Holdings) would also strengthen the case for interdependence.

However, what we read into a classification like the above depends on how we view the relationship between the ownership and control of newspapers. This relationship has served as the main impetus of the policy debate on ownership as it evolved in South Africa.

## 3.5 THE SOUTH AFRICAN DEBATE ON OWNERSHIP AND CONTROL

### 3.5.1 The apartheid government and media ownership

Barely two years after the former National Party government came to power in South Africa, members of the government started asking questions about monopolisation. A National Party member of parliament, AJR van Rhyn, called on the government to set up a commission of inquiry (later known as the Van Zijl Commission) to investigate monopolistic tendencies in the press, internal and external reporting, and the advisability of control over such reporting (Hachten & Giffard 1984:52). The NP government was, of course, receiving a great deal of criticism from overseas for its racial policies. The government blamed the foreign press for this predicament and also condemned foreign ownership of the local press. They argued that foreign ownership allowed the moulding of black opinion by outside interests. As far as monopolisation was concerned, the Argus Group was the main target for criticism. Argus owned nine of the seventeen daily newspapers at the time and Van Rhyn suggested that this type of control limited the freedom of the press. Dr Albert Hertzog, then Minister of Posts and Telegraphs, alleged that the South African Press Association had a monopoly in the supply of news. In his view, news was first passed through London where it was filtered and sometimes twisted (Hachten & Giffard 1984:53). The Press Commission that was subsequently set up (March 1950) was charged with, *inter alia*, the investigation of the concentration of control of the press and its effect on editorial opinion and comment and the presentation of news (Hachten & Giffard 1984:54).

Two aspects stand out very clearly in the above remarks: firstly, members of government assumed that economic control also led to the control of content and, secondly, the decision to set up the commission was probably part of the effort to strengthen the position of the Afrikaner-dominated NP vis-à-vis the former imperial oppressors, that is, part of promoting Afrikaner Nationalism.

In the two reports of the Commission (tabled in 1962 and 1964 respectively), recommendations focused more on the control of the press (by the government) than on ownership. While clashes between the government and particularly the English press continued over the next 20 years, ownership did not feature prominently on the agenda. Government spokesmen did, however, on numerous occasions advocate the break-up of the ownership of the Argus and SAAN groups in this period (Hachten & Giffard 1984:77).

The issue was formally placed on the public agenda again when PW Botha appointed the Commission of Inquiry into the Mass Media (usually referred to as the Steyn Commission) in 1980. In its report of 1 367 pages, the Commission also dealt with monopolies and media control (South Africa 1981:1251–1265). The Commission was obviously very perturbed by the involvement of big business in the media. It stated:

> The restructuring of the former independent press and its absorption within the corporate womb is the death knell of a truly free press. The Commission is of the view that the stage has been reached where it must be said that the free press in South Africa is not a truly free one in the sense that the operation of big business prevents newspaper readers from having access to other newspapers which are competitors and rivals; that due to the degree of corporate control already existing in the press, much diversity has disappeared from the South African media scene. Consequently matters such as editorial comment and news reports cannot – regularly and promptly – be compared, verified and validated. The developing press monopolies are not compatible with the truly free press.
>
> (South Africa. *Report of the Commission of Inquiry into the Mass Media* 1981:1256)

From the above it is clear that the Commission also equated ownership with control, and in subsequent pages of the report a fairly big issue was made about the position of Argus and SAAN, Argus's possible control of SAAN, and Anglo-American's shareholding in these companies. The Commission recommended that the shareholding of newspapers be spread across a wide spectrum of investors. It was suggested that any individual shareholder should not be allowed to hold more that 1 000 shares, or 1 percent of the total share capital. The other possibility – that was acceptable to the Commission – was the restriction of voting rights per individual shareholder (South Africa 1981:1261).

Other recommendations on monopolies and media control included:

- An amendment in legislation so that nominees or trusts holding interests in newspaper companies would be compelled to identify shareholders.
- A period of three years for companies to get their shareholding in line with the proposed policy.
- Not allowing any further newspaper take-overs.
- The prohibition of cross-holding of shares (as in the case of Argus and SAAN) and the divestiture of such cross-holding where it already existed.
- Special efforts to establish a real black press (not owned by whites) to ensure greater diversity.

The Commission stated that all the above elements clashed with the principle of free competition and that they therefore had to be eliminated.

Although the recommendations on ownership were not transformed into formal policy by the government in power, the creation of the Media Council in November 1983 showed that the press did take notice of the commission's concerns. As Hachten and Giffard (1984:101) pointed out at the time:

> As in the case of the British Council, the Media Council is also meant to promote freedom of expression and higher professional standards. Apart from adjudicating on complaints, it is expected to keep under review developments likely to restrict the supply of information, to report on tendencies towards greater concentration or monopoly in the media, and on matters concerning the good conduct and repute of the media.

Meanwhile, the authorities were also monitoring monopolisation via the Competition Board.

## *The Competition Board*

The acquisition of newspapers by groups was monitored by the Competition Board in terms of the Maintenance and Promotion of Competition Act (no. 96 of 1979). This board functioned as an advisory body to the Minister of Trade and Industry regarding the acceptability/unacceptability of take-overs – which included newspaper take-overs – as well as monopolies.

Take-overs – or acquisitions – were defined in terms of the Act to mean the acquisition by the holder of a controlling interest in any business or undertaking involved in the production, manufacture, supply and distribution of any commodity, of such an interest –
- in any other business or undertaking so involved; or
- in any asset which is or may be utilised for or in connection with the production, manufacture, supply or distribution of such a commodity (cf. Competition Board 1994b:4).

Monopoly was defined as a situation where any person or two or more persons with a substantial economic connection, in the Republic or any part thereof, control wholly or to a large extent the class of business in which he or they are engaged in respect of any commodity (cf. Competition Board 1994b:5).

It is clear that the application of the above stipulations to the South African situation was not easy. In 1985 – when Argus wanted to take over the *Natal Mercury* – the Competition Board gave its blessing for the take-over with the proviso that Robinsons (the controlling company that wanted to sell 70 percent of its shares to Argus) maintained the power to appoint the editor. This editor also had to have complete responsibility for the editorial policy of the newspaper (cf. Competition Board 1986:15). The acquisition was also regarded as being in the public interest because the alternative would have been closure of the newspaper. The latter is in line with the thinking of the Cartel Office in Germany, referred to in section 3.2.1. The Competition Board pointed out that the survival of the newspaper would ensure some form of competition between the two daily newspapers published in the Durban area and would also safeguard the employment of 70 percent of the *Natal Mercury's* staff.

At the same time, however, the Board expressed its dissatisfaction with the degree of concentration in the South African newspaper industry that has been further exacerbated through the involvement of this industry in the electronic media (M-Net).

The Board also published findings on the take-over by Argus of the *Cape Times* and the sale of Argus to Independent Newspapers in 1994 (Competition Board 1994a:38–40). In this case it was clear that, in terms of the existing legislation, the board could not bar a foreign company from taking over the biggest press group in South Africa. In terms of Independent's absence from involvement in the local market prior to the take-over, the deal did not constitute an acquisition. The board was also not empowered in terms of the Act to instruct the companies (Anglo/JCI) to sell their shares to anyone else, such as members of disadvantaged communities or other people who were interested in buying the shares. Although the Board conceded that the take-over by Argus of the *Cape Times* would lead to a monopoly of the English press in Western Cape, assurances of continued editorial independence for the publication and a separate board of directors that would include members of the local community seemed to secure the go-ahead for Argus at the time.

In May 1996 it was announced that Competition Board chairman Dr Pierre Brooks would probably be replaced. It was reported (Competition boss Brooks ... 1996a:1) that

Dr Brooks would become the first victim of the government's tougher approach to competition policy. Although the news report did not mention media transactions as (possibly) one of the reasons for not renewing his contract, the stand taken by the senior partner in government (the African National Congress) with regard to media monopolies has been well publicised. We can also deduce from the views of the ANC on monopolisation in general that tougher action to curb media monopolies could follow in future.

### 3.5.2 The ANC and media ownership

The official position of the African National Congress (ANC) on ownership and control became part of the South African public agenda when they stated at a conference in Zambia in 1989 that they were opposed to what in general terms amounted to:

- a lack of pluralism (diversity) in the South African media;
- the prevalence of the formation of media monopolies; and
- the restriction of the free flow of and access to diverse information (Louw 1989:117–119).

These objections were addressed in the ANC's draft media charter some three years later (cf. African National Congress 1992a). In this charter, it was stated, *inter alia*, that the structure of ownership of media resources undermined access to information by the majority of the population. In view of this situation it was suggested that diversity of ownership of media production and distribution facilities be guaranteed. In the final draft of the charter, it was stated that ownership of media resources, production facilities and distribution points should be subjected to antimonopoly, antitrust and amalgamation legislation. It also made provision for the introduction of affirmative action in the media. In its charter the ANC declared that affirmative action had to be taken with regard to race and gender as far as access to and control of media institutions were concerned.

The ANC's Reconstruction and Development Programme (RDP) published in 1994 was also very specific about the concentration of media ownership. This RDP document stated in section 5.14.5 that measures would be taken to limit monopoly control of the media. Cross-ownership of print and broadcast media would also be subjected to strict limitations, and unbundling of existing media monopolies would be encouraged in both the areas of publishing and distribution (African National Congress 1994:133–144). In addition, an affirmative action programme would also be put in place to give disadvantaged communities access to the resources needed to start newspapers and to train them to exercise their media rights.

In the same year, the competition policy of the new ANC-led Government of National Unity was spelt out in a White Paper dealing with the Reconstruction and Development Programme. This White Paper was also very specific about monopolisation. In section 3.8.1 of this document it was stated that the South African economy should be opened to allow greater ownership participation by a greater number of South African people.

The government undertook to introduce strict antitrust legislation to create a more competitive and dynamic business environment. The central objectives of such legislation would be to discourage the system of pyramids that led to overconcentration of economic power and interlocking directorships, to abolish numerous anti-competitive practices such as market domination and abuse, and to prevent the exploitation of consumers. In addition, it was postulated that existing government institutions and regulations concerned with competition policy would be reviewed in accordance with the new antitrust policy. The government also undertook to establish a commission to review the structure of control and competition in the economy, and to develop efficient and democratic solutions. To that end, changes in regulation or management in addition to antitrust measures would also be considered. Other aspects covered by the White Paper (1994) concerned the removal of the distorting effects of economic concentration, corporate conglomeration and collusive practices; curbing the economic power of enterprises in a dominant position; the identification and elimination of practices that restrict the entry of competitors into the market; and the identification and elimination of illegal practices such as price-fixing and collusion. The restructuring of the Competition Board was also foreseen.

While the above measures would naturally also be applicable to the newspaper industry, it was clear that the government felt strongly about newspaper ownership in particular. Closer scrutiny of remarks made by government leaders reveals that the ANC-led government also equated ownership with control, just like their predecessors. For example, in 1995 the premier of Gauteng, Mr Tokyo Sexwale, attacked foreign ownership of the media and, in no uncertain terms, related such ownership to control. He said that because of the influence of the media in shaping opinions, the country had to guard against the concentration of ownership in the hands of a small group of people. He went on to say that limits on foreign ownership were required and that South Africa needed South African media to tell the South African story. Ensuring South African ownership and control is the best way to make sure that this happens, Mr Sexwale said (Sexwale hits out ... 1995:13).

In 1996 it was the turn of the so-called ANC/Cosatu (Confederation of South African Trade Unions)/SACP (South African Communist Party) alliance to address the issue of ownership and control from a more socialist perspective. The then Minister of Posts, Telecommunications and Broadcasting, Mr Jay Naidoo, blamed the media for the weakening of the value of the rand and criticised the media for undermining democracy. He told a meeting of the alliance that, as long as they did not have access to the media, Cosatu would always be criticised and their actions seen as irresponsible. Mr Naidoo said that the same companies that owned the newspaper groups also owned the factories in which Cosatu members worked. That is why the media wanted to put all the blame for the problems of the country on the workers. The secretary of the SACP at the time, Mr Charles Nqakula, said that the interests of the people were unfortunately not served by the media that were not under the control of the people. The media served the big business companies that owned them (Jay blameer die media ...1996:1).

The above arguments about the influence of the press and the relationship between ownership and control were again fairly similar to those championed under the previous dispensation.

By 1996 a task force, named COMTASK, which was set up by then Deputy President Thabo Mbeki, was also looking into ownership of the media. Although this task force's main brief dealt with the role of the South African Communication Service, it was also investigating ownership and control of the media and how it affected government communications (Team to take ... 1996). Legislation to control media ownership was being called for by some members of this task group, among them Tshepo Rantho. Specific legislation dealing with media ownership was therefore considered to be a possibility at the time.

## *The Competition Commission*

In 1998 the Maintenance of Promotion of Competition Act (no. 96 of 1979) was replaced by the Competition Act (no. 89 of 1998). This Act requires notification of all mergers or acquisitions. The Act has jurisdiction over all economic activities but excludes those provided for in other public regulation. This means that telecommunication and broadcasting are excluded but that all mergers in the newspaper arena fall within the jurisdiction of the Act.

The new Act makes provision for the prohibition of anti-competitive conduct. In terms of this stipulation, horizontal practices (like price-fixing by colluding firms) as well as vertical relationships (e.g. one firm buying control in the paper industry to drive out competitors in the newspaper business) are prohibited. If these practices, however, result in technological, efficiency or other pro-competitive gains that outweigh the anti-competitive effects, the Act allows for defences.

The new Act does not investigate monopolies as such, but rather prohibits the abuse of dominance as defined in terms of market share. Such abuse would include charging excessive prices; refusing to grant access to an essential facility (which could include a printing works); engaging in exclusionary acts (e.g. convincing a supplier not to deal with a competitor); or engaging in price discrimination (charging some people more than others) to the effect that it lessens competition. Provision is made for defences of exclusionary acts under the same proviso as that for anti-competitive conduct (technological efficiency and pro-competitive gains that outweigh anti-competitive effects).

In terms of the Act, the Competition Commission (that replaced the old Competition Board) must be informed of all mergers and acquisitions. These include vertical or conglomerate acquisitions as well as joint ventures (all above a specific threshold as determined by the Minister by way of notice in the *Government Gazette*). Concerned trade unions (employees or employee groups) should also be notified. This Commission has primarily an investigative function but can approve or prohibit intermediate mergers.

In terms of the new Act, the Minister of Trade and Industry has less power. He/she is only involved in merger proceedings of a public interest nature and cannot overturn the findings of the Commission – but may appeal them. A decision by the Commission may be appealed to a Tribunal – a competition court of law – by either the complainant, the respondent or the minister). Tribunal decisions can be appealed to a special Appeal Court – specifically dedicated to competition cases. The tribunal can also levy administrative fines and penalties and has primarily an adjudicative function. The tribunal handles larger mergers that have been referred to it by the Competition Commission.

## 3.6 OWNERSHIP AND THE FUTURE

It is difficult to say how the debate on ownership and control will develop in South Africa in the future. What is, however, important to note is that it is a very complex issue and students (as future policy formulators) would be well advised to take note of all the variables that are involved.

We showed above that policy formulation on ownership is introduced in democracies to ensure diversity of opinion or pluralism. Future policy formulators should therefore ensure that their policy attains the goal of ensuring pluralism within the realities and constraints of the South African situation. Newspaper editors, like the *Sunday Times'* former editor Ken Owen, have argued that the newspaper market in South Africa is not only open, but also fluid and dangerous to existing media products that do not keep pace with its demands. Owen has remarked that the restrictions on press ownership – as practised in other countries – have done little good or harm and that he would not be against such restrictions.

Although we could debate the openness of the South African newspaper market (as Anton Harber did after the closure of the *Daily Mail*), we should also take note of the economic realities of the newspaper business in South Africa. Escalating production costs, decreasing advertising revenue and competition from the newer information media have led to the disappearance of several newspaper titles in the 1990s. The latter means that the risk for potential investors in the print media has increased. Foreign investors could therefore play a meaningful role in increasing diversity if they invest in the local media. Ivan Fallon (at the time group editorial director of Independent Newspapers) has pointed out that, instead of being a threat to media diversity, Independent Newspapers has launched new titles, such as *Business Report, Sunday Life*, and *The Sunday Independent* to compete with Times Media. This type of competition (between the two groups) did not exist before. Although this competition could be viewed as competition directed towards the upper end of the market, it represents competition none the less.

Other flagging titles, such as the *Cape Times, Natal Mercury, Saturday Star, Diamond Fields Advertiser*, and the *Pretoria News* were redesigned, repositioned and relaunched. These papers have therefore been improved. In terms of empowerment, Fallon in addition has noted that the group was appointing blacks to editorial positions which they have never held before (cf. Foreign investment in the press ... 1995).

A former editor of the *Mail & Guardian*, Anton Harber, has urged the government to take the economic realities of escalating production costs, decreasing advertising revenue and competition from new forms of information services into account before acting on foreign owners. The *Mail & Guardian* (70 percent owned by the Guardian Group in London) made an operating loss of over R1 million in 1994/1995 and expected an even greater loss for the following year. The fact that the Guardian Group purchased 70 percent of the shares gave the newspaper an injection of R3,5 million which probably saved it from closing (Creamer 1996:86). Just as the Competition Board did in the past, we should probably ask the question here whether international involvement to secure the survival of the newspaper is not preferable to closure. The Cartel Office in Germany has taken a similar position. From the vantage point of promoting pluralism, such an argument would make a lot of sense.

The above does not, of course, mean that foreign ownership could not have negative effects on the newspaper industry or, for that matter, on the promotion of pluralism. These companies do, naturally, expect a return on investment. When the Independent company took over Argus, a major rationalisation programme was, for example, put into place. The first newspaper to bear the brunt of this programme was the *Pretoria News* where 100 printers and seven journalists were retrenched. This followed the moving of the Pretoria newspaper's printing operation to the Newspaper Printing Company in Johannesburg, jointly owned by TML (Emdon 1996:197).

In the case of group ownership, there is in addition, always the possibility of standardisation of content. In this regard Louw (1993:166) noted that previous newspaper take-overs by Argus have also led to the homogenisation of content and what he refers to as an "uncontroversial bland greyness in representation". Tendencies to standardise content would, indeed, have negative implications for the promotion of diversity.

The influence of chain-ownership or monopolies on the market, on the other hand, should not be taken for granted. As Picard (1989:79) has noted:

> Given demand theory and market structure expectations, one would expect consumers to benefit economically from competitive situations and to be harmed by monopolies. One would expect competition to improve the media content and monopoly to harm it. The evidence in this regard is mixed.

Although it has been shown that programming and price decisions can be influenced by oligopolistic interdependence in television, Picard (1989:79–80) says that there is little evidence in the newspaper industry that market structure has any significant effect on news and editorial content.

According to Picard (1989:80), most studies that have compared newspapers operating under different market structures have concluded that professional norms and journalistic standards were more important determinants of content or lack of diversity of different newspapers (also McQuail 1992:120) than the market structure (e.g. a monopoly situation versus a situation where newspapers compete). In terms of pricing,

Picard found that the newspaper industry paid little attention to economics and marketing knowledge in making decisions about advertising rates. They relied more on hunches than data in making price decisions. Contrary to expectation, Picard found that competing newspapers had higher actual rates (when not adjusted for circulation) than monopoly newspapers. However, in places where monopolies developed (after the demise of a competitor), customers were charged more for advertisements. Other studies did indicate higher advertising rates in monopoly newspapers (Picard 1989:82).

Although the above research is not necessarily valid in terms of South Africa, some of these findings sound a warning to critical students not to take the assumed effect of concentration of ownership – especially on content – for granted. On the other hand, it is also imperative to take note of the unique shortcomings of the market in South Africa. As Emdon (1996:193) has noted, apartheid denied blacks access to the media in the past. Today other barriers to entry in the market still exist. The main barrier is probably the prohibitive costs of launching and sustaining a competitive product under the present market structure. According to Emdon (1996: 194), the launch of *The Citizen* in competition with the *Rand Daily Mail* in the 1980s cost R38 million in the first eighteen months. Two alternative weeklies, namely *Vrye Weekblad* and *Sunday Nation* – both operating on a much smaller scale – needed R2,5 million each in grants to stay in the market from mid-1993 to December 1994. *Sunday Nation* was subsequently taken over by Independent and *Vrye Weekblad* closed.

What is also striking, but quite understandable in terms of South Africa's history, is the total absence of positive policy stipulations to promote diversity of opinion or pluralism, such as subsidies or tax concessions (Oosthuizen 1991:41). There are also no reductions of tariffs for transport or telecommunications for newspapers, no special facilities for granting loans at low rates for attaining new printing equipment, and so forth (Emdon 1996:194). As Emdon points out, the absence of these promotional mechanisms also represents less obvious barriers to entry in the market. Other aspects that make it more difficult for people to enter the newspaper market include the heterogeneity of the population, illiteracy (as high as 83 percent in some regions), and the high percentage of street sales (Emdon 1996:195–196; Oosthuizen 1991:46). Apart from these aspects, the sustainability of alternative and black-owned newspapers has also been negatively influenced by the lack of management capacity and infrastructural support (such as printing, marketing, and distribution facilities) (Emdon 1996:198).

In the light of the absence of real promotional mechanisms to increase diversity, the formation of the Independent Media Diversity Trust (IMDT) in 1993 was widely welcomed. The main aim of the Trust is to support diversity of the media in South Africa with the emphasis on independence of ownership (independent of government or major commercial interests).

It has been involved in rescue operations for two independent newspapers (*Sunday Nation* and *Vrye Weekblad*) in the past. However, the main focus of the IMDT shifted to the kick starting of community media in 1995 (newspapers/magazines and radio stations). It is very important to note that the (mainstream) newspaper industry contributed

R850 000 of the corporate South African grants of R1,45 million during the first eighteen months (from July 1993 to December 1994) of the Trust's existence; the rest of this grant was made up of contributions from M-Net and JCI (holding company of TML). The bulk of the contributions during this time came from the European Union (R5 million).

Four national and regional publications (historically part of the alternative press); six magazines from the Independent Magazine Group, eight community newspapers and three agencies were the beneficiaries of these contributions which took the form of financial and development assistance. (IMDT played a role in establishing the Independent Magazine Group from a merger of publications such as *Work-in-progress, Speak, Challenge, Labour Bulletin, Shopsteward*, and *Learn and Teach*.)

The contributions to the IMDT from the (mainstream) press, M-Net (jointly owned by all the press groups at the time) and owners of TML (at the time JCI), seem to suggest that these interest groups were not insensitive to the promotion of diversity in the media market. By the end of the century the IMDT was winding down what was mostly described as capacity building for local community radio stations. A lack of financial support was hampering IMDT activities and more and more media observers were looking to the Media Development and Diversity Agency (MDDA) of the Government Communication and Information Service (GCIS) – previously the South African Communication Service – to carry the torch for independent media.

According to Duncan (2000:11), the government was in the process of establishing such a (statutory) agency at the time of writing. In her view, the setting up of a common carrier (distribution facility) for new (independent) media; securing low interest loans for (future) commercial media; as well as the provision of grants for (existing) commercial media were some of the challenges facing the MDDA.

There are of course also other issues that governments must consider. The assumption of governments that ownership inevitably leads to control does not always hold water. It is true that the former editor-in-chief of *The Star*, Richard Steyn, resigned in 1994 because of reservations about editorial autonomy under the new Independent management structure. Under this structure editors were expected to report to regional managing editors. This was unacceptable to Steyn. His resignation would, therefore, seem to support the idea that ownership leads to control. At the same time, however, it underscores the fact that he had such independence under the previous Argus structure. The former National Party government did not seem to agree! The editorial independence of Argus newspapers was also confirmed during interviews with two previous editors of the *Pretoria News*, Mostert van Schoor and Deon du Plessis, in 1989 and 1992 respectively. Meanwhile media mogul Tony O'Reilly has also undertaken to ensure the editorial independence of his newspapers. Some of Independent's employees were however very quick to point out that editorial content was increasingly influenced by the companies owners and advertisers alike. In one such instance editorial staff was apparently instructed to carry this country's Olympic bid on a more prominent position in local Independent newspapers. However, one can probably only challenge the principle of such editorial interference and not the intention.

This somewhat confusing state of affairs underlines the necessity for local research to establish the extent to which newspapers really are independent.

On a last critical note, we could also argue that there is a vague possibility that government will seize the opportunity of using the issue of ownership to address other issues at the expense of the real promotion of pluralism. Affirmative action and the support (or lack of support) for government policy decisions in the press are two of these issues that come to mind.

Affirmative action was also discussed at the Arniston conference of government communicators in 1995. Thami Mazwai (editor of *Enterprise* magazine) suggested that the government should use its advertising as an incentive to stimulate affirmative action in the industry. The idea would be to direct advertising to newspapers that have implemented affirmative action policies.

Affirmative action as such, though morally justifiable, will not necessarily lead to the promotion of pluralism. As Ken Owen has pointed out, editors who have not been trained extensively at a particular newspaper will probably lose readers once they start editing that newspaper. If we take this further, we could argue that if a newspaper loses enough readers, it could lead to the closure of that particular newspaper and a subsequent decrease in pluralism (titles). Pluralism in titles and content should therefore not be confused with the plurality of the staff component.

Governments should also get used to the idea of having an adversarial relationship with the press. This is the natural result of the watchdog role of the press in a democracy and part of its responsibility to its readers. This relationship also stimulates diversity of opinion, because different sections of the press usually take different viewpoints on the same issues. Linking conflict between the government and the press to ownership is dangerous because there is not necessarily a direct correlation between the two (Oosthuizen 1995:2).

## Summary

In considering media policy issues, in this unit we looked at two structural approaches to ownership and control, those of the democratic and Marxist positions. Against the background of the media operating as capitalist ventures in a democratic country, we distinguished between various levels of monopoly formation and discussed the development of the ownership debate in South Africa. We concluded by looking at the implications of structural, economic and political variables for the future debate on ownership and control in South Africa.

## Research activities

1  Make a list of the newspapers that are sold in your community and establish which group/company controls them.

2 Based on the different market structures that were discussed above, decide which market structure is functioning in South Africa.
3 Start a scrapbook and throughout the year collect press reports that relate to the debate about ownership and control of the mass media in South Africa.
4 Draw up a document of five pages in which you put forward your recommendations regarding policy formulation on ownership and control of newspapers in South Africa. Base your recommendations on:
- The demands of the new democratic structure in South Africa.
- The economic realities of the market.
- Research findings dealing with the relationship between ownership and the content of newspapers.
- The media ownership policy of the present government.

## Further reading

African National Congress. 1994. *The reconstruction and development programme. A policy framework.* Johannesburg: Umanyano.
Bagdikian, BH. 1983. *The media monopoly.* Boston: Beacon.
Emdon, C. 1996. South Africa, in *Media ownership and control in the age of convergence,* edited by V MacLeod. London: International Institute of Communication.
Hachten, WA & Giffard, CA. 1984. *Total onslaught. The South African press under attack.* Johannesburg: Sage.
Humphreys, PJ. 1990. *Media and media policy in West Germany. The press and broadcasting since 1945.* New York: Berg.
Litman, B. 1988. Microeconomic foundations, in *Press concentration and monopoly,* edited by RG Picard, ME McCombs, JP Winter & SL Lacey. Norwood, NJ: Ablex.
Louw, PE. 1993. *South African media policy debates of the 1990s.* Bellville: Anthropos.
McQuail, D. 1992. *Media performance.* London: Sage
Oosthuizen, LM. 1989. *Media policy and ethics.* Cape Town: Juta.
Picard, RG. 1989. *Media economics. Concepts and issues.* Newbury Park, CA: Sage.
Tunstall, J & Palmer, M. 1991. *Media moguls.* London: Routledge.

## Bibliography

African National Congress. 1992a. African National Congress draft media charter in *Free, fair and open. South African media in the transition to democracy.* Papers, recommendations and resolutions: Part 1. Johannesburg: Campaign for Open Media.
African National Congress. May 1992b. *ANC policy guidelines for a democratic South Africa*:67-71.
African National Congress. 1994. *The reconstruction and development programme. A policy framework.* Johannesburg: Umanyano.
Annual Report MIH Holdings Limited. 1999. Randburg.
Annual Report Electronic Media Network Limited (M-Net). 1999. Randburg.
Bagdikian, BH. 1983. *The media monopoly.* Boston: Beacon.

Berger, G. 2000. *Deracialisation, democracy and development: transformation of the South African media 1994–2000.* Paper delivered at The political economy of the media in Southern Africa – conference, 25–29 April 2000 in Durban.
Burns, Y. 1990. *Media law.* Durban: Butterworths.
Competition Board. 1986. *Report No. 16.* Pretoria: Government Printer.
Competition Board. 1994a. *Fifteenth annual report.* Pretoria: Government Printer.
Competition Board. 1994b. *Report No. 49.* Pretoria: Government Printer.
Creamer, T. 1996. Ownership and control of the South African press: exploring the implications for policy formulation in South Africa. BA Hons project, University of South Africa, Pretoria.
De Bens, E & Østbye, H. 1998. The European newspaper market, in *Media policy: convergence, concentration & commerce,* edited by D McQuail & K Siune. London: Sage.
Dennis, EE & Merrill, JC. 1984. *Basic issues in mass communications. A debate.* New York: Macmillan & Collier.
Duncan, J. 2000. *Talk left, act right: what constitutes transformation in Southern African media.* Paper delivered at The political economy of the media in Southern Africa – conference, 25–29 April 2000 in Durban.
Du Plessis, D. 1992. Personal interview. Pretoria.
Emdon, C. 1996. South Africa, in *Media ownership and control in the age of convergence,* edited by V MacLeod. London: International Institute of Communication.
Fisher, H & Merrill, JC. 1976. *International and intercultural communication.* New York: Hastings House.
Gallagher, M. 1982. Negotiation of control in media organisations and occupations, in *Culture, society and the media,* edited by M Gurevitch, T Bennett, J Curran & J Woollacott. London: Methuen.
Grange, H. 1990. Why did the "Daily Mail" fold? Verdict: not good enough. *The Journalist* November 6–7.
Hachten, WA & Giffard, CA. 1984. *Total onslaught. The South African press under attack.* Johannesburg: Macmillan.
Hardt, H. 1979. *Social theories of the press. Early German and American perspectives.* Beverly Hills: Sage.
Hiebert, RE, Ungurait, DF & Bohn, TW. 1991. *Mass media VI. An introduction to modern communication.* New York: Longman.
Holmes, D. 1986. *Governing the press. Media freedom in the U.S. and Great Britain.* Boulder, CO: Westview.
Humphreys, PJ. 1990. *Media and media policy in West Germany. The press and broadcasting since 1945.* New York: Berg.
Litman. B. 1988. Microeconomic foundations, in *Press concentration and monopoly,* edited by RG Picard, ME McCombs, JP Winter & SL Lacey, Norwood, NJ: Ablex.
Louw, PE. 1993. *South African media policy, Debates of the 1990s.* Belville: Anthropos.
Louw, R. 1989. *Four days in Lusaka. Whites in a changing society.* Excom: Five Freedoms Forum.
Marshall, PG. 1990. *Editorial Research* 1 (31):478–490.
Martin, JL & Chaudhary, AG. 1983. *Comparitive mass media systems.* New York: Longman.
Mazzoleni, G. 1991. Media moguls in Italy, in *Media moguls,* edited by J Tunstall & M Palmer. London: Routledge.
McGregor Information Services. 1995. *McGregor's stock exchange handbook December 1995–June 1996.* Johannesburg: Profile Media.
McQuail, D. 1987. *Mass media theory. An introduction.* London: Sage.
McQuail, D. 1992. *Media performance.* London: Sage.
Meier, WA & Trappel, J. 1998. Media concentration and the public interest, in *Media policy: convergence, concentration & commerce,* edited by D McQuail & K Siune. London: Sage.

Naspers Annual Report 1999.
*Omni Media Corporation Limited.* 1995. Annual report. Johannesburg: Omni.
Oosthuizen, LM. 1989. *Media policy and ethics.* Cape Town: Juta.
Oosthuizen, LM. 1990. Ideologie, media en Afrikaner-nasionalisme. *Communicatio* 16(1):38–48.
Oosthuizen, LM. 1991. Suid-Afrikaanse mediabeleid: die media se bondgenoot is soek. *Communicatio* 17(1):38–48.
Oosthuizen, LM. 1992. Issues in mass communication. *Only study guide for CMN 311–3.* Pretoria: University of South Africa.
Oosthuizen, LM. 1993a. Die internasionale debat oor die media en terrorisme: beleids- en etiese implikasies vir owerhede en die media. *Communicatio* 19(1):27–47.
Oosthuizen, LM. 1993b. Media en terrorisme: dominante navorsingparadigmas en bevindings. MA thesis, University of South Africa, Pretoria.
Oosthuizen, LM. 1995. Media policy on ownership. *Dialogus* 2(2):1–2.
Picard, RG. 1989. *Media economics. Concepts and issues.* Newbury Park, CA: Sage.
Profile's stock exchange handbook, Jan 2000–Jun 2000. Profile Media: Johannesburg.
Robertson, G. 1983. *People against the press. An enquiry into the Press Council.* London: Quartet.
Roelofse, JJ. 1983. *Towards rational discourse. An analysis of the report of the Steyn Commission of Inquiry into the media.* Pretoria: Van Schaik.
Ruddock, R. 1981. *Ideologies. Five exploratory lectures. Manchester Monographs* 15. Manchester: Department of Adult and Higher Education, University of Manchester.
South Africa. *Report of the Commission of Inquiry into the Mass Media, PR 89(3).* 1981. Pretoria: Government Printer.
*Sunday Times.* 1998. [O].
   Available: http://www.suntimes.co.za
   Accessed on 1998/06/28
Tunstall, J & Palmer, M (eds). 1991. *Media moguls.* London: Routledge.
Tunstall, J. 1983. *The media in Britain.* New York: Columbia University Press.
*White Paper on the Reconstruction and Development Programme, No. 1608* 23 November 1994. Pretoria: Government Printer.

## Newspaper articles

Competition boss Brooks to get the axe. 1996a. *Sunday Times Business Times,* 5 May:1.
Foreign investment in the press should be welcomed: it's created new titles, jobs, and embraced the new SA. 1995. *The Sunday Independent,* 1 October.
Jay blameer die media vir dalende rand. 1996. *Beeld,* 2 Mei:1.
Sexwale hits out at the "Independent". 1995. *The Citizen,* 29 September:13.
Team to take foreign media control to task. 1996. *Mail & Guardian,* 12–18 January.

# The External Media Policy Framework: From Restrictive Policy to the Democratisation of Communication

*Lucas M Oosthuizen*

## Overview

In this unit we discuss the following:

- the values of freedom, equality and order as the basis for media policy frameworks;
- media policy regulators: governments, norms, pressure groups, advertisers, consumers, and the media profession itself;
- the media policy framework under the National Party government in South Africa;
- the media policy framework under the ANC (African National Congress) government in South Africa;
- the implications of regulation;
- telecommunication as policy domain with specific reference to universal service; and
- codes of conduct.

## Learning outcomes

After completing this unit you should be able to

- describe how values form the basis of and inform external media policy formulation;
- determine which values in a democracy inform media policy;
- explain how expectations about the functions of the media in society inform media policy;
- isolate the main differences between the National Party and the African National Congress' (ANC) media policy frameworks in South Africa and the results of these frameworks as far as legislation is concerned;
- evaluate the National Party and the ANC's media policy frameworks in terms of the value criteria: freedom, equality and order;
- provide your own examples of the following forms of regulation: norms, pressure groups, advertisers, consumers as regulators, and the profession itself as regulator;

- demonstrate awareness of the content of codes of conduct; and
- give examples of where you think journalists have transgressed a code of conduct.

## 4.1 INTRODUCTION

In the previous unit we have dealt with the issues of ownership and control of the media. The institution or promulgation of a law or Act – like the Competition Act (no. 89 of 1998) – is a typical example of policy formulation by the government. Where such regulation affects the media – in the sense that it specifically restricts the media in some or other way – we are dealing with media policy in the traditional sense. The government, through its legislative framework, is probably the most important regulator on this level. But it is not the only one. Media institutions or organisations are part of society. Viewed from this broader societal context, policy that affects the media directly or indirectly is therefore made by the various interest groups in society which also interact with one another (cf. Oosthuizen 1989). For purposes of definition, this societal context is referred to as the external framework.

## 4.2 THE EXTERNAL MEDIA POLICY FRAMEWORK

Media institutions function within specific societies. The nature of any particular society, for example the South African society, provides the framework for the expression of expectations about media functioning (what the media should or should not do). These expectations are based on the fundamental values prevalent in a society and form the basis of the external framework. Fundamental values are in turn articulated by a particular system of government (like a democracy or autocracy) which results in concrete policy formulation (e.g. legislation). As a result, policy becomes a determinant and co-indicator of the social functions that the media fulfil, or ought to fulfil, and also influences their content (Oosthuizen 1989:4–6).

By way of clarification, we use democracy as an example. Democracy – as a system of government and an ideology – articulates certain fundamental values such as freedom, but also, as part of the external framework, sets specific expectations for the media, giving rise to distinctive media policy.

### 4.2.1 Democracy

Democracy is commonly associated with the liberal tradition (cf. Rudock 1981). In terms of this tradition human beings are regarded as free individuals with the right to self-determination. Freedom afforded to people in terms of this tradition includes freedom of speech, religion, movement, as well as the freedom to form economic associations. As Roelofse (1983) points out, the whole point of democracy as an ideology is therefore to promote the social and political conditions where people can exercise their choice and become even freer.

But democracy also implies that the individual has the duty to tolerate the views of others and that individuals and groups have the responsibility not to jeopardise each other's liberties (Roelofse 1983:4–5).

From the above it should be clear that the basic or fundamental values articulated by a democracy, are values like freedom, equality and order. But how would these values be translated into policy formulation? A reworking of McQuail's (1993) media performance norms can provide us with an indication.

## Freedom

Freedom is provided for in democracies by largely exempting the media from censorship and legislation that curtails the acquisition of information. The media in democracies are therefore also typically free to observe and criticise the actions of a government. They can, in other words, fulfil a watchdog role. People also have the liberty to run a mass medium economically (for example, start a newspaper). A constitution that ensures the freedom of the media in a particular country, would be a typical example of a policy measure that articulates the fundamental value of freedom. So would a *Freedom of Information Act* – that compels government to make information available to the populace – and a *Government in the Sunshine Act* which compels authorities to conduct their affairs in public under the scrutiny of the public media.

## Equality

Equality would in broad terms, concern the levelling of the playing fields in democratic society. In other words, all people should be able to exercise their rights equally in a democracy. In terms of media policy, this value leads to the introduction of measures to ensure equal access to information – both as users and suppliers of such information. The introduction and maintenance of a public broadcasting system would be one of the measures a government could introduce to ensure such access to the broadcasting system. Policy to promote the diversity of opinion, viewpoints and information in democratic society would also be relevant here. An act that prevents the formation of media monopolies would be a typical policy measure to ensure diversity – equality. Other measures would include subsidies to struggling news media, exempting them from value-added tax (VAT), and so forth.

## Order

The value of order expresses the commitment to ensure that freedom in a democratic society is not exercised at the expense of other individuals, groups or society as a whole. Provisions to protect children against violent media content or pornography; stipulations barring hate speech in the media; and constitutional provisions to protect the privacy of individuals would be good examples of media policy formulation that addresses the value of order.

### Expectations, functions and codes of conduct

As you would have seen in the previous unit, the articulation of the fundamental values of a particular ideology (like democracy) does not only lead to explicit policy formulation – such as legal restrictions – but also leads to certain expectations in terms of how the media should function in society. These expectations could lead to implicit policy formulation.

Codes of conduct are good examples of implicit policy formulation. In democracies these codes are indicative of the fact that the media are prepared to regulate themselves – in line with societal expectations. In other words, the media accept their responsibility to, for example, not only inform the populace, but also to do so responsibly (accurately and truthfully).

In a democracy, because the media are accountable to society such codes usually also make provision for the avoidance of reportage that could lead to crime, violence or public disorder. Policy formulation – on this implicit level – is therefore also clearly the result of the articulation of specific fundamental values in democratic dispensations. In this particular case, the value of order forms the basis for such articulation and eventual policy formulation.

Now that we have taken note of the broad context (external framework) in which media policy is formulated, we will take a closer look at the people or institutions that determine the specific policies that affect the media.

### 4.2.2 Policymakers in the external framework

As Snyman (1985:5) points out, the most decisive source of policy formulation (clearly on a national level) is the state. Within the jurisdiction of the state, political parties (in multiparty systems) can formulate their policies on information and the communication media (Oosthuizen 1989:8). When a party comes to power, its policy becomes the official policy of the country and may be embodied in legislation. Such legislation can award rights to the media, but could also restrict them. It is this restrictive legislation (regulation) that is usually perceived as media policy by the media themselves (Tunstall 1983:200; Oosthuizen 1989:9).

Although governments can be regarded as the most important regulator of the media, they are by far not the only one. Ultimately, all institutions or individuals outside the media – and in the position to regulate the media in some or other way – could explicitly and implicitly lay down media policy in the external framework. These parties may simply be referred to as regulators. They include such groups or institutions as governments, advertisers, pressure groups and the expectations of the journalistic profession itself. Let us take a closer look at these regulators within the South African policy context.

## 4.3 REGULATORS

Regulators function within the external framework and are institutions or measures that determine or codetermine media content from the outside. In other words, although these people or institutions stand outside the media, they deliberately influence the material published in the media. Regulators are usually tolerated; as Hiebert, Ungurait and Bohn (1991:14) put it, no one wants to incur their wrath. Governments are by far the most important regulator (also see Van Heerden's discussion of regulators in Oosthuizen 1996).

### 4.3.1 Government as regulator

The nature of the relationship between a national government and the media is decisive for what the media are allowed to publish. The main reason for this is that the media are legally, normatively and structurally subject to the control of political institutions (Gerbner 1977: 263). Gallagher states that the key relationship that links the media to society, is that between the media organisations and the government of a country (Gurevitch, Bennett, Curran & Woollacott 1985:160). Holmes (1986:1) adds that the media of a nation, more than any other kind of institution, are shaped by the prevailing type of political power. But, what does this mean in practice?

Governments control the media through legislation (legally). In addition, they also have specific expectations about how the media should fulfil their role in society. These expectations are in essence normative pointers that governments provide to the media and could, of themselves, become forms of intrinsic regulation. In other words, the media will tend to act in a certain way, because the government expects them to behave like that. If the media deviate from such expectations, they usually get negative feedback from the government in question (such as, for example, criticism and threats). If this feedback results in corrective action by the media, it serves as an indirect form of control.

But from where do these expectations that governments use to gauge the performance of the media emanate? They basically evolve from the articulation of the public interest by individual governments in the countries that they govern (a specific territory). In a democracy, the articulation of the public interest would theoretically be in line with the interests of the majority of the people. However, what the media can do, and what they are expected to do can be radically different in other types of political dispensations. The type of political power can therefore have a profound effect on the nature of the media system in a country and in particular on

- the rights afforded to the media;
- the restrictions that are placed on them; and
- expectations about how they should behave in order to best serve society.

To illustrate how all of the above translates into action, we take a closer look at the South African situation during and after apartheid.

### *The South African policy context during apartheid*

Although National Party and government leaders referred to South Africa as a democracy (Oosthuizen 1989:32), the South African State did not closely approximate a democratic system during that dispensation. The majority of the South African population had no say in the legislation that applied to them because they had no representation in parliament; the executive had wide discretionary powers, which included the right to prohibit publications; and no Bill of Rights (in keeping with the principle of human rights) was in place (cf. Viljoen 1989; Oosthuizen 1989). By 1984 South Africa displayed the essential features of a racial aristocracy (Van der Vyver 1994:16). This aristocracy consisted of whites, Indians and coloured people nominated to a legislative assembly (in a Tricameral Parliament) headed by an elected executive state president. The black majority in the country had no representation in central government.

In line with the ideology of apartheid, the South African society was divided along racial lines. The ideology of apartheid also had a profound effect on the way in which the core values of this alleged democracy were articulated. In broad terms, the divisions in society and the domination of the majority by the minority were also reflected in policy formulation. Such policy included stipulations that restricted the media.

In this regard, Tomaselli, Tomaselli and Muller (1987:78) point out that the main laws that restricted press freedom in South Africa at the time, were also the ones that most effectively curtailed the activities of anti-government black groups. The spirit of the laws oscillated between co-optation and coercion. From these laws one can also deduce that the public interest was very narrowly defined under apartheid. Many of the laws only made provision for the interests of the minority and the securing of their dominant position.

In terms of the media, the National Party's constitution did not make explicit provision for any media rights such as, for example, freedom of access to government information. Although freedom of speech was provided for in the constitution, it was not enshrined in a Bill of Rights. Media freedom as such, was not explicitly guaranteed. While the constitution – at that time – did not articulate freedom very strongly, the legal framework (laws) did even worse on this score. The media had to operate in a very restrictive legal framework – with more than 100 laws that restricted the conduct of journalists as well as media content.

The most severe legal stipulations were those that dealt with internal security. In terms of these stipulations, the following:

- The government could ban organisations like the ANC, PAC and the South African Communist Party. It was also an offence for the media to quote the members of these organisations.
- The Minister of Law and Order could prohibit or suspend publications.
- A newspaper could be compelled to pay a deposit of up to R40 000, if the Minister was not satisfied that the publication would adhere to specific provisions of the law. On transgression of the law, the deposit could be forfeited.
- The media could also not quote people whose names were published on a consolidated list of prohibited persons (Oosthuizen 1992; 1989).

These stipulations obviously had the effect of excluding large parts of the South African reality from becoming news. They also led to the most drastic form of censorship with

## The External Media Policy Framework

the closing down of newspapers like *Post, Sunday Post, World* and *Weekend World*. The above stipulations made it possible for the government to curtail the voices of anti-government groups. It reached a climax in 1986 when the emergency regulations effectively ruled out the publication of "unrest" related news, if such news did not emanate from Cabinet, government ministers or government spokesmen (Oosthuizen 1989: 41). The government also had the right to ban publications and to insist on the prior approval of media content before publication. It led to the banning of mostly alternative newspapers, for periods ranging from one to three months.

Legislation that dealt with the police and prisons made it an offence to publish anything untruthful about the police and prisons. In both cases the onus was on the press to deliver proof that reasonable grounds for the veracity (truth) of information existed. As far as prisons were concerned, the media were also required to prove that they had taken reasonable steps to ensure the veracity of reports on prisons. In many cases these stipulations restricted journalists to the reporting of official versions of police and prison news (Oosthuizen 1989; 1992). It obviously also made the reporting of misconduct by police and prison personnel very difficult.

Hachten and Giffard (1984:113) point out that the main purpose of most of the laws that restricted media freedom was "to close off from public scrutiny and criticism the widespread imposition of official control over the black population and the increasing activities of the police and military forces".

Not only did the government have unlimited powers to withhold information from the public, but the vague formulation of legal stipulations that dealt with subjects like state security and the combating of terrorism made it very difficult for journalists to work out when they were in actual fact transgressing the law. This insecurity ultimately led to self-censorship (cf. Hachten and Giffard 1984).

From the above it should be clear that regulation of the media was done strictly in accordance with the dictates and interests of the ruling power under apartheid. The articulation of the values of freedom, equality and order was done accordingly. There was little or no *freedom* and the media's submission to the *status quo* was enforced by a very restrictive legal framework. This framework made provision for severe forms of censorship which included the outright banning of publications. The media were not permitted to undermine the established order (by, for example, criticising or attacking the regime).

In the late eighties the South African Broadcasting Corporation (SABC) ran twenty-four radio services with broadcasts in twenty languages, as well as four television services with broadcasts in seven languages. On the surface, therefore, it might appear that the previous government made provision for *equality*, inasmuch as a public broadcasting system was in place. However, on closer scrutiny it is obvious that this system did not have the promotion of diversity in mind, for the following reasons:

- The fact that the SABC had a virtual monopoly on television news impacted negatively on the promotion of diversity (Oosthuizen 1989:32).

- Historically the National Party used the SABC to dominate its political opposition and, according to Hachten and Giffard (1984:200), its broadcasts did not truly reflect the cultural diversity of South African society.
- Tomaselli et al (1989:94–103) remarked that the main effect of the SABC as an institution was to reinforce the allocated class positions in society at the time. They argued that the policy of separate radio stations for the various black ethnic groups not only underscored the divisions between black and white people, but also the ethnic differences within the black community itself. The inherent aim behind this strategy was to divide and rule.
- The content of these black radio stations also provided listeners with a model of subservience, Tomaselli et al (ibid) argued.
- Government interference in the affairs of the SABC also made it impossible to uphold its charter as a public broadcaster. As Potter (1975:49) remarked, "The corporation long ago abandoned any pretence at upholding the principles of its charter to act as an impartial public body, and has been used extensively – both inside and outside South Africa – to disseminate the views of the National Party Government."

Although the National Party government made provision for the curtailing of monopolies in the press, they had no additional policy in place to promote the diversity of ownership in this sector. No direct or indirect subsidies were made available for press development. As a result, the so-called "black press" was mostly white-owned. However, white ownership did not deter the government from singling out this sector as a target for special scrutiny and action.

Policy of the previous government also made provision for the articulation of *order*. The Publications Act (no. 42 of 1974), for example, made provision for censorship based on the concept of undesirability. A film, magazine, book, pamphlet or newspaper not affiliated to the Newspaper Press Union could be deemed undesirable as soon as it – or any part of it –

- was judged to be indecent or obscene or offensive or harmful to public morals;
- was regarded as blasphemous or offensive to the religious convictions or feelings of any section of the population of the Republic;
- brought any section of the population of the Republic into ridicule or contempt;
- harmed the relations between any sections of the population of the Republic;
- was prejudicial to the safety of the state, the general welfare or the peace and good order (Oosthuizen 1989:27).

If found to be undesirable these media could be prohibited, which made the distribution or possession of any of these items an offence. The application of this Act not only led to the censorship of pornography and violence (which would have been acceptable in a democratic framework), but it also led to the banning of political content that was deemed to threaten the *status quo* (the dispensation of apartheid). The Publications Act therefore neatly slotted in with those acts in the regulatory framework that had the same effect (Driver 1980:10; Brink 1980:18; Oosthuizen 1989:80–82).

The narrow articulation of the public interest – in terms of the value of order – is also quite evident here. Racial distinctions were made in the application of censorship; for instance the release of certain films was specified in terms of racial groups (Harvey 1970–12). This meant that one group (for example, whites) could see a film, but another group (for example, blacks) could not, or vice versa. The lives and liberty of black writers were more directly endangered (Brink 1980:23). They also had greater difficulty in getting their works published, since the chances of prohibition were greater than in the case of white authors (Hachten & Giffard 1984:173).

From the above one could conclude that the public interest (seen in terms of freedom, equality and order) was very narrowly defined or articulated under apartheid. This narrow articulation was also clearly reflected in the regulation of the media.

Apart from laws and regulations such as those mentioned above, the South African Government also had other ways of exercising its influence. These methods can be regarded as an extension of government regulation of the media. The following are examples of the type of regulation that occurred over the years in South Africa:

- *Direct confrontation with reporters*: Direct confrontation with the press occurred for many years in South Africa and there were many altercations with reporters, especially foreign correspondents. In the eighties a number of foreign journalists were denied visas to visit South Africa and the government refused to renew the work permits of several other correspondents (Hachten & Giffard 1984:279). In 1989, in another example of how the government directly confronted journalists, Mr Ken Owen, then editor of *Business Day*, was questioned in connection with an article that alleged that the police were incompetent to maintain law and order (cf. Oosthuizen 1996). In 1992, the police started to use court orders to restrain newspapers from publishing information about their activities. Because of such action *Vrye Weekblad* could not, in one instance, publish a report at all and in another case *Weekly Mail* had to delete names and place references before publication (cf. Oosthuizen 1996).
- *Interference in the affairs of the SABC*: The manner in which SABC-TV handled the resignation of Mr Allan Hendrickse from the cabinet in 1987 provoked considerable speculation about government interference. In 1989 a letter from the then State President, Mr PW Botha, was published in which he interfered in the affairs of the SABC by writing to Mr Alwyn Schlebusch, the ex-Minister responsible for the SABC. More recently, in 1995, the National Party accused the ANC of such interference.
- *Appeals to the press to show greater responsibility*: An appeal to practise consensus journalism made by former Minister Chris Heunis aptly illustrates how the government tried to appeal to the press to show greater responsibility. In 1988, Mr Adriaan Vlok, ex-Minister of Law and Order, asked the media not to disseminate lies about the police and security forces.

By contrast, we now consider the present dispensation.

## *The South African policy context after apartheid*

On 2 February 1990, former State President Mr FW de Klerk announced, *inter alia*:

- the unbanning of political organisations such as the African National Congress (ANC), South African Communist Party (SACP) and Pan Africanist Congress (PAC);
- the release of political prisoners;
- the abolition of the media emergency regulations.

These three steps had far-reaching implications for the media:

- formerly "prohibited" organisations were free to publish their ideas – even in their own media;
- formerly "prohibited" persons could be quoted freely in the media;
- coverage could again be given to unrest in the country.

Owing to these changes, the government reconsidered some of the country's legislation. The old Internal Security Act (no. 74 of 1982) was repealed in June 1991 and replaced with the Internal Security and Intimidation Amendment Act (no. 138 of 1991). This step enhanced the free flow of information in the country considerably, in that:

- It was no longer an offence to quote Communists, members of the ANC, PAC and others.
- The Minister of Law and Order could no longer prohibit or suspend publications for a period or warn a publication that it may not public specific actions or propagate particular views.
- The Minister could also no longer compel a publication to pay an amount of up to R40 000, if he was not satisfied that a publication would adhere to specific provisions of the law.
- The media were no longer prohibited from quoting specific persons (in the then consolidated list of prohibited persons).
- Restrictions on all persons (including journalists) to attend gatherings or to enter or leave specific regions were lifted.

The amendment of other Acts followed, which included the scrapping of the veracity clauses in the Police Act (no. 7 of 1958) as amended (article 27 (b)) and the Prisons Act (no. 8 of 1959) as amended (article 44 (1)).

The ANC emerged as the leading political party during subsequent negotiations. In its draft media charter the organisation confirmed that South Africa was in transition towards a democracy and that such a democratic society would be founded on the free flow of information and a culture of open debate. It aspired to promote the principles of freedom of the media, and, in so doing, to contribute to the democratic process. According to the ANC, the basis of this process would be maximum openness within the context of a democratic constitution and a charter of human rights (ANC policy guidelines for a democratic South Africa, May 1992:68).

This vision was addressed in the preface to the charter in which it was stated that:

1 Access to information and conflicting opinions would be essential for informed decision making in a democracy.

# The External Media Policy Framework

2 For the majority of the population, access to information, has been undermined in the past by:
   - legal restrictions on the flow of information
   - the structure of ownership of media resources, skills, language policy and social deprivation.
3 Freedom of the media in itself would not be sufficient; it had to be endorsed by equitable distribution of media resources, development programmes and a conscious effort to promote a culture of open debate.

The ANC also accepted the following specific policy guidelines:

1 **Freedom of the media**
   - That all people should be free to disseminate information and should have free access to information and opinion.
   - That no institutional or legislative restriction should be placed on the free flow of information and that there should be no censorship measures.
   - That all people should have the right of access to state information (excluding restrictions imposed by the constitution).

2 **Democratisation of the media**
   - That the different types of media should make provision for the diversity in communities.
   - That steps should be taken to provide all communities with access to the technical means of receiving and disseminating information, such as electricity, telecommunication and other facilities.
   - That communities should also have access to skills required to receive and disseminate information – including reading and writing.
   - That diversity of ownership of media production and distribution facilities should be guaranteed.
   - That affirmative action should be taken to make financial, technical and other resources available to the sectors of society that have so far been denied these facilities.

3 **Public media**
   - That those sources of the media that are in the hands of the state should be used to promote and strengthen democracy.
   - That the state should maintain a public broadcasting service that will serve society as a whole and will provide a mouthpiece for all sectors of society.
   - That this public broadcasting service should be independent of the ruling party and administered by structures that are representative of all sectors of society.

4 **Media workers and society**
   - Under this section it is, *inter alia*, stated that media workers should be protected from intimidation and coercion that may prejudice their work.
   - That media workers should be protected by law from disclosing their sources of information.

- That they should have the right to establish and belong to trade unions, political and other organisations of their choice.
- That organisations, institutions and citizens should have the right to react to information and opinion published about them.
- That the right to privacy of citizens – as well as other liberties entrenched in the charter of human rights – should not be violated.

5 **Education and training**
- Under this section it is, *inter alia*, stated that the state and media institutions should provide facilities for the training and upgrading of media workers.
- Provision must be made for affirmative action in favour of those previously discriminated against.
- Communities must be trained to allow them to publish and broadcast.
- The state and media institutions must aspire to inform citizens of their media rights – as well as the rights of media workers.

6 **Promotional mechanisms**
- Independent structures should be instituted for the different sectors of the media to realise and promote the above principles.
- That structures should be representative of the media owners, workers, political parties, civilian society, knowledgeable persons and others.
- That, where codes of conduct are required for the application of the above principles, they should be formulated according to democratic process in which the various media role players should be involved.
- That an ombudsperson should be democratically appointed to deal with complaints related to the violation of the above principles.
- That society should have the right to challenge decisions of all these structures and persons in court.

(African National Congress Draft Media Charter 1992a:1-4; Oosthuizen 1992:21-26)

This draft charter corresponds largely with the ANC's media policy that was ratified as part of its policy guidelines for a democratic South Africa at its national conference held on 28-31 May 1992. However, there were important additions. Amongst others, that with regard to basic rights and liberties, all media should sign a Standard of Practice and/or Code of Conduct approved by all producers and distributors of public information, communication institutions and advertisers. In the same section the ANC declared that no restrictions, apart from the accepted constitutional restrictions and technical regulations deriving for legislation controlling the media, should be placed on private broadcasting initiatives.

Another important addition was that ownership of media resources, production facilities and distribution points should be subject to antimonopoly, antitrust and amalgamation legislation. The ANC affirmed that media resources of the state would be used to promote democracy. Provision was also made for the monitoring of the media for sexual and racial prejudice (ANC 1992b:67-71).

# The External Media Policy Framework

The policy framework has led to new media policy formulation that includes the following:

- A new constitution with a Bill of Rights that not only guarantees media freedom, but also the freedom to receive and impart information and ideas as well as freedom of artistic creativity (cf. Constitution of the Republic of South Africa, Act 108 of 1996). As in most social democracies, media freedom is not an absolute right in the sense that it could be limited by any law of general application (see section 36(1)). Furthermore, propaganda for war, incitement to violence and the advocacy of hatred based on race and ethnicity, are also specific exclusions (cf. section 32(2)). The Bill of Rights also protects people's right to privacy (cf. section 14).
- In addition, the Bill of Rights also makes provision for the right of citizens to any information held by the state, or held by other persons – and is deemed necessary for the exercising or protection of that persons' rights (cf. article 32 (1)). This gave impetus to the drafting of an Open Democracy Act Draft Bill in 1997. In effect, such an Act would compel government to divulge information to the citizenry – and also to the media. In 2000, this Act was promulgated as the Protection of Access to Information Act (no. 2 of 2000).
- New broadcasting policy (*inter alia*, promulgated in the form of the Independent Broadcasting Authority Act (no. 153 of 1993) has led to the freeing up of the airwaves in South Africa. This resulted in the SABC selling some of its regional radio stations, such as Highveld. Broadcasting was also extended to include commercial and stereo community radio stations. Apart from that there has been a reassessment of the role of the SABC. The SABC is now more representative of South African society on a management level (in terms of the compilation of the SABC Board) as well as in terms of staffing and programme content.
- The introduction of so-called telecentres started in 1998 and resulted from the promulgation of the Telecommunications Act (no. 103) in 1996. This government initiative – supported by the statutorily formed Universal Service Agency (USA) – is geared towards providing people of previously disadvantaged communities with access to the Internet, fax and other telecommunication facilities. At the time of writing, in the region of 12 government telecentres were up and running.
- In line with ANC policy, the Competitions Board has been restructured and is now known as the Competitions Commission. As you would have seen in Unit 3 on media ownership, legislation to regulate competition has also been amended.
- A general movement away from the control of the media by government – to self-control – has taken place. The press is now regulated by an Ombudsman, while the Broadcasting Complaints Commission of South Africa (BCCSA) looks after the affairs of broadcasting. Both of these institutions regulate media conduct through the application of voluntary codes of conduct.
- The formation of the Government Communication and Information Service (GCIS) with a Media Development and Diversity Agency (MDDA) forms part of the media development plans of the new government. The MDDA will promote media skills and development among previously disadvantaged communities.

- An investigation into racism in the media (conducted on the behalf of the Human Rights Commission) culminated in a report that was released in 2000, discussed in Unit 1. In this report especially the print media were castigated for promoting racial stereotypes. The ownership structure of the media in South Africa was also criticised.

From the above it should be clear that the ANC government has gone a long way to apply in practice what is inherently a democratic media policy.

If one looks at the three criteria of freedom, equality and order, it also becomes clear that we are dealing with a much wider articulation of the public interest under the new dispensation.

Freedom of expression forms an integral part of the new Bill of Rights which, *inter alia*, also makes provision for the right to send *and* receive information. Regulation through legislation is now minimal and on par with restrictions in other social democracies. This does not mean that the relationship between the present government and the press has been altogether a happy one.

Some legal restrictions still cause problems. Section 205 of the Criminal Procedures Act (no. 51 of 1977) is one of them. Under this section journalists can be compelled to divulge their sources or other information in a court case if that is deemed to be relevant to solve an alleged offence.

In 1996 journalists were subpoenaed to hand over photographic material taken during the gang leader Rashaad Staggie's torching in Cape Town. Since then, an agreement about the application of section 205 to journalists has been reached between the South African National Editors Forum (SANEF) and the Ministers of Justice and of Safety and Security – as well as with the National Director of Public Prosecutions. Other Acts, such as the Internal Security and Intimidation Amendment Act (no. 138 of 1991), still pose problems in terms of interpretation. As in the case with stipulations about terrorism, it is very difficult to ascertain if and when you are in fact transgressing the stipulations about intimidation (cf. Webber Wentzel 1992; Oosthuizen 1992). Interpretational problems have, in the past, led to self-censorship (cf. Oosthuizen 1989). Where such problems exist, it could therefore theoretically have the same effect in future.

At the time of writing, indications were that the old Internal Security Act (no. 74 of 1982) would be brought back into operation. Subpoenas on journalists (in terms of the Criminal Procedures Act, no. 51 of 1977) continued.

In addition to legislation, journalists have also had other problems. During Mr Nelson Mandela's term of office, for example, especially black journalist were criticised for promoting the interests of white-owned media. Other points of criticism that emanated from government leaders and in government circles included:

- allegations that the media were too critical of the government, and
- that the media did not give enough coverage to achievements such as the Reconstruction and Development Programme (cf. Oosthuizen 1996).

Calls by political leaders for greater responsibility by the media started coming from the ANC soon after they came to power in 1994. For example, in 1995 Dr Pallo Jordan,

Minister of Posts, Telecommunications and Broadcasting, appealed to the media to look at themselves with a critical eye and said that it was a pity that newspapers did not give enough attention to the transformation process in South Africa (Van Heerden 1995:8).

Mr Mandela's meetings with the South African National Editors Forum (SANEF) also did not go unnoticed. To what extent Mr Mandela was able to influence the approach of editors during these meetings, is not quite clear. If he did, in fact, it would be a good example of regulating.

There has also been direct confrontation with reporters. The editor of *Die Volksblad*, Jonathan Crowther, had to learn that the government was not impressed by the way his newspaper reported the massacre at Tempe military base near Bloemfontein in 1999. He "got the message" when the Minister of Defence and senior army officers paid him an impromptu visit at his office in Bloemfontein to air their grievances! The South African military establishment was again under the spotlight when it surfaced that the defence force was trying to recruit journalists for what was generally viewed as becoming agents/spies for them. The same sort of thing happened during the previous dispensation. Shortly afterwards, the Minister also announced that the communication function of officers at military bases would be reassessed – after they had communicated information of which he was not even aware, to the public.

Some sectors of the media also severely criticised the investigation into racism under the auspices of the South African Human Rights Commission (SAHRC). It was felt that the researchers went out with a brief to prove that there was racism in the media, and that they did just that with the aid of questionable methodology. This exercise was also equated with the previous dispensation when government officials were intent on finding a Communist behind every bush. It was argued that Communists had now made way for racists.

Equality is clearly articulated in the ANC policy about the role of public broadcasting services in the South African society. However, there has been some criticism about the restructuring and role of the SABC under the new government. It included allegations – ironically from the National Party – that the ANC was interfering in the affairs of the SABC. Other points of criticism that have surfaced, centre around the role of the SABC as public broadcaster. It has been pointed out that the SABC could not really fulfil its role as public broadcaster as long as

- it did not get its income solely from public funds, and
- adequate steps were not taken to ensure the quality and editorial independence of programmes.

The SABC was, for example, severely criticised when it came to light that companies were paying large sums of money to get coverage on SABC-televison programmes in the year 2000. As a result, the editorial independence of the SABC was again strongly questioned.

Order is also wider articulated under the present dispensation. Since reform started in the early nineties, previously banned books – of mostly political nature – have been unbanned. We have also witnessed a more liberal application of the Publications Act (no. 42 of 1974). Calls by the government for affirmative action in the media; the eradication of racism; and changes to media ownership all articulate the variable of order. Behind these calls is a conception of what the media should do in society. If this conception turns out to be the promotion of a new South African nationalism, it will again underscore a commitment to the democratic articulation of the public interest. However, if order is utilised to promote group or party political interests it will place a big question mark behind government intent in this regard.

There can, however, be little doubt that the policy context – also as far as regulating is concerned – has changed dramatically from the previous to the present political dispensations.

Because of the broader articulation of the public interest, South Africa has clearly moved to a public philosophy of communication that has resulted in the type of media regulation one will find in most social democracies. The previous authoritarian approach has clearly made way for social responsibility. The media are obviously now exercising mostly self-control – and are not primarily regulated by the government. The media are, however, accountable to society. They must therefore avoid anything that could cause crime, violence or public disorder. The latter stipulations are clearly reflected in the exclusions on freedom of expression provided for by the new Constitution under section 32(2). As part of this public philosophy, it would also be expected of the media to reflect the pluralistic diversity of society in their content. Because the government – like its predecessor – has historically equated ownership with control, it possibly explains why ownership has played such a dominant role in the discourse about media diversity in this country. It is also interesting to note that Independent Newspapers – publishers of papers like *The Star* and *Pretoria News* – have lately gone out of their way to give detailed coverage about local events that the government would probably regard as being of national interest. This included fairly wide coverage of the summit of the Non-aligned States as well as the international conference on Aids that was held in Durban in 2000. This could be an indication of the impact of the ownership debate being felt by Independent – an Irish-owned private company. If so, it would also be a good example of indirect regulation of content by the government. Governments are, however, not the only regulators that can influence media content. Some of the others are considered in the next section.

### 4.3.2 Norms as regulator

Norms (Oosthuizen, Faure & de Wet 1991:122) can be defined as "the unwritten rules of conduct that apply within a community". For the news media this means that – as far as their content is concerned – there are certain rules governing what ought to be published and what may not be published. These rules act as regulators of newspaper content.

The key issue is often whether or not something is in good taste, that is, whether it is acceptable or unacceptable to the recipients of media content. Cultural differences could play a role in this regard. Readers of *Die Volksblad* may find a picture of a topless woman unacceptable, while it might well be perfectly acceptable to readers of the *Sowetan* when such a photograph depicts an initiation ceremony. You must, however, remember that norms are not rigid rules to which society adheres: they change over time. A lot of things that are acceptable to publish today – such as photographs of models in revealing swimsuits – were not acceptable many years ago.

Norms are thus reflected in what the media choose to publish. Norms are therefore responsible or co-responsible for what ultimately appears in the media. A good example of the influence of societal norms is found in the amount of violence shown in news photographs. The publication of explicit photographs of a terrorist who killed himself with his own explosive device at a theatre complex in Pretoria in 1988 drew so much reaction from readers of *Rapport* that, in its next edition, the newspaper had to explain its decision to publish the photographs. Since then more horrendous photographs have appeared in many newspapers and as visual footage in the broadcast media – without eliciting any official response from the public. These included:

- Pictures published on the front page of *Beeld* of a man that gruesomely burned to his death in the townships. This horrific incident was depicted in stages.
- Close-ups of the corpse of Mr Chris Hani (charismatic leader of the Communist Party) after his assassination by rightist extremists in 1993.
- Close-ups of the corpses of members of the AWB (Afrikaner Weerstandsbeweging, a right-wing resistance movement) slain by a soldier in the previous homeland of Bophuthatswana in the town of Mafikeng (Oosthuizen 1994:3).

This state of affairs might be an indication that people in South Africa have got used to the level of violence in the country or, alternatively, that they have given up on their ability and duty to influence media content. Whatever the reason, such an apathetic attitude has definitely impacted negatively on the standard of journalism in the country. It will be the responsibility of media users in future to rectify this problem by ensuring the media give them the type of content that they deserve.

The news media often use the excuse that they have decided to publish content that is not in good taste in order to have a specific impact on media users. The moment they become vague about what precisely the impact was that they had in mind, it is usually a good indication that such a decision was taken purely for sensational and/or circulation reasons.

## 4.3.3 The influence of pressure groups as regulators

Pressure groups can also influence the content of newspapers. Hiebert et al (1991:107) point out that the voice of an individual fades as the media become larger. As a result, people organise themselves into groups in order to be heard. Groups usually apply pressure to force journalists to change the news or to omit a story, which constitutes censorship, or they apply pressure to induce journalists to use self-censorship (cf. Oosthuizen et al 1991).

Good examples of the kind of groups that bring pressure to bear on journalists include those that represent gay and lesbian rights, and women's rights. In recent years such groups, especially in the USA, have campaigned for more balanced news coverage. They also exert pressure on media organisations not to discriminate against women or homosexuals in the employment of staff.

Political parties also often act as pressure groups. In past years, leaders of the Conservative Party (CP) have often made statements about the SABC and certain newspapers from public platforms. Daily newspapers such as *Beeld* have come under fire. It is uncertain, however, to what extent such statements influenced news about the CP on television and in the press. In some instances, this type of action might even have had the opposite effect than what the party had intended.

Another form of pressure exercised by pressure groups is the strategic release, withholding or compilation of news (Oosthuizen et al 1991:123). In 1985, for instance, a pressure group at a Pretoria school leaked information about certain irregularities at the school to an Afrikaans afternoon newspaper shortly before a school board election. This exclusive story was given considerable prominence. Parents later alleged that it was an attempt by the group to assume control of the school board. This technique of releasing certain information was also used from the mid-eighties by – at that stage still banned – black groups as part of their struggle against oppression (Oosthuizen et al 1991:141).

### 4.3.4 Advertisers as regulators

The West (Oosthuizen et al 1991:123) is often accused, in Marxist circles, of allowing advertisers to determine the content of newspapers. According to the Marxist view, advertisers in the West insist on a particular type of news presentation and will withdraw their advertising should the newspaper fail to comply. Allegations of such flagrant manipulation are probably somewhat exaggerated. Nevertheless, it is true that advertisers are guilty of subtle or indirect manipulation or influencing of news content.

In view of present economic demands, a newspaper will, however, think twice before publishing a story that will annoy its largest advertiser. Hiebert et al (1991:106) point out that the advertiser's power of regulation depends on the degree to which the medium is dependent on income from advertisements. Newspapers are greatly dependent on advertisements for their survival. Since the early eighties there has been a worldwide tendency to follow a marketing approach in the newspaper business. This means that newspapers have primarily become vehicles between readers and advertisers. As a result of this approach, one could argue that the potential influence of advertisers has increased. Chris Vick, in charge of journalism training for the Independent group in the late nineties, concurred that advertising pressure on newspaper content was mounting. The potential for influence in broadcasting is of course also there – even in the programmes of the SABC – as we have seen earlier.

It should be remembered that advertisements are also subject to regulation under the code of conduct of the Advertising Standards Authority (ASA). The code stipulates, amongst other things, that advertisements should be legal, decent, honest and truthful and should conform to the principles of fair competition (Oosthuizen 1989:48).

Examples of the direct regulation by advertisers of media content do exist, but usually such regulation is exercised with the consent of the newspaper concerned. The "write-ups" done for advertisers in supplements are an example of such regulation. The use of write-ups is a common practice in community newspapers and amounts to advertisers buying newspaper copy.

Newspapers also have to take into account that they reach a particular type of reader who represents a specific market for the advertiser, thus a newspaper can lose advertisers if it suddenly changes its content to cater for a different type of reader. It can be seen, then, that changing of content is another form of indirect regulation. The demise of the *Rand Daily Mail* is an example of what happens as a result of this type of regulation. This newspaper (Oosthuizen et al 1991:124), under the editorship of Allistar Sparks, progressively increased its coverage of news events in the black community. For advertisers, however, the black community represented a market with a small per capita disposable income. The *Rand Daily Mail* therefore lost many of its advertisers and ultimately had to close down.

Payola is seen as the worst form of manipulation by advertisers (Oosthuizen et al 1991:124) and is, in essence, a form of bribery. Journalists receive gifts and perks from advertisers in return for publicity and good reviews of meetings, performances, products, and so forth. Such gifts and perks vary from presents (for instance liquor at Christmas), to complimentary tickets to performances for reviewers and promises of free cars for motoring journalists. In its worst form, payola involves cash payments to journalists. This practice, however, is restricted by the profession itself and, therefore, only occurs in secret.

## 4.3.5 The profession as regulator

Media workers or journalists do not differ much from other professional people such as doctors and attorneys. They have to make complicated decisions in their daily work, and they use ethical codes to guide them in making these decisions. These codes and the journalistic conventions or professional standards of the media workers are important determinants of newspaper content. Nevertheless, journalism differs from other professions in that journalists do not lose their jobs if they fail to observe these codes.

In South Africa, both the Broadcasting Complaints Commission of South Africa (BCCSA) and the Press Ombudsman (PO) have similar codes of conduct which broadcasting and press industry people respectively and voluntarily adhere to. The inception of these bodies in the middle of the nineties represented a clear shift from government-influenced self-regulation (the practice during apartheid) towards regulation by the profession itself – with the aim of serving the interests of the public (the result of the new dispensation).

Self-regulation by the profession can influence content on two levels. Firstly, by adhering to a code, journalists undertake to *do* certain things when they report (such as writing the truth, in an objective and balanced manner). They also undertake not to do certain things (such as, for example, not to publish the names of rape victims). If journalists don't adhere to their own codes, it militates very strongly against professional recognition in the society that they serve. It could also give a government an excuse to introduce formal regulation (Oosthuizen 1998:19).

### 4.3.6 The consumer as regulator

In the West, where capitalism forms the basis of the economy, the consumer (or reader) and the advertiser are probably the main regulators of the press. The operative principle here is supply and demand and this principle, together with the audience characteristics, determines the content of the newspaper.

It follows that a newspaper that fails to fulfil the needs of its readers will simply lose its readership and consequently its advertisers, until it is forced to close down. In 1987 it was calculated that daily newspapers in South Africa were dependent on advertisements for between 70 to 80 percent of their income (Oosthuizen et al 1991:124).

Newspapers therefore cannot afford to ignore the preferences of their readers. Hiebert et al (1991:110) point out that, apart from the fact that consumers use laws and courts to keep the media on their toes (and thus also to regulate them), most consumer regulation takes place in the market itself when the consumer decides which newspaper to buy. Publications that sell, remain in business.

The *Rand Daily Mail* is a good example of a South African newspaper that did not survive, partly because it did not fulfil the needs of its readers and advertisers (Jackson 1993:76). Years later, consumer resistance to the high selling price of the independent *Daily Mail* also contributed to the closure of this newspaper in 1990 (Oosthuizen 1996).

In terms of the marketing approach referred to earlier, a mass medium would typically investigate the needs of listeners, viewers or readers (the audience), and adapt content to serve these needs. Marketing research results of audience expectations could therefore influence the nature of news that a particular news medium chooses to publish.

Greater sensitivity to the market has also led to shorter news stories and better packaging of these stories (e.g. more colour and diagrams) in, for example, the print media. As a result there has been less space to address things like background. The focus has shifted to events – or an event orientation. Some people would argue that this tendency has short-changed readers on the background that they need to really understand what is going on around them.

## 4.4 THE IMPLICATIONS OF REGULATING

Regulating of the mass media can change the original or intended message of a particular medium. As we have seen, the role of governments is of particular importance in this regard. By using legislation, governments can

- exclude large parts of reality from the scrutiny of the press;

- confuse reporters with vague formulation of acts that could lead to self-censorship; and
- pressurise journalists into becoming less critical or not to report about controversial issues.

In its severest form (for example, as practised during apartheid) it results in a badly informed public that is not really in the position to make informed and/or quality decisions.

It should thus be clear that the government as regulator can seriously inhibit media freedom. The government restricts the media directly, by laying down penalties, and indirectly, through self-censorship by the media. In South Africa, prior to 1990, the media were powerless to do anything against the government's regulation and could, as a result, not fulfil their watchdog function properly (Oosthuizen 1989:45).

Besides the government, the other regulators also force the media to operate within certain constraints. Direct and indirect regulation takes place as a result.

### Case Study 4.1: Regulation: The telecommunication policy context in South Africa

The narrow articulation of the public interest by the previous government was also clearly reflected in telecommunication policy formulation and the implementation of this policy under apartheid. Although the values that have been used for the articulation of the public interest in the telecommunications sector differ slightly from that in the other media, freedom to have access to this sector as well as equality have also featured strongly in policy discourse here.

Initially, economic regulation (interference in the free market) played an integral part in global policy formulation in the telecommunication sector. Such regulation was instituted because it was deemed to be in the public interest. It was argued that – as in the case of water and electricity supply – the provision of telecommunication services (initially telephones) would be very costly. The main reason for this was the enormous cost of infrastructure roll-out in this sector (for example the installing of lines and exchanges). It was felt that because of these prohibitive costs, consumers would not necessarily derive the same benefits if competition between operators were allowed. If operators, for example, only concentrated on the more lucrative sections of the market (like more densely populated areas) people in rural areas would not necessarily get access to the telephone system – or would have to pay more for it. Post and telecommunications companies (and other sectors regarded as public utilities) were therefore awarded monopoly status to ensure efficient service at affordable prices on an equitable basis.

Regulation was therefore initially done on these grounds. The argument was that a better telephone service (using financial and social indicators) could be provided when more people had access to telephones. As a result, the whole idea of providing a universal telephone service became a key component in private and public telephone administrations and served as the determining principle for the management and regulation of the sector by different governments (cf. Oosthuizen 1997).

The provision of a universal telephone service – often just referred to as universal service – in broad terms made provision for the following:

> The provision of universal geographical access to telephones; on an equitable basis (minorities, for example, also had to get access); that would be affordable to all (at a fair price); that adhered to universal technological standards (so that systems could link up with one another – which also referred to the efficiency of the service) and would consequently ensure universal participation.

Because of the narrow articulation of the public interest in South Africa during the previous political dispensation, the application of universal service as a policy instrument reflected the historical inequities of this society. When the ANC came to power in 1994, in the region of 60 percent of the population still had no access to telephones. Access previously secured was done along racial lines with the consequence that most whites had access to telephones, and most blacks did not.

In terms of new legislation (policy) a Universal Service Agency is now in place that must ensure the promotion of universal service and universal access to telecommunication services in the country. As a result, twelve Telecentres are now up and running. Telkom's monopoly as a fixed line operator has also been extended. The rationale behind this is the same as monopoly provisions that were originally made for other telecommunication operators in other parts of the world. The idea is to give Telkom the opportunity – without having to worry about competition – to fast track the roll-out of expensive infrastructure as well as the installation of telephones to previously disadvantaged communities. In other words, this represents a catch-up exercise on universal service and access provision that is in line with the articulation of the public interest in democratic societies. Telkom has also been allowed to bring in equity partners to finance this venture and to assist with roll-out (Southern Bell (SBC) from the United States and Malaysia Telecom).

Meanwhile, the basis for telecommunication policy formulation in the Western world has moved away from equity and affordability to efficiency. South Africa has also had to take cognisance of the international trends that have led to this shift. These included the deregulation of telecommunications (as well as broadcasting); the phasing out of monopolies to become more efficient (once acceptable levels of equity had been attained); a reassessment of the role of the market versus the state; a shift towards longer-term goals and the growing emphasis on the needs of consumers. In terms of the growing globalisation of the world economy, South Africa – as for all other countries – will also have to make provision for the increasing impact of international role players on the local telecommunication policy context.

As a result, privatisation and competition are seen as inevitable policy directions in the global arena. Telkom's monopoly officially expires at the end of 2003 and moves were already afoot in 2000 (by companies such as Johnnic) to get into the fixed line operating business once competition is allowed. Once this sort of competition becomes a reality, one can expect improved emphasis on efficiency that should translate into better service to consumers and improved tariffs.

The telecommunication policy context underscores a point that is also of great relevance to traditional media policy formulation. That is that policy is never static and that it is formulated in a specific context. Present policy formulation in South Africa has obviously been influenced by the previous political dispensation but will also increasingly have to make provision for new trends in the international arena. Meanwhile technological developments – like the convergence between broadcasting and telecommunications – have also impacted on the regulation of both sectors. In South Africa it has resulted in the formation of the Independent Communications Authority of South Africa (ICASA) that will in future regulate both broadcasting and telecommunications in the country.

## Summary

In this unit we discussed the external policy framework of the media. We dealt with the nature of this framework in a democracy and discussed the role of regulators and how they articulated the public interest during the previous political dispensation. This position was compared to the present policy context. We concluded this unit by looking at the variables that are used for the articulation of the public interest in the telecommunication policy context.

## Research activities

1. Analyse a media policy issue. Collect newspaper reports or any information that you may find from other media, institutions, or the government, on the policy issue, recommendations and/or legislation. For example, a policy issue related to the public broadcasting service, or the ownership of the print media, or advertising regulation, or the Internet (ICTs), or telecommunications.

    a) Describe the policy issue and debate about it in detail.

    b) Analyse the policy issue you have selected in terms of the following value criteria:
    - Freedom: whether proposed policy complies with and will contribute to the freedom of expression, information, and so on.
    - Equality: whether policy will contribute to the levelling of the playing field for all stakeholders and to improved access to the media and information for the public.

- Order: whether the kind of regulation emanating from proposed policy is fair and what the execution of such policy will involve and cost.

2. Provide one of your own examples for each of the following forms of regulation with the purpose of indicating how these forms of regulation can impact on the media in general and on media content in particular:
   - Norms: an example of where the media, according to you, have displayed bad taste.
   - Pressure groups: an example of any pressure group complaining about and/or pressurising the media to change their reporting about the group and/or an issue.
   - Advertisers: any example about a controversy about an advertisement and/or advertising campaign and the media's reaction to it.
   - Consumers: any example of consumers (media audiences: readers, listeners and viewers) complaining about any aspect of the media.

3. Write, on the basis of the above exercises, a five-page essay in which you express your views on external media policy, in other words, regulation of the media from the outside.

## Further reading

Baran, SJ, McIntyre, JS & Meyer, TP. 1984. *Self, symbols & society: an introduction to mass communication*. Reading, MA: Addison-Wesley.

Bell, Dewar & Hall (Attorneys). 1990. *Kelsey Stuart's The newspaperman's guide to the law*. 5th edition. Durban: Butterworths.

DeFleur, ML & Dennis, EE. 1994. *Understanding mass communication*. 5th edition. Boston: Houghton Mifflin.

Gans, HJ. 1979. *Deciding what's news*. New York: Pantheon.

Hachten, WA & Giffard, CA. 1984. *Total onslaught. The South African press under attack*. Johannesburg: Macmillan.

Hiebert, RE, Ungurait, DF & Bohn, TW. 1991. *Mass media VI. An introduction to modern communication*. 6th edition. New York: Longman.

McQuail, D. 2000. *McQuail's mass communication theory*. 4th edition. London: Sage.

Oosthuizen, LM. 1989. *Media policy and ethics*. Cape Town: Juta.

## Bibliography

African National Congress. 1992a. African National Congress draft media charter in *Free, fair and open. South African media in the transition to democracy. Papers, recommendations and resolutions: Part 1*. Johannesburg: Campaign for Open Media.

African National Congress. May 1992b. *ANC policy guidelines for a democratic South Africa*:67-71.

African National Congress. 1994. *The reconstruction and development programme. A policy framework*. Johannesburg: Umanyano.

Brink, AP. 1980. Censorship and the author. *Critical Arts* 1(2):16-26.

Burns, Y. 1990. *Media law*. Durban: Butterworths.

Driver, D. 1980. Control of the black mind. *South African Outlook* 110 (1308):10-13.

Gerbner, G (ed). 1977. *Mass media policies in changing cultures.* New York: John Wiley.
Grange, H. 1990. Why did the *Daily Mail* fold? Verdict: not good enough. *The Journalist* November 6–7.
Gurevitch, M, Bennett, T, Curran, J & Woollacott. 1985. *Culture, society and the media.* London: Methuen.
Hachten, WA & Giffard, CA. 1984. *Total onslaught. The South African press under attack*: Johannesburg: Macmillan.
Harvey, CJD. 1970. The problem of censorship: by an ex-censor. *Bolt* 1(2&3):8–13.
Hiebert, RE, Ungurait, DF & Bohn, TW. 1991. *Mass media VI. An introduction to modern communication.* 6th edition. New York: Longman.
Holmes, D. 1986. Governing the press. *Media freedom in the U.S. and Great Britain.* Boulder CO: Westview.
Jay blameer die media vir dalende rand. 1996. *Beeld,* 2 Mei:1.
Marshall, PG. 1990. *Editorial Research* 1(31):478–490.
McQuail, D. 1987. *Mass media theory. An introduction.* London: Sage.
McQuail, D. 1993. *Media performance.* London: Sage.
Oosthuizen, LM. 1989. *Media policy and ethics.* Cape Town: Juta.
Oosthuizen, LM. 1990. Ideologie, media en Afrikaner-nasionalisme. *Communicatio* 16(1):38–48.
Oosthuizen, LM. 1991. Suid-Afrikaanse mediabeleid: die media se bondgenoot is soek. *Communicatio* 17(1):38–48.
Oosthuizen, LM. 1992. Issues in mass communication. *Only study guide for CMN 311–3.* Pretoria: University of South Africa.
Oosthuizen, LM. 1994. Blood and guts: ethical standards under pressure. *Dialogus* 1(2):3–4.
Oosthuizen, LM. 1995. Media policy on ownership. *Dialogus* 2(2):1–2.
Oosthuizen, LM (ed). 1996. *Introduction to communication – course book 5: journalism, press and radio studies.* Cape Town: Juta.
Oosthuizen, LM. 1997. Universal service: the South African context. Unpublished lecture. Pretoria: University of South Africa.
Oosthuizen, LM. 1998. Towards an ethical framework for the analysis of journalistic conduct in South Africa: *City Press* reporting Colin Chauke.
Oosthuizen, LM, Faure, C & De Wet, L. 1991. *Enigste studiegids vir CMN 207–4.* Pretoria: Universiteit van Suid-Afrika.
Potter, E. 1975. *The press as opposition: the political role of South African newspapers.* London: Chatto & Windus.
Robertson, G. 1983. *People against the press. An enquiry into the Press Council.* London: Quartet.
Roelofse, JJ. 1983. *Towards rational discourse. An analysis of the report of the Steyn Commission of Inquiry into the media.* Pretoria: Van Schaik.
Ruddock, R. 1981. *Ideologies. Five exploratory lectures.* Manchester Monographs 15. Manchester: Department of Adult and Higher Education, University of Manchester.
Snyman, PG. 1985. Informasie- en kommunikasiebeleid. Ongepubliseerde lesing. Potchefstroom: Potchefstroomse Universiteit vir CHO.
South Africa. 1958. *Police Act, no. 7 of 1958 (as amended).* Pretoria: Government Printer.
South Africa. 1959. *Prisons Act, no. 8 of 1959 (as amended).* Pretoria: Government Printer.
South Africa. 1974. *Publications Act, no. 42 of 1974.* Pretoria: Government Printer.
South Africa. 1977. *Criminal Procedures Act, no. 51 of 1977.* Pretoria: Government Printer.
South Africa. 1981. *Report of the commission of inquiry into the mass media.* Pretoria: Government Printer. Chairman: M Steyn.

South Africa. 1996. *Constitution of the Republic of South Africa, Act 108 of 1996.*
South Africa. 2000. *Promotion of Access to Information Act, no. 2 of 2000.* Pretoria: Government Printer.
Tomaselli, K, Tomaselli, R & Muller, J. 1987. *Narrating the crisis: hegemony and the South African press. Addressing the nation.* Johannesburg: Richard Lyon.
Tomaselli, R, Tomaselli, K & Muller, J (eds). 1989. *Currents of power: state broadcasting in South Africa. Addressing the nation.* Bellville: Anthropos.
Tunstall, J. 1983. *The media in Britain.* New York: Columbia University Press.
Van der Vyfer, JD. 1984. Persvryheid en die toekoms. *Saambou ASPU-bundel '84*:1–18.
Van Heerden, MM. 1995. Mediamonitor: April 1995-Julie 1995. *Dialogus* 2(2):6–8.
Viljoen, H. 1989. Noodtoestand en die wet. *Insig* Maart 1989.
Webber Wentzel. 1992. Submission on legal considerations for a free media in the transitional period, in *Free, fair and open. South African media in the transition to democracy. Papers, recommendations & resolutions: Part 1.* Johannesburg: Campaign for Open Media: Johannesburg.
*White Paper on the Reconstruction and Development Programme, No. 1608* 23 November 1994. Pretoria: Government Printer.

# 5
# The Internal Media Policy Framework

*Lucas M Oosthuizen*

## Overview

In this unit we discuss the following, as applied to the South African media:
- the concepts "gatekeeper" and "gatekeeping";
- charters, mission and/or vision statements, and news and programme policies as the basic documents of internal media policy;
- the influence of the external media policy framework on the internal media policy framework;
- the different internal gatekeepers: directorates, boards and group managers; editors, directors and managers, journalists and professional practices; and
- the implications of gatekeeping.

## Learning outcomes

At the end of the unit you should be able to write a critical essay in which you present your view, with examples, of the following factors playing a role in media gatekeeping:
- your understanding of the concepts "gatekeeper" and "gatekeeping";
- the impact of external media policy on internal media policy;
- the role of charters, mission and/or vision statements, news and programme policies as the basic documents of internal media policy;
- the role of directorates, boards and group managers in the process of gatekeeping;
- the role of editors, directors and departmental managers in the process of gatekeeping;
- the role of journalists in gatekeeping; and
- the impact of temporal and spatial factors, location, and sources on the content of news.

## 5.1 INTRODUCTION

The internal media policy framework refers to the policy made within the media by the media themselves. Although it is discussed as a separate entity in this unit, internal policy can obviously not be divorced from the external framework that we have

# MEDIA STUDIES

discussed in the previous unit. Internal policy is always formulated within the parameters of the external framework, and hence under the influence of the particular sociopolitical structure that is in place in a particular country (Oosthuizen 1989:13).

As Lee (1976) indicates, the media are linked to the economic and political structure (and also other features of the social structure) of a country. Media performance can, therefore, lead to policy formulation by a government. On the other hand, internal media policy is also influenced by external factors – such as a government decision to introduce subsidies, an advertiser's decision to withdraw advertisements and the broad expectations of media users in a particular society.

Internal media policy formulation takes place within the structure and operation of a medium itself. Gatekeepers are generally responsible for policy formulation on this level. Policy formulation can be spelt out explicitly, or can form part of implicit expectations – usually described as the right way of doing things in a particular organisation. The organisational structure and method of operation of the media set certain requirements for information and determine the value attached to that information (Oosthuizen 1989:14). Individual journalists learn to adhere to those requirements in their daily work. We will return to gatekeeping in more detail later. First a closer look at what we are going to discuss in this unit.

In this unit we will deal with the following:

- Where policy formulation features in the internal framework
- How the external framework influences internal policy formulation
- The role of gatekeepers and how they influence the content of the news media.

## 5.2 INTERNAL POLICY FORMULATION

We have already seen that the media can explicitly spell out internal policy. But where do we find it – or look for it? As in the case of the previous unit, the emphasis in our discussion in this regard, will be on the news media.

### 5.2.1 The charter, mission or vision statements

The broad policy of a mass medium is usually set out in a charter, credo, declaration or statement of intent. In media management terms one would, therefore, also find policy of this nature in the mission statement of a media organisation.

A mission statement usually states why the medium is being established and, either directly or by implication, whose interests it will serve. Such interests could include those of shareholders, advertisers, the personnel of the company and the public – or media users.

Policymakers on this level include control boards in the case of broadcast media, and boards of directors and trustees in the case of the print media. They often have "allocative control" – in the sense that they have the power to determine the overall objectives and scope of the media institution and how its productive resources are to be developed. "Thus they lay down the overall policy and strategy of the medium, decide on expansion and rationalisation, develop its basic financial policy and control the distribution of profits" (Oosthuizen 1989:14).

Not all mass media spell out their policy in the same manner and detail. In some instances a medium might not even have a charter or a mission statement. Policy principles emanating from top management can be decided upon in the course of a meeting or simply be communicated downwards by the managing director (or chairman of the board). Policy can also be integrated as part of the conditions of service of individual journalists.

A charter or mission statement can also reflect a perception of communication and of the way in which the medium – radio, newspaper and television – is to be used in society. Naturally the envisaged role of a medium in society can also change or be revised. A good example is the values and vision statement of the Board of the South African Broadcasting Corporation (SABC Board) that was published just before democratic elections took place in this country in 1994. It clearly articulated a move away from alignment with the former National Party government (cf. Oosthuizen 1989) towards a role more in line with the position of a bona fide public broadcaster.

The Board formulated the following values:

- Accountability to the full spectrum of the South African public for providing accessible, high quality broadcasting services.
- Commitment to the truth.
- Impartiality, equitability and fairness to all people without regard to any divisive features or characteristics.
- Sensitivity to the diverse nature of South African society and the need for justice and healing.
- Compassion and concern for human dignity, the people, life and the environment.
- A common "South Africanness".
- Integrity, transparency and trust in all relationships.
- Professionalism in quality, efficiency, reliability, management and financial accountability.
- Equity and equal opportunities in all employment programmes and practices.
- Commitment to independence and autonomy of the SABC.

Based on these values they came up with the following vision:

> South Africa, deeply divided and emerging from an apartheid structure, is striving for democracy and the elimination of discrimination on the basis of race, gender, age, disability, religion, class or language. In this context, a public broadcaster has to play a prominent role in supporting that process.

Accordingly the SABC will:

- Be an impartial public broadcaster that continually develops its independence and autonomy while being responsive to the needs of the public to which it is accountable.

- Be fair and just to all the peoples of South Africa, irrespective of any divisive features or characteristics. To this end it will be affirmative in its approach in addressing historic imbalances, and will consciously address itself to playing a positive healing role and developing a common "South Africanness".
- Deliver accessible broadcasting services of equal quality to the full spectrum of its audience.
- Meet the challenge of growing local and international competition where it is a threat to the general interests of the South African public.
- Be stable and "sustainably" funded in order to comply with its accountability to the broader public interest.
- Maintain an editorial policy and ethos that corresponds to its values and vision and through which society is portrayed consistently to itself, in its diversity.
- Have a culture and mindset consistent with its values and vision.
- Be a fair employer with exemplary labour practices, with staffing at all levels being reflective of South African society and maintaining appropriately high levels of competence.

(South African Broadcasting Corporation 1994:3-4)

### 5.2.2 News and programme policy

Policy on this level deals with the content or composition of a news medium. Such policy is often expressed in terms of concepts such as news policy (in the case of the print media) and programme policy (in the case of broadcasting) (Oosthuizen 1989:14-16).

This policy usually determines what a medium will present (for example the different subjects focused on in news) and how it will be presented (prominence or angle). News or programme policy is based on the intentions expressed in the charter, mission or vision statements. Such policy is not necessarily codified; it could, for example, be formulated on an ad hoc basis during meetings and communicated downwards in the form of directives.

Were a medium's charter to promise support for a certain political party, for example, this support would usually be reflected in the medium's content. This will then manifest in the nature of coverage given to the party (probably mostly positive coverage) and the prominence given to its activities by way of placement and layout (more prominence than other parties) (Oosthuizen 1989:15). Such political allegiances of the media are of course not always published.

When internal policy stipulations are published, they often form part of the standard editorial guidelines of that specific medium. In the case of the SABC, editorial guidelines make provision for the following:

- Acceptance of editorial authority, control and responsibility over the content of all programmes broadcast over its facilities.
- Practical guidelines for journalists which include:
  1. Non-interference with the free dissemination of information.
  2. Verification of the accuracy of facts and the reliability of sources.

# The Internal Media Policy Framework

    3    Protecting the confidentiality of sources.
    4    The clear labelling of opinion and commentary as such (not presenting it as news).
    5    The full and prompt correction of errors.
    6    Not misleading the public by staging or rehearsing material and presenting it as spontaneous news.
    7    Making every effort to present all sides of an issue.
    8    A provision for the analysis of situations without including personal opinions on people, events and ideas.
    9    A restriction on ties with any political or financial organisations.
    10   A restriction on journalists to accept gifts or favours of any sort in the course of their professional duties.

- A general adherence to the principles of accuracy, fairness, balance and impartiality as well as to the public's right to know (which also makes provision for the diverse interests of the whole population).
- Compliance to the laws of the country.
- A reasonable discussion of conflicting views – which includes the right to reply – during the reporting of politics and elections. The equitable and fair treatment of all political parties – with "particular attention" to major political parties and views. This section also has guidelines for the reporting of specific programme formats.
- Maintaining acceptable production standards. This section includes guidelines pertaining to the reporting of opinion polls, the handling of privacy issues, the protection of sources, the rights of interviewees, payment for news, the warning of people prior to publishing offensive of disturbing material, and so forth.
- Guidelines for investigative reporting – which include the legal and ethical care that should be taken during such endeavours.
- Other issues pertaining to journalists – like the handling of conflict of interests, promotional activities and so on.
- A referral system to deal with difficult editorial issues.

(South African Broadcasting Corporation 1994:16–120)

The above editorial guidelines (internal policy formulation) were the result of contributions by many individuals and organisations. These included the journalists of the SABC, the South African Union of Journalists, the Public Broadcasting Initiative, the Campaign for Open Media, and the Institute for the Advancement of Journalism, the Canadian Broadcasting Corporation and the Australian Broadcasting Corporation.

    Internal policy formulation does not always result from such a broad input base. On a more operational level, the principal policymakers of news and programme policy could also be individual editors (print media) and directors general or chief executive officers (in the case of broadcasting). They typically serve as links between their respective boards and the editorial staff and must, therefore, see to it that the objectives set by the directors/control board are achieved. Internal policy formulation could then be used to this end. On the other hand, policymakers are also typically responsible for policy formulation in the specific medium on a day-to-day basis – which they issue downwards. These policy stipulations could vary from instructions on which, how many and in what way political meetings will be covered before an election, to decisions on how topics such as terrorism, obscenity and violence are treated in or by a medium (cf. Oosthuizen 1989).

The treatment of the topics mentioned here underlines the impact of the external framework on the internal framework. We will now take a closer look at the effect of the external framework on internal policy formulation.

## 5.3 INFLUENCE OF THE EXTERNAL POLICY FRAMEWORK ON THE INTERNAL FRAMEWORK

It is important to understand that internal policy formulation takes place within the parameters of the external policy framework. Let us again use the SABC as an example. As we have seen in the previous section, a new political dispensation clearly impacted on the expected role of the SABC in South African society. This, in turn, led to a new value and vision statement – which is an example of internal policy formulation. Broad societal expectations – articulated in and by a new political dispensation (part of the external framework) – therefore impacted directly on the internal policy formulation of South Africa's public broadcaster.

The new political dispensation also led to changes in the legal framework in this country. As we have seen in the previous unit, the media were severely regulated under apartheid. These restrictions (part of the external framework) directly impacted on what the media could and could not publish on a daily basis (their internal policy formulation). The unbanning of political organisations and political leaders in February 1990 had an immediate impact on internal media policy. A newspaper like *New Nation* for example, could openly lend its support to the African National Congress (ANC) and the South African Communist Party (SACP). It did so by commenting under the banners of these two organisations in a special cover page of its edition of 2–8 February 1990. A week prior to State President FW de Klerk's groundbreaking speech in parliament on 2 February 1990, this would not have been possible.

Since then many of the laws that restricted the media have been scrapped or amended (see the previous unit), resulting in a more liberal working environment for the media and individual journalists. The media must, however, still take the legal framework into consideration in their day-to-day operations. As we have seen in this section, the SABC's editorial guidelines also make explicit provision for adherence to the laws of the country. Non-adherence could lead to formal prosecution – a possibility of which all media organisations must take cognisance. As a general rule, legal advice is sought when media managers are in any doubt as to whether a report transgresses the law. If this is not done, it could lead to costly and time-consuming court cases.

In the case of internal policy formulation, non-adherence does not lead to formal prosecution. It could lead to internal action being taken against individual journalists who have transgressed editorial policy – for example disciplinary steps or even informal castigation. In other instances management could allow non-adherence when they, for example, deem it to be in the public interest.

The formulation and publication of internal editorial guidelines by a media concern is indicative of the professionalism and social responsibility of that particular media company. Non-adherence could unfortunately have the opposite effect. A public broadcaster, in particular, should take cognisance of this fact because it is accountable to the full spectrum of the public that it serves.

Violations and potential violations by the SABC of its own internal policy under the new political dispensation have not gone unnoticed. The following incidents have raised eyebrows:

- The dismissal of Max du Preez, presenter of the programme *Special Assignment*, in 1999. The Freedom of Expression Institute (FXI) argued that the dismissal was unfair and that various transgressions of editorial independence preceded his dismissal. In a press release (cf. FXI 1999, 6 May) the organisation argued that the broadcaster, in its dealings with Du Preez:

  1 compromised the values and vision of the SABC – and in particular the commitment to truth, transparency, balanced coverage and accountability to viewers and listeners;
  2 failed to give him the opportunity to state his case before dismissing him. In their view his dismissal constituted an unfair labour practice and was indicative of the plight of many SABC staffers who have been treated in this manner;
  3 used the public broadcaster to settle their own petty fights with Du Preez – denying him a say and pressurising those who chose to present fair and balanced reports on the alleged dispute;
  4 punished those who worked with him, in particular black documentary filmmakers of a "pulled" (not aired) witchcraft programme for *Special Assignment*. The filmmakers were allegedly "blacklisted" and told that they "would never work for the SABC again" (FXI 1999, 6 May:1–5).

- A refusal of the SABC to provide information to the FXI in a subsequent editorial independence inquiry. They FXI stated that it was appalled at the refusal and that it showed that the SABC was not prepared to allow public scrutiny of employment practices that could have a direct impact on the editorial freedom and independence in the news room (FXI 1999, 23 July:1).
- Dissatisfaction with the findings of the SABC Task Team that dealt with this matter (the editorial independence inquiry). Cutting and pulling of stories were dismissed as common editorial practice by the task team, while it in actual fact boiled down to internal censorship by management, the FXI said. The institute cited an example where a story that involved the Minister of Welfare and Pensions was "corrected" by editorial management after the Minister phoned the SABC to complain about the coverage of the story (FXI 1999, 4 November:1).

MEDIA STUDIES

- In June 2000 it was reported that the SABC Board intended to refer three senior appointments – including the appointment of the Chief Executive Officer (CEO) of the SABC – to the Cabinet for approval. Opposition parties said that they would challenge the proposal (cf. *Mail & Guardian*, 6-12 October 2000) because it would put the Government in the position to exercise political control over the SABC. The Freedom of Expression Institute warned that the SABC's right to pursue journalistic, creative and programming independence could not be protected if Cabinet was allowed to appoint people to such key positions. The Institute said it could lead to interference in the affairs of the corporation and compromise the integrity of the Board.

The last of these examples again underlines the (potential) influence of the external framework on internal policy formulation. As a whole, these incidents could also negatively impact on the role of the SABC as a public broadcaster.

In the previous dispensation the SABC clearly deviated from its mandate as public broadcaster. The SABC at that time:

- Represented the ruling group.
- Became the public relations mouthpiece of the government.
- Preferred to scrap programmes if there was any doubt as to their acceptability to the government.
- Had to cope with numerous instances of direct government interference (Oosthuizen 1989:56-61).

As a result, the SABC – although it was modelled on the British Broadcasting Corporation's public broadcasting model – had more in common with broadcasting services in the rest of Africa, where the utilisation of broadcasting for party political purposes is quite common.

The deviations from its own internal policy framework in the present dispensation should therefore be of serious concern to all media scholars. It is imperative that a public broadcaster, like the SABC, does not lose sight of its values and vision and accountability to the broad public. If it does, it could very easily lose credibility as an unbiased server of the broader public interest.

The internal policy formulation of the SABC that we have dealt with here is a good example of explicit policy formulation. The SABC has formulated values, a vision and editorial guidelines that you can read and evaluate. Not all policy formulation in the media is explicitly codified – as we have remarked earlier. It can also be formulated implicitly. The people, parties or institutions that influence the content of the media from the inside – known as gatekeepers – can be responsible for both implicit and explicit policy formulation. Let us take a closer look at what gatekeeping is about.

## 5.4 GATEKEEPING

Gatekeeping can be defined as the process through which certain information passes a series of checkpoints (gates) before being finally accepted as news material. Gatekeepers are the people or groups that have an impact on this process. They are part of the news organisation and their influence can also extend beyond the daily tasks of news identification, newsgathering and publication.

As far as news, in particular, is concerned, gatekeepers primarily decide what is going to appear and how it is going to appear in the media. On the issue of "what" will be published or presented, gatekeeping could be regarded as essential. Most news media receive more news than allowed for in terms of space (newspapers) or time (radio and television). From this glut, only that which is regarded as the most important is selected and, in the process, some of the news is discarded or left out. As a result, readers, viewers and listeners are presented with only a part of daily reality.

Once gatekeepers have selected the news events that they want to publish, they allot varying amounts of space (in newspapers) or time (on radio and television) to news items. This leads to the emphasis or de-emphasis of certain news events. If they allot more space or time to an event, it means that they regard it as being more important. In the case of radio and television, the chronology of events is also important. The main or most important news is always presented first. Less important events are dealt with later. In the case of newspapers, the most important news – in the view of the particular news medium – is published on page one.

Apart from selection and emphasis or placement, gatekeepers can also delete from and insert material into existent news reports. For all these actions, they use a variety of standards – aesthetic, financial, or those stemming from a professional or organisational code (cf. Hiebert, Ungurait & Bohn 1991:14). The actions of gatekeepers could be guided by (or lead to) explicit or implicit policy formulation. In addition, the external framework could also influence gatekeeping.

The following types of gatekeepers are discussed below: directorates, boards and group managers; editors, directors general and departmental managers; administrative-hierarchical gatekeeping, certain temporal and spatial factors, location and sources.

## 5.4.1 Directorates, boards and group managers

Directorates, boards and group managers can intervene in the content of a news medium – if they want to. It is, however, not viewed or accepted as common practice in most democracies. Directorates and boards usually restrict themselves to giving certain broad guidelines to editors (or heads of broadcasting stations or programmes) about the operation of the particular medium.

As DeFleur and Dennis point out (1994:403), "the owners or their corporate representatives at the top seldom exert direct control over specific news stories, but they set broad guidelines as to which styles of journalism are to be emphasized and where the organization will locate itself along a liberal to conservative continuum" (cf. Van Heerden 1996).

Boards or similar structures are therefore likely to perform their financial and managerial functions and leave it up to the editor or people in similar positions to determine the content of a publication or station. There is at least one very obvious reason for this practice. In most democracies, privately funded news media are seen as independent purveyors of news – because of the fact that the news is reported and managed by media professionals. When owners or managers interfere in media content, this independence as well as the credibility of the medium comes under pressure – because of the outside interests that (potentially) interfere with the news. In such instances, conflict between journalists and management is not uncommon. Even interference with advertising policy is viewed as undesirable.

An excellent example to illustrate the effect of management interference is that of when the managing director of the Independent (newspaper) Group in Western Cape Province, Shaun Johnson, decided to give free advertising space to the Government to promote its controversial views on HIV/Aids in October 2000. It sparked off a row between editors and management and led to a meeting between disgruntled editors and the CEO of the company, Ivan Fallon. Fallon flew in from London to attend the meeting. The decision to give free advertising space to the Government raised serious questions about the relationship between Independent and the Government (*Mail & Guardian*, 13-19 October 2000:1, 5).

In a leader article the *Mail & Guardian* made the following very relevant remarks about this incident:

- The management of the group showed an inability to understand the concept of editorial freedom.
- Editors carry overall responsibility for the presentation of a newspaper to the public – which includes advertising content. In this instance, the management of the Independent group did in some instances not even inform editors that the advertisements were going to be published in their newspapers.
- The fact that the advertisements coincided with a debate in parliament (about the Government's stand on the Aids-issue) suggested further abuse of the editorial function by the management of Independent Newspapers.
- It could be interpreted as a joint effort by management and the Government to seize editorial space and control at the expense of editors and editorial staff and to secretly manipulate public opinion on this issue.
- The attempt (of the executives of the group) to curry favour with the Government, boded ill for the independence of the group from government interference (*Mail & Guardian*, 13-19 October 2000:26).

The above incident could also be an indication of the Government's (potential) influence as regulator (see the previous unit) in the external framework, on gatekeeping in the internal framework. The Government's reservations about foreign ownership of the media have been widely published in the past. Whether this stance led to the decision by the Independent group management to award them the free advertising space, is an open question.

During the previous dispensation (potential) political influence by boards of directors on newspaper content was structurally more apparent. During the seventies, for example, it was common practice among Afrikaans newspapers to appoint members of the Cabinet to their boards of directors and this sometimes led to the politicisation of the content of certain newspapers.

Examples of members of the Cabinet who served on Perskor's board of directors during the seventies were Minister Ben Schoeman, who was the chairman of the board, and ministers MC Botha, Connie Mulder, Fanie Botha, Hendrik Schoeman and Marais Viljoen. At the same time, Cabinet ministers who served on the board of Nasionale Pers were PW Botha – then Minister of Defence – and ministers Piet Koornhof, Fanie Botha and Dr Nak van der Merwe.

The way in which these two press groups and their directorates handled the Information Scandal (Muldergate) was very different. The scandal was revealed in 1978 by English newspapers such as the *Rand Daily Mail* and the *Sunday Express*, and concerned the covert and illegal activities of the Department of Information and some government ministers. Vast sums of government monies were used "to win friends and to punish the enemies of South Africa both at home and abroad" (Hachten & Giffard 1984:6). In one instance an estimated R32 million was used to fund *The Citizen*, a newspaper that had to provide editorial support for the National Party (cf. Hachten & Giffard 1984:229-261 for more detail on the Information Scandal). In the process, the government became a direct regulator of content and – one would assume – also influenced the appointment of this newspaper's management.

The way in which Perskor's newspapers (e.g. *Die Transvaler*) reported on the scandal made it obvious that the group was much more sympathetic towards cabinet ministers involved in the scandal than the directorate of Nasionale Pers was (Oosthuizen, Faure & De Wet 1991:126). One of the reasons for this type of gatekeeping could have been that Information Minister Connie Mulder was a director of Perskor at the time.

Fortunately there was a visible decline in the eighties in the tendency of South African newspapers to nominate politicians to their boards of directors. In comparison with previous years, the content of certain newspapers, such as *Die Transvaler*, was noticeably less politicised in later years. According to Jackson (1993:101), Nasionale Pers also relaxed the political and ideological guidelines that influenced its activities. He states that when Nasionale Pers bought *City Press*, a black weekly newspaper in Johannesburg, it left the staff free to pursue their own editorial policy and that Percy Qoboza, the newspaper's editor until 1988, was known as one of the government's most articulate critics (cf. Van Heerden 1996).

However, the same group did not show the same leniency with some of its other publications. In 1987 Dene Smuts, the editor of *Fair Lady*, resigned after Nasionale Pers barred her from publishing an article on Dr Dennis Worrall, an independent candidate in the election (Oosthuizen et al 1991:127). Worrall stood against a Government minister, Chris Heunis, and won the seat.

To conclude this section, it is important to note that the potential influence of financial interests on media content has markedly increased over the last twenty years. The reason for this tendency has been the introduction of the marketing approach –

where a news medium is primarily viewed as a link between advertisers and consumers. The strategy has been introduced to ensure the financial survival of the media in an increasingly competitive environment. As a result, the authority of financial managers and their influence on the content of publications and stations have increased. Managers now play a far greater role to ensure that media content optimally serves the respective interests of media users and advertisers. The approach has not only led to a change in media content but also to a decrease in editorial autonomy of individual journalists (cf. Underwood 1993).

Historically, financial and political influence on media content has obviously gone hand in hand in this country. As Tyson (1993:366) points out, the bottom line is, of course, "that no political party newspaper is going to tolerate political deviation from policy – and no owner of a commercially independent newspaper is going to leave an editor to his own devices if it means losing millions of rands" (cf. Van Heerden 1996). For this reason the directorates and managers of media companies will remain major potential gatekeepers of media content. Proving such influence empirically is always fairly difficult.

### 5.4.2 Editors, directors general and departmental managers

The structure of the print media and broadcasting differs markedly on this level. We will therefore discuss these structures separately.

*Print media*

The editor of a newspaper acts as a link between the directorate and the editorial staff (journalists). It is the editor who ultimately determines the policy of a newspaper and who has to make sure that this policy is carried out. The actual responsibility for the newspaper is thus lodged with the newspaper's editor (Gans 1979:85). As a result, the editor of a newspaper is usually the one who is held responsible for a newspaper's rise or fall, for its successes or failures. Because the editor is also the one who must answer to the newspaper's directorate, he or she is often made a scapegoat if something "goes wrong" (cf. Van Heerden 1996).

Editors should thus perform their tasks in accordance with the broad guidelines laid down by their board of directors. If they do not keep to these guidelines, it can lead to conflict. In the past South African editors such as Allistar Sparks of the *Rand Daily Mail* and Willem de Klerk of *Die Transvaler* have been dismissed because they have clashed with their boards of directors (Tyson 1993:366).

As Gans points out (1979:85), news organisations are not democratic and the editors, and sometimes their assistants, have the power to decide what gets into print. It is therefore obvious that editors can act as strict gatekeepers and that they can discard or ignore stories or news items that do not conform to their own beliefs or policies. In this way news can be distorted. As Rothman and Lichter (1984:47) argue, editors' perceptions of the world "help filter reality for the rest of society".

Although editors are usually only responsible for the writing of editorial comment or articles on the editorial pages of the newspaper, their influence is also evident in other parts of the newspaper. For instance, the change of editors of the now defunct *Die Transvaler* in 1987 was accompanied by a dramatic change in the appearance of the newspaper. The newspaper received a new nameplate, headings were set in upper case, and a new series of "exclusive articles" appeared in the newspaper (Oosthuizen et al 1991:127). When Allistar Sparks became editor of the *Rand Daily Mail* in 1977, his influence was very clearly seen in, amongst other things, the policy of the newspaper, which remained liberal despite the board's wishes for a more conservative line. According to Mervis (1989:473), this editor was dictating to the board (cf. Van Heerden 1996). The taking over of Perskor by Caxton in the late nineties culminated in the appointment of a new editor, Tim du Plessis, to head their daily newspaper *The Citizen*. His appointment coincided with gradual changes in the editorial content of the newspaper to cater for the needs of its majority black readership.

## *Broadcasting*

In the case of broadcasting, directors general fulfil a similar role to that of editors in the print media. When there is direct government influence on a public broadcasting system, the position of a director general can become quite precarious. Under the previous dispensation Wynand Harmse (director general of the SABC in the eighties), for example, pointed out that political news policy at that stage specified that the SABC would not offer a platform for revolutionary groups or promote extra parliamentary politics: "In the event of the SABC's interpretation of the national interest corresponding with the actions of government, the corporation will naturally be inclined to reflect this in its programmes," he remarked (Harmse 1989:30–31). According to Harmse it was difficult to cross swords with the government of the day, since they appointed the board of control that determined SABC policy (Oosthuizen 1989:59). If the appointment of the CEO of the SABC will have to be approved by Cabinet in future (see the previous section), the incumbent will probably be in a worse position than previous directors general when it comes to independent decision making. The potential influence of the external framework on internal policy formulation could therefore increase as a result.

The management of different programme genres in broadcasting, obviously leaves more room for the managers of those genres (like news) to exert influence on programme content. On this score recent developments at the SABC have also been alarming. In its response to the findings of the SABC Task Team into editorial independence and other matters, the FXI pointed out in 1999 that it was surprising that the report vindicated the "unhealthy practice" of editorial managers like Snuki Zikalala and Phil Molefe acting as journalists at the same time. In a press release the FXI stated:

> Their (the Task Team's) motivation for vindicating this practice is that other broadcasters allow it. We have spoken to trade unions and management in both the BBC and the Australian Broadcasting Corporation, and they have roundly

condemned this practice on the basis that editorial managers are simply too close to management to be able to act as journalists in an unbiased manner. The fact that the report glosses over the deep problems inherent in blurring the lines between editorial and management is alarming.

(Freedom of Expression Institute 1999. Press release, 4 November)

In the above instance the managers in question did not only serve as gatekeepers, but were actively involved in the creation of content. In terms of the public broadcasting model, this is clearly not deemed desirable.

### 5.4.3 Administrative-hierarchical gatekeeping: journalistic and professional practices

Gatekeeping is often affected by journalists' own desire for promotion and their need to protect their jobs and avoid conflict. These personal needs sometimes force journalists to conform to the organisational culture (ways of doing things) that employs them. Journalists also tend to work for publications whose policies broadly correspond with their own views (Oosthuizen et al 1991:127). In this regard their performance is often guided by "the right way of doing things around here".

Journalists whose reports do not conform to the norms and standards of the institution that employs them can expect opposition and trouble, especially from their superiors. The news editor plays an important part with regard to reports, and many journalists can attest to incidents where unacceptable reports were published either inconspicuously or not at all.

Other members of a news medium's editorial hierarchy, for instance the chief sub-editor and sub-editors, play similar gatekeeping roles. They can change a report beyond recognition and can even insist that it be rewritten. As gatekeepers, sub-editors can change the emphasis of a report by assigning it a particular position, using a certain size of heading (in the case of the print media), and combining it with other reports (cf. Oosthuizen et al 1991).

Journalists do not control story selection and, although they can suggest stories or propose dropping them if the necessary information is lacking, their main role is story production (Gans 1979:85). News editors and sub-editors therefore both supervise and influence the work of the journalists (cf. Van Heerden 1996).

### *Temporal and spatial factors*

Temporal and spatial factors can also serve as gatekeepers. These factors come into play during both newsgathering and news construction which will be dealt with in more detail in Unit 14 on the critical assessment of news.

Let's first take a look at the influence of time. The general rule in the news media is that old news is no news. For this reason, time is very important in the selection of news. A recent or fresh news story has a much better chance of appearing in the news media than an outdated story.

Time is also part and parcel of news production. In the case of newspapers, we distinguish between morning, noon and evening newspapers. These newspapers all have specific deadlines for different pages, and these deadlines have to be met to ensure uninterrupted production. A report that is finished after the deadline cannot be considered for publication. In this way deadlines contribute to story selection (Gans 1979:109) or act as gatekeepers.

The centre pages of a newspaper usually have to be ready first. Because fresher and more important news appears at the front of the newspaper, these pages, and the corresponding back pages, are published last. An event that occurs after midnight will probably not be covered in the rural edition of a morning newspaper. In this case, time acts as a gatekeeper because it excludes certain news from a particular edition.

The deadline for front-page news in a noon newspaper could be approximately 10:00. News received after 10:00 would normally be covered in the second edition, or the first edition would merely contain a brief reference to it (Oosthuizen et al 1991:128). However, a scoop is often more important to a newspaper than any other factor when deciding on the selection and prominence of news (cf. McQuail 1987:164). Newspapers are always on the lookout for a scoop because it is news that will be published in advance of rival newspapers. For this reason a deadline could be extended to accommodate a scoop. If the scoop takes up a lot of space, other news items will be omitted.

In the case of a radio station with hourly news bulletins, news can of course be updated on a regular basis and can provide for the latest news – events that have occurred during the last hour. However, as with television, time is a huge constraint.

There is only limited time available for a newscast. As a result, news stories on radio basically only provide for the broadcasting of news headlines – in other words much shorter news stories. Television news is also limited by the time allotted to the newscast in the programme schedule. In both instances (radio and television) time therefore has a direct influence on the number and scope of stories that can be presented as news and will lead to omission of certain news events.

In the case of newspapers, space fulfils an important gatekeeping role. The number of advertisements often determines the size of a newspaper because "advertising is an important source of financial support for newspapers" (DeFleur & Dennis 1994:80). If many advertisements are placed in a newspaper, more space is available for news as well. The editor may, for instance, have enough news to fill 125 columns, but because of the lack of advertisements, only 75 columns of space may be available for the publication of news. This means that news is selected – and some news consequently omitted – because of limited space (cf. Van Heerden 1996).

## *Location*

The significance of location in newsgathering and selection should not be overlooked. The place or location where newsworthy events occur is often an important gatekeeper. According to McQuail (1987:164), the planning of news coverage involves a set of presuppositions about where news is likely to happen, which will have a certain self-fulfilling tendency. Certain places have over the years become established as sites for events and these places are usually well covered by the gatherers of news. The capitals of countries are, for instance, better covered by journalists than small, unknown villages in remote areas. News is thus not as readily reported from locations where sudden or unexpected events occur (cf. Van Heerden 1996).

In recent years the rationalisation of editorial staff – for economic reasons – has increased the potential influence of location as gatekeeper. A panel of South African newspaper editors therefore concurred during a conference in the middle nineties that as a result of staff cutbacks no newspaper of record existed in South Africa any longer. *The Citizen* was cited as the only possible exception. The reliance of the latter newspaper on news agency copy, however, raised questions about the influence of news agencies on *The Citizen's* content.

Physical proximity is another important factor in the selection of news. Newspapers and national broadcasters tend to pay more attention to events that are close to home than to events that occur far away from their readers or audiences. The argument is that "the nearer the location of news events is to the city, region or nation of the intended audience, the more likely it is to be attended to" (McQuail 1987:165).

Coverage of local events sometimes also differs from the coverage of similar events that happen in other countries. In the reporting of terrorism, for example, countries tend to stick to official versions of such events (as described by government ministers or security personnel) when they happen at home. When such events happen in other countries, they sometimes deviate from the official perspective by, for example, elaborating on the reasons why terrorists are perpetrating their acts of violence in that particular country.

Cultural proximity can also be an important gatekeeper. According to Hartley (1982:77), events that correspond with the cultural background of the audience and the news gatherers are regarded as more meaningful than others, and will therefore be more likely to be selected as news. We will deal with these and other factors that influence news selection in more detail later when we discuss the phenomenon of news.

## Sources

A prestigious or authoritative source of news – for instance a political leader or a famous academic – often acts as the first gatekeeper of news. Such a person's judgement of what should be disclosed at a press conference, a meeting or in an interview is already selective. According to Gans (1979:116), the news is usually also weighted towards sources which are eager to provide information.

Furthermore, "each newspaper prefers to quote certain people rather than others as sources of news" (Oosthuizen et al 1991:128), either because journalists have built up good relationships with certain contacts or because staff and time are in short supply. Journalists, therefore, actively pursue only a small number of regular sources that have been available and suitable in the past (Gans 1979:116). According to McQuail (1987:157), some sources are also more powerful than others or they have more bargaining power because of their status, market dominance or intrinsic market value. McQuail (1987:163) says that news "is often reports of what prominent people say about events rather than reports of the events themselves".

Editorial staff will seldom question the statements of sources that have acquired a certain status with their newspaper. Such sources would, therefore, be in a better position than other sources to distort or withhold information from the newspaper. Such sources can thus act as gatekeepers because they can personally influence the news that originates from them. For this reason a journalist's preference for a certain source can also lead to gatekeeping. Because journalists use their own or their newspapers' trusted sources and are reluctant to approach other sources about the topic in question, news reports can be influenced and distorted, and biased information is sometimes published (cf. Van Heerden 1996; Oosthuizen et al 1991).

## 5.5 IMPLICATIONS OF GATEKEEPING

The primary effect of gatekeeping, and also of regulation, is that it changes the media's original message in some way. What readers read in a newspaper – or hear or see on radio and television – is thus seldom an accurate reflection of reality.

Though gatekeeping is introduced by the media themselves, it also seriously influences the content of newspapers. It leads to the evaluation of news and the creation of news reality. With regard to gatekeeping, Hiebert et al (1991:91) say that "most media regulation starts internally, and that media's self-censorship can often be more crucial than outside pressures".

The main implications of gatekeeping in the media are that certain events are selected to be published as news and that the details of these events are published in a certain way. The individual preferences of, for instance, news editors and journalists are important in gatekeeping. Such gatekeeping can, however, never be at odds with the value system of the institution – that is, the newspaper or station – concerned. Gatekeeping remains a necessity so long as it is not used consciously to obscure facts or slant the perception of the reader or audience. When used deliberately to mislead, gatekeeping becomes unacceptable (cf. Van Heerden 1996).

# Summary

In this unit we have looked at the nature of the internal media policy framework. We have identified the different spheres where such policy formulation takes place and used the internal policy formulation of the SABC as an example to explain internal policy formulation in media institutions. We concluded this unit with a discussion of the various people and groups (gatekeepers) that influence internal policy formulation in the news media.

## Research activities

1. Obtain three different morning newspapers of your choice that appeared on the same day. Compare the stories and pictures on page 1 of each of the newspapers by using the following criteria:

   a) Identify the stories that all the newspapers have covered (stories about the same event). Compare the contents of these stories and identify the information that these stories have in common. Now take a look at the information that the stories don't share. How does this information alter your understanding of the news events reported in each of the newspapers?

   b) Based on this exercise, write an essay of three pages about the possible influence of gatekeepers on readers. Also take the stories into consideration that were unique to each individual newspaper. Use the contents of this unit as general background to substantiate your views.

## Further reading

Croteau, D & Hoynes, W. 1999. *Media/Society: industries, images and audiences.* London: Sage.
European Research Group. 1998. *Media policy: convergence, concentration and commerce.* London: Sage.
Gans, HJ. 1979. *Deciding what's news.* New York: Pantheon.
Jackson, G.S. 1993. *Breaking story. The South African press.* Boulder, CO:Westview.
Manning, P. 2000. *News and news sources: a critical introduction.* London: Sage
Tyson, H. 1993. *Editors under fire.* Sandton: Random House.
Thompson, K. 1997. *Media and cultural regulation.* London: Sage.
Underwood, D. 1993. *When MBA's rule the newsroom. How the marketers and managers are reshaping today's media.* New York: Columbia University Press.
Van Heerden, MM. 1996. Gatekeeping and regulating, in *Introduction to Communication: journalism, press and radio studies,* edited by LM Oosthuizen. Cape Town: Juta.

## Bibliography

DeFleur, ML & Dennis, EE. 1994. *Understanding mass communication.* New York: Random House.
Freedom of Expression Institute 1999. Press Release, 6 May.
Freedom of Expression Institute 1999. Press Release, 23 July.
Freedom of Expression Institute 1999. Press Release, 4 November.
Gans, HJ. 1979. *Deciding what's news.* New York: Pantheon.
Hachten, WA & Giffard, CA. 1984. *Total onslaught. The South African press under attack.* Johannesburg: Macmillan.
Harmse, W. 1989. SABC builds understanding. *RSA Policy Review* 2(1):27–48.
Hartley, J. 1982. *Understanding news.* London: Methuen.
Hiebert, RE, Ungurait, DF & Bohn, TW 1991. *Mass media VI. An introduction to modern communication.* New York: Longman.
Jackson, GS. 1993. *Breaking story. The South African press.* Boulder, CO:Westview.

Lee, JAR. 1976. *Towards realistic communication policies: recent trends and ideas compiled and analysed.* Pretoria: University of South Africa.
*Mail & Guardian*, 6-12 October 2000.
*Mail & Guardian*, 13-19 October 2000:1&5.
*Mail & Guardian* Leader article, 13-19 October 2000:26.
McQuail, D. 1987. *Mass communication theory: an introduction.* London: Sage.
Mervis, J. 1989. *The fourth estate: a newspaper story.* Johannesburg: Jonathan Ball.
Oosthuizen, LM. 1989. *Media policy and ethics.* Cape Town: Juta.
Oosthuizen, LM. 1992. Critical issues in mass communication. *Only study guide for CMN 311-3.* Pretoria: University of South Africa.
Oosthuizen, LM, Faure, C & De Wet, L. 1991. Print media. *Only study guide for CMN 207-4.* Pretoria: University of South Africa.
Rothman, S & Lichter, R. 1984. Personality, ideology and world view: a comparison of media and business elites. *British Journal of Political Science* 15:29-49.
South African Broadcasting Corporation 1994. *Ethical code and editorial guidelines for editorial staff March 1994* (unpublished).
Underwood, D. 1993. *When MBA's rule the newsroom. How the marketers and managers are reshaping today's media.* New York: Columbia University Press.
Van Heerden, MM. 1996. Gatekeeping and regulating in *Introduction to Communication: journalism, press and radio studies*, edited by LM Oosthuizen. Cape Town: Juta.

# Part B
# Media Theory

**Unit 6**
Mass Communication Theory

**Unit 7**
The Role and Functions of the Media: Functionalism

**Unit 8**
The Effects and Power of Mass Communication

**Unit 9**
Media and Ideology

**Unit 10**
Media and the Production of Meaning: Semiotics

**Unit 11**
Media and Culture

**Unit 12**
Feminist Media Theory

# Mass Communication Theory 6

*Pieter J Fourie*

## Overview

In Part A, the focus was on media institutions. Before we look at specific theories in units 7–12, the purpose of this unit is to
- define mass communication;
- discuss some of the issues related to the complexity of mass communication as a phenomenon;
- give an overview of some of the models of mass communication;
- explain what theory is;
- briefly discuss the main paradigms in mass communication theory and research; and
- situate mass communication in the context of public communication culture.

## Learning outcomes

After you have completed this unit you should be able to
- define mass communication with a critical awareness of issues related to
  - the communicator in mass communication
  - the nature of the medium in mass communication
  - the concepts "message", "text" and "media content"
  - mass communication audiences
  - the concept "mass"
  - the media as public sphere
  - the concept "mediation"
  - the nature of mass communication's media culture
- describe the main features (transmission, feedback, gatekeeping, interpretation, context, perception and individualism) of three mass communication models;
- explain, with examples, McQuail's (2000) typology of mass communication models;
- design your own mass communication model taking into account the gaps in the three models discussed and against the background of the focal points in our definition of mass communication;
- describe the value, goals and building blocks of theory and the criteria for the evaluation of theory;
- apply this knowledge (on the basis of your acquired knowledge of what theory is) to your own theory of the media based on your everyday experience of the media;

- give an overview of the main paradigms in mass communication theory and research with reference to empirical, critical and technological theory and research;
- critically reflect on the nature and value of our present day public communication culture with specific reference to commodification and commercialism.

## 6.1 DEFINING MASS COMMUNICATION

Mass communication can be defined in a number of ways, especially against the background of the latest developments in information and communication technology (ICT). ICT has increased the number and kinds of media involved in transmitting messages of various kinds and in various formats to bigger, increasingly heterogeneous and global audiences.

Mass communication can also be defined from various perspectives, each with its own emphasis on one or another aspect of mass communication. McQuail (2000:7) distinguishes four theoretical perspectives, from each of which mass communication can be defined. These theoretical perspectives are:

- Media-culturalist perspective: In definitions of this kind the emphasis is on the content, reception and environment (context) of the communication. For example, definitions of mass communication from a media-culturalist perspective will emphasise the nature of media content (information, entertainment, propaganda, and so on) and how the content is received and interpreted by different audiences in different circumstances, for instance in rural versus urban circumstances.
- Media-materialist perspective: The emphasis is on the technical aspects and how the technology of a medium impacts on the nature of media messages and audiences. For example, it is possible to differentiate between radio and television as media of mass communication because each medium involves different technologies, encodes their messages differently, and (can) reach different audiences who relate differently to the different media.
- Social-culturalist perspective: In this perspective the influence of social factors on media production and reception and the functions of the media in social life is emphasised.
- Social-materialist perspective: The media and their content are mainly seen as a reflection of the material conditions of a society. For example, media and media audiences in developed countries may differ from that in developing and in poor countries. Such differences will effect definitions and perceptions of what mass communication is, and can be. Given South Africa's development needs we may define mass communication differently from definitions (and perceptions) attributed to it in Europe.

Whatever the perspective and emphasis in a definition may be, certain focal points are always present (Berger 1995:4). The focal points are the communicator, the medium, the message, the recipient or audience, the public nature of mass communication, and the diverse content of mass communication. Around these focal points it is possible to at least formulate a working definition such as the following:

> Mass communication involves the production of a large variety of messages (usually) by an institutional group or a collective communicator. The messages are distributed and transmitted (usually) by means of technological media (channels) to reach large, heterogeneous and widely dispersed audiences who may interpret the messages in a variety of ways. The content of mass communication is a mix of information, views, entertainment and advertisements. The purpose is to mediate meaning and understanding, either overtly and/or covertly. By achieving this, the media create a unique kind of public sphere, are seen to be one of the primary producers of mass/popular culture and a culture in and for itself. An outstanding feature of mass communication is its publicness compared to the private nature of other forms or levels of communication.

This may sound like a simplistic definition, but it raises a number of questions and issues that have been and are debated in critical media studies. In the following section we will briefly discuss *some* of these issues with the purpose of making it clear that a single definition of mass communication is not easy to formulate. We will do this by way of asking a number of questions.

Our discussion of these questions and possible answers do not pretend to cover every aspect or to pre-empt the issues.

## 6.1.1 Questions related to a definition of mass communication

### Who is the communicator?

In interpersonal and group communication it is not that difficult to identify the communicator. In mass communication, however, the communicator is usually a collective body. In other words, a group of people responsible for the production of programmes, news bulletins, films, a newspaper, Web sites on the Internet, and so on. For example, although the names of individuals (the director, the designer, the camera operator, and so forth) responsible for a television programme are shown in the credits at the end of a programme, it remains difficult to pinpoint a single communicator. Apart from the people responsible for the production of a programme, one might well ask whether the communicator(s) is not the presenter(s) of a programme. Furthermore, one must also consider the managers and owners of the television station. Although they may not be overtly involved with the production and presentation of a programme, they are responsible for policy. In the case of newspapers, and although a journalist's name may be published with his/her story, the journalist forms part of a group consisting of editors, managers, a board of directors and other journalists who are expected to support a newspaper's values, ideology and codes of conduct.

The issue of identifying a single communicator in mass communication can have far-reaching implications when questions of responsibility, objectivity (in the case of news and comment), liability and other such matters arise. Without pinpointing a single communicator, public service broadcasting, for example, is often blamed collectively for being the mouthpiece of a ruling government. All individual journalists and programme producers are then labelled as being "government agents".

From an artistic point of view it is also difficult to credit the real artist (communicator) in film, television and radio. In the so-called high art forms such as literature, poetry, music, and so on, it is easy to subscribe the work of art to the intellect and skills of a single person. In film, television and radio this is more difficult and one of the reasons why these symbolic forms of expression are often not seen as art but rather as popular culture. For example, who is the artist (communicator) of a film? The director? The cinematographer? The sound engineer? The costume designer? The author of the screenplay? Or the producer (manager/ financier)?

## What do we mean by "medium"?

In mass communication, the medium (plural media) is, for example, radio, television, film, newspapers, magazines, the Internet, videos, CDs, and sound cassettes. The medium is usually of a technical nature and can involve complicated production and distribution technologies and techniques. It also requires that audiences or a member of a media audience must have the technological means to receive the transmitted messages, for example, a transistor radio or a television set, as well as the financial means to buy a newspaper or a magazine, a computer, a video player, and so on. In using the term "medium" we also mean the channel through which the media content is transmitted and distributed. In short, a single description of the medium in mass communication is much more complex than in the case of other forms of communication, such as for instance interpersonal communication. In interpersonal communication the medium is the human body and all its communicative facilities. With the latest technological developments, multimedia are also increasingly utilised within a single medium. In this regard we referred in Unit 2 to the SABC's radio station, Radiosondergrense. This radio station is no longer just a radio station communicating through the technology of radio, but it is also available on the Internet, satellite television and so on, and is thus making use of the technologies of all these media.

## What is the message?

The message has both concrete and abstract form. It is concrete in the form of the content being produced: the newspaper story you can see and read, the television programme you can see, the radio programme you can hear, and so on. Put in another way, the concrete content of the media is a whole range of stories in a newspaper varying from political commentary to sport, crime, economy, leisure, recipes, cartoons, disaster reports and the like; different television and radio programmes; different films on a whole range of topics, themes and genres; and the overwhelming content of the Internet. Thus, the concrete message is referred to as the text and/or media content. The message is abstract in terms of the meaning encoded in the content by the communicator and the meaning you attach to and derive from the content through your own interpretation of the content. Message thus also refers to signification (see Unit 10 on semiotics and the production of meaning). From the above it is clear that in mass communication you should always be very specific when you use the concept "message". Do you refer to the concrete content or to the meaning(s) entrenched in the content which can be different to different people?

## What do we mean by "audience"?

The audience is the listeners, viewers, and readers. Media audiences in mass communication are heterogeneous and usually unknown to the communicator. With the latest developments in interactivity, all this is, however, beginning to change (cf. the Radiosondergrense example already referred to). At the most the communicator can target a specific group, for example a specific language group, regional group, income group, or age group, but it remains a broad group within which numerous differences as far as education, culture, taste, political views, needs, opinions and perceptions exist. Media audiences usually receive and use media messages either as individuals (one person reading a newspaper, looking at a film, viewing a television programme, listening to a radio programme, surfing the Net) or within a small or larger group (for example a family or group of friends watching a television programme, or an audience in a film theatre). With the development of ICTs, media audiences are increasingly global. For example, multinational media corporations produce media content such as films, television programmes, magazine articles, comics, and so on, to be read and viewed by audiences from all over the world. Lately a newspaper from a specific country, for example South Africa's *Mail & Guardian* can be read on the Internet in almost any place in the world. The same applies to the availability of radio programmes on the Internet and the distribution of radio programmes on international radio channels such as the World Radio Network which you could access, at the time of writing, on the frequencies of the SABC's English radio service SAfm after midnight.

## What do we mean by the "mass" in mass communication?

The concept "mass" is controversial and has been debated and thoroughly discussed in social and mass society theory (cf. O'Sullivan, Hartley, Saunders, Montgomery & Fiske 1994:173). From an élitist point of view, "mass" carries negative meanings. The negative connotation to the concept "mass" originated in the 1930s from cultural and literary critics who were sceptical about the impact of industrialisation and urbanisation on humankind and society. It was believed that the industrialisation of labour (the move from the production of primarily agricultural products to the formalised and mass production of consumer goods in a goods economy) and its associated urbanisation (from rural communities to cities), created a citizenry

- made up of a vast workforce of atomised, isolated individuals without traditional bonds of locality or kinship
- alienated from their work because of its repetitive and unskilled tendencies (usually associated with factory work) and
- subject to the totalitarian ideologies of employers (the ruling class), political leaders, and propaganda from the media.

It was furthermore believed that the mass (created by the above conditions) couldn't think for themselves and were to be educated. Such education and what it should involve was to be defined by the élite.

The media and the growth of the media were seen to be part and parcel of industrialisation and urbanisation, and the disciples of the ruling class. (It was in this period that public service broadcasting, with its patriarchal top-down communication approach to "educate" people, originated.)

With the growth of modern and postmodern society, the growth of economic and educational upliftment, the growth of democracy, and against the background of globalisation, the concept "mass" with its associated negative connotations has fallen in dispute. As far as the media are concerned, research has proven that media users are not powerless victims of media messages (cf. Unit 8 on the effects of the media). To the contrary, the media are increasingly seen to be a pillar of democracy in the sense that the media (can) provide people with a wide range of (critical) opinions on matters of public interest.

Nevertheless, the term "mass" communication remains. There is, however, a scholarly debate as to whether it should not be replaced with "public communication".

## What do we mean by "communication" in mass communication?

Strictly speaking, communication means dialogue towards mutual understanding. It means a two-way exchange with mutual feedback between a communicator and a recipient in reciprocal roles. Against the background of such a definition of communication, mass communication isn't communication. It is mainly one-way communication from a (collective) communicator to a recipient(s) unseen by the communicator; to a recipient(s) in a different physical environment; different mental frame of mind; different contexts and circumstances; and not known to the communicator. "One-way communication" is understood to mean the dissemination and distribution of information and entertainment from a source to multiple recipients. In mass communication, feedback existed only in the form of letters to newspapers, and telephone calls to radio and television stations.

However, the above view of mass communication as one-way communication is changing rapidly with the development of ICTs, the introduction of new genres (or programme types), and a general change in the ethos of mass communication from a patriarchal top-down approach to participation with and between communicators and recipients. The development of information and communication technologies has introduced the possibilities of interactivity. Especially, the Internet has created platforms for continued feedback between communicators and recipients and communication among recipients. Via the Internet, recipients can enter into electronic newspaper debates on numerous topics, cast their votes on numerous topics related to matters of public interest, and come into contact with one another by joining Internet chat rooms. (Whether computer-mediated communication is "real" communication is a complex topic of scholarly debate and investigation.) Radio and television have introduced popular programme formats such as talk shows and phone-in programmes in which viewers and listeners can air their views on numerous topics. Furthermore, it seems as if there is a general trend in newspapers to provide more space for the publication of readers' letters and by so doing creating platforms for public debate. Lately some newspapers also publish the e-mail addresses of their journalists who can then be contacted by members of the public.

In short, against the background of the development of ICTs it is obvious that the concept of "feedback" will gain new meaning and that the lack of feedback in mass communication will no longer be a distinct characteristic of mass communication.

Closely related to the discussion of the nature of mass communication as communication, are the issues of the media as the public sphere, the concept "publicness", and the role of mass communication in democracy. It seems as if the most distinct characteristic of mass communication will be its publicness.

## What do we mean by "public sphere", "publicness" and "democracy"?

If we argue that one of the outstanding characteristics of mass communication is its publicness, then this concept and its relatedness to the concepts public sphere and democracy, needs further explanation.

By "publicness" we mean the act of making something public, which is one of the primary tasks of the media. By making something public (whether it is the exposure of corruption, the exposure of increased violence and crime in a society, political debates, economic developments, and even the private affairs of a public figure) the media claim to contribute to democracy and even to be a pillar of democracy. The media provide a platform for public debate and the formation of public opinion. The space, area or terrain in which, by whom, and on what topics public opinion is formed, is called the public sphere.

To be an authentic public sphere, there are several requirements:

- open access
- voluntary participation
- participation outside institutional roles
- the generation of public opinion through assemblies of citizens who engage in rational argument
- the freedom to express opinions
- the freedom to discuss matters of the state

- the freedom to criticise the way state power is organised.
  (Thompson 1997:37)

For the media to be an authentic public sphere, the above prerequisites mean that the media must be open to all people who voluntarily want to participate in the formation of public opinion, who can do so despite their standing or position in society, who must be free to associate with whomever and whatever opinion they want to and to express their opinions, free to discuss matters of the state, and free to criticise the way state power is organised, or whatever else may be criticised.

The constitutions of most democratic societies guarantee that these requirements can be met. However, although the role of the media to make public and to contribute to informed public opinion(s) is acknowledged and valued, much disillusionment exists about

- how the media sometimes go about making something public, and
- whether everything claimed by the media to be of public interest is really of public interest.

Against the background of such criticism the German social scientist, Jürgen Habermas argues that the media often contribute to the disintegration of the public sphere. Briefly and here simplified, Habermas (1984) argues that saloons and coffee houses in Paris and London of the late seventeenth and eighteenth centuries became the centres of public discussion and debate. Here private individuals discussed issues of public concern. The discussions were facilitated by the publication of news sheets and newspapers, which in themselves became the forum of political debate where people could criticise the actions of government. Habermas argues that this public sphere

- embodied the idea of a community of citizens
- coming together as equals in a forum within civil society
- distinct from the authority of the state and the private sphere of the family
- capable of forming public opinion through rational debate (cf. Thompson 1997:37).

Thus, for Habermas, "public sphere" first of all, and ideally, means a domain of our social life in which such a thing as public opinion can be formed. Access to the public sphere is in principle open to all citizens. A portion of the public sphere is constituted in every conversation in which private persons come together to form a public. They are then acting neither as business or professional people conducting their private affairs, nor as legal consociates subject to the legal regulations of a state bureaucracy and obligated to obedience. Citizens act as a public when they deal with matters of general interest without being subject to coercion; thus with the guarantee that they may assemble and unite freely, and express and publicise their opinions freely.

Lately, instead of facilitating public opinion on matters of public interest, the media rather *produce*, *manage* and *guide* public opinion in a certain direction in an institutionalised way. By "institutionalised way" we mean that only a few people control what goes into the media, what we get to read, listen to and see on television. These

# Mass Communication Theory

people produce a media-manufactured public opinion. It is a public opinion that Habermas labels as *ersatz* public opinion and which has the following influence:

> Whereas at one time publicness was intended to subject persons or things to the public use of reason and to make political decisions subject to revision before the tribunal of public opinion, today it has often enough already been enlisted in the aid of the secret policies of interest groups; in the form of "publicity" it now acquires public prestige for persons or things and renders them capable of acclamation in a climate of nonpublic opinion. The term "public relations" itself indicates how a public sphere that formerly emerged from the structure of society must now be produced circumstantially on a case-by-case basis.
>
> (Habermas in Rheingold 1997:404)

The public sphere and democracy (see above requirements for the public sphere to exist) were born at the same time and from the same sources. But now, the idea that public opinion can be institutionally, centrally and globally *manufactured*, and the fact that electronic spectacle can capture the attention of a majority of the citizenry, damages the foundations of the public sphere and with it the foundations of democracy.

Chronologically, the media's role in the decline of the (ideal) public sphere can be described as follows:

- The print media of the nineteenth century gained more and more power to reshape the nature of public discourse – in other words a platform for discussing public issues.
- The birth of advertising and the public relations industry began to undermine the public sphere by inventing a kind of buyable and sellable phoney discourse that displaced the genuine kind of public sphere.
- In the twentieth century the telephone, radio and television became vehicles for the simulation (and therefore destruction) of authentic discourse, the "quantum leap" into the society of the spectacle, and the world's slide into hyper-reality.
- Apart from the above, commercialisation and commodification of public discourse, we are now faced with the effects of the Internet on public discourse, the public sphere and democracy. To many authors the greatest threat of the Internet to the public sphere is the so-called electronic or computerised democracy it prophesies, and the problem of privacy (cf. Rheingold 1997; and Unit 19 on globalisation).

A less pessimistic author about the media as public sphere and the relationship between media and democracy is Thompson (1995). He acknowledges the threat of media conglomerates and globalisation to the freedom of expression, but he nevertheless argues for a re-invention of our conceptualisation of "publicness", and thus for a re-invention of what we understand as the "public sphere". He contends that our ways of thinking about politics have been profoundly shaped by a certain model of what public life should be. This is a model derived from the assemblies of the classical Greek city-states in which individuals came together in the same spatio-temporal setting to discuss issues of common concern. Apart from the differences between classical Greek society and complex modern societies, the development of the mass communication media has created a new kind of publicness.

We should rather acknowledge how modern media and its communication have created new forms of publicness: a publicness not localised in space and time, and which is non-dialogical in character. This means an investigation of the new kind of publicness created by the media and an analysis of its characteristics. Such an analysis, as Thompson argues, will open up new possibilities as far as the nature and role of the media (cf. Unit 7) in the development of democracy are concerned.

The author then distinguishes between representative, participative and deliberative democracy and the role of the media (mediated democracy) contributing to what he sees as the ideal form of democracy (against the background of the failures of representative and participating democracy), namely deliberative democracy. In a deliberative democracy, the central role of the media as the modern public sphere can and should be acknowledged. In other words, instead of facilitating or manufacturing public opinion, the role of the media in a deliberative democracy could be one of providing a platform of deliberation and negotiation and of playing a role in such deliberation and negotiation. According to Thompson (op cit) media policy and regulation should have as its primary concern the empowerment of the media to play such a role.

## What do we mean by "meaning", "understanding" and "mediation"?

The concept "meaning" is dealt with in more detail in Unit 10 on semiotics. The units on ideology (Unit 9), culture (Unit 11) and representation (Unit 15) also deal with meaning. These units explain how the media as mass communication produce meaning by making use of specific codes in order to provide us on a daily basis with an interpretation of what is going on in reality; by focusing on certain topics and ignoring others, and by presenting a picture of reality to us in a certain way. By "reality" we mean the crime, politics, economics, arts, entertainment, fashion, sport, government, education, and so on, taking place in real life. In the unit on ideology it is argued that the media form our ways of thinking about and experiencing reality. Much of what we, as ordinary citizens, know about, for example politics, economics, crime, and so on, in South Africa, and what and how we think about what is going on in our society, we derive from media content. In Unit 6 (Volume 2) on reception theory, the emphasis is on the ways we as audiences of the media interpret media messages and in so doing how we ourselves create meaning by interpreting media messages in certain ways. Each of these above-mentioned units emphasises a specific approach to meaning and the relationship between the media and meaning.

What all of them have in common is the mediating role played by the media. By mediation (cf. Grossberg, Wartella & Whitney 1998:14–15) we can mean all of the following:
- The media provide a medium or a channel through which people send their messages; for example the government uses the media as a channel to send messages about its decisions to the citizenry.

- The media mediate between people and groups and thus provide a platform for mediation, occupying a middle position between people and groups in an attempt to reconcile. For example, through the media politicians explain their actions to the citizenry; the media provide an interpretation thereof by consulting and publishing the views of other spokespersons, interest groups and so forth. In turn, the citizenry can make their views known to the government by writing letters to newspapers, phoning radio stations, participating in television programmes and debating on the Internet.

However, at the same time mediation also means that the media

- replace the real with a representation and interpretation of the real. In other words, we should always keep in mind that a report by the media on whatever it may be is never the real thing. For example, a report about a disaster or a debate in parliament is not the real accident or debate, but a representation thereof.

By so doing, the media

- create a new a space of experience, interpretation and meaning, and
- a unique kind of relationship between producers (of media messages) and the consumers of these messages (readers, listeners, viewers).

Grossberg et al (1998:15) therefore rightfully argue that the notion of mass communication through the means of media embodies a number of senses of the term "mediation":

- reconciliation, the difference between reality and an image or interpretation of reality
- the space of interpretation between subject and reality
- the connection that creates the circuit of the communication of meaning.

This complexity helps to explain the apparently contradictory effects of communication in society; but it also helps us to understand why it so difficult to arrive at a singular understanding of the process of [mass – PJF] communication.
(Grossberg et al, op cit)

## What do we mean by "mass/popular culture"?

The concepts "culture" and "media culture" are explained in more depth in **Unit** 11 (Media and culture). Here, it suffices to say that the media as an institution is often explained and criticised as being a culture of its own and for itself and that media culture (the culture created by the media) can be explained as being a popular/mass culture often with all the negative connotations associated with the concepts "mass" and "popular". Hereafter we will only refer to popular culture. We base our explanation mainly on the work of Gitlin (1981) and Hartley, Goulden and O'Sullivan (1985).

Popular culture, compared to other forms of culture, is seen as the product and direct result of technologisation, industrialisation, urbanisation and commercialisation. Compared with the popular culture of earlier societies, which was spontaneously developed and used by people, today's popular culture is known by the fact that it is produced in bulk by a complex and multibillion-dollar industry. This complex production process is particularly relevant to the so-called information and entertainment industry, which aims to sell itself to the masses for mass consumption (also see Hartley et al 1985:7–12).

Unlike other earlier societies, popular culture in today's society is, therefore, purposefully produced as a product, with mass consumption envisaged.

Gitlin (1981) shows that through the ages all societies have had popular culture. People have always articulated meaning in some or other symbolic form. In the Neolithic society (the final period of the Stone Age), people in Europe, India, Africa and Australia spontaneously started creating artistic work (e.g. cave art) for functional and artistic purposes. In Greek and Roman times, the theatre, street shows and gatherings, ballad singers, troubadours, and so on, expressed social and political issues of the day in prose form. Today these forms of expression are regarded as art or *high* culture.

According to Gitlin (1981), early popular culture was characterised by meanings that were aesthetic and at the same time religious, political, or simply incarnations of everyday sentiment. Early popular culture exhorted, celebrated, cautioned, and denounced; it embodied morality and provided release from it; it gave pleasure and attached that pleasure to particular symbolic constructions. Because its artefacts were concrete, popular culture could make values stand forth to be recognised, appreciated, refined, and if need be, rejected. Social identity, whether of class, region, nation, community, religion, people, or political ideal, could become publicly manifest when it was embedded in the stone and glass of cathedrals, in the rituals of dance and passion of play, in song and in story (Gitlin 1981:202).

Although the same qualities might apply to contemporary popular culture, it is distinguished from previous forms of popular culture at the following levels:

- Popular culture is (usually multinationally) centrally and corporatively produced for private consumption by members of the mass society. An example is Hollywood, known as the world's entertainment industry par excellence. Hollywood produces entertainment that is used by individual members throughout the world, without these members having any part in the production of the entertainment and/or the meaning of this entertainment itself. These products do not address or symbolically reflect individuals' personal, cultural values and issues, as was the case in earlier societies.
- Contemporary popular culture is accessible to all and even enters the private domain. For example: today television is accessible to almost everyone, it is easily available, cheap and has practically become standard equipment and entertainment in private homes. The earlier forms of popular culture were, for example, limited to the town square, the regular carnival and/or the marketplace, traditional ceremonies and the church, and were only physically accessible to those who could attend, participate and afford it.
- Popular culture is known by rhythmic and cyclical mass production based on style and fads for the sake of maximum and continued income for the producers. An

appropriate example is found, for example, in pop stars' music and their influence on fashion fads.
- Popular culture is recognised by its secular nature. Unlike the popular culture of earlier societies that testified to spiritually and religiously symbolic meanings, popular culture today mainly aims at the secular and the here and the now. The meaning of popular culture is mainly ideological by nature. However, the viewer is seldom conscious of these meanings, and neither is it expected of the viewer to be conscious of ideological and other meanings (cf. Hartley et al 1985:8–9).

## Summary

In the above section we raised some issues debated in media studies about mass communication. We focused on some of the problems in:
- identifying the communicator in mass communication;
- the complexity of the concept "medium" in mass communication;
- the different meanings of the concept "message";
- the nature of the concept "media audiences" and how the nature of media audiences is changing against the background of the development of interactivity;
- the negativity attached to the concept "mass";
- how mass communication was traditionally seen to be one-way, top-down communication and as such not "real" communication, but how, with the development of ICTs and the growing possibilities of interactivity and new ways of feedback, this is changing rapidly;
- the importance of publicness as a distinct characteristic of mass communication and the role of the media in fabricating a public opinion instead of providing a public sphere in which a public opinion can be deliberated;
- the mediating role of the media and the different interpretations that can be given to the concept "mediation"; and
- the media as popular culture and as a producer of popular culture.

We conclude that mass communication and its media are complex phenomena that can hardly be defined in a single definition. This is especially true with the rapid development of ICTs and their impact on traditional mass media: their modes of productions, their content, their relationships with audiences, their technologies and the changing nature of media audiences themselves.

In the next part of this unit the focus is on mass communication models.

## 6.2 MODELS OF MASS COMMUNICATION

The purpose of the previous section was to provide you with a definition of mass communication and to draw your attention to some of the theoretical (and practical) issues related to different aspects of mass communication. The purpose of this section is to provide you with graphic representations of the elements involved in the process of mass communication, in other words, with models of mass communication.

Models are usually graphic representations of the key elements in a process with the purpose of showing the links between the different elements. Mass communication models focus on the links between, for example, media institutions, communicators, messages, recipients (audiences) and society.

Usually a model is based on or the result of a specific theory and research. At the same time models provide a basis for research and the kind of questions that can be asked related to one or more of the elements listed in a model. Put in another way, all theories involve models, but not all models are theories. Models may only suggest ways of viewing communication phenomena or suggest, without mandating, specific theoretical predictions (cf. Perry 1996:39).

The value of models is that they

- help us to visualise abstract ideas,
- guide our analytical thinking, and
- help us determine what to study and research.

In the case of mass communication there are many models based on many theories developed by many researchers and theorists over a period of time (cf. for example Berger 1995; Littlejohn 1992; McQuail 2000; McQuail & Windahl 1993; Wood 2000).

These models range from simplistic linear models such as

Source → Message → Channel → Receiver

to complex convergence models such as the Kincaid and Schramm model (1975) which concludes that although understanding is the aim of all communication, perfect understanding cannot occur (cf. Perry 1996:45).

What is important to remember is that each model usually emphasises something different in the process of mass communication, and as such contributes to our better understanding of the mass communication phenomenon.

For the purpose of this unit we refer to only three almost classic (from historical and foundational interest) models of mass communication, each emphasising a different aspect of mass communication. They are:

- Shannon and Weaver's (1949) mathematical model in which the transfer of information is emphasised
- Westley and MacLean's (1957) model in which feedback is emphasised
- Gerbner's (1967) model in which interpretation and context is emphasised.

### Shannon and Weaver

One of the first models used to describe mass communication research graphically, and an example of a linear (one-way) model, was Shannon and Weaver's mathematical model (1949).

## Mass Communication Theory

|Information source | Transmitter | | Receiver | Destination |

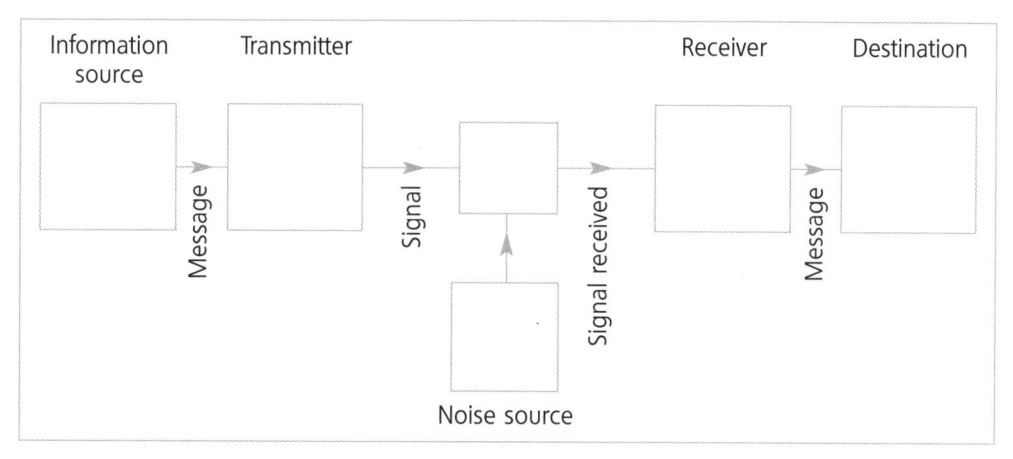

Figure 6.1 Shannon and Weaver's (1949) information theory model

The above graphic representation means the following:

A source expresses a message chosen from many possible messages. The message is sent through a transmitter which changes the message into a signal which is carried through a channel (that may encounter some noise – interference) to a receiver that translates the signal back into a message which is carried to a destination who interprets it.

Applying this model, for example, to radio communication, the model will look as follows:

A source (*radio journalist*) expresses (*formulates*) a message (*news story*) chosen from many possible messages. The message (*formulated in, for example the English language*) is sent through a transmitter (*transmission technology*) which changes the message into a signal (*sound waves*) which is carried through a channel (*signal distributor*) (that may encounter some noise – interference – *atmospheric interference*) to a receiver (*transistor radio*) that translates the signal back into a message which is carried to a destination (*the radio listener*) who *interprets* it.

This model was applied for many years to any situation of information transfer, whether by humans, machines or other systems. For many years it guided research about what information (compared to communication) is, how information is transferred, what the obstacles are in the transfer of information, and how information is interpreted by recipients. However, a gap in the model is that it doesn't provide for feedback – in other words feedback from the recipient to the communicator.

### *Westley and MacLean*

Westley and MacLean's (1957) model is still widely used. It emphasises feedback, the sequence of events in mass communication, the relationship between the elements in the process of mass communication, and the fact that mass communication is part of a larger social system (McQuail 1984:171).

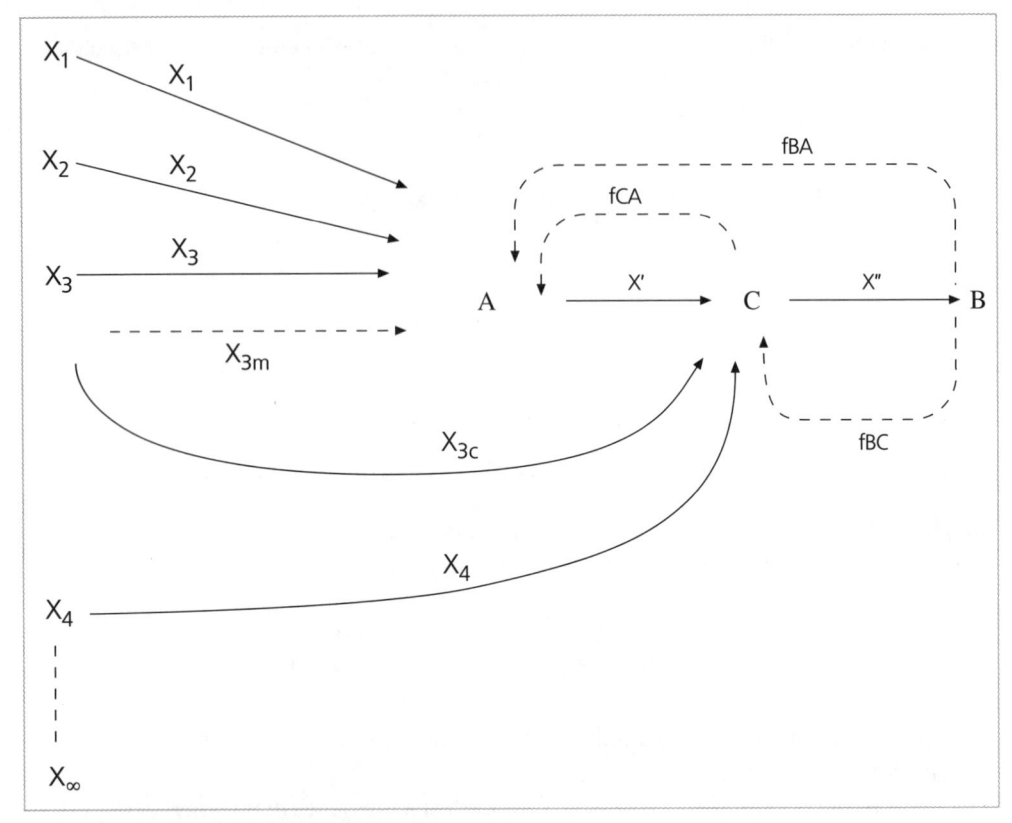

**Figure 6.2 Westley and MacLean's (1957) model of mass communication**

The symbols in the model mean the following:
A: the would-be communicator or "advocate"
B: the audience member (recipient)
C: the mass communication organisation and its agents who control the channel
X: any event or object in the environment of A, B, or C which is a subject of communication
f: feedback

McQuail (1984:172) explains the model as follows: The model illustrates how the messages C transmits to B (X') represent his selections from both messages to him from A's (X's) and C's selections and abstractions from X's in his own sensory field (X3c, X4,) which may or may not be Xs in A's field. Feedback not only moves from B to A (fB A) and from B to C (fB C ) but also from C to A (fC A). In mass communication a large number of Cs receive from a very large number of As and transmit to a vastly large number of Bs, who simultaneously receive from other Cs.

This model recognises that mass communication involves the interpolation of a "new communicator" role (namely the role of the journalist in a media organisation) between society and audience. In other words, mass communication is something between society and an audience (recipients). The sequence of communication is thus not simply: (1) sender, (2) message, (3) channel, (4) many potential recipients; but rather:

1. events and "voices" in society: something happens in society and different opinions exist about it
2. channel/communicator role: a journalist interprets the event or takes over the opinion/view of someone else about the event (but not all opinions), and adapts it for the purposes of being conveyed by a channel (be it a newspaper, radio, television, Internet)
3. messages: the interpretation/opinion is formulated in a message (media content), which is
4. interpreted by a recipient.

According to McQuail (2000:57), Westley and MacLean's model is important because it acknowledges

- the fact that the mass media themselves do not usually originate messages or communication
- that they rather (i) relay their own account of a selection of the events occurring in an environment in the form of messages to a potential audience, and/or (ii) give access to the views or accounts of others (advocates/critics) of an event to be relayed by the media (or a specific medium)
- the selecting (gatekeeping) role of mass communicators (journalists, photographers, and so on)
- that the selection of events is on the basis of what they (the mass communicators) think the audience will find interesting and/or important
- that the media usually do not purposefully persuade, educate and inform
- that mass communication is a self-regulating process guided by the interests and demands of an audience that is known only by its selections and responses to what is offered and is thus shaped by feedback (in one or another form – usually ratings) from the audience (McQuail 2000:53).

For McQuail (1984:171–172), the main implication of the model is to show mass media organisations and the people who work in them as occupying an intermediary position between the audience on one hand and, on the other, either the events of the world which some people (advocates) wish to convey to the audiences (or part of it). The intermediary position is characterised by the authors as a gatekeeper role and can be either purposive or non-purposive. Purposive when it involves conveying messages from an "advocate" with a particular audience or public in mind; non-purposive when it is a matter of conveying the unplanned events of the world to an audience. For example, purposive if the media are invited to a political meeting with the purpose of getting them to report the ideals and views of the specific political party; non-purposive in the case of disasters.

## George Gerbner

In George Gerbner's (1967) model, much more attention is paid to individualism, perception, reaction and context.

> Someone
> perceives an event
> and reacts
> in a situation
> through some means
> to make available materials
> in some form
> and context
> conveying content
> with some consequences.

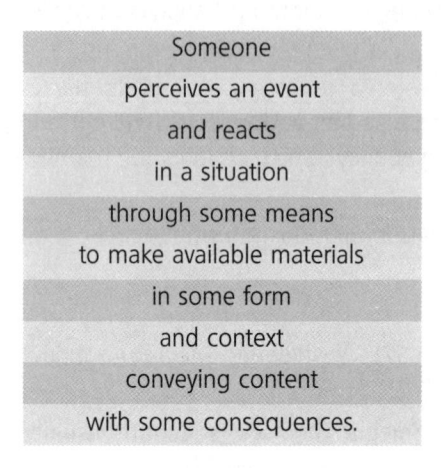

**Figure 6.3 George Gerbner's cultivation model**

The "someone" refers to the communicator(s), "perceives an event" refers to perception, "reacts" to interpretation, "situation" to the context of the event, "through some means" to the channel, "to make available materials" to the content, "in some form" to the media (the specific medium), "context" to the context of the communicator, "conveying content" to the message, and "with some consequences" to meaning and effects of the communication.

What is important in this model is the emphasis placed on the fact that mass communicators interpret events within the context of the event, meaning the broader context of, for example, the society within which the event takes/took place; that communicators' interpretations are further moulded by contextual ideology(ies) and professional work practices within which they work (the media institution); and by the specific medium through which they communicate (for example the differences between press, radio and television and how these differences impact on the formulation (format) of the message). Furthermore, Gerbner emphasises the interpretative role of the recipient and the openness of meaning in the sense that he emphasises *some* consequences – leaving the interpretation and meaning of the message open to the recipient(s).

### 6.2.1 A typology of models

As said above, there are numerous other models of mass communication, the latest emphasising the new possibilities of feedback, modes of production and dissemination of information created by new ICTs.

# Mass Communication Theory

McQuail (2000:52-59) offers a typology of models based on the orientation of both the communicator and the recipient. In other words, on the basis of the orientation of the communicator and the recipient he lists the following four groups of models:

- transmission models
- ritual or expressive models
- publicity models
- reception models.

In transmission models the communicator is emphasised as providing a so-called neutral service contributing to the work of other social institutions. From the media's (communicators') perspective the media provide society with information, orientation, entertainment, education, and so on, without which society will not be able to function effectively. Recipients are free to use, interpret and understand the information and entertainment as they wish and for whatever purposes. As McQuail (2000:53) points out, this is a free market perspective of mass communication which would not accurately fit a state-run media system, for example, in some developing countries where the media are perceived to play a very specific role. In this group of models, mass communication is essentially seen as service provision. Westley and MacLean's model can be seen as an example of a transmission model.

In ritual or expressive models, the emphasis, in the case of the communicator, is on the processes of creating media content and the satisfactions related to it, and in the case of the recipient on the pleasures derived from using media content, whatever the use may be. Mass communication becomes essentially a way of expressing ideas, feelings, emotions, moods, beliefs, and so on, and for the recipient it is a way of sharing or not sharing these expressions. Mass communication is essentially seen as a symbolic form of expression more or less similar in its purpose and nature to other symbolic forms such as theatre, literature and ritual.

In publicity models the emphasis is on the nature of mass communication and its communicators to draw and hold attention on something for a certain period of time, and for recipients to use the media as a form of diversion: to draw their attention away from themselves to something else. Mass communication is thus essentially seen as a process of attention-drawing and spectacle.

Finally, in reception models the emphasis is on the stages of transformation through which media messages pass on the way from their origins to their reception and interpretation. In other words, the emphasis is on the communicator's interpretation of reality or of an event, how this interpretation colours his/her encoding of the event in a specific form (media content) and how the message is interpreted by the recipient who is free to interpret it in whatever way. These models emphasise the interpretative nature of mass communication.

In conclusion and to summarise: models of mass communication highlight in a graphic way certain qualities, characteristics and the nature of mass communication. In many instances they form the basis of research in the sense that they often emphasise the shortcomings in the processes of mass communication, or such shortcomings become apparent from the models. This then provides a platform for new investigation.

## 6.3 MASS COMMUNICATION THEORY

In the previous section we argued that models are not theories but may suggest ways of perceiving communication phenomena and may suggest specific theoretical predictions.

Theories, in their turn, are ways of looking at and describing phenomena usually from a specific point of view or paradigm. In the following units of this volume and in Volume 2 of this series you are introduced to specific theories of the media. However, it is first of all necessary to ask the question: What is theory?

The purpose of this section is thus

- to explain what theory is
- to provide you with a classification of media theory, and
- to briefly summarise the basic assumptions of groups of theories.

### 6.3.1 What is theory?

In her book, *Communication theory in action* (2000), Julia Wood provides us with a comprehensive answer to the above question. The section below is based mainly on her explanation.

### *The value of theory*

Wood (2000:2–5) explains that apart from having a scientific value, theory always has a practical value (see below). Theory's scientific value is that it teaches us how to *describe, interpret, understand, evaluate* and *predict* a phenomenon, such as, for example, the mass communication media as a phenomenon. It also provides us with an overview of the development of a discipline, its relation(s) with other disciplines and its possible future developments. For example, although it may not be the explicit purpose of media theory to provide a historical overview of the discipline, if we study media theory as it developed over time and as it focused on different issues in different historical periods, then it reveals much about the development of the discipline. A good example is the effect theories discussed in Unit 8. Effect theories started by focusing on the effect of the media on personal behaviour and then developed into a more holistic approach to the effects of the media on society and culture in general. It thus began with simplified assumptions about the power of the media and gradually developed into complex and multiple assumptions, saying a lot not only about the media but about society and humanity as such. The same applies to other branches of media theory.

As far as the relation with other disciplines is concerned, effect theories started from a behaviourist perspective closely associated with the positivism and behaviourism of the social sciences in the first part of the 1900s and then moved on to the more critical approaches presently practised in the social sciences. Present theories related to the information society and globalisation include a good deal of predictions of how media theory may develop in the future, and for what we should be on the lookout.

Apart from its scientific value, theory also has a practical value. If theory teaches us the skills of describing, interpreting and understanding, evaluating and predicting a phenomenon, such skills can become entrenched in the way(s) we deal with reality. Simple everyday problems such as tense relationships between colleagues can be solved by carefully describing the problem and the reasons responsible for the problem, interpreting them, evaluating the importance of the different reasons for the conflict and then predicting and deciding on solutions for the problem. Reading a newspaper story or watching a television programme can become a descriptive, interpretative, evaluative and predictive exercise, all leading to better understanding, enjoyment and critical awareness. Theory building skills, once entrenched in one's way(s) of dealing with reality, can thus be applied to dealing with one's finances, interpersonal relations, group relations, and so forth.

## *The goals of theory*

Theory can be defined as a human account of what something is, how it works, what it produces or causes to happen, and how that something can be changed, if necessary (Wood 2000:33). Actually, all of us are theorising beings. When we tell someone how something happened, why it happened, what our reactions to it were, what we should have done, and how the issue or event could have been avoided or directed in another way, we are in fact theorising about that circumstance.

From this definition it is clear that being a human account of something, theory cannot be objective, or necessarily true. At the most it provides us with different points of views about the same thing. In media studies, like in all other social and human studies, we therefore have different theories about the same thing: different theories about the power and effects of the media; different theories about how audiences use, interpret and understand media content; different theories about the nature of media content, and so forth. Each (new) theory may however, add and/or emphasise a different aspect of the phenomenon and as such contributes to our better understanding of the phenomenon.

The goals of theory are then to:
- describe: before we can comment on how something works, we must first describe that something
- explain: before we can understand, predict and/or change something we must first explain how something works
- understand, predict and control: description and explanation lead to understanding on the basis of which certain predictions of how something works and how it can be controlled can be made

- reform: description, explanation and understanding with the purpose of predicting and controlling can lead to changing something.

For example, say that the "something" is the media's portrayal of race. A theory about this will have to

- describe how the media report race
- explain why the media report race in a specific way
- from this description and explanation come to an understanding of why the media portray race in a specific way and thus why such reporting can be predicted and controlled
- on the basis of this understanding suggest ways of reforming the media's way of reporting race.

Many scholars believe that theory does not need to reform something. The act of describing, explaining and understanding something is in itself enough. However, critical scholars and critical theory (especially in the social sciences with its goal to improve society) emphasise the need to reform. In other words, a theory about the media's reporting of race and racial issues should lead to media practitioners changing their ways and habits of reporting race, even if it is only to be more sensitive about reporting race and racial issues.

Obviously description, explanation, prediction and reform can be done in different ways and by using different analytical techniques. This will depend on the theorist's (and researcher's) ontological and epistemological points of departure, which brings us to the building blocks of theory.

## The building blocks of theory

The building blocks (Wood 2000:54–68) of all theory related to human behaviour (of whatever kind) are:

- ontology
- epistemology
- purpose, and
- focus.

One may also say that a theory about something will depend on how you see something (ontology), how you investigate something (epistemology), your purpose and your focus.

How does one formulate a theory? A theory begins with a question or questions about a specific phenomenon in the mind of the theorist (or group of theorists). For example, can the media frame a person, a group, an event or a topic in a certain way so as to influence public opinion about a person, group, event or topic in a specific direction? Underlying an answer to this question, as to all questions dealing with humanity (its behaviour, products, thinking, and so on), will be the theorist's view of human nature (keeping in mind that media content is a product of human activity). Thus we say that all theory in the human and social sciences begins with a view of human nature.

In the philosophy of science this view of human nature is called ontology. As far as ontology is concerned we distinguish between two broad views of humanity: a deterministic view or determinism and a liberal view or humanism. The point of departure in determinism is that human behaviour is governed by forces beyond individual control. A deterministic point of departure to the question about media framing will thus be: yes, the media *will* frame people and events and *will* influence public opinion about people and events in a certain direction. The point of departure in humanism is the belief that people have a free will and that they make choices about how to act. A humanist answer to the question about media framing will thus be much more cautious about an outright yes, and would rather be: yes, the media *may* frame people and events under certain circumstances and given certain conditions including the various conditions of the media audience(s), and *may* influence public opinion in a certain way.

| Ontology ||||
| --- | --- | --- |
| Do the media frame people and events to influence public opinion in a specific direction? |||
| Ontological point of departure | Determinism | Yes |
| Ontological point of departure | Humanism | Not an unqualified yes; it will depend on circumstances, conditions and the free will of people |

The second building block that underlies theory is epistemology. This means *how we know what we know*, or in philosophical terms, the science of knowledge. Broadly, we can distinguish between two schools of thought about this: those who believe in objective truth and those who believe in subjective experience, perception and understanding. Put in another way, I know what I know because the phenomenon I'm investigating and/or theorising about exists objectively, independent from my understanding, perception and experience. Or, I know what I know because I (myself) can experience, think, understand and perceive. The first school can be called objectivism and the second subjectivism. The first believes that reality is material and external to the human mind, independent of feelings, and the same for everyone (Wood 2000:60). Theorising can therefore also be objective, uninfluenced by values, biases, personal feelings, and other subjective factors when perceiving material reality. The second school does not believe in objective truth. They assume there are multiple views of reality, no one of which is intrinsically more true than any other (Wood 2000:61).

In the case of the media framing a person or whatever, the first school will believe that there are objective ways of investigating this that will lead to objective conclusions. The second school will believe that there are different ways of looking at this issue leading to different opinions; none of them being either true or untrue.

| Epistemology ||| 
|---|---|---|
| Do the media frame people and events to influence public opinion in a specific direction? |||
| Epistemological point of departure | Objective investigation | Yes or no |
| Epistemological point of departure | Subjective investigation | Not an unqualified yes or an unqualified no. It will depend on circumstances, conditions and the free will of people |

The third building block concerns the purpose of theory. What is the purpose of my theory about the media framing people and events? Is it to discover and formulate universal laws about the nature of the media, in other words to be able to say that the media always function in this or that way, or is the purpose to discover patterns of media behaviour that may prevail under certain conditions and in certain circumstances? Again we distinguish two schools: universalists and situationalists. The first believe that it is possible to generate universal laws of human behaviour. The second believe that it is not possible and that theory can only articulate rules that describe patterns in human behaviour, rather than laws.

| Purpose of a theory |||
|---|---|---|
| Do the media frame people and events to influence public opinion in a specific direction? |||
| To discover universal laws | Universalism | Laws about how and when the media frames people and events can be described and are universal |
| To discover patterns of behaviour | Situationalism | Given certain conditions and circumstances the media may frame people and events in different ways |

Finally, and as the fourth building block of theory, the focus of a theory has to be considered.

Again it is possible to distinguish between two broad schools. As in the case of ontology, epistemology and purpose, it is important to keep in mind that the schools are not necessarily exclusive of each other. Theorists belonging to a certain school or point of departure may share some of the beliefs and points of departure of the other school. It is often a matter of degree. In other words, the degree in which a theory is deterministic or humanistic, the degree of objectivity and subjectivity, the degree of supporting the idea of discovering universal laws or situational rules.

Nevertheless, as far as focus is concerned the two broad schools are behaviourism and humanism. Simply defined, behaviourism focuses on observable behaviour. Behaviourists believe that only concrete behaviour, such as the things people actually do and say, are relevant. Behaviour as such is the determinant and therefore the proper focus of theory. Contrary to this, humanists believe that the *meaning* of behaviour should be the focus of theory and that meaning may differ from circumstance to circumstance and from condition to condition. Humanism emphasises the fact that people have free wills, the ability to make choices and the capacity to create meanings. It is not so much a specific behaviour that is important, but rather the reasons why people behave in certain ways. External behaviour is only a sign of deeper psychological and physiological processes. What we perceive, think, and feel directly affects what we do and what we assume it means (Wood 2000:67).

| Focus of a theory |||
|---|---|---|
| Do the media frame people and events to influence public opinion in a specific direction? |||
| The media behave in a certain way | Behaviourism | The media behave in a certain way therefore the media frame people and events |
| Why do the media behave in a certain way? | Humanism | For specific reasons the media may create certain meanings in its covering of people and events and may thus frame people and events in a certain way in the minds of certain people who are free to interpret the media's framing as they wish |

To summarise this part: theory and theory building always depends on
- a basic point of departure about humanity and its activities (ontology) which can range from being deterministic to humanistic
- a preferred way of looking at or investigating humanity and its activities (epistemology) which can range from being objective to subjective
- the purpose of the theory which can range from being to discover universal rules to discover patterns
- the focus of a theory which can range from being behaviourist to being humanist.

| Ontology | Epistemology | Purpose | Focus |
|---|---|---|---|
| Determinism | Objectivity | Discover universal rules | Behaviourism |
| Humanism | Subjectivity | Discover patterns | Humanism |

## Evaluating theory

How do we evaluate a theory? Wood (2000:41–47) suggests five criteria:

- scope
- testability
- parsimony
- utility, and
- heurism

In evaluating the scope of a theory we have to establish how much and how well a theory describes and explains. Some theories claim to describe and explain almost every aspect of mass communication including the communicator, the medium, the content and the recipient of media messages. They claim to offer a theory of mass communication in general. These are so-called grand theories, such as, for example, McLuhan's "the medium is the message" theory and Gerbner's "cultivation" theory. Other theories offer a description and explanation of only one aspect of mass communication, for example feminist theories which, although they can cover the whole domain of mass communication, often only focus on media content and the portrayal of women in media content.

When deciding how well a theory describes something, we thus have to distinguish whether a theory describes all the essential aspects of a phenomenon, or if it only provides a partial description. For example, does a theory focus on all the aspects of the mass communication process (communicator, medium, messages, recipient), or only on one or two of these. Both are acceptable.

As far as explanation is concerned we distinguish between two broad types of explanation, namely *law-based explanation* and *rules-based explanation*. The first argues that if this happens this will follow. If I send this kind of message this will be the audiences' reaction. In other words, the explanation is causal or correlational. Rules-based explanation identifies rules that explain why certain things happen. It aims to identify patterns rather than laws, to describe and explain what may happen under certain conditions.

A second criterion for evaluating theories is testability. Can a theory be investigated to determine whether it is accurate or not, or is it so farfetched that it does not even need to be tested.

Thirdly we look at parsimony. Parsimony refers to simplicity. A theory doesn't need to be complex. To the contrary, some of the best theories are simple and allow for clear description and explanation. A good example is Roman Jakobson's theory of communication functions: namely that we communicate to refer to something, express our feelings about something, to make contact, explain something, and to draw attention to something. This theory can and has been applied in numerous ways by numerous researchers to analyse components of mass communication.

The fourth criterion is utility. People tend to think of theory as being esoteric and academic. This need not be the case. Theories need to have a practical value in terms of our understanding of a phenomenon with the purpose of controlling the phenomenon and improving the phenomenon. A theory helping us to understand how mass communication works can lead to our control of this phenomenon to the benefit of people and society.

Finally we evaluate a theory in terms of its heuristic value. Does the theory lead to new thinking? Does it contribute to our knowledge of something and does it provide us with the potential of further investigation?

## 6.4 MEDIA THEORY AND RESEARCH

In the previous sections we looked at some of the difficulties in defining mass communication, models of mass communication as graphic representations of the components of mass communications, and at the question what is theory: its value, goals, buildings blocks, and parameters for evaluating theory. On the basis of ontology and epistemology it is possible to describe at least four broad paradigms or approaches to media theory and research. They are:
- administrative theory and research
- critical theory and research
- technological deterministic theory and research
- information society theory and research.

These will be discussed later on in this section.

As in the case of models, there are many theories of mass communication (media theory) and approaches to mass communication research. Similarly, to the number of theories and research approaches there are different ways of trying to group media theories and their associated research approaches.

Certain authors such as Littlejohn (1992:341-374) distinguish between macro and micro theories and research: macro being those theories and approaches which investigate and explain the link between the media and other institutions (cf. for example, political economy referred to in Unit 2); and micro being those theories and approaches concerned with the link between the media and audiences (for example, effect theories and research discussed in Unit 8). The link itself may be the content of the media that is investigated and explained in numerous content theories and analysis.

McQuail (2000:61-162), on the other hand, distinguishes between theories and approaches concerned with the relationship between media and society, with the relationship between media and culture, and a third branch of new theories and approaches concerned with the relationship between new media and the information society. He emphasises that the "distinction" between society and culture, including the so-called information society, is not distinct and clear-cut and that theory-formation does not follow a systematic and logical pattern but responds to real-life problems and historical circumstances. He says:

> There is no neat system for categorizing the available theories. These [typologies – PJF] are fragmentary and selective, sometimes overlapping or inconsistent, often guided by conflicting ideologies and assumptions about society.
> (McQuail 2000:68)

# MEDIA STUDIES

In other words, it is difficult to say that a theory and its research is only concerned with, for example, the relationship between the media and other institutions such as politics or the economy. The same theory and research will also have to concern itself, to a certain extent, with media content, because media content reflects this relationship, and with audiences' responses to the content, because response determines the outcome of the relationship between media and other institutions.

Nevertheless, we can say that all media theory research concerns itself in one or another way with the description, interpretation, explanation and evaluation of

- the power of the media to integrate people into society, and
- the media's role in changing society.

In doing this the emphasis in media theory and research is on

- the relationship between media and society, for example theories and research about the media's political economy (cf. Unit 2), the functions of the media (cf. Unit 7), media and culture (cf. Unit 11), media and globalisation (cf. Unit 19), feminist media theory (cf. Unit 12)
- media content, for example genre theory and analysis (cf. Unit 2, Volume 2), narrative analysis (cf. Unit 4, Volume 2), semiotics (cf. Unit 10, this volume), ideological theory (cf. Unit 9, this volume)
- media audiences (cf. Part C, Volume 2), for example reception theory and analysis, ethnography, psychoanalysis, and so forth.

It is also important to remember, as has already been said, that it is usually difficult to say that a theory and research only concerns itself with, for example, content, only with the audience, or only with the relationship between media and society. Media content always signifies something about a society and its media audiences, as audiences always signify something about content and society. The relationship between media and society always signifies something about the media content and its audiences.

Despite the difficulty of a clear typology of media theories it is almost customary in media studies, as has already been mentioned, to distinguish between four broad paradigms: the administrative paradigm, the critical paradigm, the technological/deterministic paradigm and the information society paradigm.

## 6.4.1 Administrative theory and research (paradigm)

The purpose of empirical theory and research is usually to gain a better understanding of exactly how the media work in order to plan the more effective use of the media with specific outcomes in mind. The emphasis is thus on the

- working and management of the media
- the production of media content
- functions of the media, and the
- effects of the media on people and society.

# Mass Communication Theory

In general, one could say that the empirical approaches see the media as instruments (in the hands of their owners) that can and should be applied to achieve a certain goal. Theory and research therefore focuses on the functions and effects of the media.

The functions are seen to be the provision of information, entertainment and education. Insofar as effects are concerned, the argument runs more or less that greater knowledge of the effects of the media will result in a more effective fulfilment of the functions of the media.

With these assumptions as background, innumerable studies of the effects and consequences of the media, the individual and social functions of the media, the ways in which the media are "used" by recipients (uses and gratification studies) and quantitative content analyses and market research (who is the recipient?) have been and are being done.

Typical research questions will, for example be:
- What effects do political news have on the media user's voting behaviour?
- What effects do the portrayal of violence by the media have on the behaviour of people?
- What effects do, for example, television, have on communication within families?
- What effects do the media have on children's learning?
- How many people watch a specific programme?
- Why do they watch it?
- What are the functions of the media in, for example, developmental projects?
- How best can the media contribute to education?
- What is the content of the various media?
- Does news coverage of, for example, acts of terrorism contribute to increased acts of terrorism?
- What is the public's opinion (about any matter)?
- How is the public's opinion formed?

The point of departure in the empirical approaches is a perception of the media as neutral tools, capable of serving a wide range of purposes. Research takes as given the purposes of media users, or would-be users, and then collects the information intended to promote the realisation of those purposes. This might include studies of people's media preferences, their exposure patterns and the various content forms made available to audiences, as well as studies of media impact, effects, influence or power under diverse conditions of presentation and reception.

In short, the empirical approaches are guided by the almost classic question of Harold Lasswell (1948): Who, says what, in which channel, to whom, with what effect?

From an ontological and epistemological point of view one can say that administrative theories and research are grounded in positivism, functionalism and behaviourism.

## Positivism

In positivism the emphasis is on scientific method (logical processing of experience) – in other words, on knowledge derived from scientifically processed experiential data without recourse to metaphysics. The purpose is to arrive at a scientific description of the world and of individual phenomena (such as media).

In media theory and research positivism crystallised in the previous century in the work of Robert E Park, a member of the influential Chicago School of Sociology. Park was influenced by and followed in the footsteps of European sociologists such as Emile Durkheim (1858–1917), Max Weber (1864–1920) and Talcott Parsons (1902–1979). Park's disciples include the founders of modern communication science, such as Paul F Lazarsfeld, Kurt Lewin, Bernard Berelson and De Sola Pool. A central assumption in their work was that the media help to shape public opinion and in this way may trigger and influence social change. The mass media can function and must be used to improve society.

## Functionalism

Functionalism is a theoretical perspective associated with the sociology of Durkheim and Parsons. It views society as an integrated, harmonious, cohesive whole in which all parts (for example institutions such as the school, the church, economic, political and cultural institutions) function to maintain equilibrium, consensus and social order. In other words, society can be viewed and analysed similar to a human body consisting of different organs all functioning together. Should one of the organs become sick of dysfunctional, it affects the whole body. In the case of mass communication, functionalism sees the media as one of the instruments in society that should contribute to the harmonious and cohesive functioning of society (cf. Unit 7 for a more in-depth discussion of media functions).

Functionalism has been subject to criticism on many levels. As a perspective it overemphasises consensus between groups in society, thus absenting conflict from social relations. It also fails to provide an adequate account of social change and transformation (O'Sullivan et al: 1994:124–125).

## Behaviourism

Behaviourism concentrates on experimental analysis of behaviour – hence on the observable actions of a subject (person/group) as opposed to concealed cognitive processes underlying behaviour. In mass communication theory and research, behaviourism is associated with, for example, the mass communication model of Shannon and Weaver (1949). As already referred to, they developed this model in an attempt to construct a mathematical theory of information dissemination which would be applicable to a variety of situations in which information is transmitted, whether by human, mechanical or other systems. Within the framework of their model of transmission these authors identify three levels of problems in the analysis of information: level A (technical), level B (semantic, i.e. the meaning emanating from the transmitter's mode of address) and level C (effectiveness, measured in terms of the recipient's reception and understanding of the message). Their model was constructed mainly with a view to solving level A problems, the assumption apparently being that the resolution of technical problems through improved encoding of the message will *ipso facto* improve matters at levels B and C.

To a great extent this model still underlies the analysis of communication problems as executed within the framework of administrative media theory and research.

For examples of administrative theory and research see the units on functions and the effects of the media. Some of the classic examples include Walter Lippmann's *Public opinion* (1922), Paul F Lazarsfeld, Bernard Berelson and Hazel Gaudet's *The people's choice* (1948), Harold D Lasswell's *The structure and function of communication in society* (1948), Robert K Merton's *Social theory and social structure* (1949), Elihu Katz and Lazarsfeld's *Personal influence* (1955) and Joseph T Klapper's *The effects of mass communication* (1960) (cf. Lowery and DeFleur (1983), *Milestones in mass communication research*, for an overview of the nature and influence of these works).

However, and against the background of our earlier argument that a clear distinction between administrative and critical theory is not always possible, it is important to take note that the above-mentioned works dealt with the formation of public opinion as much research in critical theory deals with public opinion. The difference lies mainly in the purpose of research. In the aforementioned work the purpose of investigation is to understand the processes of public opinion formation (and its concurrent effects), whereas in critical theory the purpose is to criticise the ways in which mass communication forms public opinion and the quality of such public opinion.

## 6.4.2 Critical media theory and research (paradigm)

Compared to empirical theory and research, which for many years was the dominant approach in especially North American mass communication research, a more critical stance on mass communication was adopted from the start by European researchers.

The development of critical thinking on mass communication has a long history. Since the earliest times there have been complaints about the abuse of the media for political purposes: in classical times the complaints concerned the use of Greek theatre (as a form of mass communication) to propagate their political ideals and in the Middle Ages the flysheet and the bard aroused controversy. However, for our purpose, modern critical thinking about the role of the media can be traced back to the "élitist" social (including media) criticism and the work of the influential Frankfurt School whose work gave rise to what is known as the critical theories on mass communication. It was also from their work that the influential British cultural studies approach to the study of mass communication media developed. (Note that critical theory, the Frankfurt School and British cultural studies are also discussed and/or returned to in Units 9, 11 and 12.)

Briefly, critical theory/theories on mass communication amount to the following. The media are seen to be the most pervasive ideological agent in late twentieth and early twenty-first century society. There is hardly a person who does not come into contact with media of one or another kind and the ideas and values they convey, be it newspapers, radio, television, advertisements, popular music or the Internet. Small wonder then that the media are referred to as the consciousness industry – a description with far-reaching philosophical implications concerning the possible influence of the media on human beings, their thinking and existence.

Within the context of mass society theories it was concern about the possible ideological implications of the media that gave rise to critical media theory. Mass society theories were formulated at the turn of the twentieth century as a critical reaction to the rise of technology that in turn gave rise to industrialisation, urbanisation and what is referred to as the "mass man" and "mass society". Radio, film and the press of the day, and after the Second World War, television, were seen by critics on both sides of the political spectrum as products of technology used by a minority to manipulate the majority.

## Élitist criticism

Originally élitist critics (see Kornhauser 1949) and élitist criticism were concerned about the atomisation of individuals in mass society, with a resultant destruction of traditional ties and relationships between people, the destruction of political and other hierarchies, the alienation of traditional tasks and duties, and the commercialisation of culture.

Typical examples of élitist criticism can be found in the work of social theorists and critics such as Matthew Arnold (1822–1888), Ortega Y Gasset (1883–1955), John Stuart Mill (1806–1873) and Hannah Arendt (1906–1975), to name but a few. Their attacks on mass society and the role of the mass media as a creator of mass and/or popular culture are characterised by a pessimism about industrialisation, urbanisation, the rise and development of democracy, the accessibility of education for all and the growth of the mass media.

Mill, for instance, argued that democratic forms of government could lead to a new kind of despotism – namely the tyranny of the majority. He pointed to the danger that a self-assured and complacent middle class poses to the morality and intellectual authority of the high class. According to Ortega Y Gasset, the development of democracy, the media and free and accessible education disturbed the natural balance between the élite and the mass. These developments erased the traditional distinction between social classes. The earlier clearly defined subordinate state of the masses became obscured. The masses, although they may have access to information through the mass media and education, do not possess the ability to give and take the moral and intellectual lead in society. Yet the masses claim the right to lead.

Theorists such as Matthew Arnold shared the concern that the disintegration of the traditional distinction between different classes could lead to moral and intellectual decline. In much the same vein Hannah Arendt argued that there is a relationship between the thinking and social conditions of the masses and the rise of totalitarian social and political movements. The rise of Nazism, Stalinism and other totalitarian political trends can, according to her, be attributed to the entry of the masses in politics and an acceptance of mass man's thinking as the only acceptable norm.

In short, according to these and other "élitist" critics, the rise of mass society, and the development and role of the mass communication media in this society, have various ghastly consequences in and for society, including the rise and development of mass/popular culture.

The élitist way of thinking about mass society, mass man and the possible negative role of the media in this society can be seen as some of the earliest modern acknowledgements of the possible ideological role of the media. In critical media studies, the ideological role of the media has become the basis of critical theory and investigation.

A next step in the development of critical media theory can be found in some of the research and writing of members of the influential Frankfurt School.

## *The Frankfurt School*

The Frankfurt School or Institut für Sozialforschung at Frankfurt am Main (Germany) was established in 1923 to conduct sociological research. Eminent social scientists that were associated with this School included Theodor Adorno (1903–1969), Max Horkheimer (1895–1973), Walter Benjamin (1892–1940) and Herbert Marcuse (1898–1979). In 1933 the School was closed down by the Nazis. Its leading lights emigrated to the USA, where they continued their work at Columbia University.

The ideas of the Frankfurt School are epitomised by Horkheimer's critical theory. His original aim was to demonstrate the presence of contradictions in existing theories of society (and in society itself). What is said to be democratic society is in fact not democratic. So-called objective positivist science (administrative research) is in fact anything but objective.

With this as their primary concern, the 1950s saw members of the Frankfurt School such as Habermas, Adorno, Marcuse, Fromm and Benjamin rebelling against modern society and the media as creators and bearers of contemporary culture and ideology.

Where the élitist criticism was concerned with the influence of industrialisation, urbanisation and the mass media on the preservation of the organic society and culture, the Frankfurt School presented a vision of a new Utopian society, free from class and domination.

The Frankfurt School's criticism of the mass communication media was that they hamper the road to such a Utopian society and that the media stand in the way of change. By *selectively* presenting reality, including aspects of culture, education and entertainment (in which bourgeois values enjoy priority) the media confirm and support dominant capitalist ideologies and thus maintain the *status quo* at the cost of the working class, which is represented by the masses.

## *Critical theory*

Unlike the so-called élitist critics, but in line with the thinking of the Frankfurt School, critical theorists are concerned about the media's ideological manipulation of the mass and the utilisation and exploitation of the media by capitalist considerations (see Hartley et al 1985:5).

Critical theory was influenced by the ideas of Hegel, Marx and Freud, but unlike these scholars, both early and contemporary critical theorists are not intent on designing an alternative model for society and even less on devising a strategy for political action. Their premise is rather that the social sciences should be *engagé* (morally committed). In this way they can strive for a just society and the eradication of prejudice.

In order to understand how ideology and hegemony invades and pervades our common sense, we have to describe as closely as possible the signification, power and production means and instruments of society, of which the media is one of the most important instruments.

> ### Ideology defined
>
> The concept "ideology" is central in much of media studies and you will encounter it in many of the units of both volumes of this book. We therefore provide you here with a brief introduction to the concept.
>
> A straightforward definition of the concept "ideology" is that it consists in the patterns of ideas, belief systems and interpretive schemes found in a society or among specific social groups.
>
> Scientific interest in ideology has a long history. As early as in the works of Niccolò Machiavelli (1469–1527) and Francis Bacon (1561–1626) there was a clear relationship between "ideology" (as a concept) and the way people think (or the way they think about something). The term "ideology" was first coined during the French Revolution by Antoine-Louis-Claude Destutt de Tracy (1754–1836) to describe the "science of ideas". At the end of the eighteenth century and in the *Age of the Enlightenment*, "ideology" was known to mean the study of systems of ideas (the suffix -ology meaning "study of").
>
> The first negative use of the term "ideology" stems from the work of Karl Marx (1818–1883) who used the term to characterise the influence of idealism in German philosophy (e.g. GWF Hegel 1770–1831) and as an aspect of the critique of religion (e.g. Ludwig Feuerbach 1804–1872) (cf. Hall 1982). Marx (and Friedrich Engels 1820–1895) argued that material processes and socioeconomic relations form the *bases* and ideas the *superstructure* of society. With this as the underlying premise, further key issues in Marx's arguments concerning ideology are:
>
> - It is not the consciousness of w/men that determines their being, but social being that determines consciousness.
> - In bourgeois society ideas are linked to class position and class interests.
> - Political economy is the common-sense ideology of capitalism. Ideology therefore legitimates capitalist exploitation.
> - Ruling classes maintain their position through their monopoly over cultural institutions that produce ruling ideology.

- Subordinate classes, whose ideas do not reflect their true class interests, have been deceived into false consciousness.

These standpoints gave rise to the theory of *class struggle* and the birth of ideology as a theory of partisan interests: that is, the view that the ruling class favours best those ideas which preserve its own property and power by persuading everybody else that things are just fine as they are, and that the ideas, values and frame of mind which suit them so well suit everybody else at the same time (cf. Inglis 1990:78).

Ideology is then nothing but a *false consciousness* created by the ruling bourgeoisie to keep the working proletariat in place.

Against the background of the Industrial Revolution and the economic issues of the nineteenth century, Marx regarded the class struggle as principally a struggle between the (capitalist) bourgeoisie and the workers (proletariat) of the time. For this reason Marx described "ideology" as the ideas of the ruling capitalist bourgeoisie and the attempts by the bourgeoisie to force their ideas, customs and values on others.

Today, the concept of "ideology" is no longer only associated with Marxist criticism of capitalism, but applies to all forms of power domination.

Other pioneering social scientists of the nineteenth century who concerned themselves in one or another way with ideology were:

- Karl Mannheim (worldview or *Weltanschauungen*)
- Max Weber (the role of Puritan thinking in the rise of capitalism)
- Auguste Comte (thought stages)
- Emile Durkheim (the social basis of the thinking and religions of various groups and the normative function of this thinking in the ordering of social behaviour)

Two modern philosophers who played an influential role in critical theory in communication and media studies and in the shaping of critical thought concerning media and ideology are Antonio Gramsci (1891–1937) and Louis Althusser (1918–).

Gramsci is associated mainly with the concept *hegemony*, which he regarded as synonymous with ideology. Briefly, hegemony refers to the way in which we think and feel about things. According to Gramsci, this way (hegemony) is created and maintained by power structures in society. These are structures such as the school, the state, the church, political parties, cultural bodies and the mass media, which teach us how and even what to think.

The French neo-Marxist philosopher, Louis Althusser, described the above power structures (governments, schools, churches, media) as *Ideological State Apparatuses* (ISAs). He argues that all these institutions are bits of apparatus for the state to use in order to manage the consent of society. He described ideology as consisting of concepts, symbols and images representing the ideas and ways of thinking of the dominant ruling class.

The usefulness of these and other ideas of critical theory with its emphasis on ideological and hegemonic analysis is that it teaches us to be suspicious. It permits us to study the strictly structural weight of social institutions such as the media upon our thought and living (see Inglis 1990:82).

Underlying *assumptions* of critical media theory are:

- Critical theory sees the media as forms of symbolic expression. This means that, like other forms of expression, they are media in and through which the communicator expresses, in a structured manner, his/her values, beliefs and attitudes in respect of a particular topic (subject) or person. In this way the communicator assigns meaning to reality or some aspect of reality.
- Viewed thus, the media and its different forms and genres (e.g. news reports, commentary, soap operas, documentaries, and so on) can be read as texts (like a novel). The recipient understands and interprets this text in his/her own distinctive manner, the meaning that he/she attaches to it being a result of a confrontation between viewer and text (what the viewer sees on screen, hears over the radio or reads in the newspaper).
- Apart from seeing the media and its messages as a text(s), critical theory stresses the *circumstances of the communicator*: the influences and pressures to which he/she is subject, the powers beyond his/her control and how these conflict with his/her ideology and worldview. In particular it is concerned with how the ideologies of proprietors (owners) of media industries influence the eventual media content that is produced.
- Critical media theory is concerned with the *relation between the media and underlying production conventions*. For example: how does an underlying ideology influence the production and the eventual content, form and meaning of media products?
- In critical theory it is argued that the media mainly support the interests (political, economical, social) of one group at the cost of another group. This criticism has led to the media being seen as:

    ... not as an autonomous organizational system, but as a set of institutions closely linked to the dominant power structure through ownership, legal regulation, the values implicit in the professional ideologies in the media, and the structures and ideological consequences of prevailing modes of newsgathering.

    (Curran, Gurevitch & Woollacott 1982:16)

In order to perform this ideological role, the media manipulate and institutionalise language (cf. Unit 3, Volume 2) and visual codes (cf. Unit 1, Volume 2) for the sake of the transfer of an ideology(ies).

Related to the above it is clear that a central issue in critical theory is meaning – ideology is related to the processes of the creation of meaning and the attachment of meaning to reality. Questions then asked are:

- How do the media create and convey meaning for the sake of maintaining an ideology?

# Mass Communication Theory

- How does the meaning given by the media to events and the underlying meaning(s) of fictional media content such as in films, television series, cartoons, advertisements, and so on, support a specific ideology?
- What are the structural relationships between the political and economic powers in society and the media and what is the influence of these relationships on the creation of meaning and the maintenance and conveyance of ideology by the media?
- How does the user (or recipient/subject) of the media understand this meaning and personalise it?

Because meaning no longer depends on how something actually is, but rather on how, from an ideological perspective, meaning is given to an event, critical theory comes to the conclusion that meaning is *produced* by the media in a specific way. The assigning of meaning is a *process*. A process presupposes the transformation of the raw material of a product – a transformation that takes place through a specific kind of labour. In order to give expression to an ideology (which is, for instance, supported by an editorial in a newspaper), an event and the significance of the event is produced by means of the manipulation of language and visual signs and codes. In this process of media labour, the meaning of the event thus undergoes a transformation.

In order to support the above-mentioned assumptions, critical research focuses on the following:

- the analysis of the formal qualities and latent meaning of media content (media discourse)
- the analysis of the relationship between media content and the political economy of the media
- the analysis of media content within the context of the entire society and culture
- an analysis of the structural relationship between the media and other societal structures, for example those found in the political, educational, economic and religious spheres.

## Criticism against critical theory

In contrast to critical theory, *pluralist media theories* (*pluralism*) argue that the above-mentioned élitist and critical theories of the media

- offer no explanation of why certain uplifting and positive changes have taken place in mass society
- do not acknowledge the uplifting role of the media in mass society
- do not acknowledge the informative, educational and democratising role of the media in society
- do not acknowledge the tremendous entertainment value the media have for billions of people
- make too rigid a distinction between those with power and the masses
- are too often ignorant of audiences (and the individual media user's) ability to judge and be critical.

# MEDIA STUDIES

The concept "pluralism" refers to the variety of media (in democracy). The underlying premise in pluralist media theory is that in view of the variety of media (various newspapers, television stations, radio stations, films, videos, publishers, advertising agencies, all looking at reality from different perspectives) it is impossible to make one-sided and limited claims about the way the media function. If one newspaper or television station adopts a particular ideological perspective, another newspaper or television station is perfectly free to propagate an opposing ideology. Furthermore, media users are free to be selective about their exposure to the media and the ideologies that may be propagated. Critical theory ignores this variety or focuses its attention specifically on undemocratic societies.

Critical theory's reply to this is that although there may be a variety of media, they are all owned by a few people. For example, although a number of newspapers of widely differing ideological persuasions may be published in South Africa, and although there may be independent television and radio stations in addition to the public service broadcaster (SABC), the media, as in other countries, remain in the hands of a few and that the majority of the voices of the populace are still silenced, not represented or misrepresented.

### Case study 6.1: The South African media is racist

A good example of South African media research done within the context of the critical paradigm is the South African Human Rights Commission's research on racism in the South African media (South African Human Rights Commission: 2000). Although this research and its main finding that the South African media is racist can be criticised from a methodological perspective, it addressed some of the issues that are of pertinent concern in critical theory. This includes topics such as the relationship between media and racism, media and ideology, the representation of racial groups, white dominated ownership of the media, and discrimination within media institutions. Although nobody can claim that there aren't incidents of racism in the South African media, be it in their institutions and/or content, criticism against the report, its finding and recommendations can be made from a methodological point of view. If one wants to state categorically that the South African media are racist, and if such a statement comes from an important and prestigious institution such as the Human Rights Commission who claims that its finding is based on research, then one should make sure that such a finding can be backed up with sound empirical proof. Although there may be some examples of such proof in the Commission's research, an overall impression, as is often the case with critical theory and research, is that the research itself has been conducted from a specific ideological point of view which originated in neo-Marxist thinking about the media, and that examples of the media being racist were looked for and analysed haphazardly from this ideological point of view. The Commission's research and finding are thus nothing more but a subjective, hypothetical and deterministic claim, again, as is often the case with critical theory and research. To nevertheless recommend on the basis of such research that further control of the media is necessary, is unacceptable. To send a message to the world that the SA media are racist, based on this research, is irresponsible, dangerous, and even unethical. Many examples of efforts in the SA media to break down the myths and stereotypes of apartheid and how the media as such are contributing to a less racist society, can be cited. Furthermore, the research, its finding and recommendations do not thoroughly take into account the complexity of the media as a commercial product, but at the same time being a cultural product. In this regard the research could have distinguished in a clearer way between

- racism in the media as a social institution with its different media organisations (all operating from different ideological perspectives and as such adhering to the principle of pluralism), and
- racism in the content of the media and in different kinds of content.

The research could have acknowledged in a more informed way

- the complexity of media markets and of the media as a business enterprise
- the political economy of the media
- the complexity of media audiences' uses and gratifications of media.

It could have acknowledged in more depth that there are different ways of doing research about media and racism and that different kinds of research will come up with different findings.

Because of the "untidiness" of the research the only value of this particular investigation is that it may contribute to more awareness and sensitivity about the topic of racism in the media (also see Unit 15 on representation).

## 6.4.3 Technological determinism (paradigm)

A third broad theoretical and research paradigm is technological determinism. In this approach the focus is on the nature of the technology associated with specific media and how such technology determines the nature of mass communication and the role of the media in society. The best example of such a theory is that of Marshall McLuhan which we discuss in the next section.

In determinism of whatever kind, the basic claim is that a single cause or phenomenon determines all other aspects of (Wood 2000:244; O'Sullivan et al 1994:82–83).

For example, in economic determinism it is believed that all social and cultural processes are reducible to underlying economic and material relations. In biological determinism it is believed that biological or natural drives and needs determine all behaviour. In technological determinism it is believed that technology and technological innovation drive social change, culture, economics, politics, and so on.

## MEDIA STUDIES

### Marshall McLuhan

One of the best examples of technological determinism in media theory is Marshall McLuhan's theory "the medium is the message" and the ideas of his mentor Harold Adams Innis. Both these Canadian theorists saw the media as the essence of civilisation and the course of history as a manifestation of the dominant media of the age (Littlejohn 1992: 342-345).

Innis believed that developments in each historical period are directly related to the dominant public communication culture (see 6.5) and the media (channels) of that period. For example, he argued that:

- Early media such as stone or clay were time-binding and facilitated communication from one generation to another. A good example were the early media of Africa.
- Paper and papyrus were/are space-binding. They fostered empire building, large bureaucracies and military interests and facilitated communication from one location to another. A good example were the media of early Egypt.
- Speech as medium encourages temporal thinking, values knowledge and tradition and supports community involvement. Here one may think of the high emphasis on rhetoric in early Greek societies and the oral communication culture of Africa.
- Writing as the dominant medium (or channel of communication) produced strong space-binding effects such as the growth of empires during the Middle Ages and early Renaissance.
- According to Innis, the invention of the printing press was the essence of early Western and modern culture. It did, however, contribute to spatial bias and the monopolisation of knowledge and the development thereof. In other words, it restricted knowledge to those countries that knew the art of printing and developed it (Littlejohn 1992:343).

Taking it from here, McLuhan argued that every medium is an extension of people's senses or some human faculty. For example:

- The wheel is an extension of the foot.
- The book is an extension of the eye.
- Clothing is an extension of the skin.
- Electric circuitry is an extension of the central nervous system.

He then argues as follows:

Tribal people were primarily hearing-oriented – hearing was believing. The invention of the printing press changed this and sight started to dominate. This forced people into a linear, logical, and categorical kind of perception and reasoning. It encouraged the habit of perceiving things in visual and spatial terms. The electronic media (radio and television) changed this and the aural started to predominate again. Printing, being space-bounded, separated people and societies from each other. The electronic media, not being space-bounded, bring them together in a "global village".

| Tribal Epoch | Literate Epoch | Print Epoch | Electronic Epoch |
|---|---|---|---|
| | 2000 BC | AD 1450 | AD 1850 |

**Figure 6.4 Media epochs in human history** (Wood 2000:245)

According to McLuhan, the fact that the electronic media (as channels of communication) make it possible for us to listen to radio programmes from all over the world and watch television programmes from all over the world, and in terms of how this effects our perception of reality and how we think about reality, *space* and *time*, is more important than the *content* of these media. Therefore he argues that the medium as such is the message and not the content. The fact that electronic media, despite their content, have became so all-pervasive and part of our everyday existence makes the medium as such more important than the content.

He then goes on to distinguish between "hot" and "cool" media in terms of how they involve people perceptually. "Hot" media, such as film, are those that give us everything and leave little to one's own imagination and participation. The image projected on the screen is complete in every detail and does not require the viewer to fill it in perceptually. Compared to this, television is a "cool" medium and requires the viewer to participate perceptually by filling in missing data. It provides the viewer only with a sketch through the illumination of tiny dots. It actually only provides a stimulus to which the viewer must respond (Littlejohn 1992:345). Cool media such as television thus involve the viewer perceptually and on a sensory level, more so than hot media. Therefore, McLuhan argues, television is changing the very fabric of society in the sense that it changes our ways of seeing things.

From this distinction between "hot" and "cool" media it is clear that McLuhan was far more involved with the medium and the nature of the medium as being determinant in the quality of the communication, than with the actual content conveyed by the medium.

According to Wood (2000:249-251), the main criticism against technological determinism, and McLuhan's theory as an example thereof, is that his theory

- lacks empirical support: convincing research to support his ideas has not been produced
- does not acknowledge other research, for example, from the perspective of film theory his theory of "hot" and "cold" media can be rejected on the basis of the visual quality and richness of images
- is hyperbolic speculation: for instance, it proclaims the death of literacy while writing and reading are still major activities
- proclaims linear logic and thought as inferior while logic has given rise to some of the most important developments in the world
- overestimates the power of the media while research questions such overestimation

- is overly deterministic in asserting that human consciousness is controlled and determined by the media: at the most, the media can contribute partially to our awareness and consciousness
- ignores the fact that only a small portion of the world's population has access to media and/or uses media to such an extent that it may have a powerful effect on their consciousness (cf. Wood, op cit).

### 6.4.4 Information society (paradigm)

The last paradigm to be referred to here concerns theories and research about new media and ICT (information and communication technology). Aspects hereof are discussed in more depth in Unit 19 (Globalisation).

Here we suffice with a summary of some of the key issues in the three broad fields of enquiry in this paradigm:

- defining new media and the information society
- describing the nature and impact of the information society
- new media and communication policy.

In this paradigm, numerous studies concern themselves with a definition of the new media and the information society. Authors emphasise the following as characteristics of the information society:

- increase in the production and flow of information of all kinds largely as a consequence of reduced production costs following miniaturisation and computerisation
- reductions in costs of transmission
- decreasing sensitivity to distance
- increasing speed and volume
- increasing interactivity.

The above characteristics describe the *production* and *flow* of "information" compared to the production and flow of information in pre-information society.

The diversity of new media (the media of the information society) complicates a summary of the characteristics of new media as such. However, certain dimensions or variables can help us to differentiate "new" from "old" media, especially as seen from the individual user's perspective (McQuail 2000:127–128). They are the degrees of:

- interactivity: new media allow for far more contact between the communicator and the user/recipient
- sociability: new media allow far more contact between the user and other people
- autonomy: new media allow the user far more control over the content
- playfulness: new media allow far more enjoyment in the sense of involvement
- privacy: new media are more personalised and unique.

The second broad branch of theory and research in this paradigm concerns the *nature* of the information society. To describe the nature of the information society in comparison with earlier societies, it is, for example suggested that we rather use the concept "network society". The concept "information society" is also applicable to earlier societies in which the inventions of the printing press, telegraph and the development of electronic media such as radio had the same kinds of impact on society we today experience with the computer (digital communication). However, an outstanding characteristic of the "network society" is its interconnectedness – a distinct quality never experienced before. What new ICTs have brought about is an interconnection between people, groups, nations, and so on, on a global level.

Out of this interconnectedness develops the notion that today's society, compared to earlier societies, is a society in which information has infiltrated every aspect of daily life. Far more than in the past we have to put our trust in expert information and computer systems of all kinds for maintaining normal conditions of life. For example, ICTs have and are increasingly infiltrating banking, shopping, health care, education, entertainment, personal communication, and so forth, to such an extent that each and every one of us is increasingly aware of ICTs' role and impact on our personal lives.

For McQuail (2000:122) the *impact* of ICT on the nature of contemporary society is our increased awareness of risks of many kinds. We are bombarded with (popular) information about risks to health, the environment, and so on. This new and constant awareness of risk contributes to a general kind of anxiety and urgency in contemporary society.

Furthermore, a notable impact of ICT on society and humanity (compared to the impact of earlier ICTs such as the printing press) is on leisure-time spending. Leisure-time is increasingly dominated by a vast array of information services with interactive options.

Thirdly, theory and research in this paradigm focus on new media and communication policy. Apart from the above issues concerning the description and nature of contemporary information society, policy research centres on topics such as:

- new and improved ways of access to ICT
- the role of ICT in development
- ICTs' possibilities for economic growth
- social issues such as the possibility of a growing gap between the haves and the have-nots
- ICT and the growth and spread of democracy and its contributions to social change
- privacy issues
- regulation and control, and so on.

Old topics, one may argue, but, because of ICT's transformation of the world, topics that need to be addressed in new and challenging ways.

In Unit 19 we will return to the topic of globalisation and especially to the topic of the role of ICT in development.

In the preceding part of this unit we discussed four broad paradigms in mass communication theory and research: administrative, critical, technological deterministic and information society theories and research. We conclude this unit with a brief look at different public communication cultures.

## 6.5 PUBLIC COMMUNICATION CULTURES

The purpose of the following discussion is to emphasise that throughout humanity's history people had their "media" to communicate publicly about public matters of public interest. Many of the questions, issues and topics raised on the previous pages are thus not new. Neither can we claim to be one of the first media societies or the first media generation. Each public communication culture exposed its unique characteristics. By "public communication culture" we mean communicating about *matters of public interest in the public* compared to interpersonal communication, communication within a group and/or organisation and between organisations about personal and organisational matters.

It is possible to distinguish between three forms of public communication cultures, each being dominant in a certain era:
- a dominant oral public communication culture
- a dominant written and printed public communication culture
- a dominant electronic public communication culture.

The following is a brief summary of some of the characteristics of each culture:

### 6.5.1 The oral public communication culture

An oral public communication culture was dominant in the pre-industrial or pre-literate (before the event of writing and reading) societies. In these early societies the spoken word (and verbal sounds) was the only available means of expressing ideas, attitudes and feelings – nothing was written (the ability to write did not exist), there where no written reports, no newspapers, no television, no radio, no written records of anything. The spoken word was the only means of communication and thus defined reality and truth. The greater your facility with words and the larger your vocabulary, the greater was your credibility.

Inglis (1990:6–7) lists the following characteristics of the oral public communication culture:

- The transmission of information, knowledge and opinion was face to face.
- The meaning of language was highly specific and local, and related to everyday practical and particular concerns.
- Language was concrete and symbols were solid. There was very little possibility of "reading" meanings "between the lines". Something meant what it was supposed to mean.
- The context of oral culture was/is memory. Memory is finite. People therefore expected their memories to store and keep accessible (in memory) only what was relevant.
- The pre-literate society placed a higher value on the present tense: myth, proverb, law, belief, may all be adjusted to suit the present.

In some illiterate societies where people cannot read and/or write, and where there are little or no "modern" mass media, oral public communication is still dominant. In these societies people rely on face-to-face contact and verbal communication about public matters with their leaders and opinion leaders. Their histories are verbally told in the form of stories and myths through which their values and beliefs about what is wrong and right and about how one should behave in certain circumstances, are tested and communicated. Often these stories are closely related to human beings' experience of nature and the relationship between people and nature and to ancestry and ancestor worship. These beliefs and values are verbally passed on from generation to generation. Many tribal societies in which the oral tradition is dominant, still exist today.

### 6.5.2 The written and printed public communication culture

Visual recordings of history and messages started more or less 6 000 years ago with carvings and cave-paintings. Phonetic alphabets, and thus the possibility of recording events not only visually but also symbolically and on an abstract level, have been known for little more than 3 000 years, with the Greek alphabet, and thus writing as we know it today, dating from about 800BC. Written history therefore makes up a very small part of the more than a quarter of a million years of the history of *Homo sapiens* (cf. Inglis 1990).

In the dominant written (subsequently printed) communication culture, the spoken word was augmented by the written word. Some of the characteristics of the written and subsequently printed public communication culture are the following:

- The spoken word came to be seen and experienced as more casual and "unofficial" than the written word, which the writer has presumably pondered and verified. As a result, the written word came to be experienced as more impersonal and objective than the spoken word. It is permanent, as opposed to the fleeting, ephemeral nature of the spoken word. For all these reasons the written word was considered to be closer to the truth in the dominant written communication culture. For example, today we tend to believe that a written (or typed/printed) contract is more binding than an oral contract; that a published account of something that happened is more reliable than a verbal account. If something happens, for example a bus accident, people talk about it and there may be different verbal accounts of what has happened. Once it is recorded in print, for example in a newspaper story, we tend to belief that the written account is the official and correct version of what has happened.
- Writing makes the recording of events possible and is as such indispensable for the creation of a historical sensibility and for the existence of objective knowledge. For example, for science and rationality to be possible, we must have the principle of accurate and impartial written/printed recording. Writing makes debate about the comparative truthfulness of sources possible. Critical history is only possible with written records. A set of thought procedures like mathematics and logic is impossible without script (see Inglis 1990:8–13).

Since the emergence of the Greek alphabet it took another 2 000 years before the invention of the printing press.

In the 1450s the German, Johann Gutenberg, invented the printing press and started to develop the art of printing. This invention can be seen as the beginning of the information revolution. More than anything else, publishing contributed to the advancement of literacy among billions of people. Suddenly, documents, be they religious, legal, scientific or artistic writings were available to more people than to the previous few privileged and élite who could write and read. The increasing availability and accessibility of books and documents, the advancement of the print media as we know it today, and growing literacy over a period of three hundred years since the invention of the printing press markedly changed the ways in which politics, science, education, religion, economics, art and mass communication were to be conducted.

This was three hundred years within which human beings had been able to adapt themselves and their institutions to the revolutionary changes brought about by the printing press; within which they were able to create new institutions such as the school, new forms of government and an organised newspaper and advertising industry to regulate, control and comprehend the new information environment created by the printing press. In short, by the end of the eighteenth century the printing press had created an entirely new information and public communication culture (cf. Postman 1992).

The period of adjustment to printing, and the consequent changes in information, knowledge, society, politics and the economy, had its problems and encountered criticism similar to the criticism levelled at the media today (especially criticism about the changes brought about by the new ICTs and the effects on the quality of communication and information). Nevertheless, in the period of adjustment the emphasis on and primary purpose of public communication in the oral, written and printed communication cultures was the relevance, quality and the usefulness of information.

One can argue that early print placed a high value on the attainment of learning, meaning and reason. Furthermore, various mechanisms were developed that were intended not only to ensure that people had access to information but also, and especially, that they had control over it in the sense that they knew how to use it to their own advantage and that of their communities. Can the same still be said of print since the advent of the electronic media and lately digital media? How have the commercialisation and commodification of the media since the advent of the electronic media changed the character of public communication culture? In the following sub-section, some arguments about this.

### 6.5.3 The electronic public communication culture

Although the written and oral public communication cultures still exist today (we still have newspapers, magazines and public speeches), in the realm of public communication the electronic, photographic and digital media (radio, film, video, advertising, television and the Internet) have to a great extent became the dominant public communication culture. This process is expected to gain momentum as the electronic media and related technologies continue to develop. The old adage, "seeing is believing" is acquiring a new if not different meaning. Today it is a matter of "It is true, I saw it on TV" or "It is on the Internet". In the following segment we briefly look at how each of these electronic media contributed to the nature of our present-day dominant public communication culture. In our critical remarks we associate with one of the most prominent, albeit controversial, media critics of today, namely Neil Postman and two of his works, *Amusing ourselves to death: public discourse in the age of show business* (1985) and *Technopoly. The surrender of culture to technology* (1992).

## *The telegraph*

With the invention of the telegraph in 1837 the relationship between information and culture and between information and people began to change. This was mainly due to the fact that the telegraph initiated a dramatic change in the form, volume and speed with which information could be produced and distributed.

Before the telegraph, information was used mainly to promote an understanding of the world and other people and for the solution of specific problems. Information was therefore, in most cases, specific and purposeful and tended to be of local interest. After the advent of the telegraph, space and time ceased to be a restriction on the dissemination of information (cf. Ferguson (1990) for a discussion of the effect of the electronic media on our experience of time and space).

The invention of the telegraph laid the foundation for "contextless" information and the idea that the value of information need not necessarily be linked to a particular (cultural) function. Briefly, the telegraph launched information as a commodity. Within two years of the discovery of the telegraph, the fortunes of newspapers depended not so much on the quality and usefulness of their news, but on how much (quantity) news they could offer, on how great a distance the news had to cover and on the speed at which the news travelled (Postman 1992:68).

## *Photography, film and broadcasting*

Like the telegraph, photography and film had an incisive influence on the nature of information and public communication. After its inception during the nineteenth century the "graphical revolution" brought about a revolution in the iconography of the world. Whereas they had initially been used in support of the written word, photographs, prints, posters and illustrated advertisements began increasingly to replace the written word as the dominant means of interpreting, comprehending and testing reality. This was the start of what was known as the *image culture* in public communication. By the end of the nineteenth century advertisers and journalists had come to realise that not only was a photograph worth a thousand words, but it also brought in a thousand times more in revenue!

The discovery of the telegraph was the direct precursor of radio, and therefore of broadcasting.

After the invention of radio it was still to take about fifty to seventy years before the world felt the full influence of media technology on public communication culture. This had to wait for the coming of television, which marked the beginning of the media period described in postmodern theory as the fragmentation of the boundaries between image and reality. We can summarise the nature of television in contemporary dominant communication culture in the following remarks:

- According to several media critics the advent of television was the beginning of the media's contribution to the dismantling of organic culture. It was said to have introduced the media period in which the media, and especially television, integrated people into a corporate world as consumption units, instead of integrating them into society as political citizens of a nation state (see Elliot 1982:243). In other words, the new culture was one in which people were seen and experienced as little more than consumers, with public communication contributing to this view of human beings and perhaps even instigating it.
- To what can we ascribe these changes? The views of Kubey and Csikszentmihalyi (1990) support those of Postman (1992). They conclude that the reason is that television has become purely a consumer commodity (a commercial product), and in the process has lost its value as a cultural product, so that it no longer has much to offer that could contribute to our mental, cultural and psychological growth. As a consumer product it forms part of the postmodernist condition, with the high value it places on materialism.
- The availability of television programmes on the international market, international news networks and satellite communication and the influence of this on the dissemination of information have begun to expose viewers in all parts of the world to divergent cultures and ideological stances and opinions or meanings. In brief, the advent of television (with all its advantages) was the beginning of Marshall McLuhan's (1964) "global village".
- As a result of television's ability to bridge time and space, the *boundaries between cultures* have been broken down and a continual cross-pollination between various cultures and subcultures has been taking place. In consequence, television has contributed to the fact that there is no longer any question of a single contemporary society with a single culture and a single agreed hierarchy of values, but instead, of various cultures and subcultures.

There is no objection to this in itself. The criticism is that in and through its programme offering, television has taken on an international character and in so doing has become a culture on its own and for itself, so that it has become detached from the culture in which and for which it functions. For example, does South African television differ from American television, or do American television programmes

dominate the world to such an extent that we can no longer (or ever could) really speak of indigenous television.
- Television, it is argued, is a communication culture which, in attempting to reach the largest (international) audience, has become trivialised and commercialised. Briefly, it is a communication culture in which the media as a consumer culture dominate the media as a cultural product, and in which television has increasingly become part of the late twentieth century postmodern condition.

Since industrialists have started marketing their products directly to the public (via television), and since programme offering and content have become increasingly dependent on this, television has emerged very strongly as the *marketer of material values*. Differently stated: television has increasingly begun to replace the church, the family and the school (the traditional socialising agents of traditional values) as the purveyor of values, and these values are mainly materialistic ones (cf. Postman 1992).

Materialism (and also consumption) is reflected not only in advertisements, which suggest that human welfare depends on the way you look, smell, how you feel at a particular moment and what you own, but is also reflected in the programme content as a whole. Television is a form of entertainment which is neatly packaged and structured as a consumer commodity, and television stars (and the characters they play) dictate to us on virtually every aspect of life – love, marriage, religion, grief and so on.
- In news bulletins, topical programmes and commentaries, the presenters, journalists or television personalities have become the oracles of our time, and they often have far more popularity and authority with the public than politicians, ministers, teachers, parents and academics. This is evidence of the fact that television poses a threat to the church, school and family as a socialising agent (cf. Postman 1985; 1992).
- Furthermore, what television offers is merely substitute experience – the experience of joy and sorrow of popular television characters, and even the secondary experience of pain and misery that we glean from certain news images. The viewer's experience of this is also related to contemporary consumer culture. Just as consumption does not involve much trouble and effort (certainly not in affluent societies), television and the secondary experiences it has to offer do not require effort either. Because the content of television usually consists of "bits of novelty safely packaged in a familiar context" (Kubey & Csikszentmihalyi 1990:186), it requires very little intellectual effort. If television content and form demanded more of the viewer, the medium would fail in its "therapeutic" function of offering recreation and escape and would lose popularity.

This is a disturbing situation – a situation which, in conjunction with various other factors indicates that twenty-first century society is one in which people shy away from complex intellectual challenges. People tend to prefer rather bland forms of recreation and activities that do not really contribute to self-enrichment. Kubey and Csikszentmihalyi (1990) consider television viewing to be an activity of this kind and one that therefore fits in with the prevailing spirit of postmodernism.

# MEDIA STUDIES

Much of what have been said above about television as our dominant public communication culture is speculative and needs to be tested through research. However, it does provide some critical thoughts about the role of the media and especially the electronic media in today's society. The influence of the Internet on public communication is increasingly also becoming an area of investigation and concern.

To conclude: in the above sections we briefly looked at some of the characteristics of different dominant public communication cultures over time. For the student of media and the media practitioner it is important to take note of the impact of the unique qualities of each culture on the quality of communication.

## Summary

In this unit we discussed some of the issues related to the complexity of defining mass communication as a phenomenon. Your attention was specifically drawn to matters such as

- the communicator in mass communication
- the nature of the medium in mass communication
- the concepts "message", "text" and "media content"
- mass communication audiences
- the concept "mass"
- the media as public sphere
- the concept "mediation"
- the nature of mass communication's media culture.

Thereafter we looked at some models of communication and emphasised the importance of taking cognisance of the impact of ICTs on mass communication and the growing role of interactivity in mass communication, which in turn will determine future models and theories of mass communication. Using Wood (2000) as a point of departure we then explained the building blocks of theory before we looked at four paradigms in media theory and research, namely administrative, critical, technological deterministic and information society theory and research.

We concluded the unit with a brief look at the characteristics and the impact of the characteristics on the quality of communication in the oral, written and printed, and electronic public communication cultures.

## Research activities

1  Compose a portfolio consisting of the following:
   a) Identify the communicator in:
      - a newspaper story
      - television newscast

# Mass Communication Theory

- radio documentary
- Internet Web site
- a television soap opera
- a film you have recently seen.

b) Illustrate the similarities and differences in the concepts "message", "text" and "media content" with examples from media content.

c) Describe the characteristics of media audiences and how the nature of media audiences is changing against the background of the impact of ICTs on traditional mass media.

d) Against the background of your study of the above unit, write a one-page essay in which you argue for or against the retention of the concept "mass" versus "public" in mass communication.

e) What do you understand by the concept "public sphere"? Illustrate your answer with your own example from the media.

f) What do you understand by the concept "mediation"? Illustrate your answer with your own example from the media.

g) Provide examples from media content in which you illustrate the following:
  - the media as a disseminator of popular culture
  - media content as popular culture
  - the media as a culture in itself and for itself.

h) Models are graphic representations of the processes of mass communication. Design your own mass communication model for Internet communication in which you provide for the communicator, content, message, medium, transmission, receiver, feedback, interactivity and any other feature you want to include in your model. Apart from the graphic design of the model, briefly describe the role and importance of each of the features in your model.

i) Develop your own theory of mass communication. Describe the value, goals and building blocks of your theory and the criteria that can be used to evaluate the theory.

j) You are invited by a special interest group to lecture them on the state of art in mass communication theory and research. Prepare a lecture in which you explain the underlying assumptions and point of departure in administrative, critical, technological deterministic, and in the evolving group of information society theories and research.

k) Write a critical one- to two-page essay in which you express your own ideas about the nature and value of our present-day public communication culture with specific reference to commodification and commercialisation.

## Further reading

Branston, G & Stafford, R. 1999. *The media student's book.* 2nd edition. London: Routledge.
Grossberg, L, Wartella, E & Whitney, DC. 1998. *Media making. Mass media in a popular culture.* Thousand Oaks, CA: Sage.
Gurevitch, M, Bennett, T, Curran, J & Woollacott, J (eds). 1982. *Culture, society and the media.* London: Routledge.
Inglis, F. 1990. *Media theory: an introduction.* Oxford: Blackwell.
McQuail, D. 2000. *McQuail's mass communication theory.* 4th edition. London: Sage.
O'Sullivan, T & Jewkes, Y. 1997. *The media studies reader.* London: Arnold.
Postman, N. 1992. *Technopoly. The surrender of culture to technology.* New York: Knopf.
Thompson, JB. 1995. *The media and modernity. A social theory of the media.* Cambridge: Polity.
Thompson, K (ed). 1997. *Media and cultural regulation.* London: Sage published in association with the Open University.
Webster, F. 1995. *Theories of the information society.* London: Routledge.
Wood, JT. 2000. *Communication theories in action: an introduction.* 2nd edition. Belmont, CA: Wadsworth.

## Bibliography

Berger, A. 1995. *Essentials of mass communication theory.* Thousand Oaks, CA: Sage.
Curran, J, Gurevitch, M & Wollacott, J (eds). 1977. *Mass communication and society.* London: Open University/Arnold.
Curran, J, Gurevitch, M & Woollacott, J. 1982. The study of the media, theoretical approaches, in *Culture, society and the media,* edited by M Gurevitch, T Bennett, J Curran & J Woollacott. London: Methuen:11–29.
Curran, J & Gurevitch, M. 1996. *Mass media and society.* 2nd edition. London: Arnold.
DeFleur, M & Dennis, E. 1994. *Understanding mass communication. A liberal arts perspective.* 5th edition. Boston: Houghton Mifflin.
Dorfman, A & Mattelart, A. 1971. *Para Leer al pato Donald: Comunicacion de masa y colonialismo.* Buenos Aires: Siglo Veintuno Argentian Editores.
Elliot, P. 1982. Intellectuals, the information society and the disappearance of the public sphere. *Media, Culture and Society* 4(3):243–53.
Ferguson, M (ed). 1990. Electronic media and the redefining of time and space in public communication, in *The new imperatives. Future directions for media research,* edited by M Ferguson. London: Sage.
Fiske, J. 1990. *Introduction to communication studies.* London: Routledge.
Fourie, P. 1988. *Aspects of film and television communication.* Cape Town: Juta.
Fourie, P (ed). 1996. *Introduction to communication – course book 3: communication and the production of meaning.* Cape Town: Juta.
Fourie, P (ed). 1997. *Introduction to communication – course book 6: film and television studies.* Cape Town: Juta.
Gernber, G. 1967. Mass media and human communication theory, in *Human communication theory,* edited by F Dance. New York: Holt, Rinehart & Winston.
Gitlin, T. 1978. Media sociology: The dominant paradigm. *Theory and Society* 6:205–253.
Gitlin, T. 1981. Television screens: hegemony in transition, in *Cultural and economic reproduction in education: essays on class, ideology and the state,* edited by M Apple. London: Routledge.

Grossberg, L, Wartella, E & Whitney D. 1998. *Media Making. Mass media in a popular culture*. London: Sage.

Habermas, J. 1984. *The theory of communicative action, vol 1, Reason and rationalization of society*. Boston, MA: Beacon Press.

Hall, S. 1982. The rediscovery of ideology: the return of the repressed in media studies, in *Culture, society and the media*, edited by M Gurevitch, T Bennett, J Curran & J Woollacott. London: Methuen.

Hartley, J, Goulden, H & O'Sullivan, T. 1985. *Making sense of the media. Popular culture and the teaching of media studies*. London: Comedia.

Inglis, F. 1990. *Media theory: an introduction*. London: Blackwell.

Kornhauser, W. 1949. *The politics of mass society*. New York: Free Press.

Kubey, R & Csikszentmihalyi, M. 1990. *Television and the quality of life. How viewing shapes everyday experience*. Hillsday, NJ: Lawrence Erlbaum.

Lang, K. 1980. The critical functions of empirical communication research. Observations on the German-American influences, in *Mass Communication Review Year Book*, Volume 1, edited by GC Wilhout & H De Bock. Beverly Hills, CA: Sage.

Lasswell, H. 1948. The structure and function of communication in society, in *The communication of ideas*, edited by L Bryson. New York: Institute for Religious and Social Studies.

Littlejohn, SW. 1992. *Theories of human communication*. 4th edition. Belmont, CA: Wadsworth.

Lowery, S & DeFleur, ML. 1983. *Milestones in mass communications research. Media effects*. New York: Longman.

McLuhan, M. 1987 (1965). *Understanding media. The extensions of man*. London: Routledge.

McLuhan, E & Zingrone, F. 1997. *Essential McLuhan*. London: Routledge.

McQuail, D. 1984. *Communication*. 2nd edition. London: Longman.

McQuail, D. 2000. *McQuail's mass communication theory*. 4th edition. London: Sage.

McQuail, D & Windahl, S. 1993. *Communication models*. 2nd edition. London: Longman.

O'Sullivan, T, Hartley, J, Saunders, D, Montgomery, M & Fiske, J. 1994. *Key concepts in communication and cultural studies*. 2nd edition. London: Routledge.

Perry, DK. 1996. *Theory and research in mass communication. Context and consequences*. Mahwah, NJ: Lawrence Erlbaum.

Postman, N. 1985. *Amusing ourselves to death: public discourse in the age of show business*. London: Methuen.

Postman, N. 1992. *Technopoly. The surrender of culture to technology*. New York: Knopf.

Rheingold, H. 1997. Disinformocracy, in *The media studies reader*, edited by T O'Sullivan & Y Jewkes. London: Arnold.

Shannon, CE & Weaver, W. 1949. *The mathematical theory of communication*. Illinois: University of Illinois Press.

South African Human Rights Commission. 2000. Research Report commissioned by the South African Human Rights Commission as part of its Inquiry into Race and the Media. Johannesburg: HRC.

Thompson, JB. 1995. *The media and modernity. A social theory of the media*. Cambridge: Polity.

Thompson, K (ed). 1997. *Media and cultural regulation*. London: Sage published in association with the Open University.

Westley, BH & MacLean, MS. 1957. A conceptual model for communication research. *Journalism Quarterly* 34:31–38.

Wood, JT. 2000. *Communication theories in action*. 2nd edition. Belmont, CA: Wadsworth.

# The Role and Functions of the Media: Functionalism

*Pieter J Fourie*

## Overview

We all know and have experienced how the media are often blamed for almost everything that can go wrong. Politicians frequently accuse the media of misinterpreting them, of framing them, of lying, of wrongfully criticising them, and of not doing what they wish the media to do or achieve. Similarly, celebrities and even ordinary people once faced with the media are often disillusioned that "the story didn't turn out to be what they wanted it to be". Organisations often complain that the media only focus on the negative. They then go on to criticise the media.

In this unit we are concerned with criticism like this and the ongoing debate about what the functions of the media are and what their role in society should be. To explain this difficult topic we specifically look, by way of example, at the role of the press and the functions of film. We have chosen the press because much of what has been written about the functions and roles of the press applies to all the other media. Also, much of what has been written about the press concerns the media's information, surveillance and political functions. In film, the emphasis is on the other main function of the media, namely entertainment. Much of what is said about the entertainment functions of film equally applies to television.

We begin by setting the problem within the context of the theoretical framework of functionalism. We provide you with a typology of media functions. We then take a closer look at six theories about the role of the press in society. The functions of film are then examined by means of taking a closer look at exactly what we mean by entertainment.

## Learning outcomes

After studying this unit you will be able to

- contribute to the ongoing debate about the functions and role of the media in society;
- define functionalism as the main paradigm (way of thinking about the role of the media) from which research about the functions of the media is done;
- list and explain the main limitations of functionalism;

# The Role and Functions of the Media: Functionalism

- explain with examples from the South African media McQuail's (2000) typology of media functions;
- explain the concept "pluralism" with reference to the political functions of the media;
- define normative theory and explain the basic assumptions of six theories about the functions and roles of the press in society;
- explain the complexity of the entertainment function of film (electronic moving images); and
- explain the social, education and propaganda functions (or nature) of electronic moving images.

## 7.1 INTRODUCTION: FUNCTIONALISM

Since the beginning of the academic study of mass communication and mass media, scholars concerned themselves with descriptions of exactly what the functions of the mass media are or should be. This was done under the influence of key sociologists such as Emile Durkheim (1858–1917) and Talcott Parsons (1902–1979) and within the context of the sociological paradigm known as functionalism or structural functionalism at the end of the nineteenth century and the first part of the twentieth century.

The bottom-line of functionalism is a view of society as being integrated, harmonious and a cohesive whole consisting of different social systems. All parts of society, be it government, welfare institutions, educational institutions, the military, economic institutions and cultural institutions function to maintain equilibrium, consensus and social order. The goal of sociology is to describe and analyse these different social systems in terms of their functions and functioning towards equilibrium, consensus and social order (O'Sullivan, Hartley, Saunders, Montgomery & Fiske 1994:124). The same applies to the media system in a society. As powerful socialisation instruments they should function towards integration, harmony and cohesion, whether it is through the information, entertainment and/or education they provide.

Some of the first communication scholars to provide functionalist analyses of media were Lasswell (1948), Lazersfeld and Merton (1948), and Merton (1957). Merton was one of the first to distinguish between latent and manifest functions and the fact that what might be functional to one group may be dysfunctional to another.

More recent, but now almost a classic model for the study of the functions of the media is that of Wright (1975) who proposed the following inventory of questions (see Table 7.1) (cf. O'Sullivan et al 1994:125).

In this model Wright argues that the main functions of the media are to inform and entertain people, and that through such information and entertainment the media contribute either manifestly or latently to cultural growth for both individuals and society as such. However, this is, as are many other functionalist models, a rather simplistic model which does not provide for other manifest and/or latent functions of the media, especially when it comes to the political functions of the media, which we will show later in this unit (see 7.2).

## Table 7.1 Wright's model of functions

| Model of functions |
|---|
| *What are* <br> 1   the manifest <br> 2   latent <br> 3   functions and <br> 4   dysfunctions <br><br> *of mass communicated* <br> 5   surveillance (news) <br> 6   correlation (selection) <br> 7   cultural transmission <br> 8   entertainment <br><br> *for the* <br> 9    society <br> 10   individual <br> 11   subgroups <br> 12   cultural systems? |

Some of the main objections to functionalism (O'Sullivan et al 1994:95–96) are that functionalism often:

- Tends to oversee the fact that the media do not necessarily have the same functions for the same people or groups in a society. It takes consensus as granted and disregards conflict in social relations. In other words, functionalism takes it for granted that the media will have the same functions for all the people in a society. This is not necessarily the case. What might function as information for one, might be disinformation to others. What some people might experience as entertainment might offend others.
- Fails to account adequately for social change and transformation. Media functions in well-established democratic societies might be dysfunctional in societies in a process of change, development and transformation. In such societies the emphasis on the media's perceived role may be more on its role in development and less on, for example, surveillance.
- Neglects to provide for feedback and the fact that feedback modifies both the message and the context. Put another way, functionalism often tends not to acknowledge the importance of context – social, political and cultural – as an influence on all stages of the communication processes (Watson & Hill 1984:149).

Nevertheless, as McQuail (2000:79–80) argues, functionalist models and discussions of the functions of the media provide us with *basic ideas* about the role of the media in society. As such they provide a structured framework for our continued and important discussions and reviews of the significant tasks of media as key socialisation and ideological instruments in society.

For this introduction, McQuail's (ibid) summary of media functions (slightly adapted in the table) suffices.

**Table 7.2 McQuail's typology of functions** (McQuail 2000:79–80)

| Functions/tasks of the media |
|---|
| **Information:** the media (can)<br>• provide information about events and conditions in society and the world;<br>• indicate relations of power;<br>• facilitate innovation, adaptation and progress.<br><br>**Correlation:** the media (can)<br>• explain, interpret and comment on the meaning of events and information;<br>• provide support for established authority and norms;<br>• socialise;<br>• co-ordinate separate activities;<br>• contribute to consensus building;<br>• set orders of priority and by so doing signal the status of a topic.<br><br>**Continuity:** the media (can)<br>• express the dominant culture and recognise subcultures and new cultural developments;<br>• forge and maintain commonality of values.<br><br>**Entertainment:** the media (can)<br>• provide amusement, diversion and the means of relaxation;<br>• reduce social tension.<br><br>**Mobilisation:** the media (can)<br>• campaign for social objectives in the sphere of politics, war, economic development, work and sometimes religion. |

## 7.2 THE POLITICAL FUNCTIONS OF THE MEDIA: THE CASE OF PLURALISM

As far as the political functions of the media are concerned Van Cuilenburg, Scholten and Noomen (1992:317) argue that in a democracy the media has the following political functions:

• to inform about political developments and decisions

# MEDIA STUDIES

- to guide the public opinion about political developments and decisions
- to express different views about political developments and decisions
- to criticise political developments and decisions.

In order to empower the media to perform the above political functions

- media policy should ensure media pluralism
- media content should reflect social plurality.

By social plurality (or social pluralism) we mean the acknowledgement of political, social, cultural and economic differences between people and groups in a society.

By media pluralism we mean (1) the acknowledgement of social plurality and (2) the reflection thereof in a diversity of media content, for instance reflecting different political views, as well as (3) the existence of different media, for instance different newspapers, radio stations, television stations, a variety of magazines, films, and so on, catering for and reflecting the views of different groups within a society.

Van Cuilenburg, Scholten and Noomen (1992:327) distinguish between internal and external plurality. Internal plurality refers to the differences within the information and entertainment content of, for instance a single newspaper, radio station and/or television station, within which there should be a balance between information, entertainment and the like; different opinions must be offered, and so forth. External plurality concerns the difference between different newspapers, radio stations and television stations.

The authors also distinguish between three levels of plurality: *macro- meso-* and *micro-plurality*.

Micro-plurality concerns each medium on its own and is thus internal. For instance the South African Broadcasting Corporation (SABC) and its plurality in terms of content, or the plurality available in a newspaper such as *Mail & Guardian* or within the *Sowetan*. Meso-plurality concerns media categories, in other words are there different newspapers available, different television stations, radio stations, different film companies, different magazines, and so on, in a country. For example, how many radio stations are there in a country and what is the nature of diversity in their content? Macro-plurality concerns all the available media, regardless of category, available in a society. In other words, one may have only newspapers and radio stations, but no television stations and no film companies. Macro-plurality thus concerns the availability or lack of availability of the whole range of media. To explain the above difference, the following applies:

- Micro-plurality: the availability of plurality within a newspaper such as *Mail & Guardian*.
- Meso-plurality: the availability of plurality between *Mail & Guardian* and the *Sowetan* (newspaper categories).
- Macro-plurality: the availability of plurality between *Mail & Guardian* and other media such as television, radio, film, and so on.

In short, in a democracy the question about media functions is closely related to the principle of pluralism. A single newspaper with its own ideology and political stance might have an informative function for a certain group, but at the same time it might be disinformative to other groups and/or individuals. For this reason the question of pluralism is emphasised in democratic societies. The ideal is that there should be as many radio and television stations, newspapers, magazines and films as possible, for as many people and groups in a society as possible. Only by and through acknowledging the plurality of political views and tastes in entertainment can the media be in position to function for as many people and groups as possible in a society, and play a democratic role.

With this as an overall prerequisite for the media to function free and democratically we now look specifically at the role of the press.

## 7.3 THE FUNCTIONS OF THE PRESS: NORMATIVE THEORY

Theories and research about the functions, often referred to as "the role of the press in society", have culminated in what is generally known as the so-called normative theories of the press. By normative theory we mean ideal views (from different perspectives and within different conditions) about the role of the press in society. In short it means "the press should or could do this or that". Keep in mind that although we call them normative press theories they also apply to other media in society.

Roelofse (1996:48–60) argues that since governments generally have the power to restrict newspapers' criticism of government, and since the press usually assumes a surveillance role on behalf of civil society, tensions and conflicts between these two institutions are natural and to be expected. The power that governments claim for themselves usually conflicts with the democratic right of freedom of speech, a right which is important to newspapers as it enables them to perform their functions properly.

Normative theories are thus mainly concerned with the freedom of, or restrictions on, the newspaper industry (media) in various situations and how this impacts on the functions of the press (media) in society.

This was the premise of a study (conducted in 1956 by Fred S Siebert, Theodore Peterson and Wilbur Schramm) of the different press systems in the world (cf. Siebert, Peterson & Schramm 1963). They developed the following four theories:

- The authoritarian theory
- The libertarian theory
- The social responsibility theory
- The Soviet communist theory.

The first and second theories are regarded as the main or basic press theories, while the third and fourth are variations on these theories.

A fifth theory, the development theory, was formulated to accommodate conditions in developing countries. A sixth and last theory, the democratic-participant theory, is a description of a new kind of press-government-public relationship which has in recent years developed in reaction to deficiencies, such as corruption and abuse of power, in traditional democratic, free-market societies.

The following overview of these theories is based mainly on the interpretations of Roelofse (1996) and McQuail (1987).

### 7.3.1 The authoritarian theory

The authoritarian theory prevails in dictatorial societies, but can also surface in less authoritarian societies when, for example, the freedom of the press conflicts with the interests of the state or society in general, for instance when there is a danger of terrorism or in times of war. Authoritarianism can also be exercised with regard to one medium in contrast with other media – in some countries television is subjected to greater control than the newspaper industry, for example. The authoritarian theory, therefore, is not merely that of historical or descriptive importance, or simply an extraordinary deviation from established democratic norms, it continues to justify government suppression of the press (Roelofse 1996:50).

McQuail (1987:111-112) identifies the following basic assumptions of the authoritarian press theory:

- The press should do nothing to undermine vested power and interests.
- The press should be subordinate to vested power and authority.
- The press should avoid acting in contravention of prevailing moral and political values.
- Censorship is justified in the application of these principles.
- Editorial attacks on vested power and authority, deviations from official policy and the violation of moral codes should be criminal offences.

A good example of how the press was expected to play a role such as described above, was under the rule of Milosevic in Yugoslavia. Part of the popular uprising against his rule in October 2000, was to attack media institutions which had no other function but to publicise Milosevic and his government's propaganda.

One can conclude that under authoritarianism the only function of the press is to publicise and to propagandise the government's ideology and actions. In other words the press is nothing else but an instrument and mouthpiece of government.

Roelofse (1996:51) draws our attention to the fact that some of the most significant communication and political events in the past century took place in authoritarian societies. The fascism (the philosophy and practice of the absolute power of the state and the subservience of the individual) found in Hitler's Germany, Mussolini's Italy, Franco's Spain, South Africa's apartheid regime and in many African and communist countries, is and was rooted in authoritarianism and/or totalitarianism, which gave much freedom to the rulers, little or no freedom to the ruled, and which defined press freedom as a right vested in the state.

## 7.3.2 The libertarian theory

Roelofse (1996:51–53) shows how developments such as the rise of democracy, religious freedom, the expansion of economic freedom and the general philosophical climate of the Enlightenment undermined authoritarianism and led to a new view of the press as a mass medium. The emphasis on personal freedom and democracy that emerged in the late seventeenth century and flourished in the nineteenth century, gave rise to the libertarian theory in reaction to the authoritarian theory.

According to the libertarian theory, people are rational beings capable of distinguishing between truth and falsehood, and between good and evil. The search for truth is regarded as an inalienable natural right. In terms of these beliefs the press is seen as a source of information and a platform for the expression of divergent opinions, informing people about government affairs and other issues and enabling them to monitor their government and form their own ideas about policy. The press should be free from government control and government influence, and there must be a free market for ideas and information (Roelofse 1996:52). The USA and Britain have had this type of press for approximately 200 years. The press has been encouraged to act as a *fourth estate* along with the legislative, executive and judicial authorities in the governing process (Siebert et al 1963:3–4).

However, the application of the idea of a free press is not simple. Referring to this, McQuail (1987:114) comments as follows:

> The question of whether [a free press] is an end in itself, a means to an end, or an absolute right has never been settled.

Once freedom is abused, it is no longer freedom and should be restricted. Absolute freedom is in fact anarchy. Libertarian societies therefore all more or less agree with Mill's (1964) contention that the freedom of the individual is defined – and thus constrained – by the freedom of other individuals. Put simply: my freedom ends where yours begins (Roelofse 1996:52).

Most societies that recognise freedom of the press sought the solution to this dilemma of determining the boundaries of freedom without infringing the rights of the individual in:

- the abolition of censorship on the one hand; and
- the introduction of press laws designed to protect individual rights.

The protection of reputation, privacy, the moral development of individuals or groups and the security and even the dignity of the state were recognised in common law and enshrined in statutory laws – which often caused these rights to override the right of the press's freedom to publish (McQuail 1987:114).

McQuail (1987:115) identifies the following basic assumptions of the libertarian press theory:

- The press should be free from any external censorship.
- Publication and distribution should be accessible to any individual or group without a permit or licence.

- Editorial attacks on governments or political parties should not be punishable.
- There should be no coercion to publish anything.
- False reporting is viewed in the same light as publication of the truth.
- No restrictions should be placed on the acquisition of information through legal channels.
- There should be no restriction on the export and import of messages across national borders.

### 7.3.3 The social responsibility theory

Exponents of this theory attempt to reconcile the ideas of freedom and independence with responsibility towards society (Roelofse 1996:53–54). The social responsibility theory is based on the following premises (McQuail 1987:116–118):

- The media have an important function to fulfil in society, especially with regard to supporting democratic political principles.
- The media are under an obligation to fulfil their social functions, especially with regard to the transmission of information and the creation of a forum for different viewpoints.
- The independence of the media should be emphasised in relation to their responsibility towards society.
- The media should meet certain standards.

The theory offers two types of solutions to the problem of reconciling freedom with social responsibility. These are:

- the development of public institutions, independent of government, for the control of the broadcasting industry, for example institutions such as the Independent Communications Authority of South Africa (ICASA) and the Independent Broadcasting Complaints Commission (IBCC)
- the continuing development of professionalism, which should advance and nurture balanced and impartial news presentation (compare for instance the plight and recommendation of the South African Human Rights Commission for the development of professionalism and training in South African journalism).

McQuail (ibid) identifies the following basic principles of the social responsibility theory about the media:

- The media should accept certain responsibilities towards society.
- The media should fulfil their responsibilities mainly by setting professional standards with regard to the supply of information and the truth, accuracy, objectivity and balance of their reporting.
- In order to be responsible, the media should apply self-regulation within the framework of the law and established institutions.
- The media should avoid publicising information that can lead to crime, violence or social disruption, as well as information that can offend ethnic or religious minorities.

# The Role and Functions of the Media: Functionalism

- The media collectively should represent all social groups and reflect the diversity of society by giving people access to a variety of viewpoints and the right to react to these viewpoints.
- Society is entitled to expect high professional standards and intervention is justifiable if the media fail to meet these standards.

## 7.3.4 The Soviet communist press theory

Until the fall of communism and the disintegration of the former Soviet Union there was probably no press system in the world as strictly controlled as the communist system. Western notions of freedom of the press were rejected as being fundamentally "unfree", because the Western media are controlled by capitalist economic interests which prevent them from publishing the Marxist *truth* (Siebert et al 1963:5, 125). The communist press, on the other hand, had no profit motive. McQuail (1987:118–119) and Roelofse (1996:55–56) identify the following basic assumptions of the Soviet communist theory of the media:

- The media should act in the interests of and be controlled by the working class.
- The media should not be under private control.
- The media should perform positive functions for society such as socialisation (to make people conform to desirable norms), education, the supply of information, motivation and the mobilisation of the masses.
- The media should respond to the desires and needs of their recipients.
- Society has the right to use censorship and other legal measures to prevent and punish antisocial publication.
- The media should reflect a complete and objective view of the world and of society in terms of Marxist-Leninist principles.
- The media should support progressivistic (communist) movements everywhere.

Much has changed since the fall of communism. However, there are still many countries in the former Soviet Bloc, in Africa and Asia that are battling to obtain media freedom.

---

**Freedom of the media Web sites**

See the following Internet sites to follow the continued struggle for media freedom:

(South African) Freedom of Expression Institute (FXI): http://www.fxi.org.za

Media Institute of Southern Africa: http://www.misanet.org

Campaign for Press and Broadcasting Freedom: http://www.keywords.dsvr.co.uk/freepress/index.html

Freedom Forum: http://www.freedomforum.org

## 7.3.5 The development theory

The developing countries advocate the positive use of the media to promote national development, autonomy and cultural identity. The most important principle of the development theory of the media is that the ideals of economic development should be emphasised. Certain liberties of the media should be made subordinate to the achievement of these ideals. At the same time, common objectives are given priority over individual freedom (Roelofse 1996:56-58). McQuail (1987:119-121) identifies the following basic assumptions of the development theory of the media:

- The media should make a positive contribution to the national development process.
- The state should be able to restrict the media if economic interests and the development needs of the society are at stake.
- The media should give preference to information about national, cultural and language issues.
- The media should also give preference to information about other developing countries that are geographically, culturally and politically akin to one another.
- Journalists have both responsibilities and liberties in obtaining and distributing information.
- To protect development objectives, the state has the right to intervene by restricting and censoring the media. State subsidies and direct control are therefore justifiable.

With regard to the role of the media in development it is important to take note of the South African government's plan in November 2000 to set up a Media Development and Diversity Agency (MDDA) to promote access to the media by marginalised groups and to enhance media pluralism. See in this regard the following Web site (at the time of writing) for the position paper on the MDDA: its objectives, functions and proposed budget:

http://www.polity.org.za/govdocs/discuss/mdda/index.html

## 7.3.6 The democratic-participant theory

This theory is primarily a reaction to the trends towards commercialisation and monopoly-formation in privately controlled mass media, and towards centralisation and bureaucratisation in public broadcasting. The practical realisation of this theory is encountered primarily in developed societies (Roelofse 1996:58-60).

The democratic participant theory supports and emphasises the importance of the following:

- the multiplicity/diversity of media
- the small-scale use of media
- the local nature of media
- the deinstitutionalising of the media
- the reciprocal role of communicator and recipient
- horizontal communication
- interaction and involvement.

McQuail (1987:121-123) summarises the basic principles of the democratic-participant theory as follows:
- Individuals and minority groups should be able to claim:
  - the right of access to the media, and
  - the right to have their needs served by the media.
- The organisation of the media and the content of messages should not be influenced by political or bureaucratic control.
- The existence of the media must be justified in terms of the needs and interests of recipients, and not exclusively in terms of those of the media organisations, professional media workers or advertisers.
- Groups, organisations and communities should have their own media.
- Small-scale, interactive and participatory forms of media are regarded as more beneficial than large-scale, unidirectional media which are used only by professional media workers.
- In general, social needs are neglected by established media.
- Communication is regarded as too important to be left to professionals.

### 7.3.7 A revision of the press theories

The above normative theories (or perceptions about the functions) of the press are presently revised by Nordenstreng, Christians, Glasser and McQuail (Nordenstreng 1997:97-109).

They argue that theories of the functions and roles of the press fall into two types of theory: those *prescribing* openly normative tasks for the media in society (such as the theories summarised above), and those *describing* the *real* role of the media in society. The latter approaches the issue from the "objective" angle of media sociology, while the former deals with the "subjective" conceptions held by various players (including public opinion leaders, government officials, cabinet ministers, and so on) about the mission of the media. In other words, we should distinguish between *ideal* theories and *real* theories, or *normative* and *sociological* theories.

In their revision, each media system (for instance the South African media system) is not placed in any one category (or within the confines of one of the above theories). Instead, Nordenstreng et al suggest that each national media system and individual medium, even each individual journalist, can have a combination of roles. Instead of formalising specific theories to classify the role of a media system one should rather classify the kind of arguments about media roles (functions) within the framework of a specific paradigm. They distinguish between five such possible paradigms, here briefly summarised:
- Liberal-individualist paradigm: arguments about the role of the media in which the emphasis is on individual liberty as the cornerstone of democracy and on the public's interest. The media's overall role is to contribute to and uphold democracy. Therefore the state should have a minimal role in media affairs.

- Social responsibility paradigm: arguments about the role of the media in which the emphasis is on active citizenship, instead of abundant information. The media should contribute to the upliftment of society and its citizens.
- Critical paradigm: arguments about the role of the media in which the emphasis is on the potential of the media to emancipate the masses. The media should question prevailing and oppressive ideologies.
- Administrative paradigm: arguments about the role of the media in which the emphasis is on the point of departure being the objectivity of information and the efficient transmission of reliable information to as many people as possible – the emphasis is on professionalism and technocratic excellence.
- Cultural negotiation paradigm: arguments about the role of the media in which the emphasis is on the rights of subcultures with their particular values, inter-subjective understanding and a real sense of community. Media serve both communitarianism and cultural negotiation between conflicting values, aiming at mediations through drama (confrontation between issues) rather than news.

From the perspective of these paradigms Nordenstreng et al then argue that the media can play one or more of the following roles:

- Collaborative: a role the media plays when a nation-state is young and insecure. In other words to collaborate towards development ideals, nation building and national interest. This is usually the role governments want the media to play and is the role the SA government wants the South African media to play.
- Surveillance: the media plays an adverse role, acts as a watchdog and agenda-setter. The media exposes violations of the moral and social order. The media informs by bringing important issues to the attention of the community. This is usually the role played by the media in established democracies and often the reason for its unpopularity with governments.
- Facilitative: the media seeks to create and sustain public debate. This is the essence of the public or civic journalism movement.
- Critical/dialectical: journalists examine in a truly radical way the assumptions and premises of a community. The media's role is to constitute public debate about, not within, the prevailing political order.

### Case study 7.1: Civic journalism defined

Civic journalism is about providing people with the news and information they need to allow them to function as citizens, to make the decisions they are called on to make in a democratic society.

Fouhy (2001) explains the aims of civic journalism in the following way:

- It is an effort to reconnect with the real concerns that viewers and readers have about the things in their lives they care most about – not in a way that panders

to them, but in a way that treats them as citizens with the responsibilities of self-government, rather than as consumers to whom goods and services are sold.
- It takes the traditional five w's of journalism – who, what, when, where, why – and expands them to ask why is this story important to *me* and to the *community in which I live*?
- Civic journalists are trying to plug back into their communities, to cross the gap that has opened and widened between the news media and their constituents – their readers and viewers.
- Plugging into the community is hard. It's much harder journalism than dealing with the same old sources, the experts, the media-savvy advocates of the same old tired points of view, the self-serving talking heads, always available for the interview, always ready with conventional wisdom or a cynical one-liner.
- Civic journalists broaden their agenda from the usual overwhelming focus on political and governmental news to aggressively ferret out issues of interest to citizens who are not members of the élite. That means things like the education of their children, the security of their families, and the economic future they face. That means covering an agenda that is set more by citizens, by the people, and less by those who would manipulate them.
- That means thinking about the news not only from the standpoint of conventional journalistic practice but taking it a step further and thinking about a subject from the standpoint of the public and public interest.

Source: *Civic Journalism: Rebuilding the foundations of democracy* by Edward M Fouhy (2001). Executive Director: Pew Centre for Civic Journalism.

From the above it is clear that the emphasis in the press theories is on the role the media can or should play in the dissemination of information and the formation of public opinion.

There are no clear answers. From an academic point of view we can only try to group the different arguments in terms of their underlying assumptions and to identify them within the framework of a specific paradigm. If one accepts that the media is, can be and should be a pillar of democracy, then the only solution to the problem of defining the media's role, is to acknowledge the importance of pluralism.

In the next section we look at the functions of film, in which the emphasis is on the role of entertainment. We have selected to focus on entertainment, because, second to the media's crucial role of informing the public and to participate in the formation of public opinion, is its entertainment role. Through its entertainment it can be argued that media have became the most dominant entertainment industry in our time.

## 7.4 THE FUNCTIONS OF FILM: THE CASE OF ENTERTAINMENT

The entertainment function can be approached from many perspectives. We decided to do it from the perspective of posing the question: What is entertainment? Finding

# MEDIA STUDIES

answers to this question can contribute to our understanding of entertainment in general and more specifically understanding film and television as entertainment. Our focus is furthermore on the feature or fiction film and not on genres such as news and the documentary (obviously they also entertain). Furthermore, where we refer to film you may also understand television as we are dealing with the moving image, which applies to both these mediums.

## 7.4.1 The entertainment function of film

Usually one would argue that the primary function of film is to entertain. The entire history of film demonstrates that this medium has an almost magical fascination, because the fictional (sometimes idealised) world it creates offers people an escape, however fleeting, from their routinised worlds. But, at the same time it must be kept in mind that the entertainment provided by film can also serve to orient people in society (socialisation) and to influence and educate them in certain ways. Inherently, and although the emphasis is on entertainment, film thus also has an educational function, or plays an educational role and can act as an ideological agent.

### *Identification and projection*

To understand film's entertainment function we must begin by asking: How does a film entertain us? There are different answers from different perspectives. It suffices for us to say a movie must get the viewer to do two things:
- to identify with the content, characters and action on screen, and
- to project his/her own feelings, values and the like onto these events.

Identification and projection are two essential features of the social and emotional life of human beings. In order to stimulate such identification and projection, and to fascinate the viewer, a film must satisfy three requirements:
- First, the nature of the theme, content and action should be of a kind that makes viewer identification easy and pleasurable. To this end, feature films follow a recipe which Lindgren (1963:47) summarises as follows:

    > The function of fiction in general, then, and of the fiction film in particular, is to present an imaginary story of the thoughts and actions of individual human beings. We must, therefore, expect to find the unity of a work of fiction deriving, not from a subject or an idea or argument, but from the human activities which are its characteristic material; one should be able to summarise the essence of a work of fiction, in other words, in some statement about its action.

    In other words, action is equivalent to what people (the characters) do. The primary business of a feature film, then, is to show events in a course of action.
- The second requirement is that the characters (cast/stars) must be such that people can identify with them and what they do. This applies especially to the character of

the protagonist(s). Viewers must be able to identify with the character of, for example, James Bond and the star who portrays James Bond, as well as with what James Bond stands (and fights) for.
- Thirdly, the film must make a visual impact on the viewer. To do so, it has to synthesise various communication sign systems, such as language (dialogue) words, acting, costuming, composition, music, camera and editing techniques, lighting and colour. Failure at any one of these operative communication levels means failure of the film as a whole. In effect it implies that without a good script, good photography, good cinematography, perceptive editing, good acting, imaginative lighting, mood-creating special effects and music, the film as a whole will fail to have the desired emotional impact on viewers. This is the art of film production: to synthesise all the operative communication systems, which together impart meaning to a film.

Because film communicates through the simultaneous use of different sign systems (cf. Unit 5 on film theory and criticism in Volume 2), it commands and grips the viewer's full attention, thus creating emotional involvement: it entertains.

The above are the prerequisites for identification. But what is identification? In simplistic terms identification is the human ability to *pick up another person's "vibes"*, to empathise with others. Such feeling is based on shared values, a common background, education, culture and the like – in fact, everything that makes inter-subjective fellowship possible.

Identification proceeds in two ways: those of introjection and projection. Introjection means that the recipient assumes or adopts the feelings of the other party (e.g. of fictional characters); projection means that the recipient projects his own feelings onto the other party (character/s).

Apart from identification and projection, research also indicates that in the case of film, people usually have some emotional predisposition towards a work which in itself may give rise to identification. This predisposition is referred to as *couche constituante* – the phenomenon of pre-existing emotions stimulating people's imaginations. Translated into practice it is reflected in the phenomenon of the viewer who watches a particular film or television programme with certain expectations. People expect to laugh (be entertained) when they watch a comedy. These expectations are raised partly by external factors such as the publicity preceding the programme or the actors (known to viewers) appearing in it, and partly by personal taste which in turn depends on the viewer's cultural, educational, intellectual and social background. In other words, if publicity tells us that a specific actor whom we like, plays the lead in a film, one is already inclined to identify with the film. If you know the work of a specific director (knowledge) and you like his/her work, then you may already be inclined to identify with the film. Or if you know and like a specific genre, such as science fiction, then you may already want to see a new science fiction film, despite who the actors are or what the story is about. If you don't like this genre, you will in any case not go and view a science fiction film despite the actors, story, and so on.

## Distance and play

Although viewers may experience film as a pleasurable catharsis, and despite the fact that they identify with the characters and their imaginary world (mainly on the strength of built-in rhetorical motifs), they always maintain a personal distance. This is probably the real reason why they experience the film product as gratifying or entertaining.

It should be borne in mind that the emotions experienced by viewers are directed to a fictional object and can therefore not be regarded as genuine emotion. Even though viewers become emotionally involved, they realise that it is an ephemeral experience from which they could dissociate themselves if they so wished. They know that the experience of these emotions cannot do them permanent harm (e.g. lasting sorrow) or afford abiding pleasure or joy. The crux of the experience is the distance that the viewer maintains despite possible emotional involvement with the events on screen. The viewer never becomes wholly part of them but preserves a safe distance, so to speak. This enables the viewer to experience even tragedy, violence and horror as entertaining. Film fiction affords viewers the opportunity to see, experience and identify (or otherwise) with themselves and other people in the vicissitudes of the characters and the events in which they are caught up. In this process, however, they are always outsiders – observers rather than participants. They are the "peeping toms", the "quasi voyeurs". To the voyeur, peeping is a pleasurable experience leading to gratification and sublimation.

What we have said about the preservation of distance applies not only to the viewer but also to the producer, the director, and the actors. The same applies to all forms of photographic communication, be it documentary, film or fiction. In the case of news, for example, the editor, journalists, announcer/television newsreader, the interposing of a camera between the communicator and reality (e.g. in the case of news) or an imaginary reality (e.g. in fictional film and television) at once creates a distance between the communicator and that (imaginary) reality. The result is a type of uninvolved involvement: reality is viewed from the security afforded by the camera lens. In the case of an imaginary reality (fiction), it is actually created by the camera (and other visual and sound codes). The end result is therefore a manipulated reality. In the case of film and television fiction, the scriptwriter, the director, actors and other members of the production team have to step outside reality, as it were, in order to create an imaginary world.

In view of all this, film fiction and the experience of it as entertainment can be described as a game (cf. Huizenga 1950). The characteristics of any game (and play) are:

- It is always voluntary.
- It is always imaginary (not reality itself but a step-out-of reality).
- It always has rules and one must understand the rules.
- It always has a specific duration and end within a given length of time.
- It always has a social nature.

One can also argue that the act of viewing a film, like any form of play, is always voluntary. The viewer knows that what he/she is watching and identifying with is not reality but an imaginary world; the viewer understands the dramatic structure of the programme and the use of certain codes, together with their meanings (e.g. flashbacks). In other words, the viewer is familiar with the rules of film or a specific genre; indeed, the viewer is usually aware of the stereotyped structure of a comedy, a thriller, a drama, soap operas, family series, situation comedies and the like. In addition, the viewer knows that a film will end within a given length of time. Watching a film constitutes a spatio-temporal interruption of the viewer's daily routine and the performance of his/her daily work, and is usually a social occasion.

As far as *content* is concerned film fiction professes, like play or a game, to be reality. It is, like play or a game, manufactured according to institutional rules and conventions, which often dictate the content and form as well. Consider in this regard the success recipe, stereotyped content and production patterns and the fact that a film has a certain length and that the content is enacted within specific spatio-temporal confines. True to the social nature of games and the fact that they are social occasions, film fiction always in some way reflects prevailing social values, norms and behaviour.

## *Recreation and leisure*

Under film's entertainment function we also understand recreation and leisure. The emphasis is on social activity.

Apart from getting people emotionally involved, film is also par excellence recreation: going to the movies fulfils the need for a particular type of social activity. Going to the movies represents an opportunity to "go out" and experience emotions collectively. Watching a television programme in the privacy of the home does not necessarily fulfil this social function. Films are aimed at entertaining people outside their homes and thus afford an opportunity for social relaxation.

The nature of the recreation provided by film is characterised by the following combined elements (Eidsvik 1978:15):

- physical passivity of the viewer
- emotional involvement of the viewer
- anonymous viewing
- collective experience
- accessibility (relative easy accessibility of movie theatres and at a relative low cost) insulation from distraction (dark enclosed room)
- ritualised behaviour (of all the viewers).

In addition to recreation, film is also a way of spending one's leisure time, compensating for personal shortcomings and alleviating loneliness. With reference to leisure-time occupation, White (1971:26) says that modern people want to spend their leisure in a comfortable and relaxed way: free time is being consumed in predominantly ocular activities and, within that category, in the pictorial variety – picture magazines and film screens – rather than in the kind that involves an intermediate step of deciphering, like reading.

## What is entertainment?

Having said the above, the question remains: But what is entertainment? There are many and complicated answers to the question, and answers can be provided from many disciplinary perspectives such as psychology, biology, sociology, and so on. It suffices to say that entertainment is a value-judgement attached to a work by an individual recipient. In other words, the recipient decides for him/herself, independently of the communicator's intention, whether or not he/she is experiencing a work (e.g. a film) as entertaining. This happens against the background of the viewer's own knowledge, education, culture, expectations, experience and taste.

Therefore it is possible for different people to experience different things as entertainment, thus making it possible to experience news, sport, educational programmes, commentary, even tragedy or *high* art, as entertaining. Because entertainment is a value rather than an intrinsic quality of a programme, it is indefinable as a phenomenon or even as a specific genre.

If, on the other hand, one considers the value of entertainment to relate to an experience of pleasure or a sense of gratification, then one could try to establish what element of a film or a television programme causes the recipient to attach the value of entertainment to a film or programme. In other words, the question as to what is entertainment changes to what is it that causes a sense of enjoyment/gratification that allows one to attach the value – it is entertainment (or something is entertaining) – when I watch a film or television programme. Again there are many possible answers to this question. One such an answer will suffice, namely that film and television have certain intrinsic rhetorical motifs that lead the viewer to decide whether he/she is experiencing something as entertainment.

In their extensive and searching analysis, Rosenfield and Mader (1984:475–544) show how one can identify five rhetorical motifs which are prerequisites for the pleasurable or gratifying experience of communication and thus of a work as entertainment. The motifs are the following:

- Knowledge about identity, that is those facets in a work (e.g. a film) which offer the viewer answers to the question: Who am I? Rhetorically, this question is only answerable in terms of an analysis of the individual's relation with and to others, including his/her role, place and function in society. Film usually focuses on human relations.
- Knowledge about ability: when a work manages to demonstrate possibilities to the recipient (e.g. how to solve a difficult problem) and to show him that he, or others, have the ability to achieve something, the recipient experiences gratification and liberation.
- Knowledge about survival: by making the recipient aware of eternal values (e.g. love, friendship, generosity and fellowship) he/she is freed from basic anxiety about destruction and, ultimately, death.
- Knowledge about and an understanding of reality: a work (e.g. a film) should enable the viewer to transcend the stress of reality by giving him/her an opportunity to view it objectively from the outside (as an outsider).

# The Role and Functions of the Media: Functionalism

- The final motif comprehends all the preceding ones in that it relates directly to knowledge. The knowledge gleaned from the responses to questions about identity, ability, survival and reality is in itself liberating and is therefore experienced as pleasurable and gratifying.

According to Rosenfeld and Mader (ibid), the presence of these motifs facilitates and encourages recipient identification with a work. Content analyses indicate that these motifs keep recurring in the content of films and popular television genres such as the situation comedy, family drama, soap opera and police and action drama. These genres, popular as they may be and often criticised by high-brow critics for being meaningless and "a waste of time", invariably contain some sort of information about values, attitudes, ideas, customs and behaviour towards which viewers have to orient themselves in their daily lives. One could therefore say that these genres, like film, directly and indirectly convey knowledge and understanding about identity, ability, survival and reality. Awareness of all these (albeit at a latent experiential level) affords the viewer knowledge of him/herself as a person in relation with others and to society. Such knowledge is reassuring, at any rate to most viewers, and they therefore can experience these works as pleasurable and thus as entertainment.

### Case study 7.2: Rhetorical motifs in popular television genres

Soap operas and family series (for instance *Egoli*, *Isidingo*, *The Cosby Show*), police dramas (for instance *Miami Vice*, *Magnum p.i.*), action dramas and situation comedies are sufficiently intimate to portray dramatic interaction, yet generalised enough to reflect personal and social norms and values. Notwithstanding the portrayal of violence and themes of decadence and even amorality – usually on the part of the antagonists, particularly in police and action dramas – content analyses indicate that socially accepted norms, values and behaviour invariably triumph at the end of a programme and/or series.

**Family series:** In the numerous family series on television the family circle offers the communicator a symbolic background which can be constructed in any way he/she chooses in order to portray all sorts of characters and their moral values. To most viewers the family is one of the most familiar and readily comprehensible of worlds, thus permitting ready identification. These series present, in a very direct way, a number of ideals and (to viewers) desirable attitudes towards virtually every aspect of interpersonal behaviour and social responsibility. Consider the stories and themes of a series such as *The Cosby Show*. They present a diversity of problems, particularly the interpersonal kind that confronts every family at one time or another, together with commendable and socially acceptable solutions to these.

**Police and action dramas:** Police and action dramas also portray ideal behavioural models. These programmes are usually explicitly concerned with the maintenance of law. Violent and often-unrealistic portrayals are in fact intended to dramatically emphasise the contrast between socially acceptable and socially unacceptable behaviour, favouring the former. Although these series are undeniably violent, one need merely call to mind written press reports of crimes to realise that they are not particularly unrealistic. In fact, crime reporting in the daily press presents far more violence than does television, which moreover offers it in fictional story form, and more acceptably in that justice always prevails.

**Situation comedy:** Situation comedies may be described as a form of institutionalised humour. When these series poke fun at individuals, groups and organisations, they do so in order to indicate what constitutes proper, acceptable behaviour. The power of comedy as a social corrector, with laughter as its main weapon, has been known since ancient times. As long ago as the fourth century it was known and accepted that comedy is a fable that teaches people how to behave. Comedy (and humour) is a socially sanctioned instrument to ridicule the sacred cows of society. It is used as a weapon against authority and serves as an outlet for frustration with authority. Grote (1983:31) puts it thus:

> There is no doubt that over the centuries, comedy and humor have been used as the bludgeon with which to assault the rigid, authoritarian and hypocritical aspects of society. Plautus attacked the core of all Roman society. The Commedia dell' arte took on all fathers, intellectuals, old men, soldiers and judges. Shakespeare ridiculed the money-mad Jew. Molière personified greed, religious hypocrisy, social and intellectual pretensions and doctors' ignorance and pomposities. The Restoration took on the social foibles and pretensions of the day. Shaw, of course, took on everything and everyone. And the most persistent method was exposure, peeling away the public face and holding up to public laughter the reality behind.

In South Africa one can think of Pieter-Dirk Uys' satirical persona Evita Bezuidenhout and how she (he) "gets away with murder".

### 7.4.2 The orientation, integration and social functions of film

The feature film, no matter how fictional, visualises the behavioural models of a society to which viewers have to conform in daily life. It provides information on social value systems and holds up ideals with which the viewer can identify. In an entertaining way, films enable people to orient themselves towards prevailing behavioural models, norms and value systems, and show them how to relate to these.

In this regard Jarvie (1978a:128) lists the following socialisation functions of film:
- Motion pictures provide a frame of reference to enable viewers to understand other people and lifestyles in their society and across societies and cultures. A good example is South African film since the 1990s, which often has as an objective to visualise intercultural relations in South African society. As far as television is concerned, good examples are the series *Isidingo*, *Egoli* and *Madam & Eve*.

# The Role and Functions of the Media: Functionalism

- Motion pictures instil a certain degree of status aspiration. For example, sometimes viewers may want to be like a character in a film with which they identify. They want to have the same lifestyle, attitudes, behaviour, and so on. Put in another way, films can promote anticipatory socialisation by putting lower socio-economic and educational groups in touch with other lifestyles. These people may then attempt to adopt the value systems and status symbols of the higher educational, economic and social class. For example, some viewers may want to adopt the lifestyle of James Bond.
- Motion pictures also contribute to the entrenchment, questioning and erosion of values. These functions are the reason for film censorship. Because films reflect the values of a society, there is always considerable criticism of their portrayal of violence, sex, political themes and the like. Some researchers and critics argue that film contributes a lot to the adoption of new attitudes concerning divorce, same-sex-relations, the adoption of new fashions both in clothing, hairstyles, interior decoration, and so on.

Socialisation is an ongoing process through which the individual learns how to interact with others in that society. In this respect the film helps our society to run smoothly by adding substantially to the things which people hold in common. Socialisation, on a large scale, helps people in a variety of different societies and cultures to know and understand each other better.

## 7.4.3 Film as an educational and a propaganda medium

Finally, the inherent and structural characteristics of the film (and television) make it an eminently suitable and powerful medium for educating people (see Unit 15, Educational media: television, in Volume 2). At the time of writing, some of the best examples of educational television in South Africa were (Oliphant 2001:6):

*Soul City*: Produced by Soul City Institute for Health and Development Education and licensed to the SABC, this series deals with a variety of topics, such as Aids, domestic violence, TV and disability, in an educational but entertaining manner.

*Khululeka*: This programme was designed to tackle serious issues, like human and social rights in a very funny and entertaining manner. In its last season, it dealt with voter education, local government elections, and why people should vote.

*Soul Buddyz*: The lives, struggles and joys of 8-12-year olds in our changing society are closely reflected in this programme. The story revolves around a group of children from different races who hang out in a park after school. They find an old abandoned taxi and make it their headquarters. Here they laugh and cry and live their young lives to the full and their slogan is "Tomorrow is ours".

*Yizo Yizo*: This is an educational drama designed to awaken the South African public to the reality and problems facing students and teachers in the majority of schools. It is also intended to promote a national dialogue about education. The series brings to light, amongst other things, issues such as leadership, reading, technology, corrupt teachers, rape and school safety.

As far as propaganda is concerned, the following:

Film (and television's) structural characteristics make it an ideal medium for (the misuse of) propaganda. The structural characteristics, as already referred to, are the following.

A filmic image is a synthesis of various sign systems and codes that appeal simultaneously to the senses. This image is composed of verbal (linguistic) and nonverbal (meta- and paralinguistic) signs, articulated and emphasised by means of the camera and editing.

The net result is that the camera exposes everything, enabling the director of a film to create certain connotative contexts for the viewer. By means of camera and editing techniques, the director can add to reality a further dimension of meaning not necessarily intrinsic to that reality. Viewers are so much under the sensory impact of the image that they are unaware of the fact that they are looking at (imaginary, filmic) reality through the "eyes" of a camera operated by a camera person. What they see is not their own perception of reality, but that of someone else (the director or camera operator) who constantly causes things to be seen in a specific way by manipulating viewers' perceptions. Through the use of camera and editing techniques, the director fully controls both what the viewers see and the way in which they see it. The potential for influencing and propaganda is obvious.

A condition for a politically successful feature film is that viewers must be able to project themselves and identify with it. From studies of Nazi propaganda films, it appears that viewers identify more readily with fictional films than with documentaries or educational films. Examples of Nazi fiction films include *Triumph of the Will* (1935), *The Wandering Jew* (1940), *Uncle Kruger* (1941) and *Kolberg* (1945). In all these films, the message is never overtly conveyed but is transmitted covertly through the attitudes and dialogue of the characters who, as secondary communicators, convey the message of a specific group or authority. In the visualisation of the action and the dialogue, these attitudes are diametrically opposed to those of the antagonist.

Besides the structural characteristics of the filmic image and the ideological narrative structures that may characterise a feature film, its principal value, both as propaganda and educationally, is its firm commitment to providing entertainment and recreation.

The positive association with recreation has the effect that viewers are more ready to project themselves onto the filmed events and hence to assume the attitudes communicated on screen. A fundamental characteristic of fictional propaganda films is that they appeal to the emotions rather than the intellect of the viewer. The technique used for this purpose is to relate the theme of a film to some situation that is already associated with a specific social issue.

## Summary

We started this unit by saying that we all have experienced how the media is often blamed for almost everything that can go wrong. This is because people subscribe certain ideal roles to the media. In this unit we introduced you to some of the more formal and academic arguments about the role and functions of the media in society.

They range from providing information to entertainment. We specifically looked at the so-called normative theories of the press. Thereafter we posed some questions about the nature of (media) entertainment.

We conclude this unit by saying that questions concerning the roles and functions of the media will always be debatable, because they relate to people's expectations. As long as the media stand in the midst of democracy and the struggle for democracy this will rightfully be the case.

## Research activities

1 Write a one-page essay in which you define functionalism with reference to its limitations.
2 Apply McQuail's (2000) typology of media functions to one South African mass communication medium, for example the press or radio. Provide clear examples of the information, correlation, continuity, entertainment and mobilisation functions of the medium you have selected.
3 Write a two-page essay in which you argue the state of pluralism in the South African media. Give examples to motivate your answer, for example, refer to the number of radio and television stations available to listeners and viewers and in the kind of available radio programming.
4 Compare the basic assumptions of the six press theories. Explain on the basis of this comparison the present role of a specific South African medium, for example South African radio, and whether you think the medium you have selected is functional in terms of South Africa's development and nation-building needs.
5 Write down your own views about the role (functions) of the media in society. Thereafter, "classify" your view in terms of one or more of the paradigms identified by Nordenstreng et al.
6 Interview five people about how film or television entertains them. How do they define entertainment? What entertains them? Why are they entertained by what they say entertains them? How do they experience introjection and projection? What are their main leisure activities and where does film or television fit into their programme of leisure?
7 Analyse an episode of a television situation comedy in terms of the presence or absence of rhetorical motifs in it.

## Further reading

Branston, G & Stafford, R. 1996. *The media student's book*. London: Routledge.
Downing, J, Mohammadi, A & Sreberny-Mohammadi, A (eds). 1995. *Questioning the media*. 2nd edition. London: Sage.

Grossberg, L, Wartella, E & Whitney, D. 1998. *Media making. Mass media in a popular culture.* London: Sage.
Levy, MR & Gurevitch, M. 1994. *Defining media studies. Reflections on the future of the field.* London: Oxford.
McQuail, D. 1992. *Media performance: mass communication and the public interest.* London: Sage.
McQuail, D. 2000. *McQuail's mass communication theory.* 4th edition. London: Sage.
O'Sullivan, T & Jewkes, Y (eds). 1997. *The media studies reader.* London: Arnold.
O'Sullivan, T, Dutton, B & Rayner, P. 1994. *Studying the media: an introduction.* London: Arnold.
Potter, W. 1998. *Media literacy.* London: Sage.
Silverstone, R. 1999. *Why study the media.* London: Sage.
Stevenson, N. 1995. *Understanding media cultures. Social theory and mass communication.* London: Sage.

# Bibliography

Crowther, B. 1977. Magic, myth and monotony: a measurement of the role of movies in a free society, in *Mass media and the popular arts*, edited by F Rissover & D Birch. New York: McGraw-Hill.
Eidsvik, C. 1978. *Cineliteracy: film among the arts.* New York: Random house.
Fouhy, EM. 2001. *Civic journalism: rebuilding the foundations of democracy.* [O].
    Available: http://www.cpn.org/cpn/pew_partnership/civic_partners_journalism.html
    Accessed on 2001/03/08
Fourie, P. 1988. *Aspects of film and television communication.* Cape Town: Juta.
Fourie, P. 1992. Televisie, tegnopolie en postmodernisme. *Communicatio* 19(1):2–14.
Fourie, P. 1996 (ed). *Introduction to communication – course book 3: communication and the production of meaning.* Cape Town: Juta.
Fourie, P. 1997 (ed). *Introduction to communication – course book 6: film and television studies.* Cape Town: Juta.
Grote, D. 1983. *The end of comedy. The sit-com and the comedic tradition.* Connecticut: Archon.
Huizenga, J. 1950. *Homo ludens: a study of the play element in culture.* London: Temple Smith.
Jarvie, I. 1978a. *Movies as social criticism. Aspects of their social psychology.* London: Scarecrow.
Jarvie, I. 1978b. *Towards a sociology of the cinema. A comparative essay on the structure and functioning of a major entertainment industry.* London: Routledge.
Lasswell, H. 1948. The structure and function of communication in society in *The communication of ideas*, edited by L Bryson. New York: Harper & Row.
Lazersfeld, P & Merton, R. 1948. Mass communication, popular taste and organised social action, in *The process and effects of mass communication* (1971), edited by W Schramm & D Roberts. Champaign: University of Illinois Press.
Lindgren, E. 1963. *The art of the film.* London: Allen & Unwin.
McQuail, D. 1987. *Theories of mass communication.* 2nd edition. London: Sage.
McQuail, D. 2000. *McQuail's mass communication theory.* 4th edition. London: Sage.
Merton, R. 1957. *Social theory and social structure.* New York: Free Press.
Mill, JS. 1964. *On liberty.* Harmondsworth: Penguin.
Nordenstreng, K. 1997. Beyond the four theories of the press, in *Media and politics in transition. Cultural identity in the age of globalization*, edited by J Servaes & R Lie, Leuven: Acco.
Oliphant, L. 2001. TV sugars the learning pill, in *Saturday Star*, 17 February 2001.
O'Sullivan, T, Hartley, J, Saunders, D, Montgomery, M & Fiske, J. 1994. *Key concepts in communication and cultural studies.* 2nd edition. London: Routledge.

Roelofse, J. 1996. Press theories in *Introduction to communication – course book 5: journalism, press and radio studies*, edited by L Oosthuizen. Cape Town: Juta.

Rosenfield, L & Mader, T. 1984. The functions of human communication, in *Handbook of rhetorical and communication theory*, edited by C Arnold & J Bowers. Boston: Allyn & Bacon.

Siebert, F, Peterson, T & Schramm, W. 1963. *Four theories of the press*. Urbana: University of Illinois Press.

Van Cuilenburg, J, Scholten, O & Noomen, G. 1992. *Communicatiewetenschap*. Muiderberg: Coutinho.

Watson, J & Hill, A. 1984. *A dictionary of communication and media studies*. London: Edward Arnold.

White, D. 1971. Mass culture revisited (II), in *Mass culture revisited*, edited by B Rosenberg & D White. New York: Van Nostrand Reinhold.

Wright, C. 1975. *Mass communications: a sociological approach*. New York: Random House.

# The Effects and Power of Mass Communication

*Pieter J Fourie*

## Overview

When we consider the effects of the media, in other words how the media affect people's behaviour and thinking, immediate examples that spring to mind are the occasional public outcry about the possible effect of a violent film or television programme on children's behaviour, the effect of the media's portrayal of sex on people and society's morals, or the effect of the media's portrayal of acts of terrorism on instigating further acts of terrorism. In South Africa we are also deeply concerned about the media's contribution to racism through the use of racial stereotypes, the role of crime reporting in giving criminals new ideas, and the quality of AIDS reporting on the spread of the disease. The above are just a few examples.

Apart from these possible macro impacts of the media on people and society, each and every one of us is affected on a daily basis by some media content. For example, we get information about the weather, what's on in the theatre and what's happening in sport. We are informed about the latest international and national political developments, developments in the economy, and we are made aware of disasters all over the world. But, we also listen to music, watch soap operas and dramas, go to the movies, and, through advertisements, learn about the latest products on the market. Surely, all this must have some kind of influence on our thinking and behaviour.

Potter (1998:259–260) compares the media with the weather. Although we may not be directly influenced by the weather or even constantly aware of it, it is always there. Like the weather, the media is pervasive and all around us. Like the weather the influence of the media is difficult to predict because many and complex variables play a role. However, there is also a big difference between the weather and the media. In the case of the weather we can immediately recognise its influence. We may feel hot or cold, dry or wet, and we can see the devastation of a storm, a heat wave, and so on. Media effects, however, are difficult to recognise.

For many years, scientists, making use of various research techniques, have investigated media effects. The results are still not clear-cut. At the most we can categorise different kinds of possible effects and postulate that after exposure to media content over a long period of time the media have certain cognitive effects on our thinking.

# The Effects and Power of Mass Communication

The purpose of this unit is to create an awareness of the different kinds of possible media effects. Despite the fact that there are no clear-cut answers and proofs, the fact remains that the media are pervasive and do have an influence of some kind on our existence; this underlines the importance of continued effect research.

As present and future communication workers, knowledge of past and continued research is of strategic, scientific and ethical importance.

- Strategic importance: even although we cannot predict the effect of media content with precision, a knowledge that some kinds of messages, structured in specific ways may have a specific kind of response under certain circumstances, is strategically important, for example, in political, social awareness, marketing and advertising campaigns.
- Scientific importance: the quest for knowledge about a pervasive phenomenon such as the media makes knowledge and continued research about media effects scientifically important. They can contribute to the increased beneficial use of the media for the improvement of people's circumstances and society in general.
- Ethical importance: finally, it is an ethical responsibility of present and future communication workers to know about the possible consequences of their work on the lives of people and society.

We begin the unit with two typologies of different kinds of effects. This is followed by an overview of the assumptions of different short-term and long-term effect theories. The unit ends with a brief note about the complexity of effect research.

## Learning outcomes

At the end of this unit you should be able to

- motivate why effect research is necessary and important;
- differentiate between different kinds of media effects;
- describe the assumptions of different short-term and long-term effect theories;
- test the assumptions against the background of your own experiences with media messages and among your friends, colleagues and family;
- find your own examples that illustrate the different media effect theories; and
- formulate your own views about media effects against the background of criticism against media effect theory and research.

## 8.1 INTRODUCTION: CATEGORISING MEDIA EFFECTS

Based on research findings, many scholars have categorised media effects more or less in the same way. Grossberg, Wartella and Whitney (1998:278–284) suggest that we distinguish between the following different kinds of media effects.

- Behavioural effects which include the following:
  - Cognitive effects: media messages or a single message (story/article/programme)

can impact on our knowledge and thinking about something, for example, our thinking about racism.
- Affective effects: media messages or a single message can affect our feelings about something, for example about child abuse, terrorism, violence.
- Conative effects: media messages or a single message can affect our behaviour towards something or someone, for example it can contribute to political uprising against a government and/or a specific politician.

- Manifest and latent effects: media effects can be overt or implicit. In other words, we may be aware that media messages or a single message have overtly caused us to think or act in a certain way, or we may not be aware that we have implicitly been influenced by media messages.
- Intended and unintended effects: closely related to overt and implicit effects is the fact that effects may be intended by the media or unintended. In other words, it may have been planned by the media to achieve a specific effect, or not planned. For example an AIDS-awareness campaign in the media may be intended to warn people against the disease and to stop its spreading. It may also have unintended effects in the sense that it may teach certain people how to spread the disease.
- Time-scale effects: effects may occur on different time scales, that is after:
  - Short-term message exposure: exposure to a single message, for example exposure to a single television programme can have an effect on a person while the programme lasts or while a person reads a story in a newspaper. After that, the person forgets about it. For instance, a person can be affected emotionally while watching a movie or reading an article. A media user may even decide to take a certain action based on what he/she is seeing in a movie or reading in an article, but in reality never takes such an action. While reading an article on slimming or physical fitness, we may take the "serious" decision to go on a diet and/or to start exercising. However, shortly after reading the article or watching a programme we may completely forget about it.
  - Intermediate message exposure: exposure to a series of related messages such as a product campaign, a social awareness campaign, and so on, can influence our thinking about a matter and our behaviour. For example, after exposure to a number of articles and radio and television programmes about the dangers of smoking, we are fully aware of the dangers of smoking, or of the dangers of obesity and of not exercising. Although media messages over a period of time may have changed our thinking about these (and other) matters we may, nevertheless, continue smoking, overeating, and so on.
  - Long-term message exposure: many cumulative exposures to related messages over time, for example media violence, pornography, but also positive topics such as an awareness of environmental issues, and so on, contribute to our disgust with topics such as violence, pornography and the like. Exposure over a long period of time to anti-smoking campaigns can eventually contribute to our decision to quit the habit.

## The Effects and Power of Mass Communication

Similarly, McQuail (2000:424) suggests that we distinguish between the following main kinds of media-induced effects:

- The media can cause intended change.
- The media can cause unintended change.
- The media can cause minor change (form or intensity).
- The media can facilitate change (intended or not).
- The media can reinforce what exists (no change).
- The media can prevent change.

Any of these changes may occur at the level of the individual, society, institution or culture. They can be located on two dimensions, that of time, namely short-term and long-term, and that of intentionality, namely planned effects and unplanned effects.

As an example, the following can be listed under planned effects:

- Propaganda: a strategically planned and ongoing campaign to influence people's minds by focusing on the negative aspects of an opponent (person, group, institution, topic) by making use of various techniques including the withholding of positive and objective information about a person, group, institution, topic, from the public.
- Media campaigns: for example, an advertising campaign to promote a specific product or to inform people about AIDS.
- Media development communication campaigns: for example an ongoing campaign in the media on literacy and educational development (see for example the *Sunday Times*' supplement *READ*).
- The distribution of knowledge by the media: for example on a new topic such as the Human Rights Bill, about which people (initially) knew little but which is important for the functioning of the South African society.
- Agenda-setting, framing, and diffusion of innovations (see discussion further on).

These effects can either be over a short or a long-term.

The rest are unplanned effects. These include the media's contribution to:

- Cultural change (e.g. the cultural change presently taking place in South Africa – moving from a dominant Western culture to an African culture).
- Socialisation (e.g. information about different cultures).
- Reality defining (e.g. the media's interpretations of the realities with which we are confronted daily and how we should understand them).
- Institutional change (e.g. the media's role effecting changes in the organisation of civil service by, for instance, emphasising corruption in the civil service).
- Collective reaction (e.g. the public's outcry about match-fixing in cricket).
- Media "violence" (e.g. if a film or television programme causes violent behaviour in an individual or amongst a group).

These effects can also be over a long- or short-term.

The above are only two examples of typologies of the kinds of media effects. In the following overview we discuss specific effects and their related theoretical assumptions.

## 8.2 AN OVERVIEW OF EFFECT THEORIES

The emphasis in this overview is on the historical development of effect research with the purpose of showing how the emphasis in effect research and findings has moved from short-term to long-term effects. The overview is primarily based on DeFleur and Dennis' (1994:533-606) comprehensive discussion of effect theories.

### 8.2.1 Short-term theories

There is almost general agreement that the media may have, only under extreme circumstances, a direct effect on people's behaviour. The circumstances may include war, when disaster of whatever kind strikes, in circumstances of social upheaval, or in the case of media content such as advertisements which are intentionally designed to have a specific kind of effect, namely to persuade potential consumers to buy a specific product. These kinds of effects are (usually) short-term effects. Under short-term effects we can list the following theories:

- the *hypodermic needle theory* (ies), also referred to as the magic bullet theory
- the *two-step-flow theory* (ies), also referred to as the mediating factors theory
- the *uses and gratifications theory* (ies)

### *The hypodermic needle theory*

In the 1930s and 1940s it was generally accepted that the media have a strong effect on the behaviour, thinking and attitudes of media users. Isolated research during this period (mainly on radio) largely supported this hypothesis. This research and its results are today known as the hypodermic needle theory.

This theory equates the influence of the media with the effect of an intravenous injection: certain values, ideas and attitudes are *injected* into the individual media user, resulting in particular behaviour. The recipient is therefore seen as a passive and helpless victim of media impact.

Among the best-known studies supporting the hypodermic needle theory is that of Cantril (1940) on the 1938 CBS (American radio station) radio broadcast of a dramatisation of HG Well's novel, *War of the Worlds*. The producer and actor Orson Welles's intention with this radio play about the invasion of planet Earth by warriors from Mars was to entertain. Listeners who tuned in and did not recognise it to be a play, panicked. The unintended effect of the broadcast was, as reported the following day in newspapers, a tidal wave of panic and terror that swept the USA.

Cantril's study underscored the power of radio to cause panic and incite individuals to instantaneous action.

However, today, and seen within context, it is accepted that research results that support the strong-effect hypothesis should be interpreted against the background of their time of origin – before, during and shortly after World War II. This was a period when people were often exclusively reliant on radio for information, when there were few rival media and when the media (specifically radio) enjoyed remarkable credibility. It was a period when social scientists were critically scrutinising existing social structures and voicing grave concern about the influence of modernisation, technology and urbanisation on the spiritual and cultural development of human beings.

Strictly speaking, the hypodermic needle theory is not applicable to television, the press, and film. Nevertheless, the sudden rise of modern concern about the effects of these media (which we experience from time to time, such as for example in 2000/2001 the media/public concern about the effect of the popular television series and video game *Pokémon*) is reminiscent of the underlying assumptions of the hypodermic needle theory, namely that the media has a strong influence on people and society.

During the sixties, when television emerged as the dominant public communication medium, concern about the influence of the radio made way for growing anxiety about the effect of violence and sex portrayed on television (and film) in particular.

Despite the fact that, most of the time, studies since the days of the hypodermic needle theory have shown that such concern is unfounded and despite the fact that film and television differ from radio and other media, such concern still flares up periodically, especially among moralists and politicians who use moral issues for their own political strategies. Often concern is also blown out of proportion by the media themselves. As a rule, none of these parties offers any scientific substantiation for their statements.

Moralists' concern relates to the concept of moral panic, which Watson and Hill (1984:109) describe as individuals and/or groups who perceive certain activities as seriously subverting the mores and interests of the dominant culture. Such reactions are disseminated by the mass media usually in a hysterical, stylised and stereotypical manner, thus engendering a sense of moral panic. In the social sciences the concept moral panic is usually associated with the concept "anomie". Anomie refers to a state to which a group or individuals become prone when they feel that their accepted values, norms and culture are threatened. It usually manifests itself when societies are in the throes of change.

One should also consider the finding of Howitt and Cumberbatch (1977:9–30), namely that public debate and concern about media effects are public only inasmuch as they are expressed and initiated by the media themselves; the viewing public, while condemning, for example violence in principle, in fact enjoys programmes that feature it. (This finding underscores the artificiality of surveys which seek to probe subjects' reactions to television programmes by means of questionnaires and experimental methods, and then present their findings as an honest reflection of people's experience of television to substantiate the view that the public is concerned.)

## *Two-step-flow theory*

During the 1950s it was realised that, because of the large number of mediating factors involved, reliable measurement of media effects is extremely difficult. This gave rise to the two-step-flow theory. During this period (the fifties) a prominent communication

# MEDIA STUDIES

scientist, JT Klapper (1960) pointed out that studies of media effects should always take account of the following factors which codetermine human behaviour and attitudinal change:

- Media users are not at the mercy of the media but selectively expose themselves on the basis of their own knowledge, experience, background, education, culture, expectations and the like. In other words, people expose themselves selectively to media content with which they agree, prefer, understand, and so on.
- The group (family, colleagues, friends) in which media users are situated can filter media users' interpretation and experience of media messages and in a sense acts as a buffer against one-sided interpretations. For example, often you discuss what you have read in a newspaper or have seen on television with friends or family or colleagues who also air their opinions.
- Societies and people themselves have certain opinion leaders (e.g. parents, teachers, politicians, clergymen) to whom media users (e.g. children) defer when moulding their behaviour, developing their attitudes and ideas. These opinion leaders can represent a further filter and buffer in the interpretation and experience of media messages.
- In a commercial (capitalist) media system characterised by free-market competition, the media themselves provide divergent and competing interpretations. For example, different newspapers and different radio and television stations provide us with different interpretations of the same topic.

Against this background Klapper (op cit) came to the following conclusions about the nature of media effects:

- As a rule media communication in itself is not a necessary or sufficient *cause* for behavioural change. At most it operates in conjunction with and via certain mediating factors and influences as discussed above.
- It can, however, *contribute* to behavioural change and *reinforce* existing behaviour.
- In cases where mass communication does change behaviour, there are no mediating factors or, if there are, these factors themselves operate in the direction of change. For example, in authoritarian societies or in developing societies where the media are expected to play a leading role in transforming society.
- The effect exercised by the media is itself subject to such variables as situation, circumstances and context.

Klapper's and other corroborative research confirmed Bernard Berelson's familiar statement about the nature of media effect:

> Some kinds of communication on some kinds of issues, brought to the attention of some kinds of people under some kinds of conditions, have some kinds of effects.
> (Berelson 1949:500)

The two-step-flow theory thus acknowledges that mass media users are not passive isolated individuals, but members of a structured society to which they belong. They form part of different groups – groups which themselves attach various interpretations (meanings) to media messages.

The critical question of the hypodermic needle theory was: *What does the media do to people?* In the two-step-flow theory the question changed to: *What do people do with the media?* The latter question in turn formed the basis of the uses and gratifications theory.

## *The uses and gratifications theory*

The uses and gratifications theory(ies) proceeds from the needs of users and the probable gratifications that they derive from media use. Research is based on questions such as, What do people do with the media? What do they use the media for? and What do they get from their media use? In general the following conclusions where drawn (cf. O'Sullivan, Hartley, Saunders, Montgomery & Fiske 1994:326; McQuail 2000):

- Diversion: People use media content to escape from their daily work and other routines, and from a wide variety of problems that confront and constrain them. The gratification is emotional release, albeit of a temporary nature.
- Personal relations: Media provide content that gratifies the needs for companionship and sociability. People use media to keep them company and even experience media personalities and fictional characters (for example, the characters in television soap operas) as personal friends. Media use also provides a focus for interaction with others (people discuss with others what they have read, seen or listened to).
- Personal identity: Media content is used to explore, challenge, adjust or confirm personal identity. People use media content to compare themselves and their situations and values with those of others.
- Surveillance: The media gratifies the need for information about the immediate and distant world and circumstances. Media users need and get information about issues that can effect them directly or indirectly.

Although there are methodological critiques against uses and gratifications research, today it still forms the basis of many theories and continuing research about the ways in which and the reasons why people use media. Lately much research about the use of the Internet is done against the background of the assumptions of uses and gratifications. One of the main methodological objections is the absence of a theoretical basis. Critics maintain that it is an a-theoretical approach arising from an underlying tautology, namely that use necessary leads to the gratification of needs. Being a-theoretical, uses and gratifications do not really explain the complex cognitive processes involved in the experience and interpretation of media content.

To summarise the short-term effect theories, DeFleur and Dennis (1994:566–567) come to the conclusion that the numerous studies done within the context of and against the background of the hypodermic needle theory, the two-step-flow theory and the uses and gratifications theory revealed only weak effects. The hypodermic needle theory no longer holds true. Before empirical studies began, it was believed that the mass media produced direct, immediate and powerful influences on all individual members and audiences. The earliest research findings did little to challenge this prevailing belief, and, in fact, seemed to confirm it.

The selective and limited influence theories replaced the hypodermic needle theories and the factors causing people to expose themselves to the media were found to be individualistic, as part of social categories (age, education, gender, and so on) and as part of social relationships (family, friends, colleagues).

Finally, the uses and gratifications theories exposed the fact that media users are active and not passive in selecting media content for personal uses and gratifications.

DeFleur and Dennis (1994:567) come to the conclusion that

> ... the preponderance of evidence about the effects of mass communication that emerged from these theories and decades of research, led to the general conclusion that the mass media are quite limited in their influences on people who select and attend to any particular message. In short, six decades of research revealed an overall picture of weak [short-term] effects.

### 8.2.2 Long-term (or cognitive) theories

The underlying assumption of long-term (cognitive) theories is that the media do not have an immediate impact on behaviour and people's way of thinking, but can affect it over a longer period of exposure to media content. Under long-term theories (as an umbrella term) we include the following theories:

- accumulation theory
- diffusion of innovation theory
- modelling theory
- social expectation theory
- meaning construction theory
- stereotype theory
- agenda-setting theory
- framing theory
- spiral of silence theory

All of them are closely related and can be termed cognitive theories. By cognitive we mean our faculty of knowing and understanding something in a specific way and how we base our behaviour and thinking on such knowledge. Research provides evidence that the media have a (strong) impact on our knowledge and understanding of the world and its peoples, and thus affect our behaviour.

#### Accumulation theory

In accumulation theory it is believed that if the media focus repeatedly and in a relatively consistent way on an issue(s), this can over a long period of time change people's attitudes and behaviour. If the various media corroborate each other by presenting the same interpretations, significant changes can take place in people's beliefs, attitudes and behaviour.

DeFleur and Dennis (1994:579) list the following as the basic propositions of the accumulation theory:

- The mass media begin to focus their attention on and produce messages about a specific topic (problem, situation, issue, for instance race discrimination, the environment, social habits, crime and so forth).
- Over an extended period, they continue to do so in a relatively consistent and persistent way and their presentations corroborate each other.
- Individual members of the public increasingly become aware of these messages, and, on a person-by-person basis, a growing comprehension develops of the interpretations of the topic presented by the media.
- Increasing comprehension of the messages regarding the topic supplied by the media begins to form (or modify) the meanings, beliefs, and attitudes that serve as guides to behaviour for members of the audience.
- Thus, minor individual-by-individual changes accumulate, and new beliefs and attitudes slowly emerge to provide significant changes in norms of appropriate behaviour related to the topic.

One can, for example, argue that the accumulation theory provides an explanation for the role of the media in changing people's attitudes about topics such as divorce, sex, style, politics, and so on, over a period of time. If all the South African media, over a longer period of time, report in the same way about race relations in South Africa, either positive or negative, such reporting can have an impact on people's perceptions of race and race relations.

## Diffusion of innovation theory

In modern and postmodern society there is a consistent flow of new products, ideas, solutions to problems, new interpretations and other kinds of innovations. As DeFleur and Dennis (1994:92–93) say, these can range from trivial, such as a new hairstyle, to the profound, such as a new political ideology. Whatever the innovation may be, sociologists have proven that every innovation is taken up by people in a particular society in a rather regular process that can be described by the diffusion of innovation theory.

This theory applies to mass communication in two ways: the innovation of news media products and the role of the media in spreading the innovation of new innovations, ideas, fashions, beliefs, fads, and so forth.

First of all, the media itself is an innovation. With each development in media technology new forms of communication are established. These new forms must be adopted by people. Recent good examples are the cellular phone and the Internet.

The printing press brought about a massive change in public communication culture and created a completely new information environment. The same happened after the invention of the telegraph, photography, radio, television and satellite. Today, we are adopting the changes brought about by the development of information and communication technology such as the fax machine, computer, Internet, e-mail, cellular telephones, and so on. The theory of the diffusion of innovation can explain the ways in which people adopt these new media.

Secondly, the innovation theory is important to the study of mass communication, because the media, in modern society, are often largely responsible for bringing new items (products, ideas, interpretations, beliefs) to the attention of people who eventually adopt them.

DeFleur and Dennis (1994:93) summarise the basic propositions of this theory as follows:

- The adoption process begins with an *awareness stage* in which those who will ultimately adopt an innovation learn of its existence (often from the mass media), but lack detailed information about it.
- Awareness is followed by an *interest stage*. People interested in the innovation begin to seek additional information on it. The media often provide the additional information.
- This is followed by an *assessment stage*. People interested use the additional information obtained to evaluate the innovation in terms of their expected and future situations.
- The fourth stage is called the *trial stage*. A small number of the people interested acquire and apply the innovation on a small scale to determine its utility for their purposes (this, of course, can also be a political theory or an attitude towards a specific kind of behaviour, for instance, premarital sex).
- Finally, in an *adoption stage*, the innovation is acquired and used on a full scale by a few people. After that, increasing numbers adopt it and accumulation of users follows a characteristic S-shaped curve that has started slowly, but rises quickly and then levels out.

It is important to remember that not all adoptions and innovations necessarily go through all the stages. Some innovations are adopted rapidly, some virtually overnight, by many people, while the adoption of others are spread over longer periods by a smaller proportion of the population. Some innovations are not adopted at all.

## Modelling theory

The modelling theory is based on the social learning theory developed in psychology. In this theory it is argued that in some cases some media users can adopt the media's depictions of people's behaviour. In other words, in some cases some people can adopt media-portrayed behaviour as a model for their own behaviour. Because of their rich visual nature showing and exposing actions in detail, especially film and television are believed to may have this kind of effect.

The assumptions of the modelling theory (DeFleur & Dennis 1994:585) are:
- A media user encounters a form of action portrayed by a person (model) in a media presentation. (A model can be a sport personality, a movie star, but also a policeman, a politician, an ordinary person, and so on.)
- The individual media user identifies with the model and believes that he or she is like, or wants to be like the model.
- The individual remembers and reproduces (imitates) the actions of the model in some later situation.
- Performing the reproduced activity results in some reward (positive reinforcement) for the individual.
- Thus, positive reinforcement increases the possibility that the media user will use the reproduced behaviour again as a means of responding to something or someone or in a situation.

Remember the outcry of parents after it was revealed that the South African cricket captain, Hansie Cronje, was involved with match-fixing. They claimed that many of their young boys' dreams were shattered because their model, Hansie, misled them. The same media that portrayed Hansie as a hero also had to portray his fall from grace. Many Afrikaners' political ideals, thinking and behaviour were modelled on the ideology and political styles of their leaders such as previous prime ministers Verwoerd and Vorster and the former state president De Klerk. They were portrayed by the Afrikaans media as God-fearing, highly principled leaders. These images were shattered after the brutalities and inhumanity of apartheid became known and exposed by the media. Many black children and young adults are now modelling their behaviour on that of South Africa's new political leaders, black stars, sport personalities, and so on, who are now for the first time visible in the South African media.

## Social expectation theory

By watching television, going to the movies, reading newspapers or listening to the radio, we can, over a period of time, learn the societal norms and roles expected from and adhered to by certain groups, people and organisations in society (cf. the socialisation function of, for example film, in Unit 7). We can learn from the media how, for example, medical doctors are supposed to behave, how newly-wed couples behave, how elderly people in old age homes behave, and so on. Through the media we get an image of how police stations function (e.g the many police dramas), how courtroom procedures are followed, how bills are debated in parliament (how politicians behave), and so on. Often these images are idealised. This is called the social expectation theory. Compared to the modelling theory, which is more concerned with personal behaviour, the emphasis in the social expectation theory is on social norms and roles. DeFleur and Dennis (1994:591) list the following as the assumptions of this theory:
- Various kinds of content provided by the mass media often portray social activities and group life.

- These portrayals, even if they are fictitious (soap operas, comedies and the like), are representations of reality that reflect, accurately or poorly, the nature of many kinds of groups in a society.
- Individuals, when exposed over a period of time to these representations, receive information, one can even say unintended lessons and education, about the norms and roles that prevail within the groups.
- The experience of exposure to portrayals of a particular kind of group results in incidental learning of behaviour patterns that are expected by others when acting within such a group.
- These learned expectations concerning appropriate behaviour for self and others serve as guides to action when individuals actually encounter or try to understand such groups in real life.

The social expectations theory can also be useful in explaining, for instance, the role of the media in multicultural societies where one group is expected to understand the social norms and values of another group and to act accordingly, when mingling or working with such a group. Think, for example, how we in South Africa learn or can learn through media portrayals about the different cultural groups in South African society and how different cultural and social norms and values portrayed in, for example, soap operas such as *Isidingo* and *Egoli* can contribute to such knowledge.

### *Meaning construction theory*

In many theories it is argued that we act and understand something and that our behaviour is based on and defined in terms of:

- what we know (our knowledge of something/somebody); and/or
- what we believe.

In these theories the emphasis is on how the media condition us to attach certain meanings to objects, words, and concepts. These theories are known as meaning construction theories.

They claim that often we obtain our knowledge and what we believe something means from how the media define that something. In our present information society, much of what we know (our basic information), and on which we base our beliefs, is derived from the media as a social source. This applies especially to new phenomena we have to confront. The media not only expose us to the known, but also to new developments, concepts and ideas to which the media apply certain meanings, which we adopt. Think of concepts and their meanings such as "star wars", "car hi-jacking", computer "bits", "chips", "software", "hardware", "globalisation", "unit trusts", "cultural transformation", "ozone layer" and so on. A few years ago we did not know or frequently use these terms. Today, the majority of people use and understand these terms and concepts by way of what they have learned about them from the media and in terms of how they are used and defined in and by the media.

DeFleur and Dennis (1994:595) summarise the basic stages of the meaning construction theories as follows:

- The media describe objects, events, people or situations in ways that link labels (language symbols, such as words) to meanings.
- A member of the media audience is exposed to such a label and undergoes some change in his/her personal interpretation of the meaning(s) of the label or has a meaning already attached to it, stabilised.
- He/she now communicates with others using the label and its media-influenced meaning. By doing this, such media-derived meanings are further shaped and/or stabilised among other members of society.
- Eventually, through the communication of media-derived meanings, strengthened in and through the means of interpersonal communication, such meanings become social convention and are thus adopted as the real and/or only meaning of a concept, action, person, and so on.
- Thus, individual behaviour toward objects, situations, or events is guided by the meanings people hold for them. In this way the media have played an indirect but significant long-term role in shaping people's thoughts and actions.

Take for example the label or concept "ozone layer". By far the majority of people attach the media's defined meaning(s) to this concept and not the far more complicated meaning scientists attach to it or which can be learned in geography texts. Often the meanings the media attach to concepts and phenomena are oversimplified and one-sided.

## Stereotype theory

The role of the media in creating and sustaining stereotypes (stereotyping) of certain people, organisations and groups (for example, of women, white people, black people, Jews, Afrikaners, gays, financial institutions, political parties, politicians, professions), and how these stereotypes affect our perceptions of people, groups and institutions, are dealt with in depth in Unit 15 on Representation.

Here, the following suffices: it is believed that through stereotyped portrayals, the media reinforce existing patterns of attitudes and behaviour toward specific individuals, groups, and institutions, especially minority groups. DeFleur and Dennis (1994:599) express the essential ideas of this theory in the following way:

- In entertainment content, and in other media messages, for instance in the way social and political journalism portray an event related to a specific group, the media can repeatedly present us with negative portrayals of, for instance, a specific ethnic group.
- These portrayals tend to be consistently negative, showing such people as having undesirable attributes and fewer positive characteristics than members of the dominant group in which the media function.

- Such portrayals are similar among the various media – providing corroboration.
- These portrayals provide constructions of meaning for media users, particularly for those who have only limited contact with actual people of the stereotyped group.
- Viewers, readers and listeners incorporate these meanings into their memories as relatively inflexible schemata – stereotyped interpretations – that they use when thinking about or responding to any individual of a portrayed category, regardless of his/her actual personal characteristics.

We have already referred to the South African Human Rights Commission's report on racism in the South African media. In essence this report is about stereotypical portrayals (written, verbal and visual) of black people by the South African media. Against the background of the proven role and means of the media to convey and sustain stereotypes, many of the findings of this report, although flawed with methodological mistakes, must be taken seriously. The report and investigation can serve to sensitise South African media workers and media users about the issue of stereotypes and how stereotypes serve to sustain an ideology.

## Agenda-setting theory

The basic assumption of the agenda-setting theory is that, whether consciously or unconsciously, the media create a particular image of reality. The media confront us on a daily basis with events that are, according to the media, important. Every day the media releases a list of topics (issues on which the media focuses) – similar to the agenda of a meeting. The omission of certain events and issues, and the overemphasis of others, establish a particular way for media users to think about reality. For example, at the time of writing, stories about crime, corruption and AIDS filled the columns of many South African newspapers, creating the image of South African society being nothing else but a crime- corruption- and AIDS-ridden society and country.

The attention given in news coverage to items or issues such as the above, influences the rank order of public awareness and attributes to the significance of an issue (McQuail 2000:426).

Agenda-setting thus focuses on *what* topics the media present to an audience and secondly on *how* information on the selected topics is presented. It relates to the dynamics of news coverage: the spectrum of viewpoints, symbols and questions that are selected to construct the news and how they are ranked or accorded legitimacy and priority. Finally agenda-setting is concerned with *how* the media's legitimisation of issues and events *affects* our perceptions of reality (O'Sullivan et al 1994: 8).

Apart from applying the hypotheses of agenda-setting to everyday issues, the theory is of particular importance in analysing the effects of political reporting (especially during times of elections) on people's political views and voting behaviour. In other words, on which issues does the media focus during times of elections in order to prioritise certain topics compared to others.

## Framing theory

Closely related to agenda-setting is framing. As a media effect, framing describes the influence on the public of the news angles used by journalists. Angles is understood to mean the interpretative and ideological frameworks from which journalists report about an issue and the contextualisation of news reports within a specific (ideological) framework. In other words, it involves the way in which the media report about a matter, a person, a group or an institution. For example, the media in general, or a single newspaper, radio station or television station, may decide to report about a person, topic, group or institution in a certain way – they may only focus on the negative attributes of a politician, a financial group, a gang or a proposed new law. The results are that the public, being exposed only to negative aspects in such reporting, have negative perceptions of such persons or issues. We often hear about people, organisations, groups, and so on, complaining that the media, through its negative reporting, has framed them and as such has influenced, for example, a court's rule about them.

## Spiral of silence theory

Finally, a note about the spiral of silence theory. Although evidence to support this theory is weak and inconsistent from one context to another (cf. McQuail 2000:463) it nevertheless should be kept in mind, especially in studies about the formation of public opinion during political campaigns. The main assumptions of the theory are:

- Society threatens deviant individuals with isolation.
- Individuals experience fear of isolation continuously.
- This fear of isolation causes individuals to try to assess the climate of opinion at all times.
- The fear of isolation affects their behaviour in public, especially their willingness, or unwillingness, to express their opinions openly (McQuail 2000:461–463).

The above means the following and has the indicated consequences:

Although the media pretend to represent the majority view or align themselves with what is perceived to be the dominant public opinion, it may in fact not be the case that public opinion is reflected accurately in the media. Many people's opinions may differ from that expressed by the media, however, because of their fear of isolation they remain silent, which gives the impression that they go along with opinions expressed by the media. Their silence has the spiralling effect of suggesting that the opinion(s) expressed by the media is the dominant public opinion. For example, the South African media may claim that public opinion is against the view that AIDS is caused by poverty (not a virus). However, many people may believe this, but are afraid to air such a view. The result is that the media's opinion gains support as being the dominant public opinion. In the same way, the media may present criticism against a political party as being the dominant criticism (public opinion) of the public. Although people may agree with the criticism, they nevertheless vote for the same political party against whom the criticism is expressed out of fear of isolation within their group. Predictions about election results based on what the media present as the public opinion is thus risky.

From the above it is clear that there is a correspondence between the different long-term or cognitive effect theories. They all support the view that over a longer period of time the media can affect our perceptions of reality and our understanding of things. However, each of the theories emphasises or focuses on a different aspect:

- accumulation: how corresponding or corroborative representations by different media on the same issue, person, group, and so forth, affect our perceptions of issues, people, groups
- diffusion of innovation: the process of bringing something specific under people's attention and how media users adopt such an innovation
- modelling: how people model themselves and their behaviour on media representations
- social expectation: how social values and morals are spread by the media
- meaning construction: how we accept media interpretations as our own knowledge of something
- stereotypes: how the media's negative representations affect our perceptions of issues, people, groups
- agenda-setting: how the media's prioritising of events and topics affects our perceptions of reality
- framing: how the media's deliberate framing of a person, topic, event, and so on, affects our perceptions of that person, topic, event
- spiral of silence: how the media create a specific image of what the public opinion is and how media users accept that to be the public opinion.

## 8.3 A CAUTIONARY NOTE ABOUT EFFECT THEORIES AND RESEARCH

From the above overview it is clear that the media have some influence on our thinking and in some instances on our behaviour. We end this unit with a brief note about the complexity of effect research.

- From a methodological point of view, effect research is difficult to undertake and must usually be done over a long period of time.
- Research is conducted mainly by means of surveys (questionnaires), interviews and experimental methods. However, it must be kept in mind that in contrast to the rest of nature, human beings – their experiences (including media experiences), thinking and behaviour – are not easily quantifiable or measurable by only quantitative and experimental methods (cf. the units on reception theory and ethnographic research in Volume 2 of this book). So far these methods have had difficulties to conclusively establish a direct causal relation between media and behaviour and media and thinking, be it voting behaviour or people's thinking about, for example, violence in society.

## The Effects and Power of Mass Communication

- Findings and conclusions must be contextualised. The effects the media may have in the USA and other parts of the world are not necessarily the same in South Africa where different contexts, circumstances and patterns of media use and exposure to media prevail. For example, in a developing country such as South Africa, people (or the majority of people) have far less exposure to media compared to people living in developed countries with higher levels of literacy and more and diversified media.
- Most effect studies are in fact based on certain limited assumptions such as: the media user is helplessly exposed to and at the mercy of the media. In other words, the media user is helplessly caught up in a (behaviourist) stimulus-response relationship with the media. Such an assumption is based on two behaviourist theories: the catharsis theory and the mimesis theory. Catharsis theory postulates that the portrayal of, for example, violence by the media, can result in a release of aggression in the viewer, thus acting as a safety valve for such negative emotions, or the release of sadness and grief when one watches a sad movie, and so on. The key postulate of the mimesis theory is that the portrayal of, for example violence, causes media users to imitate violent behaviour in real life and to regard it as sanctioning their own aggressive conduct. The same applies to the imitation of other emotions, behavioural patterns or the adoption of values and mores portrayed by the media. Despite extensive research, neither of these theories has been conclusively proved or refuted on scientific grounds.
- Finally, it must always be kept in mind that media users (including children with the necessary guidance) are not helpless victims of the media. Apart from users' free choice to expose themselves to media as they wish, their personal values, norms, human relations and cultural and educational background act as a buffer against media effects. Several variables are thus at play, which make it difficult to ascribe specific behaviour and thinking to the effects of the media.
- In short, people's behaviour, attitudes, notions of the world, themselves and other people are codetermined by several other variables such as their personal, cultural and socio-economic background. It is therefore difficult to argue, for example, that a specific film or television programme, or even that the exposure to specific kinds of media content such as for instance crime movies and television programmes over a longer period of time, are responsible for a specific act of, for example, violence, or a specific way of thinking and behaviour. In the same way it is difficult to argue that a specific newspaper's political reporting is responsible for a person's political thinking and (voting) behaviour.

Gauntlett (1998) lists ten points of criticism against the effects model:

- The effects model tackles social problems "backwards": Gauntlett argues that one shouldn't start with an analysis of the media's portrayal of social problems such as crime, violence and pornography, and then try to deduct from such analysis what the effects of the media's portrayal will or could be on people's behaviour and understanding. Rather, one should start with an analysis of the social problem as such. What comes first: the chicken or the egg?

- The effects model treats children as inadequate: he concludes that cognisance should also be taken of research which seeks to establish what children can and do understand about and from the mass media. Such research has shown that children can talk intelligently and indeed cynically about mass media and that children as young as seven can make thoughtful, critical and "media literate" video productions themselves.
- Assumptions within the effects model are characterised by barely concealed conservative ideology: for example, the condemnation of generalised screen "violence" by conservative critics can often be traced to (political/ideological) concerns such as "disrespect for authority" and "anti-patriotic sentiments".
- The effects model inadequately defines its own objects of study: definitions of concepts frequently used in effect studies, such as "anti-social", are often value judgements based on conservative ideology. Furthermore, *how* and *who* define concepts and categories of analysis such as "verbal aggression", "act of violence", and the like.
- The effects model is often based on artificial studies: this concerns the unnaturalness and artificiality of the situations and contexts in which the research is conducted, for example in a laboratory test in which viewers are decontextualised from their natural media use circumstances and environment.
- The effects model is often based on studies with misapplied methodology: in other words, the wrong or inappropriate techniques of research are used.
- The effects model is selective in its criticisms of media depictions of violence: why just focus on violence as portrayed in fictitious programmes such as police dramas and so forth, and not on violence as portrayed in, for example, news broadcasts? Why are the same kind of "anti-social" acts portrayed in news not seen in the same negative light as the acts in fictitious media content?
- The effects model assumes superiority to the masses: those who conduct the research almost never say that they (or their close relations) have been affected in the ways they propose the media affects people. In other words, are the researchers superior to ordinary media users?
- The effects model makes no attempt to understand meanings of the media: effects research often assumes that the medium holds a singular message which will be carried unproblematically to audiences. It ignores the polysemic nature of media content and the findings of, for example, reception theory – how people "read" and interpret media messages in different ways.
- The effects model is not grounded in theory: the effects model is substantiated with no theoretical reasoning beyond the bald assertions that particular kinds of effects *will* be produced by the media. The basic question of *why* the media should induce people to imitate its content has never been adequately tackled.

## Summary

In this unit we discussed the different kinds of media effects and distinguished, amongst others, between behaviour, manifest and latent, intended and unintended (or planned and unplanned) and time-scale effects. We then looked at specific effect theories. Under short-term theories we distinguished between the hypodermic needle theory, the two-step-flow theory and the uses and gratifications theory. Under long-term theories we distinguished between accumulation, diffusion of innovation, modelling, social expectation, meaning construction, stereotyping, agenda-setting, framing and the spiral of silence theory. Finally we concluded with some warnings about the complexity of effect research, and criticism against the effects model. We emphasised that media users are not helpless victims of the media.

## Research activities

1. Write a short (two-page) essay in which you argue the strategic, scientific and ethical importance of effect research and whether you agree with its importance or not.
2. Distinguish between behavioural, manifest and latent, intended or unintended (planned or unplanned) and time-scale effects and give your own examples of these different kinds of effects.
3. Use the assumptions of any two of the short-term theories to design two questionnaires, in other words a questionnaire for each of the two short-term theories you have selected. Conduct an interview with five respondents (friends, colleagues, family) in which you test the assumptions of the two short-term theories you have selected. Compare their responses. For example, have any of your respondents acted on the basis of a media message (hypodermic needle theory) and if so, how and why. Or, test whether your respondents discuss media content (for example, a soap opera or news) with others, and if so how such discussions contribute to their understanding of media content (two-step-flow theory). Or, use your questionnaire based on the assumptions of the uses and gratifications theory to test your five respondents' use and gratification of media, for example, their use of the Internet (why and how do they use the Internet) and which gratifications do they get from it.
4. Use the assumptions of any two of the long-term theories to design two questionnaires, in other words a questionnaire for each of the two long-term theories you have selected. Conduct an interview with five respondents (friends, colleagues, family) in which you test the assumptions of the two long-term effect theories you have selected. Compare their responses. For example, ask your respondents about how they became aware of the cell phone as a new technological phenomenon and how they adopted or rejected the cell phone as a means of communication (diffusion of information theory). Or, interview your respondents on how they arrived at the meaning of a concept such as the "ozone layer" (meaning construction theory), or any other concept.
5. Write an essay of two pages in which you formulate your own views about media effects.

## Further reading

Curran, J, Smith, A & Wingate, P (eds). 1987. *Impacts and influences. Essays on media power in the twentieth century.* London: Methuen.

DeFleur, ML & Dennis, EE. 1994. *Understanding mass communication. A liberal arts perspective.* 5th edition. Boston, MA: Houghton Mifflin.

Dickinson, R, Harindranath, R & Linné, O (eds). 1998. *Approaches to audiences. A reader.* London: Arnold.

Glynn, CJ, Herbst, S, O'Keefe, GJ & Shapiro, RY. 1999. *Public opinion.* Boulder, CO: Westview Press.

Grossberg, L, Wartella, E & Whitney, DC. 1998. *Mediamaking. Mass media in a popular culture.* Thousand Oaks, CA: Sage.

Hiebert, RE. 1999. *Impact of mass media. Current issues.* 4th edition. New York: Longman.

McQuail, D. 2000. *McQuail's mass communication theory.* 4th edition. London: Sage.

Potter, WJ. 1998. *Media literacy.* Thousand Oaks, CA: Sage.

Shoemaker, P. 1991. *Gatekeeping.* Thousand Oaks, CA: Sage.

## Bibliography

Berelson, B. 1949. What missing the newspaper means, in *Communications research: 1948–1949*, edited by P Lazarsfeld & F Stanton. New York: Harper.

Cantril, H. 1940. *The invasion from Mars.* Princeton: Princeton University Press.

DeFleur, ML & Dennis, EE. 1994. *Understanding mass communication. A liberal arts perspective.* 5th edition. Boston, MA: Houghton Mifflin.

Gauntlett, D. 1998. Ten things wrong with the 'effects model', in *Approaches to audiences. A reader*, edited by R Dickinson, R Harindranath & O Linné. London: Arnold.

Grossberg, L, Wartella, E & Whitney, DC. 1998. *Mediamaking. Mass media in a popular culture.* Thousand Oaks, CA: Sage.

Howitt, D & Cumberbatch, G. 1977. *Massamedia en geweld.* Utrecht: Spectrum.

Klapper, J. 1960. *The effects of mass communication.* New York: Free Press.

McQuail, D. 2000. *McQuail's mass communication theory.* 4th edition. London: Sage.

O'Sullivan, T, Hartley, J, Saunders, D, Montgomery, M & Fiske J. 1994. *Key concepts in communication and cultural studies.* London: Routledge.

Potter, WJ. 1998. *Media literacy.* Thousand Oaks, CA: Sage.

Watson, J & Hill, A. 1984. *A dictionary of communication and media studies.* London: Edward Arnold.

# Media and Ideology

*Stefan Sonderling*

## Overview

The purpose with this unit is to provide you with an understanding of ideology and the relationship between ideology and the mass media; to identify some of the theories of ideology; and explain how ideology is produced by powerful groups in society through the manipulation of language and the mass media in order to serve their interests.

## Learning outcomes

At the end of this unit you should be able to

- identify the various definitions of ideology;
- explain the difference between neutral and critical theories of ideology;
- explain how ideology is produced by language and the mass media;
- recognise how ideology operates and creates meaning and experiences of reality;
- identify and describe the different ways people accept, evaluate or reject ideology;
- analyse media texts to identify ideology; and
- apply your knowledge to evaluate your own experience of ideology.

## 9.1 INTRODUCTION

The ideas people have in their heads or the beliefs or ideologies they say they support are not simply a matter of abstractions. "*Ideas*", as John B Thompson (1990:2) puts it, "do not drift through the social world like clouds in a summer sky, occasionally divulge their contents with a clap of thunder and a flash of light; ideas circulate in the social world as utterances, as expressions, as words which are spoken or inscribed". This points to the fact that the ideas that people have are very real and powerful when they are communicated and motivate people to take action, for example, ideas about equality and freedom motivated the African Nation Congress to revolt against the domination of the white minority in South Africa. Ideology has a close connection to language and to the mass media that are the main means for the communication of ideology in society and manipulating people.

In the most general way we can say that ideology is concerned with study of ideas and how people and societies think. However, there are many definitions of ideology, for example, the term ideology is used to describe

- a general system of beliefs held by a particular social group, such as the beliefs of a Christian or Muslim religious group;
- a system of false ideas, for example the ideas of people who believe that the HIV/AIDS disease is not caused by a virus;
- a process for production of meanings to support social domination of one group over another, for example, such a process includes the ideas about the superiority of the white races produced by the former apartheid regime and promoted by the mass media, system of legislation and social institutions.

In this unit we will introduce you to the different theories of ideology and will concern ourselves with explaining how ideas, attitudes, values, and belief systems held by a group of people or a society are used to guide their understanding of the world and enable them to function effectively. That is, *ideology* explains how a society is able to exist and maintain itself by reproducing its institutions, social relations, and the things needed for the people to exist, such as the resources to produce food and material goods, the labour force that is needed for the economy to operate. Ideology also produces people with the correct attitudes and beliefs that enable them to take their given social positions. For example, how poor people come to believe that they are unable to change or improve their situation. Such ideas keep indigent people in their poverty and make them accept their dependence on the affluent people in society. This shows us that a society is divided into different groups of people, some poor and some rich, and such a social arrangement is called a social structure whereby people are organised into different groups. How a society comes to organise its people is not simply a peaceful matter performed by some neutral disinterested scientists, professional administrators or gods. The problem that faces every society is how to maintain its social structures and relationships that are also relations of power, inequality and domination, and compel people and make them accept unequal relations of power and oppression as legitimate.

One method to maintain social stability is the use of force or violence to control people and compel them to conform to the demands of society. For example, if a government uses the police force and the army to intimidate its citizens they will be afraid to express their dissatisfaction and will do what they are told to do by the government. However, the use of violence is not the best way to control people. A more effective method for exertion of such control to make them accept their position, respect their government and the social order is to communicate to them ideas and images, or *ideology*, that present their society's structures and relations of inequality as the natural order of the world. For such a purpose, every government considers the mass media as important means for manipulating the ideas and opinions of the people. Governments believe that through the communication of ideology by the mass media people will be convinced that they must accept and do what they are told to do.

## 9.2 A POPULAR VIEW OF IDEOLOGY

While the concept ideology is important for understanding society and the mass media, it is also one of the most hotly contested concepts in the social sciences and most difficult to define. Today, when we use a concept such as *ideology* in our everyday discussions or in the social sciences, we encounter a concept that is illusive and has different uses and shades of meaning. The problem with the concept is that in everyday popular use it acquired a negative connotation and is used to denigrate and criticise ideas, attitudes, values, belief systems or worldviews that are held by a particular group of people that one does not like.

Thus, to characterise an idea or view as ideological is already to criticise and condemn it for being an illusion or untruth. For example, Christians refer to their religion as *Christianity* rather than *Christianism* and express their disguised criticism of other religions by naming these as Hinduism, Buddhism, or Paganism and other forms of "misguided" religious "isms" (where the use of -ism suggests a basis of prejudice or discrimination). Most people tend to think that their own views and ideas are not ideological; ideology is the view of somebody else. For example, I can claim that my understanding of politics is a political theory and condemn your view as political ideology. Today no person would call himself or herself an "ideologist" but rather claim to be a *conservative*, a *humanist*, a *capitalist* or a *socialist*.

For a scientific study of ideology and how it relates to society and the mass media we need a more systematic framework.

## 9.3 THEORIES OF IDEOLOGY

In the social sciences we can identify two main theories of ideology: a neutral and critical theory.

### 9.3.1 Neutral theory of ideology

A neutral theory of ideology regards ideology as a system of thought, system of belief, ideas and values of a particular group of people or whole society. From this perspective, every group in society has its own ideology, a set of ideas that provides a selective interpretation of reality and serves as an action-oriented framework for the group to operate effectively in the world. For example, during the apartheid period people in South Africa were classified according to their skin colour and it was believed by many white people that blacks were inferior.

All ideologies can be considered as equal and there is no attempt to criticise one ideology or promote another. It is also assumed that it is possible to study ideology from a neutral and nonideological position such as offered by science. From the perspective of this theory, ideology refers to the way attitudes and beliefs are organised into a coherent pattern. For example, let us assume that we know a person who holds certain attitudes toward young people and who believes that young people should be conscripted by the army for national service because such an experience will give them strong character and solve all the social problems. From such knowledge we could also predict the sort of attitude that person will hold on other issues such as crime, death penalty, law and order, social class, race and gender. Such a person, one could assume, has authoritarian or right-wing ideology that provides a coherent framework to link his or her attitudes on the different issues.

However, such a neutral concept of ideology is not very useful. If all ideologies are equal then how could we compare and evaluate them? How could we explain that a particular ideology, such as capitalism, for example, is more successful in motivating many people in the world while communism has fallen from grace? How can we explain the fact that many people accept particular ideas about their inferior position in society even when these ideas are against their best interest and maintain their own oppression?

### 9.3.2 Critical theories of ideology

A more critical view of ideology that provides important understanding of the role of the mass media in society was developed from various Marxist's theorists.

The concept ideology is made of two words: *idea* and *logy*, or science. The term ideology was first used in the eighteenth century by the French philosopher Destutt de Tracy in 1796 to describe a new science that would be concerned with the systematic study of ideas or how people think. But the term quickly acquired negative connotations when Napoleon used it to accuse the philosophers for distributing ideas that were responsible for undermining the French society. In the nineteenth century German philosopher Karl Marx took the concept ideology with its negative connotations and developed it to its present form.

#### *Marx's realist theory of ideology*

Marx wanted to explain how ruling minorities or a small group of people were able to dominate large masses of people and hold on to power without using force and why the majority of subordinated people accept their subordination. Marx came to a conclusion that those in power were able to construct and communicate a dominant vision of society that justifies their rule and the subordination of others and have such a vision accepted by those that were dominated. When such an image of society is accepted by the majority of the people as legitimate, the power of the ruling minority becomes secure and the use of force is unnecessary (cf. Grossberg, Wartella & Whitney 1998:181). For example, most people believe that the ANC government has the best ideas about running the country and accept these ideas and policies as true and legitimate. Such people become annoyed when an opposition party criticises the ideas of the government.

Marx suggested that ideology in a particular society was always produced by a ruling minority or the élite holding power, as he put it: in every society the dominant ideas are the ideas of the dominant class. Because the dominant class has power, owns the means for the production of material goods and controls the economy in a society and profits from it (this is termed the material base of society), such material or economic reality determines the consciousness of the people. Marx explained that ideology was false consciousness because the dominant class was able to dominate the majority of people in a society by explaining that the existing relations of domination were the natural order of things and have such an explanation accepted by the dominated majority. Obviously such interpretations of the existing social arrangements present a false picture and create false consciousness because they prevent the dominated from seeing their own real situation of oppression. As such, ideology always presents a limited view and prevents people from thinking about other ways of arranging society.

In Marx's views, ideology can be considered as a social cement that glues together different social classes and groups who assume that their own views of society are the only possible way to think about reality. In short, for Marx ideology was always determined by the material and economic conditions and it always was a distortion of reality. For example, apartheid ideology in South Africa justified the domination of the majority of the black people by a powerful white minority as a natural social order that was created by the gods. Because it was evident, when one looked at the reality of the South African society where one could see blacks dominated by whites, many people, including those dominated accepted such an explanation or ideology even when it was against their own interests. Another example is the ideology of patriarchy (male domination) that assumes that men are stronger and superior over women who are weak by nature. In some societies women are thought of, and represented in traditional stories, legislation, and the mass media as passive and in a subservient position to men. In these societies women accept their position of domination as natural.

Marx's view on ideology could be described as a realist theory of ideology because it assumes that a person's social position within the economic and social relations directly determines his or her ideology. According to this theory, if we know a person's social class situation then we could predict that person's ideology. For example, a person belonging to the working class, such as a labourer, would hold views that are based on his experiences and relationships and we could predict that such a person would be a member of a trade union such as COSATU, will consider capitalism as an oppressive system, and supports labour reforms like the demands for minimum wages and the right to strike.

According to this theory the mass media function as important agencies of social control and reinforce domination by communicating the ideology of the dominant class, provide legitimacy to the existing social *status quo*, manipulate and control the ways of thinking of the dominated groups and are responsible for creating false consciousness. It is assumed that because the mass media are usually owned by politically and economically powerful minority groups in a society, the mass media purposefully communicate false information and create false consciousness in order to support their owners. For example, it is assumed that a male-dominated mass media would produce reports that propagate male domination, or that white South Africans journalists working for the mainly white-owned mass media are racists and produce racially biased reports, as was the finding of the Media Monitoring Report of the South African Human Rights Commission in 1999.

Marx's and the orthodox Marxist theory have some shortcomings and their views on ideology seem to provide a simplistic explanation. The shortcomings are the following: By defining ideology as false consciousness it is assumed that there is true consciousness and that it is possible to understand reality from an objective point of view. However, human consciousness is influenced by culture and meaning, for us "reality" and how we understand depends on our language and meanings we acquired from our society (see the discussion on how language influences the way we see reality in Unit 3, Volume 2). Marx's views are also simplistic as they assume that only the economic and material interests directly influence a person's ideology and they neglect to consider people's personal experience and how such experience influences their views of the world. For example, Marx would assume that if you are a factory worker you would always believe that you are exploited by your bosses. Marx's theory also fails to explain how different and contradictory ideologies can coexist in a society, for example in South Africa newspapers owned by whites consider affirmative action as racism while newspapers written by blacks report that whites who oppose affirmative action are victims of their own racist ideology.

In order to overcome the limitation and the economic determinism that reduce ideology as reflection of the economic base, neo-Marxist and cultural studies theories have extended Marx's views in an attempt to provide a better understanding of ideology.

## Neo-Marxist critical theories of ideology

The French philosopher Louis Althusser revised Marx's ideas of ideology and rejected his assumption that ideology is always determined by the material and economic conditions. Such a view is a distortion of reality. Althusser suggested that there need not be such a direct and determining connection between the material conditions and the ideas and beliefs people have. He suggested that ideology was produced by the Ideological State Apparatuses (ISAs), which consist of institutions such as the following:

- family
- school
- church
- politics
- language
- mass media.

These institutions socialise and prepare people to accept their society as it is. For example, children at school learn how to become members of their society and what types of jobs they could hope to have when they grow up. ISAs, economic conditions and Repressive State Apparatuses (RSAs), such as the military and police that use direct

# Media and Ideology

force, together promote the social norms, values, beliefs and ideas that make people conform to their society. For example, you learn at school about religion and in church you learn about how you should behave as a religious person.

For Althusser, ideology is *the system of representation in which people live their imaginary relationship to the real conditions of existence.* What Althusser means by this is that it is not possible to have a direct understanding of any real relationships, but rather people can only have meaningful interpretations and experience of their relationships. This means that people cannot have a direct and an objective view of a reality as there is no way that one could step out of ideology to some nonideological position and measure how ideology distorts and misrepresents true reality. People live, experience and give meaning to their world and society by using a system of representations such as language, pictures and the mass media. For example, many people in South Africa have not been victims of crime but they believe that crime is a major problem because they read this in newspapers. It is as if people live in a *symbolic universe* (see Unit 3 in Volume 2 on language, for more explanations of the concept "symbolic universe"). Ideology is a system of signs and meanings which explain and guide people about how they should experience their world, and it is within such a meaningful world that people live or live their relationship to a reality. For example, people with a religious ideology believe that their world is directed by gods.

To give you an example that it is not possible to understand reality without meanings and interpretations, please read the following short case study.

## Case study 9.1: Perspectives

One Monday morning I read the following report in the newspaper:

"The city police report that they found a young man lying unconscious in a park in the city. The man's head was bleeding and it seems that in a state of drunkenness he fell to the ground and injured himself."

Later that day I met a friend who told me the following story:

"I was walking with my husband in the park in the evening and as we passed next to a bench a young man looked at me, jumped up and grabbed my husband by the sleeve and asked if he had a light for a cigarette. Having been annoyed that the man looked at me, my husband pulled away and banged the man over the head with a walking stick and the man fell to the ground."

An hour later I met the husband and heard his story:

"I was lucky last night and escaped being robbed. My wife and I were walking in the park when a man accosted me. I had a walking stick in my hand and hit the man on the head. Otherwise, we would have been robbed. It was obvious to me that we were threatened when a man accosts us in a dark spot, grabs hold of my arm and asks for a light."

That evening I met another friend whose head was bandaged. He explained that he was attacked by a lunatic last night, and told me his story: "Last night I was

sitting on a park bench for a while, I wanted to light up a cigarette but realised that I had no matches or a lighter. Then I saw a man and a woman go by, and the man was smoking a cigarette. I got up, walked up to them, touched the man on the arm and politely asked him for a light. Suddenly and without reason this madman banged me on the head with a walking stick. I woke up in the hospital the next morning with my head aching and bandaged."
(Adapted from a short story by A Averchenko as told by Charon 1979:1–2).

As the case study above suggests, there is no nonideological position from which we could evaluate reality or compare different representations of reality to discover how they distort reality. The writer of the newspaper report accepts the story as told by the police because journalistic ideology dictates that official police reports are true, while each person involved in the incident believed that their story was the only true interpretation of the events.

There is no such nonideological position because we live in systems of meanings, for example the language of our community is one such system. Language as a system of representations defines how we experience the world as a meaningful place and so defines for us what is real, what is true and what should be accepted as the common sense or natural order of things. In the end, ideology produces our experience.

Althusser suggests that ideology works by providing a place for each individual to identify himself or herself within the representations, for example, we identify with heroes in the movies. Such a process of identification he terms *interpellation*. Interpellation means that the individual is positioned or inserted as the subject for his or her own statements and experiences. Such interpellation provides each individual with the sense of identity. For example, language, film and television provide positions of identity for individuals. In language the word "I" can be used by anyone to refer to themselves, and when I read text written in the first person I identify with the "I" in the text as if it is me; it is as if the text provides me with a position into which I can insert myself and experience the world as it was experienced by the original writer. In taking such a view I also accept the meanings and beliefs, interpretations and ideology presented to me. Althusser explains that interpellation is similar to the act of "hailing". For example, you are walking down the street and you hear someone behind you saying "Hey, You!". On hearing these words you turn around because you recognise that possibly it is you that is being hailed or called. In a similar manner, film and television position you as a viewer, the television announcer is speaking to you and you recognise yourself as the subject or individual. In viewing a film you are presented with a position that provides you with a particular fixed view on the action. When we accept such a position and the ideas represented in the texts that are produced by powerful social groups who control the mass media, we are in fact cooperating in the production of ideology.

## Hegemony

People's cooperation in production of the dominant ideology is termed *hegemony* by the Italian philosopher Antonio Gramsci. Hegemony is the way the powerful ruling class in a society can maintain domination without the need to use force to subordinate the less powerful people in a society. The ruling class gains the approval or consent of the dominated classes to accept the existing social positions. The dominated classes are co-opted into social institutions that support the power and authority of the ruling class. For example, the people are conscripted to the army or join the police force that serve to protect the interests of powerful groups and help maintain their wealth, however, the people believe they are protecting the whole society or the country against enemies. Once again we can see that ideology seems like social cement that makes a hegemonic consensus. For example, you are watching a detective story on television and identify yourself with the policeman who protects a rich industrialist against the gangsters or members of a trade union.

## British cultural studies

Extending on the ideas of Althusser and Gramsci, British cultural studies theorists proposed that society is not a unified collection of people that accept one particular ideology. Society is more dynamic and characterised by many conflicting *ideologies* rather than a single ideology. For example, in South Africa there are different groups of people with different ideologies, such as the religious ideologies of Christians and Jews, capitalists and socialists, ideology of right-wing whites, and black power ideology.

The production of representations and meanings are processes that take place in a social context and therefore involve relations of unequal power. The production of meaning and ideology involves the power of a particular social group to represent its own views and images or its representations as the reflection of reality and propagate its own meanings as the real experiences. Such a process involves conflict and challenges from other groups who have constructed different ideologies. For example, the new law on Capital Gains Tax that will make rich people pay more tax is considered by the South African government as a means to make taxation more evenly spread among the people. Rich people on the other hand see the extra tax as an assault on free enterprise and capitalism. Each group would like to promote their view as the real meaning of the new tax. Obviously, the government as a group with more power is in a better position to propagate its ideas as the true meaning of the new tax.

Ideology refers to the ways in which meaning serves to establish and sustain relations of power and domination. From the cultural studies perspective a more comprehensive definition of ideology would be *meaning in the service of power* (cf. Thompson 1992:7). This implies that ideology is always connected to systems of representations such as language and the mass media that communicate dominant meanings and serve the interests of power. For example, most newspapers and television programmes in the Western World report on the events in Iraq as seen from the

American ideology which describes Iraq's leader, Sadam Hussain as a ruthless dictator and terrorist and justifies American military attacks against Iraq.

Thompson (1992:60-66) identifies five modes through which ideology is imposed on society by dominant groups in order to promote their interests:

- Legitimation – Relations of domination can be established and maintained if they are represented as legitimate and worthy of support. Domination is justified as *rational*, and the interests of the ruling class are claimed to be *universal* and represent the interests of everyone in society, and the mass media construct stories that present the existing social inequalities as timeless and unchanging. For example, during the apartheid era the churches described the separation of the races and exclusion of blacks from many social activities as having been decreed by God.
- Dissimulation – Relations of domination are established and maintained by being concealed, denied or obscured. Dissimulation works by *displacing* attention from relations of domination and focusing attention on other issues, for example media criticism of the excessive payment made to black members of a university council is described by a black trade union as attacks by white racists on deserving blacks. Another example is the criticism of Zimbabwe's president Robert Mugabe by the mass media, while such criticism is described by the Zimbabwe government as a sign of disrespect for all African leaders. Dissimulation also works by the use of *euphemisation* that describes relations and institutions in different words or metaphors, for example the harsh South African prisons are described as "rehabilitation centres".
- Unification – Relations of domination are maintained by constructing stories that unify individuals into collective identity regardless of their differences, for example, that of creating one black nation in South Africa regardless of the differences between different black groups. *Standardisation* is an example of unification, for example constructing one national language in South Africa.
- Fragmentation – Relations of domination are maintained by fragmenting individuals and groups that may be able to challenge the dominant group. Such fragmentation is caused by promoting disunity in the political opposition, emphasising the differences between those groups that opposed power of the ruling group. For example, mass media reports on differences of opinion within the African National Congress regarding the situation in Zimbabwe. Such reports attempt to create conflict within the ANC.
- Reification – Particular relations of domination within a society are the product of changing history and are not permanent; through reification they are represented as natural, permanent and eternal and outside of history. For example, for years the mass media presented apartheid as the natural order of life in South Africa.

Through such modes, the ideology of the powerful groups in society is communicated by the mass media and then accepted by the majority of the people in a society as the taken-for-granted, common-sense view of the world. The mass media excludes other

# Media and Ideology

alternative ideologies or ideas by not communicating them. As a result of such exclusion of alternative views the ideology of the dominant group becomes the dominant ideology and serves their interest and manufactures consent and consensus. For example, criticism of the South African government over the arms deal reported in an alternative newspaper such as *Mail & Guardian* are denounced by other media as misguided.

## 9.4 IDEOLOGICAL STRUGGLES AND CONFLICTS OF INTERPRETATIONS

While the dominant ideology manufactures consent and is taken as the common-sense view of the world, it is also challenged and resisted by other ideologies. Resistance and challenge arise because a society is not entirely unified and different groups compete to promote their own ideologies and there are always different and competing ways to describe reality, for example, socialists and capitalists interpret labour relations differently.

Ideologies are also not entirely coherent systems of meanings but are fragmentary and contain contradictions; for example, many conflicting ideas about God could be extracted from the Bible. Furthermore, individuals can interpret ideological texts and create their own meanings and resist the dominant ideology. Such struggles over meaning occur in domains such as language, mass media and culture where ideology is produced as different groups attempt to promote their ideas and definitions of the social reality. For example, we may find different interpretations of the economy being propagated by trade unions such as COSATU and business organisations: trade unions demand that workers be paid fair wages to be able to buy basic necessities, however such a demand is interpreted by business organisations as excessive cost. The capitalist ideology is shared by mass media journalists and owners of factories and businesses and this would explain why it is common for the media to present labour disputes over living wages as unjustified and criminal acts that are "costing the country millions of rands". For example, a South African radio talk-show host described all attempts by labour to organise strikes as "crimes" and "acts of terrorism".

As the dominant ideology is produced and circulates in society in text and images produced by the mass media, these are also challenged by the individual who receives such ideological messages, interprets them and attributes different meanings to them – according to his or her own social and material conditions. Mass media texts, such as reports in newspapers or television programmes are polysemic as they have multiplicity of meanings for different people. For example, if you are a factory worker and read a story about labour disputes you may agree with the views expressed by your trade union; however, a factory owner who reads the same story would disagree with the views of the labour union.

### 9.4.1 Preferred reading

British cultural studies scholar, Stuart Hall suggests a theory of "preferred reading" that explains the conflict of interpretation of ideological texts. Hall identifies three social

# MEDIA STUDIES

positions that readers may take in relation to the interpretation of the dominant ideology:

- Dominant reading – A person that shares the views of the dominant ideology accepts the ideology and the interpretations of reality that are presented in the mass media texts. For example, a member of the South African Communist party would accept the party's views on the economy and reject criticism as being inspired "capitalist ideology".
- Negotiated reading – A person who does not entirely accept the dominant ideology, attempts to negotiate or compare the meanings presented in media text to his or her own situation. Such a person may only accept some ideas of the dominant ideology. For example a Unitarian who, as a member of a religious body, maintains that God is not a Trinity but one person, advocates freedom from formal dogma and doctrine and thus embraces ideas from various religions and ideologies.
- Oppositional reading – A person who is entirely opposed to the dominant ideology, rejects the meanings and interpretations presented by the mass media. For example, a person who considers abortion as murder of unborn children, rejects as misguided a television programme that explains that abortion may be necessary under certain conditions.

While Hall's classification explains how different ideologies lead to different interpretation, his three reading positions are much too limited because we could find other and more complex ways people interpret meaning. Hall's theory nevertheless shows that ideological texts allow for a variety of interpretations and the dominant ideology cannot be entirely imposed on all the people in society.

### 9.4.2 Discursive practices

The ideological meanings that are represented in mass media are only potential meanings as they can only become meaningful to particular readers who interpret and mediate such meanings through their own knowledge, experiences and views. To account for more complex ways people interpret text that extend beyond the preferred, negotiated and oppositional reading suggested by Hall, we could suggest that people interpret from their various social positions and dispositions (knowledge, prejudices, and so forth) they have acquired as members of different *discursive practices* in society. A discursive practice is any formal and institutionalised group of people, such as journalists, doctors, lawyers, for example, who have a specialised and rule-governed way, such professional ideology of journalists, scientific method of scientists, slang of gang members, and so forth – for using language and interpreting reality. (Discursive practice is discussed in more depth Unit 3, Volume 2 on media and language.) The interpretation of media text then becomes a dynamic negotiation between ideology in the text and the various ideologies and positions a person may have as the result of being a member in a number of such discursive practices. For example, a lawyer may interpret a text from a professional position and combine this with a political ideology.

# Media and Ideology

In the previous sections of this unit we looked at different theories of ideology and how ideology operates in society. Understanding ideology, its nature and ways of operation in society are important for our encounters with the mass media that have become the most visible and important social and cultural institutions. Such positions place the media as the main battlefields for the production and communication of ideology to define social reality. We conclude our discussion with the following case study.

## Case study 9.2: How the mass media promote ideology

The way ideology of the mass media *legitimates* a particular view by providing *rationalisation* and justification for a narrow perspective from which to interpret reality, while at the same time such an ideological perspective blinds or conceals other interpretations of reality can be found in many newspaper editorials.

For example, an editorial opinion article in the *Mail & Guardian* (26 May 2000), begins with a headline: "*A war that goes beyond reason*" and declares that "The chances of quickly resolving the senseless, inexplicable, insupportable conflict between Ethiopia and Eritrea look slim". The editorial then continues: "The sheer, reckless imbecility of the war between Ethiopia and Eritrea is breathtaking. The fighting, which began in 1998 and flared again last week, seems totally pointless". The editorial writer wants us to accept or identify with his or her pacifist (anti-war) ideology that assumes that all wars are pointless and unreasonable.

Having established that war is unreasonable, the editorial writer thus presents himself or herself as a reasonable person and representing the voice of universal reason. From such a perspective the writer then goes on in the next few paragraphs to uncover the causes of this unreasonable war, and writes that its "ostensible cause is a dispute over demarcation of the two countries 1 000 km border. To the extent that there is a half comprehensible explanation for the conflict, it appears to be friction over trade and Eritrea's decision to have its own currency, valued independently of the Ethiopian birr." The editorial then briefly explains that Eritrea's decision to have its own currency increased Ethiopia's oil and transport costs considerably and that there also was a dispute over demarcation of the ill-defined border between the two countries, and that Ethiopia is landlocked and its only access to the sea is through Eritrean territory. These *unreasonable* causes and Ethiopian aggression lead to that "we now have a war, which has achieved a momentum and gravity wholly out of proportion to the original dispute".

What is important for us to note as reader of the article is that logically and reasonably there are good reasons and justifications for the war – all major nations have gone to war at one time or another for the same reasons. However, such facts are not presented by the writer who insists and emphasises the *unreasonableness* of the war. Such presentation distracts the reader from thinking differently; the editorial writer's own ideology prevents him or her from seeing that there are good reasons to justify the war.

The writer of the editorial article then goes on further and suggests that both Ethiopia and Eritrea have many things in common: a colonial past, they were liberated by the British who have "thrown out" the Italian occupiers of these countries. However, the fact that the British used military force and waged a war against the Italians during the Second World War is *euphemised* and evaded by the writer, who says that Italy was simply "thrown out" by the British who had "non-altruistic reasons" to do so.

Then the editorial writer points out other similarities and some differences between Ethiopia and Eritrea:

> There are ethnic and religious differences, although Christianity and Islam predominate in both countries. But there are no great riches at stakes, no oil wells or diamond fields. Indeed, both antagonists are pathetically poor. There is no great ideological or political gulf. So what exactly is the present-day casus belli?

The editorial writer's pacifist and anti-war ideology seems to suggest that war is a game reserved for the rich.

The article then proceeds to make the point:

> What, then can justify the recurring carnage which has claimed up to 70 000 lives in the past two years? What can possibly excuse the creation of yet more refugee armies in a region where millions are already suffering the cruel deprivation of drought and famine? Nothing excuses it. This war is reprehensible as it is futile ... It is beyond reason.
>
> (*Mail & Guardian,* 26 May 2000)

The editorial article shows us how ideology conceals facts and opposing interpretation and only presents facts that support the ideology or fixed ideas of the editorial writer.

## Summary

In this unit we identified a number of definitions of ideology and explained the difference between the neutral and critical theories of ideology. We recognised how ideology is interrelated with language and the mass media, and explained how people accept, evaluate or reject ideology. We applied our knowledge of ideology and its operation to analysis of media texts.

## Research activities

1. Select a number of editorial opinion articles in different newspapers and do the following:
   a) Identify the ideology of the writer of the editorial article.
   b) Using Hall's theory of reading, explain what reading position the writer of the editorial article intended to communicate to the audiences.
   c) Identify the reading position that is taken by the writer of the case study.
   d) Identify the ideology of the writer of the case study.
   e) List other reading positions that you as the reader could adopt when reading the editorial opinion article.
   f) Explain whether you agree or disagree with the interpretation of the editorial article as given by the author of the case study above.

## Further reading

Fowler, R. 1991. *Language in the news: discourse and ideology in the press.* London: Routledge.
Grossberg, L, Wartella, E & Whitney, DL. 1998. *Media making: mass media in a popular culture.* Thousand Oaks, CA: Sage.
Thompson, JB. 1992. *Ideology and modern culture.* Cambridge: Polity.
Tolson, A. 1996. *Mediations: texts and discourse in media studies.* London: Arnold

## Bibliography

Bourdie, P. 1992. *Language and symbolic power.* Cambridge: Polity Press.
Charon, JM. 1979. *Symbolic interactionism.* Englewood Cliffs, NJ: Prentice-Hall.
Fowler, R. 1991. *Language in the news: discourse and ideology in the press.* London: Routledge.
Grossberg, L, Wartella, E & Whitney, DL. 1998. *Media making: mass media in a popular culture.* Thousand Oaks, CA: Sage.
Thompson, JB. 1990. *Studies in the theory of ideology.* Cambridge: Polity.
Thompson, JB. 1992. *Ideology and modern culture.* Cambridge: Polity.
Tolson, A. 1996. *Mediations: texts and discourse in media studies.* London: Arnold.

# Media and the Production of Meaning: Semiotics

## 10

*Pieter J Fourie*

## Overview

In this unit we discuss the following:
- a definition of semiotics
- structuralism as the origin of semiotics
- the founding fathers of semiotics and the distinction between the concepts "signifier" and *signifié*/"signified" and between the concepts "langue" and "parole"
- the characteristics of a sign
- different kinds of signs
- the functions of signs
- different kinds of codes
- the characteristics of codes, and
- different kinds of meaning.

## Learning outcomes

After completing this unit you should be able to explain the following with your own examples taken from media content:
- what semiotics is;
- semiotics' history and what structuralism is;
- the distinction between the concepts "signifier" and *signifié*/"signified", and between the concepts "langue" and "parole";
- the characteristics of a sign;
- the arbitrary, iconic, symbolic, and indexical sign;
- the functions of signs;
- different kinds of codes;
- the characteristics of codes; and
- the concepts denotation, connotation, ideology, and the polysemic nature of television.

## 10.1 INTRODUCTION: THE FIELD OF SEMIOTICS

How do the media communicate? In semiotics it is argued that we, including the media, communicate with signs. Signs are combined according to the rules of codes. With the

# Media and the Production of Meaning: Semiotics

use of signs and codes we convey meanings. Semiotics is thus the science of signs and codes and the meaning they convey.

The point of departure in media semiotics is that media content is not reality itself, but a representation and an imitation of reality. In these representations, signs and codes are combined in a structured way to convey specific meanings the media wish to distribute about reality. The media are thus a symbolic form of expression similar to other forms of symbolic expression such as drama, theatre, dance, myth, literature, music, and so on.

But the media are also a very specific sign system in the sense that media accommodate numerous other sign systems. By this we mean that the media include linguistic sign systems (language), nonverbal sign systems such as clothing (costumes), body language, visual (pictorial/imagery) sign systems such as moving and digital images (film, television, the Internet) photographs, graphics, verbal sign systems (voice, articulation, register) and so on.

The aim of media semiotics is to sharpen our critical awareness of the ways in which the media reflect, represent and imitate reality or aspects of reality with the purpose of conveying a specific meaning usually in support of an underlying ideology, point of view, ideal, argument and attitude.

Semiotics embraces four principal areas of study:

- The *sign*: this involves the study of the sign itself. What does a sign consist of, which different types of signs are there, how are signs related to reality, how are signs related to the users? For example: what is a linguistic sign (words) and how does it differ from a pictorial or visual sign (such as a photograph)?
- *Sign systems*: this involves the study of how signs collectively form a sign system. Language is an example of a sign system, television (which consists mainly of audio-visual signs) is a sign system, nonverbal communication (gestures, facial expressions) is a sign system. Further variants are found within a particular sign system. For example, Zulu, Xhosa, Afrikaans, English and Sotho are variants of language as a sign system. The national costumes belonging to different cultures and peoples are variants of clothing as a nonverbal sign system; the different culinary styles of various peoples and cultures are variants of culinary practices as a sign system.
- *Codes*: this involves the study of how signs are related to one another by means of codes which are understood by the users, and how the various sign systems are related to one another by means of various codes. For example, how are words (verbal signs) related to one another in a language by means of grammatical sentence constructions (codes) to form sentences? How are words (for example the dialogue in a film) and the images of the film related to one another in a film by means of the use of the camera and editing techniques (codes)? How do these codes develop and what is the role of culture and cultural conventions in the creation, use and comprehension of codes?
- *Meaning*: what is meaning and are there different kinds of meaning?

© JUTA & CO

# MEDIA STUDIES

In the following parts of this unit we will return to each of these areas of study in more detail. In this unit we will not do a semiotic analysis as such. For this you are referred to Unit 1 in Volume 2, namely Text analysis. Here the purpose is to acquaint you with the basics of semiotic concepts and instruments. You will also note that semiotic concepts will be referred to and in some cases applied in many of the units of this volume and in Volume 2. This is because semiotics is, to a certain extent, an underlying point of departure in this book and a prominent approach to the study of media in both volumes.

Before we take a more detailed look at signs, sign systems, codes and meaning, some brief notes about the history of semiotics.

## 10.2 THE HISTORY OF SEMIOTICS

Since Greek antiquity, philosophers have been interested in the concept "sign" and the fact that a sign represents something to someone in some respect or capacity. The fact that a sign is not reality as such, but replaces reality or an aspect or a concept of reality, so that it is a substitute for the original, has raised searching questions throughout history about the anatomy of reality and even about the existence of reality.

The hypothesis that the entire universe is perfused with signs, if it is not composed exclusively of signs, forms, for example, the basis of a period in German philosophy known as Idealism, and specifically conceptual idealism. An eminent representative of this school was the German philosopher Immanual Kant, who held that our view of reality, namely our *Umwelt*, entails an essential reference to mind (*Gemüt*) in its constitution. Based on this point of view it is argued that raw experience is unattainable. Before we can apprehend experience it must first be steeped in, strained through, and seasoned by "a soup of signs" (Sebeok 1991:20).

Taking the preceding paragraphs as an indication of how far back people's thinking on the sign and the relationship between the sign and reality really goes, we shall next proceed to examine twentieth century structuralism, which is the origin of modern and postmodern semiotics.

### 10.2.1 Structuralism

It is generally accepted that present-day semiotics had its origin in structuralism. But what is structuralism?

Defined in its simplest form, structuralism is

> ... an intellectual enterprise characterised by attention to the systems, relations and forms – the structures – that make meaning possible in any cultural activity or artefact.
>
> (O'Sullivan, Hartley, Saunders, Montgomery & Fiske 1994:225)

## Structuralism as a philosophy

Throughout the centuries, the practice of science has been influenced by the thinking and models of the "dominant" science of the period. For example, Medieval thinking about man, society, politics, ethics, aesthetics and the like, was mainly dominated by theological concepts and thinking. Consequently, one could say that theology was the dominant paradigm in medieval "science" practice.

In the nineteenth century it was mainly the natural and medical sciences that influenced human beings' way of thinking about their existence and reality. The practice of the humanities and social sciences – sociology and psychology for example – was therefore heavily influenced by the natural sciences, which accounts for the intensely behaviouristic nature of the social sciences in the nineteenth century.

It can be argued that language and the study of language (especially structural linguistics) have been a dominant paradigm in the twentieth century. Structural linguistics, and particularly the work of the Swiss linguist Ferdinand De Saussure (1857–1913), directed for the greater part of this century most of the humanitarian and social scientific thought about humankind.

Thus, structuralism (as defined by and practised in linguistics) was, at least for part of the last century, one of the main and dominant paradigms in the human and social sciences.

With his distinction between *langue* and *parole* De Saussure points to the underlying structure (langue) (a code or grammar) on which language usage (parole) is based and which underlies the use of language. The ordinary user of language is hardly aware of this underlying structure. The structure becomes visible only through linguistic analysis and description; only through such an analysis and description can one gain knowledge about the nature, working, power and possibilities of language. Likewise, it is argued, an underlying structure directs and supports a person's thinking, behaviour and values, as well as the functioning of society.

According to the philosophy of structuralism, the purpose of scientific analysis should then be to lay bare these underlying structures. Only through knowledge of how these structures are constituted and how they work can people obtain knowledge about their own ways of thinking and behaviour and about the functioning of society.

Thus: the purpose of structuralism in, for example,

- psychoanalysis is to lay bare the underlying structure which dictates behaviour – the unconsciousness is then seen as the underlying structure of behaviour;
- economics is to lay bare the underlying objectives and modes of production of capitalism or socialism;
- sociology is to lay bare the underlying structures of power and control and to show how these structures dictate and direct the functioning and/or disfunctioning of society;
- anthropology is to lay bare the ways in which social taboos, archetypes and myths direct the behaviour of a person as a social being as well as the collective unconsciousness of a society, and in

- media studies is mainly to lay bare the underlying structures of media production and its resultant messages; the relation between these messages and other power, social, cultural and economic structures in society, and the way the media represent and reflect all the above-mentioned structures.

To put it another way: according to structuralism, the surface structure (in other words what we see and hear) of literature, the fine arts, film, television, radio, the press, myths, politics, the administration of justice, the economy, society, the human psyche, is based on a *deep structure*. Therefore, Karl Marx's economic, political and social theories are a structuralist exposure of the deep structure of capitalism. In this case the deep structure is based on class difference, dispute and conflict. Sigmund Freud's psychoanalysis is a structuralist analysis of a person's unconsciousness, which forms the deep structure of his or her behaviour and mind.

As a philosophy, structuralism differs radically from, for instance, existentialism. In existentialism the individual and his or her freedom to determine his or her own fate and identity are emphasised. In contrast to existentialism, structuralism depicts the individual (humans) as no more than another structural component of reality: an object among other objects. Even a person's thinking is only regarded as one object among various others in reality, and is actually nothing more than the result of the collective unconsciousness or deep structure of society.

## Structuralism as a method

Apart from its underlying philosophy, structuralism also refers to all those methods applied to investigate, describe and explain the underlying or deep structures of different sign systems.

We distinguish the following stages (cf. Dethier 1993:490) in the history of the development of structuralism as a method:

- Linguistic structuralism and the origin of semiotics: Ferdinand De Saussure and the publication of his book in 1916, *Course de linguistique généralé*, and the American philosopher, Charles Sanders Peirce. Although Peirce had been theorising about the sign around the end of the nineteenth century, it was not until 1931 that his writings were published as the *Collected Papers of Charles Sanders Peirce* (produced by Hartshorne & Weiss). See our subsequent discussion of De Saussure and Peirce.
- Russian formalism (between 1910 and 1920): The leading proponents include Tomasjevskij, Sklovskij and Eichenbaum. Formalism is concerned with the formulation of a distinct literary and aesthetic theory. A work of art (such as a novel) is regarded as an autonomous text and analysed as such. The sociological and psychological context of the work, and bibliographical data about the artist (writer), his/her world and philosophy, are not considered relevant. Russian formalism laid the foundation for the structural narrative analysis of for instance Vladimir Propp (cf. Unit 4, Volume 2 on narrative analysis). Even today, Propp's work can be regarded as one of the influences that shape narratology – narrative

analysis as applied to the analysis of narratology in for instance cinematic art, the analysis of television programmes, and so forth. Propp also had a strong influence on the work of Claude Lévi-Strauss and Roland Barthes.
- The Prague circle: Founded around 1930 by well-known figures such as Roman Jakobson. The aesthetic isolation of Russian formalism was interrupted and the work of art (literary text) was seen and studied in its social context.
- Parisian structuralism: Structuralist activity was extended to anthropology (Lévi-Strauss), philosophy (Foucault), sociology (Aron) and psychoanalysis (Lacan).

The first stage was important for communication and media semiotics in the sense that it formed the basis for semiotic theory/theories on meaning. Russian formalism and the Prague circle were especially important for the development of literary theory and its application to literature and later to film and television. The last stage and its influence on modern thinking on the media as a symbolic form of expression is especially important in communication science and semiotics.

What is important as far as structuralism as a method is concerned are the rules that developed out of structuralism for the analysis or any process of organisation – meaning, for example organisation (structure) in an organisation, to the ways in which a recipe is organised (structured), a soap opera, a newspaper story, or a news bulletin, and so on. Put in another way: in the application of structuralism as a research method the principal concern is the discovery of one or more of the following rules in a sign system. Here we mention only some of these rules:

- the rule of immanence: the discovery of whatever is peculiar to a specific structure, for instance an organisation, newspaper, or a recipe
- the rule of pertinence: whatever is striking in a structure
- the rule of displacement: what happens when one structural element in a structure is replaced by another?
- the rule of compatibility: which structural elements in a structure are compatible?
- the rule of linkage: how are structural elements in a structure linked?
- the rule of synchronism and diachronism: what is the nature of a structure at a given moment and how does it change?
- the rule of functioning: how does a structure function?

These rules can be made applicable to literally all structures: the press, broadcasting, political structures, the social and health structures in a country, education as a structure, the structure of interpersonal communication, organisation structures, the structure of communication in an organisation, and so on.

From the above it is clear that semiotics originated out of structural philosophy and method in the sense of semiotics' emphasis on signs and codes as structural elements of sign systems, and their role in the production of meaning within a given sign system or its combination with other sign systems. Let us now turn to the origin of modern semiotics.

## 10.2.2 De Saussure, Peirce and the emergence of semiotics

The Swiss linguist Ferdinand De Saussure (1857–1913) and the American philosopher Charles Sanders Peirce (1839–1914) are regarded as the founders of modern semiotics.

One of De Saussure's premises was that language should be studied as a system of signs. He was intimating at the same time that he did not consider linguistic signs to be the only kind. In fact, in De Saussure's view, linguistics is the study of a particular kind of sign (language) which is subordinate to the study of a general theory of signs, or semiology.

His most important contribution was to describe the distinction between

1. signifiant/signifier (SA) and signifié/signified (Sé) (cf. the later discussion of the sign), and
2. langue (linguistic system/sign system) and parole (language usage/use of signs) to which we shall return at a later stage.

It was not until several years later, after the publication of *Course de linguistique générale* (1916) that his proposal regarding a general theory of signs was followed-up by linguists. The result was a form of semiology that was strongly influenced by linguistics.

Between 1931 and 1935 the first six parts of Peirce's work, *Collected Papers of Charles Sanders Peirce* (Peirce 1960) were published posthumously.

His conclusion that people think in signs is rooted in his knowledge of and work in the field of logic. He became increasingly convinced that everything could be reduced to signs. In consequence it became important for him to establish the function(s) of a sign/signs. He argued that the essential function of a sign is to make "ineffective" relations "effective" – whether this means communicating with others by means of signs, or using signs to improve our thinking about and understanding of the world.

According to Peirce, communication and an improvement in our understanding of the world take place through what we (invisibly) believe (think) and visibly capture or express. The capture of (invisible) beliefs/thought takes place through verbalisation and visualisation (including cognitive visualisation) with the aid of signs. For example: I am thinking of my mother. My thinking about my mother is determined by (i) the mental and cognitive image (sign) I have of her and (ii) the expression of this image in a linguistic sign, indicated in Afrikaans by the letters "ma", in English by "mother", in Zulu by "úmama", in Sotho by "Mme" and in Xhosa by "Umame". The use of signs such as these is destined to create mutual understanding of the world (effective relation). If I had not had a sign (whether visual or verbal) for the concept "mother", I would not have been able to capture/express my feelings, thoughts and comprehension of "mother" or communicate these to anyone else.

For Peirce, the value of semiotic concepts such as "sign" and "code" lies in the fact that they make us more aware of our own habitual beliefs (the way we use signs to verbalise and visualise the invisible – that which we know and believe) and the beliefs of others, and in consequence make us more aware of our conduct and thinking, and that of others. This is related to his view of the three approaches to our comprehension of the world (cf. Van Zoest 1978:17–20).

He refers to these three approaches by means of the concepts "Firstness", "Secondness" and "Thirdness".

- Firstness is related to concepts such as "property", "feeling", "probability character", "essence". Firstness is the conception of what is, without referring to anything else. This is the conception of the possible and potential.
- Secondness is related to concepts such as "confrontation with reality", "the outside world", "what happens". Secondness is the conception of the way things are in terms of another or a Second, but without reference to a possible Third. This is the conception of what exists.
- Thirdness is related to concepts such as "a rule", "a law", "a pattern of behaviour", "an element of generality in our collective and individual experience". Thirdness is the conception we arrive at by relating what has been brought about by a Second to a Third. It is the conception of the generally valid.

Various developments have taken place in semiotics since the time of De Saussure and Peirce and various streams or movements have emerged. The following is a concise account of the most important of these:

- the "communication" semiology of thinkers such as Buyssens (1967), Preito Mounin (1970) and especially Umberto Eco (1976) with the emphasis on the literal meaning of a sign and on formalism (the description of the visible relationship between the signifier and the signified)
- the connotative semiotics of which Roland Barthes (1967) is a leading proponent (see discussion in Unit 15, Representation), with the emphasis on the social and ideological relationship of and between signs and codes
- the expansive semiotics of Julia Kristeva (1974), for example, in which the emphasis falls on the production of meaning, semantic practices and ideology, and which relies largely on Marxist and psychoanalytical theory.

With this brief introduction to the history of semiotics, we return to the four areas of study in semiotics, namely the study of the sign, sign systems, codes and meaning. In the remainder of this unit we will look at each of them separately.

## 10.3 THE SIGN

Semiology distinguishes between different kinds of signs. A sign is never the real object. It is not reality, but represents and serves as a means of referring to reality. In their daily communication people use linguistic signs in order to refer to things, to express their feelings, desires, thoughts and attitudes. How could one refer to something like a dog, for example, unless one knew the linguistic sign D-O-G? One could draw a dog, but that would simply be to use a pictorial or iconic sign as opposed to a linguistic one. In short: without signs it is impossible to communicate. Imagine a situation without the linguistic and/or nonverbal means of referring to something.

### 10.3.1 The characteristics of a sign

Basing our analysis on Peirce's work (see Peters 1974; Van Zoest 1978; Fourie 1983; Leeds-Hurwitz 1993), we can identify a number of characteristics of the sign.

- If it is to function as such, a sign must be physically perceptible, that is to say it must in some degree be visible, audible or tangible, or we must be able to smell or taste it.
- A sign always refers to something, and therefore it has a representative character.
- The representative character of a sign is indissolubly linked to its interpretative character. A sign is always interpreted. This interpretation gives rise to a second sign in the mind of the interpreter.

To sum up: three elements determine the presence of a sign. These are: the perceptible sign itself, what the sign refers to, and the other sign that is created in the mind of the recipient. There is a relationship between the sign and the referent; that is the sign has a representative character. A sign is followed by interpretation; it must be interpreted if its meaning is to be understood. Perceptibility, representation and interpretation therefore characterise the sign (see Van Zoest 1978:23).

### 10.3.2 The components of a sign

For the purpose of this unit we only focus on De Saussure's distinction between signifier, referent and signified. For De Saussure, a sign consists of three components: a signifier, a referent and a signified. The signifier is the physical quality of a sign such as a word, a traffic light, a cloud, a crucifix, a photograph or a television image. These signs are physically observable, often tangible and concrete. The signifier stands in the place of, refers to and/or represents something, which is called the referent. The referent is the object/concept/idea the sign is referring to. Between the signifier and the referent there can be different relations, on the basis of which different groups and kinds of signs can be distinguished, as will be discussed later on. The signified is the meaning attached to the signifier by the recipient: it is abstract, impalpable and may vary from one person to the next. This distinction is explained in our explanation of the different kinds of signs, below.

#### *Types of signs on the basis of the signifier/referent relationship*

On the basis of the relationship between the signifier (sign) and its referent one can differentiate between various kinds of signs. We confine ourselves to *arbitrary, iconic, symbolic* and *indexical* signs.

- Arbitrary sign: The best example of an arbitrary sign is a linguistic sign, such as a word. Here there is no resemblance between the signifier (sign) and the referent. The sign D-O-G ("dog") bears no resemblance to a real dog. In order to understand the sign D-O-G, users of that language have to agree to attach a certain meaning to it – they have to *learn* the meaning of the word. To a Frenchman the sign D-O-G will

mean nothing; he will not spontaneously attach the same meaning to it that an English speaker would, unless he knows English as a sign system.
- Iconic signs: The best examples of iconic signs are pictorial images or visual images (paintings, film images, photography, and the like). Here the signifier (sign) resembles that to which it refers (the referent) in the sense of corresponding with it visually. A photograph (or television image) (sign) of a dog looks like a dog. It is immediately recognisable and the recipient does not need any special knowledge to interpret the sign. Speakers of all languages will attach the same literal (denotative) meaning to the iconic sign. Because of the directly identifiable resemblance between an iconic sign and its referent, it is possible that the recipient will treat the iconic sign as the real thing, especially in film and television. This might explain the power of television and film. People believe television news more readily than press bulletins, lending fresh significance to the old adage, "seeing is believing".
- Symbolic signs: As in language there is no outward correspondence or correlation between the sign and its referent. This applies to linguistic and literary symbols no less than to pictorial symbols. To many people a picture of a cross symbolises Christianity; a picture of a skull symbolises danger. Whence do these meanings derive? The answer is that the meanings of symbols are culturally determined and that people belonging to a particular culture learn these meanings.
- Indexical signs: In the case of indexical signs there is a causal (cause-effect) relation between the sign and its referent. Natural signs are the best examples: clouds signify rain; smoke signals fire.

It is important to remember that the referent (that is, whatever the sign refers to) need not be a concrete object (such as a person, a house, a garment, food); it may well be abstract (such as thoughts, ideas). The referent may be something that existed in the past (take the example of a deceased person), or something that does not yet exist (e.g. an object in science fiction or a sketch of an unborn baby). The referent may be conceivable (such as life) or inconceivable (such as death). According to Van Zoest (1978:30), any imaginable or unimaginable thing could possibly become the referent of a sign.

Collectively, the distinction between these four types of signs forms the basis of semiotics and embraces more or less all the signs available to human beings for the purposes of communication.

In practice, however, it is not always possible to draw rigid distinctions between the signs. Furthermore, the same sign can have different meanings in different cultures and more than one type of sign can operate in a sign system. For example, in television and film iconic signs (the images), indexical signs (the actions) and symbolic and arbitrary signs (the dialogue, but remember that an image – icon – may also be symbolic) occur at the same time and interact with each other to convey meaning. What is more, the same sign could be an index, a symbol or an icon in different circumstances. Take the example of religious relics (a body part of a saint or an object which has been in contact with a saint's body and which is worshipped or venerated). The significance of such a relic would depend on a person's beliefs and culture; it would be seen as a different kind of sign in different religions and different cultures. In some cases it would be an icon, in others a symbol and in yet others an index, or all three.

### 10.3.3 Sign functions

For the purpose of this discussion, one of the last questions to be asked about the sign is the following: What are the functions of signs? Here we cite the structuralist model of the Russian-American linguist, Roman Jakobson (1896–1984), who distinguished six linguistic functions, or in other words contended that language (as a sign system) has six functions. Today these functions are generally cited as the functions of signs and sign systems and are organised into a systematic communication model. That is to say, signs have the following functions, or we communicate by means of signs because signs enable us to:

- refer to something (referential function)
- express and communicate our attitudes/views/ways of understanding about something or someone (expressive function)
- express something in a *specific way* (poetic function)
- find particular ways of shedding further light or explaining what we have expressed (metalinguistic function)
- persuade or convince others (conative function)
- make contact with others (phatic function)

```
                    Context
              (Referential function)
                       |
                    Message
               (Poetic function)
                       |
Communicator ──────────┼────────── Recipient
(Expressive function)  |          (Conative function)
                       |
                    Contact
               (Phatic function)
                       |
                     Code
            (Metalinguistic function)
```

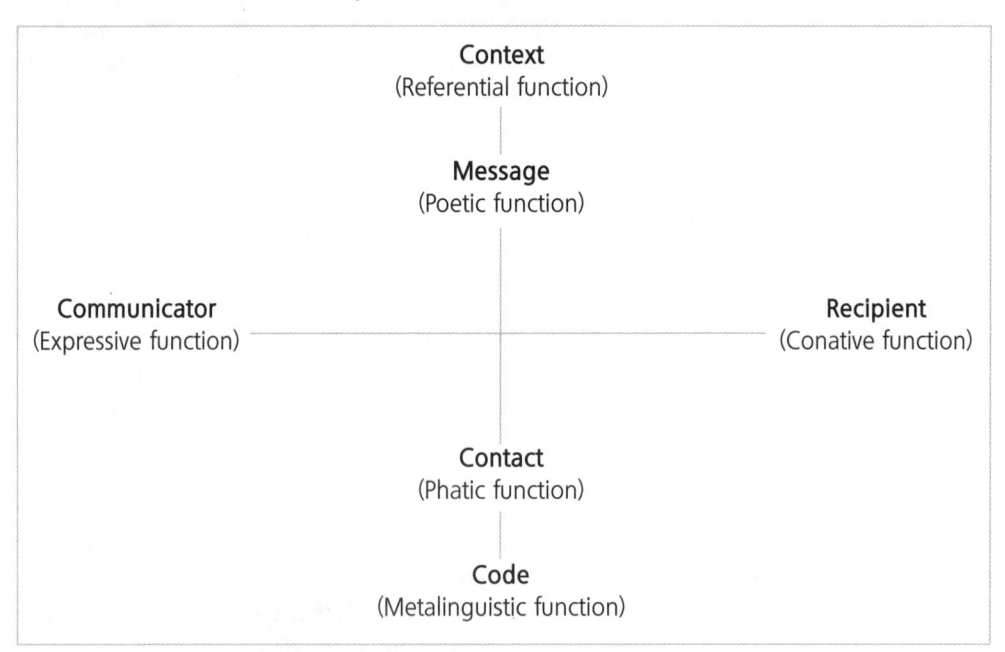

Figure 10.1 Jakobson's communication model (functions)

The referential function relates to the content and context of the communication. This is what the communication is about, the *subject*. One could also see this function as relating to the observed and imaginary world to which both the communicator and the recipient are able to refer. The keyword is *content*. The question is: Which signs are used to represent the content of the message?

The expressive function refers to the *communicator*. The expressive function embodies the expression of the subject and incorporates the attitude of the communicator regarding the subject of the communication. In a political report the expressive function would be what a politician had to say about a topic such as provincial boundaries, for example, as well as the journalist's opinion on the matter. The keyword is *attitude*. What signs does the communicator use to convey his/her attitude about the matter in question?

The conative function refers to the *message* that is intended to influence the recipient and persuade him or her to adopt a particular point of view. In what form is the message intended to reach the recipient? What signs in the message are specifically intended to persuade the viewer, to catch him or her? In a cigarette advertisement intended to convert people to a particular brand of cigarette, these signs usually take the form of attractive models, tropical or other luxurious settings, and so on. However, it is not only in advertisements (which openly set out to persuade) that signs have conative functions. Political communication, in the form of speeches and reports on speeches, newspaper editorials, or political commentaries on radio or television, also contains built-in rhetorical techniques, which may be consciously or unconsciously used, and are intended to persuade the recipient. When it comes to the conative function, the keyword is *persuade*. The question is always: What signs in the message play a conative role? Dethier (1985:85) points out that the expressive and conative functions are directly related: I/you.

The poetic function relates to the *form* or the "how" of a message; which signs are used and how are they used to express the content of the communication in a *particular way*. The poetic function of signs is generally directly related to the *nature* of the medium. Each medium has its own way of expressing a particular message; the message might be the same but it would take on a different form in television as opposed to the printed media. As recipients of messages we are seldom primarily aware of the way the message is shaped, or the poetic functions. This aspect becomes apparent in a field such as art photography, where we are explicitly aware of the communicator's use of camera techniques, camera angles and lenses; or in art films, where there is a deliberate and visible use of camera and editing techniques to express a particular point of view; and frequently also in film advertisements. But since most mass media messages aim to reflect reality as faithfully as possible, there is no attempt to make the recipient aware of the poetic functions. In television news broadcasts, which are intended to be as "slick" as possible, the viewer is not intended to see the deliberate creative and structuring processes that are fundamental to news broadcasting. The keyword is *form*. How are the signs by means of which we communicate created, selected and combined (given a particular form) so that they can embody a specific meaning?

# MEDIA STUDIES

The phatic function refers to those signs in the message that are specifically intended to establish *contact* with the recipient. In pictorial communication the phatic function would refer to the things in a photograph or television image which immediately attract the attention of the viewer. In the printed media such signs would be the layout and typography, such as the letter type and the size of the headings, the placement of a report on a specific page and at a specific point on a page; in language we would be referring to usages such as cries of joy, exclamations of astonishment, shock, greeting or anything else intended to draw the attention of the listener or reader to something specific. The keyword is *contact* and the question is: Which signs in the message are specifically intended to attract the attention of the recipient?

The metalinguistic function refers, in simple terms, to those signs in the message which are intended to throw further light on, explain or emphasise the subject matter that has been communicated. In pictorial communication (photographs, television images, film images) such signs would be the linguistic text, for example captions to photographs and commentary on the content of television or film images. The intention is to make certain that the viewer understands the photograph or television image. In language some examples of metalinguistic signs would be aspects such as intonation, articulation, projection, and also gestures, physical attitudes and so on. The keyword is *illumination* and the question is: Which signs in the message are principally intended to explain the message and make it more accessible to the viewers? It is important to remember that these sign functions do not occur in isolation. Although a sign may have a specific and/or dominant function in a message, it could also have more than one function. For example, the tropical scene in a cigarette advertisement may be referential, expressive, phatic and conative at the same time. Furthermore, the same sign could be seen by different recipients as having different functions in a message.

In any event, Jakobson's six-function classification is a valuable model, the uses of which extend beyond semiological analysis. It is also a valuable aid in the planning and practical formulation of professional communication messages (advertisements, film images, television images, newspaper reports and articles) and in communication campaigns. How effectively do you as a communicator use signs in terms of their functions in the message you are formulating? The questions set (above) at the end of the discussion of each function should serve as a yardstick. If you are able to use signs effectively in terms of their functions, then you have made considerable progress on the road to effective communication.

## 10.4 SIGN SYSTEM

Apart from the individual signs, one can also distinguish between different types of sign systems. A sign system is a group of signs with much the same character, integrated by the same rules or grammar. Examples include language, style of dress, traffic signs, mathematics, music, physical movements (kinaesthetics and proxemics), television, film and photography (the electronic visual media). Based on their similar iconic nature, film and television can be described as a unique visual sign system. The newspaper, using symbols (language) and icons (photographs), is a sign system, just as nonverbal communication, a particular language, maths and music are unique signs systems, each with its own rules, grammar, syntax or codes.

Note that in communication we seldom use a sign system in isolation. In communicating we generally use several sign systems simultaneously. During a conversation we use not only language as a sign system, but also gestures, facial expressions, and metalinguistic components such as intonation, articulation and projection. People also communicate by the way they dress; for example the clothes someone is wearing would probably say something about the communication situation – whether it is formal or informal – and might also provide an indication of the profession or group the person belongs to. Television communicates by means of language, images, nonverbal communication, sound and music, and often by all of these simultaneously.

## 10.5 CODE

Like "sign", "code" is a central concept in semiotics. A code is the "recipe" or technique according to which signs are combined in order to convey meaning – that is, the grammar we use in our everyday linguistic formulations (written or spoken), the rhetorical techniques in public communication, the camera and editing techniques in film and television, all the codes in printing, designing, architecture, theatre, poetry, prose, music and culture in general.

Meaning is generated not only from the raw material of signs and the relationship between a signifier and the referent, but also from the relationship between various signs. The relationship between signs is determined and directed by codes. A code is therefore a group of signs and the rules for their use.

### 10.5.1 Code typology

Based on the work of numerous scholars, Fiske (1982:68–89) provides a rather comprehensive typology of communication codes. The following paragraphs are based on this typology, as well as on previous work on codes done by Fourie (1983;1988).

### *Codes of behaviour and signifying codes*

Almost every aspect of our social behaviour is codified. Behavioural codes govern behaviour such as table manners, the way we dress for various occasions, the way we conduct ourselves at various social occasions, the way we behave towards our superiors and inferiors, the way we obey traffic signs, the way we queue in an orderly fashion at a bus stop or box-office, the way we behave at a soccer match or a tennis tournament, at a pop concert, a wedding, a funeral or in church, and so on.

Such behaviour is governed by what we call codes of behaviour, which are the result of the prevailing norms and values in a society and of cultural traditions and customs. These are handed down from one generation to the next, but are modified over time in response to political, economic, social and cultural changes. In a society we agree to behave in a certain way in terms of these codes of behaviour in given social situations. Without such codes of behaviour there would be social chaos.

In the case of the media, internal policy and codes of conduct (cf. Unit 5) can be seen as codes of behaviour – "the way things are done" at a certain newspaper or radio station.

In contrast, signifying codes are codes that function in specific sign systems such as language, film and journalism. These codes are specifically intended to fulfil a particular communication function, in the sense that they have and convey a specific meaning. Examples of signifying codes include the editing techniques of fade, dissolve and cut in film and television – each has its own quality and meaning and can give a specific meaning to a scene, depending on how it is used by the communicator (cf. Unit 1, Volume 2). The tenses in a grammatical system are another example of a signifying code. The use of tenses differs from one language to another. Tenses have specific meanings and when used incorrectly they turn language into a grammatical chaos.

## Analogue and digital codes

The best illustration of a digital code is provided by comparing a digital watch with an analogue watch. A digital watch tells the seconds and minutes one by one, whereas a conventional watch does not indicate each second and each minute.

Clear distinctions are a feature of digital codes, like digital watches. In the case of digital codes the distinction is between the signifier and the referent. Language provides a good example of digital codes – there is a clear distinction between signifier and referent. Arbitrary codes (based on convention, consent and agreement) are digital and therefore easy to record (like music and mathematics). The dance, on the other hand, is an example of an analogue code. The dance functions through gestures, posture and distance and these are continually changing and are therefore more difficult to record. Whereas culture is principally a digital code, nature, which changes continually without any intervention on the part of humans is an analogue code.

## Presentational and representational codes

A further important distinction is that between presentational and representational codes. Texts (a newspaper article, a television programme, a film, a radio programme, a legal document, a novel, a play, a cartoon strip, and so on) may be considered to be inherently representational codes. They stand for something else; they were created with a specific purpose, to convey something specific in a controlled and orderly fashion, to comment on something or express something. Representational codes are usually iconic and symbolic. By contrast, presentational codes function in and for the thing itself, and

## Media and the Production of Meaning: Semiotics

they are related to the communicator's present social situation. Presentational codes are indexical. Nonverbal communication is a good example of presentational codes; it depends on gestures, eye movements, vocal quality and so forth. Another feature of presentational codes is that they function in the present (here and now), with the object of controlling and directing interaction. For example, my tone of voice or facial expression may reveal the way I feel about something at that particular moment; but they cannot send a message about what my feelings were last week. Presentational codes are restricted to face-to-face communication or communication when the communicator is present (see Fiske 1982:68–89).

### Elaborated and restricted codes

We can also distinguish between restricted and elaborated codes. In the area of language it has been found that people from a lower socio-economic class have more limited linguistic abilities (vocabulary, powers of expression and comprehension) than those from higher socio-economic classes (although exceptions will always be found). This may be ascribed to educational opportunities and social factors. The former group is considered to be people with a restricted language code; and the latter group as people with an elaborated language code.

This distinction may be extended to almost all social phenomena. In semiotics it is used mainly to distinguish between the restricted codes of particular organisations/occupations/bodies/people and explain their influence on meaning. For example, the accepted rules in a subcultural group such as the skinheads constitute a restricted code. The same applies to the legal profession – if one is not familiar with the rules and regulations (restricted code) that govern court procedures, one is excluded from that world. This is equally true of the restricted codes of the army, parliament, journalism with its codes of behaviour, the medical and health care professions, and so on. The purpose of semiotic investigation is to determine the exact nature of these restricted codes and how they ultimately determine and direct the behaviour of these groups/people and the content and meaning of their communication.

One could also argue that apartheid, with its laws, rules and regulations, was a restricted social code, and that since the demise of apartheid South African society is tending to function in terms of elaborated codes such as the Declaration of Human Rights.

### Logical, aesthetic and social codes

The best examples of these three codes are:
- Logical codes (science): for example, mathematics, Morse code, the alphabet, road signs
- Aesthetic codes (art and symbolic forms of expression such as the media): for example, drama, the opera, prose, poetry, fine art, sculpture, architecture, television, film, radio

# MEDIA STUDIES

- Social codes (society): for example, clothing, foods and cookery, objects, social conduct, conventions, rituals, sport, furniture, games

These codes do not occur in isolation. For example, we cannot speak of the media as merely an aesthetic code; they also constitute a social code and frequently a logical one as well. But because the media's representation of the world includes a deliberate and structured creative process, the media are regarded as principally an aesthetic code.

## Codes of content and codes of form

The distinction between codes of content and codes of form embraces all the above codes, which may be either codes of content or codes of form, or both. The distinction between codes of content and codes of form can readily be illustrated by referring to examples from the visual media.

The techniques that are used to unite the components of an image to enable them to convey meaning jointly may be described as codes of content. These include aspects such as composition (levels and lines in the image), the combination of colours, costume, the actors and their acting techniques, objects in the image, such as furniture, props, scenery, buildings and streets. All of these could be described as codes of content.

Codes of form, on the other hand, are the aspects associated with the way the camera looks at the content and the manner in which the various shots are combined in editing.

Take as an example a battle scene in a film. Before the "shoot", that is the recording of the shot on film, the director composes the sequence of shots. He/she might decide to arrange the actors on horseback with a hill in the background, for example. They would be wearing uniforms and a great variety of people, colours, sounds, trees, weapons and other objects typical of a battle scene would be visible. In one shot the camera would focus on the hero. The next shot would show the wounded hero falling off his horse. In the following shot the horse would be falling on top of the hero, and so on and so forth. All the above represent codes of content. These codes may be logical, aesthetic and/or social.

The content of these shots is *viewed* in a particular way by the camera or group of cameras. The director may now decide to capture the whole scene in a wide-angle shot, show the pain on the hero's face in a close-up, show the horse's hooves in another close-up, add a bird's-eye-view of the scene from the air, and so on. The *way (or ways)* in which the content is reproduced by the camera constitutes the codes of form.

Similarly, the director may decide to link the various shots in different ways. In battle scenes, film producers often use a rapid succession of shots, but the shots may overlap (dissolve). The way in which the shots are *linked* is also a code of form.

The same distinction between codes of content and codes of form may be found in language and other sign systems. If a writer were to describe the same battle scene in a newspaper article for instance, the soldiers, the battlefield, the weapons, the horses and so on would be the content of the article and therefore the subject. The codes of

# Media and the Production of Meaning: Semiotics

form would be the way in which the writer gave the content form: he/she might decide to tell the story in verse or to use other stylistic techniques to give expression to the content.

## 10.5.2 Characteristics of codes

Codes have certain typical features, of which the following are singled out for mention:

- Codes exist only in and through the way people *use* them. They have no existence outside someone's head. Unlike signs, which have an objective existence outside the human mind (take as an example the sign "tree" for something with leaves and branches and roots, which has a meaning that can be recorded in a dictionary), codes do not exist as an objective phenomenon. Only when one uses a code such as the camera point of view is it and can it be described as a code. What, for instance, is a close-up? You can't touch it, or see it as an independent object; it has no inherent meaning, you can't read, smell or hear it. It has no sensory existence. Only when it is used does it acquire a meaning. The same applies to grammatical codes, stylistic codes and social codes. On the subject of social codes, a code (which we could just as well call a custom or convention) such as a man rising when a woman enters a room, or in other cultures of remaining seated when a woman enters a room, has no objective existence. It is merely a custom that exists and acquires a meaning through the fact that it is used.
- By implication, codes are linked to culture and context. The above example of rising when a woman enters a room is relevant here. In some cultures this is the acceptable social code but exactly the same code is considered unacceptable in other cultures. Similarly, every language employs grammatical codes in a unique way. Even the codes related to the use of technology may differ from one culture to another. To cite one example, there are often distinct differences in the ways in which Easterners and Westerners make films. The use of codes in various cultures bears a relationship to those cultures' prevailing attitudes and views on matters such as reality, family relations, relations between the sexes, ancestors, religion, time and space.
- Codes function intertextually. One learns to understand and interpret a code through other codes that are used in other media, behavioural forms, cultures and so on. For example, if I were to drive a car in Kuala Lumpur, their traffic safety practices (traffic code) would not be entirely unfamiliar to me, and I would soon learn this code by comparing it with my own (South African) traffic code.
- Codes act as filters for our perceptions of and about the world, people, things and events. Codes form what may be called the skeleton of our cognitive comprehension of something, and allow us to condense and understand an enormous amount of data and information. Fiske (1987:4) speaks of *encoding* and *decoding* information. For example, my comprehension and understanding of and/or attitude towards someone are directed by a social code. For instance, we are taught (codified) to treat handicapped people in a certain way, and think about and behave towards them in

a particular way. This is a code in terms of which people think and behave when they come into contact with a handicapped person. (See our subsequent discussion of stereotypes in Unit 15.) The same applies to our thinking and actions regarding race, gender, homosexuality, ethnic groups, countries and political systems. One can also argue that the media as such, and the codes operative in the media, are filters of our experience of reality. They provide us with specific interpretations of reality and in the process filter how we think about reality.

- In accordance with their culture-relatedness and their function as filters in our structuring of reality, codes function as markers for social classes, groups, cultural groups and subcultural groups. (See previous discussion of restricted and elaborated codes in this unit.) By using codes in a particular way and creating new codes, a sign or group of signs can undergo a change of meaning in a particular subgroup, for instance in a subculture like the punks. By transforming (codifying) the signs associated with Christianity to fit in with their own views, satanists give radical new meanings to Christian symbols. When different garments are combined (codified) in a certain way, they become associated with particular subcultural groups, such as the hippies.

  The Nazis provide a further example. One could argue that the genocide for which they were responsible was a direct result of their codes of behaviour, which also formed the basis for their view of humankind, and which differed radically from accepted social norms and views of humankind.

  A last example of a code as marker is to be found in for instance Venda art. As soon as we see the symmetrical patterns and characteristically bright colours painted on a house we immediately associate them with the Venda people and their culture.

- A last, and an important, characteristic of codes is that they change. This is evidence of the fact that some or our customs and conventions differ from those of our ancestors. In many cases we also think differently from the way they did. For example, people are less critical of divorce these days; they are less rigid in their ideas about marriage; views on birth control have changed, as have views on women's place in society. It is frequently argued that the media are responsible for and in the forefront of the changes in codes and perceptions. For example, the more liberal way of thinking about something such as divorce or sex is often ascribed to the media's liberal attitude towards these issues. Another example would be apartheid and all the customs, conventions and ways of thinking that went with it. Since April 1994 there has clearly been an entirely new set of codes in South Africa, both in terms of people's thinking and in terms of the way in which they behave towards one another.

Having now looked at the sign, sign system and codes as three of the main areas of semiotic study, there are also other semiotic aspects that can be discussed, such as paradigms and syntagms, and synchronic and diachronic semiotic analysis. However, for the purpose of this introductory unit we now continue with the fourth main area of semiotic study, namely, the study of meaning.

## 10.6 MEANING

Since the earliest of time, scholars from various academic disciplines have been intrigued with the complex issue of how people attribute and understand meaning.

In language studies, for example, a distinction is made between seven varieties of meaning (cf. Leech 1974:10-27). Here we only briefly mention them:

- Conceptual meaning (sometimes called "denotative" or "cognitive" meaning): the basic and central meaning in linguistic communication.
- Connotative meaning: the communicative value that an expression has by virtue of what it refers to, over and above its purely conceptual content.
- Stylistic meaning: that which a piece of language conveys about the social circumstances of its use.
- Affective meaning: language reflecting the personal feelings of the speaker including his/her attitude to the listener or attitude towards something he/she is talking about. It is explicitly conveyed through the conceptual or connotative contents of the word used. For example "You're a vicious tyrant and a villainous reprobate and I hate you for it" (Leech 1974:18), leaves little doubt as to the feelings of the speaker towards the recipient. Keep in mind that there are less direct ways of disclosing attitude. Examples in the media, especially on television where not only language is used but also all other forms of nonverbal communication, are numerous.
- Reflective meaning: the meaning that arises in cases of multiple conceptual meaning, when one sense of a word forms part of our response to another sense. "On hearing, in a church service, the synonymous expressions 'The Comforter' and 'The Holy Ghost', both referring to the Third Person of the Trinity, I find my reactions to these terms conditioned by the everyday non-religious meanings of *comfort* and *ghost*" (Leech 1974:19).
- Collocative meaning: consists of the associations a word acquires on account of the meanings of words that tend to occur in its environment. *Pretty* and *handsome* share common ground in the meaning "good-looking", but may be distinguished by the range of nouns with which they are likely to co-occur: girl = pretty/ boy = handsome; village is pretty/ typewriter is handsome (Leech 1974:20).
- Thematic meaning: what is communicated by the way in which the speaker or writer organises the message, in terms of ordering, focus, and emphasis. It is often felt, for example, that an active sentence such as "Mrs Bessie Smith donated the first prize" has a different meaning from its passive equivalent (where the subject undergoes the action of the verb) "The first prize was donated by Mrs Bessie Smith", although in conceptual content they seem to be the same.

See Unit 3, Volume 2 "Media and language" for a more in-depth discussion of language and the role of language in the media.

In semiotics the main distinction is between denotative and connotative meaning. In addition, present-day media semiotics emphasises ideological meaning.

## 10.6.1 Denotation and connotation

Denotation is the literal or dictionary meaning (conceptual meaning) attached to a sign. For instance, the linguistic or verbal sign D-O-G means "any four-legged flesh-eating animal of the genus *Canis*, of many breeds domesticated and wild, kept as pets or for work or sport."

Without being able to attach a denotative meaning to for instance the colour red, or a table, or a facial expression, or a uniform, or to the pictorial signs (representations) of these signs, meaning and communication would be impossible.

In contrast to denotation, connotation is the communicative value a sign and/or code has by virtue of what it refers to over and above its denotative meaning or conceptual content. Connotation is the subjectively personal meaning assigned to a sign/code. It is the "real world" (Leech 1974:15) experience one associates with an expression or sign when one hears, reads or sees it. The linguistic sign D-O-G now not only means "any four-legged..." animal but the user of the sign also attaches to and brings to the sign his/her own experience and cognition of a dog based on his/her experience with a dog as either a pet, a flesh-eating, biting and/or working animal.

The same distinction applies to other kinds of signs such as for instance visual signs. A television image (sign) of a dog, will be identified by all viewers as a dog, but in addition to this denotative meaning, each viewer will attach a subjective, personal meaning to it. One can therefore state categorically that a television programme, advertisement, news flash and/or a film – despite the fact that they are all pictorial and iconic presentations and representations – will not necessarily convey the same meaning to all viewers. Viewers assign meaning to images (signs) and experience them in terms of their own knowledge, background and experience.

Therefore, and for the purpose of this discussion, one can conclude that connotative meanings are relatively unstable: they can vary considerably according to culture, historical period, and the experience of the individual.

## 10.6.2 Ideological meaning

It is important to read this component in conjunction with the sections on critical theory in Unit 6 (Mass communication theory) and Unit 9 (Media and ideology).

In the previous unit we discussed ideology. Here just a few notes about its importance in media semiotics. Media semiotics is concerned not only with the denotative and/or connotative meaning of a sign/code, but also with the way in which the meaning of a sign/code is shaped and determined by the media to produce, convey, support and uphold an ideology.

More specifically, the focus in media semiotics is on:

- The ideological functioning of the media as a symbolic form of expression and thus on media texts (or media content). Text in this context refers to newspaper reports (or a newspaper in its entirety), films, television programmes, structured speeches (such as radio talks), speeches, radio programmes, news bulletins, soap operas or

# Media and the Production of Meaning: Semiotics

sportscasts, to give a few examples – in brief, *text* is taken to mean media texts. How do these texts produce, reproduce and disseminate ideologies?
- The ideological functioning of the media as a social institution. This is what is known as the institutional approach. By this we mean the study of the media as an institution of power similar to the schools, the state and the church – the media as the "Fourth Estate". For example, how do certain sectors of the media in this country or the South African media as a whole go about establishing, reproducing and maintaining, or adopting a critical stance towards an ideology or ideologies? (Cf. the units on ownership, and internal and external policy as examples of the institutional approach.)
- The public's interpretation of and contact with ideology as produced and reproduced by the media and media texts. In recent semiotic investigations the emphasis has shifted from an analysis of signs and codes as such to a description of the relationship between the user/recipient of signs/codes or the relationship between subject and text and the meaning that is generated by this relationship. (Cf. the units on reception theory and ethnography as examples of the importance of the subject (or recipient/media user) of media messages.)

Originally it was argued by semioticians (see Umberto Eco, 1976) that a sign system such as television communicates according to a set of "grammatical" rules. In the case of television the accent was placed on the nature of the image as an iconic sign and the way in which the camera and editing codes produce meaning.

Lately, although still necessary for a basic understanding of the "technical" working of a sign system, media semiotics is no longer concerned with the formal qualities of a sign/code (such as for instance camera angles and editing techniques), but in meaning as *produced* in the *exchange* between subject (reader, listener, viewer, audience) and a set of signifiers (see Lapsley & Westlake 1988; also see Unit 5 on film theory and criticism in Volume 2).

In the tradition of post-structuralism, semiotics has also accepted that meaning is not at all the stable relationship between a signifier and a referent presumed by De Saussure. What *fixes* meaning is the punctuation of the signifying chain by the action of the subject – in other words, how the media user subscribes meaning to a media text.

This "new" insight based on the contention that the analysis of texts can no longer afford to ignore the role of the subject within signification, has forced semioticians to re-evaluate their former writings on the formal nature of a sign, code and sign system and to follow Julia Kristeva (1974) in her call for a theory of the speaking subject constituted within a text. The emphasis is thus on the relation between the subject (media user) and the text (media content), and on the text's power to determine the subject's response. In other words, the emphasis is on:
- How do I (as the reader/subject) interpret for example the newspaper story I'm reading, or the television programme I'm watching?
- Which properties in the newspaper story or television programme are responsible for the fact that I may interpret (and understand) the newspaper story or television programme in a specific way?

Watching a film, reading a newspaper, looking at television, listening to radio necessarily entails adopting the spectator (subject) position that is inscribed in the text. In accordance with this dictum the second (present) phase of the "new" semiotics is concerned with the following question: How do the codes in a sign system (for instance the use of the camera and montage in film and television) position the subject? To answer this question semiotic analysis has shifted away from the text as a system towards the text as a process; away from "the object media" towards the "operation media".

In conclusion, as far as the move from formalist semiotics to what can be termed social semiotics is concerned, it is argued (see Lapsley & Westlake 1988) that semiotics in its original approach to and emphasis on the formal qualities of sign systems has risked blocking an understanding of how communication (and mass communication) is related to other practices, as well as the more general relations between signification, ideology and history.

Formalist semiotics itself ran the risk of becoming an obstacle rather than the road to the analysis of the text's ideological functioning. To circumvent this danger, a conception of communication and media as a "specific signifying practice" is now proposed in media semiotics.

"Signifying" indicates the recognition of media as a system or series of systems of meaning – of media as an articulation of an aspect of reality. The term "practice" entails that a medium (such as television) is not a neutral medium transmitting a pre-given ideology, but is the active production of meaning. The term also carries the further implication that, since media produces meanings, the question of the positioning of the spectator enters into the analysis of media.

With questions such as:

- How do mainstream media contribute to maintaining the existing social structure? and
- What is the appropriate form for an alternative media that will break the ideological hold of mainstream media and transform media from a commodity to an instrument for social change?

media semiotics can now be fully situated within the realm of critical theory (cf. Unit 6) as practised in media studies, its main point of reference being Althusser's ideological theory.

As a specific signifying practice, media is now not only studied in terms of langue and parole but also of discourse, thereby implying a subject. Under such a conception, media is furthermore viewed as one of a number of "machines" generating ideology: through its mechanisms the recipient or subject is moved, and related as subject in the process of that movement (see Lapsley & Westlake 1988).

Media is seen as a work of semiosis; a work that produces effects of meaning and perception, self-images and subject positions for all those involved, communicators and recipients.

# Media and the Production of Meaning: Semiotics

To conclude this unit we take a brief look at some of the main "new" semiotic-based arguments about television and the production of meaning.

## *Television and the production of meaning*

We select television because it is the dominant medium of our time.

One of the most outstanding characteristics of television is that it is an active producer of meaning. What do we mean by this statement? (When we speak of television we are referring to the variety of television genres: news and documentary genres, sport, discussion programmes, children's programmes, games and so on. Although different methods may be employed, meanings of and relating to the topic(s) in question are created by means of the codes of television.)

Because of their iconic nature (the fact that the image is always a recognisable semblance or representation of reality), television images create an illusory reality which most viewers experience as the correct version and/or as *the truth*. The average viewer fails to appreciate that what he/she is watching is the outcome of a *conscious creative endeavour* on the part of the communicator.

This creative process entails the conscious selection of certain images from real life, removing them from their overall context and presenting them by means of selective, expressive use of such codes as camera point of view, editing, sound and commentary. Because of the speed at which the images flash by, even experts and critical viewers have to be extremely practised to be continually aware of the manipulative effect and use of codes in each image. They have to distance themselves from the content of the images in order to become aware of the form and the technique used. This rarely happens.

Studies of the perception aesthetics of television indicate that television exercises a fascination over viewers, leaving them little time or opportunity to interpret and reflect for themselves. This characteristic of television derives partly from its technology and partly from the institutionalised production conventions or codes which are standard practice. With regard to medium technology, one cannot alter the fact that television is able to present a mimetic representation of reality, which makes it a very powerful medium. The critical theorists maintain, however, that one can and should change the institutionalised production patterns that correlate directly with the ownership, management and control of television networks.

Critical theorists raise the following objections in this regard: owners of television networks and their employees consciously select aspects of reality that highlight and reflect their ideology and therefore they create a structured image of reality. This permits one to distinguish between three articulations of meaning:

- 1st articulation: the selection of topics, thus elevating the ones that are selected to a meaningful level and degrading those not selected to the level of meaninglessness (for example, the choice to report one crime in a news bulletin, but not another)
- 2nd articulation: the choice of techniques (e.g. camera techniques, costumes, décor) to depict the selected topic/material (one can also call it the treatment of the topic selected to be covered)

- 3rd articulation: the choice of editing techniques to place the selected, depicted material in a particular spatio-temporal context (one can also call it the contextualisation of the topic within the framework of other topics covered and treated in specific ways).

From the above it is clear that before something appears on our television screens, be it news, documentaries, entertainment, advertisements, or whatever, the topic has been worked with and has been treated in a number of ways. Television rightly claims to present a windowscape of reality, but, against the background of the above, it should be borne in mind that a windowscape is a limited perspective: everything beyond the window frame is out of sight.

Another important aspect related to television and meaning is the polysemic nature of television. "Polysemic" refers to multiple meaning. By this we mean the following:

- The same programme content may have different meanings for different people.
- Programmes contain not only explicit information on the topic of the communication but also implicit and often unintended information on values, attitudes, modes of behaviour and so on. For example, a news item on violence in South Africa, in addition to showing images of violence, also contains implicit information on the values current in South African society; a situation comedy not only contains information on or deals with a comic subject, but also tells us about the values, attitudes and patterns of behaviour of the society from which the characters in the situation comedy are drawn, and gives us information on matters such as the city in which the situation comedy is set, the mode of dress of the community, new fashions, the style of interior decorating.

Although the polysemic nature of television can and may be a positive attribute in some cases, as for example when it serves to pass on democratic values to undemocratic countries (see Lull's [1991] research on the role of Western television in China and the way it led to the uprising in Beijing), various authors point out the dangers of this polysemy. They express particular reservations about the fact that the world market is chiefly dominated by American television news and programme networks. Smaller and developing countries are therefore in danger of being overwhelmed by American values and ways of thinking and doing, in fact by the "American Dream", to the detriment of home-grown culture.

## Summary

In the preceding section of this unit you were introduced to the nature of the media as symbolic forms of expression from a semiotic perspective. The point made was that the media offer a treatment of reality and not reality itself. This premise is investigated in media semiotics by focusing on the media as a sign and a combination of sign systems that communicate according to different kinds of codes in order to convey specific meanings. Media semiotics is furthermore interested in the relationship between media users and media content and the ways in which media content are structured in order to obtain a specific effect.

We looked at a definition of semiotics and structuralism as the origin of semiotics. We considered the founding fathers of semiotics and the distinction between the concepts "signifier", "referent" and "signified" and between the concepts "langue" and "parole". Next we examined the characteristics of a sign, different kinds of signs and their functions. In the same way we looked at different codes and their characteristics, as well as different kinds of meaning.

## Research activities

1. Write a paragraph in which you explain semiotics and its emphasis on the use of signs to your own life-world. In other words, what is the importance of signs in your own life and interests.
2. Write a paragraph in which you explain how the media articulate meaning, for example, in a story about a political speech, or a fashion show.
3. Explain the origin of semiotics as a structuralist development.
4. Explain with your own examples the following concepts: signifier, referent, signified, langue and parole.
5. Explain the characteristics of a sign with your own examples taken from media content.
6. Provide an example for each of the different kinds of signs, namely for the arbitrary sign, the iconic sign, the symbolic sign and the indexical sign. Select your examples from media content to explain the relationship between the signifier and the referent in each case.
7. Explain sign functions. We suggest that you look for an artistic and imaginative advertisement in a magazine that will lend itself to the identification and description of the referential, the expressive, the conative, poetic, phatic and metalinguistic functioning of signs. For the sake of clarity concentrate on visual (iconic) signs, except for the description of the metalinguistic function.
8. Compare this advertisement with a less artistic and imaginative advertisement in which the sign functions have not been used to their full, or some of them may even be absent.
9. Explain each of the following codes with an example from media content:
    a) codes of behaviour and signifying codes
    b) analogue and digital codes
    c) presentational and representational codes
    d) elaborated and restricted codes
    e) logical, aesthetic and social codes
    f) codes of content and codes of form

10 Briefly explain the characteristics of codes by providing an example for each of the following:
   a) codes exist only in and through the way people use them
   b) codes are linked to culture and context
   c) codes function intertextually
   d) codes act as filters for our perceptions of and about the world, people, things and events
   e) codes function as markers for social classes, groups, cultural groups and subcultures
   f) codes change
11 Give explanations of the following concepts, using examples from media content: denotation, connotation, ideology and the polysemic nature of television.

## Further reading

Barthes, R. 1967. *Elements of semiology.* New York: Hill & Wang.
Eco, U. 1976. *A theory of semiotics.* Bloomington: Indiana University Press.
Fairclough, N. 1995. *Media discourse.* London: Arnold.
Hawkes, T. 1977. *Structuralism and semiotics.* London: Methuen.
Hervey, S. 1982. *Semiotic perspectives.* London: Allen & Unwin.
Hodge, R & Kress, G. 1988. *Social semiotics.* Cambridge: Polity Press.
Leeds-Hurwitz, W. 1993. *Semiotics and communication: signs, codes, cultures.* Hillsdale: Erlbaum.
Peters, J. 1974. *Pictorial communication.* Cape Town: David Philip.
Rice, P & Waugh, P (eds). 1989. *Modern literary theory: a reader.* London: Arnold.
Sebeok, T. 1991. *A sign is just a sign.* Bloomington: Indiana University Press.
Sturrock, J. 1979. *Structuralism and since: from Lévi-Strauss to Derrida.* Oxford: Oxford University Press.

## Bibliography

Barthes, R. 1967. *Elements of semiology.* New York: Hill & Wang.
Barthes, R. 1977. *Image, music, text.* Glasgow: Fontana.
Barthes, R. 1982. *Selected writings.* Glasgow: Fontana.
Buyssens, E. 1967. *La communication et l'articulation linguistique.* Paris-Bruxelles: PUF.
Culler, J. 1976. *Saussure.* Glasgow: Fontana.
De Saussure, F. 1916. *Cours de linguistique générale.* Paris: Payot.
Dethier, H. 1985. *Semiologie.* Kursusteks: Vrije Universiteit van Brussel. Brussel: VUB.
Dethier, H. 1993. *Het gesicht en het raadsel. Profielen van Plato tot Derrida.* Brussel: VUB.
Eco, U. 1976. *A theory of semiotics.* Bloomington: Indiana University Press.
Fiske, J. 1982. *Introduction to communication studies.* London: Methuen.
Fourie, PJ. 1983. *Beeldkommunikasie. Kultuurkritiek, ideologiese kritiek en 'n inleiding tot die beeldsemiologie.* Johannesburg: McGraw-Hill.
Fourie, PJ. 1985. Betekenis en betekeniskonstruksie in beeldkommunikasie. *Communicare* 4(1):33–40.
Fourie, PJ. 1988. *Aspects of film and television communication.* Cape Town: Juta.

Fourie, PJ (ed). 1991. *Critical television analyses: an introduction.* Cape Town: Juta.

Fourie, PJ. 1992. Diskoersontleding as 'n metode in die sosiale wetenskappe. *Communicatio* 18(1):19–29.

Fourie, P (ed). 1996. *Introduction to communication – course book 3: communication and the production of meaning.* Cape Town: Juta.

Fourie, P (ed). 1997. *Introduction to communication – course book 6: film and television studies.* Cape Town: Juta.

Guiraud, P. 1971. *Semiology.* London: Routledge & Kegan Paul.

Hawkes, T. 1977. *Structuralism and semiotics.* London: Methuen.

Hervey, S. 1982. *Semiotic perspectives.* London: Allen & Unwin

Hodge, R & Kress, G. 1988. *Social semiotics.* Cambridge: Polity Press.

Jakobson, R. 1960. Closing statement: linguistics and poetics, in *Style and language*, edited by T Sebeok. Cambridge: MIT.

Kristeva, J. 1974. The system and the speaking subject. *Times Literary Supplement*, 12 October:1249.

Lapsley, R & Westlake, M. 1988. *Film theory: an introduction.* Manchester: Manchester University Press.

Leech, G. 1974. *Semantics.* Harmondsworth: Penguin.

Leeds-Hurwitz, W. 1993. *Semiotics and communication. Signs, codes, cultures.* Hillsdale, NJ: Lawrence Erlbaum.

Lull, J. 1991. *China turned on. Television, reform and resistance.* London: Routledge.

Lyons, J. 1977. *Semantics I.* London: Cambridge University Press.

Mounin, G. 1970. *Introduction à la sémiologie.* Paris: Minuit.

O'Sullivan, T, Hartley, J, Saunders, D, Montgomery, M & Fiske, J. 1994. *Key concepts in communication and cultural studies.* 2nd edition. London: Routledge.

Peirce, C. 1960. *Collected papers of Charles Sanders Peirce.* Cambridge, MA: Harvard University Press.

Peters, JM. 1974. *Principes van beeldcommunicatie.* Groningen: HD Tjeenk Willink.

Sebeok, T. 1991. *A sign is just a sign.* Bloomington: Indiana University Press.

Sturrock, J. 1979. *Structuralism and since. From Lévi-Strauss to Derrida.* Oxford: Oxford University Press.

Van Zoest, A. 1978. *Semiotiek. Over tekens, hoe ze werken en wat we ermee doen.* Baarn: Basisboeken.

# Media and Culture

*Jennifer Lemon*

## Overview

In this unit we briefly investigate the relationship between media and culture, which can be interpreted in two ways: media as culture and media as a reflection and portrayal of culture. The point of departure is that the media portray different forms of culture such as religion, architecture and the built environment, sport, theatre, music, fashion and style. We then look at the concepts of "culture" and "ideology" and the relationship between culture and ideology.

Finally, we address the basic assumptions of the cultural studies approach to the study of communication and media.

Please take note that the topic of ideology also features in other units of this book, specifically in Unit 9 (Media and ideology), Unit 12 (Feminist media theory) and in Unit 6 of Volume 2 (Reception theory). Given the importance and centrality of ideology in critical media studies, such overlap is almost inevitable.

## Learning outcomes

At the end of this unit you should be able to explain the following with your own examples from media content:

- the relationship between the media and culture;
- a definition of culture;
- different forms of cultural expression;
- the theoretical assumptions of cultural studies;
- the concepts: hegemony, polysemy, open texts, dominant reading, negotiated reading oppositional reading, and intertextuality; and
- do an ideological analysis of a media text.

## 11.1 INTRODUCTION

In the previous units and in following units of the book, the media are discussed as our dominant forms of public communication, as symbolic forms of expression, as a culture in its own right, and as typifying late twentieth and early twenty-first century popular culture. The point this unit wants to make is that the media are "surrounded" by other forms of culture such as religion, architecture, sport, theatre, and so on. In its own right, each can be described as a form of communication and each communicates and produces meaning in a unique way. However, in its content, whether factious or fictitious, the media reflect and portray all these and other forms of culture. It is therefore important for us to understand culture and cultural products in the broader sense of the word. Such knowledge is essential for a critical understanding of the media as part of culture and as a culture in and of itself.

Communication does not only take place by means of verbal, nonverbal and mass communication (e.g. television, radio, film, the press). Communication takes on many forms of expression, from graffiti on the walls in public toilets and railway stations to the grand facades of monuments, museums and corporations; from the fickle nature of fashion and fads, to the often noisy nature of popular music, and so on. These social and cultural forms of expression are the means by which we give expression to our culture – our values, beliefs and common experiences. As such, communication is an ontological fact of human existence. Put simply, this means that we live in and through communication. Communication is the medium through which our existence and experience (our daily lives), that is, our culture, finds its expression.

Clearly, there are many examples of social and cultural forms of expression – or culture – to be found in any society. You will undoubtedly be able to identify a whole range of examples from your own environment (e.g. meanings conveyed by designer furniture, political rhetoric, craft art, shebeens, clubs, flea markets, fashion, computer and other games). However, for the purposes of this unit, we examine only a few examples by way of illustration. The purpose of this unit then, is simply to make you aware of the fact that there are many forms of communication and that everything around us communicates, whether implicitly or explicitly. Against this background, we attempt to define culture and ideology, and discuss the underlying assumptions of a cultural studies approach to the study of communication.

## 11.2 CULTURE AND COMMUNICATION

One of the most important advances in human existence in the last century is the multiplying means and forms of communication. Technological development and modern communication (e.g. film, television, interactive video, computer technology) have drastically altered traditional frames of reference, experiences, values, beliefs, structures and social relations. Today we live in a world in which the constant circulation of social and cultural forms of expression expressed as "culture" play a fundamental and increasingly important role in the definition and redefinition of our culture(s). Each day we are confronted by literally thousands of images (whether visual or verbal). We read or interpret these images as texts, which become part of our collective consciousness, our common experience, ultimately contributing to the evolution of our culture(s) (cf. Thompson 1990).

The academic and scientific discipline of communication is directed at the study of all social behaviour as meaningful action, that is, it is concerned with all forms of expression as sign systems of communication. The products of these actions (productions or artefacts as material culture) are organised into sign systems (visual, verbal, nonverbal and/or sensory codes), and expressed in the form of texts (discourses) which can be read or interpreted differently by differently socially situated readers. You and I will therefore read the messages inscribed in these texts or discourses in different ways because of our individual differences (e.g. age, sex, education, attitudes or values).

In South Africa we have a particularly complex multicultural and multilingual society (e.g. Xhosa, English, Zulu, Sotho, Afrikaans, Indian, Muslim, and so on), and many diverse forms of communication (or sign systems) which give expression to our different cultures. This makes our cultural context particularly complex, and provides fertile ground for the analysis and study of various forms of social and cultural expression. Think, for example, of industrial theatre, township jive and traditional folk songs, tales and dances, not to mention so-called tribal or native art and crafts, flea markets and "boere" music, amongst others, as forms of expression which reflect and affect our cultural values. Sometimes we "cross over" and identify ourselves with a culture to which we do not necessarily belong. Think for example of how popular Miriam Makeba's music is to both black and white South Africans. This example can be applied to a range of other phenomena.

## 11.3 SOCIAL AND CULTURAL FORMS OF EXPRESSION

In short, this unit demonstrates that all cultural practices, objects and artefacts (that is, texts) have meaning. Everything that is cultural communicates, just as culture is created, maintained and perpetuated by means of communication.

In the section to follow, we illustrate this point with a brief discussion of a few examples of social and cultural forms of expression.

### 11.3.1 Religion

Religion is a pervasive and influential social and cultural practice in most societies. As Patte (1990:3) points out:

> ... all human beings, whether they are religious (in the common contemporary sense of the term), agnostic, or atheistic, have an 'ultimate concern' (the definition of faith proposed by Paul Tillich). In contemporary Western culture, this ultimate concern is often secular and finds expression in non-religious behaviour, but it remains a faith.

There are many definitions of religion. However, we may broadly define religion as the belief that supernatural forces influence human lives. Durkheim (1969:62), whose definition of religion is probably one of the most frequently cited, wrote that

> ... religion is a unified system of beliefs and practices relative to sacred things, that is to say, things set apart and forbidden – beliefs and practices which unite into one single moral community called a Church, all those who adhere to them.

Religion is expressed by means of faith or belief in a set of morals, values, norms and/or rules. Faith affects all aspects of human experience, both public and private, and embodies what we believe about our reality, our experience, and the meaning of life. Here we are not talking about the church itself, but rather of the institutionalisation of religious belief, recognising that there are many religions. Ritual is basic to religion. Through the repetition of particular symbolic acts, worshippers are reminded of the supernatural and are unified in a common belief with others sharing in the ceremony. Other signs and codes that may be studied include icons, idols, proverbs, shrines, pilgrimages, testimonies, miracles and the like.

Historically, the organised church formed the foundation of many societies, exercising virtual control over the creation and maintenance of social and cultural life. In fact, the church can be regarded as the first mass communication medium. For most people in pre-industrial societies, the church was the largest social organisation or gathering of which they were a part (cf. Hitchcock 1979:178). The church was the primary source of information and education, providing the only comprehensive view of life to which people were exposed. The meaning of life was powerfully conveyed to recipients by means of the signs and codes of rituals, symbols, moral injunctions, and the customs and laws propagated by the church, which saturated social life.

The emergence of Protestantism and the concomitant splitting of the medieval church coincided with one of the greatest technological revolutions of the West – the invention of the printing press. This is a fascinating and perhaps causal relationship. The easily produced and relatively inexpensive books destroyed the communication monopoly enjoyed by the Catholic Church, permitting the dissemination of heterodox opinion (often viewed as heresy by the Church). The printing press put the Bible within reach of all people, making it possible for people (such as Martin Luther) to invalidate or question the version of truth provided by the Church on the grounds of infidelity to some other source (such as the Bible). This dramatically altered the nature of the Church and the practice of religion.

The 1980s have seen a significant resurgence of interest in religion in the form of the rebirth of Christian fundamentalism, Islam fundamentalism, the charismatic movement, and importantly, the rise of the electronic church and televangelism as highly popularised forms of religion (cf. Hadden & Swann 1981; Oberdorfer 1982; Stuart 1985; Fore 1987). Religion has been increasingly endowed with entertainment value, offering its recipients attractively packaged, mass-mediated religion. In response to the rise of a consumer culture, an electronic church has emerged which offers many new forms of religious expression and experience – from breezy Christian talk shows on radio and television, to Gospel rock and other religious music genres, religious magazines, clubs, and audio-cassettes offering advice on the Christian lifestyle. The commodification of religion has resulted in mass-marketed religion, and many new forms of social and cultural expression, from T-shirts to bumper stickers, portraying a whole range of values and beliefs (e.g. the morality of stable, happy families, monogamy, or healthy living) (Luke 1989:129–158).

# MEDIA STUDIES

To summarise, in recent years a number of authors have pointed to the extent to which mass communication media (and television and film images in particular) have begun to operate as a kind of visual catechism, transforming the traditional practices of religion, and popularising religion as entertainment. Thus, with the development of technology and the rise of the mass media, there is an interesting interface between the mass media and the practice of religion. Within the context of the study of communication there is renewed interest in the meaning of the signs and codes of religious practice and ritual.

## 11.3.2 Architecture and the built environment

Among the more pervasive elements of society's reality are the physical structures and spaces that constitute our environment. As Ruben and Soleri (1979:214) point out:

> ... human history is fundamentally a saga of the manipulation of the physical world to produce myriad forms, small and large, private and public, lasting and ephemeral, humble and flamboyant, functional and symbolic.

The built environment includes architecturally designed structures, such as houses, office blocks, parks, schools, shopping centres and malls, entertainment centres, public libraries, recreation halls and museums, or functionally built structures, such as tin shacks, that is, all those structures and spaces created to facilitate human shelter and activity (Budd & Ruben 1979:212).

Architecture and the built environment have from the time of the earliest civilisations been a physical manifestation of culture. An important relationship exists between human beings and their physical and contextual environment. Architecture and built structures and spaces are an important medium of communication through which human beings express their needs, attitudes, values and social and cultural norms. As such, architecture and the built environment are important forms of social and cultural expression. From the buildings in which we conduct basic human functions, like sleeping and eating, to the structures which house society's most complex institutions, such as the houses of parliament, multinational corporations, municipal libraries and museums, the role of the physical and contextual environment in our daily lives is substantial. Irrespective of the origin of a building, we are affected in some way by its form and appearance (Ruben & Soleri 1979:212).

Our physical and contextual environment is so pervasive in its influence that it is a much taken-for-granted form of social and cultural expression. Human beings mould, shape and alter their physical environment to reflect and suit their needs, values and expectations. For example, think of the different architectural styles reflected in some of the major cities in South Africa -Johannesburg, Soweto, Cape Town, Kimberley, Bisho, Bloemfontein and Pretoria. Think of the vastly different architectural styles that dominate and provide atmosphere and character in Soweto and in Sandton, for example. Or think of the homesteads made of mud built by people living in rural areas, with different spaces for men and women as well as public and private spaces, or of the geometric and colourful paintings on Ndebele huts made from mud and thatch. In contrast, think of the values communicated by the architectural styles of corporate headquarters in major cities like Johannesburg. Think of what values these architectural structures communicate or express (e.g. capitalism, materialism, concern for the environment, poverty, progress or decay).

The structures and spaces of our environment (whether public or private) regulate our conduct insomuch as they influence what behaviour is considered appropriate or inappropriate in particular places, spaces and cultures. For example, in some cultures it is considered inappropriate to talk loudly in an art museum, a temple or a church. In some cultures, we are obliged to take off our shoes in a church (e.g. in Muslim holy places). A busy restaurant or a doctor's waiting-room are similarly not considered appropriate places for a private argument. You can no doubt think of your own examples. Moreover, certain structures or spaces in our environment affect how we feel in them, and thus how we behave. A picturesque park with many trees, gardens and lawns, may engender a feeling of tranquillity and peace, despite the fact that if may be situated in the centre of a large city. Large corporate headquarters made of steel and glass may seem cold and austere, or even overwhelming, in their magnificence.

Our environment is an important source of information and an important example of nonverbal communication, whether sensory, auditory, and/or olfactory (relating to the sense of smell). All architecture or less formally built structures carry messages which will be read differently by differently socially and culturally situated recipients. The messages and meanings of architecture and the built environment can be studied according to various sign systems and symbols, including spatial analysis and organisational arrangement of places (indicative of proximity), direction (suggesting continuity) and areas or spaces (defining enclosure). As Ruben and Soleri (1979:225) point out, notions about direction and movement are crucial to space utilisation and architectural design. For example, aspects of religious architecture may reflect the relationship between the vertical and the sacred, as seen in the prominent steeples of many of the Dutch Reformed churches centrally situated in numerous towns in South Africa. Depending on their context, their placing, these structures can take on very different meanings. Look at Figure 11.1, for example. How can the context or setting of the church be read or interpreted differently by people of different races, ethnic groups, nationalities and religions?

**Figure 11.1 The built environment and the significance of context**

# MEDIA STUDIES

Now look at the examples of architectural styles and the built environment in Figure 11.2. How can the built environment affect the living conditions and lifestyles of the people who live or work there?

**Figure 11.2 Examples of architectural styles and the built environment**

Architecturally designed structures or buildings and their placement play a major role in shaping the reality within which we organise our experience. What we learn in response to the physical and contextual environment varies from home to home, from region to region and, most dramatically, from culture to culture.

Cultural and social structure plays a major role in the evolution of the built environment, and vice versa. If one looks at the landscape of Lesotho, for example, it is obvious which homes are made from traditional materials (e.g. round huts made from mud with thatch roofing), and which have been more recently built by migrant workers from the urban areas (e.g. rough bricks built into tiny rectangular homes with tin roofs). Can one argue, for example, that the influence of the men who have been living in South Africa, many working on the mines, is clear in the development of the homes into small brick structures with steel windows, typical of the houses provided for workers in South Africa?

In short, the divisible nature of architecture and design renders it a legible language of structural elements and symbols – the language of architecture as nonverbal communication. However, the visual and nonverbal characteristics of architecture and the built environment are also irrevocably linked to concepts of aesthetics and subjectivity. The role of the recipient in the perception and interpretation of the signs, symbols, auditory and sensory stimuli from the environment is important.

### 11.3.3 Sport

Sport as the enjoyment of physical activity and competition is clearly a pervasive and popular cultural practice in all societies. As such, it is an important form of social and cultural expression. With the development of technology, and the mass media in particular, sport has become a mainstay of everyday life. Indeed, the degree of fanaticism engendered both by participation and spectator sports, the excitement, enthusiasm and dedication, is indicative of the pervasive and penetrating nature of sport in society. Enormous amounts of time, money, energy and emotion are invested in sport, suggesting that these games are far more than frivolous, inconsequential activities or surface rituals (cf. Leonard 1984). Sport relates to the entire fabric and structure of society and, as such, is a social institution, carrying with it many potential meanings and value systems (Sage 1990:1-2).

**Figure 11.3 Sport as a form of social and cultural expression**

In simple terms, sport is a game. It is about play, about a social ritual, which encompasses norms, values and language (that is, signs and codes). Sport is therefore governed by sign systems, with rules that govern their use, for example, the so-called rules of the game which are used to regulate behaviour and construct the dynamics of the game.

It would be naive to attempt to study sport outside its historical, economic, political and cultural context. The world of sport, like that of religion or politics, is not value-free or ideologically neutral. According to Leonard (1984), sport functions as an important social institution that both affects, and is affected by, other social institutions. Indeed, there are important links between sport and other significant social institutions and cultural practices (such as politics and the economy). An example of the link between politics and sport is the sporting and cultural boycott imposed on South Africa during the 1980s. Clearly, sport can be used, and is used, both to reveal and to conceal material and cultural exploitation and oppression (cf. Sage 1990). It is worth noting that this could be interpreted in a number of ways. White South Africans may have thought of this as damaging to South African sport, while black South Africans may have interpreted this as an important opportunity to rejoice since it represented some international support for their cause to end apartheid.

As Kovecses (1990:139) points out, perhaps the most studied aspect of sport is its symbolic value – that is, what makes sporting activities meaningful to people. The values implicit in many sporting activities include character building, discipline, loyalty, competition (and, more specifically, winning), physical and mental fitness, religiosity and nationalism, amongst others (Leonard 1984:65–72). Indeed, it may be argued that many sporting activities may be seen as a modern form of warfare, where the sports arena becomes a modern battleground. Think, for example, of the degree of violence and aggression engendered by many sports, such as rugby or boxing.

It is clear that sport has many codes in common with other important social institutions (such as the church and politics). The ritualised nature of sport is evident from the fact that sporting activities are contained within the limits of ritual time and ritual space, and there are definite sets of rules and conventions that govern play. These rules and conventions represent various value systems, such as notions of fairness and sex role demarcations, amongst others. Sport offers a structured experience, with rituals signalling the beginning, the middle and the end. Insofar as the recipients' response is concerned, most fans are knowledgeable about the rules of the games, strategies of play, the roles of each player and of the spectator-recipients, and the skills required to excel in a particular sport.

An interesting link exists between sport and Gramsci's (1971) concept of hegemony, which refers to power, dominance and coercion. A more critical analysis of the role of sport in society exposes the dominant power interests of governments, business and the economy, the mass-communication media (and television, in particular), and the important role of sport in education and in maintaining the social, political and cultural *status quo* (cf. Sage 1990). Think, for example, of the ways in which sport expresses the norms and values of race, class and gender (e.g. prejudice, discrimination and gender socialisation).

What is of greater interest, however, is the ideological significance of sport. While some theorists argue that sport is, in fact, an expression of sociability and collective activity, others argue that sport may be regarded as the opiate of the masses, generating and intensifying hostility between people. The latter argue that sport is exploited by the state for economic control or used as a tool for social coercion, and that it is used to promote commercialism, materialism, nationalism and militarism, as well as classism, racism and sexism (cf. Calhoun 1987).

Against the background of this discussion, it is clear that sport has many complex ideological functions in modem societies. It may be used as a political tool, a sociopolitical mirror of a society's problems, a socialising agent (e.g. sex roles and stereotypes), a propaganda showcase, an outlet for national pride or aggression, and/or an economic showcase (Leonard 1984:290). In short, politics is endemic to sport. Sport is intimately related to the capitalist interests of the mass media, government, business, and political leaders who recognise its potential for making profits, disseminating propaganda and eliciting national pride (Eitzen 1989:3).

Sporting activities often mirror and/or shape the complex dynamics of a particular culture or community, whether that be conflict, unity, injustice or prejudice. In South Africa, sport has been used both to divide and to unite. Think, for example, of the way in which particular groups were intentionally excluded from national sporting events during the years of apartheid, and of the ways in which individuals and cultures have subsequently been brought together by sporting events, despite their hostilities and divergent interests. Think also of some of the violence that one sees associated with large sporting events.

### 11.3.4 Theatre

Theatre is another important form of social and cultural expression, representing a crossroads of culture(s) where foreign discourses and artistic and technological effects are manipulated to create what may be regarded as a collage of languages (as sign systems) or discourses. From medieval morality plays to modem theatrical productions, popular theatre and drama (unlike film, which requires expensive equipment and technical skill) are more readily accessible and more flexible in communicating to large numbers of recipients with little, or no, previous experience of this medium of communication (Shiach 1989:141).

Some theatre productions may be a site for developing critiques of the dominant culture, or attempts to construct politically progressive, generally accessible forms of so-called popular culture. While some theatrical productions may be polite propaganda for the establishment, others may provide a space for challenging and undermining the definitions and assumptions of the dominant ideology. This is why theatrical productions sometimes elicit such heated debate and moral outrage from the establishment, which may attempt to censor, or even ban, them in an alleged attempt to protect its recipients from dissenting ideas or voices. Theatre therefore has enormous potential as a creative form of expression that can emancipate and unite people, providing for alternative or dissenting views of social reality.

Like other forms of social and cultural expression, theatre brings together a wide range of codes, for example, settings, acting, costume, décor, lighting, sound, and language (both verbal and nonverbal). These codes intersect to create meaning – the dramatic text and the performance – that is, all that is made visible or audible on stage.

### 11.3.5 Music

Music pervades and permeates all areas of social life, both public and private. We hear music in supermarkets, pubs, in public lifts (e.g. elevator music), airports, in restaurants and at home on the radio, sound system or television. Indeed, it may be argued that music has become a global language, representing a mediated reality that can be experienced either alone or with others. In the words of James Lull (1992:1):

> Music is a passionate sequencing of thoughts and feelings that expresses meaning in a manner that has no parallel in human life. It is a universally recognized synthesis of the substance and style of our existence – a blending of personal, social, and cultural signification that is confused with no other variety of communication. Music promotes experiences of the extreme for its makers and listeners, turning the perilous emotional edges, vulnerabilities, triumphs, celebrations, and antagonisms of life into hypnotic, reflective tempos that can be experienced privately or shared with others.

There is a wide range of musical forms of expression, each with its own unique characteristics. Think, for example, of the wide range of musical classifications from classical music and opera to music genres such as punk rock, acid rock, new wave, rock and roll, American swing, kwela, rap, reggae, hip hop, techno, disco, folk, heavy metal, or Christian rock, amongst others.

According to traditional views of forms of social and cultural expression, classical music may be regarded as so-called real or high art, while other classifications (that is, genres) are merely popular art, and are thus regarded by élitist critics as creatively and culturally inferior. However, the lines between classical music and popular music shift constantly. Think, for example, of the renditions of Vivaldi's *Four Seasons* by the punk violinist, Nigel Kennedy, and of the popularity of Gregorian chants, which have now become international best-sellers.

Popular music has always been, and still is, regarded as controversial, eliciting much-heated debate regarding its influence or effects. Despite this controversy, the recording industry is one of the most powerful and influential media for social and cultural expression the world over. Censors, governments and lobby groupings have criticised the lyrics of popular music which are seen as immoral, obscene and corruptive, promoting sexual licentiousness, violence, drug abuse, and even such evils as Satanism, amongst others. Critics and censors have reported the use of subliminal messages and back-masking, which they argue are unconsciously heard. They suggest that this has a negative and/or destructive effect on the recipient. Such accusations add to the controversy regarding contemporary music.

The lyrics and performance of much popular music also implicitly and explicitly poses a threat to dominant ideologies, with lyrics dealing with the grim realities of war, hatred, racism, and the complexities of human relationships (e.g. the music of Bob Dylan, Paul Simon and John Lennon, and more recently in South Africa, Johnny Clegg, Jennifer Ferguson and Johannes Kerkorrel, amongst others).

**Figure 11.4 Music as a form of social and cultural expression**

Like theatre, music has many levels of meaning. It may serve as a unifying force, promoting universal consensus on values and taste, or it may promote fragmentation, diversity and alienation. Deena Wienstein (1991) in her research, for example, offers a cultural/sociological analysis of heavy metal.

Few cultural phenomena elicit such heated debates as those provoked by the brash and aggressive form of music known as heavy metal. Wienstein (1991) suggests that the negative attitudes that heavy metal frequently elicits result from the fact that people do not understand the so-called culture of heavy metal. She argues that the predominant theme of heavy metal is its exuberant challenge to respectable society, communicated by its irreverent lyrics and disharmonious sounds. These conclusions are drawn from an in-depth analysis of the social history and the cultural sociology of the musicians, artists, and the audiences and mediators such as sponsors or managers. She studies the broader public discourse about, but predominantly against, heavy metal, as well as the implicit and explicit values and ideological assumptions they express; the themes, musical lyrics and diverse styles of heavy metal.

However, despite the controversies surrounding the messages and values of popular music, the recording industry is a rapidly growing commercial enterprise with immense sales figures recorded every year. Popular music is clearly a powerful and extremely popular form of cultural and social expression in all societies.

### 11.3.6 Fashion and style

Within the context of a burgeoning consumer culture, fashion and style have become an important part of personal self-expression and identity formation (cf. Ewen 1988). Fashion and style have become important purveyors of social and cultural meanings in modem societies. Clothing represents far more than the biological necessity of covering our bodies or of protecting ourselves from the elements; it increasingly creates and conforms to social and cultural beliefs and customs.

Fashion and style can be studied as important forms of nonverbal social communication (Lemon 1990:19). Adornment of the body and a preoccupation with fashion and style are indulged in by all culture groups and societies and, as such, can be said to be a universal pursuit. Solomon (1981:183) argues that because dress provokes and evokes such widespread social reaction, whether admiration, tolerance, indignation or moral outrage, it is an important form of social and cultural expression. While dress is concerned with a basic human need, its expression in fashion and style goes far beyond simple biological necessity, and is intimately related to aesthetic, social and cultural factors and influences.

According to Solomon (1981), the need of the whole of society for clothing links fashion directly to the structure of society. We may then argue that a closer analysis of clothing (dress) and fashion can provide an opportunity for understanding human beings and human communication which goes far beyond mere outward appearances. Clothing permits and facilitates individual and social expression and, as such, is an important medium of communication. The expressive and communicative functions of fashion and style are twofold, namely, accommodation and reaction. Accommodation refers to the need to express group affiliation or the values and standards of the group. This is seen, for example, in the wearing of uniforms by people in the medical field or the military. Reaction refers to the need to express individuality by stressing unique physical features or unique aesthetic taste; that is wearing particular clothing to make a statement. There are many other expressive functions of fashion and style. Perhaps you can think of a few examples yourself. For example, why you choose particular styles of clothing and not others.

The concept of style is undeniably a popular term in contemporary societies. The word "style" and its expression can be seen in glossy magazines, on the pages of popular publications on nearly every imaginable topic ranging from news, fashion and architecture, to music, interior design and sport. The phenomenon of style is a transient one, however. Finding an adequate definition is problematic, since the concept of style is often informed by a current and changeable fad, fashion or mode of behaviour which render the concept elusive and fickle. Style registers different meanings to different people, at different times and among different communities. Style has to do with the way people express themselves, with the way they conform and the way they rebel (cf. Ewen 1988).

The signs and codes of fashion are able to imbue a simple pair of blue jeans with multiple meanings. Consider the many meanings associated with the following styles of blue jeans: bell bottoms, stove pipes, ripped jeans, tight-fitting versus loose-fitting jeans, and so forth. As the social history of denims, more popularly known as jeans, provided by Ewen and Ewen (1992) demonstrates, blue jeans have moved from being clothing worn by the so-called workers to being a part of a statement, a rejection of post-war suburban society, moral rebellion, a commitment to an emerging social struggle in the student rebellion and anti-war movement, an explicit rejection of conventional sex roles by feminists, and a sign of freedom or of high fashion.

Fashion and style and their implicit and explicit meanings also have many ideological implications. They are infused with the symbolic meanings and values of a culture or society. Norms linked to fashion and style often indicate social values such as the sexual division of labour and/or sex role demarcations in society (cf. Ewen & Ewen 1992: Chapter 4). For example, in many societies women are expected to dress in a stereotypically feminine way, while men are expected to dress in a typically masculine way. However, modern fashions have increasingly begun to blur the boundaries between what is regarded as masculine and feminine, with men wearing styles of clothing traditionally or stereotypically associated with femininity (e.g. clothing with soft lines and colours), and women dressing in clothing traditionally or stereotypically worn by men (e.g. trousers, shirts, and ties).

## 11.4 MAKING SENSE OF CULTURE

From the preceding discussion, it is clear that culture and its expression take on many forms and that culture and communication are in many ways interlinked. This brings us to the question: What is culture?

### 11.4.1 Defining culture

There are many different and often divergent definitions of culture, making this a contested domain. As Hebdige (1993:359) points out, culture is a notoriously ambiguous concept that has acquired a number of often contradictory meanings over the decades. Culture may be defined as everything from the cultivation of civilisations, human faculties or manners, the improvement of the intellect by means of education, to the cultivation of plants or animals (Hebdige 1993:358). Popular definitions define culture broadly as including everything that occurs in a society, that is, all the customs, beliefs, values, norms, ideas and practices, as well as the material artefacts, objects and instruments handed down from one generation to another (Thompson 1990:129). These definitions are largely descriptive in nature and are often marked by an attempt to quantify culture. These associations are however the most common meanings attached to the concept of culture (Billington, Strawbridge, Greensides & Fitzsimons 1991:5-6).

Clearly, culture cannot be defined and described as one, unchanging aspect of human experience. Culture is not homogenous or static. It changes and evolves as the historical, economic, political and social beliefs, values and circumstances of groups and individuals change. Against this background we can define culture as

> ... the pattern of meanings embodied in symbolic forms, including actions, utterances and meaningful objects of various kinds, by virtue of which individuals communicate with one another and share their experiences, conceptions and beliefs.
>
> (Geertz 1973:44)

The implicit and explicit link between culture and communication is clear in this definition. Within this context, culture may be seen as a "whole way of life" (Williams 1981:13) and as a signifying system through which meaning is constructed. Culture is a "historically transmitted pattern of meanings embodied in symbols" (Geertz 1973:44), and may be seen as a series of texts or discourses which can be read and interpreted differently by different individuals (Thompson 1990:132). Within this context, culture, and its manifestation in all forms of social and cultural expression, are seen as language systems (that is, discourses). Our common cultures, the experiences we share, often become the dominant cultures to which we subscribe.

Culture is not a neutral concept. All forms of social and cultural expression as social discourses are essentially dialogues, which vary according to the kinds of social institutions and practices within which they operate. These discourses are produced in struggles between different groups in society (e.g. struggles between classes, ethnic, racial or gender groups), and emerge from conflicting ideological positions. Consequently, power struggles occur as contests over social and cultural meanings and the values attached to these.

These meanings give expression to the social, political, economic and historical power relations in a particular society. They are produced by individuals or groups who have access to certain resources and who are endowed with varying degrees of power and authority. Moreover, as Thompson (1990:135) points out, these forms of expression are circulated, received, perceived and interpreted by other individuals or groups in particular socio-historical, political and economic contexts, drawing on their experience and resources in an attempt to make sense of (or interpret) the phenomena concerned.

Social and cultural forms of expression thus express relations of power. Indeed, John Fiske (1987a:255) defines culture as "a struggle for meanings ...". Against this background it is evident that, in order to define culture more completely, one must of necessity define and explain the notion of *ideology*.

## 11.4.2 Defining ideology

With the development of theories on culture and meaning from more descriptive definitions, to the more recent debates on culture, ideological questions have come to play a more important role in communication and media studies. Indeed, it may now be argued that the notion of ideology is central to any discussion of culture.

Ideology, like culture, is a highly contested and notoriously elusive concept that resists easy definition. However, in order to gain a clearer understanding of ideology, some of its basic characteristics can be identified by looking briefly at the theoretical and historical development of this concept.

According to its popular definition, ideology refers to the ideas, attitudes, values, belief systems or interpretive and conceptual frameworks held by members of a particular social group (Geuss 1981:5). Ideology thus refers to the assumptions according to which individuals, groups or societies conceptualise the values and beliefs that express their culture (Dupre 1983:240). Ideology can also be broadly defined as the total system of beliefs that selectively provide limited perceptions of reality. In this sense every individual, group, society or culture has an ideology or speaks from a position that is informed by ideological assumptions – consciously or unconsciously.

The definition of ideology has a long history, and we will very briefly follow this trail in the sections that follow, beginning with the classical Marxist definition of ideology.

## 11.4.3 The classical Marxist definition of ideology

The classical framework for theorising and conceptualising ideology arises from critical Marxist theories of culture and society. Within Marxist theory, however, there is a wide range of varying perspectives on culture and ideology and, as White (1987:136) points out, the particular approach to ideology which we adopt will vary according to our position within Marxism. In broad terms, two main approaches to Marxism can be identified, namely, *classical* or *orthodox Marxism*, and *contemporary, neo-Marxist* conceptions of Marxist theory, best illustrated by the works of Althusser (1971; 1977) and Gramsci (1971).

Simply stated, classical or orthodox Marxist theory defines ideology negatively as delusion or *false consciousness*. According to this theory, social and cultural forms of expression, as the cultural products of a society, serve as carriers of the dominant ideology. These media serve the interests of the minority grouping of ruling élites. The so-called masses, who uncritically accept the meanings contained in these messages, fail to recognise that the values and belief systems propagated do not serve their true interests, but, in reality, reflect the interests of the ruling class (Geuss 1981:14). Within this context, all social practices and institutions are seen to be peddling false consciousness to duped masses who unwittingly participate in their own oppression (White 1987:137).

Against this background, classical Marxist theory contends that all forms of expression function as agencies of social control and legitimation, and play a strategic role in reinforcing dominant social norms and values which legitimise the existing social system, thereby propagating false consciousness (Gurevitch, Bennett, Curran & Woollacott 1982:26). By presenting the views of the dominant and élite classes as the only legitimate views, these social and cultural forms of expression help to perpetuate and maintain the social and political *status quo*. They thus perpetuate various forms of subordination (of class, race or gender) by encouraging people to accept inequalities as if they were natural. In this way social and cultural forms of expression assist in the hegemonic process, functioning as ideological instruments in the hands of the powerful ruling class (Gurevitch et al 1982:22). Classical or orthodox Marxist theorists are thus essentially concerned with questions concerning the structure, ownership and control of the culture industry in an attempt to subvert this dominance structure.

However, there are a number of problems with the basic assumptions of a classical Marxist definition of ideology. Firstly, the definition of ideology as false consciousness erroneously assumes that true consciousness exists as an objective, empirical truth. Clearly, as Fiske (1987a:256) points out, consciousness is never the product of truth or reality, but rather of culture, society and history. "Truth must always be understood in terms of how it is made, for whom and at what time it is 'true'" (ibid).

Secondly, classical Marxist theory fails to take into account the social and historical context within which social practices and institutions operate. It fails to provide an adequate theory of social subjectivity, emphasising the institutional and economic nature of these practices and institutions at the expense of individual, social, cultural and historical factors (White 1987:138; Lemon 1991:28).

Thirdly, as White (1987:138) points out, the definition of ideology as false consciousness fails to explain how or why people so readily adopt ideas that differ from their own, and that they know to be contrary to their own true interests. In this sense, we may argue that classical Marxist theory implicitly adopts a deterministic perspective with regard to influence, suggesting that we, as recipients, are passive victims of the meanings offered to us by others (Lemon 1991:28).

We may ask, for example, how does the minority grouping of power élites assume a position of power over the majority grouping in society? How do they control recipients? And how is it that contradictory and inconsistent ideologies exist in society? These questions, problems and limitations point to the inadequacies of the classical Marxist definition of culture as false consciousness, and have led to the development of a number of alternative, neo-Marxist conceptions of ideology (White 1987:138; Lemon 1991:8).

### 11.4.4 Neo-Marxist definitions of ideology

The neo-Marxist definitions of ideology, best illustrated by the writings of Althusser (1971; 1977) and Gramsci (1971), developed from the research and writing of the Frankfurt School and from critical theory (Fourie 1988:100–103). These definitions make allowance for a more complex understanding of the relationship between society, culture and ideology, and acknowledge the coexistence of contradictory and competing ideological positions within society (White 1987:138; Lemon 1991:8).

Simply stated, Althusser (1971) reconceptualises the notion of society through a revision of the classical base/superstructure model, and provides a context for understanding ideology as a social practice (White 1987:137). While recognising the importance of the mode of production in determining the nature of society, Althusser rejects the notion that the economic base of society determines the whole cultural superstructure. He argues that society comprises a variety of interrelated social and intellectual activities or practices – the political, economic and the ideological – each having relative autonomy from the others, in that there are no overt connections between them. Together these practices comprise the social formation (Althusser 1971:127–186; Clarke, Seidler, McDonnel, Robins & Lovell 1980:159). Within this context an attempt is made to understand how social meanings are produced, distributed and received in society.

A central concept in Althusser's theory is the Ideological State Apparatuses, which refer to social institutions such as the family, language, the education system, politics, the church or the mass media (Althusser 1971:136–137). The Ideological State Apparatuses are an important part of the social formation, and together with the Repressive State Apparatuses, which include institutions such as the defence force, the judiciary, and the police force, function to propagate social conformity, influencing people's behaviour and thoughts (Gurevitch et al 1982:31). According to Althusser (1971), all social and cultural forms of expression propagate social norms and values that are intended as mechanisms of social control. While presenting themselves as socially neutral and objective, these norms and values are in fact ideologically determined, in the sense that they serve the interests of those who possess social power. Furthermore, these social norms and values function to maintain particular sites of power by naturalising them as the only legitimate positions for the location of power. Antonio Gramsci (1971) coined the term "hegemony" to explain the complex ways in which the dominant or ruling class maintains control over society, and to describe the general predominance of particular class, political and ideological interests. A second central concept in Althusser's (1971:156) theory is that ideology always has a material existence and is inscribed within the Ideological State Apparatuses and its practices. Within this context, rather than being imposed from above, ideology is the medium through which people experience the world. Ideology provides the framework for understanding through which human beings interpret and make sense of their reality. Ideology is thus an essential element of every social formation, and is defined as the lived relations between human beings and their world.

According to Althusser (1971:160–173), individuals are all constituted as subjects in, and subject to, ideology by the Ideological State Apparatuses, which

> ... not only constitute the sense of the world for us, but they also constitute our sense of ourselves, our sense of identity, and our sense of our relations to other people and to society in general.
> (Fiske 1987a:258)

Ideology is then not a static set of ideas imposed upon the subordinate classes "but rather a dynamic process that is constantly reproduced and reconstituted in practice – that is, in the way people think, act, and understand themselves and their relationship to society" (Fiske 1987a:256). Within this context, there is no such thing as being outside ideology. For Althusser, all ideology functions to constitute individuals as subjects, which is a social construction, not a natural one. All forms of social and cultural expression play an important role in the construction of the subject, that is to say, in the reproduction of ideology in people.

A third central tenet of Althusser's theory is his contention that ideology is not simply a set of illusions, but a system of representations about the circumstances in which people live. Thus, within an Althusserian framework, all social and cultural forms of expression play an important role in the functioning of the social formation, and essentially operate through ideology. Thus, the effectiveness of social and cultural forms of expression does not lie in an imposed false consciousness or in changing attitudes, but in the unconscious categories through which conditions are represented and experienced. The power of social and cultural forms of expression is then not simply rooted in their economic bases, but in ideology.

Clearly, all forms of social and cultural expression communicate fundamental beliefs, attitudes and values by means of their images or artefacts. In this sense all forms of expression are in some way ideological, and function as the cultural lens through which we perceive, interpret and understand our own social reality.

Forms of cultural and social expression offer ideological positions in a number of ways. First, they reflect or reveal existing (dominant) ideologies by reproducing (whether consciously or unconsciously) the myths, values and beliefs of a particular society. Secondly, they create their own ideologies, their own unique expressions of reality, by reinforcing, undercutting, creating or contradicting specific ideologies. In short, all cultural products are ideological and political insomuch as they are determined by the ideology that produced them, and inevitably present a particular ideological position, or point of view for the viewer.

All cultural artefacts (whether items of clothing, craft art, popular music, flea markets or modern shopping malls) are produced and created in specific social, historical and political contexts, by and for specific social groups. Moreover, they express and promote the meanings (values, beliefs and ideas) of the society or culture from which they emerge. According to Althusser (1971), all social practices propagate social norms and values which are intended as mechanisms of social control, but which present themselves as socially neutral and objective common sense. These social norms are, in fact, ideologically determined in the sense that they serve the interests of those who possess social, political and economic power. As such, social and cultural forms of expression as media of communication serve as important sites of struggle in which meanings are created, contested, debated and negotiated.

Althusser's reformulation of a theory of ideology clearly indicates an important shift in Marxist thinking, and marks a definite move away from the notion of ideology as a distorted reflection of reality or as false consciousness. Althusser's theory provided an important theoretical foundation for the recent cultural studies approach to the study of communication by focusing attention on individuals as social subjects who both construct and are constructed by systems of representation. In the next section we discuss the underlying assumptions of cultural studies.

## 11.5 CULTURAL STUDIES

Structural semiotics, neo-Marxist interpretations of ideology (that of Althusser in particular) and post-structuralist theory, have been the principal influences in the resurgence of work within Marxist cultural studies. One of the most notable examples of research and theorising in the discipline of communication is being undertaken by the Centre for Contemporary Cultural Studies in Birmingham, where the term "British cultural studies" was coined.

Cultural studies is an increasingly influential approach in the study of communication. It is marked by a far more positive approach to the products of the mass-communication media, and by an attempt to understand the meanings and value of these forms of expression within a postmodern society (cf. Hall, Hobson, Lowe & Willis 1980). Cultural studies is therefore centrally concerned with so-called marginal discourses, such as the products of popular culture, which were traditionally not regarded as legitimate objects of academic and scientific study.

An important aspect of the theoretical assumptions of cultural studies is that it does not represent a single monolithic approach, but includes aspects of various theoretical approaches, such as semiotics, psychoanalysis, feminism, ethnography, anthropology, and Marxist (ideological) analysis, amongst others. Cultural studies therefore represents a blending of approaches, and is essentially interdisciplinary. Cultural studies does not merely refer to the study of culture, but to the study of all forms of self expression as manifestations of culture. Society is seen as a totality that forms the basis for explanations of cultural practices. By looking at the whole of society, we can begin to understand cultural practices. Cultural studies is therefore not a homogenous, monolithical field which is clearly delimited by theoretical programmes and models. It is formed and adapted in the society in which it is practised. The three central terms that are of importance when talking about cultural studies are "meaning", "knowledge" and "power". Cultural practices are often regarded as a site of struggle for meaning – a struggle for the right or power to ascribe meaning. This struggle is an ideological one, since it is about the power to decide which meanings or ideas are dominant in a society.

In broad terms, cultural studies is fundamentally concerned with the problem of contradictory and competing ideologies within society (Hall et al 1980:15–47). Cultural studies stands opposed to the merely reflective role assigned to culture, and instead regards culture as a socially constructed phenomenon, a signifying practice which is interwoven with all other social practices within a particular society. As is the case with the neo-Marxist approach, cultural studies concentrates less on the economic and structural determinants of ideology, affording a greater degree of independence to ideology from its economic base.

A distinctive and important aspect of cultural studies is that the social production and reproduction of meaning is not only a matter of signification but also a matter of power (Ang 1990:145). In cultural studies, the study of all forms of social and cultural expression and the question of power constitute an ideological question. This brings us to the concept of *hegemony* which is central to a cultural studies approach.

### 11.5.1 Hegemony

The term *hegemony* was coined by Antonio Gramsci (1971), and is used to explain the complex ways in which the dominant or ruling class maintains control over society. This concept also helps us understand the general predominance of particular class, gender, political and ideological interests, propagated by the mass-communication media and all forms of social and cultural expression.

Stated simply, hegemony is another way of referring to, or explaining, power. It refers to a type of domination, by which the ruling classes try to win the voluntary approval or active consent and cooperation of the subordinate classes to the very system that ensures their subordination (cf. Larrain 1983:80; Rojek 1985:131).

For Gramsci (1971:164), hegemony

> ... works through ideology, but does not consist of false ideas, perceptions, definitions. It works primarily by inserting the subordinate class into key institutions and structures which support the power and social authority of the dominant order. It is, above all, in these structures and relations that a subordinate class lives its subordination.

According to Gramsci (1971), hegemonic rule is mediated through social institutions such as the mass-communication media and all other social and cultural forms of expression. These institutions, which are spread through society, are the locations for the transmission of hegemonic rule, and are the key sites of power struggle within society.

Hegemony is not a static power relationship, according to Gramsci (1971), but a constant process of struggle between those with and those without power. Fiske (1987b:41) writes that

> ... hegemony is a constant struggle against a multitude of resistances to ideological domination, and any balance of forces that it achieves is always precarious, always in need of re-achievement.

Within the context of a cultural studies approach, hegemony is thus constantly confronted by resistance. Because the social experience of material things constantly reminds us of the disadvantages of the subordination of others, we may in time build up resistance to domination and inequality. This resistance constitutes a constant threat to the dominant group, who must constantly work at retaining the cooperation and consent of the subordinate classes. Thus, despite the power of ideology and the hegemonic forces of the ruling classes, individuals are able to create their own meanings within, and often against, those provided by culture industries (Fiske 1987a:286). Within this context, culture is the arena in which the battle for ideological supremacy between those with and those without power is waged (Larrain 1983:81; Fiske 1987a:259; Hall et al 1980:36).

For example, the ideal of romantic, heterosexual love may be said to be the myth most prominently communicated by some soap operas, advertisements, magazines and music videos. However, other music videos, styles of dress, or feminist ideas expressed in magazines or advertisements pose both an implicit and explicit challenge to these portrayals of social reality which pretend to be the norm for everyone in society. Think, for example, of the gender-blending styles of dress in many music videos or advertisements. These so-called new ideas represent a challenge, and thus a threat, to the hegemonic order.

The basic characteristics of hegemony may be summarised as follows:

- Hegemony is difficult to detect because it masquerades as normal, natural and commonsense (produced and distributed as popular beliefs).
- Hegemony can be regarded as silent domination and is therefore not overt coercion (that is, it functions as a form of indirect rule).
- Hegemony is constantly under threat by those who question, challenge, negotiate, oppose or resist it (e.g. as seen in the lyrics of popular music such as heavy metal, rap, punk rock, and alternative genres).
- Hegemony is dynamic and constantly changes because it has to be constantly renewed, recreated, defined and modified.
- Hegemony works through ideology, and is a means of ideological domination or control.
- Hegemonic ideology (as the dominant beliefs of a society) is produced and distributed through social institutions, including the family, the school, the mass-communication media, and all forms of social and cultural expression.

According to the cultural studies approach, social and cultural forms of expression are replete with many potential meanings, which may be read in different ways by differently socially situated recipients (cf. Fiske 1987b). Thus, an essential characteristic of social and cultural forms of expression is that they are polysemic, that is, they possess a number of possible meanings. Simply put, this means that social and cultural forms of expression do not have only one meaning, but are relatively open texts which can be read or interpreted in various ways. Indeed, in view of the heterogeneous nature of recipients, it is inevitable that different meanings will be attributed to various forms of expression. And, as Fiske (1987b:66) argues, in order to be popular, social and cultural forms of expression must necessarily be open to multiple readings, that is, they must be polysemic, in order to facilitate the widest range of potential interpretations possible.

Because various forms of expression may function as agents of the dominant ideology, the structure of the text typically tries to limit its meanings to ones that promote that ideology (e.g. patriarchy, capitalism, or democracy). However, tension may develop between the structure of the text and the social situations of the recipients whose opinions do not necessarily accord with the dominant ideology, thereby positioning them at odds with that ideology. This inevitably leads to conflict of interests. However, the polysemic nature of the text establishes forces that challenge and oppose this ideological domination or closure, and facilitates the possibility of oppositional or negotiated readings. The hegemony of the text is thus never total, but must constantly struggle to impose itself against the diversity of meanings that recipients will produce.

The concept "hegemony" plays a central role in the cultural studies approach and provided the inspiration for Hall's theory of *preferred reading*, which attempts to explain this conflict of interest.

### 11.5.2 Hall's theory of preferred reading

According to Hall's theory of preferred reading, culture is a constant site of struggle between those with and those without power. Hall argues that while social practices and all forms of expression may offer a variety of meanings, their structure generally prefers a set of meanings that works to maintain the dominant ideology (e.g. the ideals of what is regarded as appropriate behaviour for men and women and the conventional distinctions drawn between masculinity and femininity). What is significant in this theory, however, is that these meanings cannot be imposed, only preferred.

Hall proposes three reading positions that recipients may occupy in relation to the dominant ideology: the *dominant*, the *negotiated*, and the *oppositional*.

A dominant reading is produced by a recipient who agrees with and thus accepts the dominant ideology and the meanings that it offers. Accordingly, viewers whose social situation, particularly their class, aligns them comfortably with the dominant ideology, would accept its preferred meaning(s). Such a recipient takes message and decodes them in the same way in which they were encoded, thereby operating within the dominant ideology (Morley 1980; Hall et al 1980:137; Fiske 1987b:64). For example, we may accept the preferred reading of the vast majority of magazines' messages about what is regarded as appropriate behaviour for men and for women.

A negotiated reading is produced by recipients who fit into the preferred reading of the dominant ideology in general, but who need to modify it to meet the needs of their specific social situation. These recipients will adjust the dominant ideology to fit their particular view of reality in accordance with their own needs, experience and context. For example, we may accept the meanings offered by many advertisements about the respective roles of men and women in general, but intentionally adapt them to fit our own personalities or values, thereby adjusting or negotiating the preferred meanings of these messages.

Oppositional readings are readings produced by those individuals whose social situation and experience puts them in direct opposition to the dominant ideology, and who understand both the literal and connotative meaning of the text, but intentionally decode or deconstruct it in a contrary or subversive manner. An example of an oppositional reading would be that we could intentionally ignore the preferred meanings of the text, rejecting and even subverting the roles and requirements expressed as appropriate behaviour for men and women.

The value of this theory is that it frees the text from complete ideological closure, making the text open to many different interpretations. Moreover, it shifts the focus away from the text towards the recipient as the site where meanings are ascribed or attributed. Morley (1980), however, suggests that Hall's three categories of reading are too simplistic, and that a wide range of readings resists simple categorisation. In reality, there are few purely dominant or purely oppositional readings (Fiske 1987b:64). Individuals generally engage in a continuous process of negotiation between the text and its potential meanings. In this way the balance of power lies with the recipient. Morley (1980:163–173) proposes a model based on discourse theory. Discourse is a language or system of representation that develops socially in order to create and circulate meanings. These meanings serve the interests of the section of society within which the discourse originates, and work ideologically to naturalise those meanings into "common sense" (Fiske 1987b:15).

Morley (1980) suggests that the text is a social discourse. As recipients, our experience is similarly made up of a number of discourses or texts (that is, beliefs, ideas, attitudes or experiences) through which we make sense of our reality. Reading a text is defined as the moment when the discourses of the recipient meet the discourses of the text. Reading, or interpretation, therefore becomes a constant process of negotiation between the meanings inscribed in the text and the meanings ascribed to it by its recipients.

Within this context, the text is seen as having many potential meanings (that is, it is polysemic), which will be read according to the discourses (knowledge, experience, prejudices, attitudes and/or political views) of the recipient. Reading becomes a complex and dynamic process of negotiation between the recipient and the text in an attempt to reconcile the apparent conflict of interests. In other words, we are not passive recipients of predetermined meanings, but rather active participants, interpreting the message to produce meanings that correspond with our own experience. Moreover, we are able to actively resist or oppose the dominant ideology.

Textual devices, such as the use of irony as a rhetorical device, metaphor, humour, contradiction, exaggeration, myth, fantasy and parody, open the text as a form of expression to polysemic (multiple) meanings. These devices work against the attempted ideological closure of the text and allow for oppositional or perverse readings. This allows for a multiplicity of voices and meanings (or discourses) often in conflict with one another. In this way the text becomes a site of struggle for meaning, in which meanings are negotiated and constructed. Thus, according to cultural studies, the text is essentially intertextual. The idea of intertextuality proposes that the text is read in relation to other texts, and must be seen within their social, economic, political and historical context.

### 11.5.3 A model for an ideological analysis of cultural texts

Now that we have outlined the basic underlying assumptions of cultural studies, the following broad steps can be identified in a critical analysis of various forms of social and cultural expression.

- Identify the primary text and situate it within a social, political, economic and historical context.
- Identify the textual devices that open the text to polysemic readings. How do these devices work against ideological closure?
- How are meanings generated by the text?
- How are sign systems, myths and symbols used to convey meaning?
- How is ideological meaning unified and/or contradicted through the use of irony, metaphor, humour, contradiction, exaggeration, parody and/or fantasy?
- Identify all intertextual relations in terms of the following:
  - the formal qualities of the text;
  - the socially situated recipient and the process of reading;
  - the impact of the social, political, economic and historical context of both the text and the recipient.
- Identify the values and ideological points of view expressed in a particular social and cultural form of expression in terms of the following:
  - Identify the potential preferred reading as the dominant ideology.
  - Identify the three possible types of readings of the text suggested by Hall, namely, the dominant, the negotiated and the oppositional.
  - Identify whether the text is polysemic or open to a number of possible meanings or interpretations.

In following these broad steps it becomes apparent how a particular social and cultural form of expression functions as an ideological instrument within society, inevitably reflecting and creating a particular ideological point of view. The ultimate objective of this analysis is to expose the underlying ideological positions offered in various forms of expression in order to establish to what degree they support, contradict or question the ideologies of the society which produced them.

## 11.6 THE CULTURAL STUDIES APPROACH – A SUMMARY

The cultural studies approach, while recognising the power of ideology and the hegemonic forces of the ruling class, sees individuals as able to create their own meanings within, and often against, those provided by the dominant classes (Fiske 1987a:286).

A cultural studies approach is therefore centrally concerned with marginal discourses, such as the products of popular culture, and attempts to explain how these discourses play a role in integrating and subordinating potentially deviant and oppositional elements in society (Gurevitch et al 1982:262; Hardt 1989:587). Cultural studies is thus concerned with the social construction of meanings and their distribution in heterogeneous, industrial societies. It assumes that meanings and their construction are indivisibly linked to the social structure and therefore takes the historical, cultural, economic and social context into consideration.

Within this context, ideology may be defined as shared systems of belief, and is intimately related to the use of power in society (that is, hegemony). Essentially, ideology operates through discourse, which refers to a socially constructed way of speaking or of representing something. Within the context of cultural studies, discourse is the expression of ideologies, the battleground upon which struggles for power are waged. Culture is a systematic way of constructing reality and is expressed and reflected in forms of expression such as various forms of art, dress, architecture, dance, drama, sport and any other human activity or behaviour.

Cultural studies

- sees that cultural processes are intimately connected with social relations, especially class relations and formations, with sexual divisions and racial structuring (e.g. racism, classism and sexism);
- regards culture as inextricably related to the uses and abuses of power (that is, hegemony) and helps to produce asymmetries in the abilities of individuals and groups to define and realise their needs (e.g. negotiation of meaning);
- regards culture as neither autonomous nor externally determined, but as a site of social difference and struggle;
- is centrally concerned with marginal discourses and with social and cultural forms of expression as signifying practices.

In this section it became clear that ideology and ideological assumptions are fundamental to *all* forms of social and cultural expression as communication. Moreover, it is clear that the potential meanings inscribed in any event, image, product or artefact, are incredibly diverse. Clearly there are countless examples of social and cultural forms of expression or communication. Indeed, culture is ultimately a form of expression, and is the means by which we create, maintain, perpetuate and challenge our cultural values.

## Summary

In this unit we demonstrated that besides verbal and nonverbal communication, there are many more forms of communication. To illustrate this view we briefly discussed religion, architecture and the built environment, sport, theatre, music, and fashion and style as social and cultural forms of expression. We also discussed the concepts of ideology and culture, as well as the basic assumptions of a cultural studies approach to the study of communication.

MEDIA STUDIES

## Research activities

1. Explain in a paragraph what is meant by social and cultural forms of expression. Refer to your own examples to illustrate.
2. Study the definition of culture provided earlier. How is culture defined? What adjectives are used to define culture, and what values are ascribed to these adjectives?

    *Culture is the process of developing and ennobling the human faculties, a process facilitated by the assimilation of works of scholarship and art and linked to the progressive character of the modem era* (Thompson 1990:126).

3. Think of an example of one social value which is presented as a natural and common-sense value in your culture (such as getting married and having a family or that men should perform certain roles and women others). Think of how you could challenge those values, thereby disrupting the hegemonic power of the *status quo*.
4. Give an example of a social and cultural form of expression where the hegemonic *status quo* is challenged (e.g. with reference to fashion, sport, politics, music, religion, or architecture and the built environment).
5. Define culture and mass communication and explain the relationship between them in your own words.
6. Define the concept of *hegemony* in your own words, and give an appropriate example.
7. Study Figure 11.5 and then answer the following questions.

**Figure 11.5 Reading religion**

a) What is the preferred reading of this photograph? How do you know this is so? Substantiate your argument by referring to the photograph.

b) Identify a potential dominant, negotiated and oppositional reading to this photograph as a text.

## Further reading

Barker, C. 2000. *Cultural Studies: theory and practice.* London: Sage.
du Gay, P, Hall, S, Janes, L, Mackay, H & Negas, K. 1997. *Doing Cultural Studies. The story of the Sony Walkman.* London: Sage.
During, S (ed). 1993. *The cultural studies reader.* London: Routledge.
Featherstone, M. 1992. *Cultural theory and cultural change.* London: Sage.
Hernadi, P. 1995. *Cultural transactions: nature, self, society.* Ithaca: Cornell.
Oriard, M. 1993. *Reading football: how the popular press created an American spectacle.* Chapel Hill: University of North Carolina.
Swingewood, A. 1998. *Cultural theory and the problem of modernity.* Hampshire: Macmillan.
*The Polity reader in cultural theory.* 1994. Cambridge: Polity.
Titon, JT. 1994. *Early downhome blues: a musical and cultural analysis.* Chapel Hill: University of North Carolina.
Wiredu, K. 1996. *Cultural universals and particulars: an African perspective.* Bloomington: Indiana University.

## Bibliography

Althusser, L. 1971. *Lenin and philosophy and other essays*, translated by B Brewster. New York: Monthly Review.
Althusser, L. 1977. *For Marx.* London: New Left.
Ang, I. 1990. Culture and communication: towards an ethnographic critique of media consumption and the transnational media system. *European Journal of Communication* 5:239–260.
Billington, R, Strawbridge, S, Greensides, L & Fitzsimons, A. 1991. *Culture and society. A sociology of culture.* London: Macmillan.
Budd, RW & Ruben, BR (eds). 1979. *Beyond media: new approaches to mass communication.* New Jersey: Hayden.
Calhoun, DW. 1987. *Sport, culture and personality.* 2nd edition. Champaign, Ill: Human Kinetics.
Clarke, S, Seidler, VJ, McDonnel, K, Robins, K & Lovell, T. 1980. *One-dimensional Marxism. Althusser and the politics of culture.* London: Allison & Busby.
Dupre, L. 1983. *Marx's social critique of culture.* New Haven: Yale University.
Durkheim, E. 1969. *The social foundation of religion.* London: Allen & Urwin.
Eitzen, DS. 1989. *Sport in contemporary society.* 3rd edition. New York: St Martin's.
Ewen, S. 1988. *All consuming images. The politics of style in contemporary culture.* New York: Basic.
Ewen, S & Ewan, E. 1992. *Channels of desire. Mass images and the shaping of American consciousness.* Minneapolis: University of Minneapolis.
Fiske, J. 1987a. British cultural studies and television, in *Channels of discourse: television and contemporary criticism*, edited by RC Allen. London: Methuen.
Fiske, J. 1987b. *Television culture.* London: Methuen.
Fore, WF. 1987. *Television and religion. The shaping of faith, values and culture.* Minneapolis: Augsburg.

Fourie, PJ. 1988. *Aspects of film and television communication.* Cape Town: Juta.
Geertz, C (ed). 1973. *The interpretation of cultures: selected essays.* New York: Basic.
Geuss, R. 1981. *The idea of a critical theory: Habermas and the Frankfurt School.* Cambridge: Cambridge University.
Gramsci, A. 1971. *Selections from prison notebooks.* New York: International.
Gurevitch, M, Bennett, T, Curran, J & Woollacott, J (eds). 1982. *Culture, society and the media.* London: Routledge.
Hadden, JK & Swann, CE. 1981 *Prime time preaching. The rising power of televangelism.* London: Addison-Wesley.
Hall, S, Hobson, Lowe, A & Willis, P (eds). 1980. *Culture, media, language.* London: Hutchinson.
Hardt, H. 1989. The return of the "critical" and the challenge of radical dissent: critical theory, cultural studies and American mass communication research, in *Communication Yearbook 12,* edited by JA Anderson. Belmont, CA: Sage.
Hebdige, D. 1993. From culture to hegemony, in *The cultural studies reader,* edited by S During. London: Routledge.
Hitchcock, J. 1979. We speak that we do know: religion as mass communication, in *Beyond media: new approaches to mass communication,* edited by RW Budd & BD Ruben. New Jersey: Hayden.
Kovecses, Z. 1990. Sport and semiotics, in *Semiotics in the individual sciences,* edited by WA Koch. Bochum: Brockmeyer.
Larrain, J. 1983. *Marxism and ideology.* London: Macmillan.
Lemon, J. 1990. Fashion and style as non-verbal communication. *Communicatio* 16(2):19–26.
Lemon, J. 1991. Ideological criticism and analysis, in *Critical television analyses: an introduction,* edited by PJ Fourie. Cape Town: Juta.
Leonard, WM. 1984. *A sociological perspective on sport.* 2nd edition. Minneapolis: Burgess.
Luke, TW. 1989. *Screens of power. Ideology, domination and resistance in informational society.* Urbana: University of Illinois.
Lull, J (ed). 1992. *Popular music and communication.* 2nd edition. London: Sage.
Morley, D. 1980. Texts, readers, subjects, in *Culture, media, language,* edited by S Hall, D Hobson, A Lowe & P Willis. London: Hutchinson.
Oberdorfer, DN. 1982. *Electronic Christianity.* Minnesota: John L. Brekke & Sons.
Patte, D. 1990. Religion and semiotics, in *Semiotics in the individual sciences,* edited by WA Koch. Brochum: Brockmeyer.
Rojek, C. 1985. *Capitalism and leisure theory.* London: Tavistock.
Ruben, RW & Soleri, P. 1979. Architecture: medium and message, in *Beyond media: new approaches to mass communication,* edited by RW Budd & BR Ruben. New Jersey: Hayden.
Sage, GH. 1990. *Power and ideology in American sport. A critical perspective.* Champaign, Ill: Human Kinetics.
Shiach, M. 1989. *Discourse on popular culture. Class, gender and history in cultural analysis. 1730 to the present.* Cambridge: Polity.
Solomon, MR (ed). 1981. *The psychology of fashion.* Lexington, MA: Lexington.
Stuart, AP. 1985. *The Bible and popular culture in America.* Pennsylvania: Fortress.
Thompson, JB. 1990. *Ideology and modern culture: critical social theory in the era of mass communication.* Cambridge: Polity.
White, M. 1987. Ideological analysis and television, in *Channels of discourse: television and contemporary criticism,* edited by RC Allen. London: Methuen.
Wienstein, D. 1987. *Heavy metal. A cultural sociology.* New York: Lexington.
Williams, R. 1981. *The sociology of culture.* New York: Schocken.

# Feminist Media Theory 12

*Lynn Parry & Beschara Karam*

## Overview

The media have always been at the centre of feminist criticism because of the power of the media to impart *patriarchal* (rule of the father, subordinating the female to the male) and *ideological* (how men of all classes and races use the media to oppress women) messages. The negative portrayal of "women as women" in the media has resulted in a backlash, particularly from radical feminists, who seek separatism from male dominance. Feminists are of the opinion that most theories of communication are inadequate because they misrepresent women's beliefs, attitudes and experiences. In the feminist view, male theorising has often resulted in intimidation, oppression and justification of the *status quo*, leading to divisions between *those who know* (men) and *those who do not* (women) (cf. Van Zoonen 1994). In other words, many feminists maintain an active hostility to theory, which is viewed as a male form of discourse, based on a narrow conception of reasoning.

In this unit we outline the basic assumptions and terrain of feminism. We then provide you with various feminist theoretical perspectives, such as liberal, Marxist and socialist, radical, psychoanalytical, and postmodern perspectives. We also give you examples of film and television programmes with regard to each theoretical perspective. A case study based on the film *The Piano* (1993), which falls under the psychoanalytical feminist perspective is also provided. This case study will enable you to study and apply feminist concepts, such as the *Other* (woman as the realisation of the male objective, rather than as an individual in her own right), *gaze* (woman as a spectacle to be looked at by the male audience), *Subject* (man as Subject views woman as inferior by nature) and *Object* (woman as object of the male gaze), *fetishism* (woman as object of male sexual pleasure) and voyeurism (looking in on the private world of women which emanates from a masculine perspective). We end this unit with a brief synopsis of feminism and feminist media criticism in South Africa.

## Learning outcomes

At the end of this unit you should be able to

- describe the assumptions and terrain of feminism;
- describe the various feminist theoretical perspectives;
- apply the knowledge you have obtained in this unit by providing your own critical examples of film and television programmes with regard to the feminist theoretical perspectives;

# MEDIA STUDIES

- answer the question on the case study of the film *The Piano* with the purpose of understanding the concepts of the Other, the gaze, Subject and Object, fetishism and voyeurism;
- analyse the image of women in advertising;
- evaluate the current situation of feminism in South Africa in the context of what is covered in this unit; and
- conduct your own research by studying the portrayal of South African women on television and in media in general.

## 12.1 INTRODUCTION: BASIC ASSUMPTIONS

Feminism broadly means the advocacy of the rights of women. There is no one single accepted definition of feminism and, generally speaking, feminism incorporates the struggle for political and legal rights, equal opportunities, sexual autonomy and the right of self determination. The feminist movement started with the recognition of the subordination of women, from the existence of discrimination and inequality based on sex/gender. Feminism has never been a unified single movement, but has comprised different tenets that may unite behind a single campaign. Feminism can be categorised into different types of feminism, such as liberal, Marxist and socialist, radical, psychoanalytical and postmodern feminism (Tong 1992).

*Feminist criticism* is concerned with women as writers and women as readers of texts, and although the heading of this unit is Feminist media theory, we focus on the visual film and television programme as *text*. For example, in the television soap opera *Days of our Lives* currently on SABC1, the majority of women do not work and spend their days scheming on how to make their men happy because they cannot live without them. Conversely, most of the women in this soap opera who have successful professions are without men in their lives. As readers or viewers of this text, we should ask ourselves whether there no happily married women with children who are also successful in their careers? Feminist criticism is significant because it has established the importance for women to secure their own space in which to speak and express themselves freely. For instance, *Lebone* (Women on the Move) a magazine programme currently on SABC2, deals with women's issues about successful women in the corporate world and is produced by women for women. Another example is the *Oprah Winfrey Show*, a talk show currently on e.tv. Oprah Winfrey has her own production company, Harpo, and (although there are some male employees) it is essentially run by women, staffed by women and produces content for women.

A crucial aspect of feminist criticism is the examination of the fact that "women as women" are rarely represented in film and television. Recognition of this fact unites all attempts at a feminist critique of film and television. According to Sharon Smith (1999:14) "women in any fully human form, have almost completely been left out of film ... That is from its very beginning they were present, but not in characterizations any self-respecting person could identify with". The female image in the media is frequently presented in one-dimensional stereotypes, such as nurturing mother, whore, vamp, dutiful wife, girl Friday or frigid career woman. *Women and Film's* Naome Gilbert postulates that the cinematic and televisual female image represents the male Other, with man's fears and desires imposed on a female aesthetic (Gledhill 1985:818). Thus the fundamental questions of feminism focus on issues of cultural identity and position. What does it mean to live as a woman? To what extent does gender – our own identities as male and female, our ideas about what that might mean – shape our experience of the culture around us? What about the need to explore and examine the roles and representations with regard to any difference in how black and white South African women are portrayed in television and film? (Parry 1991:112.)

## 12.2 THE TERRAIN OF FEMINISM

It is crucial to recognise that *feminist theory* itself is a complicated and contested term. Although the popular media, including television, tend to define it as monolithic, there are many different types of feminism (and therefore of feminist criticism and theory) incorporating a wide variety of attitudes and assumptions. However, both popular and academic writers often divide feminism into general categories that represent a fairly narrow range of political perspectives and cultural analyses. For instance, Marxist feminism looks closely at how gender is connected to the reproduction of the labour force, while radical feminism often concentrates on issues related directly to sexuality. Whilst these categories are frequently viewed in isolation, we must realise that they are not mutually exclusive. In fact, critiques by women of colour, lesbians and others have demonstrated that these and other familiar versions of feminism share not only a set of common interests but certain common flaws as well, including a tendency to impose white, Western, middle-class, heterosexual women's experiences on all women. Do all women share the same problems or perspectives? Is there an inherent social or cultural perspective rooted in biological femininity (essentialism)? These urgent critiques have inspired many women who feel excluded from mainstream feminist theory to develop new analyses that look more seriously at the experiences of marginalised and non-dominant groups (Myers, Anderson & Risman 1998).

Other disciplines have also reshaped feminist approaches to popular culture. After a substantial critique of its biases towards male experience, many feminist scholars have also found *cultural studies* (by this we mean investigation of the production and circulation of meaning) important. More recently, other innovative forms of criticism and theory have developed, such as post-structuralism and postmodernist feminisms, which base their analyses of gender on new understandings of the operations of language, sign systems and discourse. Other theorists have extended the principles of interdisciplinarity to methodology itself, employing an eclectic mix of approaches rather than identifying themselves with a single school or position (Mumford 1998).

We now consider some of the most important theoretical perspectives of feminism.

## 12.3 LIBERAL FEMINISM: A THEORETICAL PERSPECTIVE

Liberal feminism has the most influence on feminism in the United States in its demands for individual autonomy and equality of opportunity. According to Jaggar (1983), liberal feminism is grounded in the application of the principles of liberal political philosophy (as explained by Locke, Kant, Mill and others) to political and economic bias experienced by women. Jaggar (1983) links the 300-year history of liberal philosophy with the history of capitalism and capitalist demands for equality of opportunity. Liberal theory assumes that rational and mental development is the highest human ideal and that the state should act to ensure equal opportunities for both women and men in pursuing this goal. Although early liberal feminists worked for women's right to vote and to own property, contemporary liberal feminists are particularly interested in changing laws to promote women's opportunities for intellectual and professional success and they fight for issues such as equal pay for equal work. They assume that rational argument and legal efforts will allow women to move toward equity with men in the workplace. This line of reasoning adopts the view that equal opportunities for women rest on the acceptance of the existing capitalist, socio-economic system. Therefore liberal feminists are committed to major economic reorganisation and redistribution of wealth, since equality of opportunity will lead to both.

Other liberal feminists borrow ideas from cognitive theory and socialisation theory. For instance, cognitive theorists, such as Kohlberg (1966) assume that once children realise their own genders are constant, they maintain cognitive consistency by imitating those of the same sex. Conversely, social learning theorists like Bandura (1977) emphasise the importance of rewards in children's modelling behaviour. Both perspectives stress the importance of modelling and reinforcement by parents, teachers and the *media* in the acquisition of sex-role behaviours.

The negative aspects of liberal feminism are that it was essentially a movement of white middle- to upper-class women who felt themselves excluded from the economic rewards the system had to offer, and whose concerns were to get women (themselves included) into the corridors of power and money. We can also criticise liberal feminism in that it does not address the origin of gender differences, however in recent years liberal feminists have recognised their tendency to accept male values as human values and their inclination to place more importance on a gender-neutral humanism instead of a gender-specific feminism (Steeves 1987).

### 12.3.1 Liberal feminism and film and television criticism

Liberal feminist film and television analyses centres chiefly on *quantitative content analyses, historical* and *processor studies* and *effect studies*. In the following section we describe what these analyses and studies mean in terms of feminist criticism.

#### Quantitative content analyses

Generally speaking, quantitative content analyses of television programmes aim to assess *television sexism* and merely count the numbers and types of men and women portrayed in order to reflect changes in the status of women, particularly in non-traditional and professional roles. Early studies of the techniques of content analysis to prime-time television dramatic programmes with the purpose of measuring the roles and status of women in society revealed the following:

McNeil (1975:259-271) applied the techniques of quantitative content analysis to prime-time television dramatic programmes in the United States. On the strength of her research she concluded that

- Male characters outnumbered female characters by almost three to one implying that females are less important.
- Marriage and parenthood are more important to a woman than to a man. For instance, 46 percent male characters exhibited an indeterminate marital status, 53 percent an indeterminate parental status; conversely, for female characters the figures were 11 percent and 19 percent respectively.
- Men were traditionally portrayed as breadwinners and women as homemakers. For instance, 72 percent of the males and 44 percent of the females were lucratively employed.
- Female characters were more personally and less professionally oriented than male characters. For example, professional-to-professional relationships between men accounted for 23 percent while between women for a mere 8 percent. Marital and family relationships constituted 41 percent of women's interactions and only 8 percent of men's.
- Female characters showed more passivity than male characters in problem solving. For example, 48 percent of women's problems as opposed to 35 percent of men's were resolved entirely by other people.

A more recent look at a quantitative content analysis of 40 television advertisements broadcast on SABC1, 2 and 3 between 17:00 and 21:00 over the period of the first week in July 2000 had the following results:

- 75 percent of all the advertisements using women were for products found either in the kitchen or bathroom.
- In 30 percent of the advertisements women were depicted in the home, whereas only 15 percent of the advertisements showed men in the home.
- 35 percent of women in the advertisements were housewives.
- 18 different occupations were shown for men and 10 for women.
- 30 percent of the advertisements used female voice-overs, whereas 70 percent of the advertisements had male voice-overs.

Content analysis as a method of research in liberal feminism is also apparent in the American situation comedy *The Nanny*, currently on SABC2. There are eight different types of stereotypical women in this show. For example, Val plays the ever-popular dumb blonde, whereas Nanny Fine is portrayed as a nanny in charge of Mr Sheffield's three children and when she is not looking after the children, she is "hunting" for the perfect man. Nanny Fine is stereotyped as a typical Jewish woman in search of a rich husband who will feed her grapes and drape her in gold. CC is Mr Sheffield's secretary and she and Nanny Fine fight continuously for his attention and admiration.

## Historical and processor studies

Historical studies of women in mass media are numerous and most of these studies rest on liberal assumptions revealed in praising notable achievements by women irrespective of class, race or sexual preference. When discussing historical studies of women in television you could take note of the remarkable achievements of South African women such as Liz Khumalo a veteran award-winning journalist recently nominated for *Lebone* SABC2's achiever award, Nothembo Madume the first female presenter of sport on SABC1, Tinky Pringle the first female presenter of sport on M-Net and Ruda Landman of Carte Blanche on M-Net. Other examples of successful achievements of South African women in television are Kim Cloete of SABC TV news who in 1999 won the CNN African Journalist of the Year Award and CNN World Report Award, and Felicia Mabuza-Suttle who has her own talk show currently on e.tv.

Processor studies often imply inequalities in numbers and opportunities for women in media professions. A 1988 survey of 451 network television journalists in the United States showed that a mere third were women. Another result of the survey found that although 39 percent of network news producers were women, a mere 15 percent were bureau chiefs and only 6 of 29 network news vice-presidents were female. This study also emphasised that male television anchors are employed on the grounds of their journalistic experience, whereas female television anchors are chosen by men according to cosmetic appearance (Smith, Fredin & Nardone 1989:228). When considering processor studies, you could take the situation in South Africa into account. For example, think of young and attractive SABC newsreaders like Nadia Levin and Khanyi Dhlomo-Mkhize. Are there any older or more mature female television anchors on SABC TV?

## Effect studies

Some twenty-five years ago a study by Drabman, Hammer and Jarvie (1976) in the United States showed that research can be confounded by children's already well-informed *stereotypes*. In this research on children's accounts of sex-role stereotypes on television, the children were shown videotaped visits to Doctor Mary and Nurse David and then asked to recall the names of the doctor and the nurse. Only a fraction gave a woman's name for the doctor and a man's name for the nurse. Liberal feminism has concentrated largely on the effects of television on children in order to determine their perceptions of male and female stereotypes. A further study by Durkin (1984) about how children between the ages of four and nine perceive stereotyped television excerpts confirmed that even at this early age an understanding of stereotypical, gendered behaviour was displayed.

In terms of television programmes and effect studies, we can refer to the popular American sitcom, *Roseanne* currently on e.tv. Roseanne runs a fast-food outlet, which must be very tiring and when she gets home she is expected to cook, and attend to the children's needs, and keep the peace. This does not seem out of the ordinary because most of her time is spent serving people either at work or in the home. We do, however, see Roseanne's sister, Jackie as unusual because she is a young woman who lives alone and is single. This tends to strike us as abnormal, instead of perhaps wondering why Roseanne is not entitled to have some of her "duties" reduced. Children watching this sitcom will make stereotypical assumptions about gender behaviour, such as that although Roseanne works, a woman's place is in fact in the home attending to her children's needs.

With regard to film there are numerous films depicting a liberal feminist point of view that coincides with effect studies. For example, *Pretty Woman* (1990) directed by Gary Marshall and starring Richard Gere and Julia Roberts purports to be light entertainment, and is about a love affair that develops between a prostitute/sex worker with a heart of gold, and a cold but wealthy businessman who hires her as a paid companion. However, on a deeper level feminists were appalled by the film because it reinforces the notion of male supremacy and reduces the heroine to a sex object needing to be rescued by a Prince Charming, who will make her life meaningful. Imagine the effects of this film on youths' perceptions of stereotypical behaviour?

## 12.4 MARXIST AND SOCIALIST FEMINISM: A THEORETICAL PERSPECTIVE

Marxist and socialist feminism focuses on the class system under the capitalist mode of production, which plays a major part in *women's oppression*. For Marxist feminists, feminism like Marxism is "a confrontation, a struggle, a political intervention in institutions and in the practice of everyday life" (De Lauretis 1984:3). Orthodox Marxist feminists claim that class oppression is at the core of women's oppression and devaluation, and focus on the dominant ideology instituted by the capitalist system. Marxist-influenced feminism opposes both radical and liberal perspectives. Marx rejected the idea of an essential, biologically determined human nature, which contradicts one of the assumptions of radical feminism. He also rejected the liberal assumption that individuals can autonomously develop their potential while living in a class society where wealth and power are controlled by a few.

Friedrich Engels (1985) initiated Marxist feminist arguments in *The origin of the family, private property and the state 1845*, where he claimed that the subjugation of women to men did not exist prior to capitalism, private property and monogamous family forms. He used anthropological data to show how primitive kinship groups were disrupted as production was moved away from the home and class divisions were created. As a result of these changes the tendency was for male wage earners to provide and control the capital for nuclear families. Although most Marxist feminists acknowledge Engels' contribution as the first materialist explanation of women's oppression in the nuclear family structure, his work has been criticised for his erroneous assumption that *proletarian* (those dependent on labour and without capital) women were not oppressed (Steeves 1987).

Marxist feminists have been criticised for saying too little about women's oppression by *men*. When Marxist feminists speak about women's oppression, they argue that capital is the primary oppressor of women as workers, and that men are the secondary oppressors of women. Marxist feminists also rarely discuss issues related to sex and when they do they tend to compare sex to work, for instance by comparing the husband-wife relationship to the bourgeois-proletariat relationship as if male-female relations in marriage were exploitative in exactly the same way as those in employer-employee relationships. Marxist feminists draw these analogies because they want to link the Marxist treatment of women's sex-specific oppression with Marxism's main theoretical system, incorporating domination both by class and by gender in the same framework. However, Marxist feminists cannot make this link because, although there are similarities, exploited workers do not suffer in the same way as do oppressed wives (Jaggar 1983).

Although socialist feminists have much in common with Marxist feminists, at least one major difference divides these two perspectives. Whereas Marxist feminists believe that class ultimately accounts for women's status, socialist feminists believe that gender and class play an equal role in women's oppression. Furthermore, socialist feminists are influenced by Althusser (1971) and emphasise that although ideology plays an important role in defining classes, the inequalities of sexism and gender, race, language and cultural background should be taken into account. Althusser (1971) argues that societies consist of three levels: the economic, the political and the ideological. Each level has its own relative autonomy, however the economic is ultimately the determinant. He assumes that classes are the major social formations of capitalist society and that ideology is important in sustaining class distinctions necessary to capitalism (cf. Steeves 1987).

Socialist feminists also share points of agreement with other feminist perspectives. For example, they agree with radical feminists that gender inequality is fundamental, however they criticise radical feminists' general use of the term patriarchy to describe all gender oppression. Many socialist feminists doubt that radical feminism is a realistic solution in its separatism and argue that women should align themselves with sympathetic political factions, for example, the socialist left.

Socialist feminists have yet to develop a theory that accounts for the various ways that patriarchy and capitalism interact to oppress women of different economic circumstances, both in the home and in the workplace. For instance, some socialist feminists believe that an integrated theory of capitalist patriarchy should be developed, which distinguishes women in terms of their economic status at home and at work, while other socialist feminists argue that describing two systems (capitalism and patriarchy) in continual interaction with each other is preferable to an integrated framework (Tong 1992).

### 12.4.1 Marxist and socialist feminism and film and television criticism

Both Marxist and socialist feminists advocate the use of *critical research* methods although they concede that not all research questions can be answered by qualitative means. By following the cultural studies approach the focus is on how television and film reinforces ideology in terms of *class, gender* and *race*. In other words:

- How is class represented?
- How is gender represented?
- How is race represented?
- How do class, gender and race intersect?

Feur (1984) turns to the television soap opera as a feminine narrative form in her analysis of prime-time American television soap operas like *Dallas* and *Dynasty* in terms of class and gender portrayal, and observes that the major characters in both soap operas (for instance JR Ewing, Miss Ellie, Blake Carrington and Krystle Carrington) belong to the capitalist élite or ruling class, and are juxtaposed against minor characters, such as secretaries and servants, who do not belong to this social milieu. Although the women in these soap operas, like Sue Ellen (*Dallas*) and Krystle Carrington (*Dynasty*) are dominant in their economic power, these positions of power occur because of marriage or inherited wealth. In *Dallas* and *Dynasty* both married and single women are depicted as obsessed with the men in their lives (Krystle over Blake in *Dynasty* and Pam over Bobby in *Dallas*) and use their sexuality to compete for male attention, whereas the men are portrayed as career-orientated.

Another example is the music video, which may be viewed from a Marxist and socialist (class, gender and race perspective). The video *She works hard for the money* by Donna Summer, an African-American, serves to negotiate class, gender and race inequalities. This video champions working-class women's rights and points to the fact that women derive minimal financial or spiritual satisfaction from both their work and personal lives. Consider the following words from this music video:

> She works hard for the money ...
> So hard for it, honey ...
> She works hard for the money ...
> So you better treat her right ...

In this music video the woman represents all working-class women in that she is presented as a waitress, a seamstress, a cleaning woman, and a housewife at home with her children. The narrative of this video allows the viewer to assume that she is a single mother with rather undisciplined children. The video opens with a slow-motion shot of the swirling protagonist, an image revealed as a dream when she is awakened by an alarm clock calling her to work. A photograph of the protagonist as a younger woman in dance pose illustrates her unfulfilled ambition of becoming a dancer. Its strategic placement in a scene with her two unruly children contextualises the failure to meet her goal in her female sacrifice for love and family.

Furthermore, in the video the woman is featured in various sexist and physically gruelling scenarios. The viewer sees men patting her rear in her role as waitress, and her bowing her head from physical exhaustion as a seamstress bent over her sewing machine. A certain nobility, however, is revealed through the woman's communication with fellow workers as she goes to clean offices in the morning. Then there is a dissolve and a pan from the woman's bed to a New York street and after that the video is divided into three structural parts. First the heroine is viewed washing a floor, next waitressing and finally working as a seamstress. The latter part of the video depicts the woman's home life. The viewer sees the woman walking towards the camera, carrying two bags of groceries, thus emphasising the harshness of her existence. She is wearing high-heeled shoes, and stumbles over the dirt and rocks near the railway line. Her every movement appears fruitless, or at best difficult. There are also shots of the roughness of her work in both workplace and at home (Holdstein 1984).

A rock music video that is an example of the Marxist and socialist feminist perspective is Pat Benatar's song *Love is a Battlefield*, which encapsulates her tough-woman outlook. This video exposes the limitations of the nuclear family, the heroine, portrayed by Pat Benatar herself, is thrown out of her home at the very beginning and reveals a woman's vulnerability in the big city. Ending up as a prostitute/sex worker the heroine nevertheless takes action against the pimp oppressing her friend. The women side with one another, marching bravely out of the brothel to engage in a warlike, threatening dance on the street before they part company and go their separate ways. In this music video dance represents a vehicle for the women's militancy. The women's chest thrusts and kicks combine a wild sexual energy with self-defence moves to mock and threaten the pimp figure (Kaplan 1988:148).

Other television and film examples with regard to *class, gender* and *race* include the following:

## Class

In our local soap opera *Generations*, currently on SABC1, Archie Moroka, the Managing Director of New Horizons, an advertising company, lives in a mansion in an élite suburb, and is admired by everyone in the advertising world and society. On the other hand, Margaret Mashele lives in a squatter camp in poor conditions. Her link to Archie is that they have an illegitimate daughter conceived during their teenage years, and do not belong to the same social milieu or class system. Other women in *Generations*, for example Ntsiki, Queen, Zinzi and Zoleka all want to marry Archie (after all he is a Moroka) because of his status, *class* and money. Zinzi, Zoleka's twin sister (Archie chose to marry Zoleka) is even prepared to compromise her relationship with her sister to get Archie.

Another example of the representation of *class* in a television text is an episode from the American situation comedy, *The Golden Girls*. This situation comedy is about the interactions of four well-to-do divorced or widowed women living together in a house in Florida in the United States. In one particular episode, the women, Dorothy, Sophia

# Feminist Media Theory

(Dorothy's mother), Rose and Blanche compete for the attention of a doctor. This episode focuses on Doctor Clayton Elliott, an eligible divorcé, who makes a house-call to check on Sophia. The women flirt openly with him and are almost willing to sacrifice their friendship over such a "catch". The fact that he is a doctor implies the desirability of a certain gradational class.

An analysis of the American situation comedy, *Frasier* reveals that women are portrayed in a negative light with regard to class and professional capabilities. The main characters, Doctors Frasier and Niles Crane are both psychiatrists. Their father is a retired police officer. The main female characters are Ros and Daphne. Ros is an unmarried mother who holds a mediocre job at a radio station where her position is not prestigious or at management level; Daphne is the father's nurse and occupies a general housekeeper's position. Daphne is the object of the affections of Dr Niles Crane who is besotted with her. She is slim and pretty and although not very intelligent she retains his interest and admiration.

In the film *Titanic* (1997) the so-called lower class and the upper class do not mix. People belonging to the upper class "well-dressed ladies and gentlemen" are placed above the deck of the boat and have luxurious cabins as well as the best of food and entertainment. Those belonging to the lower class are put below the deck of the boat, in shabby sleeping quarters with meagre food and no entertainment.

## Gender

The representation of *gender* can be seen in *The Simpsons* currently on M-Net. In this cartoon series, Bart Simpson's mother (Marge) is portrayed as the subservient wife who does not work but looks after the home and the children. Bart Simpson's father (Homer) is the breadwinner and the dominant figure in this show. *The Simpsons* therefore creates the outdated stereotype of a mother who does not work but merely runs the home and looks after the children, while the father is the partriarchal, powerful figure who supports his family.

A further example of the representation of *gender* comes to the fore in our local soap opera *Generations*, where Karabo who is married to Mandla is dominated by him. He tells her what to wear, she is not allowed to wear revealing clothes (but must appear in baggy clothing) because men might be attracted to her beautiful body. She is also not allowed to use any facial make-up. Karabo wants to register for a course in psychology to stimulate her intellectual capacity, however Mandla strongly disapproves of this.

## Race

The representation of *race* in a television text was seen in the South African sitcom *Suburban Bliss*, where Thando was portrayed as a muddle-headed bimbo, continually being put down by her neighbours and mother-in-law. Her tight-fitting clothing was stereotypical of a feather-headed woman, and her ambitions and attempts at building a career as a black woman were nullified, while the males in the show were the breadwinners and in charge of all situations.

The race issue is also evident in the American sitcom *Dhama and Greg*. Greg's mother Kitty is a pompous socialite who treats her Hispanic maid as though she were stupid and inferior, when in fact *she* runs the home and knows more about the family's affairs and secrets than Kitty does.

Another example of the portrayal of *race* on television is in the local soap opera *Generations* where Ntsiki a domestic worker sleeps with her employer's son Simon Rossouw, a white man. Ntsiki falls pregnant and tells her employers who decide to fire her. They give her a sum of money based on an agreement that she should disappear. On the other hand, Simon is prepared to accept his child and agrees to go for a blood test. Furthermore, in yet another local soap opera *Isidingo – The Need* currently on SABC3, evidence of the race issue is portrayed. Derek Nyati a black man is raised and adopted by a white woman who provides him with everything he wants, such as a private school education. Derek is also voted in as mine manager at The Deep, a position formerly held by Pierre de Villiers (a white man). However he is told that his biological parents were no good, especially his father who was an alcoholic. This leaves Derek hostile towards his black parents.

In a recent First National Bank advertisement on SABC TV a white woman is advised by a black woman to place her crying and irritated baby on her back. She takes the black woman's advice and after putting her baby on her back, the baby stops crying, much to the amusement of the black woman. Yet another illustration of the issue of racial interaction.

## 12.5 RADICAL FEMINISM: A THEORETICAL PERSPECTIVE

One of the first radical feminists to insist that the roots of women's oppression are buried in patriarchy's sex/gender system was Kate Millet. In her book *Sexual politics* (1970) she argues that sex is political because the male-female relationship is the paradigm for all *power* relationships.

To eliminate male control, men and women have to eliminate gender, specifically sexual status and role constructed under patriarchy. Patriarchal ideology exaggerates biological differences between men and women, ensuring that men always have the dominant or masculine roles and women always the subordinate or feminine ones. Arguments which treat biology as fundamental and which play down socialisation have been used mainly by men to keep women "in their place". Millett (1970) suggests an *androgynous* future (that is an integration of separate masculine and feminine subcultures), however she insisted that this integration must evaluate the desirability of all masculine and feminine traits. For instance, *obedience* should not necessarily be celebrated as a desirable feminine trait, and *aggressiveness* not necessarily viewed as a desirable masculine trait. Furthermore, *androgyny* (from the Greek *andros* meaning 'male' and *gune* 'woman') is not a physical state, and does not refer to the sexual orientation of a person, but ascribes a socio-psychological state or the gender integration of a person (cf. Du Preez 1996:3).

# Feminist Media Theory

The origins of radical feminism are also linked to Simone de Beauvoir's *The second sex* (1952) in her description of man as *Subject* and woman as *Other*. De Beauvoir (1952) documents her argument with the notion that women have been made inferiors and their oppression has been compounded by men's belief that women are inferiors by nature. Radical feminism assumes that men and women are born with different natures and use the term *patriarchy* to include all the ways that men dominate women. According to radical feminists, women were historically the first oppressed group; women's oppression is the most widespread in most societies; women's oppression cannot be removed by the abolition of class; women's oppression causes the most suffering to its victims both quantitatively and qualitatively; and women's oppression provides a model for understanding all other forms of oppression (Tong 1992).

Radical feminism thus assumes biologically inborn differences between the sexes and is less concerned with explaining the origins of women's devaluation than with promoting radical alternatives. Radical feminists argue that separatism and women's need to constitute a separate class, culture and their own language forms and meanings offers a solution (Gledhill 1999). Furthermore, radical feminism assumes that control over women's reproductive processes is the major factor for sustaining *patriarchy*. There are radical feminists who support a biological revolution, for instance, the necessity for women to become lesbians or to establish sperm banks to free themselves from male oppression, or even to practice celibacy (Hinds1997).

However, radical feminists have been criticised for the following reasons:

- conceiving of biology as unchanging and fixed; for example sex differentiation is sometimes minimal in some social groups where women are tall, broad-shouldered and narrow-hipped
- their identification with lesbianism and a refusal to have anything to do with heterosexuality
- their opposition to male culture thereby defining *that* culture as the norm from which to deviate
- radical feminism's association with abortion and the dissolution of the nuclear family

In conclusion, although radical feminism is not a feminist perspective without flaws, feminists owe much to it, in that if it were not for radical feminists we would have been slow to understand the connections between not only pornography, prostitution, rape and sexual harassment, but also between contraception, abortion and artificial insemination by donor. Radical feminists have shown us how women's bodies can be used by men against women, and also how to celebrate women's nature.

## 12.5.1 Radical feminism and film and television criticism

Radical feminists are of the opinion that research on women in film and television should be carried out exclusively by women and advocate subjective approaches, such as interviewing, participant observation and qualitative interpretation. Because radical feminists seek separatism from male dominance, the implication is that, for instance, in terms of feminist television criticism separate television stations, controlled by women executives and producers with content written by and aimed at female audiences, should be established. It is interesting to note that Oprah Winfrey has teamed up with two top female executives to launch *Oxygen*, a cable television channel aimed at making television by women for women. This channel is testament to the growing power of women in the American media, not only as consumers but also as creators. The channel deals with issues facing career women and includes female oriented shows like *Cybill* and *Grace under Fire* (Oprah to make TV for women ... 1998:20).

With regard to television, in the sitcom *Friends* currently on M-Net, the fact that Monica and Rachel share an apartment is almost representative of the separatism from men that radical feminists advocate. Lesbianism is also regarded as a solution to patriarchy. In *Friends*, Ross's first wife lives with her lesbian lover and they are raising a child together. In another American sitcom *Ellen*, the actress Ellen de Generes, who "came out of the closet" and admitted that she is a lesbian, featured her girlfriend, at the time, as her lover on the show; a move in the right direction by radical feminist standards. Furthermore, the Felicia Mabuza-Suttle talk show on e.tv has devoted an entire programme to lesbians as a marginalised group in South Africa.

The following examples from films illustrate the perspective of radical feminism.

- *Fried Green Tomatoes at the WhistleStop Café* (1991): the story of an enduring friendship between two women played by Mary Louise Parker and Mary Stuart Masterton, which spans the decades and overcomes murder and revenge, ultimately developing into a love affair.
- *The Color Purple* (1985): directed by Stephen Spielberg, this film focuses on the plight of women in the African-American community. An abused woman, Celie, played by Whoopi Goldberg, gradually emancipates herself through her friendship and love affair with the worldly woman Shrug.
- *G I Jane* (1997): directed by Ridley Scott, with Demi Moore and Anne Bancroft uses aspects of radical feminism because it shows the heroine, played by Demi Moore, taking on a role in a sacred male realm – a position in the American Navy Seals.
- *Tank Girl* (1995): also shows a woman taking on a military role, although in a more tongue-in-cheek fashion. In contrast to *G I Jane*, the heroine does not try and prove herself in the male-dominated military hierarchy. Instead, she steals one of its most powerful weapons – a tank – to use against the military. The tank is a phallic symbol; its theft reinforces our perception of the heroine as an independent female rebel who appropriates the male trappings of power as she sees fit. This is emphasised by the way in which she "feminises" the tank itself by colourful decoration as a spoof on stereotypical aesthetic tastes.

## 12.6 PSYCHOANALYTICAL FEMINISM: A THEORETICAL PERSPECTIVE

Psychoanalysis offers a universal theory of the "psychic construction of gender on the basis of repression" (Weedon 1997:42). In doing so it provides a framework within which femininity can be understood with regard to the representation of women in film and television from a psychoanalytical feminist perspective.

When employing psychoanalytical feminism, feminists criticise the psychoanalytical theories of Freud, such as *penis envy* (the notion that women are inferior because they lack a penis, which is responsible for their castration complex) and Lacan's post-structuralist reading of Freud (the *phallus as a symbol of desire*) to analyse the patriarchal, cultural and psychoanalytical meaning of films and television texts. However, in Lacan's rewriting of Freud it is not the penis per se that is dominant, "but the social and cultural power it represents, the phallus" (Van Zoonen, 1994:22; Brown 1990). Psychoanalytical feminists are angered by Freudian theory because they argue that penis envy depicts an unflattering portrait of women, in that women's social position and lack of power in relation to men has little to do with female biology and much to do with the social construction of femininity. According to psychoanalytical feminists, Freud's ideas were shaped by his conservative, Victorian culture. What disturbs them is his biological determinism, in other words "anatomy is destiny" meaning that a woman's gender identity and sexual preference are determined by her lack of a penis and any woman who does not follow nature's course is "abnormal".

A core element of psychoanalytical feminism is the display of women "as a spectacle to be looked at, subjected to the gaze of the male audience" (Van Zoonen 1994:87). Although pornography (which sells the idea that women are sexually available) is the most fundamental component with regard to women's bodies as objects of desire and violence, the depiction of women's bodies as decorative elements, in for example television programmes and advertisements, also show women as a spectacle for voyeuristic pleasure. Laura Mulvey's (1975) article *Visual pleasure and narrative cinema* is considered to be the first document of psychoanalytic film theory and her approach has extended to television advertising and programmes. Mulvey's (1975; 1999) psychoanalytical feminist approach positions the female figure as an *erotic spectacle*. She observes that pleasure in looking has been split between active/male/subject/voyeur, and passive/female/object/spectacle. Her argument is that the film and television viewer is controlled by the *masculine gaze* and involved with the psychoanalytical concepts of *voyeurism* and *fetishism*.

Psychoanalytical feminists have been criticised with regard to film studies and also in terms of psychoanalytical theory in that some feminists view the distinction between *voyeurism* and *fetishism* (the two modes of active looking) as an inadequate theorisation of the male spectator vision. Furthermore, psychoanalytical feminism has been criticised for its "ahistorical nature and its powerless perspective" (Van Zoonen, 1994:92). It is argued that by negating female spectatorship of film and television programmes, psychoanalytical feminist theory collaborates in the patriarchal project by silencing women's experience of cinema and television.

Feminists have used psychoanalysis in television and film criticism in various ways:
- To investigate the oppression of women in the television soap opera as a feminine discourse.

- To research psychoanalysis for a problematisation of the notion of femininity. In other words the gaps within Freudian psychoanalytic theory becomes the site of the missing formulation of female psychical structures. This type of analysis interrogates television and film for subversive moments when television and film's unconscious elements surface in the form of repressed femininity.

### 12.6.1 Psychoanalytical feminism and film and television criticism

Tania Modleski (1997) turns to psychoanalytic theory in order to read resistances in television genres, such as the soap opera. The television soap opera is the one visual narrative form that is uniquely adapted to the woman in the home. It is in the soap opera that ideological patriarchal figures come to the fore. Men are elevated as authoritative figures, and while women may pursue a career, it is often of secondary importance when compared to their home life. The emphasis on, for example, the reading of facial expressions in close-up shots frequently establishes the *Other* as an ideal mother whose sympathies reach out to all her children. There is one exception to this – the character of the villainess; consider Alexis Carrington in *Dynasty*. Alexis is the most autonomous woman in this soap opera, who provides an outlet for feminine anger. The narrative form of the soap opera invents pleasure in the central pleasure of women's lives: waiting. Soap operas inform us about women's fantasies, the most powerful one being that of the nuclear family as a self-sufficient unit.

Another example of a television show in terms of psychoanalytic feminism is *Baywatch*. This programme is an excellent example of woman as Object of the male gaze. The significant women in *Baywatch* are sexy lifeguards who are mostly clad only in swimming costumes. A familiar and regular part of the show is the drama of the sea rescue. The women are portrayed running towards the sea in slow motion, with breasts bouncing and long hair swinging. They enter the sea and perform the rescue only to emerge again giving mouth-to-mouth resuscitation to a lucky man. The male lifeguards perform similar feats but this can be described as tokenism. The show displays patriarchy with its benevolent father figure in the form of Mitch Buchanan (played by David Hasselhoff). Even its symbols are highly significant. For example, the satisfaction of the oral urge is evident in the portrayal of ample breasts and mouth-to-mouth resuscitation. The female lifeguards are often depicted as obsessed with the males in their lives. They even fight over men; the ultimate male fantasy.

As far as film is concerned, the following case study of the film *The Piano* illustrates the psychoanalytical feminist perspective. Jane Campion's film stars the following actresses and actors: Holly Hunter as Ada; Anna Paquin as Flora, Ada's daughter; Sam Neill as Stewart, Ada's arranged husband; and Harvey Keitel as Baines. Briefly, the film is about Ada, a deaf woman, and her daughter Flora, who move to New Zealand from their native Scotland as Ada's father has pre-arranged a marriage for her to a man she has never met, Stewart. Baines is an employee of Stewart and he falls in love with Ada.

# Feminist Media Theory

**Case study 12.1:** *The Piano* (1993)

*Source:* adapted from Nelmes 1999:299–303

Jane Campion is one of the few woman directors who could justifiably be called an *auteur* director. Her early work, in particular *An Angel at my table* (1987) and *Sweetie* (1989) brought Campion's "unusual and darkly humorous films to the attention of an art house audience" (Nelmes 1999:299). It was *The Piano* (1993) though a complex, poetic film, that received international attention, gaining a number of Oscar nominations and receiving Oscars for the Best Script (Jane Campion), Best Actress (Holly Hunter) and Best Supporting Actress (Anna Paquin).

*The Piano* portrays the experiences of Ada, a deaf and dumb woman who migrates to New Zealand from Scotland with her daughter Flora. Ada's father has arranged her marriage to Stewart, a man she has never met. Ada brings her beloved piano to New Zealand, which causes conflict and tension with her new husband. An employee of Stewart, Baines shows sympathy for Ada's predicament. Ada falls in love with Baines and they eventually have a passionate affair. Ada is stubborn and wilful, yet desired by two men who try to control her. The element of control is evident at the film's climax when Stewart (her husband) severs Ada's finger with an axe in a "symbolic gesture that suggests castration" (op cit:300). Yet Ada's deafness and dumbness makes it "difficult for us to identify with her as a truly romantic heroine" (ibid). Her piano is seen as an extension of herself, which in turn becomes a fetished object of desire.

On one level the film recounts the tale of a woman at the mercy of a patriarchal society in which she has little power. Ada is forced into an arranged marriage by her father, treated as an *object* by her husband and is initially seen as a prostitute by Baines, however it is Baines who is able to transfer the relationship from one of power to one of compassion and tenderness.

"Many aspects of the film represent the female as strong-willed and powerful. Ada is determined and obstinate, even though she loses a finger, because she insists on continuing to see Baines. Flora is a replica of her mother, also feisty and determined" (ibid). Gender roles in *The Piano* are strongly defined by clothing. "Ada is shown in tight-fitting tops and waist-clenching dresses, emphasising not only how tiny and delicate she is, but also her sexuality. The whiteness of Ada's skin is contrasted by the dark clothing that she wears; her Victorian clothing seems impractical and absurd in the New Zealand climate, yet Ada often looks comfortable in her dress as opposed to her husband whose tight-fitting clothing makes him seem stiff. Baines, in contrast, is at home in this environment and his dress is loose and casual, which also reflects a shifting of his European values" (ibid). The Maoris are shown dressed in a mix of male and female clothing suggesting an ambivalence regarding their gender roles.

"Ada's underwear becomes an object of fascination for the audience and fetishisation for Baines. We frequently see Ada in petticoats and underwear, whilst playing with Flora, but especially so in her relationship with Baines" (ibid). Jane Campion undercuts conventional audience expectations of gender in her development of the relationship between Ada and Baines; "it is Baines's removal of his clothing that is startling for both the audience and for Ada who has been placed in a vulnerable, feminine position" (ibid). Ada is confronted by Baines's naked body and we see this sequence from her point of view; "we cut to a reaction shot which is at first startling, but she does not look away, in fact her eyes suggest a downward look. In this case the *gaze*, or look is not male but female" (ibid).

The act of looking, the *gaze*, takes on a complex relationship. "A key sequence that depicts this is when the relationship of Ada and Baines changes to one of mutual attraction" (op cit:301). Firstly Flora spies on the couple and this changes her relationship with her mother, an element of jealousy is brought in, but the scene also moves Flora into a new sphere; she is a *voyeur* "made aware of her mother's sexuality" (ibid). In a later scene Stewart spies on Ada and Baines making love and stays there as a *voyeur* clearly aroused by what he sees, however the scene also reflects his impotence and ineffectualness.

A later sequence reverses the traditional function of the look as instrument of the male *gaze*.

When Ada is in bed with Stewart she touches and strokes his body down to his buttocks. It is unusual in film for the male body to be explored and eroticised in this way. Stewart is bathed in a warm light and has a passive position forced upon him by Ada; when he attempts to be active, Ada rejects him.

"By the final stage of the film Ada's life has affected us so deeply (the gradual building up of empathy with Ada has been subtly woven into the film) that when the final confrontation between her and Stewart occurs we are almost as traumatised as Ada by what happens. Stewart's retribution is terrible and can be seen as a symbol of phallic dismemberment" (ibid). Stewart's aim is thus to control Ada's sexuality and spirit. In this sequence, we continually have reaction shots of Ada and suffer with her. She seems to shrink before us as she falls to the ground, punished for her transgression. Stewart has now taken on the role of the evil persecutor and the axe can be seen as a symbol of "phallic destruction" (ibid).

The landscape in this film is used to inform us about the people in the film and their characters. "The boggy undergrowth which Ada finds difficult to move in, suggests her inability to escape; she is trapped" (ibid). The forest is the limit of Ada's horizon's. She lives in a dense forest, paralleling a wild wood folk tale. Stewart's world is surrounded by grey, "half-dead tree trunks" (op cit:302). He is referred to as "old dry balls" by the Maoris and the contrasting landscapes in reference to Stewart and Baine emphasises Stewart's "impotence and inability to give love" (ibid); Baines, although living in a hut, is associated with a lush and verdant part of the forest with which he is at ease.

Ada seems to represent Western femininity in contrast with the Maori women who are coarse and loud, making lewd suggestions to Baines. Yet Ada, by her association with Baines, is different. She is able to blend in to the woods wearing garments which seem to take on the same hues of blue and green which predominate throughout the film. It could be argued that Jane Campion uses stereotypes of the "Maoris as noble natives, natural and easily able to express their sexuality, so giving a rather superficial look at the Maoris who are seen in terms of civilised versus uncivilised" (ibid).

An interesting aspect of the film is the mother-daughter relationship. The two are shown in tight, claustrophobic shots and there is a sense of "Oedipal jealousy" (op cit:303); for instance Flora is in her mother's bed whenever Stewart visits. Flora chooses the path to Stewart rather than take the piano key inscribed with words of love from Ada to Baines. Ada in fact uses her daughter as a go-between and the mother-daughter relationship is changed. In the final stages of the film, the piano has become a tie with the past and in a symbolic gesture, when Ada is on the boat with Baines and Flora, she insists the piano be thrown overboard. We think the film will end on this tragic note, however Ada releases herself and her voice-over tells us "my will has chosen life". Yet the life she has chosen with Baines (Ada will work as a piano teacher), does not seem convincing or satisfactory for women as Ada is now dominated and possessed by Baines.

*The Piano* is an exploration of sexuality and especially female sexuality. "Patriarchal filmic conventions are reversed in showing a heroine who often has control of the look, the woman is at times *subject* rather than *object*, and often it is the male who is the object of the female gaze" (ibid).

## 12.7 POSTMODERN FEMINISM: A THEORETICAL PERSPECTIVE

Feminism and post-structuralism is not discussed in this unit because post-structuralist feminism is frequently linked to *postmodern feminism* (Weedon 1997:170). Postmodern feminists reject the traditional assumptions of truth, knowledge, and power, which they believe are centred on an *absolute* male style, thus disregarding a transformative gender dimension. Postmodern feminists have criticised many general theories for their failure to see gender as a fundamental category, consisting of individuals and social relations. Postmodern feminists suggest that the criteria which theories use to establish what is "true" and "false", what is "good" or "bad" are not universal and objective. They are, instead, internal to the structures of the discourses themselves, and thus historical and subject to change. Taking this further, postmodern feminists have argued that these discourses are both *androcentric* and *Eurocentric* (Weedon 1997).

The other crucial area in which postmodern femininist concerns overlap, is subjectivity. Postmodern feminists have challenged both the nature and privileged status of the reasoning subject in the West. If Western thought has been seen as the primary human faculty which is able to transcend the limitations of a particular time and place, view the world objectively and access *true knowledge*, postmodernism suggests that reason is partial and limited. Many feminists have difficulty with the postmodern idea that neither reason or the theories which it produces offer a privileged objective position, beyond the struggle over meaning from which to base universally valid ideas of truth and morality, and the politics which follow from them. Feminists who both support and contest postmodern ideas have argued that the abstract, individual reasoning of Western philosophy is implicitly male, excluding human capacities defined as feminine. Some postmodern feminists reject any label that ends in *ism* including feminism, as they are of the opinion that labels convey the patriarchal drive to organise and rationalise the way in which we see the world.

Generally speaking, postmodern feminism is known as *French* feminism. The term itself gained acceptance in the United States, as American feminists came to understand that French writers, such as Helene Cixous, Luce Irigaray and Julia Kristeva had not only their Frenchness in common, but also their philosophical outlook, which was shared by male postmodern philosophers, like Jacques Derrida and Jacques Lacan (Tong 1992).

Common-sense views of subjectivity in the West have tended to repeat humanist assumptions that we are unique, rational, individuals born with a human potential, which given the right environment we can fulfil through education and personal development. The suggestion is that we learn about the world through experience. Experience is authentic, a source of true knowledge, which is expressed in language. Language itself is a *tool* for self-expression. Postmodern feminists have tried to develop ways of seeing feminine *otherness* as a site of resistance and transformation. A key feature of postmodern feminism is its decentring of singular centralised notions of power.

Many white feminist critics of postmodern theory claim that the Western discourses of subjectivity, historical progress and emancipation are essential to feminism. They argue that postmodernism in contesting Enlightenment discourses of subjectivity, historical progress and emancipation are essential to feminism. On the other hand, postmodern feminists stress that Enlightenment assumptions and values express the needs of white privileged Western men who have enlightenment and can afford to be critical.

Postmodern feminists maintain that it is important to recognise the nature and limitations of the *essentialist* foundations of many forms of identity politics. Feminist objections to postmodernism often rest on the assumption that to question the Western enlightenment category of the *subject* is to undermine the possibility of subjecthood. The African-American feminist critic, bell hooks (her preference to use lower case) (1991) suggests that while the critiques of subjectivity cause problems for black identity politics, it can also be liberating. hooks (1991) is of the opinion that criticisms in postmodern thinking (the critique of essentialism encouraged by postmodern thought) is useful for African-Americans concerned with reformulating outdated notions of identity. According to hooks (1991:28), we have too long had imposed on us from both outside and inside, a narrow, constricting notion of *blackness*. Postmodern critiques of essentialism which challenge notions of universality within mass culture can open up new possibilities for the construction of self.

Furthermore, hooks (1991:26) argues that postmodern theory does not merely seek to appropriate the experience of *Otherness* or to be radically *chic*, and should not separate the politics of *diversity* from the politics of *racism*. Differences in patriarchal and racist societies have always involved oppressive power relations. The need for *media texts* that are non-universal and allow for cultural and historical specificness is apparent from Third World feminism as it has developed in the United States, which brings together women from so-called Third World or developing nations, and also minority groups and people of colour living in First World countries.

The invoking of Western feminist theories, for example liberal or Marxist feminism as general theories of historical progress often leads to a denial of the specificity of black and Third World women's interests. The assertion by white critics of postmodern theory that feminism stands on Enlightenment ground is not without political consequences. Such critics assume that feminist politics is impossible from within postmodern perspectives since feminism depends on a unified notion of the social *subject woman*; a notion that postmodernism would attack.

While postmodern feminists reject essentialising theories they continue to use theory in the interests of transforming oppressive social relationships. In their view, theories have no guarantee in *truth* or *reality* but a strategic status. Postmodern feminists use categories like gender, class and race in social and cultural analyses, but on the assumption that their meaning is plural, historically and socially specific. They argue that the questioning of the possibility of objectivity and its questioning of universals, provide for theory which can avoid generalising from the experiences of Western, white, heterosexual, middle-class women.

In general, postmodern feminist theory tailors its methods to the task at hand using multiple categories and renouncing the comfort of a single feminist method (Tong 1992; Weedon 1997).

### 12.7.1 Postmodern feminism and film and television criticism

A good example of a film depicting a postmodern feminist perspective is *Thelma and Louise* (1991) with Geena Davis, Susan Sarandon and Brad Pitt, directed by Ridely Scott (a man).

*Thelma and Louise* is a film that explores the intimate bond between two best friends, whose weekend holiday takes an unexpected turn – taking them on an adventure across the United States. Thelma and Louise retaliate against a selfish husband, a boyfriend who will not commit himself, a rapist, a cheating thief and a disgusting truck driver, by using male means like violence. This film thus takes an in-depth look at issues such as marriage, work, independence, female bonding and male chauvinism. Although Thelma and Louise lose the battle in this film, it's ultimate message is their liberation as previously victimised women (Giannetti 1996).

Another example of a film with regard to postmodern feminism is *The Ballad of Little Jo* (1993) directed by Maggie Greenwald. This film tells the true story of a woman, living alone in the old American West, who disguises herself as a man in order to survive, and ends up living her entire life in this way. The film therefore subverts the traditionally male genre of the *Western*, by challenging the idea that gender roles are natural and cannot be changed. Not only does Jo successfully live her whole life in the male role of a sheep farmer, but her secret lover is a Chinese man whom she has taken on as her servant, in order to rescue him from being lynched. His position in the relationship is therefore subordinate, and in his capacity as servant, he performs the traditionally female functions of housekeeper and cook. This raises interesting issues about the relationship between race and gender (Jo is a white woman). The film also has resonances beyond feminism, in that it is an examination of the price that we must pay for personal freedom. (Jo has to hide the fact that she is a woman, and live her life in isolation so as to avoid being detected.)

Postmodern feminism is also linked to "science fiction" films, for example *The Fly* (1986) and *The Terminator* (1984) which represent the collapse of patriarchy and the "master truths" of pre-postmodern Anglo-American culture. In these films the heroes cannot distinguish reality from fantasy and this poses a breakdown between man as *subject* and woman as *object* in that the heroes cease to retain any masculine individuality (Humm 1997).

With regard to postmodern feminist television programmes, *Ally McBeal* directed by David E Kelly focuses on a young, single, female lawyer working for an eccentric firm. Ally is a 28 year-old Ivy League Boston litigator, who never seems in need of the body-concealing clothing that Northeastern American weather often requires. She spends most of her time fantasising about her ex-boyfriend who is married and sits in the next office, and manages to work references into her mangled love life in almost every summation he delivers. She has "fits" in supermarkets when she can't find enough of something she wants, and her life is always in a mess. Feminists have been outraged by this show, because although Ally has a successful career, she is bitterly unhappy since she does not have a man in her life. On the other hand, we could argue that the show realistically portrays the failure of postmodern feminism to enable career women to feel fulfilled without having a relationship with a man.

## 12.8 FEMINISM AND ADVERTISING

> Durer believed that the ideal nude ought to be constructed by taking the face of one body, the breasts of another, the legs of a third, the shoulders of a fourth, the hands of a fifth – and so on. The result would glorify Man. But the exercise presumed a remarkable indifference to who any one person was.
> (Berger 1972:74)

The relationship of male image-makers to the *female body* has a long tradition. By convention, male artists painted female nudes (or semi-nudes) in passive poses facing the spectator. These paintings were generally not available to the public. They were privately commissioned and privately enjoyed. The spectator was invariably male, as was the owner. By owning the painting, the man also "owned" the woman (Davies, Dickey & Stratford 1987:14).

Davies et al (1987:14–27) further states that the conventionalisation and stylisation of the nude, the removal of any characteristics that specify the subject of the painting, is the tradition that informs advertising. Although the models chosen are conventionally beautiful, the images introduced are in fact distortions of reality. They are distorted for precisely the same reasons as in art – to create a vision that accords with a male-defined ideal. For example, a woman is posed in an idealised context that "puts her in her place". In advertisements women succumb, wrapping their mouths around chocolates, ice-creams and coffee cups. They close their eyes and sink into foaming baths. Women either decorate a car bonnet, or photographic and computer techniques strip away blemishes, like grey hair, spots or wrinkles. Her legs may be computer generated to be made to look thinner, her waist smaller and her hair longer. It is interesting to note that the Cameo advertisements, advertising pantyhose for women use male models, as their legs are straighter and usually longer than women's legs. Furthermore, some hundreds even thousands of shots are taken of models, and only one or two are chosen. The use of harsh lighting, soft focus and many other techniques are used to produce "a look". The model herself is depersonalised and dehumanised in the process (Davies et al 1987).

As can be seen, the woman's function after all is to sell a product. Her humanness in advertising is irrelevant, only the look is important; her idealised form to drape over objects on which to hang things. She herself is objectified. She becomes part of the packaging of the product. She is woman made "perfect" in the eyes of man. Everyday we are bombarded by a plethora of these larger-than-life "perfect" images in, for example, glossy magazines, pin-ups, roadside hoardings and television advertisements. We cannot escape this fetished ideal, which is by the very nature of its construction impossible to attain. It is the representation of a male-defined ideal of a woman. Furthermore, a massive act of voyeurism is perpetuated, in that male image-makers (or women image-makers following a male tradition) portray women as objects to be viewed and consumed. We see with their eyes, not our own. As Berger (1972:76) observes:

> Men act and women appear. Men look at women. Women watch themselves being looked at. This determines not only most relations between men and women but also the relation of women to themselves. The surveyor of women in herself is male, the surveyed female. Thus she turns herself into an object and most particularly an object of vision: as sight.

Although these images are often produced to gratify male ego and desire, they are of course frequently designed specifically for a female audience. The extent to which they work is an indication of the extent to which women's minds and bodies have been colonised. Women may know logically that they will never attain a particular look of the *nirvana* promised if they purchase a specific product. However, to such a degree has the fetished ideal been internalised that women still strive, more or less consciously, to come up to scratch. The sub-text beneath it all, the covert function of the depersonalised, idealised female image, is to teach women "to know their place", to make women feel disempowered, inadequate and second-rate (Davies et al 1987).

## 12.9 FEMINISM IN SOUTH AFRICA AND MEDIA RESEARCH

The question now arises: What about the situation in South Africa? During South Africa's history, women have always played a prominent role. For example, think of the courage of the Boer women when imprisoned in concentration camps by the British during the Anglo-Boer War (1899–1902). On 9 August 1956 (now National Women's Day) thousands of women marched on the Union Buildings in Pretoria to protest against the apartheid system, and for equality for women in South Africa. These were women from all walks of life, such as Lilian Ngoyi, Helen Joseph, Dorothy Nyembe and Ray Alexander (Bam 1999:2). The Black Sash (with mainly white women adherents) was formed in 1955 and played a prominent role during the apartheid years in South Africa. These women were often harassed and arrested by the police for their anti-apartheid stance.

In an interview with Ms Zohra Khan (researcher at Gender Links Associates – Southern Africa, which is a southern African association of researchers and trainers committed to giving effect to the Southern African Development Community (SADC) on Gender and Development for the promotion and attainment of gender equality) conducted on 13 October 2000 by Ms L Parry of the Department of Communication (Unisa), the following important points came to the fore:

- Since the ANC (African National Congress) came to power in 1994 the ANC has made significant changes with regard to women's rights, in terms of the establishment of national machinery. An office on the status of women, that is located in the Deputy President's Office, has been established as has a Commission on Gender Equality, a Parliamentary Women's Group, a Committee on improving the status of women, and a Women's Empowerment Unit. In addition to national documents, South Africa has a progressive constitution in terms of the rights to Gender Equality and a number of international agreements that the South African government has signed. Of particular importance is CEDAW (the condemption of the elimination of discrimination of all women). This is an international agreement that the National Party first signed and was ratified by the then Government of National Unity in 1995, committing itself to policies and laws to protect women's rights.

    With regard to the above, the ANC-led government certainly facilitated the whole process in ensuring that gender was placed on the agenda. In addition to this, the ANC Women's League played a particularly prominent role in ensuring that there is a strong national machinery for women's empowerment.
- In terms of black and white South African women we have a particular past where

# Feminist Media Theory

black and white women were subject to very different rights. White women may have suffered as women, but certainly they were of a privileged race. On the other hand, black women were discriminated against both in terms of race and gender, so it is not surprising that black and white women have different views and ideas on what feminism is. The fact that feminism emanates from the West and is a Western construct leads many black women to be sceptical or suspicious of it, and they often see their struggle as a racial one before a gender one. This is quite sad as we now have a democratic society, where race should not be an issue anymore, yet women are still being abused at a different level. There is a general reluctance among black women to adopt a feminist position, but it has changed recently with regard to women realising that feminism is a political and ideological position, and not about a specific political party or race group; it is about being a woman. However, women differ in terms of race, class, geographical location and political affiliation, but this does not mean that women cannot empathise with other women. There is a common denominator and whilst experiences are very different, women can unite in the fact that they often experience similar challenges, problems and issues. Although there may be a shift in black women wanting to call themselves feminists, at present black women prefer to call themselves "womanists". The term "womanist" takes race issues into account as well and sees the intersection of race and gender, which is an interesting perspective. However, in South Africa there is a general lack of understanding of what feminism is. In other African countries, like Kenya and Tanzania for example, especially black women often take on the feminist cause and indigenise it according to their specific needs. This is more so than in South Africa where feminism is more politicised in terms of race than it is in other African countries, because women from further north did not have the same type of race issues to deal with.

- The impact of feminism with regard to culture plays a major role in South Africa. For instance, if we look at the major religions in the world and also in South Africa, many religions allow the subordination of women in society. Culture also plays an important part in women's oppression, as we often hear "it's my culture to do this and not to do that". Take for instance, female genital mutilation and virginity testing. The practice of virginity testing is condoned in that it thwarts HIV infection and also prevents young women from engaging in sexual intercourse. What has been discovered in research is that this practice has unfortunately increased the number of rapes in particular communities. The rationale is that there is a common myth that sleeping with a virgin cures HIV/AIDS. This has resulted in young girls being raped because they are identified in public forums as virgins. For the above reasons, culture can act negatively on feminism in South Africa and on women's rights in general, because to a large degree culture, tradition and religion provide justification for women's oppression.

- With regard to recent studies/research conducted on the way women are portrayed in the media in South Africa, there has been a particularly good piece of research done on Gender and Advertising. It was commissioned by the Commission on Gender Equality and conducted in association with the Gender Studies Unit at the University of KwaZulu-Natal. This research looks specifically at how women are portrayed in television advertisements in South Africa. The findings were generally that where women were thus portrayed, they were stereotypically depicted. For example, women were shown as wives, and mothers. Even when women were portrayed in a business environment they were shown juggling their business role with their home role, for example in the Omo (soap powder) advertisement. Whereas when men were portrayed in advertisements it was done progressively and around particular commodities, such as driving fast cars, much as to suggest that women do not drive cars. Very few men were shown in nurturing roles, such as doing washing or looking after children. A good example of stereotypes is the Ego (deodorant for men) advertisement which shows a man on an island surrounded by women who are skimpily dressed. However, there has been a general shift recently where some men are shown in nurturing roles and some women in powerful roles. Yet, in the main, women are still portrayed on television in a particular way as are men depicted in a specific way in order to maintain the *status quo*. What advertisers need to realise is that many more women have buying power now; most women work and, irrespective of the type of work they do, they thus have access to money.

In terms of further interest in feminist issues, universities and technikons in South Africa offer courses in feminist media studies. Some of the objectives of these courses are to discuss theoretical debates and critical issues in feminist media studies; to sensitise audiences to the gendered nature of the media and media messages; to problematise the role of the mass media in creating, maintaining and perpetuating the oppression of women in society; and to raise the possibilities for alternative readings of media messages.

A major issue currently confronting South Africa is violence against women. Whether of a passive or aggressive nature, violence against women must be exposed and eradicated and women must be given the necessary support to free themselves of this crime so prevalent in our country. How can the media play a role in counteracting violence against women? An example is that of the use of a genre known as "edutainment" which educates through drama and entertainment. This is our local *Soul City*, which although it comprises multimedia communication also presents a 13-episode weekly television drama (currently one hour long) presented on SABC TV. The television series consists of the use of English, and Zulu, Sesotho, Tswana, Afrikaans and Xhosa with English sub-titles. Topics dealt with in the *Soul City* series include strong messages that negate violence against women and attempt to change attitudes towards violence against women. Some of the comments received from women viewers include the following: "I would like to commend the *Soul City* producers for the well-researched and precise depiction of women abuse" and "*Soul City*, I thank you for this liberating social commentary. I am willing to offer support to other women still trapped in abusive relationships" (Usdin 2000:43).

# Summary

Feminist scholarship and film and televsion criticism is an attempt to focus on and illuminate the oppression of women within a patriarchal society. We began this unit by describing the basic assumptions and terrain of feminism. In order to create an awareness of the diversity with regard to feminism, we discussed five feminist theoretical perspectives: liberal feminism, Marxist and socialist feminism, radical feminism, psychoanalytical feminism and postmodern feminism. From our discussion it is evident that a single answer to feminism is precluded by the nature of feminism itself. After each discussion of the five feminist theoretical perspectives we provided you with examples from both film and television which illustrate these perspectives. We also discussed feminism and the role of advertising and concluded the unit with a brief overview of feminism and feminist media criticism in South Africa.

# Research activities

1. Describe in one paragraph the basic assumptions and terrain of feminism.
2. Compare all the feminist theoretical perspectives. Explain the similarities and differences among liberal feminism, Marxist and socialist feminism, radical feminism, psychoanalytical feminism and postmodern feminism. Which theoretical perspective in your opinion is the most suitable for South Africa? Discuss why you think so.
3. Liberal feminist television and film analyses centres on quantitative content analysis, historical and processor studies and effect studies. Give your own examples from either television or film of these three types of analyses.
4. Marxist and socialist feminism television and film analyses focuses on class, gender and race. Provide your own examples from either television or film of how class, gender and race are portrayed.
5. Apply the radical feminist theoretical perspective by giving your own examples from film and television programmes.
6. After you have studied Case study 12.1 answer the following question:
   Describe how Ada, Flora, Stewart and Baines are portrayed in *The Piano* with reference to the following concepts:
   - the Other
   - gaze
   - Subject and Object
   - fetishism
   - voyeurism
7. Critically analyse a film or television programme of your choice in terms of the psychoanalytical feminist perspective.
8. Give your own examples from television and film of the postmodern feminist theoretical perspective.

9 "A woman's function is to sell a product". Critically discuss this statement by referring to examples of how South African women are portrayed in television advertisements.

10 Critically discuss how South African women are depicted on television programmes and film from a feminist theoretical perspective of your choice. Refer to specific examples from television shows or films.

## Further reading

Brunsdon, C, D'Acci, J & Spiegel, L (eds). 1997. *Feminist television criticism.* Oxford: Clarendon.
Dow, BJ. 1996. *Prime-time feminism: television, media culture, and the women's movement since 1970.* Philadelphia: University of Pennsylvania Press.
Humm, M. 1997. *Feminism and film.* Edinburgh: Edinburgh University Press.
Stanley, L (ed). 1997. *Knowing feminisms: on academic borders, territories and tribes.* Thousand Oaks, CA: Sage.
Thornham, S (ed). 1999. *Feminist film theory: a reader.* Edinburgh: Edinburgh University Press.
Van Zoonen, L. 1994. *Feminist media studies.* Thousand Oaks, CA: Sage.

## Bibliography

Althusser, L. 1971. *Lenin and philosophy and other essays.* London: New Left Books.
Bam, B. 1999. Chairperson's address to Unisa Women's Forum on the occasion of the annual
Feroza Adam Memorial Lecture. *Siren News* 7(1):2–7.
Bandura, A. 1977. *Social learning theory.* Englewood Cliffs, NJ: Prentice-Hall.
Berger, P. 1972. *Ways of seeing.* Harmondsworth: Penguin.
Brown, ME. 1990. Introduction: feminist cultural television criticism-culture, theory and practice, in *Television and women's culture,* edited by ME Brown. Sydney: Currency Press.
Davies, K, Dickey, J & Stratford, T (eds). 1987. *Out of focus: writings on women and the media.* London: The Women's Press.
De Beauvoir, S. 1952. *The second sex.* Translated by HM Parshley. New York: Knopf.
De Lauretis, T. 1984. *Alice doesn't: feminism, semiotics, cinema.* Bloomington: Indiana University Press.
Drabman, R, Hammer, D & Jarvie, G. 1976. *Children's perceptions of media-portrayed sex roles across ages.* Jackson: University of Mississippi.
Du Preez, A. 1996. Current feminist debate and androgyny. *Siren News* 4(1):3–4.
Durkin, K. 1984. Children's accounts of sex-role stereotypes in television. *Communication Research* 11(3):341–362.
Engels, F. 1985. *The origin of the family, private property and the state.* Middlesex: Penguin.
Feuer, J. 1984. Melodrama, serial form and television today. *Screen* 25(1):4–16.
Giannetti, L. 1996. *Understanding movies.* 7th edition. New Jersey: Prentice-Hall.
Gledhill, C. 1985. *Home is where the heart is: studies, in melodrama and the woman's film.* London: BFI.
Gledhill, C. 1999. Pleasurable negotiations, in *Feminist film theory,* edited by S Thornham. Edinburgh: Edinburgh University Press.
Hinds, H. 1997. Fruit investigations: the case of the successful lesbian text, in *Feminist television criticism,* edited by C Brunsdon, J D'Acci & L Spiegel. Oxford: Clarendon Press.
Holdstein, DH. 1984. Music video messages and structures. *Jump Cut* 29:1–13.

hooks, bell. 1991. *Yearning, race, gender and cultural politics.* Boston, MA: South End Press.
Humm, M. 1997. *Feminism and film.* Edinburgh: Edinburgh University Press.
Jaggar, AM. 1983. *Feminist politics and human nature.* Sussex: Harvester Press.
Kaplan, EA. 1988. *Women and film: both sides of the camera.* London: Methuen.
Khan, Z. Interview conducted by Ms L Parry on feminism in South Africa, 13 October 2000.
Kohlberg, L. 1966. *A cognitive developmental analysis of sex-role concepts and attitudes.* Stanford: CA: Stanford.
McNeil, JC. 1975. Feminism, femininity and the television series: a content analysis. *Journal of Broadcasting* 19(3):259-271.
Millett, K. 1971. *Sexual politics.* New York: Avon Books.
Modleski, T. 1997. The search for tomorrow in today's soap operas, in *Feminist television criticism,* edited by C Brunsdon, J D'Acci & L Spiegel. Oxford: Clarendon Press.
Mulvey, L. 1975. Visual pleasure and narrative cinema. *Screen* 16(3):6-18.
Mulvey, L. 1999. Visual pleasure and narrative cinema, in *Feminist film theory,* edited by S Thornham. Edinburgh: Edinburgh University Press.
Mumford, CS. 1998. *Love and ideology in the afternoon: soap opera, women and television genre.* Bloomington: Indiana University Press.
Myers, KA, Anderson, CD & Risman, BJ (eds). 1998. *Feminist foundations.* Thousand Oaks, CA: Sage.
Nelmes, J. 1999. *An introduction to film studies.* 2nd edition. London: Routledge.
Oprah to make TV for women, by women. *Saturday Star,* 28 November 1998:20.
Parry, L. 1991. Feminist criticism and television analysis, in *Critical television analysis: an introduction,* edited by PJ Fourie. Cape Town: Juta.
Smith, C, Fredin, ES & Nardone, CAF. 1989. Television: sex discrimination in the TV newsroom – perception and reality, in *Women in mass communication: challenging gender values,* edited by PJ Creedon. Newbury Park: Sage.
Smith, S, 1999. The image of women in film: some suggestions for future research, in *Feminist film theory,* edited by S Thornham. Edinburgh: Edinburgh University Press.
Steeves, HL. 1987. Feminist theories and media studies. *Critical Studies in Mass Communication* (4)2:95-135.
Tong, R. 1992. *Feminist thought: a comprehensive introduction.* London: Westview Press.
Usdin, S. 2000. Intercultural, development and health communication ["Intercultural" section by Parry, L], in *Only study guide for COM 204-8.* Pretoria: University of South Africa:43.
Van Zoonen, L. 1994. *Feminist media studies.* Thousand Oaks, CA: Sage.
Weedon, C. 1997. *Feminist practice and poststructuralist theory.* 2nd edition. Oxford: Blackwell.

# Part C
# Critical Media Issues

**Unit 13**
Media Imperialism: The New World Information and Communication Order

**Unit 14**
A Critical Assessment of News

**Unit 15**
Representation: Race, Gender and Sexual Orientation

**Unit 16**
Media and Violence

**Unit 17**
Media and Terrorism

**Unit 18**
Censorship and the Media

**Unit 19**
Globalisation, the Information Superhighway and Development

# 13

# Media Imperialism: The New World Information and Communication Order

*Pieter J Fourie & Lucas M Oosthuizen*

## Overview

In this unit we focus on the origin and premises of the New World Information and Communication Order (NWICO). We consider

- the liberal and structuralist schools of thought about the NWICO;
- key documents of the NWICO;
- criticism against the NWICO;
- South Africa and NWICO issues; and
- the future of a new world information order against the background of the development of information and communication technology.

## Learning outcomes

After completing this unit you should be able to write an article about, do analyses of and debate the following topics:

- the basic concerns and premises of NWICO;
- what the democratisation of communication means within a development context
- why the United Nation's Universal Declaration of Human Rights gave impetus to the formulation of the NWICO;
- inequities in the arena of international communication;
- the liberal and structuralist approaches to the issues of the NWICO;
- why UNESCO's Media Declaration was criticised and seen by the liberal school as Marxist inspired;
- the recommendations of the MacBride Report (1980);
- USA's position on the NWICO;
- the future of the NWICO debate;
- the parallels between the apartheid government and the African National Congress' (ANC) views about the role of the media and how this corresponds with Third World claims in the NWICO about media reporting;

- follow the debate between the South African media and the ANC about the role of the media in society (or between the media and the government in the country where you reside);
- do a basic comparative content analysis of news about developing countries in two newspapers of your choice;
- do an analysis of the programme schedules of two international radio or television stations; and
- formulate your own conclusions about the future of the NWICO against the background of the development of information and communication technology (ICT).

## 13.1 INTRODUCTION

People often complain that everything on television is American, or that the bulk of television programming tends towards Americanisation. When we watch international television news channels such as CNN or BBC World, or if we watch television in a foreign country, we seldom see news about South Africa or Africa. If so, the news is seldom positive. It tends to focus on disasters, corruption, crime, and so on.

Complaints like these from developing countries have led to the formulation of the New World Information and Communication Order (NWICO). Its purpose is to address matters related to

- the imbalanced international flow of news, information and media entertainment;
- inequities in the arena of international communication; and
- the crucial role of communication in economic and social development.

In short, during the 1970s and 1980s the NWICO arose as a direct response to what is called media imperialism, a concept closely related to the concept cultural imperialism.

By media imperialism we mean the domination of mainly the Western capitalist media in the arena of international communication. Watson and Hill (1984:103) argue that crucial to the notion of media imperialism is the understanding of the relationship between economic, territorial, cultural and international factors.

In the nineteenth century, during the age of territorial and economic colonialism, the flow of information was a vital process of growth and reinforcement for the colonists. Apart from reinforcing their economic and military powers in colonised countries, they also needed to establish their own political and cultural values. This was done through education and the provision of news, information and entertainment.

Concern grew about Western media penetration as the colonised countries reached independence. In 1972, the General conference of UNESCO (United Nations Education, Scientific and Cultural Organisation) drew attention to the way the media of the richer nations of the world were a means towards the domination of world public opinion (cf. Watson & Hill op cit).

This conference was followed by a meeting of heads of state in 1973 in Algiers. At this meeting the non-aligned countries agreed to counteract media imperialism with the promotion of a fairer, more balanced exchange of information, and to release themselves from dependence on the developed countries (or their colonists). In short they agreed about the need to reorganise existing communication channels which were seen to be the legacy of the colonial past. (Non-aligned countries, read in this context developing countries often referred to as Third World countries, compared to developed countries meaning the aligned countries – Western countries, also referred to as First World countries.)

Apart from the view that Western news, information and entertainment values and practices have been dumped on developing countries (and/or ex-colonised countries), a bottom line in the notion of media imperialism is that Western media only report the bad news of what happens in their countries. This constant flow of bad or negative news about developing countries causes serious harm, especially when developing countries are in need of Western financial support and investment.

It was thus agreed that the unequal state of international communication justifies investigation. This was the beginning of the movement towards a new information order, later to be known as the NWICO.

## 13.2 CORNERSTONES OF THE NWICO

### 13.2.1 Communication and democracy

It can be argued that the NWICO is about the democratisation of communication, which relates closely to the democratisation of society. By democratisation of communication we mean:

- that all people should have equal communication rights
- equal opportunities of access to information
- equal opportunities to produce and distribute information
- equal opportunities to use communication for economic and social development.

There are many theories and definitions of democracy and the processes of democratisation.

With the emphasis on the role of communication in democracy, Winseck (1997:344–345) characterises democracy as the historical process of eliminating totalitarianism in the state, civil society and in economic practices. Obviously, communication and access to information and the formation of a strong public opinion about the values of democracy play a crucial role in this process.

Winseck argues that apart from the adoption of democratic political and legal frameworks, democracy also means and involves the processes that allow the procedures of achieving the democratic goals of society to be opened up to citizen participation through public spheres of communication. Democracy requires more than just functionally based institutions and laws equally applicable to all. To live *in* a democracy and to *live* democratically, mean that the adoption of the rules and laws of a society are

- shaped through the means (media) of public communication that are open to all

- directed towards the discovery of public rather than private interests (Winseck op cit).

In other words, it is not enough to say that we have a democratic constitution, a democratically elected government, democratic institutions, and so forth. What is further needed is to continuously debate all those issues in the interest of the public and in the interest of the wellbeing of society through the means of public communication (media).

From the above it is clear that mass communication is central in a democracy and in the processes of democracy.

### 13.2.2 Communication and human rights

Apart from the relationship between democracy and communication as being a cornerstone of the NWICO, a second and closely related cornerstone of the NWICO is the acknowledgement of communication and the right to information as a basic human right. Here we suffice with Article 19 of the United Nation's Universal Declaration of Human Rights (1948). Article 19 reads as follows:

> Everyone has the right to freedom of opinion and expression; this right includes freedom to hold opinions without interference and to seek, receive and impart information and ideas through any media and regardless of frontiers.
> (http://www.un.org/Overview/rights.html)

It can be argued that this Article provided the stimulus for a formalised discussion and investigation of loose arguments and perceptions concerning the inequities of and in international communication.

## 13.3 THE HISTORY OF THE NWICO

The emphasis on the role of communication in democracy and the acknowledgement of communication and information as a basic human right underlie the development of the NWICO and its concerns about the inequalities in the state of international communication. How can we talk about a free and just world if, according to Vincent (1997:378), inequalities in media, such as the following, continue to exist?

- The developing world has only four percent of the world's computers.
- Thirty-four countries of the world have no television sets.
- Africa (in total) has less than three newspapers per country whereas the United States has 1 687 and Japan 125 dailies.
- There are more telephone lines in Tokyo than on the entire African continent.

These figures, to mention a few, emphasise huge communication inequities in the world, especially if we want to argue that communication is crucial for economic and social development and upliftment. The NWICO tried/tries to find answers to inequities such as these as well as to inequities in the production and distribution of media content. As such it could, and ongoing efforts in this regard can be described as a first attempt towards an international communication policy.

### 13.3.1 Basic premises of the NWICO

According to Brown-Syed (1999), the basic premises of the movement for a NWICO were that:
- An imbalance existed in the direction, volume, and types of information exchanged between developed countries and the Third World. In the 1970s and 1980s the world situation was characterised by the dominance of information producing nations (North or centre nations) over those (South or periphery nations) which consume cultural and information products. This is also called the Centre-Periphery situation in international communication (Galtung 1981:165–166).
- The ethical notion that information should be viewed as a shared resource or as a social good rather than as a commodity. In other words, information should be seen as an essential and basic resource for people to develop and function well in a democracy, and not as a product that is primarily produced and distributed for the economic gain of the few who own media.

However, right from the beginning the road towards the establishment of the NWICO was characterised by a struggle between First World and Third World countries. The First World stance was led by the USA and to a lesser extent Britain. Their views about this issue are called the "liberal school of thought". The view held by mainly members of Third World or developing countries is called the "structuralist school". The former is determined by economic considerations; the latter by development needs and ideological considerations.

The labelling of the two schools as "liberal" and "structuralist" comes from Brown-Syed as used in his article "The New World Order and the geopolitics of information" published in 1993 in the journal *LIBRES: Library and Information Science Research*. This article is now also available on the Web and could, at the time of writing (4 December 2000), be accessed at http://www.valinor.purdy.wayne.edu/csyed_libres3.html. Much of the discussion that follows relies on this article.

Brown-Syed (1999) defines "liberal" not as to refer to left of centre politics (as used in the USA), but to refer to a centrist, free enterprise stance (as used in Canada and Europe). By "structuralist" is meant a socialist, social-democratic, and even neo-Marxist stance.

### Two schools, two ideologies

In the structuralist school (cf. Galtung 1981) it is argued that:
- Unprocessed information flows from developing countries to the developed countries of the West or North.
- Information users in the developed countries then interpret, process, and act upon the information they receive from their own news organisations (including their own

journalists) operating in the developing countries. They thus act upon biased information that forms their perceptions of less-developed countries, which in turn affects their responses to political, cultural and economic support.
- At the same time, the biased information is redistributed to less-developed countries that rely on dominant Western news organisations for their information. They are thus bombarded with negative perceptions of themselves.
- Concurrently, dominant news organisations from the West provide less-developed countries with more (positive) information about their own activities, cultures, and politics.
- Besides this, developing countries are dependent on developed countries for the raw materials of the communication industry, in other words equipment, hardware, software, infrastructures, training, and so on.

> Thus, the Third World nations come to be viewed through the eyes of the information interpreters of the developed nations, whose organisations control both the finances and infrastructures of the distribution system, while the developing nations never quite receive the latest information, nor the latitude of interpreting it to their own advantage. As well, in terms of pure volume of information produced and consumed, the developing nations lag far behind.
> (Brown-Syed 1999:3)

According to Brown-Syed (1999:6), Galtung's major contribution to the structuralist model is his "Centre-Periphery" typology. According to this typology, the following:

- Nations at the Centre dominate a feudal network of communication.
- The Centre owns the major news agencies.
- The Centre news takes up a much larger proportion of Periphery news media than vice versa.
- Users in the Periphery come to see with Centre eyes.
(Also see Meyer 1988:10; Galtung 1981:165–166.)

Against the background of the above structuralist model, arguments about the range of problems that had to be addressed by the NWICO included cultural dominance, concentration of media ownership among de facto cartels, transborder data flows controlled by multinational corporations, the effects of tourism and advertising, and the uneven world allocation of radio, satellite, and telecommunication technologies and infrastructures.

The NWICO proposals held that all of these relationships ran counter to the interests of the developing world and threatened their self-determination, sovereignty and economic development.

Although the notion of a revised world information structure would entail the establishment of a "free and balanced flow" of all sorts of cultural, scientific, technical, and financial information, the debate over the NWICO proposals, however, tended to focus on perceived problems with the news media (Brown-Syed 1999:6).

In the liberal school, based on the economic and development theories of Daniel Lerner and Ithiel de Sola Pool, it was/is believed that the system of free enterprise, also in the field of information and entertainment provision, is inherently liberating and would develop of its own accord. Problems related to the provision of information can be adapted to address the problems of developing countries through sufficient attention to education, technology transfer and the development of Third World infrastructures.

The liberal school sees the structuralist school as being Marxist inspired and as an inherent attack on capitalism in which news, information and entertainment are increasingly seen as being economic commodities. Providing developing countries with news, information and entertainment (programmes), as well as the raw material for the development of their own media infrastructures and the production of their own media content, even if this is in the form of co-ownership, can contribute to economic development and cultural and political liberation.

### 13.3.2 The main documents of the NWICO

The difference of opinion between the two schools led to serious conflict between mainly the USA and the non-aligned countries. It is also argued that the eventual adoption of the NWICO was one of the reasons why the USA withdrew from UNESCO (see 13.4). Nevertheless, using UNESCO as their main forum of discussion the non-aligned countries pushed ahead for the adoption of a NWICO.

On 28 November 1978, at the 20th General Conference of UNESCO, held in Paris, UNESCO issued a proclamation calling for the establishment of a New World Information Order. The document on which it was based was the *UNESCO Media Declaration of 1978*.

At the same conference, the International Commission for the Study of Communications Problems, (the MacBride Commission), which had been established by UNESCO in 1976, presented its interim report. The final draft of the MacBride Report was published in 1980. UNESCO's policies toward the media are to be found in both sources, and in attendant documents such as the 1980 Statement on Journalistic Ethics, which was reaffirmed at the 1983 Mexico select committee meeting (Brown-Syed 1999:7). The three crucial documents of the NWICO are thus:

- The UNESCO Media Declaration of 1978
- The UNESCO Statement on Journalistic Ethics (1980/1983)
- The Report of the International Commission for the Study of Communications Problems (the MacBride Commission and the MacBride Report), 1978/1980

The final report of the MacBride Commission (named after and chaired by the former Irish foreign minister, Sean MacBride, and winner of both the Nobel and Lenin prizes) was published under the title *Many Voices, One World*. This document became a standard text in debates concerning international communication issues and in the role of the media in development. Today the work of the MacBride Commission is continued by the MacBride Round Table created in 1989. This is a communications rights advocacy group. It accommodates scholars, activists, journalists and other communications experts devoted to the monitoring of world communication, legal ramifications, and information imbalances. It disseminates its findings to community groups, UN agencies, non-governmental organisations and the news media.

Let us now take a closer look at two of the documents.

## *The UNESCO Media Declaration of 1978*

The full title of this document is:

> Declaration on Fundamental Principles concerning the Contribution of the Mass Media to Strengthening Peace and International Understanding, to the Promotion of Human Rights and to Countering Racialism, *Apartheid* and Incitement to War

In it UNESCO recognises developing countries' demand for the establishment of a new, more just and more effective world information and communication order. This recognition is based on previous resolutions taken by UNESCO related to, amongst others:

- the right to freedom of opinion and expression
- the elimination of all forms of racial discrimination and the punishment of the crime of apartheid (adopted by the General Assembly of the United Nations in 1973)
- the establishment of a new international economic order
- international cultural cooperation, including the moral obligation to seek facts without prejudice and to spread knowledge without malicious intent
- the condemnation of all forms of propaganda which are designed or likely to provoke or encourage any threat to the peace, breach of the peace, or act of aggression
- the proclamation that colonialism, neocolonialism and racialism in all its forms and manifestations are incompatible with the fundamental aims of UNESCO

In its Media Declaration, UNESCO proclaimed that:

- the exercise of freedom of opinion, expression and information, be recognised as an integral part of human rights and fundamental freedom towards the strengthening of peace and international understanding
- access by the public to information should be guaranteed by the diversity of the sources and means of information available to it, thus enabling each individual to check the accuracy of facts and to appraise events objectively
- journalists must have freedom to report and the fullest possible facilities of access to information
- mass media be responsive to concerns of peoples and individuals, thus promoting the participation of the public in the elaboration of information
- mass media throughout the world contribute to promoting human rights, in particular by giving expression to oppressed peoples who struggle against colonialism, neocolonialism, foreign occupation and all forms of racial discrimination and oppression and who are unable to make their voices heard within their own territories

- journalists and other agents of the mass media, in their own country or abroad, be assured of protection guaranteeing them the best conditions for the exercise of their profession
- mass media, by disseminating information on the aims, aspirations, cultures and needs of all peoples, contribute to eliminate ignorance and misunderstanding between peoples, to make nationals of a country sensitive to the needs and desires of others, to ensure the respect of the rights and dignity of all nations, all peoples and all individuals without distinction of race, sex, language, religion or nationality and to draw attention to the great evils which afflict humanity, such as poverty, malnutrition and diseases
- mass media have an essential part to play in the education of young people in a spirit of peace, justice, freedom, mutual respect and understanding
- mass media have an important role to play in making known the views and aspirations of the younger generation
- governments should assure that the mass media have conditions and resources enabling them to gain strength and to expand, and to cooperate both among themselves and with the mass media in developed countries for the establishment of a new equilibrium and greater reciprocity in the flow of information
- mass media contribute effectively to the strengthening of peace and international understanding, to the promotion of human rights, and to the establishment of a more just and equitable international economic order
- professional organisations, and people who participate in the professional training of journalists and other agents of the mass media should attach special importance to the principles of this Declaration when drawing up and ensuring application of their codes of ethics
- the international community contribute to the creation of the conditions for a free flow and wider and more balanced dissemination of information
- bilateral and multilateral exchanges of information among all States, and in particular between those which have different economic and social systems, be encouraged and developed in order to facilitate the procurement by the mass media in the developing countries of adequate conditions and resources enabling them to gain strength and expand.

(At the time of writing (4 December 2000) UNESCO's Media Declaration of 1978 could be found on the Internet at: http://www.unhchr.ch/html/menu3/6/d_media.htm; also available at http://www.unesco.org/webworld/com/compendium/1213.html)

The Declaration was criticised and seen by the liberal school as Marxist inspired. Brown-Syed (1999:8-9) offers the following interpretations of the Declaration:

Although the Declaration appears to be a basically liberal document in its repeated support for human rights, the freedom of the press, and the free flow of information, and although it emphasises the responsibility of the media for education, the maintenance of world peace, and for more equitable distribution of wealth, the Declaration, nevertheless, contains several phrases and terms which could be interpreted

as accusatory of Western foreign policy and attributable to Marxist-Leninist inspiration. For example:
- The call for cultural protectionism carries within it the danger of censorship and monopolisation. Cultural protectionism can easily become the protection of an existing government, or of some special interest within it.
- The Declaration constituted what can be interpreted as calls for the licensing of journalists and for state control of the media. This is in direct opposition to the principles of media freedom and the freedom of expression.
- By linking the NWICO with the NIEO (New International Economic Order), the Media Declaration could be interpreted as demanding a world Socialist distribution of wealth, which is contradictory to the principles of free enterprise and holds within it a threat for private media ownership.
- To implement international protection of journalists, one must have a way of recognising them. The document therefore seems to recommend an international press accreditation scheme which is contradictory to the principles of media freedom and the freedom of expression.
- The Declaration led to fears that procuring resources for the media can mean state procurement of the media themselves and of their privately owned technological infrastructures.

Finally, it was argued, that the Media Declaration only presented a set of broad principles. It did not contain any concrete plan of action or set of regulations.

In short: on face value, the Declaration valued the basic principles of democracy and the role of a free and democratic media. A closer interpretation suggests the possibility of more stringent control of the media and of economic constraints that would hinder the economic development of the media as a free enterprise.

## The MacBride Report

Sean MacBride and his fifteen commissioners were charged with studying and identifying communication problems in society (UNESCO 1980:xvii). The Commission's brief included a mandate to analyse the state of international communication, to study problems related to the free and balanced flow of information, and to analyse communication problems within the perspective of a new international economic order (Galtung & Vincent 1992:85). During the interim report of the Commission tabled at the 1978 UNESCO conference, government intervention through the licensing of journalists was one of the proposals that caused an outcry from many in the West (Galtung & Vincent 1992:86).

In the final report, tabled in Belgrade in 1980, the anti-Western rhetoric was noticeably toned down. The report included a section with recommendations to ensure a new more just and more efficient world information and communication order. What was interesting about this report was that it tried to represent an international compromise on international world communication issues by giving the West as well as the developing countries support for their positions (Emery & Smythe 1986:446; Galtung & Vincent 1992:87).

To counter the imbalance of information, the Commission, for example, suggested the establishment and development of local communication systems in the developing world which would include the formation of strong national news agencies and cooperation between these agencies (UNESCO 1980:255, 269). Other recommendations that articulated the position of the Third World included (UNESCO 1980:253–272):

- using the media and communication for national development
- allotting more space and time in the media of the industrialised world for events in and background material about the developing world
- the right of reply by a country in the case of inaccurate or malicious reporting of international news
- training of foreign journalists in the language, history, culture, and so on, of the country they report from
- provision for more news in the media of developing countries about neighbouring developing countries or such countries in other regions.

In terms of the West, the Commission also reaffirmed international commitment to (UNESCO 1980:263–272):

- freedom of access to news for foreign correspondents (freedom of information)
- freedom of speech and of the press, the right to be informed and the right to participate in public communication
- the extension of the above communication freedoms and rights to a broader individual and collective right to communicate
- the abolition of censorship or arbitrary control of information.

However, the fact that the Commission catered for the positions of both the non-aligned states and the West did little to defuse the tension between the two. The meeting in Belgrade did have a direct positive spin-off for the developing world in the form of the creation of the International Program for the Development of Communication (IPDC), which was charged with implementing many of the objectives of the NWICO. The IPDC concentrated its efforts on four areas, namely assistance, coordination, information and financing of international communication development and the promotion of self-reliance (Galtung & Vincent 1992:88). Most of the projects of the IPDC focused on the cultivation of information flow in the Third World.

Amongst others, the IPDC provided aid for the establishment of some of the regional news agencies and broadcasting organisations in the developing world (including the Pan-African News Agency, Asian-Pacific News Network and Latin American Special Information Services) (Hiebert, Unguraid & Bohn 1988:565; Oosthuizen 1989:23). The USA was instrumental in organising the programme of the IPDC (Emery & Smythe 1986:449).

However, when the IPDC got involved in projects on ideological issues related to government control, the USA voiced its dissatisfaction. This started as early as the

Belgrade Conference itself where the so-called Venezuelan Resolution was adopted. This resolution called for a study of elements that would be part of a NWICO, attempted to create a universal definition of responsible journalism, and sought assistance for the Palestine Liberation Organisation (Galtung & Vincent 1992:88).

## 13.4 REACTION TO THE NEW WORLD INFORMATION ORDER

Western countries – and in particular the USA – had strong reservations about the MacBride proposals in general, and the agenda of the non-aligned states in particular. Apart from the objections mentioned above, let us also look at some of the other main concerns (Emery & Smythe 1986:448–449):

- It was pointed out that such a new order could lead to the sanctioning of existing government restrictions in the Third World.
- Calls for the introduction of codes of conduct, the licensing of journalists, and for greater responsibility by journalists, were seen as transparent attempts to control both national and international press systems and journalists. (The Commission placed the licensing and inter-governmental monitoring of news reporting on an agenda for further study to ensure the protection of journalists (Sussman 1990:340).)
- Countries could not expect a free and balanced flow internationally if they did not support such flows nationally. In some of the Third World countries press freedom was under constant pressure.
- Third World countries were developing their own news agencies – with the help of UNESCO and the international agencies. Most of the inflow of regional and international news was increasingly channelled through these agencies. These agencies were therefore in the position to change or eliminate offensive or unacceptable material before it went out to the mass media of that country. Third World countries could not be regarded as passive recipients of Western communication.
- Denial of access to information and the mistreatment of journalists in some of the Third World countries also made it very difficult to report fully on events in the Third World.

From a more ideological angle, the USA felt that UNESCO, with Soviet and Third World backing, was trying to gain control over the international flow of information and news (Altschull 1984:230–250; Oosthuizen 1989:23). In addition, it was held that the communist countries had, to their own advantage, convinced the Third World of cultural and communication imperialism by the West. Even in some of the African countries, journalists were highly critical of the UNESCO proposals, warning that it would lead to the curtailment of the flow of information. It was claimed that supporters of these proposals wanted to replace one kind of distortion, that of Western dominance and bias, with another based on political bureaucracies (state control) (Mytton 1983:143).

The USA (1984) and Britain (1985) subsequently withdrew from UNESCO. The USA cited trends in the policy, ideological emphasis, budget and management of UNESCO as reasons for their withdrawal (Galtung & Vincent 1992:92).

The USA pointed to the following:
- That UNESCO had been politicised.
- The unacceptable growth of UNESCO's budget ($374,4 million in 1983), a quarter of which came from the USA.
- The growth of the budget was accompanied by the unacceptable growth in the bureaucracy of the organisation.
- The proposals for an NWICO would encourage Third World countries to place restrictions on the Western press and lend support to the idea that governments have the right to control the flow of information in their own interest. As Stevenson (1987:72) pointed out, in its most extreme form the latter would mean that the media of the Third World would be mobilised for political purposes under the flag of national development. Moreover, all governments could be held responsible for the media of their countries. The USA was strongly opposed to government control of the flow of information.

The above remarks do not necessarily represent all the reasons for the American withdrawal from UNESCO (Galtung & Vincent 1992:94–95). However, it did seem to weaken UNESCO's commitment to a NWICO considerably (Lee 1989:75). As Roach (1990:286) shows, the withdrawal of the US from UNESCO did not remove the NWICO debate from the American public agenda. For example, President Reagan, in a speech to the General Assembly of the United Nations in September 1987, said that attempts to control the media and to promote censorship under the ruse of a so-called New World Information Order could not be tolerated.

## 13.5 THE NWICO TODAY

In subsequent years the emphasis of UNESCO's communication programme shifted from the promotion of the NWICO theme to more operational activities, like media training and education. This agenda seems to have been designed to avoid politically sensitive issues (Galtung & Vincent 1992:99). UNESCO's stated policy also moved closer to the position of the USA by reaffirming the organisation's commitment to:
- the promotion of the international free flow of information (not limiting or filtering information); and
- the undertaking to address imbalances by improving the capacity of all countries to communicate (Roach 1990:287–288).

Subsequent research has also started questioning the dominance of news that is dispatched from the big industrialised news services to the developing world (cf. Sussman 1990:341), as well as the effects of First World media programmes on the cultures of people in developing countries (cf. Roach 1990:293–296). Although we can accept that these findings are not necessarily conclusive, they will probably again strengthen the arguments for the promotion of free flow in the international arena.

However, we can concur with Galtung and Vincent (1992), as well as Roach (1990), that the debate about the balance of information is far from over. Economic and political differences between countries and their different national and international interests will probably ensure that it continues.

The NWICO debate has also shown that it is often difficult to overcome these differences and to transform policy into a concrete plan. The NWICO, as one observer remarked, has therefore remained more of a slogan than a plan of action (cf. Galtung & Vincent 1992:99). As Picard (1991:81) indicates, the NWICO was not a unified, well-defined programme for change in communication, but rather a philosophical approach to the role of communication that manifested itself in various international discussions and documents.

Galtung and Vincent (1992:78-104), however, argue that a NWICO could again in future become a reality if the Third World is successful with the implementation of a New International Economic Order (NIEO). If these countries could, for example, agree on better terms of trade between Third World countries, obtain more control over their productive assets (nature, capital, labour, and technology – so that import and export substitution can occur), increase economic interaction among themselves, and obtain more control over world economic institutions, these authors predict that:

- better news ratios for the Third World will follow – more news about the Third World in the First World and less about the First World in the Third
- Third World control over communication assets will increase – in terms of what First World reporters extract from the Third, and in terms of local control over local media
- more news about other Third World countries in their own media and less about the First World will be published
- Third World countries will start exerting control over the First World in terms of the events that should be processed into news, and Third World control over local media will also increase, and
- there will be some Third World control over world communication institutions.

When the NWICO debate was at its height, Galtung and Vincent pointed out that this new order (described above) was already taking shape. They argued that Third World countries have already increased their news coverage of each other substantially over the last thirty years and that the media in former colonies have also decreased their coverage of the former colonial mother countries – a process that continues today (Galtung & Vincent 1992:104-105).

What can we in South Africa, learn from the NWICO debate and issues? To begin with, it is interesting to take note of the historical similarities between the defined *role of the media* under the NWICO and the role ascribed to the media in South Africa by the former National Party government (1948-1990) and the present ANC government since 1994.

## 13.6 SOUTH AFRICA AND THE NWICO: BLAMING THE WATCHDOG CONTINUES

### In the years of Apartheid

When the National Party came to power in 1948, it introduced its policy of apartheid. As international criticism mounted against this policy, the National Party decided that the media was to blame for the Party's bad image overseas. The opposition English press was subsequently severely criticised by party members for taking part in what was described as a slanderous campaign against the, at that stage, Union of South Africa (Hachten & Giffard 1984:52).

Like the NWICO, the government saw the solution to this problem in the control of the press. We present some examples below.

In 1950, when as a member of parliament AJR van Rhyn called on the government to set up a commission to investigate the press (media), he wanted such an inquiry to focus on the monopolistic tendencies in the press, internal and external reporting, and the advisability of control over such reporting. The issue of ownership concerned mainly the position of the English language press. These newspapers were still in the control of English mining capital. As in the case of the non-aligned states later, media control by people who were sympathetic towards the interests of the former colonial power was unacceptable to the new South African government. This government's criticism of the way in which South Africa was reported overseas was similar to that later expressed by the NWICO regarding the international news coverage of their countries.

Van Rhyn, for example, accused "the British and other overseas newspapers of sensationalism, of misrepresenting South African affairs, of misleading people by false reports and also inciting public opinion overseas against South Africa" (Hachten & Giffard 1984:52). In other words, the South African government had a problem with negative international reporting long before the NWICO placed it on the international agenda!

The National Party government's other sources of frustration also included foreign journalists and news agencies. The Minister of External Affairs at the time, Eric Louw, said that much harm had been done by slanderous newspaper reports about South Africa – also quoted in the United Nations as though they were facts. He subsequently called for the deportation of foreign journalists who abused South Africa's hospitality. The then Minister of Post and Telegraphs, Albert Hertzog, had a problem with the local press agency, the South African Press Association (SAPA). He alleged that this agency had a monopoly in the supply of news, which was first passed through London where it was filtered and sometimes twisted (Hachten & Giffard 1984:53).

The issues of applying development criteria and self-regulation when reporting about South Africa, also became part of public debate in this country long before the inception of the NWICO. The then prime minister, DF Malan, during the same debate in 1950, insisted that even in peacetime comment ought to be restrained by patriotism. He lamented the fact that the South African press did not apply self-discipline and pointed out that in countries like the Netherlands journalists were registered and could be struck off the register if they did not adhere to their professional code of conduct (Hachten & Giffard 1984:54). When the Press Commission was officially set up in March 1950, its brief included the investigation of accuracy in the presentation of news in South Africa and abroad, as well as the adequacy of self-control and discipline by the press.

With the inception of this Commission, the government started a process that became the pattern of conflict between itself and the media up to 1990. On numerous occasions when the government came under pressure, it blamed the media and media reporting for its position. In other words, this was in line with the ideas of the NWICO countries about the effect of negative reporting on their countries. JG Strydom, who later became prime minister of the country, thus told a Nationalist rally in August 1954 that the English-language press was writing things that incited the Natives [sic] against the laws of the land. As Prime Minister he elaborated on this statement in 1957 by describing the English-language press as South Africa's greatest enemy. Negative local and international reports about the growing polarisation in the country as a result of the further implementation of apartheid, triggered this outburst (Hachten & Giffard 1984:56).

His successor HF Verwoerd blamed the economic depression in South Africa on the irresponsible and unpatriotic behaviour of the English media. In line with the complaints of the non-aligned states, an analysis of British newspapers by the South African Information Department in the same year purported to show that three quarters of the items published about South Africa concerned negative subjects which created an unfavourable impression on the British media user (Hachten & Giffard 1984:56).

In time, the National Party government moved from criticism of the media, to pressure on the media to institute self-censorship, and eventually also to direct regulation of the media. A taste of things to come followed after the Sharpeville massacre in 1960 when a proclaimed state of emergency restricted reporting about the crisis. By the 1980s South African media were restricted by a plethora of more than a hundred laws that severely restricted news reporting and access to information in the country (Oosthuizen 1989:30–43). The cherry on top was the so-called emergency regulations (Oosthuizen 1989:40–43) which basically placed the dissemination of information concerning the security situation in the country completely under state control.

Earlier threats by the government to restrict the media further had led to the introduction of a self-regulatory Press Council (cf. Hachten & Giffard 1984). The combination of regulation and self-regulation was, of course, in line with the basic ideas of the NWICO regarding control of the media. The South African Government also showed that it was prepared to rectify the imbalance of news about South Africa both locally and abroad. As part of its own propaganda war, the government started *The Citizen* newspaper locally and also tried to buy the *Washington Star* in the USA. These ventures were uncovered during the so-called Information Scandal and were clearly aimed at providing more positive news about the country – and in particular the government – locally and abroad. The admission of foreign journalists into the country was also strictly monitored (Oosthuizen 1989:52–53).

## Media Imperialism: The New World Information and Communication Order

Note must be taken that with references to the media (in general), we actually mean the press as such. The National Party's critique of the media was mainly against the press. Broadcasting during the rule of the National Party was mainly government controlled and in the hands of the public service broadcaster, the SABC (South African Broadcasting Corporation). One of the reasons for the late introduction of television in South Africa (only in the mid-seventies) was exactly related to one of the underlying claims of the advocates of a NWICO, namely that media users in developing countries come to see themselves through the "eyes" of the dominant capitalist Western countries.

In South Africa, government fear was that a powerful medium such as television, which especially in its initial phases relies heavily on foreign programme content, would bring South African viewers in contact with the realities and monstrosities of apartheid and would make them aware of the abnormalities of the South African society under apartheid. Of course, it wasn't worded in such a way. In parliament it was argued that South African's moral and Christian values would be "poisoned" by coming into contact with the permissiveness of Western societies.

The development theory sets out the basic philosophical tenets of the NWICO. The most significant articulation by the South African government of the principles of this theory came in the eighties in the reports of two commissions of inquiry. In 1980 a key recommendation of the Commission of Inquiry into the Reporting of Security News from the South African Defence Force and Police (the first Steyn Commission) called for the formulation of a national communication policy, which in turn would be determined and controlled by the national strategy (Hachten & Giffard 1984:91). The role of the media in relation to the state was very similar to that propagated in the development theory. In the case of conflict between the state and media interests, state interests in terms of national security (in the era of the perceived total onslaught) would be paramount. The Commission's report articulated three additional functions for the media if it was to survive as a free and independent medium of mass communication (Hachten & Giffard 1984:92):

- The media had to censor itself in the reporting of the activities of the state's internal and external enemies as defined by the state – implying the shifting of the press's watchdog role from the state to the enemies of the state.
- It had to sustain and promote a positive image of the state's security and defence agencies.
- Above all, the media had to mobilise public opinion in pursuance of the campaign for total strategy.

These sacrifices were therefore expected to be made in the name of the national interest. The national interest – as in the case of many of the NWICO supporters – coincided with the interests of the government in power that wanted to protect the political *status quo* at all costs. The second Steyn Commission of Inquiry into the Mass Media again articulated these sentiments. In addition, it contained recommendations in its report that were very much in line with the ideas expressed by developing countries during the NWICO debate.

The brief of the second Steyn Commission already implied the expected contribution of the media to the national interest. The Commission was mandated to inquire into and report on the question of whether the conduct of and the handling of matters by the mass media met the needs and interests of the South African community and the demands of the times. Some of the findings of the Commission echoed the critique of the NWICO that was levelled against the Western media in the seventies. In the second chapter of the Commission's report, which deals with the Soviet onslaught, the commissioners quoted from a study by Gann and Duigan that stated that (South Africa. *Report of the Commission of Inquiry into the Mass Media* 1981:74):

> The anti-South African bias of the liberal Western media is emphasised by the extraordinary selectivity that distinguishes their reporting.

The media also give disproportionate weight to the evils, as compared to the benefits, of white rule in South Africa; and to the lack of civil rights for Africans in South Africa as against civil rights violations in the rest of Africa. Although these comments, which were included in the Commission's report, implied that conditions were worse in Africa than in South Africa, the above critique against the Western media was very similar to that expressed by African nations in the NWICO. The commissioners came to the conclusion in this section that (op cit:76):

> The image of South Africa projected in the international and internal arena is deliberately distorted and calculated to present a one-sided and grotesquely negative picture of the government of the day and of the White population as a whole.

In its recommendations, the Commission (op cit:166–169) suggested the professional registration of local and foreign journalists – not unlike the suggestions of supporters of the NWICO before them. In addition, they recommended deregistration of journalists convicted in court of subversive activities. Such journalists would then be legally disqualified from practising as journalists. Qualifications for admission to the profession would be worked out by the profession, the media owners, the government and academics. Fortunately for the media, this recommendation of the Commission was not accepted by the National Party government. The major result of the Commission was the creation of the South African Media Council, which replaced the Press Council in 1983 (Hachten & Giffard 1984:99).

From what we have said so far, it should be fairly obvious that the previous government, particularly in the way it handled the media, had much in common with development theory in general, and with the aims and objectives of the NWICO in particular.

## Under the ANC government

Since 1990 we have seen drastic political changes in South Africa that have led to the liberalisation of the media. The country also elected a Government of National Unity

(GNU) in 1994. The National Party withdrew from the GNU in May 1996, just after the ratification of a new constitution for South Africa. In chapter 2 of the new constitution, a Bill of Rights guarantees freedom of expression. Section 16 stipulates that everyone has the right to freedom of expression, which includes freedom of the press, freedom to receive and impart information and ideas, as well as the freedom of artistic creativity. Although these rights are not unqualified (cf. section 36), the Constitution clearly makes provision for a free media and for the free flow of information (cf. Constitution of the Republic of South Africa, 6 May 1996).

However, it is also clear that, apart from the free flow of information, the new dispensation will also make provision for media development in South Africa. In a document published in 1994 by the senior partner in the GNU, the African National Congress, the party committed itself to the development of a democratic information programme. This initiative, which forms part of the Reconstruction and Development Programme (RDP), is partly in line with the more recent views that were expressed by UNESCO and the USA on media development in the developing world. In section 5.14.4 of the above document, the ANC committed itself to an affirmative action programme to empower communities and individuals from previously disadvantaged sectors of society to set up broadcasting and printing enterprises at a range of levels. The programme would also make provision for training, upgrading and civic education to ensure that communities and individuals recognise and exercise their media rights (African National Congress 1994:133).

In terms of the more recent international developments, the provisions for both the free flow of information and the promotion of media development in South African media policy herald a positive start to what could be termed South Africa's own New Information and Communication Order.

However, at the time of writing (January 2001), the views of the ANC on South African and foreign media performance, and on media control and ownership, became, like those held by the National Party government, increasingly critical of the media and reminiscent of some of the views expressed by supporters of the NWICO. As in the case of the National Party, many of the NWICO claims and premises are used in a disguised form to criticise the media for being too critical of the government. Some examples are the following:

- Government officials and ministers' increasing claims that the media do not support development.
- Increasing criticism against white-owned media (cf. Unit 3).
- Claims that the South African media are racist (cf. Unit 15).
- Disagreement between the government and the media about the proposed funding of the Media Development and Diversity Agency (MDDA). Government officials claim that the South African media do not represent the South African society; many groups still feel left out. The planned budget for the MDDA to advance diversity in the form of setting up and subsidising/sponsoring media enterprises in marginalised communities is R300 million. The media will be expected to contribute to this fund.

# MEDIA STUDIES

- From the media's side, government involvement in this form has serious implications for the freedom of speech.
- The announcement (late 2000 early 2001) of the ANC that it plans to start its own newspaper. This reminds one of the National Party who started *The Citizen* and who wanted to buy the *Washington Star* as part of its own propaganda war with the same motivation that the South African press (at that stage mainly the English press) and the foreign media were too critical of government and only focused on the negative aspects of government.
- In March 2001 the South African National Editors Forum (SANEF) and President Thabo Mbeki met to discuss the deteriorating relationship between the media and government. The possibility of setting up a media agency in the President's Office (similar to the system in the USA's White House) that will facilitate daily communication between government and the media, was mentioned.
- The launch of its own electronic journal, *ANC Today – Online Voice of the African National Congress*, on the Internet on 26 January 2001.

This electronic journal can be seen as a direct consequence of the ANC's perception, as expressed by President Thabo Mbeki (see welcoming letter below) that the white-owned media are anti-government. In his welcoming letter, published on 26 January 2001 in *ANC Today*, President Mbeki accuses the white-owned media in the same way the National party accused (mainly) the English press. Where the National Party blamed everything on British imperialism and the capitalist interests of the goldmine owners, the ANC blames everything on racism, colonialism, apartheid, and the capitalist interests of white media owners.

---

**Welcome to *ANC Today***

FIRST OF ALL, I would like to congratulate the Communications Unit on its decision to publish *ANC Today*. It is of critical importance that the ANC develops its own vehicles to communicate news, information and views to as many people as possible, at home and abroad.

Clearly, the Internet provides an added possibility to achieve this objective. It is very encouraging indeed to see an organisation as old as the ANC respond to modern challenges and possibilities with the speed and flexibility it has demonstrated by the use of the Internet.

I therefore wish this new venture, *ANC Today*, the success it deserves.

Historically, the national and political constituency represented by the ANC has had very few and limited mass media throughout the 90 years of its existence. During this period, the commercial newspaper and magazine press representing the views, values and interests of the white minority has dominated the field of the mass media.

This situation has changed only marginally in the period since we obtained our liberation in 1994. The same views, values and interests also drove the state broadcaster, the SABC. It is only now that changes are being brought about to ensure that the SABC fulfils its mandate as a public broadcaster. Much still remains to be done before this objective is achieved.

During the colonial and apartheid years, especially the latter, both the white minority regimes and the dominant economic powers pursued a deliberate policy of suppressing the media that communicated the views of our constituency, the overwhelming majority of our population. For example, both *The Guardian* and its successor, *New Age* were both banned, as was *The World* in a later period. Progressive journalists were banned and imprisoned. We also have the well-known case of the suppression of the liberal *Rand Daily Mail*.

To this day, any media that genuinely represents the interests and the views of the majority has to live with the reality that it has to overcome such obstacles as an "advertisers' boycott" and difficulties in distribution. We are faced with the virtually unique situation that, among the democracies, the overwhelmingly dominant tendency in South African politics, represented by the ANC, has no representation whatsoever in the mass media.

We therefore have to contend with the situation that what masquerades as "public opinion", as reflected in the bulk of our media, is in fact minority opinion informed by the historic social and political position occupied by this minority. By projecting itself as "public opinion" communicated by an "objective press", this minority opinion seeks to get itself accepted by the majority as the latter's own opinion.

With no access to its own media, this majority has had to depend on other means to equip itself with information and views to enable it to reach its own conclusions about important national and international matters. These have included direct contact with the leadership and membership of the ANC at public meetings. Though very important, this means of mass communication can never be adequate as a means of communicating our views and information to the millions of our people and others in the rest of the world.

*ANC Today* will make an important contribution towards filling the void of the voicelessness of millions of people, that is a direct legacy of more than three hundred years of colonialism and apartheid.

I hope the journal will make a special effort to ensure that the news and views the masses of our people are denied reach them.

Of special importance, the people must be informed of the progress we are making with regard to the social transformation of our country and continent, the obstacles and opposition we have to overcome and our programmes to achieve further progress.

The world of ideas is also a world of struggle.

*ANC Today* must be a combatant for the truth, for the liberation of the minds of our people, for the eradication of the colonial and apartheid legacy, for democracy, non-racism, non-sexism, prosperity and progress.

**The struggle continues! Victory is certain!**

(Signed by) Thabo Mbeki

**Figure 13.1 President Thabo Mbeki's welcoming of *ANC Today* – Online *Voice of the African National Congress***
(*Source:* ANC Today http://www.ANC.org.za)

The electronic journal then continues with reports about the ANC's version of the alleged arms scandal in 2000/2001 and an attack on the media that has, according to *ANC Today* "almost without exception acted as uncritical participants in fuelling this furore".

## South Africa the media imperialist

Apart from the above parallels between the NWICO's criticism of capitalist-driven media, and the National Party and ANC's criticism of the South African media, it is also interesting to note that in the field of international communication South Africa is beginning to run the risk of being accused of media and cultural imperialism, especially on the African content.

From the perspective of NWICO criticism, the expansion of the South African owned company MultiChoice, provider of DStv's (Digital Satellite Television) bouquet of channels to Africa, can easily be interpreted as a form of media imperialism. Two of the channels originate from South Africa's own public service broadcaster, the SABC. They are Africa2Africa and SABC Africa. Although the idea of a channel that broadcasts almost exclusively to Africa from Africa about Africa is commendable and in line with the original ideals of the NWICO, the fact that in 2000, seventy-five percent of Africa2Africa's programming originated from the SABC can draw criticism from other African countries.

---

**Africa2Africa**

The following is Africa2Africa's marketing of itself on the Internet:

Africa2Africa, the SABC's first ever subscription entertainment channel – and the first satellite channel to broadcast almost exclusively African programmes – was launched in November 1998 with the express purpose of establishing a channel that would bring DStv subscribers entertainment programmes produced either "for Africa, about Africa or by Africa".

The so-called "satellite invasion" of foreign images, a reference to the huge number of satellite channels now available to television viewers on the continent, can only assist in the promotion of African filmmaking and general programme production in general.

Against this background, Africa2Africa is more than just another channel in the huge bouquet available on the DStv service of MultiChoice. Africa2Africa wants to mirror Africa to all DStv subscribers – to show Africa in all its splendour and beauty. At the moment, Africa2Africa is providing alternative viewing – providing a service never available on DStv before.

The SABC's television programme archive forms the basis of the programmes broadcast on the channel (representing 75%). These are supplemented by programming from the rest of Africa (25%). The channel is broadcast in eight-hour blocks, which are repeated three times per day to complete a 24-hour cycle. For the first 14 months of its existence, Africa2Africa was distributed to DStv subscribers in southern Africa only. There are now plans to expand the channel to cover the whole of sub-Saharan Africa.

# Media Imperialism: The New World Information and Communication Order

Entertainment is the main focus of the channel, and almost 70% of the SABC-produced programmes broadcast on Africa2Africa are not currently broadcast on any of the SABC's three domestic free-to-air channels (SABC1, SABC2 and SABC3).

African dramas and documentaries are a major drawing card. Two African-produced dramas are broadcast every week (Monday and Tuesday), and represent countries such as Tunisia, Egypt, Burkina Faso, Zimbabwe, South Africa, Guinea Bissau, Cameroon and Ethiopia.

South Africans have not been part of the rest of the African continent for many years. Today, however, the situation has changed and Africa2Africa has introduced the cultures and way of life of the rest of the continent to South African DStv subscribers.

Africa2Africa provides its viewers the opportunity to experience storytelling the African way. The movies being broadcast are not all of a kind – and will certainly be a new experience for most viewers, because African filmmaking does not follow formulas made popular by Hollywood or Europe.

The African movies challenge the idea of what movies are all about. Some stories are told in very artistically challenging ways. Others tell their stories in a quite brutally direct way. African movies also challenge their own people to look at African life again, the problems the continent encounters from day-to-day and how tradition has affected Africa in many ways.

Many classic South African sitcoms, dramas, mini-series and children programmes form part of the programme schedule. They still provide excellent entertainment. Some examples include such giant productions as *Shaka Zulu* and *John Ross*, as well as *The Mantis Project, Going Up, Louis' Motors, Generations, Isidingo* and *Homeland*.

Africa2Africa broadcasts more than 20 hours of children programmes every week – seven days of the week. These include the ever popular "Cedric the Crow", "Featherfoot Farm", "Kideo" and "Pumpkin Patch", which all provide excellent entertainment while they educate the young.

A new series on DStv is the Television Environment (TVE) documentary programmes. This series, comprising international award winning documentaries, focuses on the state of our planet, people and the environment, wildlife and human rights in general. To supplement the TVE series, Africa2Africa also brings its viewers "Nature on Track", most probably the best wildlife series on African television, and the internationally acclaimed South African-produced "50/50" nature conservation series.

There are also magazine programmes for all ages and sexes. "Take-5" is for the teenager with a view to move ahead in life, while "Mamepe Africa" and "Lebone – Women on the Move" offer new insights in the ways of life of women. The programme "Issues of Faith" investigates relevant religious issues, while "Jam Alley" represents a funky and lively programme for the young at heart.

Africa2Africa also provides 12 hours of music programmes, including Jukebox Africa, African Connection, Midday Breeze, Soul Sounds and Studio Mix. These programmes not only focus on South African and African artists, but also the most prominent international musicians.

**Figure 13.2 Africa2Africa** (*Source*: Africa2Africa http://www.africa2africa.co.za/introduction.htm)

> **SABC Africa**
>
> The SABC, in conjunction with MultiChoice, offers a 24-hour news and information channel on the DStv bouquet. The objective is to
>
> - bring African news to Africa, from Africa
> - not to limit itself to catastrophe reporting, but to include development stories and good news
> - nurture and stimulate emerging democracies
> - continuously update financial reports, news and interviews, current affairs stories and people in the news
>
> SABC Africa acknowledges that at the start of this service in 2000 it would have a higher proportion of South African news stories as it introduced itself to the rest of the continent. As the newsgathering infrastructure grows, the ratio of African stories will increase. To complete the equation and to place Africa within its global context, international news stories are included in the news mix. With this service the SABC wants not only to serve as an African news provider, but also as an African news source. To provide the service, SABC Africa uses the current SABC news operation infrastructure and news sources, while some news and current affairs programming are repackaged. The SABC plans to open up avenues for newsgathering throughout the continent by setting up newsgathering bureaux and employing stringers.

**Figure 13.3 SABC Africa** (*Source*: SABC Africa http://www.africanews.sabc.co.za/home.htm)

A second example of what can be seen as a form of continued media imperialism from South Africa's side can be deducted from the research findings of the research institute, Media Tenor.

In December 2000 Media Tenor South Africa, reported its findings (cf. De Beer 2000) about the way South African media were reporting other African countries. These findings were compared with Media Tenor's research in Germany at the same time on how German media reported on Africa.

Countries that received the biggest share of reporting in South African media during the months of February until September 2000 were Zimbabwe, Mozambique, the Democratic Republic of Congo and Nigeria. In its reporting on Africa, the South African media focused on crime in these countries. This was closely followed by domestic issues and Africa's foreign affairs. Adding to the already negative topic of crime were reports about accidents and natural disasters. A positive topic, such as sport, only came fifteenth on the list of 25 news categories. On the other hand, the German media reported more on African foreign policy, followed by natural disasters and with sport in the third place of most often reported topics.

On the basis of these findings, Media Tenor came to the conclusion that for the South African media Africa is still a continent of crime.

Although many factors play a role in the selection of news (see Unit 14), and although questions can be asked about the methodological soundness of Media Tenor's investigation, including questions about the role of geographical proximity in news selection (i.e. the economic, security and social impact of crime and political unrest in neighbouring countries and why that is more important to the South African media and its users than to those in Germany), this kind of research finding can support the South African government's critique that the mainly white-owned South African media is negative about Africa. At the same time, and against the background of the claims of the NWICO, research findings like these urge the South African media to investigate their attitude towards the African continent and other developing countries. The question arises whether the South African media are not guilty of the accusations made against the media of developed countries by the supporters of the NWICO. At the same time it can be asked that if this is the nature of reporting by a developing country (South Africa) about other developing countries, what has been achieved by the NWICO?

## 13.7 CONCLUSIONS

Many conclusions about the NWICO can be drawn – what it has achieved and its future. Here it suffices to emphasise that the debate is far from over and has entered a new era with the development of new information and communication technologies (ICTs) (cf. Unit 19 on Globalisation as well as Unisa's separate Communication Science modules on international communication and new media technology). The fact that separate modules address international communication and new media technology in depth shows how the importance of these fields of study has increased.

### *A post-NWICO model*

Brown-Syed (1999:23–25) highlights the following:
- The NWICO debate has focused government attention upon information in a way as never before. It produced general agreement on the structure of the contemporary world information situation, and engendered some willingness to restructure that system for the benefit of developing nations.
- However, UNESCO politics, the rejection of the NWICO agenda by successive American administrations, and the inability of its supporters to arrive at consensus positions have been the major reasons for the difficulties which have been experienced in implementing NWICO resolutions.
- The NWICO debate tended to focus on press freedom, to the detriment of more urgently needed development information plans.

Brown-Syed (ibid) then proposes a post-NWICO model. In this model, the structuralist model with its emphasis on the inequities of information flow can remain part of the new paradigm or model. However, the new model should pay less attention to the news media, which constitute a minor percentage of all information flows across borders.

More attention should be paid to other aspects of cultural exchange such as tourism, the activities of non-governmental organisations, and ways to popularise development education schemes. In the new model, development information should be emphasised in its broadest and most practical senses.

The new model will have to take cognisance of the fact that political alliances formed after the Second World War resulted in a bipolar world divided into East and West. Meanwhile, technological and economic developments superimposed a North and South polarisation that has resulted in uneven growth and may have perpetuated the gap between affluence and poverty. The emerging political reality of the 1990s will force the adoption of a new synthesis. Brown-Syed (1999:25) argues that this synthesis must, combine the "Lerner hypothesis" (liberal school) – that "modernisation" is inevitable, with the structuralist paradigm – that inequality is a basic feature of the system. Only when both sides deal with the logic of each argument rather than the ideologies, will the dialectic of information inequality find its resolution.

## *The information superhighway*

Vincent (1997a:378-399) emphasises that the terrain of international communication has shifted from the earlier information flow concerns to the present agenda on trade. He shows how business leaders began testifying in 1980 before the US Congress that communication policy should be taken out of the "free-flow" context and situated within a trade framework. In particular, he shows how there was pressure to help protect the international leadership of the US industry in telecommunication goods and services by "advocating and adopting international communication policies which foster competition and a move toward increasing reliance on market forces, while accounting for differing national policies" (op cit:392).

This new framework forms the basis of the Global Information Infrastructure project (GII) (cf. Unit 19). It is also within this context that the NWICO has given way to the discourse of the information superhighway.

Vincent asks three questions that, according to him, will form the basis of the future discussion of the information order:

- What will the results of an information superhighway be?
- How is the information superhighway being sold in the developing world?
- Who will really benefit in the information age?

He offers the following tentative predictions:

- The notion of an information superhighway as currently offered is still ill defined and closely aligned with ideological assumptions that conflate the interests of communication corporations with the interests of citizens. When social policy objectives are merged with economic policy, any hope for a more equitable world communication system is dashed. As a result we are no closer to the objectives espoused by NWICO, and most likely even further from them than we were in the 1960s and 1970s (Vincent 1997a:397).

- The information superhighway promises Utopia for everyone – better education, stronger democracies, improved social services, global business opportunities, and so on. However, the evidence to support such claims is by no means clear or solid (ibid).
- Many anticipate that the benefits of the "communications revolution" will be equally shared by all. As argument they refer to the role of television (satellite television) in the democratising of previously authoritarian regimes such as the Soviet Union, China, Thailand, Mexico, and other countries. Although the potentials of the new communication technologies have no doubt facilitated coordinated political action and radical social changes, it must be remembered that it was people and their ideas that in the first place brought about massive changes in repressive systems of power. Although the benefits of new communications media for democracy and political change appear ambiguous, the benefits of the international move toward market and regulatory liberalisation for the US economy are clear (Vincent 1997a:398–399).

## Media imperialism and cultural imperialism

Finally, and from a theoretical point of view, the above developments urge us to rethink the concepts of "media-imperialism" and "cultural imperialism".

Media critics have to acknowledge that against the background of a new economic world order, the media are increasingly a free enterprise in which they promote themselves and their products as commodities in a competitive world market. For the time being it seems as if this process will not be reversed. Globalisation calls for a redefinition of media imperialism and for new questions about the same topics to be asked, such as questions about the international flow of news and information. One of the most important, until now neglected areas, concerns people's grassroots experiences and uses of the media within the context of globalisation.

As far as "cultural imperialism" is concerned, Sreberny-Mohammadi's (1997:49–68) argument is relevant: that this concept has also been ill defined and too broadly defined in the past debates about international communication. She shows how throughout history cultures have always influenced each other long before the advent of modern mass media. The concept "cultural imperialism" as used in media and international communication debates and research implies that a particular type of cultural development is persuasively communicated to receiving countries. The traffic is massively in one direction and has basically a synchronic mode. To name this process "cultural imperialism", she argues, is to invite two unacceptable reductions:

- it reduces culture solely to the products of the culture industry (of which the media is the most pervasive), and
- it assumes a limited cultural impact of the earlier political and military dynamics of imperialism and the fact that imperialism has been a double-edged sword, impacting, albeit unequally, both on the colonised and the coloniser.

Thus, the concept "cultural imperialism" must be used with care, which is seldom the case in its rhetorical use for political and economic benefits.

## Summary

In this unit we looked at aspects of the origin and premises of the New World Information and Communication Order (NWICO). We then discussed some of the arguments in the liberal and structuralist schools of thought and some of the recommendations in the key documents of the NWICO. From the structuralist point of view, developed countries dominate both the production and distribution of the national flow of news and information (also media entertainment). In the liberal school it is believed that the provision of news, information, entertainment, raw material for the development of their own media infrastructures, and training, can contribute to economic development and the cultural and political liberation of developing countries.

The main criticism is that although the documents and discussions of the NWICO issues appear to be liberal in the sense of supporting the freedom of the media and human rights, a closer reading reveals anti-democratic, anti-capitalist, and anti-Western sentiments that if applied oppose the freedom of the media and the development of the media as a free enterprise. It is exactly these kinds of sentiments that characterised the relationship between the South African media and the government under apartheid and presently under the ANC government.

The unit concluded with arguments about the impact of the Global Information Infrastructure project (GII project) on the future of issues such as the international flow of news and entertainment. It is argued that new questions should be asked about the flow of international news, information and entertainment and that the concepts "media" and "cultural imperialism" need to be re-conceptualised against the background of the development of the information superhighway.

## Research activities

Write an article in which you cover the following topics and report the findings of your analyses:

1. Explain in a paragraph the concerns that led to the formation of the NWICO. On the basis of your explanation formulate in a paragraph your own opinion about the occurrence of media and cultural imperialism in the country where you reside.
2. Explain in a paragraph your understanding of what the democratisation of communication means within a development context.
3. Explain in a paragraph why the United Nation's Universal Declaration of Human Rights gave impetus to the formulation of the NWICO.
4. Make a list of the basic premises of the NWICO.
5. Find your own examples from media content to add to the list of inequities in the arena of international communication.

6. Explain in one page what you understand under the liberal and structuralist approaches to or ways of thinking in the NWICO debate. Formulate and motivate your own point of view.
7. Write a paragraph in which you explain what you understand under the statement that developing countries come to see themselves through the eyes of dominant Western countries. Provide at least one example taken from media content.
8. Explain why UNESCO's Media Declaration was criticised and seen by the liberal school as Marxist inspired. Motivate your own argument about this view.
9. Summarise the main recommendations of the MacBride Report (1980).
10. Write a paragraph or two in which you summarise the USA's position on the NWICO.
11. Formulate an opinion about what the NWICO has achieved and about the future of the debate concerning news and information flow against the background of a new economic order.
12. Write a page in which you draw a parallel between (1) the apartheid government and the present South African government's views about the role of the media in promoting the government's goals, and (2) their criticism of the media and how this criticism corresponds with Third World claims in the NWICO about media reporting.
13. Collect over a period of three months newspaper clippings about the relationship between the ANC and the media and the ANC's own media plans (or about the relationship between the media and the government in the country where you reside). Summarise the latest developments in this relationship and compare the government's view about the media with the premises of the NWICO.
14. Do a basic comparative content analysis of news about developing countries in two newspapers of your choice over a period of a week. On the basis of this analysis, come to a conclusion about news selection related to developing countries in the two newspapers you have chosen to analyse.
15. Do an analysis of the programme schedules of Africa2Africa and SABC Africa (or any two international radio or television stations in the country where you reside). On the basis of this analysis support or reject the hypothesis that South African (or the country where you reside) could be accused of its own form of media imperialism.
16. Formulate three of your own conclusions about the future of the NWICO against the background of the development of information and communication technology (ICT).

## Further reading

Babbili, AS. 1990. Understanding international discourse: political realism and the non-aligned nations. *Media, Culture and Society* 12(3):309–324.

Bailie, M & Winseck, D (eds). 1997. *Democratizing communication? Comparative perspectives on information and power.* Cresskill, NJ: Hampton Press.

Brown-Syed, C. 1999. *The New World Order and the geopolitics of information.* [O]. Available: http://www.valinor.purdy.wayne.edu/csyed_libres3.html
Accessed on 2000/12/04

Galtung, J & Vincent, RC. 1992. *Global glasnost. Toward a New World Information and Communication Order.* Cresskill, NJ: Hampton.

Golding, P & Harris, P (eds). 1997. *Beyond cultural imperialism. Globalisation, communication and the new international order.* London: Sage.

Hachten, WA & Giffard, CA. 1984. *Total onslaught. The South African press under attack.* Johannesburg: Macmillan.

Roach, C. 1990. The movement for a New World Information and Communication Order: a second wave. *Media, Culture and Society* 12(3):283–307.

Salinas, R. 1986. Forget the NWICO and Start All Over Again. *Information Development* 2(3):154–158.

United Nation's Educational, Scientific and Cultural Organization. 1980. International Commission for the Study of Communications Problems. *Many Voices, One World.* New York: UNESCO.

# Bibliography

Africa2Africa. [O].
    Available: http://www.africa2africa.co.za/introduction.htm
    Accessed on 2001/03/29

African National Congress. 1994. *The reconstruction and development programme. A policy framework.* Johannesburg: Umanyano.

ANC Today – Online Voice of the African National Congress, Volume 1, Number 1. [O].
    Available: http://www.ANC.org.za
    Accessed on 2001/01/26

Altschull, JH. 1984. *Agents of power. The role of the news media in human affairs.* New York: Longman.

Babbili, AS. 1990. Understanding international discourse: political realism and the non-aligned nations. *Media, Culture and Society* 12(3):309–324.

Bailie, M & Winseck, D (eds). 1997. *Democratising communication? Comparative perspectives on information and power.* Cresskill, NJ: Hampton Press.

Brown-Syed, C. 1993. The New World Order and the geopolitics of information. *LIBRES: Library and Information Science Research.* 19 January 1993.

Brown-Syed, C. 1999. *The New World Order and the geopolitics of information.* [O].
    Available: http://www.valinor.purdy.wayne.edu/csyed_libres3.html
    Accessed on 2000/12/04

Constitution of the Republic of South Africa Bill, 6 May 1996. Constitutional Assembly Database Project.

De Beer, AS. 1989. The press in a post-apartheid South Africa: a functional analysis. *Equid Novi* 10(1&2):141–164.

De Beer, AS. 2000. Joernaliste skryf net 'oor slegte in Afrika'. *Beeld,* 30 November 2000.

Dennis, EE & Merrill, JC. 1984. *Basic issues in mass communications: a debate.* New York, NY: Macmillan.

Emery, M. & Smythe, TC. 1986. *Readings in mass communication: concepts and issues in the mass media.* Dubuque, IA: Wm. C. Brown.

Galtung, J. 1981. A structural theory of imperialism, in *Perspectives on world politics.* London: Croom Helm in association with the Open University Press.

Galtung, J & Vincent, RC. 1992. *Global glasnost. Toward a New World Information and Communication Order.* Cresskill, NJ: Hampton.

Gerbner, G (ed). 1977. *Mass media policies in changing cultures.* New York: John Wiley.

Giffard, CA. 1989. *UNESCO and the media.* New York, NY: Longman.

Grogan, J & Riddle, C. 1987. South Africa's press in the eighties: darkness descends. *Gazette* 39:3–16.

Hachten, WA & Giffard, CA. 1984. *Total onslaught. The South African press under attack.* Johannesburg: Macmillan.

Hamelink, CJ. 1979. Informatics: Third World call for a new order. *Journal of Communication* 29(3):144–148.

Hamelink, CJ. 1980. *The New International Information Order: development and obstacles.* Vienna, Austria: Institute for Development.

Hester, A. 1991. The collection and flows of news, in *Global journalism, survey of international communication*, 2nd edition, edited by JC Merrill. New York, NY: Longman.

Hiebert, RE, Unguraid, DF & Bohn, TW. 1988. *Mass media IV. An introduction to modern communication.* New York: Longman.

Kleinwachter, W. 1993. Three waves of the debate, in *The global media debate*, edited by G Gerbner, H Mowlana & K Nordenstreng. Norwood, NJ: Ablex.

Lee, C. 1989. The politics of international communication: changing the rules of the game. *Gazette* 44:75–91.

MacBride, S & Rpacj, C. 1993. The New International Information Order, in *The global media debate*, edited by G Gerbner, H Mowlana & K Nordenstreng, Norwood, NJ: Ablex.

Martin, LJ. 1991. Africa, in *Global journalism, survey of international communication*, 2nd edition, edited by JC Merrill. New York: Longman.

Masmoudi, M. 1979. The New World Information Order. *Journal of Communication* 29(2):172–198.

Mbeki, T. Speech at the Organisation of African Unity Conference. Sun City, Rustenburg, 4 October 1994.

Merrill, JC (ed). 1991. *Global journalism, survey of international communication.* 2nd edition. New York: Longman.

Meyer, WH. 1988. *Transnational media and Third World development: the structure and impact of imperialism.* New York: Greenwood Press.

Mundt, WR. 1991. Global media philosophies, in *Global journalism, survey of international communication*, 2nd edition, edited by JC Merrill. New York: Longman.

Mytton, G. 1983. *Mass communication in Africa.* London: Pitman.

Okibgo, C. 1988. Nigerian radio news and the new information order. *Gazette* 41:141–150.

Oosthuizen, LM. 1992. *Communication. Only study guide for CMN 311-3 (Critical issues in mass communication).* Pretoria: University of South Africa.

Oosthuizen, LM. 1989. *Media policy and ethics.* Cape Town: Juta.

Picard, RG. 1991. Global communications controversies, in *Global journalism survey of international communication*, 2nd edition, edited by JC Merrill. New York: Longman.

Richstad, J & Anderson, M. 1981. *Crisis in international news. Policies and prospects.* New York: Columbia University Press.

Richter, R. 1978. *Whose news? Politics, the press, and the Third World.* London: Times.

Roach, C. 1987. The U.S. position on the New World Information Order. *The Journal of Communication* 37(4):36–51.

Roach, C. 1990. The movement for a New World Information and Communication Order: a second wave. *Media, Culture and Society* 12(3):283–307.

Roelofse, JJ. 1995. The Pan-African News Agency new legal statutes. *Dialogus* 2(3):4–6.

SABC Africa. [O].
Available: http://www.africanews.sabc.co.za/home.htm
Accessed on 2000/09/04

Samarajiwa, R. 1984. The history of the new information order. *Journal of Communication* 34(3):110-113.

Servaes, J. 1986. Development theory and communication policy: power to the people! *European Journal of Communication* 1:203-229.

South Africa. *Report of the Commission of Inquiry into the Mass Media*, PR 89 (3). 1981. Pretoria: Government Printer.

Sreberny-Mohammadi, A. 1997. The many cultural faces of imperialism, in *Beyond cultural imperialism. Globalization, communication and the new international order*, edited by P Golding & P Harris. London: Sage.

Stevenson, RL & Shaw, DL (eds). 1987. *Foreign news and the New World Information Order*. Ames, IA: Iowa State University.

Stevenson, RL & Cole, RR. 1987. Issues, in *Foreign news and the New World Information Order*, edited by RL Stevenson & DL Shaw. Ames, IA: Iowa State University.

Stevenson, RL. 1987. World communications after UNESCO. *Political Communication and Persuasion* 4:71-82.

Sussman, LR. 1990. For better journalism, not more propaganda, in *Current issues in international communication*, edited by LJ Martin & RE Hiebert. New York: Longman.

Turnstall, J. 1977. *The media are American. Anglo-American media in the world*. London: Constable.

UNESCO. 1948. *Universal Declaration of Human Rights*. [O].
Available: http://www.un.org/Overview/rights.html
Accessed on 2000/12/05

UNESCO. 1978. *Declaration on fundamental principles concerning the contribution of the mass media to strengthening peace and international understanding, to the promotion of human rights and to countering racialism, apartheid and incitement to war*. [O].
Available: http://www.unesco.org/webworld/com/compendium/1213.html
Accessed on 2000/02/05

UNESCO. 1980. International Commission for the Study of Communications Problems. *Many Voices, One World*. Paris: UNESCO.

Vincent, RC. 1997a. The future of the debate: setting an agenda for a new world information and communication order, ten proposals, in *Beyond cultural imperialism. Globalization, communication and the new international order*, edited by P Golding & P Harris. London: Sage.

Vincent, RC. 1997b. Information super highway, in *Democratizing communication? Comparative perspectives on information and power*, edited by M Bailie & D Winseck. Cresskill, NJ: Hampton Press.

Watson, J & Hill, A. 1984. *A dictionary of communication and media studies*. London: Arnold.

White, RA. 1993. The new Order and the Third World, in *The global media debate*, edited by G Gerbner, H Mowlana & K Nordenstreng, Norwood, NJ: Ablex.

Winseck, D. 1997. The shifting contexts of international communication: possibilities for a New World Information and Communication Order, in *Democratising communication? Comparative perspectives on information and power*, edited in M Bailie & D Winseck. Cresskill, NJ: Hampton Press.

# A Critical Assessment of News

## 14

*Lucas M Oosthuizen*

## Overview

In this unit we focus on the phenomenon of news. To explain what news is, we look at the nature of news as language including news as signs (including signs in news), codes (including codes in news) and the role of style. The unit also contains a discussion of the news selection process and the role of news values. As far as the construction of news is concerned we pay attention to the so-called "news net", news frames, how news is constructed to make sense for the media user, and the promotion of news as a professional product. Finally we pay attention to some aspects of the influence of society on the final news product. Unless stated otherwise, our application of news is mainly to the printed press.

## Learning outcomes

At the end of this unit you should be able to

- explain the relationship between language and news;
- describe how the selection of news takes place;
- give an overview of the components that influence the construction of news;
- describe how other institutions in society influence news; and
- formulate your own definition of news.

## 14.1 INTRODUCTION

Supplying information is considered to be the media's most important function. They carry out this function by providing media users with news. But what precisely is news?

When one asks what news is the tendency is usually to start off with a definition of the phenomenon. One such definition is that of Snyman (1971) who states that news is knowledge about new, topical and contingent events that differ in the relevance and meaning they have for people. This definition could be analysed as follows. News is information

- about things happening currently (topicality)
- about events happening at a particular place and time (contingency)

# MEDIA STUDIES

- that is different from past situations (novelty)
- upon which people then constitute knowledge (knowledge)
- in which they have an interest (subjective involvement by virtue of personal interest) and in respect of which they as knowing subjects should feel responsibility because of the objective nature of the event
- in which people's interest may differ in the degree of objective and subjective involvement (meaning) (Oosthuizen 1989:71-72).

The problem with such definitions (and the media's own evaluation of their performance as providers of news) is that they do not bring anyone studying the media any closer to an explanation of news as a phenomenon. Moreover, in critical media studies, questions must also be asked as to whether the news found in media content is good or bad, objective or prejudiced, and/or serves specific or general interests. If, for example, a newspaper has a slogan "We tell it like it is" (which was previously the slogan of *The Star*), readers could get the impression that such a publication is simply reflecting reality.

Such slogans are examples of what Gassaway (1984:40) refers to as the symbolic gestures that journalists use to assure their audiences that the news report before them is complete. The same impression is, of course, also created on television when news presenters announce: "Here is the news ...". However, what people tend to forget is that the news media are telling their version of the news about events that they have selected as newsworthy. These stories are also told and presented in a particular way, which in turn affects the manner in which media users perceive the world.

To try and understand the phenomenon of news, let us first look at the principal medium or code of news, namely language.

## 14.2 LANGUAGE, SIGNS, CODES AND THE NEWS

News is in the first instance a representation of the world in language (Fowler 1991:4). The particular role of news in our lives is therefore inextricably linked to the general role that language plays in society.

Hartley (1982) postulates that language (speech) is more than the words it comprises. Through language we learn how we should act; within the framework that it establishes we find, explore and understand our own individuality, and through it we gain access to social relationships. But language is also a form of social control, because people (generally) voluntarily submit to its rules and conventions. It is also through language that we learn to accept the social forces and institutions around us as natural. Because of this role of language, it can be said that while we live through language, language also directs the way we live. News – as language in use or discourse – therefore plays an equally important role in the lives of people who make use of the news media.

Like language, news is semiotic (cf. Unit 10) in nature. This means that both language and news consist of sign systems or codes that stand between people and their experience of the world. When we consider the sign system of news – or of news discourse – the focus falls specifically on what the news message looks like and what it means. The message is composed of signs and codes. It is through the structuring of signs into codes that the news message acquires its meaning.

A sign is the smallest unit of meaning. A newspaper, like television, radio and other media, contains artificial ("man-made") signs, namely words, photographs and illustrations. These signs have certain forms (e.g. the word nanny is physically different from a photograph or an illustration of a nanny). These forms in turn refer to an idea (the idea you have of a nanny in your mind). It should therefore already be clear that signs will differ from each other in the degree of similarity between the form of a particular sign and the idea to which it refers.

## 14.2.1 Words as signs

See Unit 10 for a more in-depth discussion of semiotics. In the case of words, the relationship between the form and the idea is arbitrary. In other words, there is no similarity between the form of the sign and the ideas to which it refers (Hartley 1982:16; Roelofse 1982:48). For example, the language community has arbitrarily decided to use the letters (c-o-w) in that sequence to refer to a four-legged animal with a tail and a characteristic udder, head and horns. However, there is no similarity between the word cow and the idea to which it refers. Words obtain their meaning from their relationship to, and in particular their differences from, other words in the system (Hartley 1982:18–19). Thus, the meaning of words is socially derived.

The meaning of the words used in a news report is also socially derived. The words get their eventual meaning within the context of the report. Journalists have a choice of words (e.g. to describe somebody who has imbibed too much alcohol, they can choose between drunk, under the influence, or intoxicated). These are referred to as paradigmatic choices (Hartley 1982:20–21). Such choices are in turn incorporated into a series of words to form sentences, the composition which (known as syntagm) can reinforce initial paradigmatic choices and meaning.

However, words as such have no fixed meaning, only potential meanings. This makes it possible for the writer of a news report to give a preferred emphasis or a specific meaning to a word within the context of a particular report. According to Hartley (1982:24), however, news discourse plays an important role in assigning one single meaning (uni-accentual value) to signs. Alternative possibilities for meaning are constrained by such things as facticity (the facts of the story). Hartley (1982) maintains that one of the tasks of news discourse is to ensure that one particular meaning of events is preferred to another.

One way of ensuring the preference of one particular meaning is to choose words socially associated with particular characteristics, qualities or behaviour. In this manner, additional meanings are attached to words. By using connotation and myths, words gather additional meaning (Hartley 1982:22–30).

The choice of words is therefore very important in constructing the meaning of news. Reporting on terrorism is a good example to illustrate the point. When a journalist chooses to use the word terrorist – instead of freedom fighter – in a story, a definite negative subjective value is attached to the protagonists or actions in question. This would be an example of connotation at work. Where the word terrorist is accompanied by others which serve the purpose of classifying the event further into specific conceptual categories (Hartley 1982:26–28), we could find ourselves dealing with one or more myths that will in effect restrict or frame the meaning of the event even further.

Research about the way in which *Time* news magazine reports on terrorism (cf. Steuter 1990) is a good example of how words are used to restrict reporting on terrorism or to offer only a partial view of reality. In his analysis, Steuter (1990: 261–274) shows that:

- the way terrorism is semantically defined emphasises the importance of leftist anti-state terrorism (as opposed to right-wing suppressive state terrorism);
- the groups that are labelled as terrorists are linked to criminality through language (by using words such as murderers, thugs and assassins) and acquire a mysterious character (e.g. by referring to them as shadowy);
- headlines are used to label specific actions as terrorism (by the inclusion of words such as terror and terrorism in them), while other headlines counter this perception (e.g. by using the term freedom fighter);
- trivialisation and marginalisation of actions and objectives of terrorists take place (e.g. by referring to them as mad, describing their actions as a game, and by viewing them as agents of an international communist plot), which makes their actions seem senseless and irrational; and
- placing the emphasis on the element of violence (e.g. by stressing the fact that attacks are indiscriminate and showing sensational photographs of wounded victims and destroyed buildings) promotes the idea of fear and that all of society is threatened.

This type of reporting (and we have focused only on the language elements in Steuter's research) not only gives readers a negative perception of terrorist actions but also introduces the myth that such acts are only committed by leftist radicals. Meanwhile, in many instances, the same negative qualities are not attributed to right-wing actions or state terrorism, which are also under-reported in most countries in the West (Oosthuizen 1993a:27–47).

Although there is no universal consensus regarding the reporting of terrorism by the media (cf. Schlesinger, Murdoch & Elliot 1983), this is less important for our purposes. In other words, there could also be deviations in the language that the media use to report on terrorism. What is more important to realise is that the words used by the media imply choice, which could restrict meaning or promote a preferred meaning. Like any other discourse, the coding (the structuring of signs into codes) of news is therefore not neutral. News imposes a structure of values on whatever event it endows with meaning. Because news constructively patterns that of which it speaks, it cannot be regarded as a value-free reflection of facts (Fowler 1991:3–5).

An analysis of the way the media treat different public figures could also reveal interesting results. In another analysis of *Time* magazine it was found that *Time* subtly played on meanings of words to convey its own interpretations of the three USA presidents Truman, Eisenhower and John F. Kennedy. Adjectives, adverbs and synonyms chosen for the verb "said" resulted in the negative treatment of Truman who, amongst others, "said curtly", "barked", "grinned slyly", and the like. In contrast, Eisenhower "grinned happily", "chatted amiably" and "said warmly". His treatment was therefore more positive. Kennedy's treatment was neutral. For the most part he simply "said", "announced", and "concluded" whenever he was reported on in *Time* (Gassaway 1984:76–78).

### 14.2.2 Other signs in newspapers

Obviously the media do not only use words: they also use photographs, layout, illustrations, moving images, music, and sound effects, to name a few sign systems. Photographs, illustrations and moving images are regarded as motivated signs because there is usually a degree of similarity between the form of the sign and the idea to which it refers. For example, the form of the photograph or illustration physically resembles that to which it refers. In other words, a photograph of Nelson Mandela physically resembles the idea (the real person) to which it refers. Where there is a physical resemblance, these motivated signs (photographs and illustrations) are referred to as iconic signs.

In the media, words, photographs, illustrations and moving images are used together. This combination makes it possible for these different signs and sign systems to support each other's meaning, or jointly to change meaning (Hartley 1982:31).

### 14.2.3 Codes

Besides signs, the media naturally also use codes (cf. Unit 10 for a more in-depth discussion of codes). Language is one of these codes. Like any other code, language consists of signs (words) and the rules governing their use. Language represents the final form in which words reach media users. Newspapers, however, have a very specific style of language. As Fowler (1991:46) points out, a journalist automatically writes in a style that befits the genre of the article (e.g. an editorial or a news article), that is appropriate to the particular newspaper, and also reflects the social and economic processes in which the newspaper participates. The values and beliefs inherent in this language (e.g. ideas about patriotism, class, family life) are actively decoded by readers who over time learn to know the significance of the various journalistic codes. The reader is thus active in his/her interpretation of the newspaper's message, and meaning results from the interaction between the reader and the newspaper.

# MEDIA STUDIES

From the above it should be evident that news – like language – is a cultural product which has developed historically and which is learned by people. As Fowler (1991:6) notes, in society's cultural hierarchy great value is attached to news, especially during times of major societal events. As people learn to understand the codes and conventions of news, they become news-literate.

For example, in the case of newspapers, the reader rapidly learns that a long report in the newspaper, accompanied by a bold headline at the top of a page is more important than a brief report with a smaller heading at the bottom of a page. As a result, readers (and viewers and listeners) do not simply follow the news, they are also individually learning to interpret reality through the codes and conventions that they learn from the news. Moreover, reality is collectively created by media users, by interpreting its significance in terms of the degree of similarity between this reality and the expectations created by news (Hartley 1982:5). In other words, people who read about, for example, the political developments in the country, are cued through political reality by the codes and conventions used by newspapers. If we have a reference framework about politics, we compare this framework to the expectations created by the news in order to interpret the particular political event's meaning. Different readers (while reading about these events) therefore collectively create political reality. The potential influence of newspapers on our perception of reality naturally increases if we are reading about something of which we have no prior knowledge. Seen in this light, news has a relatively large influence on media users. It is in fact one of the factors that codetermines how we see the world, how we act and how we behave towards others.

## 14.2.4 News, language and style

What does the language of news look like? Fowler (1991:47) argues that the style of newspapers has to be lively, because newspapers offer themselves as entertainment and must also disguise the fact that this offering is actually a form of institutional discourse. Newspapers therefore adopt a personal or conversational style to bridge the gap between their own values and beliefs and those of their institutional sources on the one hand, and those of the readers on the other. This conversational style creates the illusion of informality and familiarity, and also has the ideological function of naturalising the terms in which reality is presented. It implies cooperation, agreement, symmetry of power and knowledge between the newspaper and its readers. More importantly, Fowler (1991:57) states that conversation implies a commonly held view of the world; a shared subjective reality that does not have to be proved.

From Fowler's (1991) views we can deduce that the conversational style that newspapers adopt would make it easier for readers to identify with newspaper discourse. However, the specific language used in newspapers – and also in other news media – also has essential differences from everyday colloquial language. News discourse is unambiguous. Moreover, it is also concrete and deals primarily with action. These factors could theoretically make it easier for readers to understand the news message, whilst holding their attention.

There are also specific journalistic codes. The structure of a news report can be seen as a representational code. In this case, the most important news (or climax) is given in the introduction, and followed by supporting facts. The reasons given for following this peculiar structure, called the inverted pyramid (although less and less used), are twofold. In the first place the structure grabs the attention of the reader, because the report starts with the climax. Secondly, the format allows stories to be shortened from the bottom with the knowledge that the meaning of the story will still remain intact. This type of editing is usually necessitated when there is a shortage of space on a page. Starting with the climax or "with a bang", however, also has other potential implications. An article that begins with a conclusion reflects the opposite structure of normal logic. In the case of logic, two or more assumptions are typically followed by a deduction or conclusion. A news story is therefore just the opposite. On the basis of this difference it is possible to argue that it is more difficult for the reader (viewer or listener) of news to reject the validity of the story.

This structure (inverted pyramid) is slightly different in the case of television. Stories, with the exception of those reported by the anchorperson in headline form, are often more chronological and presented as a narrative on television (DeFleur & Dennis 1985:450). In television news the event is relayed to the viewer in a new context, offering a beginning, middle, and end. Specific information, narrative, sound and pictures are selected to develop and illustrate a theme. With this format it is very easy for the viewer to become absorbed in the story, without taking note of the selection and combination of audiovisual signs (the form) that provide preferred or additional meaning to the message.

Another journalistic code that is used in newspapers is layout. In terms of this code the size of a heading, the place a report occupies on the page and whether or not it is accompanied by a photograph indicate to the reader the relative importance of the news. In time, newspaper readers learn these codes as part of news discourse.

It is obvious that the meaning attributed to news is not only determined by the language in which it is encoded, but also derives from the social forces that determine how these messages are read and understood (Hartley 1982:14). The role that journalists play in this regard should not be underestimated. Journalists work in institutions where they soon internalise the "correct" way of doing things that includes views on what news should look like. Journalists' way of doing things and of delivering a professional product is also reflected in the final news product and its meaning. Let us take a closer look at the processes that are involved, namely the way in which journalists select and construct the news.

## 14.3 THE SELECTION OF NEWS

News is not something that happens out there and which is then reported. News is primarily the events that are selected as newsworthy by journalists and which are eventually published and/or broadcast. To identify newsworthiness, journalists more or less unconsciously make use of socially constructed categories called news values (Fowler 1991:11-13). In other words, in deciding what to regard or select as news, journalists rely on specific criteria of which some are bureaucratic and others cultural in nature. Events that weather the media's selection process, almost all over the world, are determined by the following factors (F), namely those factors

F1: whose frequency coincides with the publication deadline of the newspaper (a single event is published rather than a long process because a single event coincides with the daily publication of newspapers);

F2: whose size exceeds the threshold of newsworthiness – a reference to the size or volume needed for an event to become newsworthy (e.g. the more violent the crime, the bigger the headlines);

F3: which are open to a limited number of possible interpretations (i.e. an event that is free from ambiguities in its meaning);

F4: which are meaningful in terms of the culture of the news gatherer, either in terms of cultural proximity or relevance (i.e. they are like us or what they do has implications for us);

F5: whose occurrence is anticipated or wished for (e.g. a journalist who anticipates that mass action is going to turn into violence, labels mass action as violence when it happens);

F6: whose occurrence is not anticipated (i.e. unexpected and rare – e.g. when a man bites a dog);

F7: which have already become news (e.g. a private hospital in financial trouble will probably be reported on again once it has hit the headlines);

F8: which are necessary for composition (e.g. other air disasters to report in conjunction with the Helderberg disaster);

F9: which refer to élite nations (e.g. what happens in the USA or relates to any of the other superpowers could be of great consequence to other parts of the world);

F10: which refer to élite people (e.g. famous persons such as ex-President Nelson Mandela);

F11: which may be seen as the actions of persons (personalities) rather than institutions (i.e. that are also easier for the newspaper to identify and represent, and with which the reader can identify);

F12: which are negative (bad news).

(Galtung & Ruge 1982:52-61; Oosthuizen 1989:73; Fowler 1991:12-15)

The more of these news values an event embodies, the greater its chances of being selected as news. The last four are regarded as cultural values (Galtung & Ruge 1982:56) which are particularly relevant in the USA. In critical media studies we must, of course, look at the implications of these news values for the nature of news in general, and for the readers of newspapers in particular.

## 14.3.1 Implications of news values

The first point that could be made here is that events that do not adhere to any of these news values will not become news. Apart from that, it is also fairly obvious that the average person in the street will find it difficult to become the object of news selection.

Fowler (1991:15–19), in addition, makes some damning observations about the use of specific news values by journalists. He remarks that the value (F9), which refers to élite nations, encodes a superpower ideology of the dominating status of North America, Japan, Europe and Russia in world political and cultural affairs. This ideology was, indeed, also an underlying problem that formed part of the complaints of the New World Information and Communication Order (cf. Unit 13).

Fowler (1991) sees the result of the application of the news value (F10) (dealing with personalisation) as dangerous. While the media are obsessed with people who are turned into symbols (that promote identification, empathy or disapproval), serious discussions and explanations of the underlying social and economic factors behind their behaviour are not provided. The shortage of space in a newspaper could of course also be another reason why we do not really read "why" events, like unrest and terrorism, are happening. The fact remains, however, that the focus is usually on the people involved in news events, while the official/legitimate sources often define the events.

Fowler (1991:16) contends that most of the news value factors (including the so-called bureaucratic ones – F1 to F8) are cultural in nature. The value F4 is an obvious example. Combined with the view that society is consensual in nature, Fowler shows how this value leads to a preoccupation with things and people that are "like us". At the same time, a distinction is made between "us" and "them" (groups that are unlike us, which are simultaneously regarded as alien and threatening). Fowler reckons that this causes divisive attitudes in society. In particular, the popular papers of the Right in Britain have become obsessed with putting the "them" groups in a bad light. The language they use is instrumental in this process.

During the years of apartheid – which of itself was a divisive ideology – the Afrikaans press in particular was fairly instrumental in articulating these divisions in terms of "us" and "them". Fourie (1991:4) gives some excellent examples of headings that appeared in Afrikaans papers during 1990 that articulated the rift between the National Party (in terms of the Afrikaans mainstream press "us") and the African National Congress in particular (regarded as "them").

- "FW vat ANC vas" – freely translated as: FW [de Klerk] curbs ANC
- "Magnus kap na Mandela" – Magnus [Malan – ex-minister of defence] lashes out at [Nelson] Mandela
- "ANC plan ontbloot" – ANC's plan uncovered
- "ANC uitoorlê" – ANC snookered
- "ANC leierskap geloop op kongres" – ANC leadership tackled at congress
- "Britte kap Mandela" – Britons lash out at Mandela

# MEDIA STUDIES

Fourie (op cit) points out that, while the Afrikaans papers at the time promoted the idea of peaceful negotiations with the ANC, the headings and language usage in reports confirmed the myths and stereotypes of the ANC as public enemy number one. The National Party government also played its part in strengthening this conception about the ANC and blacks in general by infusing terms such as the black danger (*swart gevaar*) and the total onslaught into the political discourse of the time.

The fact that journalists select news through news values does not mean that these values are the only variables that come into play in the selection, identification and construction of news.

## 14.4 THE CONSTRUCTION OF NEWS

Apart from the role of language in the construction of news, a further factor in the construction of news is that occurrences are turned into events and ultimately into news stories (cf. Tuchman 1978a). Thus, something only becomes news the moment it is published or broadcast. But, as we have already seen with news values, not everything becomes news. The same phenomenon reveals itself when the institutional processes that journalists use to uncover, gather or define the news on a daily basis are scrutinised more closely.

### 14.4.1 Spreading the news net

The electronic news media, especially, frequently remind us that they bring the world to our living-rooms in their news bulletins. What they usually fail to add, however, is the fact that the news we receive is produced as part of an institutional process that also influences the type and nature of the news. To cover everything in the world is virtually impossible. Consequently, the media use their reporters, correspondents and the news agencies to spread a news net to cover the events that are happening across the world. To ensure a steady flow of news and news production, this net is anchored or organised in a specific way. Through the news net, journalists try to make sense of the world out there. At the same time, however, this net frames the news that we receive – and in the process some of the news fish get away!

### 14.4.2 Frames

As Tuchman (1978a) reveals, news workers use frames to organise reality, applying variables like time, space, facticity and presentation.

- Media workers work to deadlines and their daily schedule is arranged accordingly. They learn to differentiate between types of news in terms of time. Thus hard news (which is very timely and must be acted on quickly before it becomes obsolete) is rated above soft news. The treatment of hard news and soft news will, of course, also differ in the newspaper – with the hard news typically placed on the news pages

(1, 3 and 5) and soft news treated as features further back or on verso pages. These and other typifications (e.g. whether a story is developing and can therefore be scheduled, or is an unscheduled event like "spot news") are all used by news workers to transform the daily news glut into orderly raw material that they can process and disseminate. While typification channels news workers' perceptions of the everyday world by imposing a frame upon strips of daily life (Tuchman 1978a:58), it is through this same frame that we eventually experience the world out there when we read a newspaper, watch television or listen to radio. Typification in terms of time becomes particularly interesting when one considers that what one newspaper or television station may regard, for example, as timely (hard news) another might treat as soft news. The importance that the media user will attach to the event (as a result of the eventual placement and presentation) will therefore depend on the medium he/she reads, looks at or listens to.

- News is also organised spatially. As in the case of time, the media impose a structure upon space to enable them to accomplish their daily work and to plan across days. To ensure a predictable daily flow of news, the media are tied to so-called legitimate institutions like the various state departments, the police, the courts, and others, resulting in what are known as reporters' beats. Tying reporters to institutions in effect allows news to happen at some locations. Locations which are covered by reporters naturally get more coverage than those not covered by reporters (Tuchman 1978b:295). Hierarchically, news of an institution's own reporters is preferred to that of correspondents (known as stringers) because of the financial investment of newspapers in the former. In her research, Tuchman (1978b) also reveals that editors prefer to publish material prepared by their own staff rather than by centralised agencies. This means that the status of reporters or the material produced may determine what is identified as news. Furthermore, negotiations to decide about news value also take place between the various editors and bureaux chiefs who all want "a piece of the action" for themselves and their own newspapers or news bulletins.

- By tying news to facticity, journalists ensure its significance for readers. This concept deals primarily with the way in which journalists find facts (pertinent information that is professionally validated). Tuchman (1978a:93) points out that journalists make three assumptions about their sources:
    - Sources met through institutionalised beats are regarded as being more reliable.
    - It is assumed that facts are mutually self-validating – people with more facts (like committee heads) are therefore likely to be more accurate.
    - Legitimated organisations are regarded as being inherently more correct because of the procedures they follow to protect the institution and the people who come into contact with them.

    This factual way in which journalists attribute meaning to social reality explains their preoccupation with official news sources and so-called *status quo* contacts. The professional procedure of finding facts is also reflected in the quotations that journalists use and the division of newspapers and news bulletins in specific sections. While the facts about an event, the sources, the distinction between news and comment, and the quotations all emphasise the credibility of news, these professional techniques at the same time tend to legitimise the *status quo* and also obscure the involvement of journalists in the construction of news stories (Tuchman 1978a:82–103).

The facticity of a story is, of course, not only promoted through the types of sources that journalists use; they also present news as personal, observable fact (the result of true, reliable, and accurate observation). As Weaver (1994:74–75) remarks, the emphasis on observation (combined with official accounts) not only makes facts true – they become obviously true. Narrating events in an impersonal manner also invites the reader to accept an account as true and precise.

- Finally, as far as news frames are concerned, the actual presentation of news is also a tool that journalists use to transform events into news by using specific conventions (or codes). It is these conventions that media users learn to decode over time (cf. Hartley 1982) and that codetermine media users' interpretation of an event. As we have seen in the case of *terrorism*, the narrative that is used to tell a story not only awards meaning to it but also limits meaning. Moreover, Tuchman (1978a:215) contends that if an occurrence does not readily present itself as news easily packaged in a known narrative form, that occurrence is either soft news (requiring more reportorial time and attention) or non-news.

From Tuchman's research, as well as that undertaken by Hall and others (Fowler 1991:21), it is clear that the production schedules and conventions for access to sources affect the content and presentation of news stories. Crime reporting illustrates this point well.

Chibnall (1982:78) contends that in reality the term crime reporter is a misnomer. These reporters are in actual fact police reporters who rely on the police for most of their information. A steady flow of news emanates from law and order institutions and, as a result, newspapers institute crime beats to tap this supply of news. To ensure that this news is significant to readers, versions of crime events provided by official sources are relied upon to enhance the facticity of crime stories. The spatial organisation of news and the emphasis on facticity therefore lead to a tendency among the news media to give preference to official versions of crime news.

Because of this tendency, the law and order agencies acquire a potentially powerful position. They do not only become main suppliers of information about crime, but they are also to an extent the main sources of news about their own conduct. In the process they have the opportunity to establish the parameters of the public discussion about crime and to frame it in such a way that even alternative viewpoints (if they are sought out) are reported from this point of reference (Oosthuizen 1994:81).

While the routines of news gathering ensure a supply of daily copy, it should be clear that they are also very selective. In terms of Tuchman's observations it is evident that certain parts of reality are effectively ruled out as news. For example, events which are not sufficiently topical, which cannot be covered geographically by the news network, whose facticity cannot be endorsed by élite sources or institutions, or which are portrayed as insignificant, will probably not become news. The frames that news workers use to organise reality therefore underscore the point that news is a frame on reality (which includes certain events and excludes others) and not a reflection of it.

The preoccupation with official sources, institutions and events possibly also provides a plausible reason for Hartley's (1982) observations about what is missing in the news in Britain. He says that while topics such as politics (e.g. government, parliament), the economy (e.g. performance of companies), foreign affairs (e.g. relations between our government and theirs), domestic news (e.g. what's happening in Northern Ireland), occasional stories (for example, disasters), and sport (e.g. mostly about male professional and competitive sports) are featured regularly, vast areas of social life are excluded. This seems to be the case not only in Britain but also in America and all over the world. Hartley (1982:38–39) points out that there is an overwhelming bias towards public as opposed to private life, and towards men rather than women. Little is said about the lives of ordinary people – only how the decisions made in the reported spheres of politics, and so forth, affect their lives, and these messages are conveyed by official sources. When ordinary people do enter the news arena, they enter it by some other door, for example when they happen to witness an accident or are involved in a court case (Fowler 1991:22).

This preoccupation means that we primarily read about powerful people in newspapers. In addition, it is also important to note that views of people who are regularly quoted as sources in the media (which include politicians, civil servants, directors, experts, royals and the like) also means that their formal and authoritative style of language is infused into newspaper reports (Fowler 1991:22–23). Not only does this style emphasise the credibility of the news provided by the newspaper, it contributes further to a reflection of reality that is in line with the views, tone and attitudes of the *status quo*.

To the critical student, it should therefore already be quite obvious that news does not reflect reality. Only a small part of reality and what is going on in a society are covered, with a definite emphasis on specific subjects and spheres. The diversity of interests in society is not reflected. The general ability of the press to promote pluralism can therefore be strongly questioned. We should, however, bear in mind that the press is not monolithic. Deviations from the norm can therefore take place. Newspapers, for example, sometimes deviate from their official framework for reporting terrorism. In such cases (cf. Oosthuizen 1993a) they do go into the reasons why people initiate a terrorist campaign, use terrorists as sources, and in the process question the position of the *status quo*. As can be expected, however, newspapers in a particular country usually find it easier to deviate from the official framework when they are dealing with terrorist movements of another country! Which brings us to the whole issue of how journalists ensure that news makes sense to readers.

### 14.4.3 Making sense of the news for the media user

Reporters decide in an almost automatic manner which events are newsworthy or how to make sense of the news net. In addition, they also present the news in a specific way so that it makes sense to the media user.

From our discussion of the news net, it should already be clear that events are arranged in a specific order to make sense to the reader. For this purpose journalists use cultural maps (Hartley 1982:81–86) to assign to news events their proper place in the order of things. Society is divided into specific spheres, such as politics, economics, sports, and so on. These divisions are reflected in the various sections into which newspapers are divided. Because of these divisions, we could argue – from a critical perspective – that media users would find it difficult to get an integrated picture of reality or to understand how the various spheres relate to each other. These maps also assume society to be composed of individual persons, as well as having a hierarchical nature. This brings us back to the notion of élite sources and events in specific spheres that are regarded as more important than others. As we have already seen, these people and events are consequently placed in the position where they become definers of the news reality.

Another important organising principle in news production is consensus. Consensus assumes that the interests of the population are undivided and held in common, and that the whole population subscribes to a certain set of beliefs (Fowler 1991:49). Journalists use the concept – as part of a routine mental orientation – to make sense of the world. In the process – as we saw earlier – this distinction between "us" and "them" is also used to typify certain events as negative (outside the consensus). One of the best examples of consensus at work is when a strike action takes place.

For example, newspapers – also in South Africa – usually depict strikers as "them" by focusing on the strike action itself; the loss in production; violent skirmishes between strikers and non-strikers or the police; implications for the economy, and so forth. The emphasis, as far as presentation is concerned, is on the depiction of such behaviour as dissent – or as being against "our" interest. The "them" typification is also reflected in language that articulates notions of irresponsibility, irrationality, mindlessness or violence. Terrorism usually gets the same treatment. Apart from the fact that the whole consensual model is contradictory (because there is fragmentation in society, as well as differing interests), it is also untrue. Consensus is not based on facts but on beliefs or values. But, as Fowler (1991:50) points out, whether or not the interests of workers and of capitalists do actually coincide, consensus stipulates that they do.

Using the consensual model has definite implications for the reader. The most important effect would probably be that media users would find it difficult to really understand phenomena that are based on an articulation of the consensual model. A typification based on "us" and "them" does not leave room for the explanation of an event, for example why a strike really took place. Using the consensual model also undermines the dictum that news is inherently factual. No wonder that a famous American columnist once commented that news gathering and truth seeking are quite different endeavours. He argued that the function of news is to signalise an event, while the function of truth is to bring the hidden facts to the fore and to set these facts in relation to each other (DeFleur & Dennis 1985:443).

The way in which journalists make sense of the world for media users obviously affects the meaning of news. So does the specific way in which news is conveyed to media users. The way in which media users are addressed is linked to a newspaper, television or radio station's concept of who its audience is (Hartley 1982:96; Fowler 1991:40). The tendency is to treat the sharing of news as natural or ordinary, like a conversation. Conversational style (Fowler 1991:57–58) not only closes the discursive gap between, for example, the reader and the newspaper as an institutional source, but it also constructs an illusion of informality, familiarity and friendliness. In Fowler's opinion, there is, however, a more important ideological function why newspapers use a conversational style, and that is to naturalise the terms in which reality is presented. This also includes the naturalisation of the categories those terms represent.

Various tools are used in the media to suggest the presence of speech and to contribute to the illusion of conversational style. For example, in newspapers, and without going into Fowler's (1991:62–65) discussion in too much detail, we take note of the following.

- Typography (the kind of type, as well as type size) is used in conjunction with all the other design elements on the page (such as balance and contrast) to make the text more readable, legible and, especially, lively – like conversation.
- The sentences that journalists use are short – and therefore in line with the format of speech. Seasoned journalists will, for example, often tell new reporters that a good introduction (introductory paragraph) is a short introduction. The popular press, in particular, tends to include more informal words in stories (e.g. slang, idioms and clichés). At one stage, as you would have seen earlier, it was very popular in the Afrikaans press to use the word "kap" ("lashing out") in headings whenever one politician criticised another. Using such words cues the illusion of oral mode.
- Other cues to oral mode (or conversational style) include using first names to identify people (e.g. Nelson and Magnus instead of Mandela and Malan). Expressions of modality (e.g. Mr Mandela should/will certainly/is correct/may) are often found in comment or where journalists start speculating in a story. Fowler contends that such expressions suggest the presence of individual subjectivity (a person) behind the text, which also cues the oral mode.
- As soon as a journalist starts using speech acts in his/her writing, the sense of personal interaction is also heightened. Such an act is constructed when journalists not only report (say) things but also order, question or demand – in other words "do" things. A leader article is the typical place where one would expect to find such acts (e.g. where the editor tells his/her readers to vote for a particular party during an election).

Apart from the conversational style, it is actually fairly easy for media users to make sense of the news because of the general nature of news language. Such language is concrete (not abstract, philosophical and/or intellectual); direct (informing you what has happened); refers to existing knowledge (you don't need someone else to explain it to you); and also uses popular terms (easy to understand). The language of media content is therefore accessible to the broad public. The implications of this type of language are obvious. Read in conjunction with aspects such as the consensual model of society, it makes it easier to identify with "us", because it is the language we speak. At the same time, this language also translates the sayings and doings of the élite into a familiar idiom (Hartley 1982:99) which would enhance the acceptance of official definitions of the news as reality by the media user.

From what we have dealt with so far, it is obvious that news is not a reflection of reality and, above all, it is not objective. But, to the media user, this is not always so obvious. One of the reasons, apart from those that have been discussed up to now, is the fact that journalists promote news as a professional product.

### 14.4.4 Promoting news as a professional product

When it comes to promoting news as a professional product, Hartley (1982:107–129) shows that journalists avoid propaganda, present a sense of objectivity and provide real information in, for example, television news by:

- separating objective from subjective news
- guiding viewers through the news
- using accessed voices (often élite sources) to contribute to the overall meaning and structure of the story
- using opposites for stereotyping (in particular the distinction between "us" and "them").

Newspapers also apply these promotional mechanisms of professionalism. For example, by labelling commentary on the editorial page as comment, the objectivity of a newspaper is strengthened. Comment is therefore separated from news. This implies that, as far as the rest of the newspaper is concerned, journalists are not presenting their own opinions, but simply observing on the readers' behalf.

The veracity or authority of the news itself is also strengthened by presenting decontextualised parts of reality as the truth. As we have already seen, this is done by anchoring news to so-called legitimate or élite people, or presenting it in such a way that it is indicating the facts in a narrative that is emotionally detached and impersonal (cf. Tuchman 1978a; Weaver 1994). Even official statements to the press (like press releases) are often presented as the product of the normal news-gathering process. In such cases the media user is seldom aware that this particular news was created by another institution.

The inverted pyramid structure also leads the media user through reality in a specific way. Different sources are used to tell us a story, which is often preplanned by the journalist. As we have already noted, in the case of a news report this story begins with a conclusion. In some cases the introduction reflects the journalist's own conclusions, which are later underwritten by one or more sources cited in the report. A typical example of this would be:

> Organisation X has delayed the peace process by deciding at a meeting of the executive committee this week that "...".

The use of quotation marks in news can also strengthen the impression of the impartiality of the journalist or his/her institution in the creation of news. However, quotation marks can also be used to throw suspicion on the source of a news story. Consider the following example:

> Mr X described himself as an "honest" man.

In the latter example the honesty of the person concerned is questioned by being placed within quotation marks.

The provision of news in a newspaper, just as on television, is obviously not a direct process. The journalists themselves, and the institutions they work in, play a part in creating it. Not keeping to expected forms and styles could have detrimental effects on the career of a journalist. As DeFleur and Dennis (1985:448) point out, reporters who are sent out to cover a specific story must return with a terse report that provides the "facts" about the incident. Deviating from this style and form could cost them their jobs. In addition, a deviation from the standards and views of editors and colleagues about how things should be done could also lead to reporters being ostracised. In spite of these factors that curtail the nature and scope of news, the provision of real, objective facts and all the information is still presented to media users as a newspaper, radio or television station's goal and practice.

## 14.5 NEWS AND SOCIETY

We must remember that news is not selected and constructed in a vacuum. Journalists themselves operate within the limitations, pressure, structure and norms of the larger society. The media is also a social institution that is influenced by its relationship to other institutions. The most important of these are probably governments. The reasons for the position of government *vis-à-vis* the media are quite obvious.

The media are legally, normatively and structurally subject to the control of political institutions (Gerbner 1977:263). Gallagher (1982:160) mentions that in the final analysis the key relationship linking a media organisation to society is that between the media organisations and the government of a country. According to Holmes (1986:1), the mass media of a country, more than any other kind of institution, are shaped by the prevailing type of political power. This relationship obviously gives a government a lot of potential control over and influence on the nature of news.

For example, under the National Party government, the media were restricted by more than a hundred statutes (Hachten & Giffard 1984:29). These laws restricted news reporting on a wide variety of subjects (e.g. the activities of the army and the police); banned the publication of news on specific subjects altogether (e.g. newspapers could not report on banned people and banned organisations or on unrest during a state of emergency); and in general restricted access especially to government information (Oosthuizen 1989:34–45). The government also applied the most severe form of sanctions against the press by effectively closing down newspapers like *World* and *Weekend World* in 1977 and *Post* and *Sunday Post* in 1981. During the state of emergency (1985–1990) alternative publications like *New Nation, South, Weekly Mail, Grassroots* and *New Era* were prohibited for periods ranging from one to three months. Closure meant that these newspapers could not publish any news at all.

Ultimately, however, all institutions or individuals outside the media that can consciously regulate them can influence the nature of the news. These parties are referred to as regulators and are discussed at length in Units 4 and 5. Hartley (1982) contends, however, that it is particularly governments and commercial interests that have a say in news. The relations between news and commercial interests take three forms:

- News media may be owned by private corporations.
- They operate in a commercial climate – which means that they must take note of what their competitors are doing.
- They interact on a daily basis with commercial life – organisations that also supply a lot of the information that the news media need.

Hartley says that it is therefore not surprising that information often assumes the commercial context. Although he does not profess that the media simply reproduce the ideas and ideologies of those who own them, he points out that with the profit motive in mind certain choices facing editorial staff are constrained. "They cannot overstep the commercial mark in the allocation of resources, in the appeal to mass rather than minority markets, and in the broad limits of 'acceptable' opinion" (Hartley 1982:48).

Locally, this line of thought was already reflected in, for example, the Argus Group's guidelines to editors in the late 1980s. Editors were required, amongst other things, to consistently maintain optimal editorial, technological and commercial standards, and to operate on a profit-making basis to achieve these standards (Oosthuizen 1989:66). In early 1992 a former editor of the *Pretoria News*, Deon du Plessis, made it very clear that Argus editors also accepted that there was no longer a distinction between the editorial and commercial sides of the newspaper. This meant that editors also had to accept responsibility for the commercial success of the newspaper. In addition, Argus editors were following a very clear marketing perspective at the time. This perspective meant that they adapted their news product to the needs of their consumers or market (advertisers and readers) in order to obtain an optimal financial return for their investors (cf. Du Plessis 1992).

It is therefore quite clear that commercial interests have a direct bearing on the news product for the sake of profit and economic survival. Hartley (1982:130–136) indicates that economic factors specifically also play a role in making it difficult for a newspaper to present the other side of a story – in other words, to reflect the true reality of society in the news. In this regard he points out that those media that can survive economically are largely those which are highly unlikely to criticise existing wealth and power.

In South Africa the demise of the *Rand Daily Mail* underscored this possibility. Despite having a large circulation, economic factors forced it to close. At that stage it was also one of the few newspapers to attack the political order and to carry so-called "black news".

## 14.6 CONCLUSION

Because of the specific nature of news as a sign system, the ways in which news is produced by journalists, and the influences that news and news organisations absorb as social institutions within society, news is anything but a true reflection of reality. Despite the claims of many newspapers, news is not a mirror image of reality. Rather, it is a frame or window on reality that seeks to or can only reflect part of this reality. In this process the real interests and the real conditions in society are hidden. News is thus ideological. The ideological influence does not necessarily correspond to the journalist's intention in producing the report (text). In fact, it also does not directly influence behaviour, but its influence lies in the way it structures the mediation between the media user and his/her social and physical world (Hartley 1982:138–151).

It should be clear that the mass media also reflect an image of society that is very different from the way this society is actually structured. For the student of critical media studies the question of what is not reported is, therefore, of cardinal importance. Do we, for example, read, listen to and see in-depth discussions about the reasons for the shortcomings of our society in our media? What do the media tell us about the changes that are possible or viable in our country? Once we start asking these kinds of questions we soon realise that the media not only contribute to the climate of opinion in society but also provide the cues for what are regarded as possible and acceptable modes of action and thinking. Although the news media may not have strong and direct effects in terms of influence, they contribute to our reference framework as sources of social and cultural information (i.e. how we view things). This warrants ongoing critical appraisal.

On the other hand, it should be obvious that the meaning we attach to news is also something we as recipients can actively negotiate, particularly if we are aware of the failings which exist in the representation of news.

## Summary

In this unit we looked at the phenomenon of news. News comes to media users in a specific language; thus we paid attention to the role of signs, codes and style in news. We then followed with a discussion of the news selection process and the role of news values and we concluded that in order to identify newsworthy events journalists use news values. As far as the construction of news is concerned we paid attention to the so-called "news net", news frames, how news is constructed to make sense for the

# MEDIA STUDIES

media user and the promotion of news as a professional product. In short, we have seen that media workers actively construct news and that the nature of news is also influenced by other institutions in society. News is therefore not a mirror of reality, but actively frames a particular reality for the reader.

## Research activities

1. Select a news report on any event in any newspaper that according to you explains the use of words to depict negative subjective values in the heading and body of the report. List the words and explain how the selection of these words embodies the journalist's own subjective view of the event. Now select a news report on any event in any newspaper that according to you explains the use of words to depict positive subjective values in the heading and body of the report. List the words and explain how the selection of these words embodies the journalist's own subjective view of the event.

2. Do a comparative analysis of a newspaper story on the same event in two different newspapers to ascertain the connotative meaning of the different stories. Use the following method:
    a) Analyse each sentence and write down the following:
        - Who or what (person/institution) is it about?
        - Which act or implied act is he/she/it carrying out (in other words, the verb in the sentence)?
        - Which quality is linked to this person/institution or his/her/its action (typically adverbs or adjectives – associated with the person, institution or action in question)?
        - In terms of this quality and/or action, allocate a positive, negative or neutral value to the sentence.
    b) Add up the positive, negative and neutral values at the end of each report.
    c) Based on this calculation, decide whether the report is predominantly positive, negative or neutral.
    d) You can also do a similar analysis of the headings of the reports.
    e) Now explain how the newspapers have combined signs and codes to communicate preferred associated meaning about the event or person.

3. Find a newspaper report on any political topic. Show how the journalist uses the news value F4 and consensus to distinguish between "us" and "them". In a paragraph, explain the possible implications of this type of reporting for newspaper readers.

## Further reading

Fowler, R. 1991. *Language in the news. Discourse and ideology in the press.* London: Routledge.
Galtung, J & Ruge, M. 1982. Structuring and selecting news, in *The manufacture of news. Deviance, social problems and the mass media,* edited by S Cohen and J Young. London: Constable.

Hartley, J. 1982. *Understanding news*. London: Methuen.
Lanson, J & Fought BC. 1999. *News in a new century. Reporting in an age of converging media.* London: Sage.
Manning, P. 2000. *News and news sources: a critical introduction.* London: Sage.
Oosthuizen, LM. 1989. *Media policy and ethics.* Cape Town: Juta.
Tuchman, G. 1978a. *Making news. A study in the construction of reality.* New York: Free.
Tuchman, G. 1978b. The news net, in *Approaches to media: a reader*, edited by O Boyd-Barret. London: Arnold.
Weaver, PH. 1994. *News and the culture of lying.* New York: Free.

# Bibliography

Burns, Y. 1990. *Media law*. Durban: Butterworths.
Chibnall, S. 1982. The production of knowledge by crime reports, in *The manufacture of news. Deviance, social problems and the mass media*, edited by S Cohen & J Young. London: Constable.
DeFleur, ML & Dennis, EE. 1985. *Understanding mass communication.* Boston: Houghton Mifflin.
Du Plessis, D. 1992. Personal interview. Pretoria.
Fourie, PJ. 1991. Media, mites, metafore en die kommunikasie van apartheid. *Communicatio* 17(1):2–6.
Fowler, R. 1991. *Language in the news. Discourse and ideology in the press.* London: Routledge.
Gallagher, M. 1982. Negotiation of control in media organisations and occupations, in *Culture, society and the media*, edited by M Gurevitch, T Bennett, J Curran & J Woollacott. London: Methuen.
Galtung, J & Ruge M. 1982. Structuring and selecting news, in *The manufacture of news. Deviance, social problems and the mass media*, edited by S Cohen & J Young. London: Constable.
Gassaway, BM. 1984. *The social construction of journalistic reality.* Ann Arbor, Michigan: UMI Dissertation Information Service.
Gerbner, G (ed). 1977. *Mass media policies in changing cultures.* New York: John Wiley.
Hachten, WA & Giffard, CA. 1984. *Total onslaught. The South African press under attack.* Johannesburg: Macmillan.
Hartley, J. 1982. *Understanding news*. London: Methuen.
Hiebert, RE, Ungurait, DF & Bohn, TW. 1991. *Mass media VI. An introduction to modern communication.* New York: Longman.
Holmes, D. 1986. *Governing the press. Media freedom in the U.S. and Great Britain.* Boulder, CO: Westview.
Oosthuizen, LM. 1989. *Media policy and ethics.* Cape Town: Juta.
Oosthuizen, LM. 1993a. Die internasionale debat oor die media en terrorisme: beleids- en etiese implikasies vir owerhede en die media. *Communicatio* 19(1):27–47.
Oosthuizen, LM. 1993b. Media en terrorisme, dominate navorsingsparadigmas en bevindings. MA thesis, University of South Africa, Pretoria.
Oosthuizen, LM. 1994. Crime news, the police and the press: moving away from the official orthodoxy. *Communitas* 1:79–89.
Roelofse, JJ. 1982. *Signs and significance.* Johannesburg: McGraw-Hill.
Schlesinger, P, Murdoch, G & Elliot, P. 1983. *Televising "terrorism": political violence in popular culture.* London: Comedia.
Snyman, PG. 1971. *Pers en leser.* Potchefstroom: Pro Rega.
Steuter, E. 1990. Understanding the media/terrorism relationship: an analysis of ideology and the news in *Time* magazine. *Political Communication and Persuasion* 7:257–278.
Tuchman, G. 1978a. *Making news. A study in the construction of reality.* New York: Free.

Tuchman, G. 1978b. The news net, in *Approaches to media: a reader*, edited by O Boyd-Barret. London: Arnold.
Tunstall, J. 1983. *The media in Britain.* New York: Columbia University Press.
Weaver, PH. 1994. *News and the culture of lying.* New York: Free.
Woollacott, J. 1985. Messages and meanings, in *Culture, Society and the Media*, edited by M Gurevitch, T Bennett, J Curran & J Woollacott. London: Methuen.

# 15

# Representation: Race, Gender and Sexual Orientation

*Pieter J Fourie & Beschara Karam*

## Overview

In this unit we ask the question: what are stereotypes? A number of answers and explanations can be provided to this question. We answer it from the perspective of the theory of binary oppositions and the theory of social myths. These theories lead us to conclude that stereotypes are a reflection of or the nature of people to think in terms of oppositions and differences and to think in terms of socially conditioned beliefs. We then discuss some characteristics of stereotypes and some arguments about how stereotypes originate. We emphasise the ideological and dogmatic nature of stereotypes. We argue that before we criticise the media for representing a group, person, topic or organisation in a stereotypical way, we should contextualise our criticism. We then look at some ways in which the media can contribute to the changing of stereotypes. The unit ends with case studies about the representation of race, AIDS sufferers, gays and lesbians, and women.

## Learning outcomes

At the end of this unit you should be able to

- explain and define representation and stereotyping in the media;
- form an informed opinion about the investigation of the Human Rights Commission (HRC) into racism in the South African media;
- explain the nature of stereotypes with reference to Lévi-Strauss's theory of binary oppositions and Roland Barthes' theory of socially constructed meaning and myths;
- describe the characteristics of stereotypes;
- explain how the origin of stereotypes is based on time-bound thinking, ideology and dogma;
- explain how we can change stereotypes; and
- explain why we should not be too extreme in our accusations that media portrayals are stereotyped.

MEDIA STUDIES

## 15.1 INTRODUCTION

Why do we think about certain people and groups in certain ways? Why is our collective way of thinking about certain people and groups often negative? Where do our ideas and perceptions of certain people and groups come from? Questions like these are investigated by many disciplines, including cognitive psychology, anthropology and language studies. In critical media studies we address these and related questions under one of the key topics and concepts in media studies, namely "representation".

The concept "representation" can be understood in two ways:
- how the media re-present events, and
- how the media represent (portray) people and groups (cf. Branston & Stafford 1999:125).

As far as the media's representation of events are concerned, many of the previous units have emphasised that the media can never portray an event (an accident, a conference, the opening of parliament, a disaster) or a topic (economy, politics, art, sport) in full. The media provide us with structured interpretations and views of reality. "Stories" are always constructed in certain ways and depend on interpretations. The fact that we refer to the media's coverage of topics and events as "stories" is significant. "Stories", from a basic nursery tale to a complicated novel, are always constructed and narrated in a certain way. The same applies to media stories (cf. Unit 14: A critical assessment of news).

When we talk about how the media represent specific people and groups, especially groups, we are on the terrain of stereotyping. The question of stereotyping is of special importance in South Africa – a society known for its tension and conflict between different racial, ethnic and language groups. Many people believe that much of this tension is caused by the negative perceptions people of different race, ethnic and language groups may have of each other. Should we wish to create one South African nation, these perceptions need to be changed. What is the role of the South African media in sustaining and often creating negative perceptions?

This question was addressed in 2000 by the (South African) Human Rights Commission (HRC), which commissioned an inquiry into racism in the South African media. Underlying the inquiry was a view of the media as being powerful ideological and social agents in forming and sustaining people's perceptions of and attitudes towards each other. The researcher(s) brief was to:

- investigate the handling of race and the possible incidence of racism in the media and whether such as may be manifested in these products of the media constitutes a violation of the fundamental rights as set out in the (South African) Constitution;
- establish the underlying causes and to examine the impact on society of racism in the media if such racism is found to be manifested in the products of the media; and
- make findings and recommendations as appropriate (Racism in the media ... 2000:3).

# Representation: Race, Gender and Sexual Orientation

The contentious findings of the inquiry were that the South African media are racist. The causes, amongst others, were found to be that the South African media are still largely owned by white males who present South Africans with white male dominated interpretations and views (re-presentations) of South African realities. The media products they produce are white male dominated stereotypes of race (and gender) and conflated with images and interpretations that contribute to the securement of their dominance in the media industry and to the securement of Western capitalism.

In essence this investigation was thus about stereotyping and stereotypes. It is not the purpose of this unit to analyse this investigation and its research findings. Suffice to say that it was flawed with methodological inadequacies, untested assumptions and hypotheses, sometimes far-fetched interpretations and own ideological prejudice.

What is important to us, is that the investigation made media owners, editors, journalists, advertisers, media users and media researchers acutely aware of the topic of stereotyping and the role of stereotypes in society. It emphasised the importance for critical media studies to investigate the assumptions underlying the view that the media too often portray race, as well as certain minority groups, gender, gays and lesbians in a negative stereotyped way that may contribute to people's negative perceptions of others. We will return to the problem of race, gender and sexual orientation in the case studies offered at the end of this unit, but first we need to address the question: What are stereotypes?

## 15.2 WHAT ARE STEREOTYPES?

A straightforward definition is:

> [strereotypes are] the social classification of particular groups and people as often highly simplified and generalized signs, which implicitly or explicitly represent a set of values, judgements and assumptions concerning their behaviour, characteristics or history (O'Sullivan, Hartley, Saunders, Montgomery & Fiske 1994:299–300).

For example:

- Afrikaners are inherently racists.
- Germans are inherently Nazis.
- Black people are inherently inferior to the white race.
- Jews are inherently cunning.
- Zulus are inherently ferocious.
- Women are inherently inferior to men.
- Gays are sexually promiscuous.

The above are only some of the stereotypes associated with the groups mentioned above. To us the important questions are: Why do people tend to think in these ways about groups? Why do they simplify and generalise too such an extent that these stereotypes become an unquestioned part of their way of thinking about groups and individuals? Why does stereotypical thinking form part of peoples' everyday discourse about groups and individuals? Are stereotypes and stereotypical thinking institutionalised in media content?

There are many possible answers to these questions. It is also easy to answer these questions in the affirmative. However, stereotypes, stereotyping and stereotypical thinking ask for a far more in-depth investigation, beginning with questions about how people ascribe meaning to others, organisations and things. To this question there are also many approaches, perspectives and answers. From a social science perspective we want to draw your attention to two out of many possible, here highly simplified, answers:

- the social anthropologist, Claude Lévi Strauss's view that the nature of human kind is to think, interpret and make sense of the world and others in terms of binary oppositions, and
- the French structuralist, semiotician and social critic, Roland Barthes' view that we think about and interpret our world and others according to socially constructed meanings and values.

### 15.2.1 Claude Lévi-Strauss (1908-) and the theory of binary oppositions

Claude Lévi-Strauss was born in Brussels and studied law and philosophy in Paris. He then became a professor of sociology in Brazil, where he did research on the culture of the South American Indians. He was, and still is, regarded as one of the pioneers in the field of structural analysis in Cultural Anthropology.

Lévi-Strauss draws our attention to the incidence and meaning of binary oppositions and the role of myth in human thinking.

#### *Binary oppositions*

What is meant by binary oppositions is that the meaning of something depends on its opposite: "good" and the meaning of the concept "good" is dependent on "bad" and the meaning of "bad".

His point of departure was that a collective practice of laws, rules and values direct the individual's thinking and behaviour. Furthermore, society's (or a culture's) collective existence, thinking, values and uses, shape the individual and determine his/her individuality.

According to this line of thinking we could say, "I am who I am on the basis of what society allows me to be". The individual abides by the norms and values of a collective existence. Anything that may threaten this collectiveness is experienced as negative and as an opposition. Anything that is other than the collective whole in terms of which the self is constituted, is a threat.

From this we can deduct that it is human nature to feel threatened by anything that is other from the collective whole to which one belongs. For example, anything other that

## Representation: Race, Gender and Sexual Orientation

the black race is experienced as a (potential) threat by the black race, or for that matter the white race; anything that is other from my own sexual orientation or gender group, is an inherent threat. Usually our reaction is to retreat from, to combat or to humiliate the other as experienced to be in opposition to the self and the group of which the self is part.

According to Lévi-Strauss, the purpose of structuralist analysis should then be to uncover and describe the underlying structures which determine the individual as part of a group's way of thinking about life, behaviour, values and what is right and wrong. For Lévi-Strauss a possible way of uncovering these structures was

- through the analysis of the laws of descent and the marital laws of indigenous tribes, which he did in his work *Les structures élémentaires de la parenté* (1949)
- in the analysis of totemism and the role of totemism in a society, which he did in his work *Le totémisme aujourd'hui* (1963)
- in the analysis of the myths of a society, which he did in his work *Les mythologiques* (1964).

Based on these analyses he concluded that each society could in a unique way give expression to binary oppositions (in their ways of thinking, literature/theatre, behaviour) such as good/bad, rich/poor, belief/disbelief, order/chaos, hate/love, human kind/nature, intellect/emotion, capitalism/socialism, individual/group, fascism/democracy.

In other words, each society can understand the above mentioned and other oppositions differently and can express them differently in its thinking, behaviour and values. This thinking, behaviour and values are reflected in the society's symbolic works, we may say, including in the content of its media.

In the analysis of racism in the South African media one can thus begin by investigating how the values of journalists as being part of a group (white or black, male or female) constitute their way of thinking; whether their own values as being part of a group inherently colour their interpretation of reality, defines their conceptualisation of what constitutes objectivity and hinders an openness to perceive reality from the other's perspective or not.

It can be argued that the role of collective values formed on the basis of oppositions or being in opposition to other values and to others in general, is not only manifest and latent in the political content of the media, it permeates all content. Applying the method of analysing binary oppositions in, for example, television genres such as soap operas, situation comedies and police dramas has shown how these genres constantly handle binary oppositions such as good/bad, right/wrong, hero/villain and the values which society attaches to these oppositions. A demonstration of oppositions such as these in symbolic forms of expression like the situation comedy, police drama and soap opera presents us with an image of the way a society thinks and feels about and deals with these values. In structuralist media analyses, however, we are interested in more than the demonstration and description of binary oppositions in drama texts; our interest extends to the analysis of binary oppositions in propaganda (including news and documentary programmes).

© Juta & Co

For example, how does a newspaper handle binary oppositions in its editorials? Without being explictly "in oppostion to", opposition can be implicit in terms of the perspective (value/ideology) from which an editorial is written, and implicit in the style of writing. Without being explicit in terms of oppositions in crime reporting (us/them), crime stories can and usually are written from an implicit perspective based on us/them. The us "we the victims", the them "they the criminals". The us/them could also be implicitly black/white or vice versa.

We conclude this part on binary oppositions by saying that according to Lévi-Strauss we think about others and the world, we make sense of others and the world and we define others and the world in terms of oppositions. This is done from the perspective of one's own values, which are usually rooted in the values of the group to which one belongs. If the emphasis is only on oppositions then the result is a stereotyped viewed of others and the world. If there is unwillingness to openness and to focus on similarities, then the result is a closed and restricted view of others, reality and the world.

For the purpose of answering our question "What are stereotypes?" we can thus say, based on the theory of binary oppositions, that *stereotypes are the result of emphasising oppositions.*

## Myths

A second point Lévi-Strauss made is that values derive from and are usually based on myths.

Literally the word "myth" means narrative, fable or a story without foundation, which is handed down from one generation to another, such as *Red Riding-hood* in Western culture. Lévi-Strauss analysed the myths of various cultures in order to show that although the content may differ, the structure and intended meaning is the same from one generation to the next, namely to guide and reinforce the way society thinks about a certain question, such as acceptable behaviour and what is right and wrong. Although the story of *Red Riding-hood* might be adapted from one generation to the next, the underlying purpose is to warn children right from babyhood to beware of strangers. The older one becomes, the greater the number of guises the "stranger" can put on: the "stranger" can be a member of another race, sexual orientation, gender, language group, political group, and so on. What is important is that for society, a myth such as *Red Riding-hood* spells out an accepted behaviour pattern and way of thinking: beware of strangers/the unknown/whatever is different.

In Sotho culture this warning against strangers/the unknown finds expression in fables such as *Tselane le Ledimo*. This is the story of the little girl Tselane who was warned by her mother against the giant Kgokomodumo, but who disregarded the warning and was caught by Kgokomodumo.

Briefly: Lévi-Strauss's analysis of myth and binary oppositions is intended to show that a universal logic lies at the root of our thinking.

# Representation: Race, Gender and Sexual Orientation

It can be argued that today television is one of our biggest narrators of myths. If we accept the Straussian meaning of the word we might ask whether situation comedies, soap operas and police dramas – that is, the very genres which are typical of television as a medium – do not fulfil exactly the same functions as the myths (stories and fables) of earlier cultures. Are the stories of *Red Riding-hood* and *Tselane* not being repeated in one form or another in television scripts?

From this explanation of myth we can, for the purpose of answering our question "What are stereotypes?" deduct that *stereotypes are based on myths and are mythical in nature*.

Although his work is in the same vein as that of Lévi-Strauss, Roland Barthes approached the concept "myth" differently.

## 15.2.2 Roland Barthes (1915–1980) and the theory of social myth

Barthes drew our attention particularly to the mythical character of culture, popular culture and the media. His work gave rise to media theories and analyses of the media as a myth, a narrator of myths, and as a dynamic instrument for changing myths and creating new ones.

After his initial work, which was purely structuralist (see Barthes 1967), Barthes reinterpreted De Saussure's distinction between signifier and signified. In the spirit of post-structuralism he concluded that the meaning of a signifier (sign) is "open" to many possible meanings and interpretations but that whatever the meaning of a sign, it has a "layered" structure of first-, second- and third-order meaning. The three orders are (1) denotative, (2) connotative/mythical and (3) ideological meaning. Denotation, connotation and ideological meaning have already been discussed in Unit 10. Barthes placed the emphasis on mythical meaning.

By myths and mythical meaning (as second-order meaning) Barthes meant socially constructed meaning/values. For him a myth is not so much a non-truth. Rather it is a socially constructed "truth" with an ideological meaning, aimed at maintaining a *status quo*. Societies create and maintain myths for the sake of their own survival and often at the expense of other people.

To illustrate his view, he used a series of photographs entitled *The family of man*, in which people of different nations, social backgrounds and ages are depicted. The communicator of this series of photographs wanted to convey the meaning that the everyday behaviour of people throughout the world, and despite their race and cultures, is much the same.

With this series of photographs, Barthes argued, the communicator (in this case the photographer or publisher of the magazine) is implying that birth, death, work, knowledge and play, irrespective of culture and background, are universal, and that in this respect all people are the same, almost like a large family. Barthes regards this so-called "universality of being" as a myth. The myth, however, hides the real fate and state of man: namely extreme differences in power and wealth. The series of pictures therefore serves the myth, but

> ... this myth masks the radically different social and economic conditions under which people are born, work and die.
>
> (Culler 1983:34)

According to Barthes, the meaning and uses of other objects in society, and popular culture, function in exactly the same mythical way.

> Wine, for example, is [according to Barthes – PJF] not just one drink among others in France, but a totem-drink, corresponding to the milk of the Dutch or the tea ceremoniously taken by the British Royal Family. It is 'the foundation of a collective morality'. For the French, 'to believe in wine is a coercive act', and drinking wine a ritual of social integration. In generating mythical meaning, cultures seek to make their own norms seem facts of nature.
>
> (Culler 1983:34)

For the social scientist the concern is not with the quality of (French) wine, but rather with the second-order or mythical meanings given to something such as wine in and by a specific culture, such as in France "...wine is objectively good, and *at the same time*, the goodness of wine is a myth" (Barthes 1977:158).

In South African society, for example, we have myths about Africans, Afrikaners, English-speakers, Jews, Zulus, and so on. We also have myths about matters like the place and role of women in society, the status of the family in society and the role the church should play in society. These myths are expressed in various ways in our literature, theatrical performances, television advertisements, newspaper reports and films. For example, the myths about the relationship between middle-class Afrikaners and Englishmen are reinforced every week in the Sunday cartoon published by Rapport, namely *Ben, Babsie en Familie*. The cartoon strip *Madam & Eve* (originally published in *Mail & Guardian*), deals in similar vein with various myths about the social relationship between white and black South Africans.

At the political level, the ideology of apartheid was founded on various racially based myths, such as that black people are unable to govern a country in an orderly manner. Just as the state, education and the church, with their apartheid legislation, nationalistically inspired education and early justification of apartheid on Biblical grounds, preached and reinforced apartheid, the media (as a symbolic form of expression) contributed in various ways to the entrenchment of the apartheid myths. For example, for decades the mainstream South African newspapers were fairly negative in their reporting on blacks; there was a lot of emphasis on the "swart gevaar"; black South Africans played negative roles in South African films and whites and blacks did not appear together in the same television advertisements. Because of the unfavourable publicity given to black people in the media, legislation, education and the church, the myth that "blacks are unfit to rule the country" was reinforced.

Returning to what Barthes had to say about wine as a myth, we could analyse social practices such as *braaivleis* (barbecue) and everything that goes with it, as a myth signifying many layers of meaning associated with a culture. When we see a group of people attending a *braaivleis*, or a photograph of a group of white people attending a *braaivleis* it can embody meanings associated, for example, with Afrikaner culture, Afrikaner history, and Afrikaner values including political values.

Based on Barthes' theory of myth it is argued that media analysts should always try to uncover that which is hidden in media messages; to see beyond the mythical meaning being conveyed.

The social scientist should not be concerned with the qualities and effect of something such as wine, or *braaivleis*, or *pap* (cornmeal porridge), but with the image or second-order meaning (mythical meaning) given to wine, *braaivleis* and *pap* by the social conventions of a particular culture.

In the same vein, one may argue, the communication scientist should in the case of the analysis of advertisements, not be interested in the product advertised by the media, but in the meanings associated through social convention with the product and with the meanings associated with its possession and consumption. For Barthes these meanings are usually determined by the bourgeoisie, who themselves are the victims of capitalist considerations (according to him). For instance, the possession of a certain car implies membership of a specific social class. This is why advertisements for motor cars are intended to reinforce the myths associated with a certain social class's ideas about what a fine car is like or should be like. What are the myths to which motor car advertisements appeal, and how and by means of what signs and codes is the appeal made?

What are the relationships between myths and stereotypes? How does the discussion of myth relate to our question: What are stereotypes?

The answer is that myths (social beliefs) are mainly communicated through stereotypes. Stereotypes are so much part of the culture of a particular group that members accept them unquestioningly as a kind of natural law. For example, during the apartheid years negative myths about black people, such as that they are criminal, cannot rule a country, are unskilled, cannot be educated, and so on, prevailed among the supporters of apartheid who, within the context of the culture of apartheid, including its laws and practices, seldom questioned these myths.

It can be argued that the media, with exceptions, played a role in strengthening these myths. In other words, in the apartheid years the media's mainly negative stereotyped way of portraying black people contributed to the ideology of apartheid. Newspapers, for example, would focus on blacks as criminals and barbaric. Such focus supported the myth that black people are subordinate and inferior to white people and their so-called superior culture.

Under apartheid, South African movies tended to cast black people only in the roles of clowns, servants, labourers, thieves, murderers. As such, movies fostered an image of black people as being stupid, impertinent or deceitful. In short, through stereotypes, media representations of black people implicitly and explicitly emphasised the differences (oppositions) between white and black. The exceptions in which the media questioned these myths and represented black people in a multifaceted and contextualised way, were few and far between.

Since the 1970s this began to change. Today, many examples can be cited of a more balanced media representation and even of a deliberate effort to question myths about people. This also holds for the portrayal of women and gays.

However, it is important to keep in mind that all groups tend to strengthen their myths about other groups by thinking and responding to them in terms of stereotypes. Black people also have myths and stereotypes of white people, the English speaking population of South Africa of Afrikaans people, Afrikaans people of the English, and so on. In the South African English media many examples can be found of Afrikaners being portrayed as backward, Hitlerite, overweight, bombastic, and conservative. Luckily, this is also beginning to change.

In the previous paragraphs we looked at two theories that can contribute to our understanding of the general nature of stereotypes. From these theories we can deduct that stereotypes are

- the result of emphasising oppositions and differences between people and groups, and
- have the purpose of strengthening myths about people and groups.

Now, let us take a closer look at the characteristics and working of stereotypes.

### 15.2.3 The characteristics and working of stereotypes

In critical media studies a stereotype is considered to be a scheme or a prejudice in terms of which people interpret people and groups and form particular conceptions about them. If we follow this approach, the outstanding characteristics of stereotypes are the following:

- Stereotypes depend on generalisation and *simplification*. Generalisation implies the negation of individuality; in other words a stereotype is considered valid for all the members of the group concerned: *all* Jews are wily; *all* Afrikaners are racists; all black people are lazy; *all* gays are promiscuous; *all* women are inferior to men.
- Stereotypes may be negative or positive, depending on how the group or person is assessed. Up till now we have only concentrated on negative stereotypes. It is important to keep in mind that positive stereotypes, in other words refusing to acknowledge the negative aspects of a person or a group, can also blur one's perceptions about a person or a group.
- Notwithstanding their fictitious origin and lack of foundation, stereotypes have very real and mainly negative social consequences for the group and the individual as part of the stereotyped group. For example, stereotypes in Western culture about women, Jews, gypsies, Turks, blacks, gays, lesbians, and so on can contribute to manoeuvring these groups into particular roles, including playing subordinate roles in society. Jews may tend to isolate themselves; gays may succumb to the stereotype of being promiscuous and become promiscuous, and so on. The result is a social reality that creates the impression that the stereotypes are accurate all along. In other words,

## Representation: Race, Gender and Sexual Orientation

the self-image induced by stereotypes can persuade a person or a group to whom a stereotype is applied to see himself/herself or the group in a specific role and assume or learn this role as a form of anticipatory behaviour.

The rise of black, feminist and gay liberation movements and organisations is the direct consequence of the negative stereotypes regarding these groups and the role patterns, role expectations and image formation the stereotypes have created in society and forced on the groups in question.

- With reference to the social consequences of stereotypes, a fourth characteristic is that people generally appeal to the stereotypes associated with a particular group in order to arrive at the verdict that a person or group "just is like that". Stereotypes create a vicious circle. To the critics of a particular group or person the stereotype seems "normal" and any resistance to it "abnormal". Because stereotypes form part of the social and psychological make-up of a society, criticism of stereotypes is seen as an assault on security. From this point of view, stereotypes are only a problem for those who have been stereotyped, not for the modal group(s) in the society, or the communicators of the stereotyped messages.

- A fifth characteristic of stereotypes is that those who employ them consider them to be true: the stereotype in fact becomes a kind of primordial image, and archetype or prototype. A stereotype would then be seen not as a prejudiced idea but as a true reflection of an essential characteristic of a person or a group on the basis of which the person or group should be typed. The difference between groups is then emphasised on the basis of the negative characteristics of a group. Whites differ from blacks because whites are all lazy and blacks are the opposite.

The problem with this view is that its proponents generally emphasise only the negative essential characteristics whereas there is surely an implicit obligation to take the positive essential characteristics into account at the same time, which could lead to the conversion of a negative stereotype into a positive one.

Another weakness of the argument that stereotypes are true concerns the distinction between archetypes and stereotypes. Although this is a complex distinction, we shall merely say that archetypes are primordial ideas/experiences/ opinions, which are inherited and have a genetic basis in the unconscious mind. One could also describe them as an inborn orientation that we bring into the world with us. These are Jung's primordial images; the most famous of which are probably the primordial images of the opposite sex, the Anima and the Animus. In addition there are the archetypes concerning good and evil, light and shadow, witch and god, hero and villain, and so on.

The Jungian views on the collective unconsciousness imply that a child is not born with a spirit and mind as clean as a blank sheet of paper, on which anything can be written. A child is predestined from birth to think and feel in the same way as his primeval ancestors did.

Whereas the archetype is an ancient primordial image, the stereotype has social and ideological connotations; it is variable and comprehensible. In South Africa at present we are seeing how people are changing their stereotypes about those of different races or at least how attempts are being made, in the media as well as elsewhere, to get rid of stereotypes, especially negative ones.

A last remark regarding the truth of stereotypes: anyone who contends that stereotypes are true has not taken into account the fact that there are more differences between members of a single group than there are between different groups. The stereotype of Afrikaners as narrow-minded and bucolic loses sight of the fact that there are more differences and variations within the Afrikaner group than there are differences that serve to distinguish Afrikaners from Englishmen.

To sum up, a stereotype may be defined as a prejudiced, generalised, simplified conception of a person and/or group which could be either negative or positive, but which usually implies negative consequences. It emphasises the differences between people and groups. A stereotype is considered by those who employ it to be a true conception about what the individual or group is like; it is accepted as a "normal" typing and any deviation from the stereotype is seen as a threat to personal and social security. Unlike an archetype, a stereotype is the result of and is subject to changing social and ideological views. A stereotype is therefore not a constant, but a fluid and changeable concept.

### 15.2.4 The origin of stereotypes

There are different theories about the origin of stereotypes. These vary from the complex theories of cognitive psychology, sociolinguistic theories of meaning, anthropological theories and sociological theories.

Because race is such an issue in South Africa, we look at two (popular) theories on the origin of negative stereotypes about black people. One being anthropological and the other theological in origin. Note the Western origin of both.

One of the first written records of the negative stereotype(s) of people other than of Western origin as being barbaric, savage, wild and primitive can be found in Thomas Hobbes' book, *Leviathan* (1651). In this work he describes South American Indians as a chaotic aggressive species, as *homo homini lupus*. He equates them with the Medieval description of and belief in *Homo ferus* – the so-called werewolf (cf. Pieterse [sa]:32). This image of the other ("other" meaning other than European, British and North American) was the topic of many debates and written works by authors and philosophers such as John Locke (1632–1704), Jean-Jacques Rousseau (1712–1778) and others. In these first writings about other civilisations, Africans were generally described and experienced as wild and depicted and associated with animals and animal behaviour. These views were strengthened with visual images of naked black Africans and a complete absence of Western utility articles – clothes and utility articles being Western signs and barometers of civilisation. Even the German philosopher, Hegel (1770–1831), whose work later influenced Marx (1818–1863) and Engels (1820–1895), contributed to the negative stereotypes about Africa. He wrote about Africa as "a continent without a history". This stereotype still surfaces today in the minds and thinking of many Western people.

The debates and writings gradually developed from portraying and emphasising the "other" as being barbaric, wild and savage (based on the werewolf myth, one can argue), to the origin of the concept *bon sauvage* – the noble savage, which in its turn gave moral support to the political idea and ideal of colonialism – to civilise the savage. Pieterse (sa:37) claims that the concept "noble savage" turned into *noblesse oblige* – the privilege of the "civilised" to civilise the "uncivilised". This in turn became the slogan of early socialist thinking.

In early theological writings Africans were often stereotyped as the children of Ham (Old Testament). As early as in the Church of Augustine (AD354) this stereotype provided justification for slavery. Although slavery was at this stage "colourless", the association of Ham with slavery and with the Curse of Canaan became a central theme in the Christian church's treatment of race in the sixteenth and seventeenth centuries. From hereon it was a short step to use this argument as theological justification for the use of Africans as slaves. The view of Africa as the continent of servants and to serve others can be also be related to the Dutch's theological interpretations of the Book of Genesis in the seventeenth and eighteenth centuries, and to the interpretation that although all people are descendant from Adam and Noah the continents are personified by Shem (Asia), Ham (Africa) and Japheth (Europe), and that these continents stand in a service-providing relationship to each other.

If the above paragraphs serve one purpose then it is to show how stereotypes are deeply rooted in

- people's thinking at a specific point in time
- social, political and economic ideologies, and in
- theological interpretations and dogma.

For media practitioners and critics it is important to keep the above in mind, especially when they deal with matters of race, gender, sexual orientation and the interests of all minority groups, such as for example, the physically handicapped, environmentalists, and so on. In dealing with these matters and groups they should critically reflect on their own possible prejudices and the origins of such prejudices.

### 15.2.5 The need to contextualise media representations

Similarly, media critics and media users should take care not to pre-judge media representations as being stereotyped (cf. Branston & Stafford 1999:130). Put in another way, to say that a media text is "distorted" or "unrepresentative" may ignore, amongst others:

- the unique character and nature of the medium
- the specific genre of the text in which a so-called stereotyped representation may occur
- the complex relationship between reality and representation
- the motive of the communicator
- the nature of perception and the eye of the beholder.

The *nature of a medium* places heavy demands in terms of time and space, in short, in terms of codes of production, on communicators. The nature of a medium often leads to the impossibility of contextualising a representation within the structural confines of a single story, programme, article or film, be it a representation of a view, a person or a group. Rather than blaming the communicators, one must also take into account the intrinsic shortcomings of a medium. For example, a newspaper simply hasn't got the space to publish the complete speech of a politician, or to give a full account of all the different views on a topic. Of course, responsible journalism will try doing it in the most objective way possible. This may also be done in different articles in different editions of a newspaper. Often media critics tend to ignore this and base their criticism on a single story in a single edition of a newspaper, or a single television/radio programme. The very nature of media communication, namely that they are symbolic forms of expression and as such structured representations must be kept in mind. By that we mean, amongst other things, that they are intrinsically incapable of providing "the real thing" and that we shouldn't expect them to do so.

Furthermore, the *genre of a media text* is important. For example, comedy, in particular, lends itself to the depiction of stereotypes. Criticising a television situation comedy for containing stereotyped images of people and groups is, to a certain extent, to criticise the nature of the genre (cf. Unit 7 and the functions of entertainment). A television series such as *Orkney Snork Nie* is seen by some viewers as ridiculing Afrikaners. Although *Orkney Snork Nie* undoubtedly provides us with a stereotyped portrayal of the Afrikaner, criticism of it must be within the context of the genre. Banning it because of its stereotypes will be ridiculous. The same applies to the popular cartoon strip *Madam & Eve* that communicates through the means of a stereotyped view of the relations between white people and black people in South Africa. One can also argue that editorials often tend towards stereotyping people, groups and issues. However, criticising an editorial comment as being stereotyped or not representative of reality, is to ignore the fact that the editorial (as a genre) is ideological in nature and as such based on a specific point of view.

*Advertisements* (as a genre) are often used in research about stereotypes. For example, in South Africa advertisements are used in research to illustrate race relations. In the apartheid years black people were hardly represented in advertisements of products aimed at a white market, or they were depicted in the stereotypical roles of servants, filling in the background of an affluent white population (as if the whole of the white population was/is affluent), and so on. Since the demise of apartheid this began to change. Today black people are portrayed as being affluent and white people are often portrayed in ridiculed roles, or in mixed race scenarios which is as yet far removed from the experience of the majority of people in South Africa.

What is often overlooked in research is that advertisements are in their very nature, and most of the time, abstractions of reality and thus unrealistic and idealised representations. Their communicative purpose is to create needs and desires, to act as role models towards status aspiration, and to sustain the capitalist ideology of consumption. To target the advertising industry for its portrayal of race and with the possible intention of showing that the South African advertising industry is inherently racist (cf. the discussion of the SAHRC's investigation into the South African media and race further on), as was the plan at the time of writing, should thus be handled with care. Research without taking the nature of advertisements and its genre into account will be methodologically flawed.

The above, in other words the phenomenological nature of media communication as symbolic communication (and advertising often as metaphorical communication) and the nature of genre, emphasises the *complex relationship between representation and reality* – a topic addressed by numerous philosophers and art historians and critics with no definite answers except the certainty that we cannot expect any form of expression (be it works of art, literary texts or visual, verbal and written media texts) to be an exact copy of reality. What can be unravelled and criticised in media representations is the *motive of the communicator*. Is there, through the use of stereotypes a deliberate motive to discredit a certain group, person, organisation or topic?

What, for example, is the motive of the author (and the *Mail & Guardian*) in an article published in the *Mail & Guardian* (20–25 April 2001) in which the author, who also happens to be the publisher of the magazine *Hei Voetsek*, generalises stereotypes about Afrikaners who attended the Oudtshoorn Arts Festival and happened to come across him in the following way?:

> They [festival attenders – PJF] fled with their children when I, with demonstrative verbosity, used the Cape lingua franca to the extreme by telling them that they were *naaiers* (fuckers), *fokken dom konte* (fucking stupid cunts), *varkvretende* (pig-eating) honkies and a bunch of deluded idiots for thinking that Brother Jesus even took the time to listen to meat-eating beasts who cared more for their pit bull terriers than they did for their fellow black humans ...
>
> Thick-skinned, cellulite-ridden and varicose-veined tannies would routinely mutter their "*Sies! Sies!*", only for me to berate them for not saying "*Sies*" when they and their husbands perpetrated the apartheid wars against the nation. Icy glares from double-thighed, double-chinned and double-stomached males were met with sheer arrogance and a fearlessness that scared the carcasses in their overfed bellies as I would scream, for all to hear, that there they were again, the *volk*, the *fokken volk*, eating, drinking and talking *kak* (shit) as only they could.
> (Dread 2001:5)

The author is falling back on stereotypes (among certain groups) of Afrikaners as being fat, dull, and racist. He expresses himself in a mode than can be interpreted as hate speech and bad taste. In this case, one can argue that there is a deliberate motive to belittle and humiliate Afrikaners. Even more important is the unstated reason (motive) why the *Mail & Guardian* decided to cover the Oudsthoorn Festival by means of this, what can be seen to be a derogatory article. What can one deduce from this about the *Mail & Guardian*'s attitude towards the group of people involved, the kind of cultural activity in which they engaged and whether they are of the opinion that such a report (review) can contribute to better group relations and understanding in a multicultural society? Fortunately, examples like this are seldom encountered in responsible newspaper journalism and print. Not even in known rightist newspapers, which often still perpetuate the ideology of apartheid, will attacks of this kind be found against black South Africans, Afrikaans-speaking South Africans, English-speaking South Africans, or whatever language and cultural group.

On 11 October 2001 the *Mail & Guardian* published an apology to those readers whom the article offended. This was done after the Freedom Front launched a complaint with the Press Ombudsman who requested the *Mail & Guardian* to apologise and allow the Freedom Front the opportunity to publish its reaction to the article.

However, again, one should contextualise criticism such as the above. It may be the perception of a member of the Afrikaans-speaking cultural group that the article is derogatory whilst other people, even within the Afrikaans-speaking group, may not agree with such an argument. This brings us to the complex nature of perception itself. As far as perception is concerned, it suffices to mention the art historian Ernest Gombrich's (1977) argument that in perception, or how we perceive things to be

- there is no such thing as an innocent eye (in other words, perception is seldom objective);
- the ways in which we perceive something involves intricate mechanisms of expectation, selection, and decoding (in other words, how we want and have been taught and conditioned to see things);
- we perceive things (e.g. people, reality, topics, groups) according to a definite, culturally structured mental set.

### 15.2.6 Changing stereotypes

From the above discussions it is clear that stereotypes and the act of stereotyping are complex. One can even argue that it is part of human nature. The only way in which we can change our stereotyped views of groups (for example, of gays and lesbians or of a specific race), organisation (for example a labour union or a political party), an individual (for example, an alcoholic), or a topic (for example, abortion) is

- to be critical of our own views
- to be sensitive towards the feelings of others
- to be aware of the possible harm our views and perceptions can cause to others.

When it comes to the media's representations of groups, organisations, people and topics, the same applies. The media and each journalist, programme maker, advertiser, in short, every media worker, should be

- critical of his/her own views and interpretations
- sensitive towards the feelings of others

## Representation: Race, Gender and Sexual Orientation

- aware of the possible harm his/her views, perceptions and interpretations can cause to others.

On a more concrete level, the following measures can be employed by media organisations.

People of different race, cultural, gender and sexual orientation can be employed. This involves *employment policy*. A mix of staff can counterbalance stereotyped interpretations, representations and subjective and one-sided news and programme values, policies and practices.

Policies and quotas can be introduced to reflect *planned balanced representations*: for example, policy could direct the inclusion of different races in television programming, or, as is already the case in some countries, the inclusion of people (as characters) of different sexual orientation in television programming.

Both the employees of a media organisation as well as the public must have the *right of reply* and to object to what they perceive as stereotyped representations or as derogatory. Such objections must be investigated and the outcomes thereof published and/or broadcast.

Media organisations should be encouraged to formulate *codes of conduct* with the purpose of guiding their representations. A good example is the (South African) *Sunday Times*' code of conduct for *Sunday Times* staff in dealing with issues of race, religion and cultural difference (Racism in the media ... 2000:47).

### Sunday Times staff

- Will act independently when reporting issues of race, but will take note of sensitivities regarding race, or other issues, in their work;
- Report on these issues where there is a demonstrable public interest; when race is a central issue of the story, racial identifications should be used only when they are important to readers' understanding of what has happened and why it has happened;
- Will not unjustifiably offend others in reporting on sensitive issues relating to race, religion or cultural difference;
- Will not use language or pictures which are offensive, reinforce stereotypes, fuel prejudice or xenophobia;
- Will actively seek diversity in sources which represent the whole community;
- Will be sensitive to cultural differences and values and will actively seek to ensure that reporting takes these considerations into account;
- In crime reporting, will not make mention of the race or religion of either victim or alleged perpetrator, unless that information is meaningful and in the public interest;
- Will uphold the newspaper's principles of fairness, especially when dealing with issues of race; and
- Will, in dealing with the public, be sensitive to cultural differences and not conduct themselves in any way which might unnecessarily offend.

MEDIA STUDIES

> **Race checklist for reporters and editors**
> - What is the public interest in this report?
> - Has this report been treated differently because of race? If so, why? Is this justified?
> - Is the report – even if factually correct – likely to fuel xenophobia or prejudice? If so, is this justified? Is there any way around this?
> - Is the report likely to offend people? If so, why? Is this justified?
> - What about the language used in the report? Does it unnecessarily reinforce stereotypes? If so change it!
> - What about the voices in the story? Have we actively sought out diverse opinion from ordinary people and experts alike?
> - Are there quotes in the story that are racist or possibly offensive? Are these comments balanced by others? Are we justified in using these comments? If so, why?
> - Is the report sensitive to possible cultural differences or values? How do we know? Should anything be changed to be sensitive to these differences? If so why?
> - In crime reporting, have we mentioned the race of perpetrators and victims? If so, is it information which is meaningful and in the public interest? Why?
> - Has any pressure been brought to bear in reporting this story? Has the issue of race been mentioned? If so, what and why? Do any of these arguments have any bearing on the reporting of the story? Why?
> - Have we been fair in the report to all parties?

### 15.2.7 Current issues in the study of representation

One of the main issues in present research about representation is the impact of *globalisation*, global media and global media content on *identity*. The topic of globalisation is dealt with in Unit 19. We have also seen in Unit 13 how one of the main concerns of developing (Third World) countries about media and cultural imperialism was/is how developing countries and their citizens come to see themselves from the negative perspectives about them in the media representations from developed and First World countries. It concerns the tendency to focus mainly on corruption, war, conflict and poverty in representations of developing countries.

Apart from the following features of globalisation, namely that it is about
- a new world economic order
- a new political order
- a new global society and culture
- an information and knowledge society in which the growth of information and communication technology (ICT) plays a key role,

an outstanding feature of globalisation is the growth of the *culture industry*. This is an industry in which the media and its related industries such as public relations, marketing and advertising, the Internet, and the mass entertainment industry are the most prominent role players. One can think of the media as the common carrier of all the forces of globalisation. Increasingly, multinational and transnational media corporations are responsible for what we and people all over the world get to see, listen to, and read. They are the carriers of economic messages to which markets and individuals respond on a daily basis; the carriers of political messages and interpretations that world leaders base their interpretations on; and, through their entertainment, the carriers of values in which traditions and traditional political, social and moral values are challenged with global, often liberal, values. Important questions are:

- What is the impact of global communication and its representations of cultures, ethnic groups, race, and countries on our perceptions of other cultures, groups, and so on, and on our perceptions of ourselves as a nation?
- What is the role of the mix that cultures and with it the emergence of a global society plays in the formation and conservation of own identities?

This being an introduction to the topic of representation, we end this section of the unit with these questions unanswered. However, we are fully aware of their growing importance and the need to be researched. We now turn to specific case studies on representation.

## 15.3 CASE STUDIES IN REPRESENTATION

In the following four sections Beschara Karam takes a closer look at the role of the media in the representation of race, AIDS sufferers, gays and lesbians, and women.

### 15.3.1 Race

Braham (1982) discusses how the media reports race. He argues that on one hand you have the majority of journalists who believe that the news reports itself, and that news is "immutable, unchanging and obvious" (op cit:269); on the other hand, you have critics of the media who claim that there is no such thing – rather, news is "manipulated, manufactured, shaped and suppressed" (ibid). This is an ongoing debate – do you report the news as is, or do you make it interesting and sensationalise it? Is there such a thing as objective news reporting? These are important questions – the difference between reflecting reality and reinterpreting reality. Braham does conclude, however, that the role of the media is to provide "truthful, objective and news worthy items" (op cit:265) that reflect issues accurately while still appealing to its larger audience. Although it is not the aim of this case study to look at the ethics of media reporting, we will focus on how the media represents race in South Africa. Our focus is on the recent (2000) investigation of the South African Human Rights Commission (SAHRC) into the relationship between the South African media and racism.

MEDIA STUDIES

### Case study 15.1: South African Human Rights Commission: a chronology of the media racism enquiry

In as early as 1997, three years after the ushering in of a new democratic era, South African Human Rights Commission (SAHRC) chairman Barney Pityana co-wrote an article in a South African newspaper, the *Sowetan* alleging that the media practises "subliminal racism by creating a negative image of Africans" and that "[t]he media is only patriotic to a minority section of our society. What it is doing and continues to do unchallenged is to promote the notion of European conservative superiority and excellence against incompetent and fraudulent Africans who lie their way to the top" (Barrell 2000b:1). In the same article Pityana makes the following statements concerning the media, namely that the media

- are "questioning and killing the locus standi of the African"
- are "out to damage the integrity of Africans"
- "uses the cliché of press freedom to continue to abuse its powers and the limits of that freedom"
- "has subconsciously elected not to understand the African"
- "continues with impunity to negate the African mindset"
- "columns are littered with racial innuendo and statements" (Barrell 2000b:3).

The article in the *Sowetan* on 25 August 1997 was followed up, in 1998, with the Black Lawyers Association in conjunction with the Association of Black Accountants of South Africa recommending that the SAHRC launch an official investigation into two newspapers, namely the *Mail & Guardian* and the *Sunday Times*, for "alleged violations of fundamental rights of black people" (A feebly disguised assault ... 2000:1). Later that same year, the SAHRC officially resolved to "conduct an investigation into racism in the media in general" (ibid).

Beginning this investigation was the monitoring of 1 430 news articles by researchers hired by the SAHRC, in a six-week period covering July–August of 1999 (ibid). The SAHRC concluded from this analysis that there are indeed incidents of "racism and stereotypical reporting" (ibid) in the media. The SAHRC's Interim Report, based on this research (the Media Monitoring Project and researcher Claudia Braude's reports), and citing many examples of stories that violate the human rights of black Africans (for instance, the article "African war virus spreads to Caprivi" (ibid) is cited as an example because pictures of unidentified bodies were used and this allegedly "contributed to the demoralisation of Black deaths and represented them as just another statistic") was released in November 1999. The chairman, Pityana, stated that the media has been known to play a "negative role in race relations by being used as a vehicle for hate speech ... and for hostile and racist messages" (ibid). Swindells (2000:2) reports that President Thabo Mbeki was critical of the media for failing to address the "realities of democratic South Africa" and that he has called for the founding of a government-owned national newspaper.

At the time that the Interim Report was released by the SAHRC, South African editors acknowledged that racism does exist in the media, whose ownership is still predominantly white, as is their news agenda, however, lawyers representing editors' groups at the SAHRC hearings said there was "no substance to complaints and examples submitted to the SAHRC of racism" (Swindells 2000:2). Sheena Duncan (Ngobeni 2000a:2) publicly slates the Media Monitoring Project's and Claudia Braude's reports as "ridiculous".

In January 2000 the SAHRC wrote to various editors on specific claims made in its Interim Report, and in February 2000 the SAHRC issued the first of more than thirty subpoenas ordering media organisations and institutions to attend hearings into allegations of racism in the media. These subpoenas demanded mandatory attendance at the SAHRC hearings "to testify on your product's policies and guidelines on the reporting of, and commenting on, national and international events, which impact on racism and possible incidents of racism" (A feebly disguised assault ... 2000:1). On 14 February 2000, while the ruling African National Congress (ANC) government overtly supported the SAHRC's decision to issue subpoenas, the opposition parties reacted negatively, claiming that because of these state-sanctioned subpoenas South Africa's international image "is under threat" (ibid). Four days after this, the editor of *Business Day* supported the official opposition party stance, stating that these subpoenas "could be interpreted abroad as South Africa's version of the McCarthy witch hunt in America" (ibid) and could result in the upset of foreign investment in South Africa, and especially at a time "when [President Thabo] Mbeki's government image is extremely positive nationally and internationally" (Kadalie in Ngobeni 2000b). The editorial appearing in *The Guardian* in London (Kadalie 2000:31) not only accuses the government of being "McCarthyite" but also that these actions echo those of the "worst ways of apartheid dictatorship" (ibid). The threats of demanding official minutes of meetings, threatening searches of their workplaces, forcible removal of documentation and the imprisonment of editors – simply because these editors have printed what they chose to print in their newspapers – smacks of totalitarianism. Rhoda Kadalie (ibid), a former SAHRC member, refers to the SAHRC as the "thought police" of the new South Africa. Sheena Duncan, one of South Africa's most influential liberal voices, resigned from the Human Rights Commission Trust as a result of the subpoenas that were issued, expressing her dismay at what she sees as a "violation" of the right to freedom of expression. Edward Bird of the Media Monitoring Project as well as researcher Claudia Braude distanced themselves from the issuing of subpoenas. Bird also raised his concerns that the SAHRC had "misinterpreted the researchers' analysis and used it to violate press freedom" and that his organisation did not make any allegations in its report on racism in the media. Items quoted in the Media Monitoring Project "were used as examples of racial stereotyping and in no way suggests that these reports constitute human rights violations or require censorship" (in Ngobeni 2000a:3).

From 21 February to 28 February 2000, the SAHRC met with the South African National Editors Forum and other influential newspaper owners and decided to withdraw subpoenas whilst retaining the right to reissue them if so desired. (These subpoenas included that issued to London's *Financial Times* editor Richard Lambert for its 1996 article titled *South Africa moves on Moslem militants*, about police attempts to curb violence by Islamic vigilantes. The Media Review Network, an Islamic lobby organisation, complained to the SAHRC that the story denigrated Muslims. If Lambert chose not to comply, he faces a six-month jail sentence were he ever to visit South Africa.) On 6 March 2000, the SAHRC 5-day hearings commenced.

## The SAHRC's Final Report

The final SAHRC report, issued on 24 August 2000, states that the South African media could be "characterised as racist institutions" (Taitz 2000:1). Even though the SAHRC could find no instances of the mainstream media indulging in "blatant advocacy of racial hatred or incitement to racial violence" (A feebly disguised assault ... 2000:2). The SAHRC did find, however, "much evidence of condemnation of hate speech and increasingly appropriate reporting of race crimes in our country. ... This finding holds regardless as to whether there is conscious or unconscious racism, direct or indirect" (ibid; Taitz 2000:1). The SAHRC further referred to the rather worrying "... culminative effect of persistent racist stereotypes, insensitive and at times reckless disregard for the effect of racist expressions on others" (A feebly disguised assault ... 2000:2).

## The SAHRC's recommendations

> Among the SAHRC Report's recommendations were:
> - The establishment of a statutory regulatory framework that uniformly deals with all the media
> - The aggressive recruitment and training of black staff
> - Regular workshops for journalists to promote quality and human dignity
> - The establishment of cadet training programmes for aspirant journalists which would ensure that an understanding of the Constitution and human rights was integrated into the training received.
>
> (Taitz 2000:1)

For a full account of the SAHRC's Final Report, including all the SAHRC's recommendations log on to: http://www.sahrc.org.za

## Response to the SAHRC

Although the definition of the concept "race" is extremely complex and multifaceted, and it is not the intention of this case study to give a definitive and

## Representation: Race, Gender and Sexual Orientation

all-encompassing definition thereof, we do look briefly at how the concept was dealt with at the SAHRC hearings. Lynette Steenveld, in her article *Defining the undefinable* (Steenveld 2000b:11) focuses specifically on racism as a concept, and in doing so, refers to Kwame Anthony Appiah's book *In my father's house: Africa in the philosophy of culture*. Quoting Appiah: "Talk of 'race' is particularly distressing for those of us who take culture seriously. For where race works ... it works as a sort of metaphor for culture; and it does so only at the price of biologising what is culture ..." (in Steenveld 2000b:11), which, for Steenveld, establishes that although race is a power practice, the concept of "race" as referring to races with essential characteristics is a false notion. Preferring the term "racialism", as encompassing the differences between individuals on the premise of an assumed "race", Steenveld further argues that apartheid was therefore based on a false concept, namely that people can be divided according to different "races". The result? South Africa and its citizens have been moulded by an incorrect premise, and while affirmative action may serve to correct this premise, it is in essence working within the same false concept, thereby perpetuating the view.

Looking in part to redress this view, and in part to understand it, Steenveld focuses on SAHRC panellist Margaret Legum who described contemporary racism as " ... the result of the theory or idea that white people are superior to black people" (Steenveld 2000b:11). Legum interprets this to mean that "we have all been taught racism: that means black people as well as white. Racism means that all people's relationships, even with themselves are influenced by colour" (2000b:11). She continues:

> Racism is the outworking in a culture of an ideology or a theory that one "race" or people is superior/inferior to another. Racism is at work when not only those who belong to the so-thought superior group, but also those in the so-thought inferior group, believe the ideology of superiority at some level of their consciousness. They do so because all of the manifestations of their common culture reflect that ideology, so they take it without having to think about it.
>
> (ibid)

While fellow SAHRC panelist Joe Thloloe defines race as the "behaviour towards another based on one's belief and assumptions about 'race' AND the belief that one or more 'races' are superior to others" (Steenveld 2000b:11), there is, implicit in this "definition", the view that black individuals cannot practise racism towards white individuals. This is because black people are seen (in broad historical terms) unable to enforce the cultural belief that they are superior to white people. Thus for Legum, racism is simply the "ideology of white power" (in Steenveld 2000b:11). Steenveld points out that in terms of a media critique, this would refer to any representations which contributed to notions of whiteness as superior and blackness as inferior or as less significant/powerful. This view is echoed in the South African Broadcasting Corporation's (SABC) presentation to the SAHRC prepared by Professor Dumisani

Hlope and Christine Qunta, who state that "Racism is constituted therefore, when racial prejudices are matched with the power to act on such prejudices" (ibid).

Challenging Legum's views expressed in the media, Howard Barrell (Steenveld 2000b:11) pointed out in his SAHRC submission for the *Mail & Guardian*, that Legum's view still presupposes an understanding of "race" as some essential category. Why is defining "race" so important? Referring back to Appiah's view, given that there are no "races": "there is nothing in the world that can do all we ask race to do for us ... The evil that is done is done by the concept, and by easy – yet impossible – assumptions as to its application" (ibid), we need to ask whether we need to define race before being able to identify it? Steenveld (ibid) raises the essential question about how we can, if at all, construct an "anti-racist politics", and by extension an anti-racist media? What role does the media play in this, and, most importantly, is it possible to reduce "race" to a nonessential concept?

> **Race:** the group into which people are classified on the basis of heritable and essential differences
>
> **Racialism:** the (false) belief that there are heritable characteristics possessed by members of our species that enables us to classify people into distinct groups of "races". In this view, the traits and characteristics identified constitute a kind of "racial essence" (simply a classificatory system of essential differences – but no value judgements attached to the classification).
>
> **Race discrimination:** the behaviour or practice of distinguishing between people on the basis of their presumed "race"
>
> **Race prejudice:** the attitude, belief, mental construct that makes judgements about people on the basis of their presumed "race"
>
> **Racism:** the system of beliefs and practices that people can be classified into groups on the basis of presumed differences which justifies the unequal allocation of power and privilege.
>
> (Steenveld 2000b:11)

As a result of the SAHRC hearings, one newspaper that underwent a process of introspection, was the *Sunday Times*. Immediately following the SAHRC's Final Report, the *Sunday Times* formed a Race Charter Committee, to look at how it should report news in an ever changing, dynamic society. Basically asking the same questions as Peter Braham (1982), that is, how is the media to report race, the same conclusion was arrived at. A reporter for the *Sunday Times*, Phylicia Oppelt (2000: 46) and member of this recently formed Race Charter Commission, emphasised the importance of maintaining news objectivity and independence when reporting news of political sensitivity, and while not positioning news in terms of political correctness for the sake of political correctness. Oppelt also stressed the significance of not retreating from the delicate issue of racism, but rather to address it head-on. Oppelt states that the *Sunday Times* Race Charter is essentially a code of conduct for all staff members in dealing with issues of race, religion and cultural diversity:

> ... take responsibility for what we report and the effect that it has; keep in mind that although we are now part of a democratic government, our very recent apartheid past is still prevalent especially where race and racism is concerned. While acknowledging our multi-racial and multi-cultural society we must report differences and beliefs in an unbiased and objective way.
>
> (Oppelt 2000:46)

Laura Pollecutt, at the time of writing executive director of the (South African) Freedom of Expression Institute (FXI), in her article *Freedom vs racism* (Pollecutt 2000:29), expresses the FXI's position that there should be no hierarchy of human rights, that is, no human right should take precedence over another. Essentially the FXI views itself, and the role that it plays, as part of the human rights family in its entirety, and as such desires to see the whole human rights agenda advanced, not just one aspect. While postulating that the definition of race is an ongoing one, that faces all of us, under no circumstances should we equate "covert racism with outright 'hate speech'" (ibid).

Pollecutt claims that there are many critics who wish to advance the idea that covert racism is banned by the South African Constitution. However, she emphatically states that it is overt "hate speech" that "constitutes incitement to harm" which does not have the protection of the Constitution (Pollecutt 2000:29). Covert racism and overt hate speech are two different things, legally as well as conceptually. Without fundamentally criticising the SAHRC, Pollecutt feels it is imperative that the SAHRC not give the impression that it has more power than it does: "In terms of the powers of the courts and in particular the Constitution, FXI is sure the [SAHRC] Commission will agree that it does not have jurisdiction to rule on competing constitutional rights" (ibid).

With regard to the SAHRC enquiry, the SAHRC can, and has, made recommendations, it can not however, change the law as it now stands. One right should not be alienated from other Constitutional rights and singled out. Pollecutt also feels that even if a "politically correct formula of content" (ibid) could be instituted for the media to follow, this would not change the reality of most of South Africa's population – whose economic and disenfranchised status will. Pollecutt concludes her article with the following: "Only when there is a diversity of voices will the problem of racism in the media diminish" (ibid).

While some responses to the SAHRC and its Final Report have been positive, with some praise of its recommendations, there have been critics. Ebrahim Harvey (2000) writes that in his opinion, the SAHRC Final Report is "badly flawed" (2000:29).

He argues:
- that it appears that the Commission had problems in clearly and concretely identifying racism in the media but despite that characterised it as racist
- that the Commission failed to provide a clear and comprehensive definition of racism, which satisfactorily integrates the key dimensions of race and class
- that the Commission relies on a vague United Nations definition of race and racism and ignores the vast literature on the matter.

The reason such a definition of racism is so important is that without it we cannot clearly identify its varied forms and develop strategies to combat it.

Harvey (op cit:29) asks whether racial stereotyping is necessarily racist, especially since it is largely on that basis that the media is regarded as racist? We must be careful that "black" and "white" do not in themselves become analytical categories with foregone conclusions that are a substitute for analysis. He concludes that:

> Its [the ANC's – BK] failure to focus on more critical areas adds grist to the mill of those who believe that, bad as racist stereotyping or subtle racism in the media or elsewhere is, it is being used to divert national attention from the failures of the ruling party to meet the basic needs of mainly black people. The point is not to minimise the scourge of racism but to contextualise it.
>
> (Harvey 2000:29)

## Where to now?

Lynette Steenveld, in her article "Breaking out the box" (Steenveld 2000a:43) addresses the question of "Where to now?". Steenveld ultimately comes to the same conclusion as Oppelt and Pollecutt as to how to eradicate racism from the media: through "diversity" (ibid). Beginning her argument with a definition of democracy as the "rule of the people", Steenveld identifies the single most important problem confronting the media, namely, that the media must represent all of the people. Considering that the people of South Africa are religious, culturally and otherwise, extremely diverse – how does the media achieve representation of all individuals? Steenveld's answer of "diversity" covers the following four areas: firstly, *structures of ownership and operation;* secondly, *employment equity;* thirdly, *training;* and, fourthly, *representation*.

With regard to *structures of ownership and operation*, according to Steenveld's view, it is the government's initiative to encourage diverse forms of media – from privately owned newspapers, to community newspapers, community radio, privately owned broadcasters, such as M-Net, and community based broadcasters such as the SABC, to name but a few – to instigate "freedom of expression and divergent points of view while simultaneously encouraging local culture to grow" (ibid).

Concerning *employment equity*, the role the government plays results in a diverse media staff contingent and, consequently, objective reporting. This recruitment

## Representation: Race, Gender and Sexual Orientation

policy uncovers "the social commitment of the media" which will in turn "contribute to a progressive and positive image of the media" (ibid).

The third area of diversity that this article emphasises is that of *training*. Steenveld identifies the need to train more black and women journalists – in all areas of journalism (ibid).

As far as representation is concerned, Steenveld argues that while it is the responsibility of the government to oversee and "regulate" the environment in which reporters work, reporters themselves are generally considered responsible for media content.

As already stated, only hate-speech is proscribed by the Constitution, with the rest of the content being the responsibility of the media. Once again we focus on questions already asked by Braham (1982), Oppelt (2000) and to an extent Pollecutt (2000):

- What makes news newsworthy?
- Do we reflect news as it is, or do we manipulate, suppress or manufacture news, and if this is so, do we do it deliberately or subconsciously, and what are the results?

The essential question asked here is whether the traditional list of news values is adequate, or appropriate, for reflecting our South African experiences/realities? Steenveld asks: "Are various groups and issues adequately reflected by these values, or do they privilege some groups and issues, and marginalise others? In doing so, does this contribute to the media's role of enabling democratic practices?" (Steenveld 2000a:43).

Steenveld refers to examples to illustrate her point, basing her argument on the premise that news values decide the "what", and the outline of news deals with the "how". For instance, a worthwhile news story about foreign nationalists settling in South Africa can be highlighted in numerous ways: negatively, referring to them as "aliens" taking jobs away from unemployed South Africans; positively – referring to these residents as "immigrants" adding to the cornucopia of South Africa's already rich cultural and economic heritage. Which again raises the question of whether or not news satisfactorily reflects our diverse community? Or does the media favour particular perspectives and marginalise others?

Other questions raised by Steenveld (2000a) include who sources the news, and what, if anything, is their stake in an article? Are all our demographics and political perspectives adequately covered? With regard to story assignment, are stories assigned in such a way that they enable a shared sense of citizenship for both journalists and their readers/listeners/viewers? Steenveld claims that there is a propensity towards assigning black journalists to "black" stories – based in all likelihood on the belief that the black journalist knows the black culture better than her/his white colleague, has easier access to "black" areas and is more trustworthy to black people she/he may be interviewing. This may be an entirely appropriate and efficient choice, based on the assumption that black people know more about black people than white people do, and vice versa. However, this would result in only "white" journalists covering "white" news and "black" journalists covering "black" news – which delimits journalists' coverage and perspectives and "narrow our journalists' competence and that we perpetuate laagers [encampments – BK] for white and black citizens amongst our audiences" (Steenveld 2000a:43).

Kadalie (2000:31), on the other hand, suggests that the SAHRC should attend to other rights that exist in the Constitution, such as the rights with regard to "pension and maintenance payouts, the rights of the elderly, the occurrence of deaths in custody, the violations of the rights of refugees and immigrants, and the violations of children's rights". Furthermore, Kadalie emphasises that the SAHRC should be at the "forefront in monitoring all human rights violations" as well as "promoting a culture of human rights" and tolerance in South Africa, including "the human rights of the media" (Kadalie in Ngobeni 2000b:2). Similarly, Harvey (2000) suggests that the government focus on the socio-economic rights of the Constitution, addressing poverty and the issue of meeting the basic needs of its people (mainly black).

While keeping in mind the important questions this case study has raised, we conclude with the FXI press release, issued the same day as the SAHRC's Final Report, 24 August 2000:

> Despite a finding that the South African media can be characterised as racist institutions, it is also reassuring to note that the Commission found no evidence of the mainstream media indulging in blatant advocacy of racial hatred or incitement to racial violence. We are particularly pleased to note the positive recommendations relating to training, racism awareness sessions, cultural and media diversity and the endorsement of the establishment of a media development agency. FXI will certainly be looking at how we as an organisation can take these matters forward.
>
> (Pollecutt 2000:1)

The full text of the FXI's response to the SA Human Rights Commission's final report is available on http://www.fxi.org.za/press/2000/24-8-2000.0.htm

### 15.3.2 AIDS sufferers

At the time of writing, roughly ten million of South Africa's 43 million population were HIV-positive (Human Immuno-deficiency Virus). This number is expected to increase by 25 percent this decade alone. A recent United Nations report stated that AIDS (Acquired Immune Deficiency Syndrome) surpasses malaria and war as the largest killer in Africa. Nearly half of all HIV cases in the world are in eastern and southern Africa.

## Case study 15.2: The role of the media in the representation of HIV/AIDS and AIDS sufferers

In 1997 the African National Congress (ANC), at a national AIDS conference held in Mafikeng, South Africa, in its first declaration on HIV/AIDS noted that "secrecy, ignorance and myths about the disease contribute to its spread" (Beresford, Kindra & Deane 2000:2). However, in 2000 President Thabo Mbeki called for a platform to be given to AIDS dissidents to voice their opinions, suggesting that the scientifically accepted fact that HIV cause AIDS be revisited, and that the solution to HIV/AIDS be reinvigorated.

One such dissident, Peter Duesberg of the University of California, Berkeley, holds the belief that HIV does not cause AIDS. He believes that the "orthodox connection between HIV and AIDS is nothing but a gross overblown and dangerously unrigorous myth" (Powell 2000a:1).

Although Duesberg has been discredited and his findings dismissed, his restating them, also in South Africa, led to much confusion: does HIV cause AIDS? President Mbeki and many of his Cabinet members refused to answer this question directly. Because the link between HIV and AIDS was questioned, it led to many individuals believing that they could now have unprotected sex, and many health workers in townships and rural areas have held the president and his refusal to address the question directly, as responsible for sabotaging the anti-AIDS message. This, of course, had grievous consequences for those infected, and their families. Shortly after this, in Parliament, Democratic Alliance leader Tony Leon, challenged Mbeki's stance on this issue. Mbeki acknowledged that the government's anti-AIDS strategy was "based on the thesis that HIV causes AIDS" (Barrell 2000a:1). Secondly, Mbeki acknowledged that his insistence that AIDS dissidents be given a platform on which to air their views "might have engendered public confusion and undermined the government's anti-AIDS campaigns" (ibid).

In June 2000, AIDS 2000, the 13th international AIDS conference to be held since 1985, was held in Durban. This was the first AIDS conference to be held in Africa. It is appropriate that AIDS 2000 was held in South Africa, a country with the fastest-known growing HIV epidemic. This conference airs the latest news on the medical, social and ethical aspects of HIV, as well as discussions that go beyond medicine and science into the realm of the social, political and ethical issues surrounding the AIDS epidemic. Breaking the silence surrounding the realities of AIDS was the theme of the AIDS 2000 conference. Although it was important for South Africa to host the conference, the conference will mainly be remembered for the so-called "Durban declaration": a document signed by 5 000 people testifying to their belief that HIV causes AIDS.

Another issue surrounding AIDS is the government's initial refusal to provide anti-retroviral drugs to HIV-positive mothers, health care workers or rape victims – either free or at a reduced price. The Minister of Health, Manto Tshabalala-Msimang refused to accept Glaxo-Wellcome's offer of a reduced price for anti-retroviral drugs because she believed that there is not enough proof that anti-retroviral drugs work. However, mother-to-child transmission of HIV is an area where anti-retroviral drugs have proven to reduce transmission of the disease, by anywhere from one-half to two-thirds (Nicodemus 1999b). The Minister of Health also dismissed the anti-retroviral drug AZT as too expensive, arguing that "providing the drug to nearly four million HIV-positive South Africans would break the health budget" (1999b:1). A further development has been that the government recently considered declaring a state of emergency on HIV/AIDS to secure cheaper drugs. This national emergency would allow the government to

- issue compulsory licences – as in Brazil – to local drug manufacturers authorising them to replicate patented anti-AIDS drugs cheaply
- import cheaper generic drugs, and
- copy the drugs without breaching international trade agreements because such a move would be accepted by the World Trade Organisation.

In a letter to the *Sunday Times* in March 2000, Judge Edwin Cameron expressed concern that:

> By preventing through treatment we give all people affected by the epidemic hope. And when hope returns ... the ignorance, fear and hatred will begin to subside. So, by showing how through treatment, we will also address the stigma that surrounds the disease. This message is crucial at a time when much official discourse surrounding the pandemic grows ever more confused and potentially confusing. ... statistics suggest that South Africa has the highest rate of HIV infections in the world. It is now estimated that each month about 5 000 babies are born with HIV. ... Furthermore, the government has committed itself to providing free medical care for pregnant women. Now it transpires that such care is only available to HIV-negative mothers. Surely this introduces very questionable discrimination?
>
> (Trengrove-Jones 2000:1–4)

In ideological terms, stereotyping is a means that sustains individuals of one group experiencing deferential (often discriminatory) treatment at the hands of another group (O'Sullivan in Jones & Jones 1999:105).

Some people are of the view that stereotypes represent a "blinkered mental attitude" (Barratt in Jones & Jones 1999:105). This view of stereotypes significantly involves a more general concern with the origins of attitudes and it is traditionally linked with prejudice.

In South Africa, individuals with AIDS claim that they are greatly discriminated against, and experience much prejudice. They are stigmatised because it is believed they will infect others and, that they deserve to be ill because they brought this disease on themselves through, for example, promiscuity. It is believed that the media through its reporting of AIDS and the emphasis given in reports to the role of promiscuity contribute to this perception. As one of the results of this perception we have babies abandoned at birth, while adult individuals are left to die in the street.

Stereotypes are also created through a lack of information. The stereotype is never neutral but inevitably ideological, so that the representation of the topic, individual or group appears to be "natural". In this sense it is ideological because it disempowers those with AIDS – who have become voiceless in this spiral of silence. People do not talk about it, because there is a stigma attached to having AIDS. There are also many taboos and myths surrounding AIDS – one, very prevalent myth is that if you are HIV-positive you need only have sex with a virgin in order to be cured. This has resulted in girls as young as five years old being raped – in individuals' attempts to rid themselves of the disease. Misinformation surrounds HIV/AIDS, and with the government not taking a clear line of action, confusion and ignorance continue. In this sense the media have an important role to inform the public with reliable and objective information on a continual basis.

As an expression of values, the stereotype is inevitably linked to ideology because it effectively creates divisions between groups in society; this generally leads to "this is what we think of them" – "us" and "them". Unfortunately it seems as if AIDS sufferers have become "them" and are thus discriminated against. The question is thus: What is the role of the media in creating the perception and stereotype of AIDS sufferers as being "them"?

### 15.3.3 Gays and lesbians

Gunter (1995) argues that a fundamental aspect of human social development involves learning to behave in ways deemed socially and culturally to be appropriate for one's own sex. This sociocultural normalising of displayed, acceptable characteristics and behaviour roles for males and females has been found to develop among children at an early age (Fauls & Smith in Gunter 1995:1), and may influence a child's choice of activities as early as nursery school (Fagot & Patterson in Gunter 1995:1). Spence, Helmreich and Stapp (in Gunter 1995:1) demonstrated that stereotyped beliefs were significant factors affecting how people perceived themselves and have an effect particularly on levels of personal self-esteem. Botha (in Fourie 1997) emphasises that media culture provides us with the groundwork for formulating our very identities, not only our sexuality but also our ethnicity, class, race, and nationality. With sexual orientation being formed at such an early age, it is vital that positive role models be available to children. The media can play an important role in this, also by being a source of information. Therefore, how the dominant media culture represents gays and lesbians is valuable. Ultimately the media's portrayal of gays and lesbians can also have a meaningful impact on how individual gays and lesbians perceive themselves and their relationships with and to their community.

## Case study 15.3: The media's portrayal of gays and lesbians

Dyer (in Jones & Jones 1999) identifies four prominent gay types that have been represented in the media:

- in-betweenism
- macho
- the sad young man
- lesbian feminists

"In betweenism" is characterised by the gay "queen" and "dyke". This type of representation implies a strong correlation between sexuality and gender. Gays and lesbians are depicted as caught between the male and female genders. Therefore the "queen" is portrayed as effeminate, "not a real man", while the "dyke" is masculine, "butch" and "not a real woman". These typifications are clearly underpinned by an ideology of gender that assumes true masculinities and femininities. Dyer maintains that these types are frequently portrayed in a negative light by the media because in terms of the dominant culture they have failed to achieve the status of "real men and women". Therefore they are often seen as "tragic, pathetic, wretched, despicable, comical, ridiculous figures" (op cit:134). Dykes challenge dominant ideas of gender and are therefore frequently portrayed as dangerous and threatening.

With regard to the "macho" representation, this is only applied to gay men and is an exaggerated form of masculinity. Dyer argues "in marking off the macho man from the simply straight man, this gay type retains the idea of male homosexuality implying something different in relation to gender, but here is no notion of a biological betweenism but an excess masculinity". Thus the macho type is clearly nearer to the real man, but he is defined as "other" and in opposition to this type due to his excess of masculinity, for example the body builder.

The "sad young man" is a gay type that emerged in American cinema is the 1960s. Here was an image of troubled adolescence, of soft young men, heads hung low, troubled expressions, an air of yearning. These adolescents had not yet achieved adult masculinity and were therefore not real men. The characters played by James Dean in such films as *Rebel Without a Cause* (1955) and *East of Eden* (1955), epitomise the "sad young man". In these films, the lowering of the head echoed the Christian traditions of martyrdom and suffering. Dyer argues that these types have become icons of beauty. Famous "sad young men" in film have included James Dean, Montgomery Clift and Dirk Bogarde. In a recent film *Object of My Affection* (1997), the actor Paul Rudd deals with this very issue. This image of the "sad young man" has recently also been used by advertisers to sell men's fashion and cosmetics such as Guess! and Gucci clothing, and Hugo: Dark, an aftershave for men.

Dyer argues that "liberal feminism" has portrayed lesbian culture as closer to nature and naturalness. This type of lesbianism reflects a strand of radical feminist thinking that women are closer to nature than men and that their bodies have a

# Representation: Race, Gender and Sexual Orientation

natural affinity with aspects of nature. Thus lesbians have been portrayed as hippies who are close to nature and healing and involved in craft making (worship of Mother Earth and so on) (Dyer in Lacey 1998; Dyer in Jones & Jones 1999; Wolf & Kielwasser 1991).

Dyer (in Nelmes 1999) has also pointed out the dangers inherent in thinking rigidly in terms of stereotypes when dealing with representation: "...a stereotype can be complex, varied, intense and contradictory, an image of otherness in which it is still possible to find oneself" (1999:320). Stereotypes, he points out, are not always, or necessarily negative, although some, such as the black mammy of Hollywood, are very limiting. The process of stereotyping involves power: the power of dominant groups to mould the accepted social view of themselves and of those groups that they perceive as marginal. This view can change and develop as certain social groups, such as gays and lesbians, grow in self-awareness, expression and power, so that dominant groups have to modify their available images.

## A turning point

Jones (in Nelmes 1999) recalls a turning point for gays and lesbians. In 1969, for the first time in modern history, homosexuals in a small New York bar called Stonewall fought back against a police raid. A major riot ensued and the New York Gay Liberation Front was immediately formed; soon to be followed by similar organisations across the world. Members of the new movement adopted the word "gay" for its positive connotations of happiness and because they wanted a term to describe themselves that had not been chosen by outsiders.

For "gays", the term represented a way of demonstrating pride in their identity, the power of political organisation and a distinct culture. The term was initially conceived as describing both men and women, but women soon began to feel marginalised within the movement, and the term "lesbian" came back in general use during the 1970s to signal the distinctness and strength of women. Coined as a medical term and used to describe and name a woman whose main sexual feelings are for other women, post-Stonewall the term "lesbian" was invested with new ideas of openness and liberation.

The recent crop of film and video productions on the topic of homosexuality is called the "New Queer Cinema". Lesbian and gay activists, critics, filmmakers and audiences are imbuing the previously negative term "queer" with a range of new, exciting, positive meanings in politics, literature, art and filmmaking. This process of an oppressed group reclaiming and reshaping a previously negative word or idea is known as reappropriation. Critic Amy Taubin said: "American queer cinema has achieved critical mass" (in Nelmes 1999:335) with the release of features such as *My own Private Idaho* (1991) "utilising the Hollywood star system with Keanu Reeves and River Phoenix, and with Tom Kalin's film *Swoon* (1992)" (op cit:336).

The idea behind the New Queer Cinema is
> diversity: a range of homosexualities manifested through a variety of character, situation, race, gender, sexual practice and film language. Filmmakers are questioning the attitude, developed in the 1970s, that one must promote only positive images of lesbian and gay characters and situations. Although debate rages around what many lesbians and gays see as negative images in mainstream Hollywood films such as *Silence of the Lambs* (1991) and *Basic Instinct* (1992), some lesbian and gay filmmakers see such ideas as constraints on creativity in an era where a much wider variety of lesbian and gay images is available. Gus van Sant's *My own Private Idaho* dramatises the hopeless love of a teenage male hustler for a straight college boy. In *Swoon*, Tom Kalin examines the infamous Leopold/Loeb case of 1924, where two rich, Jewish eighteen-year-olds kidnap and murder a fourteen-year-old boy. Unlike previous film versions, such as Hitchcock's *Rope* (1948), Kalin concentrates on the homosexual relationship between the two young men, and the hold which the pathological Leopold had over Loeb. In an interview, Kalin stated: "We're in a sorry state if we can't afford to look at 'unwholesome' lesbian and gay people".
> (Nelmes 1999:336).

Derek Jarman's *Edward II* (1991) "doesn't hesitate to portray England's monarch (Edward II) as weak and vacillating while his male love, Gaveston, is scheming and slimy. What both Kalin and Jarman's films do is to make the audiences aware of the political dimensions of homosexuality" (ibid).

Diversity and experimentation in film language has also characterised recent lesbian and gay film. Among the new innovators are John Greyson who mixes history in *Urinal* (1988), while Jarman deliberately clashes fourteenth century and the 1990s in *Caravaggio* (1986), and in *Blue* (1993) Jarman's one-colour screen counterpoints the emotional range of the soundtrack's meditation on his life with, and approaching death from, HIV (Jones in Nelmes 1999:337).

## Representation in television and print media

It is also interesting to see how far gay and lesbian representation has recently become part of mainstream television, rather than simply being marginalised in minority programming. In programmes such as soap operas there is some representation. The question is, are these television representations stereotypical? With regard to South African television, M-Net frequently shows films with gay and lesbian themes and characters, but the local soap *Egoli*, screened daily on M-Net, has only now after being screened for eleven years, introduced a gay character.

With regard to the print media, newspapers and magazines often report on gay and lesbian film festivals, and give reviews of gay artists and their work. The question is, how much coverage do the print media give to gay issues? How do the print media interpret and represent gay issues and is it done with sensitivity and objectivity?

## 15.3.4 Women

The representation of women has already been addressed in Unit 12. Here we suffice with only a few remarks.

### Case study 15.4: Media representation of women

Feminism has had a very significant influence on research into gender representation by the media with regard to women. Feminists have generally been highly critical of many of the representations of women by the media, but they also acknowledge that the media is not solely responsible for gender role stereotyping.

With regard to gender and television, feminists argue that from children's shows to commercials, prime time adventures and situation comedies, television proclaims that woman does not count for much. Women are under-represented in television's fictional life – they are symbolically annihilated (Tuchman in Jones & Jones 1999:109). Tuchman's concept of symbolic annihilation refers to the fact that women appear far less often than men on the small screen, and when they do their roles are very limited and/or negative. She claims that the media frequently condemn or trivialise women's activities and experiences.

Feminists have expressed concern about the limited and generally negative representation of woman in the media because they believe that it has a negative effect on attitudes towards the status of women.

Recently, concern has also been expressed about a possible link between media representation of (perceived as "ideal") women's bodies on one hand, and eating disorders and the distorted body images held by some young women on the other hand. Since the 1980s there has been increased awareness of eating disorders among young people, especially girls, and statistics indicate that the frequency of eating disorders is increasing. Some recent reports have shown that girls as young as eleven and twelve are worried about their weight and size and are striving to achieve unrealistic body sizes at very young ages (Bellos in Jones & Jones 1999:113).

The Western aesthetic is very prevalent in the media – young, white and very thin. More and more black women have eating disorders in an attempt to look like this Western ideal, as opposed to that of wide hips and big breasts usually linked with a black aesthetic of being beautiful.

Portia di Rossi, Courtney Thorne-Smith and Calista Flockhart, all appearing in the drama television series *Ally McBeal*, along with Laura Flynn Boyle (*The Practice*), Helen Hunt (*Mad about You*) and Jennifer Aniston (*Friends*), are actresses that are called "swizzle sticks" or "lollipops" on account of their being so stick thin that their heads look much larger than the rest of their bodies – and this is a trend being followed by more and more actresses. This scenario doubtless impacts negatively on young, impressionable viewers, particularly, and their perception of what an "ideal" body looks like. Thus it could be argued that the media have a responsibility to their viewers.

# MEDIA STUDIES

## Summary

In this unit we explained what stereotypes are. We did this from the perspective of Lèvi-Strauss's theory of binary oppositions and Roland Barthes' theory of social myths. According to these two theories, people think in terms of oppositions and differences and in terms of socially constructed beliefs and values. We summarised the characteristics of a stereotype as being a prejudiced, generalised, simplified conception of a person, group, organisation or topic which could either be negative or positive, but which usually implies negative consequences. Furthermore, a stereotype is considered by those who employ it to be a true conception about what the individual or group is like; it is accepted as a "normal" typing and any deviation from the stereotype is seen as a threat to personal and social security. Unlike an archetype, a stereotype is the result of and is subject to changing social and ideological views. A stereotype is therefore not a constant, but a fluid and changeable concept. We then looked at the origin of stereotypes and concluded that stereotypes originate within a particular ideological and dogmatic context. In the next part of the unit the focus was on the need to contextualise our criticism of stereotypes. In the case of the media one should keep in mind the symbolic nature of media communication, genre, the motif of the communicator and the complex relationship between representation and reality, including the complex nature of perception. Finally we suggested ways in which stereotypes can be changed. The first part of the unit concluded with a brief reference to globalisation and its possible impact on local and national identities, and the role of the media herein as the main role player in the culture industry. The unit was concluded with case studies enabling us to take a closer look at the media's representation of race, AIDS (sufferers), gays and lesbians, and women.

## Research activities

1 Write an essay of ten typed folios in which you illustrate your understanding of the following by providing your own examples taken from any media content:
   - the nature of stereotypes with reference to Lèvi-Strauss's theory of binary oppositions and Roland Barthes' theory of socially constructed meaning and myths
   - the characteristics of stereotypes
   - the origin of stereotypes
   - how we can change stereotypes
   - a context for criticising the media's representations.
2 Find an example of a race issue covered by the media. Compare two newspapers', or magazines', or radio or television channels' coverage of the same issue and decide and motivate your argument as to whether the reports are stereotyped or not.
3 Find an example of a gay/lesbian issue covered by the media. Compare two newspapers', or magazines', or radio or television channels' coverage of the same issue and decide and motivate your argument as to whether the reports are stereotyped or not.

4   Find an example of an AIDS issue covered by the media. Compare two newspapers', or magazines', or radio or television channels' coverage of the same issue and decide and motivate your argument as to whether the reports are stereotyped or not.
5   Find an example of an issue related to women and covered by the media. Compare two newspapers', or magazines', or radio or television channels' coverage of the same issue and decide and motivate your argument as to whether the reports are stereotyped or not.

## Further reading

Barker, C. 1999. *Television, globalization and cultural identities.* Buckingham: Open University Press.

Bogle, D. 1994. *Toms, Coons, Mulattoes, Mammies and Bucks: an interpretative history of Blacks in American films.* 2nd edition. New York: Continuum.

Downing, J, Mohammadi, A & Sreberny-Mohammmadi, A (eds). 1995. *Questioning the media. A critical introduction.* London: Sage.

Hall, S. 1997. *Representation. Cultural representations and signifying practices.* London: Sage in association with The Open University.

MacDonald, M. 1995. *Representing women: myths of femininity in the popular media.* London: Arnold.

Medhurst, A & Lunt SR (eds). 1997. *Lesbian and gay studies: a critical introduction.* London: Cassell.

O'Sullivan, T & Jewkes, Y. 1997. *The media studies reader.* London: Arnold.

Pines, J (ed). 1992. *Black and White in colour: black people in British television since 1936.* London: BFI.

Racism in the media. 2000. *Rhodes Journalism Review* August.

Shohat, E & Stam, R. 1994. *Unthinking EuroCentrism: multiculturalism and the media.* London: Routledge.

Tolson, A. 1995. *Mediations. Text and discourse in media studies.* London: Arnold.

## Bibliography

Accone, T. 2000. Is the Web a white place? *Rhodes Journalism Review* August:33.

Allen, A. 2001. *The dissident view.* [O].
    Available: http://www.mg.co.za/mg/news/2000mar1/14mar-aids4.html
    Accessed on 2001/02/16

Barker, C. 1999. *Television, globalization and identities.* Buckingham: Open University Press.

Barrell, H. 2000a. *What the president said about the CIA.* [O].
    Available: http://www.mg.co.za/mg/za/archive/2000oct/features/06oct-thabo.html
    Accessed on 2001/02/16

Barrell, H. 2000b. *Pityana prejudged the media.* [O].
    Available: http://www.mg.co.za/mg/za/archive/2000oct/features/06oct-thabo.html
    Accessed on 2001/02/28

Barthes, R. 1967. *Elements of semiology.* New York: Hill & Wang.

Barthes, R. 1977. *Image, music, text.* Glasgow: Fontana.

Beresford, B, Kindra J & Deane, N. 2000. *ANC tries to limit the fallout.* [O].
    Available: http://www.mg.co.za/mg/za/archive/2000sep/features/15sep-fallout.html
    Accessed on 2001/02/16

Berger, M. 2001. *Mbeki's Aids letter defies belief.* [O].
    Available: http://www.mg.co.za/mg/news/2000may1/1may-aids.html
    Accessed on 2001/02/16

# MEDIA STUDIES

Boseley, S. 2001. At the mercy of the giants. *Mail & Guardian*, 16–22 February:9.
Botha, M. 1997. Marginalisation, in *Introduction to communication – course book 6: film and television studies*, edited by PJ Fourie. Cape Town: Juta.
Braham, P. 1982. How the media report race, in *Culture, society and the media*, edited by M Gurevitch, T Bennett, J Curran and J Woollacott. London: Methuen.
Branston, G & Stafford, R. 1999. *The media student's book*. 2nd edition. London: Routledge.
Commissioners of the star chamber. 2000. *Mail & Guardian*, 18–24 February:28.
Culler, J. 1983. *Structuralist poetics: structuralism, linguistics and the study of literature*. London: Routledge & Kegan Paul.
Dickson, P. 2001. *Aids activists set up watchdog*. [O].
   Available: http://www.mg.co.za/mg/news/2000feb1/7feb-aids.html
   Accessed on 2001/02/16
Dread, Z. 2001. Arts festival or boerfest? *Mail & Guardian*, 20–25 April 2001.
Du Plessis, M. 2001. *Aids 'establishment' brooks no dissent*. [O].
   Available: http://www.mg.co.za/mg/news/99jun2/21jun-aids.html
   Accessed on 2001/02/16
Faderman, L & Gross, L (eds). 1996. *Straight news: gays, lesbians and the news media*. New York: Columbia University Press.
Fourie, PJ (ed). 1997. *Introduction to communication – course book 6: film and television studies*. Cape Town: Juta.
FXI's response to the SA Human Rights Commission's final report: *Faultlines*. 2000. [O].
   Available: http://www.fxi.org.za/press/2000/24-8-2000.0.htm
   Accessed on 2000/08/24
Gombrich, E. 1977. *Art and illusion*. London: Phaidon.
Gunter, B. 1995. *Television and gender representation*. London: John Libbey.
Gurevitch, M, Bennet, T, Curran, J & Woollacott, J (eds). 1982. *Culture, Society and the Media*. London: Methuen.
Harvey, E. 2000. Racism is a subliminal red herring. *Mail & Guardian*, 1–7 September:29.
Hills, C & Momberg, E. 2000. Citizen's editor subpoenaed. *The Citizen*, 19 February 2000.
Jones, M & Jones, E. 1999. *Mass Media*. London: Macmillan.
Jones, C. 1999. Lesbian and gay cinema, in *An introduction to film studies*, edited by J Nelmes. London: Routledge.
Kadalie, R. 2000. Defy Barney's thought police. *Mail & Guardian*, 18–24 February:31.
Lacey, N. 1998. *Image and representation: key concepts in media studies*. New York: St. Martin's Press.
Lawrence, M & Dana, M. 1990. *Fighting food*. Harmondsworth: Penguin Books.
Lawrence, M (ed). 1987. *Fed up and hungry*. London: The Women's Press.
Le Page, D. 2001. *Politicians unwilling to accept stubborn science*. [O].
   Available: http://www.mg.co.za/mg/news/2000mar1/14mar-aids2.html
   Accessed on 2001/02/16
Lévi-Strauss, C. 1962. *Het wilde denken. Over ritueel, totemisme, taboe, mytisch denken, logica, dialektiek en de 'getemde' geests*, translated by J Vogelaar & H Ten Brummelhuis. Amsterdam: Meulenhoff.
MacKie, R & Beresford, D. 2001. *Africa's Aids fate hangs in balance*. [O].
   Available: http://www.mg.co.za/mg/news/2000may1/8may-aids.html
   Accessed on 2001/02/16
Magardie, K & Le Page, D. 2001. *SA's Aids doubts baffle the experts*. [O].
   Available: http://www.mg.co.za/mg/news/2000mar2/17mar-aids.html
   Accessed on 2001/02/16

Makhanya, M. 2000. The media's oft-maligned pen is mightier than the despot's sword. *The Sunday Times*, 5 November:20.

Mankhlana, P. 2001. *What the president said.* [O].
   Available: http://www.mg.co.za/mg/news/2000apr1/3apr-aids.html
   Accessed on 2001/02/16

Mathiane, N. 2000. *Researchers fear intimidation of editors.* [O].
   Available: http://www.bday.co.za/00/0218/news/news2.htm
   Accessed on 2000/05/25

McGreal, C. 2000. *Racism inquiry calls FT editor.* [O].
   Available: http://www.mg.co.za/mg/news/2000feb2/21feb-racism_media
   Accessed on 2001/02/28

McGreal, C. 2001. *SA faces spectre of a million AIDS orphans.* [O].
   Available: http://www.mg.co.za/mg/news/99aug1/3aug-aids.html
   Accessed on 2001/02/16

Mutume, G. 2001. *Row over HIV 'cure' sets back AIDS campaign.* [O].
   Available: http://www.mg.co.za/mg/news/97jan2/29jan-aids.html
   Accessed on 2001/02/16

Nelmes, J (ed). 1999. *An introduction to film studies.* 2nd edition. London: Routledge.

Ngobeni, EWK. 2000a. *Sheena Duncan quits over racism probe.* [O].
   Available: http://www.mg.co.za/mg/news/2000feb2/25feb-racism_media2.html
   Accessed on 2001/02/28

Ngobeni, EWK. 2000b. *Kadalie takes another swing at 'curiously invisible' Pityana.* [O].
   Available: http://www.mg.co.za/mg/news/2000feb2/25feb-racism_media3.html
   Accessed on 2001/02/28

Nicodemus, A. 1999a. *Truth and lies about AZT.* [O].
   Available: http://www.mg.co.za/mg/news/99dec1/1dec-aids_azt.html
   Accessed on 2001/02/16

Nicodemus, A. 1999b. *Ministry refuses anti-HIV drug discount.* [O].
   Available: http://www.mg.co.za/mg/news/99may1/7may-aids.html
   Accessed on 2001/02/16

Niller, E. 1999. Beyond stereotype: Africa's catch 22. *Rhodes Journalism Review* December:50–51.

Oppelt, P. 2000. Tools to transform. *Rhodes Journalism Review*, August:46.

O'Sullivan, T, Hartley, J, Saunders, D, Montgomery, M & Fiske, J. 1994. *Key concepts in communication and cultural studies.* 2nd edition. London: Routledge.

Pieterse, JN. [Sa]. *Wit over zwart. Beelden van Afrika en zwarten in de Westerse populaire cultuur.* Amsterdam: Koninklijk Instituut voor de Tropen.

Pollecutt, L. 2000. Freedom vs racism. *Rhodes Journalism Review*, August:29.

Powell, I. 2000a. *The self-styled Galileo of the modern age.* [O].
   Available: http://www.mg.co.za/mg/news/2000apr1/3apr-aids5.html
   Accessed on 2001/02/16

Powell, I. 2000b. *Uproar over Aids council.* [O].
   Available: http://www.mg.co.za/mg/news2000jan2/31jan-aids.html
   Accessed on 2001/02/16

Steenveld, L. 2000a. Breaking out the box. *Rhodes Journalism Review*, August:43.

Steenveld, L. 2000b. Defining the undefinable. *Rhodes Journalism Review*, August:11.

Swindells, S. 2000. *Media racism probe gets underway.* [O].
   Available: http://www.mg.co.za/mg/news/2000mar1/7mar-racism_media/html
   Accessed on 2001/02/16

Taitz, L. 2000. Media not off the race hook, says Pityana. *The Sunday Times*, 27 August:1.
Trengrove-Jones, T. 2000. *Disarray in SA's HIV/Aids policy.* [O].
   Available: http://www.mg.co.za/mg/news/2000apr1/3apr-aids1.html
   Accessed on 2001/02/16
Van Niekerk, P & Ludman, B (eds). 1999. *A-Z of South African politics 1999: the essential handbook.* South Africa: Penguin Books.
Wolf, MA & Kielwasser, AP (eds). 1991. *Gay people, sex and the media.* New York: The Haworth Press.

## Web site articles

A feebly disguised assault on the press. 2000. [O].
   Available: http://www.mg.co.za/mg/news/98nov2/24nov-press.html
   Accessed on 2000/08/24
A former "dissident" airs his views. [O].
   Available: http://www.mg.co.za/mg/news/2000apr1/3apr-aids4.html
   Accessed on 2001/02/17
And then the subpoena came ... 2000. [O].
   Available: http://www.mg.co.za/mg/news/2000july1/07jul-aids4.html
   Accessed on 2001/02/28
Media in SA is racist, says HRC. 2000. [O]
   Available: http://www.mg.co.za/mg/za/news.html
   Accessed on 2000/08/24
Mixed HIV/Aids messages from government. [O].
   Available: http://www.mg.co.za/mg/news/2000mar1/14mar-aids1.html
   Accessed on 2001/02/16
Open letter to President Mbeki. 2001. [O].
   Available: http://www.mg.co.za/mg/news/2000may1/9may-aids.html
   Accessed on 2001/02/16
South African President addresses AIDS in Africa. 2001. [O].
   Available: http://www.washingtonpost.com/wp-dyn/articles/A40387-2000Apr18.html
   Accessed on 2001/02/16
The majority consensus. 2001. [O].
   Available: http://www.mg.co.za/mg/news/2000mar1/14mar-aids5.html
   Accessed on 2001/02/16
What the HRC wanted. [O].
   Available: http://www.mg.co.za/mg/news/2000feb2/25feb-hrc1.html
   Accessed on 2001/02/28

## Web sites

A Web site that provides lists of gay and lesbian films with distributors' addresses and phone and fax numbers: British Film Institute, Channel Four, and so forth. http://www.planetout.com
Frameline Distributions is a comprehensive, non-profit organisation dedicated to the exhibition, distribution, promotion and funding of gay and lesbian film and video. A sponsor of the San Francisco Lesbian and Gay Film Festival. http://www.frameline.org
The Department of Journalism and Media Studies, Rhodes University. http://www.journ.ru.ac.za
The Gay and Lesbian Alliance Against Defamation Web site with a movie slant. http://www.glaad.org
Web site with information on film, arts and literature of particular interest to women. http://www.feminist.org

# Media and Violence    16

*Magriet Pitout*

## Overview

In South Africa, reports on violence appear daily in newspapers and television. By just taking a cursory look at any newspaper or television news broadcast, we find graphic details of how people have been hijacked, raped and murdered in the most horrific, gruesome ways. These are grim examples of how violence has permeated the very fabric of South African society. It is indeed not far-fetched to say that at the time of writing (November 2000) a culture of violence is prevalent in South Africa. The reasons are multifaceted and complex and therefore it is beyond the scope of this unit to deal with all aspects contributing to the culture of violence. We deal rather with the portrayal of media violence, in particular television, and to what extent these portrayals may influence young children and adolescents in this country.

The debate about the destructive consequences of media violence has been raging on for centuries. To illustrate this debate, we first explain the history of media violence research and how the advent of each mass medium caused concern and moral panic. Through the years, different theoretical perspectives have been developed to explain and investigate media violence. We consider three perspectives, each with its own set of assumptions and research questions about the possible causes and effects of media violence. Furthermore, we look at research that has been conducted on television violence in South Africa and a comprehensive circular model for studying media violence. Lastly, we suggest preventative measures to avert the negative effects of television violence.

## Learning outcomes

After completing this unit you should be able to demonstrate your knowledge and understanding of

- the role of the mass media in creating moral panic in their reportage of media violence;
- different perspectives and models to study and explain media violence;
- the application of approaches and models to explain media violence;
- the complexity of variables that play a role in studying media violence; and
- ways to curb the effects of television violence.

# MEDIA STUDIES

## 16.1 INTRODUCTION

Because of the possible harmful effects of media violence, research has been done on a continuous basis over the years. According to McQueen (1998:185) more than 1 000 pieces of research covering psychology, sociology and communication have been commissioned to investigate the effects of violence as portrayed by the media. These examples illustrate why media violence is one of the most important issues in mass communication research. However, in spite of the large-scale research, there appears to be no conclusive results about whether violence on screen, in newspapers and over the radio breeds crime and violence in real life. In this unit we attempt to establish why, in spite of large-scale research, there is still a lack of empirical evidence of direct harmful effects of media violence. Our emphasis in the unit is especially on television. To put the violence debate in perspective, we first look at the history of this debate.

## 16.2 HISTORICAL OVERVIEW: MEDIA VIOLENCE DEBATE AND RESEARCH

> To get a better understanding of our discussion of media violence, first read the *Ninja Turtles* and *Yizo Yizo* case studies at the end of this unit. We illustrate the different issues pertaining to media violence in this unit with examples from these case studies.

The long-standing debate about the powerful effects of media violence has raged for hundreds of years. In the discussion below we give examples of how the introduction of each new medium and its possible harmful effects, has caused a public outcry and moral panic.

- The fear of possible harmful effects of public theatres can be traced back to the 1600s where the content of plays was strictly controlled to prevent the corruption of the minds of theatre-goers (McQueen 1998). This applies especially to Shakespearean plays that are generally characterised by violence. Thus, no banalities, extreme violence and sexual portrayals were allowed.
- In the nineteenth century, sensationalised cheap fiction, known as "penny dreadfuls" in Britain and "dime novels" in the United States of America (USA) were wrongfully blamed for many social ills that occurred during that period. At the turn of the century, street music and theatres were the scapegoats that were wrongfully accused of causing street crime and a decline in moral standards (McQueen 1998).
- With the introduction of the cinema, the first films were subjected to strict censure and censorship (especially pornographic and violent films) for fear of corrupting viewers and changing them into raging criminals roaming the streets, ready to commit copycat style violence they saw on the big screen. (The same fear has been related to crime and horror comics; paperback novels; pop music such as rap, jazz,

# Media and Violence

rock 'n' roll and so on; video games and most recently the Internet, especially with regard to child pornography.)
- The radio has also been regarded as having a great influence on listeners. An example of a straightforward stimulus response effect, is Orson Wells' often-quoted radio drama *War of the Worlds*, an adaptation of the scientific novel of the same name (see Unit 8). The broadcast of this radio drama caused havoc because many listeners missed the explanation at the beginning of the programme that what they (the listeners) were about to hear, was a dramatised version of the scientific narrative *War of the Worlds*. When listeners switched on their radios, they heard that the United States was being invaded by Martians. Wide panic ensued and according to several testimonies there were "sightings" of the Martians – even rapes by the alien invaders were reported in the media. Long before the broadcast had ended, people all over the USA were praying, crying, fleeing frantically to escape the alien invaders. In retrospect it seems that this panic had been exaggerated by the media because there were other crucial factors contributing to the night of panic and terror. For example, people were aware of the imminence of the real war, which had the listeners in a state of high anxiety anyway (McQueen 1998:181).
- The role of the media in sensationalising violent incidences is also evident in our discussion of the television programme *Yizo Yizo* (Case study 16.2). Headlines such as "... death and rape stalk SA classrooms", "TV terror comes to life at schools", create the impression that all schools in all the townships in South Africa were subjected to the influences of *Yizo Yizo*. However, when we read through the case study, we realise that only a small number of students imitated the violent behaviour in this television programme.
- Television, because of its place in the home, easy access and frequent viewing, has taken a centre stage in the violence debate. We cannot deny that television has made enormous changes in people's lives since its inception. Consequently, research has been done on a regular basis in countries worldwide to investigate the possible harmful effects television violence may have on viewers, especially young viewers. Furthermore, research has above all focused on possible causal effects in the form of violent and aggressive behaviour among children and adolescents. We discuss the results of violence research in South Africa in section 16.4 of this unit.

One of the main causes of concern about television violence, is the number of hours children spend watching television. In a recent study conducted in the United States regarding the average daily time children are exposed to television, the results are as follows:

**Table 16.1 Average daily exposure to television (hours:minutes)**

| 2 – 7 years | 8 – 13 years | 14 – 18 years |
|---|---|---|
| 1:59 | 3:37 | 2:43 |

*Source:* UNESCO 2000:7

According to Table 16.1 the child's available time increases to a peak around early adolescence, and declines during the high school years. Because a great deal of children's leisure time (that is outside school hours) is taken up by television viewing, we cannot but look seriously at what effects such large exposure to television may have, especially if the television menu includes programmes containing high incidences of violence.

## 16.3 THEORETICAL PERSPECTIVES: MEDIA VIOLENCE

We have already discussed specific theories dealing with the effects and power of the media in Unit 8. The theoretical perspectives below explain the possible effects of *media violence*, especially television, on audiences. (To define media violence, we distinguish between the portrayal of *physical violence*, e.g. beating, hitting, kicking, strangling, shooting objects, usually people and animals; and *verbal violence*, e.g. insults, swearing. In other words, verbal abuse.)

- The traditional media effects perspective which is one of the oldest perspectives to explain and investigate a causal (stimulus-response) relationship between media violence and violence in real life.
- The cultivation perspective (also called the power of culture perspective) which emphasises the role of the media as ideological agents and the effects of the media in cultivating people's perception of violence.
- The active audience perspective with its basic assumption that media users are actively and creatively involved in selecting and interpreting messages.

### 16.3.1 The traditional media effects perspective

This perspective was formulated after the success of media propaganda campaigns in brainwashing people during the First and Second World wars. This had led to the widespread belief that the media were "all powerful" and that people could be controlled against their will. A direct consequence of the world wars was urbanisation, which media critics believe had a negative impact on traditional social values and family relations. A characteristic of the new urbanised societies was a lack of close social and family ties. To compensate for this lack, members of the new urbanised societies turn to the media for moral and social guidance. Because primary family units no longer existed to soften or mediate the influence of the media, urbanites had no defences against the strong influence and power of the media.

The *first media research* on the effects of media violence was based on the hypodermic needle or stimulus-response theory with its basic assumption that if the media "inject" a message into the minds of media users, they will react immediately and in a predictable way (McQueen 1998). In other words, this theory assumes that there exists a direct causal relationship between violence on the screen and the ensuing behaviour of some viewers who watch violence. That is, viewers will become aggressive and imitate the violence they have watched. Furthermore, the stimulus-response theory regarded media users as passive and powerless to the "big" influence of the media.

Traditionally, stimulus-response research used experimental research methods to determine the influence of media violence. The procedure followed in experimental research is to select two groups of respondents – a control group and an experimental group. The experimental group is exposed to violent television programmes, while the control group watches non-violent programmes. According to Livingstone (1998:11) the results of experimental research have had some success. For example, children exposed to violent programmes were slower to seek help when they witnessed violence against other children. Furthermore, these children also showed more aggressive tendencies than did the children who were not exposed to violent programmes (the control group). However, experimental research has its definitive shortcomings, for example:

- Experimental research has been conducted in artificial, controlled conditions. That is, experimental research takes place in a "laboratory" (e.g. a classroom) where variables such as the influence of parents or other socialising agents (grandparents, teachers, church leaders and others) are absent and can therefore not soften (or intervene in) the effects of the violence that children are exposed to in an experimental situation.
- Media research using the stimulus-response framework only investigated the *short-term effects* of media violence. For example, although young children and adolescents sometimes imitate violence in the media, researchers could not conclusively establish a causal link between entertainment violence and an increase in violent crimes in real life. According to Von Feilitzen (1998:88), the main reason for the inconclusive findings about direct effects of the media was that even if the media prompt our youth to act out something they have seen on the small or big screen, these effects are most often short-term and harmless; for example, playfully acting out a violent deed immediately after watching violent programmes.

Almost all of us will remember how as children we imitated television and film characters such as Batman, Superman, Tarzan, and the Ninja Turtles. In Case study 16.1 we find evidence of how children imitate the Ninja Turtles. For example, children used paper towels to make Turtle headbands by poking holes in them for eyes, running and chasing each other, shouting "Hi Dude", "Cowabunga", and "Turtle Power". From this case study we can also deduce that these imitations were harmless. As one child said: "They (the Turtles) are not cruel because they fight against the bad guys. They only use their weapons when they are forced to do so, for example when they are attacked. They are like the police – they fight against evil and corruption." Thus, in spite of copying Turtle behaviour, it seems that the pro-social messages were more important to the children.

In the *second phase* of media effects research, which lasted from the 1980s up to the 1990s, researchers decided that media violence should be studied over longer time periods to determine long-term effects. This has led to the use of longitudinal field research where the same people (respondents) are studied over time (one to five years and longer) in order to determine causal effects of violence in the long term.

The most important findings of the longitudinal studies were that

- in more than 90 percent cases of children who developed violent tendencies over time, these tendencies were *not* caused by media violence, but by other factors (variables) such as children's and adolescents' personality traits; early aggression; family conditions; peer groups and social and cultural background (see section 16.4 of this unit for examples of these variables);
- a reciprocal causal relation, a circular or spiral effect is involved: that is, aggressive children and adolescents watch entertainment violence which reinforces aggression (Von Feilitzen 1998:89–90). We discuss the circular process model in more detail in section 16.5 of this unit.

Another long-term theory – the inoculation theory – was formulated during the second phase of effects research. This theory is based on the assumption that long-term exposure to screened violence might have a desensitising effect on viewers. That is, continuous exposure to fictional violence hardens us (makes us less sensitive) to images of real violence. However, the inoculation theory remains merely a common-sense assumption because so far no research has found evidence to support this theory (Livingstone 1998; McQueen 1998).

### 16.3.2 The cultivation perspective (powerful cultural perspective)

One of the basic assumptions of the cultivation perspective is that media output is an intrinsic part of our cultural or symbolic world, and therefore reflects the values and myths of society. Because we are exposed continuously to media messages (especially television messages – according to this perspective), we are cultivated by television to adopt certain belief systems and world views or ideologies, which then influence our frame of references to a large extent (Von Feilitzen 1998). Put differently, the media are the cultural lenses through which we view the world, the socialising and ideological agents that cultivate values, opinions, and knowledge of human beings in modern societies.

To test the above assumptions and to overcome the criticism of the experimental approach discussed above, Gerbner, Gross, Morgan and Signorieli (1986) developed the cultivation approach. Gerbner and his team focused solely upon viewers watching television in their natural surroundings over time – thus not the artificial conditions used in experimental research. They began their research by conducting numerous content analysis studies of violent television programmes. (Content analysis means that researchers count the number of violent incidences in American entertainment television programmes.) Thereafter they correlated their content analysis findings with how viewers perceive the portrayed television violence (Livingstone 1998:16).

## Media and Violence

The following are important cultivation research findings of Gerbner et al (1986):
- Heavy television viewers (those who watch television for more than four hours per day) are more likely to perceive the world as portrayed by television than are light viewers. Because heavy viewers are exposed to so much television violence, they get an exaggerated impression of the amount and types of violence in society (Livingstone 1998:16).
- Furthermore, because television viewers experience so little of what is going on in the real world firsthand, television cultivates the idea that the world is a dangerous place to live in. For fear of being a victim of crime, people – especially heavy television viewers – are too scared to leave their houses or walk alone in parks and streets (Von Feilitzen 1998). In other words, long-time exposure to television violence cultivates the images of the world as a "mean" and dangerous place. Thus, the heavier the viewing, the meaner the world inhabited by viewers becomes. According to Gerbner et al (1986), this leads to the cultivation of non-trust, that is, a negative perception is being created that we can trust nobody and because we experience so little of life firsthand (that is now violence on television), the state of affairs will simply deteriorate. When we apply these findings to the situation in South Africa, a different picture emerges: the cruel reality is that the majority of South Africans have at one or other stage been robbed, hijacked or attacked.
- Gerbner et al (1986) argued that by analysing the deeper levels of meaning – the connotative and ideological levels – we can infer that the over-representation of television violence is not really about crime, but instead about maintaining law and order. For instance, the action-adventure television genre reconstructs and reinforces our faith in law and order, and we feel safe that the good guys protect us against criminals. Therefore, our belief in social justice is reaffirmed, or as Lerner (1980; and in Livingstone 1998:17) puts it: because good always triumphs over bad (the "baddies" always get caught) viewers are conditioned to believe in a "just world". In the case study on the *Ninja Turtles*, we see that the main aim of the Ninja Turtle team is to maintain social order. The implication is that in spite of violent means to maintain order, this television programme contains pro-social messages.
- The content analysis studies of Gerbner et al (1986) also revealed that television programmes portray and therefore cultivate a "middle of the road", moderate way of life. At the centre of this way of life is an over-representation of white "well-to-do" males in the prime of their life and occupying high-profile jobs. The underlying ideology and myths of these media representations are that women and blacks are inferior to white males. As Livingstone (1998:17) says, women (and blacks) are "symbolically annihilated". We must keep in mind that the research of Gerbner et al was conducted in the 1980s. When we look at television programmes being broadcast in the new millennium, we must ask ourselves: Are females and race still under-represented in television programmes or has the position changed for the better?

The shortcoming of this approach is that although Gerbner and his team (1986) conducted numerous studies on television violence, they could not show a causal link between television violence and violence in real life. Furthermore, Gerbner's emphasis on the analyses of entertainment programmes makes one wonder why he has neglected news? As Von Feilitzen (1998:92) asks:

> Cannot news violence, as well, influence conceptions of violence in real life? In Sweden many adolescents overestimate the number of real murders and manslaughter (while they underestimate the number of traffic accidents), and believe too, that violence among young people has become more brutal – probably as a result of how the violence is presented in the news ... Press and TV news often greatly exaggerates how violent the world is ...

What Von Feilitzen's (1998) discussion boils down to is that violence in news, more than that of violence in entertainment, influences our perception of violence in real life. We can apply Von Feilitzen's (1998) statement to our own experience of news violence and violent entertainment programmes, by watching these programmes over a period (for example one week or more). We may then get an idea of whether news or entertainment programmes have the greater influence on our perception of violence in real life, especially in South Africa where incidences of violence are reported every day in television news.

Gunter (1988) supports the criticism that by merely counting the number of incidences of violence in a television programme does not explain the effects of such violence on viewers. Gunter (1988) refers to research results where the number of violent incidences in television programmes was counted by means of quantitative content analysis. One of the research findings was that television animation (cartoons) contain four times more violence than any of the other entertainment programmes being analysed. In a follow-up study, viewers' perceptions of animation violence were tested and the results showed that respondents regarded television animation as not violent at all!

Lewis (1991:586) in our case study of the *Ninja Turtles*, also says that for children, high-tech cartoon violence such as in *Masters of the Universe*, *G I Joe* and the *Ninja Turtles* is so flashy and spectacular that it is not seen as real by children. Therefore typical responses of children are "it is just a cartoon", " it's not real", and "it's fun to pretend this stuff".

However, we should always be cautious where children are concerned because the fact remains that taken collectively, these cartoons may help to create a climate where violence is a means of solving problems. And this may create problems for those children who live in a community/society where a culture of violence is prevalent, as we explain in our discussion of research on violence in South Africa (see 16.4).

### 16.3.3 The active audience perspective

The main problems with the traditional media effects and cultivation perspectives are that they look at media output as too homogeneous, the cultural influences as too negative, and the recipients as too passive (Von Feilitzen 1998). The active audience perspective on the other hand, assumes that we (media users) are actively and creatively involved in selecting and interpreting media messages. These interpretations, however, are influenced by our interests, expectations, needs and emotional involvement. Our active involvement then mediates or softens the effects of television violence. That is, we can decide for ourselves whether we want to be influenced by television violence or not.

Von Feilitzen (1998:96) gives the following examples of empirical research results on violence conducted within the framework of the active audience perspective:

- Children and adults select programmes to regulate their emotional state, for example boredom, avoiding tedious tasks, and to release stress after a hard day's work (Zillmann & Bryant 1986). Watching televised violence may help viewers to get rid of pent-up anger and frustrations (thus a positive effect of watching violence).
- Recipients who are attracted to horror movies have higher than average need for emotional and social stimulation (Lawrence & Palmgreen 1996).
- Interviews with 15- and 16-year-old boys indicate that the viewing of horror and violent movies may be a test of manliness in the circle of male peers. Jensen (in Von Feilitzen 1998) interprets the findings of his research regarding violent video games in the same vein: boys of this age are the powerless and subordinates in society and playing these games is a way of showing resistance, giving expression to masculinity and creating symbolic power and control.

Von Feilitzen (1998) concludes that sometimes and in various ways, violence plays a role in feelings of belonging to a group; playing a role in identity seeking and growing up. However, the media violence research of Jensen (in Von Feilitzen 1998) has been directed at males – female cultures have not been observed. Playing extremely violent computer games and watching films, television programmes and videos containing excessive violence, is chiefly exercised by males. Therefore, the culture of media violence is to a large extent built on male values.

The question that we should ask ourselves is whether we agree with Von Feilitzen's (1998) claims that media research on the influence of media violence on audiences has been directed only at males and that female cultures have not been observed. When we read our case study on *Yizo Yizo*, it seems that Von Feilitzen may be right: the perpetrators are the high school boys while the girls are the victims.

We conclude this section with a summary of the shortcomings of the active audience perspective:

- This perspective has been too one-sided, especially in its claim that the main causes of violence are not caused by the media. We know the media do indeed influence users in the short- and long term and both in positive and negative ways.
- This perspective does not deal with the question whether political and/or economic forces in society have an influence on media culture and violence (Von Feilitzen 1998).
- Although we are free to exercise choices regarding media and media content, too little is said about the fact that people are not unlimitedly free. Variables such as demographics (age, sex, level of education, social and cultural background, and so

forth), availability of media and personality traits do play a large role in the way we are affected by the media and media violence, as we illustrate in our discussion of television violence research in South Africa in the next section.

## 16.4 TELEVISION VIOLENCE RESEARCH IN SOUTH AFRICA

Research dealing with the influence of media violence in South Africa can be traced back to 1974, two years before the beginning of television in January 1976. South Africa was in the unique position of having access to television-naive audiences (people who have never been exposed to television before its inception) to study the effects of television. The majority of effect studies were conducted by the Human Sciences Research Council (HSRC), in Pretoria, South Africa and almost 90 per cent of these studies had been conducted among white pupils because of their greater access (at that stage) to television.

### 16.4.1 Research among white pupils in South Africa

The first longitudinal investigation into the effects of television violence on television-naive white school children was done over a period of five years. The countrywide test sample consisted of approximately 2 200 Grade 8 pupils who were followed up until their final school year (Grade 12). This investigation covered a period that extended from two years before the introduction of television transmissions on 5 January 1976 to three years thereafter. Each year the same children filled in a number of questionnaires and completed psychological tests which measured personality traits and interpersonal relationships (Conradie, Heyneke & Botha 1987). Some of the research results are:

- Television violence had made pupils more aggressive, especially with regard to verbal and physical aggression. The percentage increase in aggression for the total group however, was relatively low – only about 6% of the respondents showed a statistically significant increase in aggressive behaviour over the long term (five years).
- Pupils with a poor self-image were more influenced by television violence than those pupils with a high self-image.
- Sociability towards the opposite sex played a definite role, to such an extent that pupils with a high sociability score were not significantly influenced by television violence. However, those students with low levels of sociability, showed more aggression due to their exposure to television violence.
- As far as gender is concerned, the results were to be expected: watching television violence increased more physical and verbal aggression among boys than among girls. The girls' approval of aggression by authoritative figures diminished slightly.
- No definite pattern emerged regarding a causal relationship between intelligence and television viewing and aggression.

# Media and Violence

Conradie et al (1987) came to the conclusion that the effect of television violence was relatively small which supports research findings abroad that television is but only one of many factors that influence the aggressive behaviour of children and adolescents. Although we can argue that the respondents in Conradie's study could have been exposed to other types of media violence in 1974 to 1975 (before the introduction of television in 1976), the value of this study is that television-naive respondents were involved. Furthermore, various personality and interpersonal relationship variables were included in the research design. And, as we have already explained, these factors are often absent from overseas effect studies.

## 16.4.2 Research among black pupils in South Africa

Botha, Conradie and Mbatha (1993) conducted the most recent research on the effects of television violence on school children. The research was commissioned by the South African Broadcasting Corporation (SABC) and one of the main goals was to determine whether there exists a causal relationship between television violence and aggressive behaviour in real life. Eight primary schools from KwaZulu-Natal, Gauteng and Northern Province, were involved in this research.

The sample consisted of 348 young black children (hereafter called child respondents) in Grade 2 and Grade 3, as well as their parents/surrogate parents (hereafter called parent respondents). Interviews were conducted mainly with the male parent/surrogate parent in order to get a broader picture of the child respondent's family background and social milieu. Important findings of this study are:

- Nearly 21 percent of the parent respondents indicated that they had been traumatised by being personally threatened with a gun or stabbed with a knife while 49 percent of the parent respondents said that they had witnessed other people being victimised.
- About 39 percent of the parent respondents reported that their children had witnessed community violence such as people being stabbed, slapped, choked and beaten in the previous 12 months. It is thus clear that both the child and parent respondents had been exposed to violence in their social environment.
- Nearly 56 percent of the child respondents grew up in areas where they had little exposure to television because the majority of houses were not equipped with electricity. These child respondents watched an average of 8 hours per week, which is low in comparison to white children who watched 22 hours per week (Pitout 1985). Furthermore, the child respondents' favourite television programmes were locally produced programmes for children, with low levels of violence.
- The research results showed that television violence played *no* statistically significant role in child respondents' aggressive behaviour. Statistical significant correlations were, however, found between parents who were victimised and their consequent aggressive behaviour. This means that the more a parent respondent was the target of community violence, the more aggressively the parent behaved. Consequently, those parents used

more punitive child-rearing practices and were more rejecting in their attitudes towards their children. The results also indicate that boys who had been exposed to community violence showed high levels of aggression (Botha 1998:312–313).

To summarise: The greatest influence on violent behaviour of both parents and children (especially boys) in townships, was exposure to *community* and not television violence. And those parent respondents who were exposed to township violence were inclined to use aggressive punitive measures to raise their children. It therefore seems that children who grow up in endemic violent environments have a massive disadvantage. Add the viewing of television violence to these circumstances; we have a recipe for disaster. To illustrate the effect of television violence, we have included the case study on *Yizo Yizo* as an example of the effects of television violence on some school children in townships in South Africa.

We can further explain the influence of television violence by considering the circular process model below.

## 16.5 A COMPREHENSIVE CIRCULAR PROCESS MODEL FOR STUDYING VIOLENCE (Botha 1997)

Thus far, we have emphasised the lack of a general integrative theoretical framework to explain the influence of television violence on viewers. According to Botha (1997:295), the majority of effects studies on television violence usually add one situational or personal variable to another, without trying to determine how these networks of variables interact. What is needed is a comprehensive theoretical model that accommodates the interactive nature of the different variables in order to explain what effect television violence has in the long term.

Botha proposes a circular process model to explain the effects of television violence on children. This model is based on the theoretical and empirical data of Eron (1982) and Huesmann (1988) who have come to the conclusion that a complex causal circular pattern is concerned within which aggressiveness develops and is maintained. Although children are, to a greater or lesser degree, genetically predisposed to aggression – that is, they have inherited biological tendencies to be aggressive – the social manifestation thereof is to a large extent the result of social learning. Symbolic (role) models that we see on television are only some of the many variables that interact with viewers and which contribute to an environment conducive to cultivating aggression and violence. The circular process model explains the interactiveness of the following variables.

### 16.5.1 Social environment

- When young children are exposed to a harsh, cold, unloving milieu, the chances are good that this climate will cause or stimulate aggressive behaviour. In cases where community violence is endemic, and the parents have inborn aggressive tendencies and aggressive ways of handling conflict, a family milieu of aggressiveness is created.

In our discussion of violence research in South Africa, we indicated that children who are exposed to such an environment will probably also become aggressive, especially when they are subjected to paternal aggressive punitive measurements. And when children are continuously subjected to severe aggressive punishment and exposed to aggressive deeds towards others, the aggressor becomes their role model and they may imitate this behaviour which then leads to the reinforcement of that behaviour.
- When children grow up in an atmosphere where they are humiliated, excessively criticised and punished, the scene is set for children to acquire aggressive ways of handling their own conflicts. These children are especially vulnerable to be influenced by television violence because it fits their existing frame of reference of how to handle conflict.

## 16.5.2 Intellectual capacities

- Intellectual capacities may also predispose children to acquire violent behaviour. For example, Huesmann (1988) and Eron (1982) have found that children with low intellectual capacities are heavy television viewers, watch violent television programmes and believe that the violence on television is true to life. If parents with limited intellectual capabilities are aggressive, their children's repertoire of conflict handling is limited to aggressive behaviour.
- Furthermore, the failure to develop intellectual skills stimulates aggression and aggressive behaviour; may also inhibit the child's social interaction with peers and teachers who are needed for developing academic skills. The findings of the research regarding the influence of television on white South African school children by Conradie et al (1987), differ from those of Huesmann (1988) and Eron (1982) – Conradie et al did not find any correlation between intelligence and exposure to television violence (see section 16.4.1 above).

## 16.5.3 Cognitive and moral development

- Heavy television viewers usually also watch violent programmes and are therefore regularly exposed to television characters who solve interpersonal problems in aggressive ways. In cases where children identify with aggressive television characters, they may encode in their memory and subconscious mind aggressive ways to solve problems. According to Huesmann (1988), the social behaviour we acquire is to a great extent controlled by cognitive scripts, strategies and schemes of what we observe, and these are stored in our memories. When we have to solve problems we tap into our memories.
- Children who are constantly exposed to violence, whether in a family situation or television, are predisposed to develop and maintain cognitive scripts that emphasise that aggression is an important form of problem-solving. In addition, television

# MEDIA STUDIES

violence may also stimulate violent fantasies that are ingrained in aggressive cognitive scripts. This increases the likelihood that these scripts will be recalled and used when a conflict situation arises.
- Children who are aggressive towards peers are unpopular, have a low self-image and find it hard to fit into the school system. Research by Slabbert (1985) has shown that aggressive children feel an affinity towards gangs, probably because gang members use anti-social and aggressive ways to solve problems and thus reinforce the acquisition of such behaviour. When at home the child will rather watch television than do homework. Because of poor academic performance and social interactions these children are ostracised at home, in the playground and classroom. In the case study *Yizo Yizo*, media reports indicated that copycat gangs have sprung up acting out scenes in *Yizo Yizo* with sickening detail. And in Orange Farm, south of Johannesburg, a gang calling itself "Yizo Yizo" has been terrorising the community.

From the above discussion, we can deduce that because of poor family relations and lack of positive role models, television violence may have a reassuring function, that is television may reassure viewers that their behaviour is acceptable. Television violence may even teach viewers new coercive techniques, which they may then use in their interaction with others. Evidence of new coercive techniques is also to be found in *Yizo Yizo*. One of the attackers said he likes the bullying in the series "because it showed how boys should behave".

What is more disturbing is that children who show high levels of aggression and violent behaviour may soon find that when television violence no longer satisfies their increasing appetite for violence, they turn to engaging in stronger forms of violence such as that depicted in excessively violent films, videos and video games (Botha 1997).

## 16.6 PREVENTATIVE MEASURES: HOW TO CURB THE EFFECTS OF TELEVISION VIOLENCE

From the discussion above, we can deduce that television violence does influence some children in South Africa. Van Vuuren and Kriel (1996:36) are of the opinion that although this proportion is relatively small, broadcasters should be more sensitive to the broadcasting of violent programmes, especially in the South African situation where crime and violence are the order of the day. The case study *Yizo Yizo* shows us that there are indeed reasons for concern. Although the effects of television are not simple and straightforward, Van Vuuren and Kriel (1996:38-37) offer some suggestions as to how we can try to avert the situation.

### 16.6.1 Reduction and control of levels of violence in television programmes

The American Psychological Association has suggested that a rating system should be developed by focusing on behavioural indicators and descriptors to indicate potential harmful material to children and adolescents. A V-Chip, which is a piece of electronic technology, will enable parents to control the type of violence their children see on television. In other words, parents can set the television to "black out" programmes that they do not want their children to watch. Those of us who are subscribers to the pay channel M-Net in South Africa know that this channel, since its inception, uses the same type of technology.

### 16.6.2 Involvement of parents

Parents should be empowered to assist them in making television programme choices for their children. Van Vuuren and Kriel (1996:38) offer the following guidelines. As parents we should

- judge the amount of violence in the programmes our children view by watching several episodes over a period of time and look for the underlying messages portrayed in that programme (see the analysis of the underlying pro-social messages in the *Ninja Turtles* and *Yizo Yizo*);
- watch television together with our children and discuss the violence with them. Explain that violence is painful and destructive. Furthermore, we should provide our children with alternatives of how to resolve conflict without resorting to violence, for example
    - explain to children that entertainment violence is "faked", for example in a Bond film, Bond's helicopter crashes into a high building. Bond however, escapes unscathed. We should explain that in real life most people get killed in such an accident or will at least be seriously injured;
    - ask them how they experience the violence as portrayed by the different characters;
    - restrict watching violent videos and explain to our children why we take such a decision; and
    - encourage our children to watch programmes with strong pro-social messages where the emphasis is on cooperating, caring and helping one another. Research has shown that these programmes have a positive influence on children.

### 16.6.3 Intervention by broadcasting industries

The above guidelines for parents are useful but we also need the intervention from broadcasting industries. Van Vuuren and Kriel (1996:38) mention bodies such as the National Association of Broadcasters, and more specifically the Broadcasting Complaints Commission in South Africa. In addition, individual broadcasters themselves must also get involved in this action.

As far as the SABC is concerned, it is currently using the following set of guidelines (Van Vuuren & Kriel 1996:38):

- The SABC addresses problems relating to violence, by suggesting a "watershed time" (21:00) which is also called prime-time. Before this hour, less violent programmes are

## MEDIA STUDIES

broadcast based on the assumption that after 21:00, especially young children will be in bed. (This guideline is also used by the British Broadcasting Corporation [BBC] in Britain.)
- A second way of trying to curb the violent content, is by editing out scenes of violence. It is however, a very contentious, difficult and judgemental action, which is sometimes regarded as a form of censorship. Broadcasters are therefore cautious in the application of these guidelines.

The SABC is really confronted with a dilemma: on one hand we do not want to revert to the bad old days of strict censorship. On the other hand, parents and other critics feel that violent programmes should be curtailed.

### 16.6.4 The evaluation of violent programmes

In our case study *Yizo Yizo* we include the opinions of a group of third-year Communication students, which illustrates the value of evaluation of programmes by members of the public before programmes are broadcast – especially programmes with high incidences of violence. The views of the students are summarised below (read the *Yizo Yizo* case study again).

- Because of the graphic scenes (e.g. the rape scene) in the first three episodes, the time slot was not appropriate (20:30) and should have been moved to a later time to preclude young children from watching.
- The violence in *Yizo Yizo* was too graphic for children. One student said that although parental guidance was advised at the beginning of the programme, parents in general ignore this guideline, especially when programmes are broadcast in prime-time and *Yizo Yizo* had been broadcast in prime-time.
- Viewers should have been informed before the beginning of each episode, that *Yizo Yizo* is an educational drama which is part of the National Department of Education's campaign to restore and create a culture of teaching and learning in township schools.
- Viewers should also have been told that as the series progresses, solutions would be presented of how to solve crime in townships and how to restore and create a culture of learning.
- Crime and violence were glorified in the beginning of the series because the bullies had the upper hand over their victims and this was portrayed in grim, graphic violent detail. It was only near the end of the last episodes of *Yizo Yizo* that the educational value came through. *Perhaps*, the students said, *it was then too late – the perception had been created that violence is the only means of solving problems.*

The suggestions of the students are of great value. As has been recommended, when local programmes are produced, especially violent programmes such as *Yizo Yizo*, research should be conducted on a regular basis. This means that a television programme should be evaluated during all the phases of production – from preproduction to postproduction – by focus groups consisting of members of the target audience. The same procedure can be followed before broadcasting imported programmes with a high violence content.

## Summary

We began this unit by explaining why violence is one of the important issues in media research. We then discussed how the media contribute to moral panic by sensationalising perpetrators' copying of violent television content. In South Africa the media's reportage of the programme *Yizo Yizo* is a case in point.

We proposed three perspectives to investigate and explain violence. From our discussion it becomes clear that media content is not the only agent having an influence on violent behaviour. In fact, mental impressions we get from the media are intertwined with our own feelings, values, norms, and experiences that we acquire from our interaction with family, friends, school, church and so on. These variables are indeed of great importance when we study the influence of violence because they play a determining role in how people will respond to violence and aggression. In other words, these variables play a decisive role in increasing or diminishing the inclination to act violently. This is one reason why it is so difficult to find statistically significant relations between televised violence and children's aggressive behaviour.

Because television is but one socialising agent in the intricate interaction between various developmental, psychological, social and contextual factors that play a role in developing aggressive and violent behaviour, we proposed the circular process model to study the effects of television violence. Of particular interest is the circular pattern of causality in which violence creates the context for further violence. This, in turn, reinforces the initial violent behaviour and gives rise to a stronger inclination towards violence and aggressive behaviour (Botha 1997).

With regard to the South African context, the influence that violence has on community life, relationships between family members and the wider society, is of particular significance. As has been illustrated in our discussion of research among township children, the culture of violence in South African townships can play a major role in the development of aggression and violence on the individual and familial level. In a similar way we can assume that a cold and harsh family climate that interacts with other social forces such as television, can breed violent individuals who can, in the end, play a major role in violence associated with the larger social and political contexts. However, to address the root causes of violence one has to start at micro level – the home and family. Evidence exists that healthy, warm and supportive families breed a healthy and violence-free society (Olivier, Roos & Berg 1998:278). We concluded this unit by proposing preventative measures to curb the effects of television violence.

# MEDIA STUDIES

**Case study 16.1:** A critical analysis of *Teenage, Mutant Ninja Turtles*

(Adapted from an article by Lewis 1991:585–599.)

> Contrary to what many adults may think, the kid world of the super hero seems a kinder, gentler place with the advent of the Ninja Turtles.
> (Lewis 1991:585)

Of all the kid heroes of the nineties, the most popular were, by far, the Teenage, Mutant Ninja Turtles (hereafter called the Ninja Turtles) which started as a comic book written by Kevin Eastman and Peter Laird in the United States of America. The major characters in this comic book are the four turtles named Raphael, Leonardo, Michelangelo and Donetello, and their spiritual father Master Splinter. Together they are always up against the evil macho Shredder and his team.

The *Ninja Turtles* series came to South African television in 1990 and was immediately a hit with South African children. However, the Turtles' popularity caused a public outcry because members of the public, especially parents, regarded them as evil fighting "mean machines" and a symbol of violent rebellion against adults. The media also had a field day and soon newspaper and magazine articles appeared with headings such as "Ninja Turtles: bose invloed of gesonde vermaak?" (Ninja Turtles: evil influence or innocent entertainment?) (*Vrye Weekblad* 1990:4–5); "Storm oor 'bose' Turtles" (*Huisgenoot* 1990:89–91); "Why angry clerics hurled 'evil' Turtles into oblivion" (*Sunday Times* 1990:55–56).

Some religious groupings even went so far as to interpret the three sixes (the number of Satan) on the outfits of the Turtles as being signs of the supernatural, mysticism as well as the New Age Movement and therefore insisted that the television series should be banned. And as it happened in the USA, South African schools did indeed ban the wearing of Ninja Turtle clothes, or bringing Turtle toys to school. They claimed that children, in acting out Ninja behaviour, were hurting one another with amateurish karate chops and kicks. But this did not deter children from playing and imitating the Turtles on the playground – they just went to the bathrooms and used paper towels to make Turtle headbands by poking holes in them for eyes, running and chasing each other, shouting "Hi Dude", "Cowabunga", and "Turtle Power".

But are the Turtles ultra-violent avengers or are they loveable, cuddly creatures? When we look at the mythic nature of the violent super-hero, a very interesting picture emerges: the world of children is heavily populated with plastic representations of "super heroes" who in their very own way, create spectacular and violent means to solve problems they encounter, for example *Robocob, Masters of the Universe, G I Joe* and *X-man* to name but a few. And we all know the predictable story line of the super-hero genre: very good heroes always triumph over totally evil bad guys by blowing them away with their high-tech weapons. In the American version of the super-hero myth the victory of the hero is almost always won by violent means.

# Media and Violence

At first glance the Turtles seem to fit the same ultra-violent avenger pattern as explained above. But when we look at the narrative structure of the *Ninja Turtles* we see differences and these differences are closer connected to Gawelti's myth of individual action than the violent avenger motif. As we explain below, that although there is a lot of violence in each Turtle episode, the major focus is the social meaning of individual action and the re-establishment of social order.

### Analysis of the narrative structure of the Ninja Turtles

Each episode of the *Ninja Turtles* contains more or less the following narrative elements of Gawelti's myth of individual action:

- A crime wave caused by the evil Shredder and his team the Foot Clang, is plaguing New York and the police are ineffective to bring the criminals to book.
- April O'Neal (the Turtle's lady friend) is attacked by the Foot Clang. She is saved by one of the Turtles and is taken to their home (the underground sewers of New York) which they share with their Zen master, a giant rat named Master Splinter.
- In the course of events, Master Splinter is abducted by the Shredder and his Foot Clan.
- The Shredder and his team fight against the Turtles but they (the Turtles) lose the battle (or a series of battles) and retreat to the country.
- In the country the Turtles rest and recover mentally and physically from their beatings.
- Leonardo, the intellectual and spiritual Turtle, makes a mind contact with Master Splinter and calls together the Turtles who have been grieving for their master and are filled with guilt and self-doubt for having allowed him to have been captured. The four of them sit around the campfire and call up the image of Splinter who tells them:

    > You have learned the greatest truth of the Ninja – that ultimate mastery comes not of the body, but of the mind. Together, there is nothing our four minds cannot accomplish. Help each other, draw upon one another, and always remember the true force that bonds you, the same as that which brought me here tonight. I love you all, my sons.
    > (Lewis 1991:591)

- With their newly gained power, knowledge and mental strength they go back to the city to rescue Splinter and defeat the evil Shredder and his Clan (albeit temporarily).
- Having rid the city of its crime problem, the Turtles return happily to their hide-out in the sewer to watch television, crack jokes and eat huge amounts of pizza.

For those of us who are not familiar with the narrative of the *Ninja Turtles*, it is interesting to note that the Turtles would rather stay in their hide-out where they can enjoy eating pizzas and watching television (very much like human children). They however, have a well-developed sense of responsibility – duty before pleasure – and get involved in the conflict to save the damsel in distress (April O'Neil) and their spiritual father, Master Splinter. When the Turtles are beaten by the enemy, they remove themselves from the community to connect with the countryside in order to get a new perspective on their mistakes and to gain spiritual insight by connecting mentally with their spiritual leader, Father Splinter.

Armed with a new knowledge of themselves and united in mind and spirit, they return to New York, save Splinter, beat Shredder and his Foot Clan and retreat (vanish) into the sewers (instead of the sunset – in the Cowboy genre the hero, after defeating the bad guys, rides off into the sunset).

A variation on the mono-myth is the role of Master Splinter who is almost always abducted by his arch-enemy the Shredder, and then rescued by the four Turtles. Although they rescue April, she becomes part of the team to beat the villains and so provision is made for young liberated females. Lewis says that the abducted figure (who in the myth represents purity, innocence and love) becomes the father figure. Master Splinter raises his "sons" alone, teaching them the moral codes and skills necessary to live a good and meaningful life. Most important is that he teaches them that love, self-control, harmony and cooperation are the ultimate weapons. Furthermore, Splinter detests violence; for example he admonishes Raphael for his bad temper. Splinter can be regarded as the Turtles' socio-emotional leader which is closer to the traditional, nurturing maternal role model combined with the wise elder (a rare figure in our popular culture) than he is the macho male role model that characters such as *Robocob* represent.

What we can deduce from the above discussion, is that by means of an analysis of the underlying structures and messages in violent programmes, we gain insight into the pro-social messages, which at first glance are not apparent. The question now is: Does the Ninja world contain a kinder and gentler violence than *Robocob*, *Masters of the Universe* and *G I Joe*?

To assess the impact of television cartoons, Lewis and his colleague conducted interviews with children in preschools and elementary schools in California. The research findings were the following:

- For both girls and boys the most popular television programme was the *Ninja Turtles*, though *Batman*, *He-Man*, *Ghostbusters* were also mentioned. The reasons for the first choice were responses like "they are party dudes", "they are funny, overgrown and talented" and "because they are cute – I'd like to marry them" (Lewis 1991:597).
- All the child respondents recognised Splinter as the Turtle's dad and "he is good because he teaches them things". "He is smart and gives them advice ... they stay with him because they don't have a real home" (Lewis 1991:598). As far as

# Media and Violence

identifying the favourite part of each episode is concerned, common responses were the ending where the evil Shredder was beaten (favoured more by boys), and when the Turtles all say "Cowabunga" (favoured more by girls).
- In general the children, no matter their age or gender, did not mention the violence. They like the Turtles because they are good, funny and cool and children relate to them on a level impossible with full-grown macho figures like *Rambo, GI Joe* and even *Batman*. It might sound strange that children feel more attracted to overgrown turtles than human figures. However, this is not surprising because through fairy tales children come into regular contact with monsters, dragons and fairies. They become part of children's collective consciousness which enable them to identify with (and get used to) good friendly, cuddly and soft fairy tale animal figures. According to the co-creator of the Turtles, Peter Laird, the success of the *Ninja Turtles* can to a great extent be attributed to the fact that they are indeed nice guys; guys that kids want to be themselves.

We should mention that the television animation (cartoon) version of the *Ninja Turtles* contains far less graphic violence than that in books and the film version of the *Ninja Turtles*. And contrary to what adults may think, the kid world of the superhero seems a kinder, gentler place with the advent of the Ninja Turtles. In an interview conducted by Cristelle de Jager of the now defunct newspaper *Vrye Weekblad* (De Jager 1990:4–5) one child respondent said the following about the Turtles: "They are not cruel because they fight against the bad guys. They only use their weapons when they are forced to do so, for example when they are attacked. They are like the police – the fight against evil and corruption".

However, we should keep in mind that although children may regard these animations as "just a cartoon", "it is not real" and "it is fun to pretend the stuff", the fact remains that taken collectively, these cartoons may help to create a climate that violence is a means of solving problems. And this may create problems for those children who live in a community/society where a culture of violence is prevalent/endemic.

## Case study 16.2: *Yizo Yizo*

(Adapted from articles in *You* magazine 1999, and the *Sunday Times* 1999 on the Internet.)

> Schools gripped by fear. Survey for new drama series finds that death and rape stalk SA's classrooms
> (Pretorius 1999)
>
> Prime time portrayals of rape, drug abuse and gangsterism in school tears black communities apart

# MEDIA STUDIES

> When the first episode of *Yizo Yizo* was shown on SABC1, teachers saw the first danger signs. Now fear reigns in the schools, and hats, takkies, guns, swords, swearing and tinted hair have replaced school uniforms.
> (Prime time portrayals of rape ... 1999:22)
>
> **Horrors come to life at schools**
> (Bubesi 1999)
>
> **Switching channels won't stop playground bulllies**
> (Galombik 1999)

These were a few of the headlines that appeared in newspapers and magazines when the first episode of the SABC's new education drama *Yizo Yizo*, a 13-part drama series, had been screened in 1999 on Wednesday nights at 20:30 on SABC1. After three weeks of broadcasting, *Yizo Yizo* was the most popular programme on SABC-TV and attracted more than 6 million viewers.

To produce this series, a survey was conducted to determine what is going on in South Africa's township schools. The research results painted a scenario of schools in the grip of criminality: boys carry guns and knives to school, they rape school girls at gunpoint, abuse alcohol and drugs and highjack motor vehicles for money. Other issues identified by the survey were teenage pregnancy, schoolgirls who sleep with taxi drivers for free rides, lack of role models because teachers set a poor example by arriving late at school, abusing alcohol on school premises and after school hours, suffering from hangovers, sitting in the staff room all day drinking tea instead of attending to their classrooms. The results of the survey also showed that the rampant wave of criminality has lead to a culture of fear in schools. Teachers are desperate – when some of them want to change things for the better, they receive threatening letters warning that they will be raped (Pretorius 1999; Prime time portrayals of rape ... 1999).

The results of this survey were used for the production of the SABC's chilling new education drama *Yizo Yizo*. This drama is part of the national Department of Education's campaign to restore and create a culture of teaching and learning in township schools. The Department said that one of the aims with this drama was to suggest solutions for the crime-ridden schools in the townships and to create a culture of learning.

According to Harriet Perlman (quoted in: Prime time portrayals of rape ...1999:38), who was involved in research for the 13-part series made by Laduma Film Factory, none of the scenes in *Yizo Yizo* was invented; the scenarios are hard-core events that happen every day in township schools, such as the following rape scene portrayed in this drama:

> She pleaded for mercy as she was dragged kicking and screaming into the car ... In the township chicken coop, they pulled off her skirt and flung her to the

ground. Her pathetic screams filled the air as the teenaged thug entered her from the behind, again and again, whilst his friends egged [sic] him on ...
(Prime time portrayals of rape ... 1999:22)

This graphic rape portrayal was the most talked about scene in the series and caused such an uproar that some parents wanted *Yizo Yizo* to be removed from the SABC1 menu while others felt that it was high time that parents – and the country as a whole – took notice of what is going on in their schools and that action should be taken to do something about it. Most worrying though, are the effects of this drama: *Yizo Yizo* has developed cult followers among the black youth. Thugs with catchy names such as Chester and Papa Action in this drama have become overnight role models (idols) and school children imitate their heroes' dress code, and their way of walking and talking.

## Copycat imitations of scenes in *Yizo Yizo*

Even more chilling are the copycat scenes being acted out by school children, such as the following examples discussed in the *Sunday Times* (Bubesi 1999) and *You* magazine (Prime time portrayals of rape ... 1999:22):

- When a 20-year-old Vosloorus high school pupil, Mndaweni, flushed a fellow schoolmate's head in a toilet, he was taking the role of the antagonist ("hard guy") of the series. Mndaweni said that he got the idea from watching the series. "I was standing against the wall in the toilets smoking dagga. I saw this boy on his way to buy lunch ... and (I) said he should give me money but he said he didn't have any." Mndaweni then dragged his victim inside the toilets, taking R5 from his pocket, and forced his head into the toilet bowl and flushed. Mndaweni proudly admitted he had copied the scene from the first episode of *Yizo Yizo* and also said that "(I)f I was called to play the role of Papa Action, I would do it better. I imagine holding that gun and bossing everybody in the school".

    The head-flushing incident was also acted out at Zamukhanyo Primary School in Daveyton. According to the victim, Prince Masuku, the boys forced his head into a toilet bowl of excrement while shouting that they were baptising him in the name of Yizo Yizo and Satan. One of Masuku's attackers said that he liked "the bullying in the series because it showed how boys should behave. But after this incident I want to apologise. Now I see that the show has a bad influence because we could have hurt him or killed him if the teacher hadn't intervened."
- Copycat gangs have sprung up acting out scenes in *Yizo Yizo* with sickening detail. In Orange Farm, a gang calling itself "Yizo Yizo" has been terrorising the community.

From the media reports in the *Sunday Times* and *You* magazine, it seems that teachers and parents were divided about the effects of this series: some thought it was repulsive and that *Yizo Yizo* has started another cycle of moral decay, while others regard it as good and educational. First, we will look at a few examples of

# MEDIA STUDIES

the negative effects of *Yizo Yizo* and then give examples of pro-social (positive) effects.

## Teachers views on "bad" effects of *Yizo Yizo*

- Some teachers claimed that since *Yizo Yizo* has come to the screen, discipline in schools has deteriorated. *Yizo Yizo* became the buzzword and graffiti appeared on notice boards and blackboards. Female schoolteachers were especially the victims of schoolboys who threw paper aeroplanes at them and some male pupils openly expressed their sexual fantasies about them.
- The principal of a secondary school in Khayelitsha felt that the series should be banned before the culture of disrespect, violence and corruption spilled over to Western Cape. The view being that events as portrayed in *Yizo Yizo* happen in Gauteng and the screening of the series should be halted to prevent the culture of violence infesting schools in other provinces.
- A teacher in Vosloorus said the show made it difficult for teachers to deal with issues such as drug abuse and bullying: the series has disempowered the teachers because *Yizo Yizo* shows mostly scenes where the pupils are in control of classes and not the teachers who are trying to instil and restore the culture of teaching and learning.
- The headmaster of a High School in KwaMasuhu, KwaZulu-Natal said although no change in behaviour had been observed, the pupils were talking about *Yizo Yizo* and he suggested that schools should conduct workshops about the series.

## Views on the pro-social effects of *Yizo Yizo*

According to Nicola Galombik (1999) head of SABC Education TV that together with the Department of Education commissioned *Yizo Yizo*, the article "TV horrors have come to life at schools" in the *Sunday Times* of 21 February 1999, only highlights and sensationalises copycat behaviour and bullying in schools. The article has, however, little substance because it takes more than a television series to turn children into violent thugs. Sensationalising their anti-social behaviour distracts from the reasons for such behaviour and possible solutions to it. A case in point is the way the article dwells on the alleged self-confessed bully, Dlame Mndaweni's acting out the toilet scene from the television programme. By sensationalising this event, attention is deflected from the social reality that Mndaweni represents – a reality of a large number of youths for whom stealing, drug abuse, rape and intimidation is a way of life. Furthermore, people who imitate violent behaviour from television have a predisposition to act violently. It seems as if Mndaweni has a predisposition to bully. Bullying is not a new phenomenon that *Yizo Yizo* has brought to the screen – it is endemic in township schools. Although the breakdown of the culture of learning and the fabric of social life may not be prevalent in all schools, it is widespread enough to constitute a case for major concern in township schools. According to Galombik, the following are examples of pro-social messages in *Yizo Yizo*:

- The spiral (conspiracy) of silence around events happening in schools has been broken by *Yizo Yizo* – these events can now be addressed openly so that children do not have to live in constant fear.
- Although *Yizo Yizo* portrays the good and the bad in a realistic way, it is far more than a mere reflection of reality. It also offers solutions to problems such as how strong leadership and parental and community involvement can curb the spiral of violence and how the process of change and reconstruction can empower teachers, pupils and parents with knowledge about their rights and responsibilities.
- The problems mentioned above are complex and the solutions are not quick or easy. *Yizo Yizo* does not fall into the trap of making false promises and offering quick-fix solutions to these problems.
- *Yizo Yizo* can serve as a platform for public debate and a catalyst for social change in future television series, youth magazines, teacher supplements and workshops.

Galombik (1999) comes to the conclusion (and we agree with her) that the views of the few people being quoted in the articles cannot be regarded as representative of the wide audience for whom *Yizo Yizo* is intended. And, according to Galombik (1999), 76 percent of the audience who could vote on a vote line, express their satisfaction with the way reality in townships is reflected in *Yizo Yizo* and they would like to see more of this type of drama on television. (The question is – how many of the 6 million viewers of *Yizo Yizo* had access to a vote line? The representativeness of the 76 percent of the total viewers is thus also questionable.)

Finally, to get an idea of the views and opinions of Unisa *Yizo Yizo* viewers (between 20 and 25 years of age) an exploratory focus-group interview was conducted with a group of third-year Communication students at Unisa to hear what they had to say about this series. These students were selected because their studies in Communication provide them with enough background to evaluate the potential anti- and pro-social effects of television violence.

### The views of a group of third-year Communication students on *Yizo Yizo*: a pilot study

On 20 April 2000 an exploratory focus-group interview was conducted with Communication III students at Unisa. The aim was to determine their feelings and views about the controversy surrounding *Yizo Yizo*. During the focus-group interview, the students confirmed that the reality portrayed in *Yizo Yizo* is true to life. In other words, the incidences portrayed in *Yizo Yizo* are happening in many township schools. In fact, even worse things happen in schools than those acted out in *Yizo Yizo*. (The students did not want to elaborate on this statement.) And yes, the public should be made aware of what is going on in schools.

The students' main criticism and concern was however, that because of the graphic scenes (e.g. the rape scene) in the first three episodes, the time slot was not appropriate (20:30) and should have been moved to a later time slot to preclude young children from watching. The general feeling of the group was that the violence was too graphic for children. One student said that although parental guidance was advised, parents in general ignore this guideline especially when programmes are broadcast in prime-time and *Yizo Yizo* has been broadcast in prime-time. The students were also of the opinion that viewers should have been informed before the beginning of each episode that *Yizo Yizo* is an educational drama which is part of the National Department of Education's campaign to restore and create a culture of teaching and learning in township schools. It should also have been explained that as the series progresses, solutions would be presented of how to solve crime in townships and how to restore and create a culture of learning. According to the students, crime and violence were glorified in the beginning because the bullies had the upper hand over their victims and this was portrayed in grim, graphic violent detail; it was only near the end of the last episodes of *Yizo Yizo* that the educational value came through. Perhaps it was then too late – the perception had been created that violence is the only means of solving problems.

## Research activities

1. Do the media contribute to creating moral panic when reporting on incidences of violence? Illustrate your discussion with examples from *The Martians have Landed*, *Yizo Yizo* and the *Ninja Turtles*.
2. Which theoretical perspective (or combination of perspectives) is the most suitable to explain the moral panic hypothesis? Distinguish between short-term and long-term effects theories and illustrate your answer with examples from *Yizo Yizo* and *Ninja Turtles*.
3. The cultivation perspective assumes "that because of exposure to television violence, viewers become more fearful and develop a heightened and (perhaps) an unjustified sense of danger for the outside world". Apply this assumption to your own viewing experience and explain how often you have seen examples of violence in television programmes – news and/or entertainment – in real life.
4. What are the main shortcomings of the active audience perspective? Summarise the shortcomings and explain how this perspective can be expanded by incorporating aspects of the traditional effects and/or cultivation perspectives and/or components of the circular process model.
5. Explain in your own words why television exposure is not the only socialising agent that can influence the behaviour of children. Illustrate your explanation with research results of the effects of television violence on school children in South Africa.

# Media and Violence

6. Which processes and variables should be taken into account when studying the effects of television violence? Consider the question by explaining the circular process in which television violence affects (impacts on) the behaviour of children. Illustrate your answer with examples from the case study *Yizo Yizo*.

7. Explain in your own words which preventative measures can be taken to curb the effects of television violence. Apply these measures to your own life and indicate whether you agree/disagree with the proposed preventative measures.

8. After you have studied the *Ninja Turtles* case study, answer the following questions:
   a) Do you think the public's reaction to the *Ninja Turtles* was justified?
   b) Were the media objective and/or subjective in their reportage of the public's reaction to the violence in the *Ninja Turtles*?
   c) Do you regard the effects of the *Ninja Turtles* as short-term or long-term?
   d) What is the value of the analysis of the narrative elements? For example:
      - Did the analysis change your mind about the negative effects of the *Ninja Turtles*?
      - Do you agree that animation (cartoons) like that of the Turtles can have pro-social effects?
   e) Do you agree with the following statement?
      "Contrary to what many adults may think, the kid world of the super hero seems a kinder, gentler place with the advent of the Ninja Turtles" (Lewis 1991:585).
   f) When you were a child did you imitate the behaviour of characters in television, film, radio, storybooks and so on? If your answer is "yes" make a list of such imitations and explain your copycat behaviour as being pro-social/anti-social or both.

9. After you have studied the case study *Yizo Yizo*, answer the following questions:
   a) Did the media sensationalise the portrayal of violence in *Yizo Yizo*?
   b) Do you think that *Yizo Yizo* contributed to violence in township schools?
   c) Do you regard the effects of *Yizo Yizo* as short-term or long-term?
   d) Can the circular process model be used to explain the effects that *Yizo Yizo* had on some of the children in township schools?
   e) Do you agree that *Yizo Yizo* contains pro-social messages?
   f) Do you think that females are portrayed as victims of violence in *Yizo Yizo*?
   g) Having read the case study, what are your perceptions or first impressions of violence in township schools?
   h) What do you think are the root causes of violence in township schools?

## Further reading

Bornman, E, Van Eeden, R & Wentzel, M (eds). 1998. *Violence in South Africa: a variety of perspectives.* Pretoria: Human Sciences Research Council.

Dickinson, R, Harindranath, R & Linne, O. (eds). 1998. *Approaches to audiences: a reader.* London: Arnold.

Fourie, PJ (ed). 1997. *Introduction to communication – course book 6: film and television studies.* Cape Town: Juta.

McQueen, D. 1998. *Television: a media student's guide.* London: Arnold.

Van Vuuren, DP & Kriel, HA. 1996. Violent television: cause for concern in South Africa? *Equid Novi* 17(1):25–42.

## Bibliography

Botha, MP. 1990. Televisieblootstelling en aggressiwiteit by hoërskoolleeringe: 'n opvolgondersoek oor vyf jaar. D.Phil Thesis, University of the Orange Free State, Bloemfontein.

Botha, MP. 1997. Social issues: television violence and aggression amongst viewers, in *Introduction to communication – course book 6: film and television studies*, edited by PJ Fourie. Cape Town: Juta.

Botha, MP. 1998. Exposure to television violence and the development of aggression among children: evidence from various longitudinal studies, in *Violence in South Africa: a variety of perspectives*, edited by E Bornman, R van Eeden, & M Wentzel. Pretoria: Human Sciences Research Council.

Botha, MP, Conradie, DP & Mbatha, E. 1993. *Television violence and aggression among black children: a pilot study.* Pretoria: Human Sciences Research Council.

Bubesi, S. 1999. *Horrors come to life at schools.* [O].
Available: http://www.suntimes.co.za/1999/02/21/news02.htm
Accessed on 2000/05/08

Conradie, DP, Heynecke, M & Botha, MP. 1987. *The effects of television violence on television-naive pupils: a follow-up study over five years.* Pretoria: Human Sciences Research Council.

Eron, LD. 1982. Parent-child interaction, television violence and aggression of children. *American Psychologist* 37(2):197–211.

De Jager, C. 1990. Ninja Turtles: bose invloed of gesonde vermaak? *Vrye Weekblad*, November:4–5.

Galombik, N. 1999. *Switching channels won't stop playground bullies.* [O].
Available: http://www/suntimes.co.za/1999/02/28/insight/line09.htm
Accessed on 2000/04/28

Gerbner, G, Gross, L, Morgan, M & Signorieli, N. 1986. Living with television. The dynamics of the cultivation process, in *Perspectives on media effects*, edited by J Bryant & D Zillman. Hillside, NJ: Lawrence Erlbaum.

Gunter, B. 1988. The perceptive audience, in *Communication Yearbook 11*, edited by JA Anderson. California: Sage.

Huesmann, LR. 1988. An information processing model for the development of aggression. *Aggressive Behavior* 14:13–14.

Huesmann, LR & Eron, LD. 1986 (eds). 1986. *Television and the aggressive child: a cross-national comparison.* Hillsdale, NJ: Lawrence Erlbaum.

Jordaan, W & Jordaan, J. 1987. *Mens in konteks.* Isando: Lexicon.

Lawrence, PA & Palmgreen, PC. 1996. A uses and gratifications analysis of horror film preference, in *Horror films. Current research on audience preferences and reactions*, edited by JB Weaver III & R Tamborini. Mahwah, NJ: Lawrence Erlbaum.

Lerner, MJ. 1980. *Belief in a just world: a fundamental delusion.* New York: Plenum.
Lewis, GH. 1991. From G I Joe to the Ninja Turtles. *The World & I* 6(9):584–599.
Livingstone, S. 1998. *Making sense of television: the psychology of audience interpretation.* 2nd edition. London: Routledge.
McQueen, D. 1998. *Television: a media student's guide.* London: Arnold.
Ninja Turtles: bose invloed of gesonde vermaak? 1990. *Vrye Weekblad*, November:4–5.
Olivier, L, Roos, L & Berg, L. 1998. Violence and the individual, in *Violence in South Africa: a variety of perspectives*, edited by E Bornman, R van Eeden & M Wentzel. Pretoria: Human Sciences Research Council.
Pitout, M. 1985. *Televisiekykpatrone van standerd 3- tot 5-leerlinge.* Raad vir Geesteswetenskaplike Navorsing: Pretoria.
Pretorius, C. 1999. *Schools gripped by fear.* [O].
    Available: http://www.suntimes.co.za/1999/01/31/news/news15.htm
    Accessed on 2000/03/23
Prime time portrayals of rape, drug abuse and gangsterism in schools tears black communities apart. 1999. *You*, 4 May:22.
Slabbert, M. 1985. Violence in the cinema and television and in the streets, in *Crime and power, in South Africa: critical studies in criminology*, edited by D Davis & M Slabbert. Cape Town: David Philip.
Storm oor 'bose' Turtles. 1990. *Huisgenoot*, 14 Desember:89–91.
"Turtle-manie": versigtig met praat oor oorsake van kleutergeweld. 1990. *Beeld*, 12 Mei:9–10.
UNESCO International clearinghouse on children and violence on the screen. 2000. Nordicom: Gotenberg University.
Van Vuuren, DP & Kriel, HA. 1996. Violent television: cause for concern in South Africa? *Equid Novi* 17(1):25–42.
Von Feilitzen, C. 1998. Media violence – four research perspectives, in *Approaches to audiences: a reader*, edited by R Dickinson, R Harindranath & O Linne. London: Arnold.
Why angry clerics hurled 'evil' Turtles into oblivion. 1990. *Sunday Times*, 13 December:55–56.
Zillman, D & Bryant, J. 1986. Exploring the entertainment experience, in *Perspectives on Media Effects*, edited by J Bryan & D Zillmann. Hillside, NJ: Lawrence Erlbaum.

# Media and Terrorism

*Lucas M Oosthuizen*

## Overview

In this study we discuss the following:
- The historical relationship between the media and terrorists.
- The position of governments with regard to terrorism and how governments generally view the role of the media.
- The factors that guide media reporting about terrorism and how these factors relate to the expectations of terrorists and the media.
- How the coverage of terrorism impacts on the public.
- The need for policy formulation about the media, the government and terrorism.
- The South African situation regarding the relationship between media, government and terrorism.

This unit was written before the 11 September 2001 terror attacks on New York and Washington in the USA. Some of the views expressed in this unit might since have changed; the principles remain the same – Editor.

## Learning outcomes

After you have completed this unit you should be able to:
- Motivate a point of view about
  - the symbiotic relationship between media and terrorism
  - whether media coverage contributes to terrorists' objectives
  - the government's official view of what constitutes terrorism
  - the acceptability or unacceptability of the South African relationship between media, terrorism and the government
  - the impact of the media's coverage on the public
  - the obligation of the media to inform the public
  - criticism against the media's reporting and handling of terrorism as an event.
- Do a basic content analysis of media coverage of a terrorist event in which you account for
  - the timeliness of the reports
  - the journalists' sources
  - facts versus speculation
  - the way(s) in which the journalists framed the story.

- Test the views of a journalist or a member of the public about
  - the importance of the media coverage of acts of terrorism
  - the sensational style of coverage
  - sources of information
  - whether media coverage legitimises terrorism, sets an agenda, has an impact on violence in society, contributes to fear hysteria and rumours.
- Formulate three policy proposals related to
  - the obligation of the media to cover acts of terrorism
  - the way in which the media should cover acts of terrorism
  - the governments treatment of the media and the handling of information related to terrorist groups and acts of terrorism.

## 17.1 INTRODUCTION

The relationship between the media and terrorism is a complex one. Governments all over the world have had to grapple with the combating of terrorism. The media – as part of their information function – report about it. Official views about the relationship between the media and terrorism, and – more specifically – assumptions about how the media allegedly assist terrorists to achieve their goals, have led to media policy formulation about this issue in many countries. Such policy has mainly been directed towards:

- restricting the promotion of terrorism (also by the media) through legislation; and
- the compilation of administrative guidelines for the media on how to conduct themselves (or what not to do) during terrorist events or occurrences.

Policy formulation about the media and terrorists, therefore, usually includes three actors, namely terrorists, the media and governments (Crelinsten 1989:311). The interests of the public are naturally also at stake. These actors or components are not mutually exclusive. They will, however, be discussed under separate headings to provide you with a systematic overview of this very complex issue. Before we get to this discussion, however, we will take a closer look at what terrorism is about.

*Terrorism* can be described as the purposeful, planned, systematic and organised application of violence to achieve mostly political objectives. During this process, terror and threats are utilised to have a specific effect on victims and targets so that the terrorists' objectives (referred to above) can be promoted and achieved. As a method of war, a strategy and a tactic, it has historically been justified as the last resort to overcome tyranny – usually associated with the general curtailing of freedom.

The abnormal and inhuman nature of terrorist action is usually condemned by governments. They condemn terrorist action because it transgresses the normal conventions of warfare by – for example – targeting civilians for attack. Terrorists, which operate against governments, use publicity of their actions to coerce and blackmail their targets to consent to their demands. As a result, terrorism is often viewed as symbolic action. It is argued that terrorists primarily use their actions against victims (sometimes members of the public) to communicate a specific message to their targets (for example, the ruling government). As a result of their symbolic action, terrorists assume – or at least hope – to influence their targets to act in favour of their (terrorists') aims or demands. Terrorist actions taken against victims are often arbitrary, unexpected and unpredictable – but can form part of a planned campaign of repetitive nature that spans over a specific period of time (Oosthuizen 1993b:43–44).

Groups, movements, individuals – and even governments – can be responsible for terrorism.

## 17.2 TERRORISTS AND THE MEDIA

### 17.2.1 Historical development

Terrorism as such, is not a new phenomenon. Terrorists were already operating in ancient times. Even then, in 357BC, terrorist actions were geared towards obtaining fame or publicity (Midgley & Rice 1984:16). With the advent of the modern mass media, the ability of terrorists or terrorist movements to obtain such publicity increased.

By the 1800s, terrorists and revolutionaries were overtly utilising the media for publicity purposes. The media were, *inter alia,* used for

- making people aware of terrorist actions
- to transmit fear and intimidation; and
- in some instances even utilised to propagate the methods of terror (cf. Oosthuizen 1993).

At the end of the nineteenth century, the idea that terrorists were *using or abusing the media* to promote their own objectives was therefore already clearly established. In the 1900s, many counter-insurgency experts provided further "proof" of such abuse or misuse based on the work of the Brazilian father of (urban) guerilla warfare, Carlos Marighella.

Marighella discussed terrorism as one of the methods of guerrilla warfare in the late sixties. In his so-called *Minimanual* first published in 1969, Marighella emphasised the value of the media in such warfare (Marighella 1985). In a similar publication, an Argentinean that later rose to fame in Cuba, Ché Guevara (1962) also acknowledged the value of the media in guerrilla warfare. These two revolutionaries pointed out that the media could be used to

- obtain information about the movements of the security forces;
- get publicity for revolutionary action, for example an ambush;
- distribute, explain and legitimise the objectives and principles of the revolution;
- launch propaganda and agitation against the enemy, for example disinformation and lies about security force actions;
- put the security forces on the wrong track – thus using the media for tactical purposes; and

- to distribute information about the war as well as international support for the guerrillas.

From the above role ascribed to the media has developed a view that guerrillas and terrorists use the media to further their own goals. It is a view still held by many so-called "insiders" (terrorists and revolutionaries) as well as "outsiders" (experts on terrorism and some media scholars) today.

### 17.2.2 Outsider views

According to Alexander (1978), the using and manipulation of the media – as propagated by Marighella and other proponents of ideological and political violence – is a strategy that most terrorism movements have followed:

> They have sought not only to spread fear among the primary target, but also to publicize their discontent as well as their ideologies with a view of making their violent deeds appear heroic.
>
> (Alexander 1978:46)

Many experts on terrorism – as well as media scholars – argue that without publicity, terrorist action would not amount to much (Alexander 1978:45; Dowling 1986:14; Kelly & Mitchell 1981:271; Picard 1989:13). The basic argument is that terrorists need to publish their action in order to intimidate through fear. Apart from that, they also want to canvass support for their objectives – which they must generate through persuasion. They get the publicity they need through the mass media.

As a result, Martin (1985:132–133) argues that terrorism – as propaganda of the deed as he sees it – would only have a limited effect without the mass media. Alexander (1978:46) supports this position by stating that terrorism is more symbolic than physical in nature. Viewed from this vantage point, the violence that terrorists perpetrate would be of less importance than the communicative objectives that they want to achieve through such violent action. These objectives include:

- the transmission of fear to target groups (with the aim of influencing these groups);
- drawing attention to themselves and assuming that they will get public support for their objective/s as a result.

(See Alexander (1978) as well as Kelly & Mitchell's views (1981) on terrorism as a strategy.)

It is assumed that terrorists reach these objectives through the immediate and extended coverage of their deeds of violence in the mass media. This view is obviously in line with the role that terrorists/revolutionaries (insiders) like Marighella have historically ascribed to the media. The relationship between terrorism and the media is spelled out in a fairly deterministic fashion, which can be summarised as follows:

> ... terrorists depend on mass media to disseminate the sociopolitical message of the terror-inspiring nature of the act performed. This terror-inspiring quality, as

suggested, is not necessarily intrinsic to the act; rather, it is derivative of its impact, which in turn is largely determined by the coverage it receives from the media.
(Tan 1989:198-199)

This description of the relationship between the media and terrorism in broad terms represents what could be described as the orthodox view on the subject. As a result, many theorists and researchers have focused a lot of their attention on the communicative objectives that terrorists want to achieve through the media; which brings us to the following question: How effective are they in achieving these objectives?

### 17.2.3 Challenging the orthodoxy

Many authors concur that terrorists want to achieve three (strategic) goals, communicative objectives or aims (Dowling 1986:17-19; Alexander 1978:46-47; Vorster 1984:36):

- They want to draw attention to themselves in order to make the mass audience aware of their existence.
- They want recognition – *inter alia* that would include credibility – that they will actually do what they set out to do, that they will take risks and so forth (Dowling 1986:18; Alexander 1978:46-47).
- They also want to achieve legitimacy (acceptance of their reasons and objectives for their action – that it is good and justified – or that they are, for example, acting in the interest of the public and that they should (at least passively) be supported) (also see Vorster 1984:28). Ideally, terrorists would also strive to delegitimise the government at the same time. Legitimacy is regarded as the most important communicative objective.

Research indicates (Crelinsten 1989:316) that terrorist actions are usually effective to draw attention to themselves. Historical examples of this would include actions by groups such as Baader-Meinhof, the Japanese United Red Army, the Symbionese Liberation Army (Dowling 1986:18) as well as the Palestine Liberation Organisation or PLO (Alexander 1978:47).

Crelinsten (ibid) further indicates that terrorist action also sometimes leads to recognition, but seldom to legitimacy. Protracted terrorist events are regarded as the only exception – where terrorists sometimes get temporary legitimacy. The reason why terrorists do not reach this objective, is the specific way the media report about terrorist events. The focus is usually on the deed itself (the blood and guts of victims) and its dramatic nature (cf. Atwater 1987). This tendency is referred to as the "event orientation" of the media. As a result, the media seldom report about the reasons why terrorists commit their violent acts (cf. Kelly & Mitchell 1981; Atwater 1987). For terrorists then, the attainment of their most important communicative objective of legitimacy is, in general terms, clearly undermined (also see Nacos, Fan and Young (1989), and Paletz, Fozzard & Ayanian (1982)). Exceptions to this rule do take place, which we will come to later.

Even the ability of terrorists to gain recognition (the second communicative objective) has been questioned. Dowling (1986:20) points out that terrorists have been unable to instil enough fear into Western nations to force them to introduce repressive measures to counter terrorism in their societies. The ability of terrorists to gain credibility (recognition) can therefore also be questioned. Such credibility would theoretically enable terrorists to instil fear in target groups that could then lead to the introduction of repressive measures (like the curbing of rights and freedom in a particular country).

Terrorists are therefore not that effective when it comes to achieving their communicative goals through the media. However, the "effective" way in which they use and abuse the media, is often just accepted. As a result, the relationship between the media and terrorists is often framed in negative terms. The so-called *symbiotic relationship* between the media and terrorists is an example of this assumed relationship.

### 17.2.4 The symbiotic relationship between terrorists and the media

The basic assumption of this view is the following:

Terrorists use the media to achieve their own objectives (communicatively we have already seen that this assumption can be contested) by constructing their action in such a way (that it is sensational, unexpected and extraordinary) so that it has news value for the media (it therefore has utility value for to the media) (Kelly & Mitchell 1981:271) which the media can sell to readers, viewers and listeners. As a result, it is further assumed that the media and terrorists mutually exploit one another (Martin 1985:127; Farnen 1990:102). This would then constitute a symbiotic relationship between the media and terrorists in the sense that the one party lives off the other, and vice versa.

The typical argument that has been forwarded based on this so-called symbiotic relationship is that terrorism would not be able to survive without media publicity (Dowling 1986:22). In simplistic terms this means that if you withdraw media publicity from terrorists then terrorism as a strategy would eventually disappear. This assumption can be questioned on the following grounds:

- Numerous terrorism groups, like the Jewish *Zealots* or *Sicarii* (in the first century AD); the *Assassins* of Islam (at the beginning of the eleventh century) and the *Thugs* in India, existed and were fairly successful in modern terms, long before the mass media even existed (Crelinsten 1989:316).
- Not even all present-day terrorist groups seek publicity – but rather choose to focus on propaganda of the deed to establish awareness for their groups. In some cases they even shun the media (Picard 1989:16). The *Shining Path* movement in Peru is one such example. The media have even been targeted for attacks by this group. Their actions would refute the argument that insurgents always view media coverage as positive (Barnhurst 1991:75–89; Oosthuizen 1993a:30–31).

- Other groups, like *Hezbollah* and the Islamic *Jihad* in Lebanon, use the media, but restrict media access during, for example, hostage-taking.
- In some cases, groups also refuse to take responsibility for certain actions (cf. Picard 1989).

One could therefore conclude that terrorists can survive without the media; and that they view the media as useful, but not necessarily as essential to achieve their objectives. The media, on the other hand, can obviously also survive without publishing terrorist events.

Even though the symbiotic relationship between the media and terrorists can be challenged on the aforementioned grounds, the concept of symbiosis is still fairly widely accepted – even by the media themselves (cf. Midgley & Rice 1984). However, at the same time, many people do not realise that there is also a (and possibly a much stronger) symbiotic relationship between the media and other institutions (especially governments) (Crelinsten 1989:31). Which brings us to the role of governments in the media/terrorism debate.

## 17.3 THE ROLE OF GOVERNMENTS AND STATE DEPARTMENTS

There is a triangular relationship between governments, victims and terrorists (cf. Fourie 1989:28). Terrorists target people as victims. These victims turn to the government to protect them. Terrorists hope that governments will give in to their demands when the government in question is confronted with the plight of helpless victims. Governments are, therefore, expected to address the terrorism problem. In the case of insurgency terrorism, governments are both the eventual target as well as the party that must sort out the problem (Crelinsten 1989:311).

From the vantage point of terrorists, the publicity of their acts in the media bring their deeds to the attention of the government and members of the public with the aim of intimidating and instilling fear in both or one of these parties. This leads to the view that the success of terrorists can be measured by the amount of publicity they get; and that terrorists wilfully use and abuse the media – albeit viewed from the position of a government (Vorster 1984:5–8).

The attack by Palestinian terrorists on the Israeli team in 1972 at the Munich Olympics, therefore, led to the following typical conceptualisation of the relationship between the media, terrorists and governments:

> By creating a climate of fear in an attack on (or even killing of) unknown victims, the relatively and comparatively powerless terrorists hope to compel far more powerful state or media officials to comply to their wishes.
> (Farnen 1990:111)

As a result, the media – more often than not – find themselves in a position between terrorists (the political powerless) and governments (the political powerful) (Crelinsten 1989:312; Tan 1989:209). As we have seen in the unit on external media policy (Unit 4), governments have specific expectations about media performance in the respective countries that they govern. That includes expectations regarding the reporting of terrorism. The media are also structurally bound to the government in the country in which they operate. If a government therefore institutes anti-terrorism legislation that also curbs media reporting about the subject, the media must either adhere to these stipulations or face the possibility of prosecution. Such policy formulation can also take the form of administrative control instituted by, for example, the security forces. Because the political dispensations in countries differ, policy formulation could also vary as a result (Oosthuizen 1993a:32; Chaliand 1987:97; cf. Wilkinson 1987).

However, it would appear that the so-called official perspective is dominant in most liberal democracies (cf. Schlesinger, Murdoch & Eliot 1983; Wilkinson 1987). This perspective is clearly in line with the orthodox outsider view that has previously been referred to in this unit.

## 17.3.1 The official perspective

In terms of official thinking, the reporting of terrorist events by the mass media is extremely important and dangerous. It is argued that the media can – through their reporting of such events – legitimise the actions of terrorists by, for example, failing to report about terrorist events in criminal terms. (In other words, not depicting terrorists as thugs, criminals, murderers or terrorists, but as freedom fighters who execute – not murder – their targets – not victims.)

In terms of official thinking, media reporting could therefore undermine the efforts of governments to curb terrorism – by not taking a strong enough stand against it. As a result, popular support for government action against terrorists could also be undermined. A government's own credibility and ability to protect the social order, is therefore brought into question which, in turn, could impact negatively on its own legitimacy (cf. Oosthuizen 1993a; Schlesinger et al 1983).

The official perspective, therefore, condemns media publicity to terrorists in general terms. The following arguments typically underlie official thinking in this regard:

- Terrorists wittingly arrange their actions in accordance with the news values that news media use for selection by including elements of drama, violence and unpredictability in their actions.
- They choreograph their violence to become theatre. As a result, the media cannot resist the publication of terrorist actions. The media further accommodate terrorists by giving wide coverage to their planting of bombs, hijackings and assassinations.
- Once the standard practices of terrorists lose their news value, they must come up with new angles to get the media's attention.
- The media therefore become responsible for the escalation of violence.

This line of thinking provides the rationale behind official decisions to regulate the reporting of terrorism in democracies, if and when the media fail to apply sufficient self-regulation.

Regulation would typically come into play
- when the media report about terrorism events in positive terms – outside the discourse of criminality (e.g. using the term "freedom fighters" instead of terrorists, and so on) – or when they give coverage to terrorists' objectives or the reasons for their actions;
- when the media do not publish official versions (emanating from the police or other state departments) of terrorist events;
- when the media interview terrorists.

In terms of expectations, a counter-terrorist role is often propagated for the media. This would include giving details about the arms or weapons that terrorists use – in order to educate and mobilise the public to oppose terrorist onslaughts (Wilkinson 1987:33). The media are generally also expected not to report sympathetically about terrorists and their objectives and activities, but rather to stick to official versions of such events.

### 17.3.2 The media and the official perspective

As a result of the relationship between governments and the media in democracies, one would expect the media to adhere to the official perspective. Research confirms this expectation.

Schlesinger et al (1983) have found that the official perspective on terrorism is by far the most dominant position reported in news and actuality programmes on British television. Variations do occur in other programme formats. Research by Steuter (1990) has also confirmed the dominance of this position in the reporting on terrorists by the American news magazine *Time*. Steuter (1990:265–266) has found that

- in close to 90 percent of the stories reported over a period of a year, reporters did not use terrorists or their supporters as sources of news;
- in almost all of the articles, one or more sources of authority (such as government leaders, conservative politicians and top security personnel) were quoted;
- when alternative sources were quoted, comments from figures of authority were frequently included, which undermined the credibility of these sources; and
- even when alternative sources were quoted, their opposition still formed part of the official perspective – as forwarded by, for example, government leaders.

Research like this and other studies like the one by Paletz et al (1982) (that looked at the reporting of the *New York Times* on the Red Brigades, the IRA and the FALN) tend to refute the official assumption that the media portray the objectives and activities of terrorists sympathetically, or that the media are used and abused by terrorists.

The opposite is probably closer to the truth. Because of the fact that the media tend to prefer official sources and official versions of terrorist events, the authorities are in a much better position to use the media for their own purposes. As Farnen (1992) points out:

> By defining terrorism, any administration can control and own the problem itself, particularly if the media repeat the unquestioned assertions and afford them legitimacy as larger than life social drama with a huge public audience.

Therefore, governments generally find themselves in a fairly strong position in democracies when it comes to the reporting of terrorism. However, as a result of the official orthodoxies about the relationship between the media and terrorism, regulation that restricts coverage – or indirectly has that effect – has been introduced in countries like Canada, Britain, Germany and South Africa (cf. Oosthuizen 1993a:34).

That does not mean that the role (or possible role) of governments in terrorism has gone undetected. Crelinsten (1989:311–312) reckons that there is a growing realisation that states, themselves, can also perpetrate terrorism. This takes the form of "official" hit squads or support of terrorist movements that conduct terrorism in other countries (known as transnational terrorism). In addition, pressure has also mounted from liberal and opposition quarters in liberal democracies to scrutinise the role of the state (its actions against terrorists as well as terrorism committed by states). This is known as the alternative perspective (cf. Schlesinger et al 1983). It has also led to the questioning of media performance regarding the reporting of terrorist events.

### 17.3.3 The media and the alternative perspective

People who propagate the alternative perspective feel that the media should deviate from the official perspective. In terms of this perspective, the media

- are regarded as a tool in the struggle for the public opinion;
- are criticised for their official semantic framings of terrorism (in terms of criminality) and for the fact that they just accept and reproduce official definitions of terrorism;
- are also expected to give coverage to right-wing terrorism (and not only left-wing terrorism) as well as terrorism perpetrated by governments; and are
- expected to give more analytical accounts (explaining why) of terrorism and terrorist movements.

The alternative perspective is subordinate to the official perspective (Schlesinger et al 1983:17). This is to be expected in terms of the relationship between governments and media in democracies. The fact that governments also have better access to the media and are in a position to define terrorist events from their position as élite sources, makes it even more difficult for the media to offer alternative accounts of terrorism (Crelinsten 1989:319). State terrorism – as opposed to the actions of people opposing the *status quo* – also does not have publicity as a primary objective, but is geared more towards intimidation and control (cf. Martin 1985:35).

As a result, Noam Chomsky and Edward Herman (renowned communication theorists) have come to the conclusion that terror and terrorism have become the semantic tools of the powerful (governments) in the Western World.

However, alternative views do find their way into the media – as we will also see later in this unit (Oosthuizen 1993a:35). It depends on the place where terrorism takes place as well as on the format of the particular programme (in the case of television) or news report (if we are dealing with a newspaper report).

There are various reasons why alternative perspectives are propagated as an option that the media should consider. For one, it is argued that the publication of legitimate grievances, frustrations and despair of dissident groups by the media, could in actual fact prevent such groups from turning to violence and terrorist acts to get their message across (Picard 1986:395; Farnen 1990:132-133). In terms of this argument, the media can therefore theoretically prevent dissident groups from turning to terrorism by reflecting legitimate grievances – and not only focusing on the views of governments to start with. As an example, the question has been posed – by media managers themselves – as to whether the Palestinians would have turned to terrorism if they had had the opportunity to voice their grievances (in the media) (Schlesinger et al 1983:19).

The other argument in favour of the publication of more alternative views on terrorism in the media concerns terrorism by states. In democracies, access to information and the distribution of such information (without restriction) are usually granted to the media as rights (Oosthuizen 1989:8). Apart from that, the media also have an obligation towards their readers, viewers and listeners to fulfil a watchdog function in democracies. In order to fulfil this function they must, therefore, also report about the conduct and misconduct of governments. State terrorism would be part of such misconduct. Which brings us to the media component of the debate.

## 17.4 OBLIGATIONS AND THE NATURE OF THE MASS MEDIA

It should be clear by now that the media and terrorism are not the only components in the media/terrorism debate. We have seen that governments usually attribute a negative role to the media as far as their reporting of terrorism is concerned. Under these circumstances, the obligations of the media – that have been referred to above – can easily be shifted into the background. Let us take a closer look at these obligations and at other aspects that are relevant to media performance.

### 17.4.1 The media have an obligation to report terrorism

The information function is the most important function of the news media. As part of this information function the media also have to keep people informed about terrorism. People have the right to know about terrorist threats and the occurrence of terrorist incidents as they happen or unfold (Crelinsten 1989:320). If the media do not report these events, they could also undermine their own legitimacy as bearers of the truth in a democratic society. People do not just have a need to know in democracies, they also have the right to know.

As Petentler (1990:59) indicates, the media have a legitimate obligation to pay attention to terrorism, because it is newsworthy – and they have to report the news. Media coverage of terrorism could, of course, also have entertainment value for the recipients of communication messages. Television coverage of terrorism could fulfil such an additional function – and also movies, novels and so forth that fulfil primarily an entertainment function. Most of the debate about terrorism, however, focuses on news coverage.

During news coverage of terrorist events, the media do not only enter into interaction with governments and terrorists, but also with the public. Both terrorists and governments try to influence the public through the media. As a result, the media become the forum of political struggle between those who have power (governments) and those who want to obtain power (terrorists) (Crelinsten 1989:312; Oosthuizen 1993a:35).

### 17.4.2 The media report terrorism because it is newsworthy

It is primarily the events which are selected as newsworthy by journalists that get published as news. To identify newsworthiness, journalists (more or less unconsciously) make use of news values (Fowler 1991:11–13). If you take a closer look at these news values (cf. Oosthuizen 1989:73; Fowler 1991:12–15) you will see that terrorist events adhere to (or could adhere to) most of these bureaucratic and cultural criteria that journalists use to identify newsworthiness. Such events could, for example:

- coincide with the deadlines of the media;
- exceed the threshold of newsworthiness (as cataclysmic events);
- have limited possibilities of interpretation (violence is understood as violence);
- be meaningful in terms of a specific culture (the Palestine Liberation Organisation fighting for the rights of the Palestinian people);
- be anticipated (after an announcement that the armed struggle would be stepped up);
- not be anticipated (such as a bomb blast that occurs without prior warning);
- already be news (the media have reported about the IRA for many years);
- be necessary for composition (a whole page in a newspaper that deals with terrorism);
- refer to élite nations (American embassies being attacked);
- involve élite people (the assassination of a political leader by a terrorist group), and so on.

Terrorist events are also always the result of the actions of people (terrorists) and affect other people (victims of terrorist attacks). The type of news generated by terrorist events is usually always negative (it leads to loss of life, damage to property, and such like) – which we know is a very dominant news value.

From the above, it is clear that terrorist events have the ability to adhere to most of the news values that journalists apply for news selection. Based on that, one can deduce that terrorist events have an excellent chance of being published as news. However, contrary to popular belief, not all of these events are published. In one study that dealt with international terrorism coverage on three American television networks and in nine respected newspapers (one in New York, two in London, two in Toronto (Canada), one each in Paris, Frankfurt, Israel and Pakistan), research revealed that only a third of these events were covered (Weimann & Brosius 1991:340).

On a more local and personal level, journalists also compete for news. A terrorism event reported by one news medium, will therefore "naturally" be followed-up by other news media. Having the edge on the opposition (in terms of the latest news) could also affect the promotion of journalists in a news organisation (cf. Farnen 1990). So once journalists run with a terrorist story, they will keep on doing so.

### 17.4.3 Other reasons for the media to report terrorism

Apart from news values, there are also other reasons that motivate the media to publish terrorism events as news. In the case of television, for example, it has been argued that terrorism events are irresistible to television stations because of the visual possibilities that such events offer (Martin 1985:133). Such events are inherently dramatic and potentially spectacular and make good television footage. Altheide (1987:174) says the tendency of specifically television news to focus on the tactics and effects of terrorist action (rather than their objectives or the reasons for their actions), is the result of television format. There is a general preference for the visually dramatic in this format to ensure optimal entertainment value for the audience.

Dowling (1986) argues that viewers and readers have a need for dramatic entertainment. If news organisations do not satisfy this need, they lose their audience. Losing readers and viewers has economic implications for the media. If they lose market share, they could also lose advertising revenue (Farnen 1990:102). When the media publish terrorist events, it could have the opposite effect. When the former Italian premier, Aldo Moro was kidnapped and eventually murdered, the most important newspapers in Italy had a circulation increase of between 56 and 89 percent during the event (Farnen 1990:117).

The need for increased circulation or audience figures should of course not be seen in isolation from the other reasons for publication that we have discussed above.

### 17.4.4 Media coverage of terrorism

Not all terrorist events get the same media coverage. Longer or ongoing incidents, like hostage-taking, kidnappings and the hijacking of aeroplanes and cruise ships, tend to get dramatic and saturation coverage. According to Crelinsten (1989:315–316) this is a tendency in local coverage of such events – as well as in international coverage. Such events are of course also inherently newsworthy and spectacular (Dowling 1986:14–15; Atwater 1987:17–24; Nacos, Fan & Young 1989:108).

Bomb plantings, on the other hand, seem to get the least coverage. Bassioni (1982:130) estimates that more than 60 percent of all terrorist events that occurred between 1968 and 1978 were bomb plantings. Carpini and Williams' (1987:55) tally of bomb plantings used in international terrorism came to 46 percent over the period of 1969 to 1980. The reason why they are not covered so well is because such events are usually of a contracted nature (take place over a short period of time); people do not always claim responsibility for the bomb planting incident (in which case the news media do not have specific actors to report about – especially if there are also no victims) (cf. Crelinsten 1989). The specific nature of bomb plantings therefore undermines their potential news value.

Bomb plantings are sometimes not that dramatic; are not that unexpected (because they occur fairly frequently); cannot always be ascribed to specific people (the perpetrators are often unknown); do not develop over time and are not always that spectacular (also see Carpini and Williams 1987:56).

When they are spectacular, involve victims and can be ascribed to people, coverage of bombings of course changes. A good example is the bombing of the Hallmark building on 22 May 1983 in Pretoria. The building housed the headquarters of the South African Air Force at the time. The bomb blast killed seventeen people and close to 200 people were injured. The event got saturation coverage in most of the news media in South Africa and was clearly framed in the official perspective (see for example *Beeld* 23 May 1983:1). A more recent example was the bombing of the Planet Hollywood restaurant in Cape Town – which we will deal with in more detail later.

Meanwhile, studies have also clearly indicated that not all terrorist groups get the same coverage. In a study of *The Times* of London and *The New York Times* – research for example revealed that Palestinians as a group got by far the most coverage – as well as more prominent coverage in these two publications. The study focused on transnational terror (in other words terror perpetrated by groups in other countries) (cf. Kelly & Mitchell 1981).

Some terrorist actors, tactics, and victims also get disproportional (more) attention from the media. In terms of specifically the Western media it was found that:

- insurgents, leftist groups and Palestinians were singled out for coverage;
- hijackings, hostage-taking and sieges were the tactics that the media focused on most; and
- victims that were most often involved in coverage were tourists, passers-by and children.

State terror was not often reported, although it occurred quite often (Crelinsten 1989).

This last finding about state terrorism is clearly in line with the situation in South Africa under the previous dispensation. The mainstream media, for example, initially did not report about hit squads. It was left to the alternative press in the eighties to uncover the atrocities perpetrated by some of the members of the security forces. The full extent of these operations only surfaced during the hearings of the Truth and Reconciliation Commission in the late nineties.

Meanwhile, terrorism in some regions also gets more coverage than terrorist events in others. In the Western media the regions that have traditionally received more attention are the Middle East and Western Europe, while Latin America and Asia got less attention (cf. Crelinsten 1989). Another tendency, which has been pointed out in research done in America, is that terrorist events closer to home are also sometimes awarded disproportionate coverage (cf. Carpini & Williams 1987). The availability of personnel to cover such events – as well as traditional views on regions that are deemed as more important (such as the Middle East) – are possible reasons why events closer to home and in the Middle East get preferential treatment.

As a result of this phenomenon some regions get more coverage, and terrorism in other regions is systematically under-reported (Carpini & Williams 1987:55). The tendency not to report state terrorism could also have had an effect on the under-reporting of terrorism in Latin America – where state terrorism has been fairly common.

### 17.4.5 The views of journalists

The views of journalists about the reporting of terrorism confirm many of the reasons why the media report terrorist events – or find such events "irresistible" to report (Rowan in Midgley & Rice 1984:20–23):

- Terrorism is seen as an act of theatre. The media become the stage for these events and the press and electronic media thrive on their sensational nature. The media also show interest in the unexpected and violent nature of terrorist acts (which confirms the application of the unexpected and negativity – bad news – as news values.
- Competition between the media ensures that they follow up each other's stories. A hostage drama reported in one publication would therefore also be reported by others (which confirms the role the competitive market plays in this regard).
- The mysterious nature, fast action, tension and drama associated with terrorism also catch the interest of journalists (again confirming the application of news values).
- Journalists lastly realise that the suppression of news coverage could impact negatively on their credibility (which links up with the responsibility and expected role of the media in society).

Journalists themselves do, therefore, not necessarily deny the so-called symbiotic relationship between the media and terrorism. Some are even of the opinion that terrorists can abuse the media (Petentler 1990:60–61). The responsibility to deliver terrorist news to readers, viewers and listeners, however, overrides this concern. The media deliver such news in a particular way – which brings us to the issue of news construction.

### 17.4.6 The construction of news

The way in which journalists construct news favours the turning of terrorist events into news. Because of the timeliness of such news, it is usually identified as hard news. To ensure a constant flow of news, journalists are assigned to institutions. These institutions include safety and security institutions of the state, which then automatically become providers of terrorism news. During newsgathering, journalists must also ensure the facticity of their stories. In the case of terrorism they are provided with spokespersons of stature (officers in the police and defence force) who work for organisations that confirm the factualness of their reports. Depending on the scope, place and other variants, these events can also be presented as important news. Therefore, terrorism slots in quite neatly with the way in which journalists construct news.

News construction as such, also provides a possible explanation why journalists tend to focus on official versions of such events. Official versions result from the fact that journalists are tied to institutions (like the police and the army) that become prime providers and definers of terrorism news. Governments and government spokespersons also make it easier for journalists to access them (Paletz et al 1982:167-168) than terrorists do. Time pressure – because of deadlines – also promotes the preference for official sources. These sources are usually available. Terrorists, on the other hand, conduct their actions in secret and also face the possibility of arrest. As a result, they are usually not available to the media.

## Summary

In terms of what we have discussed in this section we can conclude that the media (Oosthuizen 1993a:41):

- are under an obligation to report terrorism;
- will identify terrorism events as news and will give coverage to them as a result of journalist's application of news values;
- find it quite easy to convert these events into news as a result of the way news is constructed. (news construction tends to favour the official perspective);
- do publish deviations from the official perspective in cases where there are geographical and ideological distances. Media diversity also makes provision for such deviations;
- will tend to follow up terrorist stories published by competitors for economic and professional reasons;
- do not cover all the terrorist events and do not afford all terrorist events and regions the same prominence;
- do not give too much coverage to terrorism events – if the total number of such incidents is taken into account.

The relationship between the mass media and governments therefore underlines the hegemonic function of the media as far as terrorism is concerned. Public consent for counter-terrorist policy and the official framework of terrorist discourse results from the preference that is given to official information and agendas. The emphasis on official sources also refutes the ideology of professional journalism about news as being an unbiased reflection of reality. Instead of balance and neutrality, the reporting of terrorism generally reflects a partial and restrictive presentation of this phenomenon that is in line with conservative values and ideology about terrorists and terrorism (cf. Steuter 1990).

Although the official perspective is clearly dominant, there are no grounds to assume that we are dealing with a universal ideological consensus in the media's reporting about this subject.

The following findings would militate against such a conclusion:
- Research in Britain about the television coverage of terrorism shows that deviations from the official perspective do take place when the physical and ideological distance from that occurrence is great. For example, a programme about the armed struggle in South Africa in the early eighties clearly deviated from the official perspective. Reports about the Irish Republican Army (IRA) (closer to home) were, however, strictly reported within the official framework (Schlesinger et al 1983:59-60). Positive framings of terrorism in countries where Israel had low political involvement were also reported in the media of that country (cf. Weimann 1985).
- The issue of state violence is also handled with greater ease (reported on) when geographical, temporal (time) and ideological distance is present. The specific format of the programme – in the case of television – also plays a role here (Schlesinger et al 1983:61). In this regard Altheide (1987) points out that news programmes in America and Britain usually focused on the event coverage (the effects and tactics) of terrorism attacks and were fairly similar, whereas documentaries were more subject oriented. In programmes of this format, provision was also made for the aims, objectives and rationale of terrorist actions.
- The heterogeneous nature of the mass media also leads to variations in the coverage of terrorism. (Crelinsten 1989:312). As the result of the watchdog function of the media – as well as the tradition of investigative reporting – legitimation of alternative perspectives do sometimes happen. The reports by *Vrye Weekblad* and *Weekly Mail* on police hit squads (state terrorism) in the eighties is a good local example. In Northern Ireland the Sinn Fein newspaper *Phoblacht* has also published a lot of stories to justify IRA action. In these reports they have focused on the social and political issues behind the conflict in this region – as well as on provocation by the security forces (Picard 1991:91-103). This type of reporting would, therefore, also represent a clear deviation from the official perspective.

## 17.5 THE PUBLIC, THE MEDIA AND TERRORISM

As we have already indicated, terrorists want to influence governments through their actions. They naturally also want to influence the public. They do so through fear and intimidation and use the media as channels for this purpose. The media are of course not the only channels at the disposal of terrorists. The nature and extent of terrorist actions can also be communicated interpersonally. Terrorist actions are also sometimes viewed as communication (cf. Crelinsten 1989:314 and Martin 1985:132 who support the idea that a terrorist deed itself becomes propaganda that is geared towards persuasion).

When the public is taken as vantage point, the media/terrorism debate focuses on the possible *effect* or *influence* that the publication of terrorist actions could have on the public. In this regard it is important to note that this impact could be anticipated or not be anticipated – or be planned on purpose or not (Crelinsten 1989:322). When it comes to effect, a few issues dominate the discourse of the media/terrorism debate. You are already familiar with some of these issues, but we will now take a closer look at them.

### 17.5.1 Legitimacy and delegitimacy

Governments, and especially their security forces, fear that publicity could legitimise terrorism. That would include the acceptance of the public that terrorists act in their interest, that such actions are good and legitimate and need to be supported – at least passively (Vorster 1984:28).

The basic argument that is usually forwarded in this regard is that the publication of terrorist actions confers status upon movements because of the fact that people become aware of their existence. In addition, the contention is that the image of terrorists, attitudes towards them and public opinion about terrorists can change (in a positive direction) as a result (Vorster 1984:29–35).

Consequently, it is usually taken for granted that the utilisation of political violence by such groups becomes more legitimate in the process. From this vantage point the argument is then forwarded that the less publicity terrorists receive, the better. Some people go as far as to assume that terrorism would disappear if no publicity is afforded to such acts (see references in Vorster 1984:35–36 as well as Crelinsten 1989:324).

We already know now that this is not generally the case in democracies. Terrorists are mostly delegitimised by the media, while the actions of governments are usually legitimised (cf. Oosthuizen 1993a, 1993b; Steuter 1991; Crelinsten 1989; Paletz et al 1982). This tendency does not necessarily have positive consequences for the public – and neither for governments that combat terrorism for that matter. In this regard the following can be pointed out:

- Dissidents who do not get their frustrations published (for example the reasons for their struggle) could be motivated to turn to terrorism (cf. Knutson 1981; Oosthuizen 1993a:42).
- The official perspective could also lead to the public sanctioning (based on the existing public opinion at the time) of extreme counter-measures by governments – which could lead to a further escalation of violence and even state terror. In this regard it is interesting to note that when the National Party government sanctioned cross-border raids on "ANC and PAC bases" in the eighties that these raids were sometimes even supported by opposition parties in parliament.

### 17.5.2 Agenda-setting

Applied to the media and terrorism, agenda-setting would come into play when the media publish terrorist events (when they become news) that would put this phenomenon – and also the threat – on the public agenda. In the case of saturation coverage such threats become real and observable to media users and do get access to the daily discourse (Crelinsten 1989:320–321). It does, however, not happen with all terrorist incidents.

We already know that:

- Some movements, areas and methods do get preferential treatment from the media (for example the PLO; the Middle East and hijacking).
- Just a fraction of terrorist events (internationally) are reported and/or emphasised by the media.
- The media's coverage of such events – because of the official perspective and its event orientation – is not very balanced (terrorists and their views only get access in exceptional cases).

In terms of this theory one can therefore deduce that terrorists are fairly ineffective to influence the media's agenda (and therefore the public agenda) in this regard (Oosthuizen 1993a:43).

### 17.5.3 Influence on violence

The debate in this instance is about whether the publication of terrorist violence actually leads to an escalation of violence among media users. The central concept to explain this phenomenon, is "contagion".

The theory about contagion is usually linked to the French sociologist Gabriel Tarde's discussion about contagious violence that took place at the beginning of the previous century.

According to Tarde, news about sensational and violent crimes led to the duplication of similar events – as a result of copy-catting and suggestion (Brosius & Weimann 1992:63). More recently, sociological studies in the 1970s uncovered increasing empirical evidence for the existence of the phenomenon of contagion (op cit:63–64).

In the case of terrorism, researchers have tried to establish whether specific terrorist events (like hijackings, for example) lead to similar events. In the case of the media, the question has been whether coverage of such events by the media leads to additional terrorist events (contagion) – which would amount to spreading terrorism in the way that the wind fans a runaway bush fire.

Research by Brosius and Weimann (1992) seems to indicate that the media are a long-term predictor of such activity. These authors/researchers are therefore of the opinion that media coverage of terrorism events contributes to the re-occurrence of terrorism in the long run (1992:72).

Finding "statistical proof" for this relationship is of course one thing; establishing a causal relationship between media coverage and terrorist events is quite another. Picard (1986) explains the problem:

> I do not mean that we should set out with our own set of biases to "prove" the media are innocent. But we do need to set out to find out just what the reality is. I suspect we will find that the media are a contributing factor in the spread of terrorism, just as easy international transportation, the easy availability of

weapons and explosives, the intransigence of some governments' policies, the provision of funds to terrorists by a variety of supportive governments, and a host of other factors are to blame.
(Picard 1986:398)

The inability of empirical research to isolate the different variables mentioned by Picard, means that findings about contagion are far from conclusive. As Crelinsten (1989) states, it is very difficult to ascertain if media coverage (or the type of coverage) as such moves people to act, or whether it is another factor that has nothing to do with coverage at all. As critical researchers have often remarked: it is possible to establish correlations between any given phenomena. But, so what?

### 17.5.4 Fear, hysteria and rumours

The last effect on the public we are going to discuss here links up with the core of the word terrorism – namely terror – which is generally associated with fear or being terrified.

Terrorists often want to spread fear, hysteria and rumours through the media. As Crelinsten (1989) points out, some of the media coverage does tend to spread false rumours – or exacerbate existing rumours – by reporting such rumours as if they were fact. He cites the so-called October crisis in Canada in 1970 as an example where any new threats were published by the media – without ascertaining whether such threats were in fact true.

The spreading of such rumours can increase circulation or viewer and audience figures because it could create a crisis atmosphere. In this particular case, the media announced that a new terrorist cell had been formed. This turned out to be untrue – but the government used this information as grounds for introducing repressive measures.

Not publishing terrorist events at all could of course have the opposite effect (cf. Bassioni 1982). In such a case, interpersonal rumours increase which could both undermine the credibility of the media and the people in power. As a result, terrorists could also be motivated to launch more spectacular attacks – leading to an escalation of violence.

From both these vantage points it becomes clear that both the media and governments have responsibilities in this regard. It also underscores the need for sound policy formulation.

## 17.6 POLICY FORMULATION, TERRORISM AND THE MEDIA

In view of what we know about terrorism, it seems that governments need to review policy about terrorism and the media's coverage of such events.
- Governments should not curtail the coverage of terrorism in the media on the grounds of shaky assumptions about the media's role in the promotion and spreading of terrorism. Restrictions on the media would only be justified when the rights of

other people in the society are prejudiced. This would apply when the media, for example, interfere with the work of law and order officials or when their actions put the lives of hostages in danger.
- Governments should also review their own role in causing terrorism. In this regard they should make sure that they make it possible for their subjects to air their grievances – also in the media. In addition, governments should also take a very close look at the legitimacy of their own armed action that they initiate against terrorists. State terrorism should be condemned as strongly as political violence perpetrated by other players.
- The media could possibly play a significant role to combat terrorism by:
  - bringing the grievances of people in society to the attention of governments
  - publishing the reasons why people turn to terrorism – in context
  - monitoring the abuse of violence by governments and holding the perpetrators accountable.
- This would mean that the media will also have to revise the way they report about terrorist actions (how they view news and do news gathering) to ensure a more balanced reflection of official and alternative perspectives, as well as between the actions of state and non-state players.
- The media and governments have a shared responsibility to reach administrative agreements. Such agreements should ensure that optimal information about terrorist events is provided to media users while also taking into account the security and interests of all parties involved in such incidents. The media can – sometimes unknowingly – obstruct the work of the security agencies and endanger the lives of victims in the process. This could, for example, happen during a hostage situation when:
  - the media allow terrorists to take over programmes
  - journalists hog telephone lines needed for negotiations
  - the media publish information about the tactics of the security forces so that the security forces lose the element of surprise as a result.

It is especially during terrorist attacks in progress where the opportunity for conflict between the interests of the law enforcement authorities and those of the media are at risk (Oosthuizen 1993a:34–37). Administrative agreements can ensure that both these sets of interests – as well as those of the victims – are protected at all times.

With the above ideas as point of departure, the media and governments can probably ensure that they do a better job of informing the public about terrorism as a phenomenon.

## 17.7 SOUTH AFRICA AND THE MEDIA/TERRORISM DEBATE

Terrorism is regulated in the external media policy framework of South Africa. The Internal Security Act (1982) prohibits terrorism and sabotage or the encouragement thereof in South Africa. Terrorism is defined as a violent act or an attempt at or encouragement in whatever manner of such an act which is aimed at:

- overthrowing or endangering the state authority;

- achieving or promoting constitutional, political, industrial, social or economic change in the Republic;
- inducing the government to do or abstain from doing something or to adopt or abandon a particular viewpoint;
- putting in fear or demoralising the general public, a particular population group or the inhabitants of a particular area in the Republic, or inducing them to do or abstain from doing something.

Although the Internal Security Act was amended in 1991 and repealed in 2000, the stipulations regarding terrorism were still in place at the time of writing.

During the previous political dispensation the media had difficulty in determining when they were contravening the Act. This was because of the Act's broad formulation. This problem would therefore still theoretically apply now. The Act as it stands at the moment, therefore could lead to self-censorship – as it did in the past. The basic motto regarding all security legislation in the past has been: when in doubt, don't publish.

The scope and nature of terrorism in this country has, however, changed tremendously since the introduction of the new dispensation. In the late eighties the South African Police's view of terrorism was clearly in line with the official perspective at the time. In an SAP publication it was stated that:

- Terrorism is both criminal and political.
- It strives to overthrow the state by means of violence and sabotage.
- To this end violence and intimidation are used.
- The African National Congress (ANC) and the South African Communist Party (SACP) are responsible for most of the terrorism in the country. They infiltrate legal organisations with a view to launching civil unrest, strikes, boycotts and other subversive actions.
- Their ultimate aim is rendering the country ungovernable and launching a popular insurrection.

The following definition of terrorism – from the perspective of the police – could be derived from the above:

Terrorism is:

- a violent method
- aimed at spreading panic and insecurity
- with the ultimate goal of overthrowing the state
- and, with the popular support and also by coercion,
- installing a new government (cf. Oosthuizen 1989:83).

Read in conjunction with the Act, this definition is clearly related to revolution and in fact shows a strong resemblance to revolution as defined by Huntington (1968:254):

> A revolution is a rapid, fundamental, and violent domestic change in the dominant values and myths of a society, in its political institutions, social structure, leadership, government activity and policies.

As far as the media were concerned, the official orthodoxy regarding the relationship between the media and terrorism was also clearly in place at the time. The Steyn Commission of Inquiry into the Media (Roelofse 1983:15) expressed itself cautiously about the reporting of terrorism. The Commission was of the opinion that overplaying and underplaying the consequences of terrorism would be equally disastrous. The Commission advocated a matter-of-fact approach, to be observed with professional responsibility, expertise and loyalty to the state and cultural values. Effective provision of information on terrorist-related matters was considered as important as any form of control. Nothing wrong with that, one could argue. However, evidence before the Commission indicated that certain government departments, the Defence Force and the Police (Hachten & Giffard 1984:78) expected the media to show greater understanding in view of the revolutionary onslaught on the country (Oosthuizen 1989:85).

Government leaders also expressed definite desires on this score. For example, the Minister of Law and Order, Adriaan Vlok (1988:63) requested the media to be wary of lies and of aiding and abetting liars (who, he said, spread untruths about the SAP and other security forces as part of the revolutionary onslaught). Ironically, Mr Vlok applied and was awarded amnesty in the mid-1990s for his part in instructing the police to perpetrate what could be regarded in hindsight as state terrorism.

Stoffel Botha, former Minister of Home Affairs (1988:69), warned the South African press that the leaders of the ANC and SACP admitted frankly that they collaborated with the mass media to promote their revolutionary struggle for a total take-over of the country. These views clearly articulated the symbiotic relationship between the media and terrorists. Both the SACP and the ANC were of course banned at the time and could therefore not be reported on – except when referred to in official rhetoric.

The media in general reported terrorist events from the official perspective in this country at the time. Deviance from the official model was not only made difficult because of the application of news selection and construction criteria by journalists, but was also made close to impossible by the nature of the legal framework. More than a hundred laws restricted the media. Deviance of especially security legislation led to journalists being questioned, harassed, and detained. Others were put under house arrest (cf. Hachten & Giffard 1984). Under these circumstances the general preoccupation of the local media with official perspectives of terrorism were to be expected. State terrorism went literally unreported until the eighties when the alternative press took the government and government security agencies to task. Meanwhile right-wing terrorism was generally not reported as such (as incidents of terror) by the mainstream media. Perpetrators were usually identified as right-wingers or members of a specific right-wing groups such as the *Afrikaner Weerstandsbeweging* (AWB) and not as terrorists.

When the ANC came to power in 1994 there was – as could have been expected – a marked decrease in terrorist incidents in the country. Since then, acts of terror have been mainly restricted to the province of Western Cape – which brings us to Pagad.

Pagad started off as a vigilante group with a name that says it all: People Against Gangsterism and Drugs. With the aim of ridding their communities of gangsterism and drugs, the movement probably came close to achieving legitimacy in many quarters. When a group of 2 000 Pagad members took the law into their own hands and shot and torched an alleged gang leader, Rashaad Staggie, in October 1998 it was widely reported by the media but not framed as terrorism.

The inquest into Staggie's death brought the state into conflict with the media when several news agencies and Cape newspapers were issued with court orders (under section 205 of the Criminal Procedures Act). The subpoenas required that visual footage of the incident – as well as information and notes – be made available for inspection by the presiding magistrate. Journalists that ignored the court orders were threatened with fines and imprisonment (cf. *Sunday Times* 30 August 1998).

The Freedom of Expression Institute (FXI) condemned the court orders on the following grounds:

- It was argued that the subpoenas could create the impression that the media were serving as informants to the police. Such an impression would not only undermine the credibility of the media, but also its independence.
- The FXI said that the step could also endanger the safety of journalists. This turned out to be a very valid fear when Western Cape journalists were subsequently intimidated and even wounded.

The general outcry from the press led to the withdrawal of the subpoenas. A subsequent agreement was reached between the South African National Editors Forum (SANEF) and the government on the application of section 205 to journalists. The agreement spelt out the steps that had to be taken before subpoenas could be served on journalists in terms of section 205 (Annual Report of the Freedom of Expression Institute 1999:6). It afforded the media the opportunity to make representations or to initiate a process of mediation and negotiation (through the office of the national director of public prosecutions) whenever prosecutors or safety and security officials wanted them to testify or to provide confidential documents (*FXI Freedom of Expression News* 26 February 1999:2).

After the Staggie incident, a bombing campaign commenced. One of the most widely reported of these events was an attack on a Planet Hollywood restaurant (an American franchise) on the Waterfront in Cape Town. This event coincided with an American missile attack on installations in Somalia and Afghanistan, which resulted in the subsequent bombings of two American embassies in Africa – in Kenya and Tanzania.

The Planet Hollywood bombing was reported in typical fashion by the media with the emphasis on the victims and the destructive effects caused by the bomb. The group, Muslims Against Global Oppression accepted responsibility for the incident and said it was in retaliation for the American attacks (*Beeld* 26 August 1998:1; *Pretoria News* 26 August 1998:1). Pagad publicly condemned the incident. However, the police later alleged that there were similarities between the bombing device that exploded at Planet

Hollywood and a device that earlier exploded at the offices of a police unit investigating Pagad in Bellville (*Beeld* 28 August 1998:2). Forensic experts of the Police confirmed this later – and added a bomb used at the Mowbray police station to the list (cf. *Beeld* 5 January 1999:2). In the Magistrates Court in Cape Town in January 2000 a member of Pagad was named as having bombed the Planet Hollywood restaurant (*ZA Now* 27 January 2000:3). It was later reported that two Pagad members had been taken into custody in connection with the bomb blast (*Beeld* 12 September 2000:2).

Things came to a head in September 2000 with the assassination of magistrate Pietie Theron outside his Plumstead home. Theron presided over many Pagad-related cases (cf. *Pretoria News* 11 September 2000:1). The same car used by the assassins was later used in a car bomb explosion that rocked the Cape suburb of Observatory. The Government openly blamed Pagad for the terror attacks and made its intention clear: to fast-track new anti-terrorist legislation through Parliament to enable it to ban Pagad.

On 11 September 2000 the Minister of Safety and Security, Steve Tshwete, said that the indications were so strong that Pagad and members of its central group, G-Force, were responsible for the terror and assassinations in Western Cape, that the Security Forces were not even considering other alternatives (*Beeld* 12 September 2000:1). On 6 October 2000 the national co-ordinator of Pagad, Abdus-Salaam Ebrahim, was charged with terrorism in the Cape Regional Court. The same Act used by the previous government to charge supporters of the ANC and PAC, the Internal Security Act of 1982, was used for this purpose.

On Press Freedom Day, 19 October 2000, the police raided media houses across South Africa after the director of public prosecutions ordered the confiscation or material relating to the activities of Pagad. The media protested that this step was in violation of the earlier agreement reached between SANEF, the ministers of justice and safety and security and the national director of public prosecutions. The public prosecutor's office argued that it had no other choice because negotiations with the media had failed to release archive material – which included material related to the death of Staggie in 1998. The Government was criticised for adopting the practices of the previous government and for sending out the signal to the rest of the world that it was not prepared to uphold and maintain the Constitutional right of freedom of expression and freedom of the media (cf. *FXI Action Alert* 22 October 2000).

The above confrontation underscores the necessity for the formulation of mutually accepted policy that makes provision for both the interests of the media and the government. Like the previous government, the present government expects the media to assist in the combating of terrorism. The media – on the other hand – fear that they could compromise the safety of journalists as well as their integrity and credibility as independent purveyors of information. The nature and scope of terrorism in Western Cape could, however, turn into a national catastrophe. The media's broader social responsibility in this regard could therefore also not be contested. In this particular case, it was also argued by Democratic Party MP, Dene Smuts, that the material in question was not of a confidential but of a public nature.

By October 2000, the bomb blast tally in Western Cape stood on close to two hundred – since the inception of the bombing campaign. An attack on the offices of the Democratic Alliance led to the rand sliding against the American dollar. It coincided with the outbreak of renewed violence between the Palestinians and Israel and the public expression of anti-Jewish and anti-American sentiments in the Cape as well as the Middle East. One of the possible reasons for the attack on the DA's office that was offered by a DA member, was that the leader of the DA, Mr Tony Leon, is Jewish. Mr Leon, as well as other opposition parties, asked for the resignation of Mr Tshwete and also challenged the Government to say who was behind the attacks.

This last incident is an interesting one. It underlines the potential national economic impact of terrorism. The value of the rand plummeted. On a local level, the spate of bombings at popular tourist spots like the Waterfront, have also severely impacted on the economic interests of retailers and tourism operators in the region. It is therefore in the national and local interest to put a stop to terrorism.

Ironically, a statement ascribed to Deputy President Jacob Zuma had an even more profound effect on the national economy. It was reported that Mr Zuma expressed approval of President Mugabe's land grab policies at a Southern African Development Community (SADC) summit. This incident saw the rand plunge to record lows two days in succession (cf. *Pretoria News* 13 October 2000). Mr Zuma later said that what he was reported to have said had been misconstrued.

However, this incident shows that there is a huge responsibility on government leaders. Statements like the above have a tremendous impact on the economic wellbeing of all South Africans. If and when such statements are made, the South African media should take a long and hard look at what these statements constitute. Theoretically such statements could, in terms of current legislation:

- endanger state security (if people start to revolt);
- lead to economic change (diminishing the real value of savings and pension funds);
- force the government to change its views (honouring policy support to neighbouring countries); and
- put fear into or demoralise the general public (because they will not be able to sustain their standard of living or they will get poorer in real terms).

Therefore, the media would theoretically be dealing with (potential) terrorism by the state – as articulated by the Internal Security Act of 1982. Viewed from this vantage point, there would then be no reason for the media not to report such incidents as acts of terror – with the proviso that they stick to the truth at all times. The incident clearly adheres to the stipulations of the Act, although the violence in question would clearly be of a symbolic nature.

Reporting state terrorism would be in line with the alternative perspective of terrorism that we discussed earlier. As you would have seen, state terrorism is usually under-reported. There have been attempts to report from this vantage point with regard to the Pagad saga as well.

These reports included:

- A report that a National Intelligence Agency (NIA) agent who infiltrated the top ranks of Pagad had been implicated in several attacks in the Cape Peninsula (cf. *Daily Mail & Guardian* 5 October 1999).
- A report in which Pagad alleged that their members were being tortured (by the police) (*Beeld* 6 January 1999:8).
- A report about a Pagad member and intelligence informer (both awaiting trial) that alleged that the police are involved in gun-running in Western Cape (cf. *Weekly Mail & Guardian* 13 August 1999).

Although the media have an obligation to report on state terrorism – or alleged state terrorism – it is obvious that journalists should be very careful when doing so. In this last instance, for example, the veracity of the allegations could be under suspicion – because both news sources were awaiting trial at the time. The journalist, however, balanced the story well by giving official sources the opportunity to respond to the allegations; from their response the reader could deduce that some doubt existed as to the truth of the allegations. In the story about alleged torturing, this was unfortunately not done.

The situation in Western Cape also clearly underlines the problems that democratic governments have to curb terrorism. At the time of writing the government was considering new legislation to handle this problem. Such policy formulation could also impact on media performance in future. We trust that you will keep on following the debate as it unfolds in the media.

## Summary

In this unit we have looked at the historical relationship between the media and terrorists and the general views held by governments about the performance of the media in this regard. We have seen that official views about the media's reporting of terrorism can be challenged. We concluded the unit with suggestions for future policy formulation on the subject.

## Research activities

1 Write a draft media policy for the reporting of terrorism in South Africa. Use the contents of this unit as a basic guideline.
2 Analyse a report of the same terrorism event in different news media. Identify the perspective/s that the media use to report such events. Write explanatory notes on the possible implications of these reports for listeners, readers and viewers.

## Further reading

Barnathan, J. 1990. *Aspects of terrorism, the police and the media. A study of communication patterns.* Ann Arbor, MI: University Microfilm International Dissertation Services.

Bassioni, MC. 1982. Media coverage of terrorism: the law and the public. *Journal of Communication,* Spring: 128–143.

Brosius, H & Weimann, G. 1992. The contagiousness of mass-mediated terrorism. *European Journal of Communication* 6.

Chaliand, G. 1987. *Terrorism: from popular struggle to media spectacle.* London: Saqi Books.

Farnen, RF. 1990. Terrorism and the mass media: a systematic analysis of the symbiotic process. *Terrorism* 13:99–143.

Fowler, R. 1991. *Language and the news. Discourse and ideology in the press.* London: Routledge.

Paletz, DL & Schmid, AP (eds). 1992. *Terrorism and the media.* London: Sage.

Petentler, CW. 1990. *The impact of American media's coverage on acts of terrorism.* Ann Arbor, MI: University Microfilms International Dissertation Information Service.

Steuter, E. 1990. Understanding the media/terrorism relationship: an analysis of ideology and the news in *Time* magazine. *Political Communication and Persuasion* 7:257–278.

Tuchman, G. 1978. *Understanding news. A study in the construction of reality.* New York: The Free Press and CollierMacmillan.

Weimann, G & Brosius, H. 1991. The newsworthiness of international terrorism. *Communication Research* 18(3):333–354.

Wilkinson, P. 1987. *Terrorism and the liberal state.* London: Macmillan Education Ltd.

## Bibliography

Alexander, Y. 1978. Terrorism, the media and the police. *Police Studies* 1(2):45–52.

Alexander Y. 1981. Super-terrorism. *Behavioral and quantitative perspectives on terrorism,* edited by Y Alexander & JM Gleason. New York: Pergamon Press.

Altheide, DL. 1987. Format and symbols in TV coverage of terrorism in the United States and Great Britain. *International Studies Quarterly* 31:161–176.

Annual Report of the Freedom of Expression Institute. 1999. Johannesburg.

Atwater, T. 1987. Terrorism on the evening news: an analysis of coverage of the TWA hostage crisis on "NBC Nightly News". *Political Communication and Persuasion* 4:17–24.

Barnathan, J. 1990. *Aspects of terrorism, the police and the media. A study of communication patterns.* Ann Arbor, MI: University Microfilm International Dissertation Services.

Barnhurst, KG. 1991. Contemporary terrorism in Peru: Sendero Luminoso and the media. *Journal of Communication* 41(4):52–89.

Bassioni, MC. 1982. Media coverage of terrorism: the law and the public. *Journal of Communication,* Spring:128–143.

Botha, JCG. 1988. Political punchlines. *RSA Policy Review* 1(1):65–70.

Brosius, H & Weimann, G. 1992. The contagiousness of mass-mediated terrorism. *European Journal of Communication* 6.

Carpini, MXD & Williams BA. 1987. Television and terrorism: patterns of presentation and occurrence, 1969 to 1980. *Western Political Quarterly* 40:45–64.

Chaliand, G. 1987. *Terrorism: from popular struggle to media spectacle.* London: Saqi Books.

Clutterbuck, R. 1983. *The media and political violence.* Hampshire: Macmillan Press.

Cohen, S & Young J (eds). 1982. *The manufacture of news. Social problems, defiance and the mass media.* Beverly Hills, CA: Sage.

Crelinsten, RD. 1989. Terrorism and the media: problems solutions and counter problems. *Political Communication and Persuasion* 6:311–339.

Dowling, RE. 1986. Terrorism and the media: a rhetorical genre. *Journal of Communication* 36(1):12–24.

Farnen, RF. 1990. Terrorism and the mass media: a systematic analysis of the symbiotic process. *Terrorism* 13:99–143.

Fattah, EA. 1981. Terrorist activities and terrorist targets: a tentative typology. *Behavioral and quantitative perspectives on terrorism*, edited by Y Alexander & JM Gleason. New York: Pergamon Press.

Fourie, DFS. 1989. Die gevorderde studie van die teorie en praktyk van interne oorlog. *Enigste studiegids vir ATHPIW-4*. Pretoria: University of South Africa.

Fowler, R. 1991. *Language and the news. Discourse and ideology in the press.* London: Routledge.

Gleason, JM. 1981. Third World terrorism: perspectives for quantitative research. *Behavioral and quantitative perspectives on terrorism*, edited by Y Alexander & JM Gleason. New York: Pergamon Press.

Guevara, E. 1962. *Ché Guevara on guerrilla warfare.* New York: Frederick A Praeger Publisher.

Hachten, WA & Giffard, CA. 1984. *Total onslaught. The South African press under attack.* Johannesburg: Macmillan.

Hecker, FJ. 1981. Contagion and attraction of terror and terrorism. *Behavioral and quantitative perspectives on terrorism*, edited by Y Alexander & JM Gleason. New York: Pergamon Press.

Hartley, J. 1982. *Understanding news.* London: Methuen.

Heyman, E & Mickolus, E. 1981. Imitation by terrorists: quantitative approaches to the study of diffusion patterns in transnational terrorism. *Behavioral and quantitative perspectives on terrorism*, edited by Y Alexander & JM Gleason. New York: Pergamon Press.

Huntington, SP. 1968. *Political order in changing societies.* New Haven: Yale University Press.

Jenkins, BM. 1981. The study of terrorism: definitional problems. *Behavioral and quantitative perspectives on terrorism*, edited by Y Alexander & JM Gleason. New York: Pergamon Press.

Kaplan, A. 1981. The psychodynamics of terrorism. *Behavioral and quantitative perspectives on terrorism*, edited by Y Alexander & JM Gleason. New York: Pergamon Press.

Kelly, MJ & Mitchell, TH. 1981. Transnational terrorism and the Western élite press. *Political Communication and Persuasion* 1(3):269–295.

Knutson, JN. 1981. Social and psychodynamic pressures toward a negative identity: the case of an American revolutionary terrorist. *Behavioral and quantitative perspectives on terrorism*, edited by Y Alexander & JM Gleason. New York: Pergamon Press.

Laquer, W (ed). 1978. *The terrorism reader. A historical anthology.* New York: New American Library.

Marighella, C. 1985. *Minimanual of the urban guerrilla.* Boulder, CO: Paladin Press.

Martin. LJ. 1985. The media's role in international terrorism. *Terrorism: An International Journal* 8(2):127–146.

Mickolus, E & Heyman, E. 1981. Iterate: Monitoring transnational terrorism. *Behavioral and quantitative perspectives on terrorism*, edited by Y Alexander & JM Gleason. New York: Pergamon Press.

Midgley, S & Rice, V (eds). 1984. *Terrorism and the media in the 1980s.* Washington DC: The Media Institute.

Nacos, B, Fan, DP & Young, JT. 1989. Terrorism and the print media: the 1985 TWA hostage crisis. *Terrorism* 12(2):107–115.

Oosthuizen, LM. 1989. *Media policy and ethics.* Cape Town: Juta.

Oosthuizen, LM. 1993a. Die internasionale debat oor die media en terrorisme: beleids- en etiese implikasies vir owerhede en die media. *Communicatio* 19(1):27–47.

Oosthuizen, LM. 1993b. Die media and terrorisme: dominante navorsingsparadigmas en bevindings. Masters dissertation. Pretoria: University of South Africa.

Paletz, DL, Fozzard, PA & Ayanian, JZ. 1982. The IRA, the Red Brigades, and the FALN in the "New York Times". *Journal of Communication,* Spring:162–171.

Petentler, CW. 1990. *The impact of American media's coverage on acts of terrorism.* Ann Arbor, MI: University Microfilms International Dissertation Information Service.

Picard, RG. 1986. News coverage as the contagion of terrorism: dangerous charges backed by dubious science. *Political Communication and Persuasion* 3(4):385–399.

Picard, RG. 1989. Press relations of terrorist organizations. *Public Relations Review* 15(4):12–23.

Picard, RG. 1991. How violence is justified: Sinn Fein's An Phoblacht. *Journal of Communication* 41(4):90–103.

Quester, GH. 1986. Cruise-ship terrorism and the media. *Political Communication and Persuasion* 3(4):355–370.

Roelofse, JJ. 1983. *Towards rational discourse. An analysis of the report of the Steyn Commission of Inquiry into the media.* Pretoria: Van Schaik.

Schlesinger, P, Murdoch, G & Eliot, P. 1983. *Television "terrorism": political violence in popular culture.* London: Comedia Publishing Group.

South Africa. 1977. Criminal Procedure Act (no. 51 of 1977). Pretoria: Government Printer.

South Africa. 1982. Internal Security Act (no. 74 of 1982) as amended. Pretoria: Government Printer.

Steuter, E. 1990. Understanding the media/terrorism relationship: an analysis of ideology and the news in *Time* magazine. *Political Communication and Persuasion* 7:257–278.

Tan, ZCW. 1989. The role of media in insurgent terrorism: issues and perspectives. *Gazette* 44:191–215.

Tuchman, G. 1978. *Understanding news. A study in the construction of reality.* New York: The Free Press and CollierMacmillan.

Vlok, AJ. 1988. Answer to terrorism. *RSA Policy Review* 1(1):59–64.

Vorster, PJ. 1984. *Terrorisme en die pers: 'n oorsig.* Sentrum vir die ondersoek na rewolusionêre bedrywighede, Randse Afrikaanse Universiteit: Johannesburg.

Weimann, G. 1983. The theatre of terror: effects of press coverage. *Journal of Communication,* Winter: 38–45.

Weimann, G. 1985. Terrorists or freedom fighters? Labelling terrorism in the Israeli press. *Political Communication and Persuasion* 2(4):433–445.

Weimann, G. 1989. The theatre of terror: modern terrorism and the mass media. *Convention papers at "Television in perspective"* 10–13 October 1989: Royal Swazi Sun, Swaziland, Human Sciences Research Council.

Weimann, G & Brosius, H. 1991. The newsworthiness of international terrorism. *Communication Research* 18(3):333–354.

Wilkinson, P. 1987. *Terrorism and the liberal state.* London: Macmillan Education.

Winn, GFT. 1981. Terrorism, alienation, and German society. *Behavioral and quantitative perspectives on terrorism,* edited by Y Alexander & JM Gleason. New York: Pergamon Press.

Wittebols, JH. 1991. The politics and coverage of terrorism: from media images to public consciousness. *Communication Theory* 1(3):253–266.

## Newspapers and articles

*Beeld,* 23 May 1983:1.
*Beeld,* 26 August 1998:1.
*Beeld,* 28 August 1998:2.

## MEDIA STUDIES

*Beeld*, 5 January 1999:2.
*Beeld*, 6 January 1999:8.
*Beeld*, 12 September 2000:1,2.
*Daily Mail & Guardian*, 5 October 1999.
*FXI Freedom of Expression News*, 26 February 1999:2.
*FXI Action Alert*, 22 October 2000.
*Pretoria News*, 26 August 1998:1,2.
*Pretoria News*, 11 September 2000:1.
*Pretoria News*, 13 October 2000.
*Sunday Times*, 30 August 1998.
*Weekly Mail & Guardian*, 13 August 1999.
*ZA Now*, 27 January 2000:3.

# Censorship and the Media 18

*Beschara Karam*

## Overview

In this unit, we will be looking at the basic concepts of censorship. It is important to take cognisance of censorship because as media students you should be aware that censorship impacts on every aspect of the media, including print, film, video, music and the Internet – all of which are central to the study of media. It is also of vital importance to understand the issues surrounding censorship in South Africa because prior to the election of Nelson Mandela as President in 1994 and the introduction of democracy into our country, censorship was the norm of the apartheid society. As part of our country's culture of censorship, freedom of expression and freedom of speech were repressed. Books were kept locked away; journalists' articles and editors' opinions banned from publication; newspapers, magazines, films and music censored; political parties banned; and political activists detained and imprisoned or, even more horrifying and of the worst kind of censorship, eradicated by assassination.

Although censorship did not completely die out with the introduction of democracy to South Africa, it is no longer predicated on the outright suppression of people's ideas. Therefore, this unit looks not only at the concept of censorship and the very issues surrounding this concept, but also looks specifically at censorship in South Africa.

It must also be kept in mind that the modern era is one of information and as such it is of the utmost importance to look at the issues involved in the free flow of information – unregulated and unrestricted.

## Learning outcomes

At the end of this unit you should be able to
- define censorship;
- identify key issues in censorship debates and explain the opposing viewpoints on these issues;
- critically analyse the major justifications given for censorship;
- critically analyse censorship in different media;
- demonstrate a critical understanding of censorship under apartheid;
- list and explain the characteristics of the new censorship laws in South Africa; and
- critically analyse current censorship issues in South Africa.

## 18.1 INTRODUCTION

In this unit we look at various topics, including freedom of expression, public good versus individual liberty, and free speech versus hate speech. Violence, sex, and political and religious opinions as the major justifications for censorship are considered. Then the focus is on censorship in the media and this covers film, video, print, music and the Internet. Lastly, we present a case study of Sir Richard Attenborough's film, *Cry Freedom* (1988) as it relates to censorship in apartheid South Africa.

## 18.2 CENSORSHIP DEFINED

Censorship may be defined in a broad or narrow sense, but in either case refers to the suppression of freedom of expression (Botha in Fourie 1997:298). Narrowly, this would mean official government interference in the freedom of expression. Broadly, it would mean interference by *anyone*, including any individual or organisation outside of the government (Grolier 1995:4; 246). This includes so-called pre-censorship, where the actual producers of messages, art and entertainment censor their own work before it ever reaches the public, such as the way in which many filmmakers avoid controversial topics (Botha in Fourie 1997:298). An example of this is the remake of the film *Lolita* (1998), based on Vladimir Nabokov's book of the same name, and directed by Adrian Lynn. This film deals with the incestuous relationship between a middle-aged man and his teenage stepdaughter. Many actors turned down the role of the stepfather as they saw the film as dealing with far too controversial topics – incest and paedophilia. After two years, British actor Jeremy Irons finally agreed to play the part – and he was ostracised and vehemently criticised for doing so. Many directors blatantly refused to work with him once the film was released. A correlation of this in South Africa is the accusation by some commentators that editors and journalists avoid taking a firm stand on various issues, such as criticising the government, for fear of being condemned as racist and anti-government.

### 18.2.1 Key issues in censorship debates

*Freedom of expression*

Article 19 of the Universal Declaration of Human Rights states:

> Everyone has the right to freedom of opinion and expression; this right includes freedom to hold opinions without interference and to seek, receive and impart information and ideas through any media regardless of frontiers.
>
> (Boyle in Article 19 World Report 1988:xii)

The Universal Declaration of Human Rights is an international document, adopted by the United Nations. As such, the rights contained within it, including the right to freedom of expression, are international rights, binding on all member states of the United Nations (i.e. the majority of countries in the world). Freedom of expression applies equally to artistic as well as sociopolitical opinion and expression. It is therefore fundamental to the development of individual maturity, as well as the maturity of human society. It is held that human beings cannot develop fully if they are denied access to a wide range of information, opinions and ideas (op cit:x–xii).

However, in practice, the right to freedom of expression is often suppressed or even ignored. Many governments engage in censorship in order to protect their own power. Even those people who are broadly in favour of freedom of expression feel that it has its limits, especially where these conflict with other human rights. Some of these conflicts will be examined below.

## Public good vs individual liberty

The primary justification for censorship is that certain messages are harmful to society, or to certain sections of society (Grolier 1995: 4:246). The key issue here is whether or not the government, or any other group, has the right to make decisions on behalf of society. In other words, should individuals be prevented from seeing or hearing certain messages, or should they be allowed to receive these messages and decide for themselves?

The answer to this question depends on whether or not you feel that individuals are fully capable of thinking for themselves. It has been argued that it is in fact harmful to society to withhold messages or information, since a well-informed public is necessary for a strong and effective democracy. The key to democracy is the participation of all citizens in the political process, and anti-censorship activists feel that such participation is impossible without full access to information (Boyle in Article 19 World Report 1988:x–xii). A further concern is the need to limit the power that a government can have over its citizens. Censorship laws may be passed with the best intentions in the world, but they do give a great deal of power to a government – power that can be misused (Shawcross in Article 19 World Report 1988:vii).

There are two censorship issues often argued as being exceptions to the above principle. The first is the need for national security, especially in wartime. This is an exceptionally difficult issue. On one hand it appears reasonable that a government should want to restrict access to strategic information so that it would not fall into enemy hands. On the other hand, governments often use national security as an excuse to introduce harsh censorship laws that protect their own interests (Boyle op cit:xii; 295). The apartheid government in South Africa was a prime example of this, where "national security" actually meant "government security".

The second supposed exception is that of the protection of children, since it is almost universally acknowledged that children are not fully capable of thinking for themselves on all issues. The usual practice is to introduce age restrictions for material considered unsuitable for children. Since the development of a child into a mature adult is a gradual process, there are usually several age categories, with fewer restrictions being imposed on older children and adolescents (Hutchinson 1999:182–185). There is considerable debate as to what age categories should exist, and what restrictions should apply to each category.

## The right to know vs the right to privacy

The public's right to be informed may sometimes clash with another right – that of the individual to enjoy a reasonable degree of privacy. In each case, the rights of the individual and the rights of the public have to be weighed up against each other.

Individuals have a right to be protected from the release of specific information that may cause humiliation, embarrassment or the disruption of their personal lives. We need to ask if the benefits to the general public outweigh the harm to the individual. In some circumstances there appears to be general agreement that the individual should be protected, for example legislation in many countries prohibits publication of the names of rape victims (Grolier 1995: 4:246). As another example, in South Africa the names and photographs of Lotto (the national lottery) winners may not be published without their consent. Other cases are more controversial, such as the recent decision by a British newspaper to publish the names and photographs of all known paedophiles in that country.

Apart from the release of accurate information, individuals have the right to be protected from the release of *false* information that paints a negative picture of the individual. This is known as defamation. Verbal (oral) defamation is called slander, and written defamation is called libel. Disagreement exists as to what exactly constitutes defamation – for example, at what exact point does a negative *opinion* about someone (as opposed to actual false *facts*) become defamatory. If the laws regarding defamation become too strict, then the media may become afraid of publishing certain information or opinions, in case this leads to expensive legal action by the supposedly defamed person. Strict defamation laws can therefore act as an informal kind of censorship (Hutchinson 1999:104–106).

## Free speech vs hate speech

Hate speech may be defined as any material likely to stir up hatred against a specific group of people. Such a group could be defined by race, gender, sexual orientation, language, culture, religion, age, or in a number of other ways. Since hate speech could possibly result in aggression and violence towards the group concerned, it is often argued that it should be banned in order to protect members of that group. In other words, freedom of expression should not include the right to cause harm.

Once again, the question is one of finding a balance. At what point does free speech end and hate speech begin? Some countries allow a great deal of free speech, such as the United States of America, which will only enforce a hate speech ban if violence is likely to result (Hutchinson 1999:106). In South Africa, with our history of intolerance and racial division, laws on hate speech are much stricter. An example of hate speech in South Africa would be the production of a poster distributed in the Muslim areas of the Cape Flats, with the controversial slogan "A vote for the DA [Democratic Alliance] is a vote for Israel" (A vote for the DA ... 2000:5). This anti-Democratic Alliance slogan intimates that the Democratic Alliance (leader of this opposition party is Mr Tony Leon, a South African Jew) supports Israel and is therefore against all Muslims. This poster, is in effect highly offensive and inflammatory, and blatantly anti-Semitic.

## *Morality*

The idea that certain messages are harmful is of course based on one's view of morality. Many societies throughout history have been dominated by a particular religion, which sought to promote its moral views and stamp out all others. Before the invention of printing, not much censorship was needed, since there were very few books. It was therefore easy to get rid of books that promoted unacceptable ideas. The advent of printing meant a sudden increase in the number of books and consequently a threat to religious monopolies on truth. Organised censorship was the result, but it failed to stop the spread of new ideas (Scammell 1988:3-5). Ever since then communications technology has continued to develop, making the flow of information and opinions almost impossible to control.

In addition, human society has grown increasingly more complex. A society such as South Africa is very diverse, with many different moral systems existing side by side. As a result, it has become increasingly difficult to say which ideas or messages are harmful and which are not. Messages that are viewed with horror by some people may be regarded as acceptable or even healthy by others. For example, devout Christians or Muslims would be opposed to pornography because it supposedly runs counter to family values, whereas some people with a more secular (non-religious) point of view would not be so opposed. On the other hand, some feminists, who might be either secular or religious, would oppose pornography on the grounds that it encourages negative attitudes towards women (i.e. it is a form of hate speech against women). Given this kind of complexity, free speech advocates would argue that pornography should not be banned, and that it should be left up to individuals to make their own choices.

In spite of all this diversity, however, there are a few issues on which almost all moral systems appear to agree. For example, child pornography is almost universally condemned, even in a diverse society like South Africa. As a result, there has been no public opposition to its banning in this country (Scammell 1988:1-16).

## 18.3 MAJOR JUSTIFICATIONS FOR CENSORSHIP

### 18.3.1 Violence

There is widespread agreement in human society that violence, especially between human beings, is generally unacceptable. It is held that violence is only permissible when there is no alternative – for example, the combating of crime, or personal or national self-defence. It is strongly believed that exposure to violence in the media can promote violent behaviour in individuals, especially children. Violence on television, and in videos and video/computer games has been the subject of special concern, since these media are easily accessed by children and adolescents (cf. Unit 16 on the media and violence). As a result, the impact of violence has possibly been studied more than any other censorship issue (Cline 1974:111). Different studies have come up with different conclusions, some of these strongly disputed (Steinfeld 1974:177–178; Watson & Shuker 1998:63). Public pressure, however, has resulted in various forms of age restriction, both formal and informal, as discussed under the headings of the various media below.

### 18.3.2 Sex

The issue of sex is more complex than that of violence. The vast majority of human beings would agree that at least some form of sex (as sexual activity) is necessary or acceptable in human life. The key questions therefore are: *what* forms of sex are acceptable; and to what extent is it acceptable to depict or refer to sex in the media?

Both of these questions have a moral dimension. Generally speaking, the more morally conservative people are, the more forms of sex they will find objectionable. Therefore opinions differ as to whether or not homosexuality/lesbianism or pre-marital sex is acceptable. There is almost universal agreement, however, that paedophilia and bestiality are unacceptable. Political ideology may also play a role – for example, in the apartheid era in South Africa, authorities considered interracial sex to be objectionable (Wistrich 1978:75–76).

Morally conservative people are also opposed to the depiction of sex, as they feel that this cheapens something that is essentially private and sacred (Wistrich 1978:76–78). As mentioned above under the heading Morality, many feminists are opposed to sexual material – not for traditional moral reasons, but because such material is invariably male-orientated and shows women as inferior beings, existing only for the sexual pleasure of men. These feminists are particularly concerned about the way in which sex is often combined with violence against women. They object especially to depictions of rape, which they see as an act of violence rather than a sexual act – that is, rape is not committed out of sexual desire, but as a way of humiliating a woman and demonstrating supposed male superiority. Some feminists feel that all sexual material should be banned, whilst others feel it should simply be reformed, with women being shown as the sexual equals of men (Wistrich 1978:81–82). In November 2000, the South African Broadcasting Corporation (SABC) refused to remove billboards depicting a woman being stabbed in the back – an advertisement for a game show – thereby rejecting the Advertising Standards Authority's order to do so (*Mail & Guardian* 2000:2).

Once again, the protection of children is a central concern, and various forms of age restrictions have been the result.

### 18.3.3 Political and religious opinions

As mentioned above, it has been common throughout history for the authorities to suppress all views conflicting with the dominant religion. The same approach has been followed with regard to all views conflicting with the dominant political ideology, and this has continued into modern times. Apartheid South Africa has of course been one of the most famous examples, but there have been many others, such as Nazi Germany and the former Soviet Union.

In many societies in recent years, especially in diverse societies such as South Africa, it has been felt that it is unjust to suppress some political or religious opinions in favour of others, and that democracy means freedom of choice. As a result, little or no censorship has been imposed on the expression of political or religious viewpoints. What restrictions there are tend to apply to hate speech. Those in favour of hate speech bans argue that just as it is wrong to suppress various political or religious opinions, so it is also wrong to belittle those opinions or the people who hold them. In other words, we are entitled to express our views on religion or politics, but not to the point where we insult opposing views.

### 18.3.4 State security

The arguments surrounding this issue have been covered in the subsection titled Public good vs individual liberty (see 18.2.1). The important thing to note here is the potential for abuse by governments, and the difficulty of determining exactly when it is actually necessary to invoke the need for state security.

## 18.4 CENSORSHIP IN VARIOUS MEDIA

### 18.4.1 Film

Film is a particularly prominent medium for censorship. Due to its visual nature, it can actually depict scenes that print media can only describe, and therefore has an especially powerful effect on the human imagination. Therefore, from its beginnings at the end of the nineteenth century, governments and other organisations have been concerned about the supposedly negative social effects of the cinema. They have been particularly alarmed by its enormous popularity and its ability to influence large numbers of people (Watson & Shuker 1998:27-28). These concerns persist to this day. As a result of this, cinema has been censored more than any other medium. Film in many countries is subject not only to outright cuts and banning, but also to restrictions based on age (Hutchinson 1999:182-185). In some countries, such as the United States of America, there is organised pre-censorship within the film industry, carried out according to an industry standard known as the Hollywood Production Code (Botha in Fourie1997:298).

It has been persistently believed, from the birth of cinema, that films have the ability to negatively influence human behaviour, to the point where some people will specifically copy antisocial acts, such as murder, that have been depicted on the screen. In recent years, there have been several cases where murderers have confessed to copying murders that they have witnessed in a film or video (Watson & Shuker 1998:11).

The question is, did the film scenes drive these people to commit murder in the first place, or would they have committed murder anyway? In other words, did the film simply give them ideas on *how* to commit a murder? The debate over this question is a fierce one, and continues to rage. There is the well-known example of a couple in the United States of America, Sarah Edmondson and Benjamin Darrus, who in 1995 went on a killing spree, patterned on the serial killers Mallory and Micky Knox; characters portrayed in Oliver Stone's film *Natural Born Killers* (1994). Because the couple claimed to have viewed the film *Natural Born Killers* more than 20 times, a court case was brought by a surviving victim (Patsy Byers) of Edmondson and Darrus' rampage. The case itself was filed against director Oliver Stone and the film studio Warner Brothers' parent, Time Warner in 1995, which produced the film. The case was based on the premise that the filmmakers intended to incite violence. The outcome of this case, at the time of writing, has yet to be resolved (Frankel, 1999). In South Africa, the South African produced television series *Yizo Yizo* (1999) fuels the same ongoing debate – can filmmakers be responsible for copycat crimes? An article in *You* magazine (The terror of real life TV 1999:138–139) reports several different *Yizo Yizo* copycat crime cases having taken place throughout South Africa. Rapes, murder and torture are all being committed as exact replicas of the scenes shown on television in the series. Others believe, however, that these are not copycat crimes, but the reverse, namely that the series reflects the crimes already occurring in the townships and schools. These differing views have split the black community, the audience at which the programme is aimed, in two.

### 18.4.2 Television and video/digital versatile disk (DVD)

In recent years, the cinema has lost popularity to television and video (including the new technology of DVD) (Botha 1997:298). Because these are also visual media, they are seen as having the same effects as cinema, and have therefore been subject to the same kind of censorship debates.

Video differs significantly from film in that it is viewed privately. As such, it is difficult to place age restrictions on video, since regulations can only control the age of the person who hires a video, and not the ages of any other people who might actually watch it. Two solutions have been implemented in various parts of the world. The first has been to place age restrictions on videos anyway, since this will act as a guide to parents as well as having some preventative effect. (Not all "under-age" viewers can find an adult willing to hire videos on their behalf.) The second has been to classify videos more strictly than films, in order to compensate for any under-age viewing that might occur (Hutchinson 1999:185). Similar difficulties face the sale of video games and computer games, and similar solutions have been sought.

Virtually all big-screen movies eventually become videos, but video stores contain a great deal of other material that has never appeared on the big screen. These are known as "straight to video" movies – that is, low-budget productions specifically designed for home viewing. Some are of a relatively innocent nature, but others fall into the category of "video nasties". These are videos of a generally shocking nature, which would probably cause a public outcry if they were shown at cinemas. They are a product of the private nature of the video medium, and have caused a level of controversy perhaps even greater than that of many films (Watson & Shuker 1998:27–28).

Television is similar to video in that it is privately viewed, but different in that it is also privately accessed. This of course poses particular problems with regard to the issue of under-age viewing. The typical strategy in the past was to impose much stricter censorship controls on television than on film or video, with more adult material only being shown relatively late in the evening (when younger viewers would be in bed), and a great deal of material being banned outright. This meant that certain films or videos were never shown on television (Bertrand 1978:180–181).

In recent years, however, the situation has become more complex with the spread of subscription television (e.g. satellite, decoder and cable television). Unlike public broadcasters (such as the South African Broadcasting Corporation [although viewers have to pay a licence fee] and e.tv in South Africa), whose material is available free of charge, subscription television uses modern technology to limit viewing to paying customers. Since this material is not available to the general public, and since only adults can subscribe to it anyway, subscription channels have been able to show virtually anything they want. In many cases, satellite television is transmitted (sometimes at no charge) to a country from outside its borders, allowing the broadcasters to ignore local censorship laws (Watson & Shuker 1998:165–168).

In order not to upset public opinion, however, especially that of their customers, some subscription channels (such as M-Net) provide comprehensive information on recommended age restrictions for programmes, in order to enable parents to restrict their children's viewing. These age restrictions are often backed up by technology that enables parents to "lock" age-restricted programmes, that is, to make them accessible only with a code. Public television also tends to provide recommended age restrictions, although of course without "locking" technology.

### 18.4.3 Print media

Printing was the very first form of communication technology capable of reaching a mass audience. As such, printed material was the very first medium to be subjected to significant levels of censorship (Scammell 1988:3–5). At first this applied mainly to books and pamphlets, but other new forms of media arose, such as newspapers, and later on, magazines and comics (Watson & Shuker 1998:115–147). Print media therefore covers a wide range of different forms of information and expression, including the artistic, the entertaining, and the sociopolitical.

Although print does not have quite the same impact on the senses as other media such as film and music, it nevertheless has powers of its own. In addition, it is relatively cheap and easy to produce and distribute; something that the authorities have been quick to acknowledge whenever they have felt that printed material was morally or politically undesirable. Although printed material has been losing out to visual media over the last few decades, the recent growth of the Internet has seen a revival in the use of the printed word, which can now be digitally produced and distributed more quickly and cheaply than ever.

### 18.4.4 Popular music

Popular music exists mainly in the form of songs, and song lyrics (i.e. the words of a song) have always been used as a way to express discontent. In the twentieth century, recording technology has meant that songs are no longer confined to particular regions or countries, but can be heard around the world. Due to pop videos and recordings of live performances, popular music has now overlapped with television and video. This massive level of exposure, together with the fact that popular music is mainly listened to by young people, has raised fears about its supposedly harmful effects, especially on young people. This of course raises the whole issue of the protection of children and adolescents (Winfield & Davidson 1999:25–26). Although concern exists about the behaviour of pop stars both on and off the stage, as well as the content of pop videos, the major concern is with the lyrics of songs. These are held to have the same kind of detrimental effect on human behaviour as certain scenes from films and videos (Budd 1999:4–7).

As with film and video, there have been several highly publicised tragic incidents blamed on the influence of popular music. Most of these incidents have been teenage suicides, supposedly inspired by the lyrics of certain songs. No clear link has ever been proven, and the question is similar to that raised by supposedly movie-inspired murders – were these teenagers already suicidal? (Watson & Shuker 1998:107–110). As well as this, there have been attempts to ban or put age restrictions on songs because of the effect that they *might* have. In 1985 an American group called the Parents' Music Resource Centre (PMRC) demanded R and X ratings on records, and Tipper Gore, wife of then Senator Al Gore, called for similar restrictions on lyrics and album covers. The Senate Commerce Committee hearings on these demands concluded that it would be ill advised for Congress to embroil itself with legislation to clean up the music industry (Foerstel, 1997). The most famous example of this debate in recent years has been the song *Cop Killer*, by rap singer Ice-T. There were widespread fears in the United States of America that the song would inspire a wave of deadly attacks on police officers – something which did not in fact happen. At stake here was of course the issue of hate speech. Was Ice-T trying to provoke violence against the police, or was he simply engaging in freedom of expression? (Winfield & Davidson 1999:22–23).

### 18.4.5 The Internet

There are two aspects to the Internet: e-mail, which allows people to send and receive messages (both text and audio-visual media) by computer; and the World Wide Web, which allows people to access information stored on other computers (collections of such information are known as Web sites). As well as being able to view material on Web sites, it is often possible for Internet users to download material, that is, transfer it on to their own computers. In addition, material such as books, videos and so forth can be ordered over the Internet. Like satellite television, the Internet knows no national boundaries. Unlike satellite television, Web sites and e-mail can be created and made public by private individuals, who are far more difficult to track down and control than the large companies needed to provide satellite television broadcasts. Satellite television broadcasts must at least be legal in their country of origin, whereas individuals can create Web sites with illegal content, knowing that their chances of being traced and prosecuted are slim (Watson & Shuker 1998:188).

Once again, the main concern is with protection of children and adolescents, who have easy private access to objectionable material. One response has been the development of computer programmes that enable parents to prevent their children gaining access to pornographic sites. At an official level, some countries have proposed various types of censorship regulations. Anti-censorship activists feel that some of these regulations go too far, and pose a threat to free speech. They also predict that such regulations will be virtually impossible to enforce (Watson & Shuker 1998:188–191). The Internet is still in its infancy, and it remains to be seen just how the situation will develop. Internet technology (IT) represents the latest and most sophisticated form of communications technology, and, as always, censorship is struggling to keep up with technological change. Legislature has not yet caught up with the Internet and as such copyright laws largely depend from which country the material originates.

## 18.5 MEDIA CENSORSHIP IN SOUTH AFRICA
### 18.5.1 Censorship under apartheid

Over the course of its stay in power (1948–1994), the National Party passed numerous laws that not only prohibited any form of expression challenging its policies, but also gave government officials the power to ban whatever media, or people, that they saw fit. The terminology used to define what was undesirable was extremely vague, and could be used to cover almost anything. For example, the very first piece of censorship-related legislation was the Suppression of Communism Act in 1950. Although supposedly enacted to fight Communism, it was used to attack any opposition to the government, whether or not inspired by Communism (Article 19 World Report 1988:40–42).

Apart from the banning, within South Africa, of any form of expression deemed hostile to the regime, the National Party also sought to restrict the flow of information from South Africa to the outside world. This was especially true of the period from 1985 to 1990, when a State of Emergency was declared, giving the authorities virtually unlimited powers as to the restriction of information. It was only legal to report information that had been released by the government, and reporters were prevented, both by legislation and by force and intimidation, from gathering or disseminating information for themselves (Article 19 World Report 1988:40-41; Botha 1997:299-300). For example, there was the first Afrikaans anti-apartheid newspaper established in 1988, *Vrye Weekblad*. This newspaper was greatly discriminated against – for instance the Minister of Justice threatened the newspaper with the Internal Security Act of 1982, two weeks after the newspaper was started, with the warning "you're not going to be on the streets tomorrow". The then state president Mr PW Botha, sued the newspaper for libel, a first in South African media history, and because the then editor of the newspaper, Max du Preez quoted a banned person in an article he was taken to court by the state, also under the Internal Security Act (Du Preez in Sperling & McKenzie, 1990). The *Vrye Weekblad* was not the only newspaper to encounter censorship from the state – *Ilanga*, the *Weekly Mail*, the *Star* and the *Sowetan* all published their newspapers with heavy black lines running through censored portions. Alternatively these newspapers used blank spaces to indicate censorship. The *Weekly Mail* of June 20 1987 used black lines and white spaces – eradicating paragraphs, an article and a cartoon. Following that, in July 1987, such evidence of censorship was in itself banned (Merrett, 1994). Merrett (1994) also mentions an example of Presbyterian minister, Reverend Abram Maja, who was jailed for 380 days for disseminating so-called subversive material in 1985.

A further government tactic that had a direct censorship impact, was the practice of banning individuals or organisations, as provided for in the Internal Security Act of 1982. Banned organisations were not allowed to legally exist in South Africa, and therefore could not produce or distribute media of any kind within the country. Banned individuals were effectively excluded from society, in that they were not allowed to publicly express themselves in any way, and had severe restrictions placed on their freedom of movement. This prevented influential opponents of apartheid from being able to express their views (Article 19 World Report 1988:41-42). Banned people included any known members of the African Nationalist Congress, such as Mr Oliver Tambo (leader of the ANC), Mr Nelson Mandela (president of the country from 1994-1998) and Mr Thabo Mbeki (successor to President Nelson Mandela). Banned journalists included Brian Sokuto, who in 1988 had already been in detention for over two years, while Vuyelwa Mhlawuli had to have an eye removed after being shot in the head by an unknown assassin. A third journalist, Zwelakhe Sisulu was placed under severe restrictions and house arrest, and Thami Mazwai, senior assistant editor of the *Sowetan*, South Africa's largest black daily newspaper, was jailed for eighteen months in 1963 for his involvement in the Pan Africanist Congress, a previously banned organisation, and a further eighteen months in 1981 for refusing to cite evidence against a friend (Mazwai in Sperling & McKenzie, 1990).

Apart from security regulations relating mainly to news reporting, the primary legislation controlling censorship in South Africa was the Publications Control Act of 1974, together with the Publications (Amendment) Act of 1986. This provided for three bodies: a Directorate; a Committee, known as the Publications Control Board, which decided on bannings, cuts and age restrictions for almost all media; and a Publications Appeal Board, which heard appeals against Publications Control Board decisions. These bodies had considerable powers of discretion, but were still subject to direct state intervention in their decisions (Article 19 World Report 1988:41–42; Botha 1997:299). They used these powers to target not only directly political material, but also any material that offended against an extremely strict sexual morality (including depictions of or references to homosexuality or interracial sex) or that appeared to attack or criticise the Christian religion (Botha 1997:299–300).

### 18.5.2 Censorship under democracy

*The new legislation*

Although the Publications Control Act stayed in force until 1996, it was enforced less vigorously from 1990 onwards, as the transition to democracy began. A task group was appointed in 1994 to put together new censorship legislation more suitable to a democratic society. The Film and Publications Act, passed in 1996, was designed to be in keeping with the new Constitution. It therefore sought to balance the rights of adults to freedom of expression and personal taste against the need to protect children (Botha 1997:300–301).

Under the new legislation, there is very little material that may not be distributed in South Africa. There are a number of age restrictions in various forms of media, up to a maximum of eighteen years. Age restrictions are based on the frequency and intensity of the following elements: strong language; use of drugs; prejudice; nudity; sex; and violence. The strongest age restrictions, applying to sexually explicit material, are X18 for film and video material and video/computer games, R18 for printed material, and F18 for periodical printed material (e.g. a monthly magazine). Not only is this material only available to people over eighteen years of age, but it must be kept away from the general public. R18 and F18 printed material must be sold in sealed wrappers, and X18 films and videos may only be shown, rented or sold in specially licensed premises that are only open to people older than eighteen (South Africa. Film and Publications Bill 1996:schedules 2–4 & 11).

Material that may not be distributed in South Africa at all is classified as XX. This covers a small range of material considered to be of the utmost offensiveness and danger to society, namely: child pornography; explicit violent sex; degrading sexual conduct; explicit bestiality (sex between humans and animals); explicit extreme violence; and aggressive material likely to promote religious hatred (op cit:schedules 1 & 6; Botha 1997:301). Material may be exempted from XX or X18 classification if it is of genuine artistic, scientific or educational merit (op cit:schedules 5 & 9).

# MEDIA STUDIES

## Table 18.1 Censorship legislation

**Film and Publication Review Board**

Primary objects of the Publications Control Act of 1974, together with the Publications (Amendment) Act of 1996: the objects of this Act are to establish a Film and Publication Board and a Film and Publication Review Board to regulate in the main by means of classification, age restrictions and consumer advice the distribution of certain publications and the exhibition and distribution of films, with due regard to the fundamental rights in Chapter 3 of the Constitution of the Republic of South Africa, 1993.

**Schedule 1**

XX CLASSIFICATION FOR PUBLICATIONS

A publication shall be classified as XX if, judged within the context of the publication as a whole, it contains a visual presentation, simulated or real, of –

(1) a child who is, or is depicted as being under the age of sixteen years, participating in, engaging in or assisting another person to engage in sexual conduct or a lewd exhibition of genitals;
(2) an explicit physically violent act or acts concurrent with explicit sexual conduct;
(3) an explicit act of sexual bestiality; or
(4) the explicit infliction or explicit effects of extreme violence in a manner which is likely to create a substantial risk of imminent ensuing violence.

**Schedule 2**

X18 CLASSIFICATION FOR PUBLICATIONS

A publication shall be classified as X18 if –

(1) judged within the context of the publication as a whole, it contains a visual presentation, simulated or real of explicit sexual conduct which, in the case of sexual intercourse, includes an explicit visual presentation of human genitals in a state of stimulation or arousal; or
(2) judged as a whole it describes predominantly and explicitly any or all of the acts defined in Schedule 1 or Schedule 2(1) of this Act.

**Schedule 3**

R18 CLASSIFICATION FOR PUBLICATIONS

A classification committee shall classify as R18 and impose any or both of the following conditions on the distribution of a publication if it is of the opinion that judged as a whole, it is necessary to protect children in the relevant age group against harmful or disturbing material in the publication –

(1) that it shall only be distributed to persons older than 18 years of age or older than a specified younger age and that the publication shall bear a distinct notice of such restriction;
(2) that it shall only be distributed in a sealed and, if necessary, opaque wrapper which shall also, if applicable, bear the notice referred to in clause (1).

## Schedule 4

### F 18 CLASSIFICATION FOR PERIODICAL PUBLICATIONS

A periodical publication shall be classified as F18 if the following six issues of such periodical publication are likely to contain material which falls within the scope of Schedule 3 and the publisher or his representative consents to such an order.

## Schedule 5

### ART AND SCIENCE EXEMPTION FOR PUBLICATIONS

The XX or X18 classification shall not apply to a bona fide technical, professional, educational, scientific, documentary, literary or artistic publication or any part of a publication which, judged within the context of the publication, is of such a nature.

## Schedule 6

### XX CLASSIFICATION FOR FILMS

A film shall be classified as XX if it contains a scene or scenes, simulated or real, judged in the context of the whole film, of any of the following:
(1) a child who is, or is depicted as being, under the age of 16 years, participating in, engaging in or assisting others to engage in sexual conduct or a lewd exhibition of genitals;
(2) an explicit prolonged physically violent act or acts concurrent with explicit prolonged sexual conduct;
(3) explicit sexual bestiality; or
(4) the explicit infliction of extreme violence which is predominantly present in the film and which is likely to create a substantial risk of imminent ensuing violence.

## Schedule 7

### X18 CLASSIFICATION FOR FILMS

A film shall be classified as X18 if it contains a scene or scenes, simulated or real, judged within the context of the whole film, of explicit prolonged sexual conduct which, in the case of sexual intercourse, includes an explicit visual presentation of genitals in a state of arousal or stimulation.

## Schedule 8

### AGE RESTRICTIONS FOR FILMS

An age restriction shall only be imposed if the classification committee is of the opinion that, judged as a whole, it is necessary to protect children in the relevant age group against harmful or disturbing material in the film.

## Schedule 9

### ART AND SCIENCE EXEMPTION FOR FILMS

An XX or X18 classification shall not be applicable to a bona fide technical, professional, educational, scientific, documentary, dramatic or artistic film or any part of a film which, judged within the context of the film, is of such a nature.

# MEDIA STUDIES

**Schedule 10**

PROMOTION OF RELIGIOUS HATRED

(1) A publication or a film which, judged as a whole, promotes hatred against the religious convictions of a section of the population of the Republic, shall be classified as XX.

(2) Clause (1) shall not apply to –
   (a) a publication or a film or a part thereof which falls within the scope of Schedules 5 or 9, as the case may be;
   (b) a publication or a film which amounts to a bona fide discussion, argument or opinion on a matter pertaining to religion, belief or conscience;
   (c) a publication or a film which amounts to a bona fide discussion, argument or opinion on a matter of public interest.

**Schedule 11**

ADULT PREMISES

(1) A publication or film classified as X18 shall be distributed or exhibited in public only by a person who –
   (a) is licensed to do such business with a licensing authority under the Businesses Act, 1991 (no. 71 of 1991); and
   (b) conducts his or her business in fixed premises.

(2) A distributor or exhibitor in terms of clause (1) shall –
   (a) not allow a person under the age of 18 years to enter the premises concerned;
   (b) display in a conspicuous manner at the entrance or entrances of the premises concerned that no person under the age of 18 years shall enter the premises;
   (c) display a publication or exhibit a film in such a manner that it can only be seen from within the premises concerned; and
   (d) not distribute a publication or film by way of postal or other delivery unless the delivery is to a person licensed in terms of clause (1)(a).

**Schedule 12**

SEXUAL CONDUCT

For purposes of these Schedules "sexual conduct" means genitals in a state of stimulation or arousal; masturbation; sexual intercourse, including anal sexual intercourse; the caressing, or touching by any object, of genitals; oral genital contact; or oral anal contact.

**Schedule 13**

ACTS REPEALED

NO. AND YEAR OF ACT TITLE EXTENT OF REPEAL

Act No. 44 of 1958 Post Office Act, 1958 The proviso in section 29(2). Act No. 37 of 1967 The Indecent or Obscene Photographic Matter Act, 1967 The whole. Act No. 42 of 1974 The Publications Act, 1974 The whole. Act No. 18 of 1977 The Transkei Publications Act, 1977 The whole. Act No. 36 of 1979 The Bophuthatswana Publications Act, 1979 The whole. Act No. 15 of 1983 The Venda Publications Act, 1983 The whole.

*Source:* Film and Publications Bill: Available: http://www.fxi.org.za/filmbill.htm Accessed on 2000/08/24

## The role of the Internet

The new legislation covers the publication and distribution of media in South Africa. However, there are considerable difficulties in applying this legislation to the Internet. As mentioned above, this is an international medium, allowing virtually anonymous access to material from all over the world. Internet issues have come to the fore in South Africa, at the time of writing, of scandals involving individuals who have been accessing child pornography on the Internet. It is of course illegal to possess child pornography, even if it is stored on your computer. It therefore follows that it is illegal to order or download child pornography from the Internet. However, is it then illegal to simply *visit* a child pornography Web site, given that you may do so unintentionally?

The other major question arising from the child pornography scandals is that of government control over Internet access – that is, is it justifiable under certain circumstances, and is it practicable? The South African government has proposed legislation aimed at service providers – the companies that manage the process whereby computer users connect to the Internet. This legislation would force service providers to monitor the Internet usage of their clients to see if they were visiting child pornography Web sites. Whilst it is unlikely that anyone will publicly endorse free access to child pornography, there is likely to be concern over rights of privacy, and fears that the government could use this legislation to intrude on citizens' privacy in other areas.

## Balancing rights in a democratic South Africa

Given the history of South Africa, it is to be expected that there be concern over balancing the right to freedom of expression against other human rights that have been violated in the past. Of particular prominence is the issue of race relations and racism. Thus far, legislation regarding hate speech has only addressed the area of religion, but a recent set of events promises to result in at least some legislation with regard to race relations and racism.

In 1998, the South African Human Rights Commission (SAHRC) decided to launch an investigation into racism in the media. Following research commissioned by the SAHRC 1999, which concluded that racism did occur in the media, the Commission proceeded to conduct hearings early in 2000. This process was at first marked by tension, with subpoenas being issued to newspaper editors to compel them to attend the hearings. After the subpoenas were withdrawn, due to the accusations that the subpoenas were a breach of the constitutional right of press freedom, the hearings began in March (McGreal 2000:1).

Finally, in August 2000, the SAHRC issued its final report, concluding that the South African media was indeed racist. The report made several recommendations for combating media racism, including establishment of a statutory regulatory framework for the media (Taitz 2000:2). The report was condemned by a number of newspapers as an attack on press freedom (Swindells 2000:4), raising the issue of freedom of expression versus protection from racial hate speech as well as the argument over what exactly constitutes hate speech. The National Conference on Racism, following almost immediately after the release of the final report of the SAHRC, promises to keep these debates alive. It still remains to be seen what the practical consequences will be for censorship in South Africa.

**Table 18.2 Laws that restrict the South African media**

| Prominent present laws that restrict the South African media |
|---|
| **Promotion of Access to Information Act (2000)** "regulates ... the control of access to information held by government and by private bodies." |
| **Organisations with codes of conduct**<br>Advertising Standards Authority – Code of Advertising Practice<br>Independent Broadcasting Authority – Code of Conduct for Broadcasters<br>Broadcasting Complaints Commission of South Africa – Code of Conduct<br>The Press Ombud's Office administers a Code of Conduct for the Press |

Now we briefly look at the case study of Sir Richard Attenborough's film, *Cry Freedom* (1988) as it relates to censorship in apartheid South Africa.

The *Cry Freedom* case is of particular interest in the study of censorship in South Africa, since it comes towards the end of the apartheid era (1988) at a time when the National Party was starting to lose the absolute control that it had previously exercised over the country. As such, the handling of this film by the South African authorities was an indication of the prevailing chaotic state of affairs.

### Case study 18.1: *Cry Freedom* (1988) – a study of censorship in South Africa

In the late eighties, sanctions and internal unrest were severely disrupting National Party rule and there was a power struggle within the party itself – between the authoritarian "securocrat" faction of then State President PW Botha and the more reform-minded faction led by FW De Klerk. As a response to unrest, the securocrat faction, then in control of the party, had declared a State of Emergency in 1985. This included tough security regulations that had a direct effect on all forms of media, and gave the authorities the power to override conventional censorship legislation. As mentioned in the section on Censorship under apartheid (18.5.1), news reportage in the late eighties was virtually crippled. Ironically, at about the same time there was an easing of film censorship. This was partly due to the appointment of Prof. Kobus van Rooyen as head of the Publications Appeal Board. It perhaps also indicated the growing influence of the reform faction in the National Party, which was determined to create a more reasonable image of the South African government in the international community – a concern not lost on the securocrat faction (Botha 1997:299; Savage 1989).

# Censhorship and the Media

Against this backdrop, the film *Cry Freedom* (1988) was constantly in the public spotlight, even before it was made. Sir Richard Attenborough, the British director of *Cry Freedom*, had already clashed with the South African government over his 1983 film *Gandhi*, which depicted the life of a political martyr (the social reformer Mohandas K Gandhi). Rumours began to circulate in 1984 that Attenborough was planning to make a similar film about South African Black Consciousness activist Steve Biko, who had died under suspicious circumstances in police custody in 1977. These rumours received negative attention from the state-run South African Broadcasting Corporation, and angry replies from Attenborough. A further war of words between Attenborough and the National Party erupted as the film went into production in 1986. Attenborough said that he did not believe the National Party would allow *Cry Freedom* to be shown in South Africa, as the film strongly criticised apartheid. He also stated that he would only allow the film to be shown in South Africa if no cuts were made, and it was only screened at multiracial venues. Statements such as these constituted a direct challenge to the censorship policies of the South African government, and put it in an awkward position. Should it allow the screening of a film that directly criticised its policies, or should it ban the film and face negative international publicity (something that would make the film more popular in other countries)? (Savage 1989).

In November 1987 the film was passed by the Directorate of Publications, without cuts. It was officially denied that the government had any say in the decision, but this was of course entirely possible, given the politically sensitive nature of the issue. The Directorate's decision was based on the belief that the film was not offensive, did not threaten the security of the state, and would not inspire violence. The Directorate also clearly stated that the screening of the film in South Africa would improve the country's image internationally. However, the controversy was far from over (Savage 1989).

Although the central controversy of *Cry Freedom* was its depiction of the death of Steve Biko, the main character in the film was in fact Donald Woods, a former newspaper editor who had known Biko, and who in 1988 was "listed" (a status similar to being banned). Advertisements for the film included quotes by Biko and Woods. Technically this was against the law, since under the terms of the Internal Security Act (ISA), it was illegal to quote a listed individual. A rumour circulated that UIP, the distributors of the film, might be prosecuted, but this was denied by the state. The possibility, of course, existed that the film itself might be banned under the ISA (Savage 1989).

Concerned about this likely new cause for banning the film, UIP requested clarity on the matter from the government, but received none. The film's release was accordingly delayed by the distributors, but was at last scheduled for 29 July 1988. At this point, the Minister of Home Affairs, Mr Stoffel Botha, exercised his powers under the Publications Control Act, and directed the Publications Appeal Board to reconsider the film. In a later statement, he said that he had thought at first that

*Cry Freedom* would not be released. He had only decided to refer the film to the Appeal Board when it became clear that it would be released after all. This strongly suggests that the government had no real intention of letting the film be shown in South Africa. It seems they had hoped the distributors would be too intimidated by potential prosecution under the ISA to proceed, and immediately moved on to the next step once this proved to be untrue (Savage 1989).

But this step also proved unsuccessful. Meeting on 28 July, the day before the film's scheduled release, the Publications Appeal Board approved the film, without cuts and with a 2-19 age restriction. They felt that security legislation was not relevant in judging the film and, like the Directorate, did not believe that *Cry Freedom* would incite violence (Savage 1989; Meyerowitz 1988:29).

Screenings accordingly went ahead, but it appeared that the government had one last move. On 29 July, the day of the screening, police swooped on all cinemas showing the film and confiscated their copies. They were acting on an order by the Commissioner for Police, General Hennie de Witt, in terms of the Media Emergency Regulations of 1988. Unlike the Publications Appeal Board, the Commissioner felt that the film would lead to violence; a belief backed up by some very convenient bomb blasts and bomb threats at a number of cinemas showing the film ("Cry Freedom" passed with age bar ... 1988:1). It appeared that security legislation had had the last word in censorship.

This rather convoluted story reveals the very interesting contradictory censorship trends that existed in South Africa at the end of the eighties. On one hand there was a trend towards reform, as exemplified by the relatively tolerant attitude displayed by the Publications Appeal Board. On the other hand, there was the heavy-handed approach of the securocrats, seemingly determined to use whatever means at their disposal to suppress the film. The Appeal Board was perhaps a little ahead of its time in acting contrary to the interests of the government – not that this mattered, since the government always had the power to intervene in the censorship process (Bauer & Johnson 1988:16).

## Summary

This unit has looked at various topics, including freedom of expression, public good vs individual liberty, and free speech vs hate speech. Furthermore, we looked at the major justifications for censorship, including violence, sex, and political and religious opinions. The unit then focused on censorship in the media, covering film, video, print, music and the Internet. Lastly we looked at censorship in South Africa. A case study was included, based on the release of the film *Cry Freedom* in South Africa.

# Censhorship and the Media

## Research activities

1. Demonstrate an understanding of the current censorship issues in South Africa by listing all the main concepts surrounding these issues.
2. Find an example of a sexist advertisement in the media (print, television, video, or even music) – one that depicts a woman or women in an inferior position to men, such as an advertisement that focuses on a woman who is "merely" a housewife or sexual object, or a woman in tight, revealing clothes, draped over a car in an attempt to sell the type of vehicle that is usually projected toward a predominantly male market.
3. Follow debates on the Internet that focus on the current debate on racism in the media. State whether or not you agree with these debates and why. Visit the following Web sites: Media Institute of Southern Africa http://www.misanet.org/ and The Freedom of Expression Institute http://www.fxi.org.za/
    - Search for discussions on racism in the media on the Internet – look for key terms, such as the Human Rights Commission Report, freedom of expression, freedom of speech, and so forth.
    - Read these articles thoroughly. List the main arguments for and against racism in the media. With each reason given – *for* the presence of racism or *opposing* the presence of racism – stipulate whether you agree with the examples and arguments given. Then stipulate why you agree or disagree.
4. Select a film or video that you want to view or have already viewed – where there are examples of violence portrayed in the film/video. Describe the film or video in a short paragraph. Think about the examples of violence in the film/video you have selected. Describe these examples in detail.
    - Having described a scene from the film/video you have selected, state whether you think that the violence depicted in the film/video is a necessary or unnecessary part of the film, and whether or not you think that the violence is central to the plot. If you think that the violence is unwarranted to the film – state why you think so. If you think that the violence is integral to the plot, state why you think so.
    - Then state whether or not the violence portrayed in the film/video is likely to induce an individual/individuals to replicate what they have seen take place in the film/video. If you believe that the effect of the violence in the film/video is likely to influence someone to behave in a similar manner, say why you think so. If you are aware of any examples where this has happened, mention them here to support your argument. If you believe the opposite, that such a scene(s) of violence does not influence an individual to behave in a like manner, then say so, and support your opinion with an argument to substantiate your views.
5. Motivate your own opinions with regard to censorship of films and music. You need to state if you think censorship of film and music is a good thing or not, and why. If you are aware of any examples, provide these to substantiate your viewpoint.

# MEDIA STUDIES

6. Analyse the debate surrounding the issue of racism in the South African media.
   - Buy a newspaper or magazine from a shop, or look through old newspapers and magazines.
   - Carefully go through the newspapers and magazine articles looking specifically for an article that deals with the issue of racism in the media in South Africa; a very current and topical issue.
   - Read the article and summarise the main points.
   - State whether or not the article supports the presence or absence of racism in the South African media.
   - Then state whether or not you agree with the conclusions of the article and why.
7. Compare different kinds of media censorship – film and advertising, film and music, or film and print.
8. Critically analyse current censorship issues in South Africa.
   - Review this unit on censorship, paying special attention to the issue of censorship in South Africa.
   - State whether or not you agree with the censorship laws in South Africa, and explain why.
9. Do you agree/disagree with the major justifications for censorship? Discuss why.
10. After reviewing the case study on *Cry Freedom*, state what your perceptions are of film censorship under the apartheid regime.

## Further reading

Addison, GN. 1980. *Censorship of the press in South Africa during the Angolan war: a case study of news manipulation and suppression.* [S.l.:s.n.]

Breytenbach, MM. 1997. *The manipulation of public opinion by state censorship of the media during the demise of white rule in South Africa (1974–1994).* [S.l:s.n.]

Brinkley, EH. 1999. *Caught off guard: teachers rethinking censorship and controversy.* Boston: Allyn & Bacon.

Cloonan, M. 1996. *Banned!: censorship of popular music in Britain: 1967–92.* Aldershot: Arena.

Coetzee, JM. 1996. *Giving offense: essays on censorship.* Chicago: University of Chicago Press.

Fuller, J. 1996. *Restricted entry: censorship on trial.* Vancouver: Press Gang Publishers.

Garry, PM. 1993. *An American paradox: censorship in a nation of free speech.* Westport, CT: Praeger.

Healey, K (ed). 1997. *Censorship.* Balmain, NSW: Spinney Press.

Hepple, A. 1960. *Censorship and press control in South Africa.* Johannesburg: [s.n.].

Lehr, SS. 1995. *Battling dragons: issues and controversy in children's literature.* Portsmouth, NH: Heinemann.

Phillips, J. 1999. *Forbidden fictions: pornography and censorship in twentieth-century French literature.* London: Pluto Press.

Selth, JP. 1993. *Ambition, discrimination, and censorship in libraries.* Jefferson, NC: McFarland.

Van Rooyen, JCW. 1987. *Censorship in South Africa: being a commentary on the application of the Publications Act.* Cape Town: Juta.

Wallace, JD. 1996. *Sex, laws, and cyberspace.* New York: M&T Books and Henry Holt.

White, H. 1997. *Anatomy of censorship: why the censors have it wrong.* Lanham: University Press of America.

# Bibliography

Article 19 World Report. 1988. *Information, freedom and censorship.* United Kingdom: Longman.
*A feebly disguised assault on the press.* 1998. [O].
    Available: http://www.mg.co.za/mg/news/98nov2/24nov-press.html
    Accessed on 2000/08/24
A vote for the DA is a vote for Israel. 2000. *Mail & Guardian,* 24–30 November:5.
Barker, M (ed). 1984. *The video nasties: freedom and censorship in the media.* London: Pluto Press.
Bauer, C & Johnson S. 1988. Friday, July 29: Cinema boss Yunus Ismael collects a "Cry Freedom" print. Friday, July 29: Cinema boss Yunus Ismael hands "Cry Freedom" to police. *Weekly Mail,* 5–11 August:16.
Bertrand, I. 1978. *Film censorship in Australia.* St. Lucia, Queensland: University of Queensland Press.
Botha, M. 1997. Censorship, in *Introduction to communication – course book 6: film and television studies,* edited by PJ Fourie. Kenwyn: Juta.
Breier, D. 1988. Biko: now SA faces world movie boycott. *Sunday Star,* 31 July:1–2.
Budd, MJ. 1999. Because of the children: decades of attempted controls of rock 'n rap music, in *Bleep! Censoring rock and rap music,* edited by BH Winfield & S Davidson. London: Greenwood Press.
Cameron B. 1988. Govt cries halt to showing Biko film. *Saturday Star,* 30 July:6.
Classification Guidelines. 2000. [O].
    Available: http://www.fpb.gov.za/classification/guideline.htm
    Accessed on 2000/07/05
Cline, VB (ed). 1974. *Where do you draw the line? An exploration into media violence, pornography and censorship.* Utah: Brigham Young University Press.
"Cry Freedom" passed with age bar but then ... State moves to curb Biko movie. 1988. *The Pretoria News,* 29 July:1.
Czarra, F & Heaps, J. 1976. *Critical issues in American government.* Belmont, CA: Allyn & Bacon.
Davis, G. 1996. *The state of porn.* [O].
    Available: http://www.mg.co.za./mg/news/96aug2/23aug-porn.html
    Accessed on 2000/08/24
De Langa, I. 1988. "Cry Freedom" a recipe for revolution: Tshungu. *The Citizen,* 29 July:5.
Du Plessis, T. 1988. Druk laai op teen SA oor verbod. *Beeld,* 30 July:1–2.
Eie Skuld. 1988. *Beeld,* 1 August:2.
Enhancing the jackboot image. 1988. *Sunday Star,* 31 July:14.
Foerstel, HN. 1997. *Free expression and censorship in America: an encyclopaedia.* London: Greenwood Press.
Frankel, D. 1999. *Natural Born Killers.* [O].
    Available: http://www.aol.eonline.com/News/Items/0,1,4444,00.html
    Accessed on 2000/11/28
Grolier Academic Encyclopaedia. 1995. Philippines: Grolier International.
Heins, M. 1993. *Sex, sin and blasphemy: a guide to America's censorship wars.* New York: The New Press.
Hutchinson, D. 1999. *Media policy: an introduction.* Oxford: Blackwell Publishers.
Hyland, P & Sammells, N (eds). 1992. *Writing & censorship in Britain.* London: Routledge.
Inglis, F. 1990. *Media theory: an introduction.* Oxford: Basil Blackwell Limited.
MacLiam, G. "Cry Freedom" a nightmare to haunt us all. *Saturday Star,* 30 July:5.
*Mail & Guardian.* 2000. 24–30 November:2.
Mathews, TD. 1994. *Censored: what they didn't allow you to see, and why: the story of film censorship in Britain.* London: Chatto & Windus.

McGreal, C. 2000. [O].
  Available: http://www.mg.co.za/mg/news/2000feb2/29feb-racism_media.html
  Accessed on 2000/07/03
Merrett, C. 1994. *A culture of censorship; secrecy and intellectual repression in South Africa.* Cape Town: David Philip.
Meyerowitz, A. 1988. Accept or dismiss it, but don't miss "Cry Freedom". *The Pretoria News,* 29 July:29.
Minervini, R. 1988. "Cry Freedom" a moving, patriotic film. *Sunday Star,* 31 July:11.
Mischke, A-M & Waldner, M. 1988. "Freedom" had g'n kat se kans. *Rapport,* 31 July:1–2.
Nelmes, J (ed). 1999. *An introduction to film studies.* 2nd edition. London: Routledge.
Nortje, M. 1988. Biko se "lot" beslis net voor fliek begin rol. *Beeld,* 29 July:1–2.
Om te weet of om nie te weet nie. 1988. *Rapport,* 31 July:3.
Phelps, G. 1975. *Film censorship.* London: Victor Gollancz.
Pretorius, W. 1988. Biko-fliek kort 'n SA vonk. *Rapport,* 31 July:1.
Savage, J. 1989. *"Asking for trouble": the South African state and the Cry Freedom saga.* [O].
  Available: http://www.und.ac.za/und/ccms/articles/freedom.htm
  Accessed on 2000/08/24
Scammell, M. 1988. Censorship and its history – a personal view, in the Article 19 World Report *Information, freedom and censorship.* United Kingdom: Longman.
South Africa. Film and Publications Bill. 1996. [O].
  Available: http://www.fxi.org.za/filmbill.htm
  Accessed on 2000/08/24
Sperling, GB & McKenzie, JE. 1990. *Getting the real story: censorship and propaganda in South Africa.* Canada: School of Journalism and Communications, University of Regina.
Steinfeld, JL. 1974. Statement of the Surgeon General concerning television and violence, in *Where do you draw the line? An exploration into media violence, pornography and censorship,* edited by VB Cline. Utah: Brigham Young University Press.
Steins, R. 1995. *Censorship: how does it conflict with freedom.* New York: Twenty-First Century Books.
Swindells, S. 2000. [O].
  Available: http://www.mg.co.za/mg/news/2000mar1/7mar-racism_media2.html
  Accessed on 2000/08/24
Taitz, L. 2000. Media not off the hook. *Sunday Times,* 27 August:2.
The terror of real-life TV. 1999. *You,* 22 April:138–139.
Van Heerden, D, Cheney, P, Jackson, D & Brooks J. 1988. Cry revenge! *Sunday Times,* 31 July:1.
Vink, M. 1988. Ons mag nie koud gelaat word. *Rapport,* 31 July:25.
Watson, C & Shuker, R. 1998. *In the public good? Censorship in New Zealand.* Palmerston North: The Dunmore Press.
Wessels, E. 1988. "Cry Freedom": Appeal Board ruling today. *Business Day,* 29 July:7.
Wistrich, E. 1978. *"I don't mind the sex it's the violence": film censorship explored.* London: Marion Boyars.
Winfield, BH & Davidson, S (eds). 1999. *Bleep! Censoring rock and rap music.* London: Greenwood Press.

## Web sites
*Mail & Guardian:* http://www.mg.co.za/news.html
Media Institute of Southern Africa: http://www.misanet.org/
The Freedom of Expression Institute: http://www.fxi.org.za/
The Universal Declaration of Human Rights: http://www.un.org/rights

# 19

# Globalisation, the Information Superhighway, and Development

*Pieter J Fourie*

## Overview

In Unit 13 the focus was on the role of the international flow of information in cultural imperialism. The argument was that through the media's content and technology, international media conglomerates create a global culture in which mainly Western interpretations of reality, beliefs and values are communicated. As a reaction to this kind of media and cultural imperialism, the New World Information and Communication Order (NWICO) project was initiated under the supervision of the United Nations Educational, Scientific and Cultural Organisation (UNESCO).

In this unit, we focus firstly on a similar kind of project, namely the Global Information Infrastructure project (GII Project). This project is a direct response to the development of information and communication technology (ICT) and the emergence of the information superhighway. Secondly we focus on the impact of ICT on progress in developing countries.

The growth of ICT holds many promises for economic and social development. However, if not managed effectively it carries within it the danger of a growing gap between developed (First World) and developing (Third World) countries and between the rich and the poor. From a cultural point of view, the fear is that the information superhighway provides the ideal platform for the creation of a global culture to the detriment of national and own cultural expressions, values and beliefs, and that it provides fertile ground for the expansion of media imperialism. More than ever the development of ICTs has made it possible to communicate across national borders at the speed of light.

The purpose of this unit is therefore to

- make you aware of some of the criticism and warnings against the unrealistic view of ICT as a magic wand that will solve all developmental needs and problems, and to
- provide you with a model for the critical analysis of policy issues related to ICT policy in developing countries.

In the following sections we briefly look at:
- a theory of globalisation and some of the characteristics of globalisation;
- key prerequisites for the GII to work;
- South Africa's information infrastructure objectives;
- criticism against the GII;
- key issues in ICT planning and policy;
- the sustainable development model as a prerequisite for ICT implementation;
- four scenarios about the impact of ICT on development; and
- a model for the analysis of ICT problems and solutions.

## Learning outcomes

After you have completed this unit you should be able to
- explain a theory of globalisation;
- list at least five characteristics of globalisation;
- define how globalisation impacts on your own life;
- present a précis about the achievability of the goals of the GII Project;
- list at least ten South African information infrastructure goals;
- evaluate the South African goals in terms of control, access, quality and participation against the background of your own experience of the availability and your use of ICT;
- describe at least five issues in ICT policy and motivate why you see the five issues as important for developing countries;
- visit an ICT Web site and obtain the latest statistics on the availability of telecommunication services or Internet services in South Africa, in Africa and in a developed country;
- motivate why the sustainable development model should or should not form the basis of ICT planning and implementation in developing countries;
- position South Africa in one of the four global scenarios for the future of information and communication technology; and
- formulate an ICT-related problem and analyse the problem according to the model for problem analysis and solutions.

### 19.1 INTRODUCTION: A THEORY AND SOME CHARACTERISTICS OF GLOBALISATION

Many disciplines, such as sociology, psychology, political science and economics concern themselves with one or another aspect of globalisation. This has contributed to a number of social, economic, cultural and political theories and research about globalisation. Some theories and research emphasise the positive dimensions of globalisation and its contributions especially to economic development, while others tend to emphasise its negative impact on humanity and society. In the fields of communication and information sciences the emphasis is on the role of the media and information and communication technologies such as telecommunications and computer technologies in globalisation. Many theorists such as Waters (1995), Castells (1996; 1997; 1998), and Giddens (1990; 1999), to name a few, have contributed extensively to our knowledge of the globalisation phenomenon. Here we look at the theory of one of them, namely that of Giddens.

### 19.1.1 Giddens' theory of globalisation

In his series of five BBC lectures, the renowned British sociologist Anthony Giddens (1999:1–5) pointed out that the global spread of the term "globalisation" is evidence of the developments to which it refers. As little as ten years ago the term was hardly used, either in academic literature or in everyday language. Now the term is almost everywhere and used by businessmen, academics, politicians and ordinary people alike. But what is globalisation?

For Giddens, globalisation is a social process involving a growing number of people all over the world whose lives are affected on a daily basis by disembedded organisations, in other words not local or national organisations. The disembedded organisations that increasingly affects our lives can range from international financial, political, governmental, educational and cultural organisations, to media organisations that provide us with information and entertainment which, in turn, contribute to our perceptions and understanding of reality and the world.

In his theory of globalisation (cf. *Globalization: Giddens' dilemma* 2000; Giddens 1990) Giddens argues that the process(es) of globalisation already started with modernisation. Modernisation (following the stage of pre-modernism characterised by traditionalism) was caused by and involved major changes in what Giddens calls four major institutional complexes (or in the ways in which people were governed, goods were produced, the economic system, and the ways in which wars were conducted). The four institutional complexes are:

- Administrative power: by this Giddens means the development of the secular nation-state. Prior to modernisation people were governed in a feudal system by kings, queens landlords, the church, and so forth. The nation-state is based upon rational and bureaucratic forms of administration, and law and order by states within the confines of national geographical borders.
- Industrialisation: the development of technology displaced traditional forms of production and products and introduced a move from agriculture to factory and industrial production.
- Capitalism: the move from agricultural to industrial production introduced capitalism and the concepts of "private ownership", "competition", "profit" and "profit-making".
- Militarism: against the background of industrialisation, the production (manufacturing) of warfare was industrialised (mechanised) and professional armies were introduced.

Giddens (cf. *Globalization: Giddens' dilemma* 2000) then explains that the changes that took place in these institutional complexes were the result of what he calls time-space distantiation.

Time-space distantiation can be explained as follows. To begin with, we distinguish between pre-modern (or traditional) society and modern society. How did people relate to time and space in traditional society compared to in modern society? For Giddens, the invention of the clock was one of the main historical moments that introduced the change from pre-modern to modern society (see Figure 19.1).

|  | Pre-modern society | Modern society |
| --- | --- | --- |
| **Time** | Linked to seasons and seasonal change. No clock and no conceptualisation of national and international time. | The invention of the clock changed people's conceptualisation of time. Time no longer seasonally linked or linked between day and night. The clock not based on seasonal time but on artificial social time. Time is linear and not cyclical. Time measured universally and not locally. This also introduced a sense of cultural distance (it is now 8.30 p.m. in South Africa, but in Europe it is 9.30 p.m.). |
| **Space** | Space confined to the local, e.g. the farm, the local village. Thus a narrow sense of space, both geographically and socially. People seldom moved beyond the borders of their particular communities. Ideas of space were fixed: people hardly knew about "other parts of the world". In other words, the majority of people (mainly peasants) were embedded in their local communities. | The invention of the clock also started to change our sense of space as communities began to calibrate its sense of time with other communities. People increasingly began to move beyond the borders of their local communities. |
| **Status** | Social status was ascribed at birth, be it a peasantry status, landlord status, royalty. There was little sense of what we today know as "a career". | The concept of "social mobility" is introduced. |

**Figure 19.1 Pre-modern compared to modern society (the concept of time, space and status)**

In short, Giddens argues that modernisation and modernity are based upon a process whereby a fixed and narrow idea of "space" as "place" (prevalent in pre-modern times) is gradually eroded by an ever increasingly dominant concept of (universal) time. Giddens describes this conceptualisation of time as the key to processes of disembedding (cf. *Globalization: Giddens' dilemma* 2000).

For Giddens (op cit), disembedding and disembedment is one of the main characteristics of globalisation. He distinguishes between two types of disembedment:
- a change in symbolic tokens and the universality of symbolic tokens
- development of trust in and reliance on expert systems.

Under symbolic tokens, money (monetary systems) can be used as an example. The economy of pre-modern societies was based on products being exchanged (bartered) for the right to live on a landlord's property, to "pay" for goods, and so on. For example, labour was exchanged for food and a house; livestock, crops and other products were given in exchange for the right to live in the house and farm the landlord's property. The keyword was exchange of goods and products. Modernisation changed these forms of "payment" and replaced it with a universal form of payment (symbolic token), namely with money. Money (as a universal symbolic form of payment) made it possible for people to move between communities and countries, which in turn made the establishment of new social, cultural and economic relations possible.

Thus, modernisation introduced the notion of a national currency, which wiped out local differences within national boundaries. Today, globalisation is beginning to wipe out differences between national currencies. For example, in Europe national currencies such as the French franc, Belgian franc or the Dutch guilder are replaced by the eurodollar. Modernisation also introduced the credit card as a universal form of payment issued by a bank in one country. The same card can be used all over the world.

By expert systems Giddens means:
- a general increase in specialisation
- universal standardised systems or models, for example a universal model for health care or a universal educational model
- a growth of trust in and reliance on science (for example medical science)
- a growth of trust in and reliance on technology, for example trust in the computerised regulation of air traffic.

To summarise the above: The processes of globalisation started with the move from pre-modern to modern societies. Modernism brought along changes in the ways in which people were governed (administrative power); the way they produced and manufactured goods (industrialisation); the way they sold goods – with profit-making as a primary goal (capitalism); and the way in which warfare was produced and armies constituted. Among many contributing factors, it was the invention of the clock which began to change people's conceptualisation of time and space from the seasonal and local to an awareness of universal time, other communities, locations and geographies. These changes also contributed to new symbolic tokens (of which we have only referred to money) and the introduction of expert systems (cf. *Globalization: Giddens' dilemma* 2000).

A further step in Giddens' theory of globalisation is to divide modernity into two phases: early modernity and late (or high) modernity. The above changes formed part of early modernity. An outstanding feature of late modernity is globalisation. What we are experiencing now, namely globalisation, is thus only part of late modernity. Some authors and theorists also refer to late modernity as post-modernity or postmodernism. According to Giddens, globalisation as a characteristic of late modernity "started" in the 1960s.

For our purpose (media studies) some of the outstanding features of globalisation discussed by Giddens are the following:

- The development of a world capitalist system dominated by Trans-National Corporations (TNCs) operating independently from nation states (e.g. the World Bank, the International Monetary Fund (IMF)). These TNCs often dictate (in the form of economic pressure and measures) to nation states. It is exactly against the development of TNCs and their impact on national economies (especially those of smaller developing countries) that Non-Government Organisations (NGOs) are increasingly protesting; for example at IMF meetings. In general there is a sense of loss of control over own economic affairs and among people and smaller nations a growing awareness of the widening gap between rich and poor.
- The growth of the so-called *culture industry*, including the growth of the media and international media corporations and all their products have created the so-called information and knowledge society. The main characteristic of this society is that the volume, spread and availability of knowledge and information (often redundant information) have increased to a level not known before in the history of humanity. This has far-reaching consequences. The accelerated availability of constantly changing information and knowledge, and with it a perceived dependence on information and knowledge for survival, has created an existential dilemma. Whereas in pre-modernity and early modernity people relied more on religion, tradition and providence, they now rely (or are made to believe to rely) on knowledge and information. People (and small and poor nations) who do not have access to knowledge and information feel left out and threatened. In short, they are often overruled and experience a loss of status. Small wonder then that Giddens calls this new reliance on knowledge and information the main existential dilemma of globalisation. As far as tradition is concerned, Giddens (op cit) argues that on the political level globalisation has exhausted the old politics of "left" and "right". In early modernity it was possible to distinguish more clearly between the traditions of conservatism, liberalism and labourism. Lately, such distinctions are blurred, as are the distinctions between class. On the cultural level there is in general a (existential) feeling of loss of space and character.
- The above, however, have contributed to a process running concurrently with globalisation, namely the processes and emergence of what is known as localisation.

Although it may seem as if globalisation is all about interrelatedness (on the economic, cultural, military and governance levels) there is at the same time a rediscovery and re-appreciation of the local. Although some people, groups and nations may experience globalisation as a threat to their own cultures, beliefs and ideals, at the same time it creates new opportunities for the globalisation of their cultures, beliefs and ideals (although these may only became part of a new world culture). For example, through the media's spread of information and knowledge we are today more than ever aware of the beliefs, practices and ideals of distant cultures, of the suffering of people and nations, of the crime and corruption of dictatorial regimes and even of the arguments of those opposing globalisation.

The above is a very brief introduction to Giddens' theory of globalisation. We will return to some of its features, trends and characteristics in the following section. Here it remains to say that his theory is not without criticism. Many authors claim that the processes now described as typical of globalisation have occurred throughout the history of human beings and that what we now call the processes of globalisation are nothing more than a continuation of processes started centuries ago as part of the evolutionary development of human control over nature. For example, what we term the "information revolution" can easily be explained as a process that started with the invention of the printing press in the fifteenth century – an invention with, at that time, the same far-reaching consequences as we are experiencing today with computer technology. The big difference is the speed with which the changes are taking place and increased geographical spread. The reason why we have focused on Giddens is, for our purpose, his emphasis on the role of information and knowledge in our times.

### 19.1.2 The characteristics (trends) of globalisation

Against the background of this brief introduction it is possible to list some characteristics (or trends) of globalisation. It is important to take into account that some of these characteristics are contradictory and that by the time of publication some of them may have changed or even moved in an opposite direction! This points to the fact that at this stage globalisation is difficult to define or pinpoint, which may be so because globalisation is still an emerging phenomenon moving in the direction of the creation of a new kind of society – the so-called global society. We list the following characteristics:

- *Globalisation is an all-encompassing phenomenon involving economic, political, technological and cultural transformation.* A new world economic order in which local economies are integrated into a global economy is developing. On the political level the ways in which nations are governed are becoming more globally transparent and nations are increasingly entering into interstate and regional agreements. All this is made possible by increased technological developments which in many ways form the foundation of globalisation and accelerate cultural diffusion creating what is called a global culture in for example fashion, entertainment, culinary habits, information sharing, and so on.

- *Communication technology and systems play a central role in globalisation.* According to Giddens (1999), new electronic ways of conveying news and information have altered the very texture of our lives. To explain this Giddens uses the example of Nelson Mandela. He argues that when the image of Nelson Mandela is more familiar to us (people all over the world) than the face of our next door neighbour, something has changed in the nature of our everyday experience. Nelson Mandela is a global celebrity, and celebrity itself is largely a product of new communications technology. The reach of media technologies is growing with each wave of innovation. It took, for example, forty years for radio in the United States to gain an audience of fifty million. The same number of people were using personal computers only fifteen years after the personal computer was introduced. It needed a mere four years, after it was made available for fifty million Americans to be regularly using the Internet (cf. Giddens 1999:3).
- *Globalisation does not only affect macro structures and institutions but also the personal aspects of our lives.* Family structures as the basic building block of a society are changing as are the relationships between the sexes and between races; minority and pressure groups are becoming more important, to mention a few of the changes we are experiencing almost on a daily basis. Smaller families and family planning are the order of the day; women are becoming more equal to men and are playing leadership roles as never before in history; relationships between homosexuals and lesbians are legalised; racial issues are pushed to the fore; and the interests and issues of minority and pressure groups (even of those protesting globalisation and its impact on the economy and culture) are on the world agenda. Giddens (1999) points to the fact that as a reaction to this, fundamentalism may seem to be growing but this is only as a consequence of the irreversible impact of globalisation on the very nature of society. The role of the media in all this is that the global media and media content have opened up discussions about these changes and groups and contribute to more liberal thinking about them; question traditional views, and point to the restrictive and discriminatory in traditional views and values.
- *Globalisation leads (contradictorily) to the revival of local cultural identities.* At the same time, and on the face of it contrary to the above, globalisation is also the reason for the revival of local cultural identities in different parts of the world. Most people think of globalisation simply as the disappearance of local communities into the global arena. This may be true, but only partially. Although nations and their governments may be more intertwined and linked than ever before (through numerous political, economic and military agreements and through their media institutions and media content), there is at the same time a move towards a rediscovery of own national and cultural identities and the recognition thereof by governments. In numerous parts of the world, liberalisation groups are at work fighting for the acknowledgement of their freedom and recognition of their independence. One can even argue that the acknowledgement of the right of the African National Congress to govern the majority of South Africa's people and the

recognition of the rights of black people in South Africa were, amongst other factors, a direct consequence of globalisation. In this regard the world media opened the world's eyes to the plight of black people in South Africa which in its turn led world leaders to pressurise for the abandonment of apartheid.

- *Globalisation is humanly inspired.* It is exactly the above that leads Giddens (1999) to emphasise that we should always remember that globalisation is not something forced upon us by nature. It is the making of human thinking. We tend to believe that economy and technology (as the two main driving forces of globalisation) are something above us, which they are not. The collapse of Soviet Communism wasn't something that just happened to occur, but was the making of human thinking inspired by the recognition of the fact that since the seventies the Soviet Union and the East European countries were rapidly falling behind the West in terms of economic growth. The ideological and cultural control upon which communist political authority was based similarly could not survive in an era of global media. Because of communication technology the Soviet and the East European regimes were unable to block the reception of Western radio and TV broadcasts. Television played a direct role in the 1989 revolutions, which have rightly been called the first "television revolutions". Street protests taking place in one country were watched by audiences in other countries in which large numbers then took to the streets themselves (cf. Giddens 1999). The same applies to the collapse of apartheid. Apart from economic sanctions against the apartheid government, the worldview against apartheid, through the globalising effects of the content of international communication and information became so overpowering that the apartheid government could no longer hold.

- *Globalisation widens inequalities.* To many living outside Europe and North America, Giddens (1999) argues, globalisation looks like Westernisation or Americanisation. No one can doubt the status of the US as now being the sole superpower. The US has a dominant economic, cultural and military position in the global order. Many of the most visible cultural expressions of globalisation are American, for example, Coca-Cola, McDonald's, big names in the fashion, industrial and financial world, the products of Hollywood, dominance in the provision of popular television programming such as soap operas, and so on. Most of the giant multinational companies are based in the USA. Those that aren't come from the rich countries. A pessimistic view of globalisation would consider it largely an affair of the industrial North, in which the developing societies of the South play little or no active part. In such a view, globalisation is seen as destroying local cultures, widening world inequalities and worsening the lot of the impoverished. Globalisation, some argue, creates a world of winners and losers; a few on the fast track to prosperity, the majority condemned to a life of misery and despair. Giddens (1999) provides the following statistics:
    - The share of the poorest fifth of the world's population in global income has dropped from 2,3 percent to 1,4 percent over the past ten years. The proportion taken by the richest fifth, on the other hand, has risen from 70 percent to 85 percent.

- In Sub-Saharan Africa, twenty countries have lower incomes per head in real terms than they did two decades ago.
- In many less developed countries, safety and environmental regulations are low or virtually non-existent. Some transnational companies sell goods there that are controlled or banned in the industrial countries – poor quality medical drugs, destructive pesticides or high tar and nicotine content cigarettes.

- *Globalisation involves a mix of nationalities (and their cultures) to such an extent that in some parts of the world one can even speak of "reversed colonialism".* One has only to look at the population of big world cities such as London, Paris, New York, Los Angeles and Brussels where there is a mix of nationalities to such an extent that it is often difficult to recognise the "true" citizens of the country to which the city belongs. This is mainly due to the relaxation of immigration laws, the relative ease with which work permits can be obtained, increased tourism, but also the infiltration of illegal workers and political asylum seekers. Eventually all this impacts on the culture and economy of the resident countries. Giddens (1999) specifically refers to the Latinising of Los Angeles.

    Apart from "cultural de-colonialisation", "de-colonialisation" also takes place on the industrial level where there is an increase of smaller countries exporting their products to the major industrialised countries. Giddens (1999) refers to the emergence of a globally-oriented high-tech sector in India, the selling of Brazilian TV programmes to Portugal, the export of African art to the rest of the world, and, as a latest fashion, the export of Eastern furniture to the West, and so on.

- *Globalisation changes the nature of the nation-state.* One of the crucial topics addressed by Giddens (1999; 2000) is the influence of globalisation on the existence of the nation-state. Is a nation-state, for example South Africa as an independent state still in full control of its own policies and governance of the South African people? Are national political leaders still powerful, or are they becoming largely irrelevant to the forces shaping the world? Against the background of internationalisation policies leading to international and regional agreements on almost every level of society, Giddens (1999) argues that nation-states are indeed still powerful and national political leaders still have a large role to play in the world. However, in their role the emphasis is no longer in terms of facing *real enemies*, but rather in terms of facing and managing strategic, economic, technological and cultural *risks*. For example, the risks of purchasing and implementing multibillion ICT systems (as will be explained later on), the risks of arms agreements, of importing and exporting, of formulating immigrations laws, of entering into international environment protection agreements, and so on. This move from facing real enemies to facing and managing risks, is a massive shift in the very nature of the nation-state and the role of national political leaders.

- *Globalisation is the emergence of a global cosmopolitan society.* Closely related to what has already been referred to as the mix of nationalities (or the fusion of nationalities and cultures), one can argue that globalisation is above all about the emergence of a global cosmopolitan society. Given the above characteristics or trends of globalisation we are experiencing the emergence of a new kind of society which differs from the known experiences of pre- early and late modernity (some critics and authors refer to this new society as post-modernity). Giddens (1999; 2000) concludes that we continue to talk of the nation, the family, work, tradition, culture, as if they are all the same as in the past. They are not. The outer shell remains, but inside all is different – and this is happening not only in the USA, Britain or France, but almost everywhere. They are what Giddens (1999) calls "shell institutions". They are institutions that have become inadequate to the tasks they are called upon to perform.

As the changes to them gather weight, they are creating something that has never existed before; a global cosmopolitan society. He then points to the fact that

> ... we are the first generation to live in this society, whose contours we can as yet only dimly see. It is shaking up our existing ways of life, no matter where we happen to be. This is not – at least at the moment – a global order driven by collective human will. Instead, it is emerging in an anarchic, haphazard fashion, carried along by a mixture of economic, technological and cultural imperatives. It is not settled or secure, but fraught with anxieties, as well as scarred by deep divisions. Many of us feel in the grip of forces over which we have no control. Can we re-impose our will upon them? I believe we can. The powerlessness we experience is not a sign of personal failings, but reflects the incapacities of our institutions. We need to reconstruct those we have [such as our economic, educational, cultural and military institutions – PJF] or create new ones, in ways appropriate to the global age. We should and we can look to achieve greater control over our runaway world. We shan't be able to do so if we shirk the challenges, or pretend that all can go on as before. For globalisation is not incidental to our lives today. It is a shift in our very life circumstance. It is the way we now live.
>
> (Giddens 1999:5)

Against the background of these introductory notes on the nature of globalisation we now turn to the specific role of ICT in globalisation and its influence on development in developing countries. We do this keeping Giddens' warning in mind, namely that we need to reconstruct our institutions appropriate to the global age, and we need to achieve greater control of our institutions, including our media and communications institutions as cornerstone institutions of the age of globalisation.

The purpose of the rest of our discussion is to show how important ICT planning is and how it should be approached cautiously in developing countries.

## 19.2 GLOBALISATION, INFORMATION and COMMUNICATION TECHNOLOGY AND DEVELOPMENT

According to O'Sullivan, Hartley, Saunders, Montgomery and Fiske (1994:130), one of the main issues in globalisation is that national culture and identity are replaced by a global-local dimension and that everyday experience of the local is now saturated with references to the global. Central to this process has been the emergence of information and communication technology and its media networks which allow for faster, more extensive, interdependent forms of worldwide exchange, travel and interaction. In communication science these concerns have led to numerous debates about media imperialism and to the formulation of a New World Information and Communication Order (NWICO) (cf. Unit 13 for a discussion of the NWICO).

Lately the NWICO is overshadowed by a new buzz-word, namely the "information superhighway" – a metaphorical concept that refers to all our contemporary means of communicating through a network of high-tech communication networks made possible by state-of-the art ICTs across borders in almost real time. The "hype" about the economic fortunes associated with ICT and the so-called possibilities of growth that ICT may create for developing countries somewhat obscures the NWICO's concerns about media content, the meanings signified by the media's content and the content's contributions to a global culture in which the emphasis is on dominant Western values and beliefs.

### 19.2.1 The Global Information Infrastructure project (GII Project)

One can argue that the information superhighway was firmly placed on our earthly map when the G-7 countries (USA, Japan, United Kingdom, France, Germany, Italy, and Canada) met in 1995 for the Brussels Summit to discuss the Global Information Infrastructure project (the GII Project). Prior to the Brussels Summit, and in preparation thereof, the then vice-president of the USA, Al Gore, declared at the 1994 conference of the International Telecommunications Union in Buenos Aires, Argentina, that "... the development of the GII must be a democratic effort... In a sense, the GII will be a metaphor for democracy itself ... I see a new Athenian Age of democracy forged in the fora the GII will create" (Gore, 1994).

A few years on and we can ask if this remark wasn't a vast exaggeration.

The purpose of the Brussels Summit was to concentrate on a regulatory framework and competition policy in the field of telecommunications and related ICTs, the implementation of information infrastructures and their accessibility for the public, and the social and cultural aspects of the information society.

The G-7 Final Declaration stated, amongst others, that key prerequisites and objectives for a global information infrastructure to work are:

- dynamic competition
- private investment
- the promotion of universal service (meaning access to the information infrastructure for all)
- dialogue on worldwide cooperation such that industrialised countries will work towards the participation of developing countries in the global information society
- democratic control of both the information infrastructure and information content provision

- the acknowledgement of access to information as a basic right of every citizen
- that the benefits of the information society should not be limited to business but should be available to society as a whole
- acknowledgement of the right of the public to be properly informed which means the right to receive a full, impartial, accurate, and independent account of events
- acknowledgement of the right of all people, including ordinary citizens to participate and be involved with policy for and the use of the information infrastructure.

Although these objectives may be praiseworthy, the question is whether they are attainable? Critics argue that much of this master plan remains nothing but political rhetoric, that developing countries do not have the financial means to achieve the ideals of the Project, and that in the end only rich countries, rich people and the big international ICT and capitalist-driven ICT industries will gain from it. We will return to this criticism later on.

### 19.2.2 The Global Information Infrastructure and South Africa: objectives

As far as the GII Project is concerned, South Africa has not been left out in the cold. In 1996 the South African government hosted the Information Society and Development Conference of the G-7 countries. At this conference a number of information infrastructure goals were proposed for South Africa, and within each a number of projects were identified and accepted. The goals are (cf. ISAD 1996):

- The setting up of integrated information systems to meet people's needs such as:
  - telematics projects in epidemiological surveillance
  - a telemedicine and interactive health network
  - interconnection of hospitals to improve access to international literature and distance diagnosis
  - natural resource management
  - regional environmental information systems
  - satellite communication to improve telecommunications services in rural and remote areas.
- Improved universal access, for example the
  - establishment of multi-purpose community telecentres
  - use of ICT in training and the empowerment of disabled people
  - use of ICT in youth development projects.
- The development of appropriate applications and content, for instance centres of excellence, expertise and resources.
- Human resource development, for instance the development of courses in ICT policy and management, the improvement of distance education, school networks and to link schools globally.
- Support for business, for instance the development of ICT trade points for the gathering and dissemination of trade-related information.

# MEDIA STUDIES

- Support for good governance, for instance a one-stop information service providing access to a range of government information.
- Cultural heritage, for instance a culture and tourism network.
- Building the ICT infrastructure, for instance satellite communications for remote areas providing a range of services.
- Reach-out services to regional countries with special circumstances, such as to those regional countries that have faced civil strive and are prone to natural disasters.

To ascertain how much South Africa has achieved in this regard since 1996 is not the purpose of this unit. This can be done through a study of the annual reports of key role players in the ICT sector, including the South African Government's Department of Communications (for this we also provide a list of Web sites under the heading Further reading at the end of this unit). It suffices to say that the South African White Paper on Telecommunications (1996) and the new Telecommunications Act (1996) provide for such developments, including for telecommunications and ICT sector reform, a working capital programme, the establishment of software centres, digitalisation, the training of skilled workers, strategic partnerships, improved ICT and basic telephony access through a Universal Service Agency (USA), and regulation by the Southern African Telecommunications Authority (SATRA), now incorporated within the Independent Communications Authority of South Africa (ICASA). In March 2000 the Government published intended telecommunications policy directions providing for, amongst others:

- changes in the market structure, including the institution of a second (to Telkom) national operator and thereby ending Telkom's monopoly
- the restructuring of the Universal Service Agency (USA)
- contributions to the Universal Service Fund
- the provision of telecommunication services to public education institutions, and so on (cf. South Africa. 2001. Department of Communications; Competitor for Telkom... 2001).

However, despite the ideals, the need for and the potential of South Africa to become a full member of the information society, care should be taken to avoid the pitfall of the euphoria accompanying the information superhighway. As has been the case in other developing countries, a real danger exists that as far as economic growth and development are concerned, only few ordinary people have gained from ICT. This is especially the case when basic needs such as housing, the provision of electricity, the provision of running water in houses, basic health care, the provision of basic telephone services, and basic educational needs have not yet been met.

As an example of needs, the statistics in Figure 19.2 and Figure 19.3 below speak for themselves. Although these figures may be dated by the time of publication, they nevertheless provide an idea of the extent of poverty and telecommunications needs in the country. Figure 19.4 provides details of Internet usage in South Africa. (For comparative figures with other developed and developing countries see, amongst others, the Web sites listed under Further reading.)

# Globalisation, the Information Superhighway, and Development

> **Poverty in South Africa**
> - 48% of households in Free State and in Eastern Cape live on R800 (the poverty line) or less per month, 38% in Northern Province, 12% in Gauteng and Western Cape, 37% in Northwest, 35% in Northern Cape, 26% in KwaZulu-Natal and 25% in Mpumalanga.
> - 12% of South African households are without toilets.
> - More than 50% of South African households have no running water in the house.
> - Almost 50% of South African houses have three or less rooms.
> - A third of South African households live in shacks.

**Figure 19.2 Poverty in South Africa**

*Source:* Poverty in South Africa (based on statistics released by Statistics South Africa (SSA)) in *Rapport,* 10 September 2000.

> **Basic telecommunication services in South Africa(1999)**
> Population: 37 000 000
> Telephone lines connected: 4 768 000
> Cellular subscribers: 2 540 000
> Telephone lines per 100 people: 11,2
> Rural telephone lines per 100 people: 2,2
> Public telephones: 127 272

**Figure 19.3 Basic telecommunication services in South Africa**

*Source:* BMI-TechKnowledge. 1999. *Communication Technologies Handbook 1999.* Johannesburg: BMI-T Group. (For updated figures consult BMI-TechKnowledge. 2000. *Communication Technologies Handbook 2000.* Johannesburg: BMI-T Group; or Telkom's latest Annual Report.)

> **Internet usage in South Africa**
> In May 2000 South Africa had 1,82-million Internet users.
>
> | Category | 1998 | 1999 |
> | --- | --- | --- |
> | Dial-up users: | 366 000 | 560 000 |
> | Corporate users: | 700 000 | 980 000 |
> | Academic users: | 200 000 | 280 000 |
> | **Total** | **1 266 000** | **1 820 000** |
>
> New users in 1999: 554 000
> Percentage growth: 44%
>
> - Taken together, these three categories amount to 1 820 000 Internet users in South Africa at the end of December 1999. Research indicates that it would be safe to forecast the number to grow to around 2,4 million by the end of 2000.

## MEDIA STUDIES

> - The rapid growth over the period between October 1997 and December 1998, fuelled by the marketing campaigns of several newcomers to the Internet, resulted in the Internet reaching a critical mass of consumers in South Africa. However, for the first time since the Internet was established as a consumer-oriented industry in South Africa, the rate of growth slowed down significantly during 1999. It is foreseen that this slow-down in the rate of growth will intensify during 2000.
> - Dial-up users: This figure, up from 366 000 at the end December 1998, amounts to 194 000 new users, representing growth of 53% in 1999 (growth in 1998 was 86%).
> - Corporate users: Growth in leased line connectivity is less rapid than in the past, indicating greater saturation of the market and slow-down of access to infrastructure. The survey showed growth of 40% over the preceding 12 months.
> - Academic users: The total student population Uninet (research and academic network) serves – and therefore potentially has access to the Internet – is more than 600 000. While a majority of these still do not use their access, e-mail has become a vital research and communications tool for more students than ever before. Based on feedback from university network administrators, the probable minimum for students actually using this access is about 250 000. Privately funded schools connectivity probably accounts for a further 30 000, bringing the total academic user base to 280 000.

**Figure 19.4 Internet usage in South Africa**
*Source*: Media Africa. 2000. *4th South African Internet Services Industry Survey 2000*. [O]. http://www.mediaafarica.co.za Accessed on 11 September 2000. (Also see http://www.southafrica.co.za/survey for updated Internet user survey figures.)

Against the background of the above figures it is important to be constantly aware of the fact that to develop an information infrastructure, to be part of the information superhighway and to gain from its possible benefits, costs billions of rands. In developing countries, often under pressure from transnational ICT companies, the question should be asked if this kind of money can't be better spent on basic needs and the alleviation of poverty.

With this question in mind we now look at some of the criticism against the GII Project.

### 19.2.3 Criticism against the Global Information Infrastructure (GII)

In technology debates we distinguish between two forms of criticism, namely liberal and Luddite critique. In liberal critique the emphasis is on the anti-social potential of ICT. This form of critique nevertheless maintains that as long as people are alert to the dangers of ICT, development will be appropriate and socially beneficial. The main focus is that the information society should be the outcome of an informed democratic process. In Luddite critique the main point of departure is that although technology itself may be neutral, it is in the hands of and managed by people and groups whose primary interest is in making money and not necessarily in the possible social good of ICT.

As an example of liberal criticism we focus on some of the arguments of Cees Hamelink (1997:415–424). For the analysis of grand projects, plans or orders such as the NWICO and the GII Project, Hamelink suggests that we ask critical questions about
- control
- access
- quality, and
- participation.

Using these four factors as criteria he shows how the NWICO has achieved very little and how the GII is following suit.

## Control

Hamelink (op cit) argues that as far as democratic and participatory control of information is concerned, the GII has, until now, not succeeded. To the contrary, there has rather been a consolidation of control over the provision of information during the 1990s. The major players are actively striving to gain control over the production of messages (ranging from digital libraries to TV entertainment), the operation of distribution systems (ranging from satellites to digital switches), and the manufacture of the equipment for the reception and processing of information. There is no indication that the major role players in the ICT sector are more willing to be held accountable than they were in the 1970s.

## Access

As far as access is concerned, Hamelink emphasises that there are different schools of thought (1997:421). One school restricts the notion of "universal service" to "*availability*". Availability means that all citizens should have access to basic communication services at affordable prices. Another school proposes that apart from availability, access also means that people should also be able to "*use*" communication services at profitable prices. In other words, the *ability* to use communication services, content and ICT also form part of access, and training towards such ability should be part of providing a universal service.

A further question that must be asked is which services should be labelled as universal. For example, only basic telephony services (a telephone line within reasonable distance), or a host of value-added services such as access to the Internet, e-mail, fax services, and so forth. In other words, where does one draw the line as far as universal service is concerned? (Cf. South Africa. 1999. Universal Service Agency's discussion paper on *The definition of universal service and universal access within South Africa, 1999.*)

The problem of access intensifies if:

- Governments, although they acknowledge their universal service obligations, want the private sector to pay for it.
- Universal service provision is left to a market driven by commercial interests.

- Third World countries without the necessary ICT infrastructure "leapfrog" into the information society as many of them are committed to do and are often pressurised to do by transnational ICT organisations and transnational agreements. This has often led to the rapid development of digital capital cities that may become part of the global network, leaving the rural populations once again behind (cf. Hamelink 1997:422).

> **Universal service in South Africa**
>
> In 2000 the South African Department of Communications defined universal service as the provision of a telephone line within a reasonable distance of 30 minutes travelling. The Universal Service Agency (USA) was launched in May 1997. It is a statutory body created in terms of the Telecommunications Act of 1996, and its objectives include advising the Minister on ways to bring about universal access and service, coordinating initiatives by service providers such as Telkom, Vodacom and Mobile Telephone Network (MTN), and to extend access to telecommunications by working with community-based organisations (CBOs), non-governmental organisations (NGOs), donor organisations and businesses. The agency manages the Universal Service Fund to which the Government has allocated R3 million in the 1997/98 financial year. The fund, which holds a percentage of funds allocated from the licences of all telecommunications suppliers, is intended to support projects that increase universal access to service.

**Figure 19.5 Universal service**

*Sources*: South African Government, Department of Communications. 2000. http://docweb.pwv.gov.za

National Information Technology Forum. 2000. http://www.sn.apc.org/nitf

## *Quality*

As far as *quality* is concerned, Hamelink (1997:423) asks if the GII will be able to deliver quality information? Isn't it more likely that the information superhighway will mainly provide opportunities for teleshopping, video games, pornography, and so on? The closest the world gets to the projected global information superhighway is the Internet which is emerging as "one of the most exciting places for doing business" and very little else, especially if one thinks about development and development needs. According to Hamelink, the Internet has been guided by the rule of sharing information free and has now been discovered as a major vehicle for commercial advertising. One may ask whether this contributes to the quality of development and adheres to development needs in, for example, education?

## *Participation*

Hamelink (1997:423) argues that just like the NWICO, the GII Project is steered by the interests and stakes of governments and corporations. It is the bilateral playing field of "princes" and "merchants", and *ordinary* people are occasionally addressed as citizens or consumers, but they play no essential role. The GII Project therefore needs to persuade people that the information society will bring them great improvements in lifestyle, comfort, and general wellbeing. This makes people important targets for marketing and propaganda; it does not make them serious partners in the project. In short, there is no serious involvement of *people's movements* in the making of the GII. There are no trilateral negotiations among governments, industrialists, and *social movements* to decide on a future that we all may want. The GII Project, argues Hamelink, is guided by a *"democratization-from-above"* and doomed to fail in making world communication more democratic (op cit:424).

In this regard one may ask whether all the different policy groups, NGOs, and movements presently involved with ICT information policymaking in South Africa aren't just a new élite? How representative are they? What is the real extent of the public's involvement and are the public's real needs addressed?

## 19.3 ICT PLANNING AND POLICY

Hamelink's criticism is one example of the kind of criticism against the prospects of the information superhighway. As we have seen, the main concern is with democratic control, access, and use.

However, despite criticism of this kind there is no doubt that the information revolution created by contemporary ICT is real and not something imaginary in the minds of technologists and economists. Statistics show that

- the diffusion of information technology is increasing worldwide
- at present no technological limits are in sight
- a global information infrastructure *is* emerging.

These developments have a remarkable influence on especially economic transformation:
- market economies are beginning to prevail worldwide
- global trade and investment are increasing
- global competition increases
- firms compete with knowledge, networking and agility, and
- industries are transforming.

It is foreseen that these economic developments will also lead to increased social transformation in the sense that they can contribute to increased:
- social reorganisation: the razing of cultural barriers and economic inequalities
- institutionalised accountability: increasing availability of information will lead to less secrecy in public affairs
- a rise in the environmental agenda: increased awareness of environmental issues
- an increased global social agenda leading to higher standards of human development in the treatment of disease and the provision of education
- increased worldwide distribution of cultural, intellectual and artistic products.

The question is how to get developing countries aboard? Talero and Gaudette (1995:20) warn that

> ... failures and horror stories litter the history of the information industry. Even the success stories, when scrutinized, reveal formidable social and technical complexities. The power of information technology, which has so much potential for social good, can also be harnessed for selfish, dangerous, or even destructive ends.

A first prerequisite for success is the planning and formulation of sound ICT policy. In the following section we provide a checklist of some of the aspects that ICT policy should take care of to safeguard the interests of the public and to contribute to development.

### 19.3.1 ICT policy: a checklist

#### *Policy should provide for sound financial planning, financial management and training*

Talero and Gaudette (op cit) emphasise that it is a fact that developing countries need to marshal substantial resources, often from abroad, to achieve ICT goals. Therefore they need to establish effective incentives and management schemes to facilitate adoption and the effective use of new systems. Apart from finding the financial resources and to manage these resources efficiently, a further important prerequisite for success is the training of qualified ICT workers, policy specialists, engineers and technical support staff to operate, maintain and produce hard- and software.

#### *Policy should prevent misallocation of scarce resources*

In the development of an ICT infrastructure there is always the possibility of waste and misallocation of scarce resources. In the absence of appropriate policy incentives, adequate quality standards, and competitive discipline, a country could allocate scarce development resources to information infrastructure investments that create waste or an increase in social inequality. Such is the case, for example, when ICT services are available only to the urban rich; when incentives favour use of technology more for recreational than productive purposes; when an excessive share of investments is directed toward military purposes; and, when there is an inadequate definition of the expected benefits and inadequate measurement of the actual results. Again, note should be taken that many of the so-called benefits of ICT are likely to be uneven and unequal and have resulted in increasing polarisation of rich and poor. The notion of "comparative advantage" became more of an ideological rationale for the *status quo* than a concern for equitable exchange relationships or commitment to social justice (cf. Talero & Gaudette 1995:220).

#### *Policy should guarantee cultural preservation versus social disruption*

ICT and the actual use of ICT go hand in hand with questions and issues related to cultural preservation versus social disruption. In this regard governments should inform themselves thoroughly of the prevailing debates about media and cultural imperialism and the need for a balance between cultural production and import. Burgelman (1994; 1995) provides numerous examples of how and where the introduction of ICT failed where developers had not considered the own cultures, needs and circumstances of societies and communities.

## Policy should prevent employment inequities

Many studies show that ICT development can lead to the loss of many jobs – people being replaced by ICT technologies and, in the face of competition, companies downsizing their human resources to become more cost-effective and streamlined. Policy should assure that this consequence of technology is limited, through, amongst other measures, the provision of education and lifelong learning in the fields of ICT.

## Policy should assure that real needs and real uses are achieved

Here we should distinguish between capacity, regional versus global needs, and grassroots needs and uses.

### Capacity

Technologically advanced ICT systems are often of little or no use for specific needs, such as the needs of a small business or a small country compared to the needs of a big business or a big country. Nevertheless such advanced systems are installed. This is a waste of money and policy should ensure that this doesn't happen. Melody (1991:29) shows how the ICT systems in technologically advanced countries are being redesigned to meet the technically sophisticated digital data requirements of high-volume, multiple-purpose global users. For traditional, simpler communications requirements, such as a basic telephone service, the new upgraded systems will serve well, but at substantially increased costs to smaller users. The ICT options available to small, localised, and even regionalised businesses often do not reflect their unique needs. But what happens is that their range of choice is dictated by the national and global needs of the larger firms and government agencies. A more efficient ICT system for the needs of smaller users is being cannibalised in the creation of technologically advanced systems.

### Regional versus global needs

If developing countries and regions are to implement ICT networks that will serve their interests in local and regional economic development, the new communication systems must promote local and regional communication and information networks within the context of the particular economic, social, political and cultural needs of the region. The new systems must increase the incentive to look first inside the region for economic activity, before going outside. Efficient domestic postal, telex, and basic voice telephone networks clearly would work in this direction. These issues require a more detailed examination of all significant dimensions of local and regional economic conditions, and the particular roles that communication and information networks do play and can play in promoting local and regional networks as a priority over international and global networks (Melody 1991:39–40).

## Grassroots needs and uses

Policy should ensure that the grassroots needs of people are met. What do we really know about the public's grassroots ICT needs? Are these needs thoroughly investigated, especially in developing countries? One rarely comes across research on the impact of or need for the new communications technologies conceptualised from the point of view of the user. In this regard the following is also important to keep in mind:

- Information technologies are mainly modelled and systems designed according to the sociocultural habitat of Western users. There may be unforeseen social consequences when applying a system engineered from Western logic into a non-Western context (cf. Lind 1990).
- Some research (cf. Metoyer-Duran 1991) indicates that the information-seeking and handling behaviour of different ethnic groups vary substantially precisely because of different cultural standards, values and practices.
- The success and acceptance of new ICTs in the professional sphere cannot be extrapolated to the private public sphere (Burgelman 1994:72; Carey & Moss 1985).
- The surplus value for the user of a new technology must be taken into account. To explain the success or failure of the introduction of a new communication technology in regions where they previously did not exist, one must look at the social or economic surplus value and/or relevance which can be realised by that new technology in terms of what the user defines to be his or her surplus value (cf. Dervin & Schields 1990).
- There is also something like an "acquisition substitution": the consumer seems to consider replacing a new technology only when it substitutes an older one with better quality and/or at a lower price. This too differs fundamentally whether the consumer wants to use it for professional or public/private purposes (cf. Van den Brink 1987).

## *Policy should ensure reasonable regulation and deregulation and achieve a balance between public service obligations and free market interests*

In the ICT sector we distinguish between the free market model and the (monopolistic) public service model. The free market model is closely associated with transnational ICT corporations which, it is often feared, do not necessarily operate in national interests (in other words, in a specific country's interest). The public service model, or the so-called PTT monopoly administrations were established in countries by governments to provide basic universal public services in post and telecommunications. This model is often criticised for not delivering. On a world scale PTTs are gradually being replaced by private companies through a process of deregulation and privatisation. Developing countries should be alerted not to privatise universal services under the pressures of globalisation and transnational corporations. Although it is recommendable that services such as cellular, paging, data communications and long distance services should be deregulated and privatised, the privatisation of these, mainly the money-making services, holds important social consequences. One such a consequence may be that even less money will be available to develop a universal service in telephony. The question arises that should public services be privatised, where will the money come from to make the necessary huge investments to provide universal services?

According to Burgelman (1994:66), the analogy that what is good for developed countries (namely deregulation and privatisation) is also good for developing countries, does not necessarily hold. He argues that deregulation started in most Western countries only *after universal service was realised and not before.* The real challenge for developing countries is then not whether they should deregulate and privatise, but *when* to deregulate and privatise – after they have made their public services more efficient, or before? One of the fears is that the movement to competitive, global conceptualised and market-orientated ICT services will benefit mainly the big professional users who can afford to pay. Although the idea is that this should finance universal service to the majority of the population, this might not be the case and there are few guarantees that this will happen.

If ICT and the purpose of ICT policy is to contribute to development (especially in developing countries), such policy should be conceptualised from the perspective of a development communication theory and model. One such a model is that of Mansell and Wehn (1998).

## 19.3.2 A theoretical model for ICT policy: sustainable development

The United Nations Commission on Science and Technology for Development (UNCSTD) underwrites Mansell and Wehn's (1998:226–239) recommendation that developing countries should have sustainable development as their goal. The sustainable development communication model is the result of many development lessons learned in developing countries. It succeeds less successful models such as the modernisation and the dependency modules. In the sustainable development model the emphasis is far more on grassroots involvement right from the beginning.

In this regard Mansell and Wehn (op cit) suggest that the bottom-goal of a national ICT strategy should be to serve the consumer and citizen. What is good for them is good for everyone including the producers of the ICT products and services. Instead of beginning with the most sophisticated users (as is often the case), the strategies of national ICT planners could be designed for the marginalised people in urban areas and rural villages.

> If national ICT decision-makers were to gear deliberations toward what people in these areas need each morning when they rise, cook, want medical attention,

seek crop prices, need weather forecasts, and seek education and jobs for their children, their ICT strategies would be more balanced.
(Mansell & Wehn 1998:239)

Furthermore, sustainable development means that

- qualified and able people must be assigned to keep abreast of the latest developments in the ICT field
- a clear vision should be formulated and clearly communicated to citizens
- a high-powered effective flexible and authoritative unit should be created for the implementation of policy
- pro-active decisions must be taken, but above all
- policy and planning for the sector should be closely *integrated* into broad economic, trade and social planning and effectively linked with other social policy initiatives such as education, welfare and a broader economic policy
- developing countries should be realistic and should not get too "hyped up" about the ICT revolution.

## 19.4 THE FUTURE OF ICT AND GLOBALISATION: FOUR SCENARIOS

We started this unit with a brief look at some of the characteristics of globalisation and Giddens' (1999; 2000) observation that the world being created by globalisation is not settled or secure, but fraught with anxieties. We then looked at goals of the GII Project, some of the South African ICT goals, the attainability of the GII goals and a checklist for ICT policy in developing countries.

In this, the penultimate section of the unit we take a brief look at the future. Whereto is ICT leading us, especially in developing countries?

The International Development Research Centre (IDRC) and the United Nations Commission on Science and Technology for Development (UNCSTD) came together in 1996 to determine whether the techniques of scenario planning could provide useful insights into the future impact of ICTs on development and how it could inform public policy choices in this regard that confront governments. At the Kelburn, Scotland Workshop (cf. Howkins & Valantin 1997) four scenarios were developed and named *The March of Follies, Cargo Cult, Netblocs,* and *Networld*.

Each scenario starts with the same certainty that technological innovation will continue for the foreseeable future. The dynamism of the information and communication industries will continue to fuel a roller-coaster ride of research, investment, development, acquisition, and wealth creation. But then, each scenario diverges according to two uncertainties:

- Will the value systems of the so-called global community become more inclusive and open, or more exclusive and closed?
- Will individual countries have a complete or partial (proactive or reactive) response to ICT acquisition and use? (Howkins & Valantin 1997:25–27.)

# Globalisation, the Information Superhighway, and Development

The outcomes of the four scenarios are briefly summarised below.

## The March of Follies

### Assumptions
- The global community is exclusive and fragmented.
- Most developing countries respond only partially and reactively to the acquisition and use of ICTs.

### Outcomes

The new world map has poles of growth where people share money, fashion, myth and power. Regions outside this network become increasingly marginalised. There is a sharp bifurcation between the élite and the rest. The rest are marginalised. Their own traditional national identity is diminished and replaced by a larger but fuzzier global identity. The gap between the nomadic wealthy and the local part is very wide, and appears unbridgeable. By 2010 the "development debate" is virtually dead. The problems of the poor and hungry, cases of mass migration, and scenes of violence, crime and war are still reported, but marginally and are no longer in the public sphere and subject to public regulation or part of public anxiety. The ICTs of the 1990s fail to live up to their promises as development aids, as was the case with the telephone, radio, satellites, and ICTs of earlier decades (Howkins & Valentin 1997:33).

## Cargo Cult

### Assumptions
- The global community is inclusive and supportive.
- Most developing countries respond only partially and reactively to the acquisition and use of ICTs.

### Outcomes

> Having a national computing centre, like having a national airline and a national satellite system is a matter of national pride, if in reality a loss to the treasury. Computers symbolize the new religion; even if they do not work well or have any useful software. Every [developing – PJF] country has a national campaign to put computers in schools, but many fail to train their teachers to operate the computers and some put computers in schools that do not have electricity or connectivity. Very few education officials have the skills that are needed.
> (Howkins & Valentin 1997:37)

- Import substitution strategies of the 1950s, 1960s and 1970s.
- Initial high-profiled ICT policies are abandoned when they fail to deliver goods and services that could compete with foreign products.
- Developing countries can buy other countries' information; but they cannot generate their own. They fail to make the connection between information and development.

They receive information and they expect to receive development, without working to make development in their own image. The result is widespread frustration. (ibid.)

## *Netblocs*

### Assumptions

- The global community is exclusive and fragmented.
- Developing countries take an active approach to the acquisition and use of ICTs and develop a complete set of policies.

### Outcomes

As a result of the spread of ICTs many people become wired into the new global information society.

- Blocs emerge, for instance OECD (Organisation for Economic Cooperation and Development) countries, Indian Ocean Rim (South Africa, the Gulf States, Malaysia, Singapore), blocs based on Islam and on Chinese script.
- Blocs are competitive and divisive.
- Blocs set up regional intranets, closed and often censored.
- Global environment breaks down into countervailing zones of exclusion.
- Not all countries join a bloc – lack resources, natural partners.

Yet at the end of this scenario, blocs have achieved much but their insistence on their own regional laws, regulations, and trading principles create centripetal forces that lead to a highly unstable situation (Howkins & Valantin 1997:38–41).

## *Networld*

### Assumptions

- The global community is inclusive and supportive.
- Developing countries have a complete and proactive set of policies toward the acquisition and use of ICTs.

### Outcomes

The OECD attitude toward developing countries is ambivalent. They find restrictive national policies (such as ownership of the media) as intensely irritating. By 2000 many corporations realise that sales to young urban élites have not produced a broad consumer base, or generated much domestic wealth. This leads to enlightened self-interest in ways of working with companies and institutions in developing countries. *Netblocs* are regarded as harmful, creating tariff and non-tariff trade barriers. Awareness in developing countries that they should work with global corporations to develop their own national information societies and economies, increases. Around 2005 intergovernmental organisations and NGOs seek new agendas, new missions, and new sources of revenue. Six "tele-towns" are established against three criteria: social and economic relevance, cultural distinctiveness, and media potential. At the end of the scenario period (2010) poverty and deprivation still remain, but the international system is not only supportive but also knowledgeable. National governments and the private sector, acting both locally and through intergovernmental organisations, work in tandem more often than not (cf. Howkins & Valantin 1997:41–44).

### Conclusions

The participants in the above scenario-planning process, being experts and policymakers, believed that *The March of the Follies* had many symptoms of the current reality. *Cargo Cult* may occur. *Netblocs* may emerge, and may exist for a considerable period. *Networld* is desirable, but its causes and the circumstances that might lead to it coming into existence are fuzzy (Howkins & Valantin 1997:45–47).

The way forward is for developing countries to enhance their national capacity to learn, identify areas where policy is appropriate, take appropriate action, and take an active part in developing the global information society. Whereas development goals are mainly set by governments, ICTs are driven by the private sector. Therefore, a prerequisite for the development of and to gain from ICT is to establish relationships between governments and global and local companies.

## 19.5 CONCLUSION: PROBLEM ANALYSIS AND SOLUTIONS

From what we have discussed in the above sections it is clear that the terrain of globalisation and the role of ICT in globalisation is complex and full of potential problems. In a developing country such as South Africa the need to approach ICT with care and good planning is of the utmost importance. Such an approach requires sound policy planning and analysis. We end this unit by providing you with a model for the analysis of problems and a checklist for the solution of problems. The model can be applied to any form of social policy, in our case ICT policy to enable South Africa to be a full member of the information superhighway, but with cognisance of its pitfalls.

The first step of policy planning and formulation is to analyse the nature of the phenomenon and why policy is necessary. Policy starts with a problem analysis and with asking questions about the cause or potential cause of the problem and the consequences of the problem should it not be addressed. The second step is to find solutions.

Let us say, for example, that if South Africa does not provide as many of its citizens as possible, especially also in the rural areas, with access to basic computing services such as access to the Internet and e-mail, then we will fail to be a member of the information superhighway. We will miss out on the possibilities ICT provides for development in, for example, agricultural growth, medical care, and education. To circumvent this, the government has formulated policy for the establishment of telecentres in rural areas. However, it seems as if this policy is not working or producing the results expected. Why not? By making use of the following model we can begin to address the problem.

## Problem analysis

**Table 19.1 Problem analysis** (Janssen 1996:347–348)

| Problem analysis |
|---|
| **A**   **What is the problem?**<br>What is the nature of the problem (managerial, financial, etc.)?<br>What is the history of the problem?<br>Since when has it occurred?<br>What developments have taken place with respect to the problem?<br>Where is the problem most acutely felt?<br>What persons or institutions are involved in the problem?<br>What is the extent of the problem?<br>Whose interests are at stake as a result of the problem?<br>What aspects of the problem seem to be crucial?<br>Who has identified the problem?<br>How does the problem relate to current policies? |
| **B**   **What are the causes of the problem?**<br>**B1** What cause(s) can be distinguished for the problem(s)/disadvantage(s)?<br>Are these causing factors inherent in current policy/policies?<br>What specific characteristics of current policy cause these problems?<br>Do these characteristics of current policy perpetuate the problem(s)?<br>**B2** Is the postulated relationship between cause and effect theoretically acceptable?<br>Do the same causes lead to similar problems in other contexts?<br>Are any other/better explanations possible for the problems/negative effects? |
| **C**   **What are the consequences of the problem?**<br>What are the negative financial, political, personal, etc. effects of the problem?<br>How do these negative effects impact on those involved?<br>How do these negative aspects impact on other aspects of policy? |

## Problem solutions

To determine and evaluate possible solutions/measures to a problematical situation it is essential that everyone in the policy team has a clear conceptualisation of the problem, the desired outcome, and of how each possible solution or measure can contribute to achieving the desired outcome or certain aspects of it.

With regard to the solution of the problem at hand, the team will have to determine the answers to the following general questions (Table 19.2):

**Table 19.2 Solutions to policy problems** (adapted from Janssen 1996:322, 342)

| Problem solutions |
|---|
| • What possible solutions/policy measures exist within the problem domain?<br>• What criteria must the proposed solutions/measures adhere to?<br>• How should the criteria themselves be prioritised?<br>• How do the various proposals/measures score on the different criteria?<br>• What differing opinions exist with regard to all the above?<br>With regard to each policy measure (X) it has to be determined, and where deemed necessary, explicated:<br>• What does solution/measure X involve/comprise?<br>• What is the purpose/aim of X?<br>• Why is X necessary?<br>• How is X implemented/operationalised?<br>• Is the implementation of X feasible or are there any economic, political, social, technical, judicial or moral impediments to the implementation of X?<br>• What effect(s) will X have?<br>• How does X solve the problem/contribute to realising the stated aims? (Is X effective?)<br>• What are X's (dis)advantages; added value?<br>• How does X score on policy criteria/adhere to contextual variables?<br>• What will X cost to implement? (Is X efficient?)<br>• Is X in line with other policies?<br>• How does X score on the stated criteria?<br>• Will X get the necessary political support? |

# Summary

Our main argument in this unit was that the development of ICT holds many promises for economic, social and cultural development. However, if not managed effectively it carries within it the danger of a growing gap between developed and developing countries and between the rich and the poor. From a cultural point of view the fear is that the information superhighway provides the ideal platform for the creation of a global culture to the detriment of national and own cultural expressions, values and beliefs, and that it provides fertile ground for the expansion of media imperialism. More than ever the development of ICTs and the related convergence of media technologies have made it possible to communicate across national borders at the speed of light and to confront all the senses of the media user simultaneously.

## MEDIA STUDIES

The purpose of the unit was to make you aware of the some of the criticism and warnings against the unrealistic view of ICT that sees it as able to solve all developmental needs and problems. We provided a model for the critical analysis of policy issues related to ICT policy in developing countries.

In the unit we introduced a theory of globalisation and some of the characteristics of globalisation; key prerequisites for the GII Project to work; South Africa's information infrastructure objectives; and criticism against the GII. We considered key issues in ICT planning and policy; the sustainable development model as a prerequisite for ICT implementation; four scenarios about the impact of ICT on development; and a model for the analysis of ICT problems and solutions.

## Research activities

1. Briefly explain your understanding of Anthony Giddens' theory of globalisation.
2. List five characteristics of globalisation.
3. Write a one-page essay on how globalisation impacts on your own life.
4. Write a one-page essay about the achievability of the GII Project goals.
5. List at least ten South African information infrastructure goals.
6. Evaluate the South African goals in terms of control, access, quality and participation against the background of your own experience of the availability and your use of ICT.
7. Describe at least five issues in ICT policy and motivate why you see the five issues as of critical importance for developing countries.
8. Visit an ICT Web site and obtain the latest statistics on the availability of telecommunications services or Internet services in South Africa, in Africa and in a developed country.
9. Write a one-page essay in which you motivate why the sustainable development model should or should not form the basis of ICT planning and implementation in developing countries.
10. In which of the four global scenarios for the future of information and communication technology and the information superhighway do you think South Africa fits? Write a one-page essay in which you motivate your argument.
11. Formulate an ICT-related problem and analyse the problem according to the model for problem analysis and solutions.

## Further reading

Baldwin, TF. 1996. *Convergence: integrating media, information, and communication.* London: Sage.
Castells, M. 1996. *The information age: economy, society and culture.* Vol 1: *The rise of the network society* (1996); Vol 2: *The power of identity* (1997); Vol 3: *End of millennium* (1998). Oxford: Blackwell.

Flichy, P. 1995. *Dynamics of modern communication. The shaping and impact of new communication technologies.* London: Sage.
Giddens, A. 1990. *The consequences of modernity.* Cambridge: Polity Press.
Golding, P & Harris, P (eds). 1997. *Beyond cultural imperialism. Globalization, communication and the new international order.* London: Sage.
Hamelink, C. 1994. *The politics of world communication.* London: Sage.
Mansell, R & Wehn, U. 1998. *Knowledge societies: information technology for sustainable development.* Oxford: Oxford University Press.
Mohammadi, A. 1997. *International communication and globalization. A critical introduction.* London: Sage.
Mowlana, H. 1997. *Global information and world communication. New frontiers in international relations.* 2nd edition. London: Sage.
Schiller, H. 1996. *Information inequality: making information haves and have nots.* London: Routledge.
Servaes, J & Lie, R (eds). 1997. *Media & politics in transition. Cultural identity in the age of globalization.* Leuven: Acco.
Sreberny-Mohammadi, A, Winseck, D, McKenna, J & Boyd-Barrett, O. 1997. *Media in global context.* London: Arnold.
Sussman, G. 1997. *Communication, technology, and politics in the information age.* London: Sage.
Waters, M. 1995. *Globalization.* London: Routledge.

### Web sites

BMI-TechKnowledge Group: http://www.bmi-t.co.za
Conducting Research on the Internet:
    http://www.unisa.ac.za/internal/deptinfo/lib/library3/inet/research.html
Department of Communications (South African Government): http://docweb.pwv.gov.za
Global Fusion 2000: http://www.siu.edu/~gf2000
Global Information Infrastructure Commission: http://www.giic.org
Info Africa: http://www.infoafrica.co.za
International Development Research Centre: http://www.idrc.ca
International Telecommunication Union (ITU): http://www.itu.int/
Internet usage: http://www.ams-ix.net
Media Africa – Reading the Mind of the Internet: http://www.mediaafrica.co.za
National Information Technology Forum: http://www.sn.apc.org/nitf
National Research Foundation: http://www.nrf.ac.za
Organisation for Economic Co-operation and Development: http://www.oecd.org
Ratings: http://www.nielsennetratings.com
South African Advertising Research Foundation: http://www.saarf.co.za
State Information Technology Agency: http://sita.pwv.gov.za
World Bank Development Forum: http://www.worldbank.org/devforum
World Bank Development Outreach: http://www.worldbank.org/devoutreach

## Bibliography

BMI-TechKnowledge. 1999. *Communication technologies handbook 1999.* Johannesburg: BMIT Group.
Burgelman, J-C. 1994. Assessing information technologies and telecommunications services: the case of developing countries. *Communicatio* 18(2):64–79.

Burgelman, J-C. 1995. *De "informatiesameleving" en de toekomstige uitdagingen voor het communicatiebeleid*. Referaat naar voor gebracht voor de Parlementaire Commissies Economie & Media van de Vlaamse Raad. Brussel: SMIT, Vrije Universiteit van Brussel.

Carey, J & Moss, M. 1985. The diffusion of new telecommunication technologies. *Telecommunications Policy*, June 1985:145–158.

Castells, M. 1996. *The information age: economy, society and culture*. Vol 1: *The rise of the network society* (1996); Vol 2: *The power of identity* (1997); Vol 3: *End of millennium* (1998). Oxford: Blackwell.

Competitor for Telkom is given thumbs-up. 2001. *Business Day*, 28 March.

Currie, W. 1996. *Regulating telecommunications in South Africa*. Conference paper, Telecommunications Conference, University of Pretoria, May 1996.

Dervin, B & Schields, P. 1990. *Users: the missing link*. Conference Paper, IAMCR 1990.

Giddens, A. 1990. *The consequences of modernity*. Cambridge: Polity Press.

Giddens, A. 1999. *Globalisation. A runaway world. BBC Reith Lectures 1999*. [O].
   Available: http://www.news.bbc.co.uk/hi/english/static/events/reith_99/week1.htm
   Accessed on 1999/07/28

*Globalization: Giddens' dilemma*. 2000. [O].
   Available: http://www.sociologyonline.f9.co.uk/GlobalGiddens1.htm
   Accessed on 2000/11/14

Gore, A. 1994. Speech to the International Telecommunication Union Conference in Buenos Aires, Argentina.

Hamelink, CJ. 1997. World communication: business as usual? in *Democratizing communication? Comparative perspectives on information and power*, edited by M Bailie & D Winseck. Cresskill, NJ: Hampton Press.

Howkins, J & Valantin, R (eds). 1997. *Development and the information age. Four global scenarios for the future of information and communication technology*. Ottawa: International Development Research Centre.

ISAD. 1996. Information Society and Development conference: Conclusions. Midrand, Johannesburg, 13–15 May 1996.

Janssen, D (ed). 1996. *Zakelijke communicatie 2*. Groningen: Wolters-Noordhoff.

Lind, P. 1990. *Computerization in developing countries*. London: Routledge.

Mansell, R & Wehn, U. 1998. *Knowledge societies: information technology for sustainable development*. Oxford: Oxford University Press.

McAnany, E. 1983. From modernization and diffusion to dependency and beyond: theory and practice in communication for social change in the 1980s. *Development communications in the Third World*, proceedings of a Midwest symposium, University of Illinois, April.

McChesney, RW. 1997. The communication revolution: the market and the prospect for democracy, in *Democratizing communication? Comparative perspectives on information and power*, edited by M Bailie & D Winseck. Cresskill, NJ: Hampton Press.

Media Africa. 2000. *Internet Usage in South Africa*. (4th South African Internet Services Industry Survey). [O].
   Available: http://www.mediaafarica.co.za
   Accessed on 2000/09/11

Melody, W. 1989. Policy issues in the evolution of ISDN, in *ISDN in Europe*, edited by JC Arnbak. Amsterdam: North Holland.

Melody, W. 1991. The information society: the transnational economic context and its implications, in *Transnational communications. Wiring the Third World*, edited by G Sussman & J Lent. London: Sage.

Metoyer-Duran, C. 1991. Information-seeking behaviour of gatekeepers in ethnolinguistic communities: overview of a taxonomy. *LISR* 13:319–346.

Moussa, A. 1995. *Information and telecommunications technologies in the public sector.* Unpublished topic paper prepared for The World Bank, January 1995.

National Information Technology Forum. 2000. [O].
Available: http://www.sn.apc.org/nitf
Accessed on 2000/09/20

O'Sullivan, T, Hartley, J, Saunders, D, Montgomery, M & Fiske, J. 1994. *Key concepts in communication and cultural studies.* 2nd edition. London: Routledge.

Pitroda, S. 1993. Development, democracy, and the village telephone. *Harvard Business Review* Nov/Dec 1993.

Pool, I de S. 1966. Communications and development, in *Modernization: the dynamics of growth,* edited by M Weiner. Washington, DC: Voice of America.

Poverty in South Africa. 2000. (Based on statistics released by Statistics South Africa (SSA)). *Rapport,* 10 September.

Schramm, W. 1979. *Mass media and national development.* Paris: UNESCO, International Commission for the Study of Communication Problems.

Servaes, J. 1997. Mass media and fragmented identities, in *Media and politics in transition. Cultural identity in the age of globalization,* edited by J Servaes & R Lie. Leuven: Acco.

South Africa. 1996. White Paper on Telecommunications Policy. Pretoria: Government Printer.

South Africa. 1999. Universal Service Agency's discussion paper on *The definition of universal service and universal access within South Africa, 1999.*

South Africa. 2001. Department of Communications. Government notice of intention to issue ministerial policy directives. [O].
Available: http://www.docweb.pwv.gov.za/docs/polity/telpoldir.html
Accessed on 2001/03/28

Sreberny-Mohammadi, A. 1997. The many cultural faces of imperialism, in *Beyond cultural imperialism. Globalization, communication and the new international order,* edited by P Golding & P Harris. London: Sage.

Sussman, G & Lent, J. 1991. Introduction: critical perspectives on communication and Third World development, in *Transnational communications. Wiring the Third World,* edited by G Sussman & J Lent. London: Sage.

Talero, E & Gaudette, P. 1995. Harnessing information for development. A proposal for a World Bank group vision and strategy. The World Bank.

Telkom. 1996. *Annual Report.* Pretoria: Telkom Group Communication.

Van den Brink, R. 1987. *Informatie over de informatie: handboek over de informatiemedia in Nederland 1938–1985.* Leiden: Stenfert Kroese.

Vincent, RC. 1997a. The new world information and communication order (NWICO) in the context of the information superhighway, in *Democratizing communication? Comparative perspectives on information and power,* edited by M Bailie & D Winseck. Cresskill, NJ: Hampton Press.

Vincent, RC. 1997b. The future of the debate: setting an agenda for a new world information and communication order, ten proposals, in *Beyond cultural imperialism. Globalization, communication and the new international order,* edited by P Golding & P Harris. London: Sage.

Waters, M. 1995. *Globalization.* London: Routledge.

# Index

## A

ability  282
access  108
access to information/ICT  605
accessing  108
accommodation  366
accumulation theory  298
acquisitions  151, 154
act of theatre (terrorism)  552
active audience perspective  516
administrative paradigm  238, 276
adspend  14, 147
adversarial relationship (government and press)  159
advertisements  482
advertisers  180, 182
advertising income  147
Advertising Standards Authority (ASA)  180
aesthetic codes  341
affective effects  292
affective meaning  345
affirmative action  152, 159
Africa-2-Africa  34
African Broadcasting Company (ABC)  7
African Consolidated Films  76
African Consolidated Theatres  76
African Film Productions  76
African Films  76
African Mirror, The  76
African National Congress (ANC)  50, 152, 172, 194, 433, 559
Afrikaans  79
Afrikaans broadcasting  8
*Afrikaanse Patriot, Die*  38
Afrikaner nationalism  77
Afrikaner Weerstandsbeweging (AWB)  560
age restrictions  574
agenda-setting  555
agenda-setting theory  304

AIDS dissidents  497
All Media and Products Survey (AMPS)  56
alternative perspective  547
alternative press  48
Althusser  371
amalgamation legislation  152
America Online (AOL)  112
Americanisation  601
analogue code  340
ANC  50, 152, 172, 194, 433, 559
*ANC Today – Online Voice of the African National Congress*  434
ANC/Cosatu (Confederation of South African Trade Unions)  153
anchor  22
androgynous  394
Anglo-American  139, 141, 150
Anglo/JCI  151
anomie  295
anti-competitive conduct  154
antimonopoly  152
antimonopoly legislation  132
antitrust  152
apartheid  429
arbitrary sign  334
archetypes  479
architecture  358
articulations of meaning  349
Arts and Culture Task Group (ACTAG)  90
Associated Scientific and Technical Societies (AS&TS)  7
attention-drawing  229
attitude  337
audience  215
authoritarian theory  270

## B

Bantu World  50, 51
base/superstructure  136

# Index

BCCSA  175, 181
*Beeld, Die*  66, 179
behavioural effects  291
behaviourism  235, 240
Berlusconi, Silvio  130
Biko  54
bilingual service  8
Bill of Rights  175
binary oppositions  472
black listeners  11
bomb plantings  550
Boniface  38
Bop-TV  13
bourgeoisie  136
British cultural studies  241, 319
broadcasters  577
broadcasting  258
Broadcasting Act (no. 22 of 1936)  8
Broadcasting Act (no. 4 of 1999)  26, 31
Broadcasting Charter  31
Broadcasting Complaints Commission of South Africa (BCCSA)  175, 181
Broadcasting Monitoring and Complaint Commission (BMCC)  21
built environment  358
*Burger, Die*  42, 66
*Business Day*  66, 72

## C

Cable News Network (CNN)  138
*Cape Argus*  41, 65
Cape Film and Video Foundation  84
Capital Radio  11, 12
capital resources  107
capitalist economic system  137
capitalist mode of production  121, 122
catharsis  280
catharsis theory  307
Caxton  67, 141, 145, 147
censorship  78, 81, 168
change (codes)  344
charter  190
circular process model  520
circumstances of the communicator  246

*Citizen, The*  45, 56, 68
*City Press*  59, 66
civic journalism  276
class struggle  245
code  339
codes  451
codes linked to culture and context  343
codes of behaviour  340
codes of conduct  166, 485
codes of content  342
codes of fashion  367
codes of form  342
coercive power  124
cognitive effects  291
cognitive theories  298
collaborative role  276
collective body  213
collective practice  472
collocative meaning  345
*Commercial Advertiser*  35
commercial broadcasting  28
commercial interests  464
commercialisation  115
Commission of Inquiry into the Reporting of Security News from the South African Defence Force and Police  431
common cultures  368
communication  216
communicator  213, 337
communicator, orientation of  229
community  54
community broadcasting  31
community radio  16
compatibility  331
competition  110
Competition Act (no. 89 of 1998)  154
Competition Board  150
Competition Commission  154, 175
competition, media  552
complex relationship between representation and reality  483
COMTASK  154
conative effects  292
conative function  337
concentration  107, 112

concentration in the SA newspaper industry 151
conceptual meaning 345
conglomerates 130
connotation 346
connotative meaning 345
consciousness industry 242
consensus 460
Constitution 178, 490
consumer 182
consumer commodity 258
consumption units 258
contact 338
contagion 556
content 337
context 228
control 149, 609
control of the press 149
convergence 114
conversational style 452, 461
Cool media 251
Cosatu 153
created meanings 349
creativity and uncertainty 106
crime reporter/reporting 458
Criminal Procedures Act (no. 51 of 1977) 176
critical paradigm 238, 276
critical research 391
critical theory/theories 241, 243, 244
critical/dialectical role 276
cross-border raids 555
cultivation perspective 512, 514
cultural artefacts 372
cultural imperialism 77, 416
cultural maps 460
cultural negotiation paradigm 276
cultural product 452
cultural studies 373, 379, 385
culture 221, 355, 367, 369, 491
culture industry 486, 598

## D

*Daily Mail* 182
*Daily News, The* 39, 41
De Nasionale Pers Beperk 43
*De Natalier* 39
*De Zuid-Afrikaan* 38
deadlines 456
deep structure (capitalism) 330
definition of terrorism 559
delegitimisation of terrorism 555
deliberative democracy 220
democracy 133, 164, 217, 219, 581
democratic participant theory 274
democratisation of communication 417
denotation 346
denotative meaning 345
desensitising effect 514
determinism 233
development theory 274, 431
diachronism 331
diffusion of innovation theory 299
digital code 340
direct competition 110
direct sales 108
directorate 200
directorates, boards and group managers 197
discourse 348
discursive practice 322
disembedded organisations 595
disembedment 597
displacement 331
dissimulation 320
distance 280
distantiation, time-space 596
distribution of films 86
divergent cultures and ideological stances 258
diversity of news 133
dominance, prohibition of the abuse of 154
dominant cultures 368
dominant position 546
dominant reading 322, 376
Dormer 41
dramatic and saturation coverage 550
dramatic entertainment 550
dramatic interaction 283
*Drum* 51
DStv 33, 34

# Index

Dube 50
duopoly 147

## E

e.tv 21, 88
early modernity 598
East Coast Radio 11
economic impact of official statements 563
economic impact of terrorism 563
economic power 123
economic transformation 611
editor 200
editorial autonomy 200
editorial guidelines 192
editorial staff 200
EDT 145
effect of gatekeeping 205
elaborated code 341
Electronic Media Network (M-Net) 143
electronic public communication culture 254, 257
electronic/digital delivery 109
élitist criticism 242
élitist point of view 215
emergency regulations 430
employment policy 485
empowerment 66
enlightenment 271
entering the market 148
entertainment 277
epistemology 233
equality 165, 169, 177
erotic spectacle 397
ethical codes 181
ethical importance (knowledge of research) 291
ethnicity 499
expert systems 597
explicit policy formulation 134
expressive function 337
external plurality 268
external policy framework 194
external reporting, control over 148

## F

facilitating public opinion 218
facilitation 218
facilitative role 276
facticity 457
facticity of news 552
Fairbairn 35
false consciousness 245, 315
fascism 270
fashion 366
feedback 216, 225
female body 404
feminism 383, 385, 386, 389, 395, 397, 401, 503
feminism, feminist theory 385
feminism, liberal 386
feminism, Marxist and socialist 389
feminism, postmodern 401
feminism, psychoanalytical 397
feminism, radical 395
feminist criticism 384
feminists 573
fetishism 383, 397
film 257
Film and Broadcasting Forum (FBF) 89
Film and Television Federation (FTF) 89
Film and Video Foundation 90
filters (codes) 343
*Financial Mail* 66
first-order meaning 475
Firstness 333
flow of news 456
5FM 32
FM 10, 12
focus of a theory 234
form 337
formal prosecution 194
Fourth Estate 347
fragmentation 320
framing 305
Frankfurt School 241, 243
free-enterprise economic system 137
freedom 165, 169
freedom of expression 133, 176, 570

Freedom of Expression Institute (FXI) 195, 561
freedom of reception 133
freedom of the press 69
frequencies 26
*Friend, The* 40
Functionalism 240, 265
functioning 331

## G

gatekeeper role 227
gatekeepers 190
gatekeeping 196
gay 500
Gaze 383
gender 503
generalisation (stereotypes) 478
genre 281
genre of a media text 482
Ghandi 50
global cosmopolitan society 602
Global Information Infrastructure project (the GII Project) 440, 604
global society 599
global village 250, 258
globalisation 120, 486, 595
Good Hope FM 32
government 463
government and media 167
Government Communication and Information Service (GCIS) 158, 175
*Government Gazette* 40
Government of National Unity 432
Gramsci 371, 374
grandfathered radio stations 29
greenfield licences 29
*Grocott's Mail* 68

## H

hailing 318
Hall 376
Harber, Anton 155, 156
hard news 456

hate speech 572
Hearst, William Randolph 130
hegemony 245, 319, 371, 374, 375, 379
Hersant, Robert 130
*Het Volksblad* 42
heuristic value 237
high culture 222
high fixed costs 106
hit squads 547, 554
*Hoofstad* 67
horizontal integration 111
Hot media 251
human rights 490
Human Rights Commission 176
human thinking 601
humanism 233, 235
hybridisation 106
hypodermic needle theory 294

## I

IBA 26, 27
IBA Act 175
IBA Act of 1993 26
ICASA 31
ICASA Act of 2000 26
iconic signs 335
ICT (information and communication technology) 252
ICT and globalisation scenarios 616
identification 278
identity 282, 486
ideological agent 241
ideological meaning 345
ideological messages 383
Ideological State Apparatuses 245, 316, 371
ideology 244, 312, 369, 379, 491
Ikwekwezi FM 28, 32
illumination 338
immanence 331
increased circulation 550
Independent 146, 147
Independent Broadcasting Authority (IBA) 16
Independent Communications Authority of South Africa (ICASA) 18, 26, 27, 118, 185

# Index

Independent Media  139
Independent Media Diversity Trust (IMDT)  157
Independent Newspapers  65, 113, 178
independent social-democrat press  55
Independent, The  65
indexical signs  335
Indian National Congress  50
indirect competition  110
indirect subsidies  134
individualism  228
industrialisation  215
information and communication technology (ICT)  114, 118, 439, 604
information function  548
information society paradigm  238
information superhighway  440, 604
Inkundla  53
inoculation theory  514
Institut für Sozialforschung  243
institutional approach  347
institutional discourse  452
institutional process  456
institutions  552
intended and unintended effects  292
interactivity  217
interconnectedness  253
interdependence  148
interest of journalists (terrorism)  552
intermediary position  227
internal censorship  195
internal media policy framework  189
internal plurality  268
internal reporting, control over  148
Internal Security Act (no. 74 of 1982)  172, 176, 558
Internal Security and Intimidation Amendment Act (no. 138 of 1991)  176
International Program for the Development of Communication  425
International Telecommunications Union (ITU)  26
internationalisation  117
Internet  578
Internet, legislation  579
interpellation  318
interpretation  221
interpretative character (sign)  334
intertextual (codes)  343
intertextuality  377
introjection  279
inverted pyramid  453

## J

Jabavu  49
JCI  141
Johannesburg Consolidated Investments (JCI)  139, 141
Johnnic  141, 145
*Journal, The*  35
journalistic codes  453

## K

Kagiso  68, 145
Kagiso Trust  145
Killarney Film Studios  77
knock-and-drop  68, 109
knowledge  283

## L

language  448
langue  329, 332, 348
late (or high) modernity  598
law-based explanation  236
layout  453
Least-Objectionable-Programme  111
left-commercial press  54
legal framework  194
legitimation  320
legitimisation of terrorism  555
leisure  281
leisure time  281
lesbian  500
Lesedi FM  28, 32
liberal critique  608
liberal pluralists  125
liberal school  421
liberal school of thought  419

liberal-individualist paradigm 275
liberalisation 116
libertarian theory 271
licence fees 108
Ligwalagwala FM 32
linkage 331
local cultural identities 600
localisation 598
location 203
logical codes 341
long-term (cognitive) theories 298
longitudinal field research 514
Luddite critique 608

## M

M-Net 14, 33, 48, 83, 88, 143, 144, 151
MacBride Commission 421
MacBride Report 421
MacBride Round Table 421
macro theories 237
macro-plurality 268
Magna Carta 36
*Mail & Guardian* 55, 64, 70, 73
mainstream press 52
manifest and latent effects 292
*Many Voices, One World* 421
marginal discourses 373
marginalisation 450
markers (codes) 344
market segmentation 110
market structure 147
marketing approach 199
Marxism 135, 369
Marxist 125
Marxist critique 135
masculine gaze 397
masks 476
mass communication 213, 215
Mass Democratic Movement 54
mass society theories 242
material base of society 315
mathematical model 224
meaning 220, 246
meaning construction theories 302

media 214
media and terrorism, orthodox view 542
media content 214
media control 150
Media Council 150
media culture 221
Media Development and Diversity Agency (MDDA) 158, 175, 433
media diversity 178
media freedom 183
media imperialism 416
media moguls 130
media pluralism 268
media semiotics 327
media technologies 600
Media Tenor South Africa 438
media texts 346
media texts, polysemic 321
media-culturalist perspective 212
media-manufactured public opinion 219
media-materialist perspective 212
mediating/mediation 220, 221
medium 214
mergers and acquisitions 154
meso-plurality 268
message 214, 337
metalinguistic function 338
Metro FM 32
Meyer Commission 12
micro theories 237
micro-plurality 268
Midi group 21
mimesis theory 307
mission statement 190
mix of nationalities 602
modelling theory 300
models of mass communication 223
modernisation 595
monopolisation 130, 148
monopolistic competition 139
monopoly/monopolies 134, 147, 150
moral panic 295, 510, 525
morality 573
Morley 377
motive of the communicator 483

# Index

Motsweding FM  27, 32
Muldergate  45
MultiChoice  33
multiple way and/or recycled (media products)  107
Munghana Lonene  32
Murdoch, Rupert  130
music  364
mutually accepted policy (media and government)  562
mythical meaning  475
myths  474, 475

## N

Nail  145, 146
Nasionale Pers/Naspers  66, 68, 113, 142, 145-147
Naspers Group  43
*Natal Mercury*  39
*Natal Witness, The*  39
nation-state  595, 602
National Empowerment Consortium (NEC)  66, 141, 142
National Film and Video Foundation  84
National Party  167
Nationalist Government  12
nationality  499
nature of a medium  482
negative social consequences  478
negative stereotype  478
negotiated reading  322, 376
network society  253
neutral theory of ideology  313
New Africa Investments Limited (NAIL)  52, 65
New International Economic Order (NIEO)  424, 428
new media  252
new media and communication policy  253
*New Nation*  55
New Queer Cinema  501
new world economic order  599
New World Information and Communication Order (NWICO)  416, 604

news  447
news net  456
news policy  192
news production  456
news values  454
news, facticity  552
news, timelines  552
news-literate  452
newsgathering  203, 458
Newspaper and Imprint Registration Act of 1971  70
Newspaper Press Union (NPU)  41
newsworthiness  454, 549
niche markets  110, 111
NIEO (New International Economic Order)  424, 428
*Ninja Turtles*  516, 523, 526
normative theories  269
norms as regulator  178
Nu Metro  86
NWICO  416, 604

## O

O'Reilly, Tony  65, 140
Object  383
objective  487
objectivism  233
observers  280
*Oggendblad*  67
oligopoly  139, 147
Ombudsman  74, 175, 181
Omni Media Corporation  141, 145
one-way communication  216
ongoing incidents, terrorism  550
Ons Land  38
ontology  233
*Oosterlig*  66
Open Democracy Act Draft Bill (1997)  175
open texts  375
oppositional reading  322, 376
oral public communication culture  254
order  165, 169, 177
organisational culture  202

organised church  357
orientation of communicator and recipient  229
origin  480
Other  383
outsiders  280
ownership  178

## P

Pagad  561
Pan Africanist Congress  53, 172
parole  329, 332, 348
parsimony  236
participants  280
participative democracy  220
patriarchal messages  383
payola  181
Pearsons  66
penis envy  397
perception  228, 484
perception aesthetics  349
perfect competition  138
perfect monopoly  138
Perskor  67, 144, 146
persuade (conative function)  337
pertinence  331
Phalaphala FM  27, 32
phallus as a symbol of desire  397
phatic function  338
photography  257
physical perceptibility (sign)  334
planned balanced representations  485
planned effects  293
pluralism  126, 248, 277
pluralism of news  133
pluralist media theories  247
poetic function  337
Police Act (no. 7 of 1958)  172
policy about terrorism and the media's coverage of such events  557
political citizens  258
political economy  121
political power  124
polysemic  350, 375, 376, 377

polysemic media texts  321
popular culture  221, 363
positive stereotype  478
positivism  239
*Post*  52
post-NWICO model  439
power  123, 374
power relations  319
practice, communication/media  348
preferred reading  321, 376
prejudice  478
presentation  458
presentation of news (terrorism)  553
presentational code  340
Press Commission  149, 430
press freedom  71, 488
pressure groups  179
*Pretoria News*  56, 65, 178
pricing  148
prime-time  110
Primedia Entertainment  86
Pringle  35
print media  577
Prisons Act (no. 8 of 1959)  172
private individuals  217
privatisation  116, 185
problem analysis  619
problem solutions  619, 620
process (text as a)  348
process of negotiation  377
production schedules  458
professional product  462
professionalism  195
programme policy  192
progressive-alternative press  54
projection  278, 279
proletariat  136
propaganda  286
Protection of Access to Information Act (no. 2 of 2000)  175
public broadcaster  191
public broadcasting  27
public broadcasting services  177
public communication culture  254
public interest  107, 171

# Index

public opinion  241, 305
public service broadcasting  118
public sphere  217
Publications Act (no. 42 of 1974)  170
Publications Control Board  80
publicity models  229
publicness  217
Pulitzer, Joseph  130
purpose of theory  234

## R

race  487, 492
race discrimination  492
race prejudice  492
racialism  492
racism  70, 488, 492, 585
radio  258
Radio 2000  32
Radio 702  11, 12
Radio Bantu  11
Radio Bop  12
Radio Good Hope  11
Radio Highveld  11
Radio Lebowa  11
Radio Lotus  32
Radio Port Natal  11
Radio Sesotho  11
Radio Setswana  11
Radio Sunshine  32
Radio Thohoyandou  12
Radio Tsonga  11
Radio Venda  11
Radio Xhosa  12
Radio Zulu  11
*Rand Daily Mail*  48, 52, 55, 65, 181, 182
*Rapport*  66, 68, 179
RARO  77
ratings  110
rationalisation of consumption  111
RDP  152, 176, 433
re-present  470
reaction  366
reality  220

reappropriation  501
reception models  229
recipient, orientation of  229
Reconstruction and Development Programme (RDP)  152, 176, 433
recreation  281
*Red Riding-hood*  474, 475
redifussion  10, 12
referent  334
referential function  337
reflective meaning  345
regulators  166
reification  320
Reith Report  8
Reith, John  8
relation between the media and underlying production conventions  246
religion  356
Rembrandt  68, 145
reporters' beats  457
representation  221, 470
representation and reality  483
representational code  340
representative character (sign)  334
representative democracy  220
Repressive State Apparatuses  316, 371
restricted code  341
restrictions on the media  557
rhetorical motifs  282
right of reply  485
right-wing terrorism  560
ritual or expressive models  229
RSG  8, 27, 32
rules-based explanation  236

## S

SABC (South African Broadcasting Corporation)  6, 8, 13, 14, 20, 84, 88, 108, 169, 171, 175, 177, 191, 268, 431, 519, 523
SABC Africa  34
SABC1  32
SABC2  33

SABC3  33
SACP (South African Communist Party)  153, 172, 194, 559
SAfm  8, 27, 32
SANEF  71
Sanlam  142, 144
Satbel  86
Satra  18, 26, 27
Schlesinger  76, 78
Schoch Commission  9
scientific importance (knowledge of research)  291
second-order meaning  475
Secondness  333
selectively presenting  243
semiosis  348
service provision  229
sex  574
sexuality  499
short-term effect theories  297
sign  333
sign systems  338
sign, characteristics  334
sign, components  334
signifiant/signifier  332
signification  215
signifié/signified  332
signified  334
signifier  334
signifiers  347
signifying codes  340
signifying practice  348
simplification (stereotypes)  478
Sithengi  84, 94, 96
situationalists  234
social activity  281
social codes  342
social discourse  377
social expectation theory  301
social learning  520
social pluralism  268
social plurality  268
social responsibility  195
social responsibility paradigm  276
social responsibility theory  272

social semiotics  348
social transformation  611
social-culturalist perspective  212
social-materialist perspective  212
socialisation  278, 284, 285
socially constructed meaning/values  472, 475
soft news  456
source of news  204
South African Associated Newspapers (SAAN)  66
South African Broadcasting Act (no. 4 of 1999)  117
South African Broadcasting Corporation, see SABC
South African Communist Party (SACP)  153, 172, 194, 559
South African Film and Video Foundation (SAFVF)  84, 91
South African Human Rights Commission (SAHRC)  70, 177, 488
*South African Journal*  35
South African Media Council  432
South African National Editors Forum (SANEF)  71, 176, 177, 434, 561
South African Native National Congress (SANNC)  50
South African Press Association (SAPA)  9
South African Scriptwriters Association (SASWA)  84
South African Students Organisation  54
South African Telecommunications Regulatory Authority (Satra)  18, 26, 27
Southern African Development Community (SADC)  56, 117
Southern African International Film and Television Market (Sithengi)  84, 94, 96
Soviet communist theory of the media  273
Soviet media theory  136
*Sowetan*  52, 65, 179
space  457
specific signifying practice  348
spectacle  229
spiral of silence theory  305
sport  361
Springbok Radio  9

# Index

Springer, Axel  130
*Star, The*  40, 48, 65, 178
state terrorism  547, 551, 554, 558, 560, 563
Statement on Journalistic Ethics  421
Station JB  7
Ster Films  86
Ster-Kinekor  78, 86
Ster-Moribo  87
stereotypes  388, 477
stereotyping  303, 470
Steyn Commission of Inquiry into the Mass Media  13, 45, 149, 431, 560
stimulus-response theory  512
strategic importance (knowledge of research)  291
stringers  457
structural functionalism  265
structuralism  328
structuralist school  419
style  366, 452
stylistic meaning  345
sub-editors  202
subject  337, 347, 383
subjectivism  233
subliminal racism  488
subscriptions  108
subsidies  134
subsidisation  108
substitute experience  259
*Sunday Express*  66
*Sunday Times*  65, 70
support for government policy  159
suppression of news  552
suppression of religious and political views  574
surveillance role  276
survival  282
symbiotic relationship (terrorists and the media)  543
symbolic annihilation  503
symbolic expression  246
symbolic form of expression  229, 327
symbolic power  124
symbolic signs  335
symbolic tokens  597
synchronism  331
system (text)  348

## T

take-overs  151
technological determinism  249, 250
technological/ deterministic paradigm  238
*Teenage, Mutant Ninja Turtles*  516, 523, 526
telecommunication policy  183
Telecommunications Act (no. 103 of 1996)  26, 175
telephone service  184
television sexism  386
Telkom  184
temporal and spatial factors  202
terror  557
terrorism  450, 539, 540, 558
terrorism reporting, alternative perspective  547
terrorism reporting, competition  552
terrorism reporting, effect/influence on public  554
terrorism reporting, official perspective (dominant position)  546
terrorism, definition  559
terrorism, legitimacy  542, 545, 555
terrorism, ongoing incidents  550
terrorism, presentation of news  553
terrorist groups  551
terrorists  540
terrorists and the media  543
terrorists, strategic goals  542
testability  236
text  214
texts  246
the medium is the message  250
theatre  363
thematic meaning  345
theory  229
theory, building blocks of  232
theory, epistomology  232
theory, evaluation  235
theory, focus of  234
theory, goals of  230

theory, ontology  232
theory, practical value  231
theory, purpose of a  234
theory, scientific value  230
theory, scope of  236
third-order meaning  475
Thirdness  333
Thobela FM  32
three-tier system of broadcasting  27
time  456
Time Warner  112
time-scale effects  292
time-space distantiation  596
timeliness of news  552
Times Media Limited  65, 141, 146
transmission models  229
transnational terrorism  547
*Transvaler, Die*  43, 67
triangular relationship (governments, victims, terrorists)  544
Triple Inquiry Report  17, 26
*Tselane le Ledimo*  474, 475
Twentieth Century Fox  78, 86
two-step-flow theory  295

## U

UIP Warner  86
Ukhozi FM  28, 32
Umhlobo Wenene FM  27, 28, 32
understanding (of reality)  282
UNESCO  416
UNESCO Media Declaration of 1978  421
unification  320
uninvolved involvement  280
Union of Black Journalists  54
United Democratic Front  54
Universal Declaration of Human Rights  418
universal service  184, 609
Universal Service Agency  175
universalists  234
unplanned effects  293

urbanisation  215
user-value  107
uses and gratifications theory  297
using and manipulating the media  541
utility  236
Uys, Jamie  77, 80

## V

V-Chip  522
*Vaderland, Die*  43, 67
value-judgement  282
Van Zijl Commission  148
vertical integration  111
video  576
Viljoen Commission  14
violence  573
visual possibilities  550
Volksbioskope-maatskappy  77
*Volksblad, Die*  66, 177, 179
*Volkstem, Die*  40
Voortrekkerpers  43
voyeurism  383, 397
*Vrye Weekblad*  55

## W

*Weekly Mail*  55
Western aesthetic  503
Westernisation  601
What is theory?  230
women's oppression  389
Wonderboom Inry Beleggings  78
words  449
world capitalist system  598
written and printed public communication culture  254, 255

## Y

*Yizo Yizo*  522, 523, 524, 530